W9-BCE-723
2540
MAXINE WHITE/SUTHERLAND...

BISON
BOOKS

The Discovery of the Oregon Trail

Robert Stuart's Narratives
of His Overland Trip Eastward
from Astoria in 1812–13

Edited by
PHILIP ASHTON ROLLINS

Introduction to the Bison Book Edition by Howard Lamar

University of Nebraska Press
Lincoln and London

♾ The paper in this book meets the minimum requirements of American National Standard for Information Sciences—Permanence of Paper for Printed Library Materials, ANSI Z39.48-1984.

First Bison Book printing: 1995
Most recent printing indicated by the last digit below:
10 9 8 7 6 5 4 3 2 1

Library of Congress Cataloging-in-Publication Data
Stuart, Robert, 1785–1848.
The discovery of the Oregon trail: Robert Stuart's narratives of his overland trip eastward from Astoria in 1812–13 / edited by Philip Ashton Rollins; introduction to the Bison book edition by Howard Lamar.
p. cm.
Includes index.
ISBN 0-8032-9234-1 (pbk.: alk. paper)
1. Stuart, Robert, 1785–1848. 2. Oregon Trail. 3. Tonquin (Ship) 4. Astoria (Or.)—History. 5. Pioneers—Oregon—Biography. 6. West (U.S.)—Description and travel. 7. Overland journeys to the Pacific. I. Rollins, Philip Ashton, 1869–1950. II. Title.
F880.S925 1995
979.5'02—dc20
95-2134 CIP
AC

Reprinted from the original 1935 edition by Edward Eberstadt & Sons. This edition is reprinted by arrangement with Scribner, An Imprint of Simon & Schuster.

The pagination of the original edition has not been changed in this Bison Book edition.

INTRODUCTION TO THE BISON BOOK EDITION

Howard Lamar

The reprinting of Philip Ashton Rollins's superbly edited *Discovery of the Oregon Trail: Robert Stuarts' Narratives of His Overland Trip Eastward from Astoria in 1812–13* is cause for celebration by scholars and all readers interested in accounts of the early exploration of the American West. Meriwether Lewis and William Clark's memorable accounts of their own trek across the continent and back between 1804 and 1806 will always remain unique first-hand narrative, but Robert Stuart's "Journal of a Voyage across the Continent of North America" and "Travelling Memoranda" are also classics that provide a cornucopia of information about the unknown western regions.

To fully appreciate the significance and value of Robert Stuart's narratives and his accomplishments as a fur trader-explorer, some context and explanation seem in order. Let us begin by following the fur trade activities of John Jacob Astor, New York businessman-entrepreneur, between the years 1806 and 1810.

When Lewis and Clark returned from their historic continental crossing in 1806 possibly no American outside of Thomas Jefferson himself was more interested in their accounts of the Oregon country, with its rich fur resources and its potential Indian trade, than John Jacob Astor. Having already amassed a fortune from the fur trade in New York State, along the Canadian border, and in the Great Lakes region, Astor soon began to devise a grand international scheme to exploit the fur and Indian trade from the Great Lakes to the West Coast. And as James P. Ronda has observed in his excellent study, *Astoria and Empire*, Astor fully expected to compete with the Hudson Bay and North West companies as well as with the Russian American Fur Company in

Alaska. He envisaged selling furs and trade goods not only to Europe but also to China, Japan, and possibly Russia via Siberia.

Astor shared his bold global scheme with President Jefferson and Secretary of the Treasury Albert Gallatin, for he felt that the federal government should be a partner in this endeavor. Fortunately, both Jefferson and Gallatin were sympathetic to Astor's plans. Indeed, at one point Jefferson declared that Astor deserved comparison with Columbus and Sir Walter Raleigh as a New World colonizer. By 1810 Astor and a number of partners had formed the Pacific Fur Company and made preparations to establish a trading post—the future Fort Astoria—at the mouth of the Columbia River.

To make Fort Astoria a reality, Astor dispatched Wilson Price Hunt, a partner and experienced trader, along with a party of partners, clerks, and trappers overland from St. Louis to the West Coast. An added purpose was to locate sites for future trading posts in the interior. At the same time he commissioned Captain Jonathan Thorne and his ship, the *Tonquin,* to sail from New York to the Oregon coast with necessary supplies and trade goods. A second group of partners, clerks, and Canadian voyageurs, many of them former employees of the North West Company, had been recruited at Montreal.

Among those on board the *Tonquin* was a young Scottish-born junior partner named Robert Stuart. Intelligent, well-educated, vigorous, with fierce eyes and a commanding presence, Stuart was soon recognized as a natural leader of men. When Thorne proved to be a tyrannical captain, young Stuart defied him and on one occasion threatened to kill him with a brace of pistols.

Stuart arrived at Fort Astoria just as fur trade operations had barely begun. Going to work with enthusiasm, he proved to be an observant trader who carefully studied the differing behavior of the Indian groups with whom he dealt. Firm but diplomatic, he believed that violence in trading must be avoided at all costs. His seniors sent him on trips along the coast and inland, and his performance was so successful that one partner described him as "prudent and brave."

Stuart's real rendezvous with destiny came, however, when the partners, in order to keep Astor informed of their activities and progress, decided to send Stuart back east, along with four men who had come overland with Hunt. Two other traders voluntarily joined them, but one, John Day, became ill and was sent back to Astoria. Stuart then proceeded with Ramsay Crooks, a fellow Scotsman; Ben Jones and Robert McClellan, two Americans; and André Valle and Françoise LeClerc, two Canadians. Ten months later they reached St. Louis, and on 23 June 1813 Stuart met Astor in New York and delivered verbal and written reports as well as his own journal account of his trip.

As Astor quickly realized, Stuart's journal was particularly valuable. The reasons went far beyond its being both an accurate account of the route taken and a description of how the six traders had survived a harrowing year in the American wilderness, plagued by hostile Indian bands, illness, near starvation, and the harsh life of a winter camp.

Among other things, the journal recorded that upon reaching the Wind River Mountains, Stuart veered from the routes formerly taken by Lewis and Clark and Hunt's party by turning southeast and crossing South Pass. To our knowledge, they were the first Americans to discover and use that historic low-lying mountain saddle which a few decades later would become the main gateway for immigrants going to Oregon and California. From South Pass, Stuart then traveled along the Sweetwater and North Platte rivers to the Missouri—also the general route of the future Oregon Trail. Unfortunately, Stuart's discovery of South Pass was never publicly reported, but ten years later James Clyman and Jedediah Smith rediscovered South Pass and it was soon part of a main highway to the Far West.

Stuart's narratives are of value to us for many other reasons as well. From the time he left Fort Astoria on 29 June 1812 to the moment he entered the outskirts of St. Louis, he took note of every distinctive Indian group he encountered—more than thirty in number. He described their relative fighting strength and differing degrees of kindness or hostility. More than once Stuart prevented his men from firing on threatening Indians, knowing full well that he and his few companions could survive only through trade, diplomacy, and the occasional loss of goods through theft or raid.

Similarly, Stuart exhibited a genuine curiosity about all animals, plants, and soils, as well as mountains and streams. James P. Ronda has called him a valuable naturalist. Stuart's vivid, even awed descriptions of the huge buffalo herds and incredible wildlife along the Platte River suggests just how bounteous the Great Plains could be in the spring.

Perhaps most significant of all, Stuart's desire for accuracy raises his narrative to a level of scientific objectivity. Romantic images, nostalgia, and evidence of favoring one companion over another are happily absent. When Ramsay Crooks, soon to emerge as one of the most distinguished fur traders in John Jacob Astor's American Fur Company, fell seriously ill on the trail, Stuart refused to leave him behind and waited patiently until he had recovered. Stuart's habitual confidence and certainty are revealed when, faced by the prospect of starvation, he wrote that for the very first time in his life he had not been able to sleep!

Fully aware of the valuable information that Stuart's narrative contained both for himself and for the government, Astor sent the journal to President James Madison and later persuaded Stuart to write a more formal version of the trip for publication in Europe. Translated into French, it appeared under the title "Travelling Memoranda," along with Hunt's "Diary" in *Nouvelle annales des Voyages* (Paris, 1821). Astor apparently wanted to be seen as a promoter of exploration and scientific inquiry, but he was also encouraged in this by his friend, Albert Gallatin, who was at the time U.S. Minister to France.

Some fourteen years later, Astor persuaded his friend Washington Irving, then America's most famous literary figure, to write up the entire Astoria story. Published in 1836, Irving's *Astoria* remains today both a valuable and delightful, romantic version of Astor's ill-fated West Coast enterprise. Irving's account made Astor himself be seen as a larger than life tragic hero who had tried unsuccessfully to expand America's empire to the Pacific only to lose Astoria to the British as a spoil in the War of 1812.

In order to write *Astoria,* Irving and his nephew, Pierre Irving, who served as research assistant, used Astor's personal papers and borrowed Stuart's "Travelling Memoranda." Washington Irving himself was so taken with Stuart's extraordinary experiences that he also made the latter, along with Wilson Price Hunt, a heroic figure. Yet even after *Astoria* had become a best seller and gone through many editions, Stuart's journal, which had been returned to him, was never published. It remained in the possession of his family until it was acquired by Frederick S. Dellenbaugh, who in turn sold it to William Robertson Coe, the noted New York collector of Western Americana. Meanwhile, Mr. Coe also acquired Stuart's "Travelling Memoranda" through an art gallery sale in 1933. It had been found in a cupboard at Sunnyside, Irving's home, by E. M. Grinnell, a grandnephew of Irving, and had remained in family hands until the time of the sale.

Mr. Coe then asked Philip Ashton Rollins to edit and publish both of Stuart's narratives. Coe could not have chosen a more ideal editor, for Rollins's own deep love for the West had begun when as a youth "he was entrusted to the famous scout and mountain man, Jim Bridger, for four months of 'tutoring.'" Later Rollins participated in cattle drives from Texas to Montana and spent time on the Cheyenne Indian Reservation. After graduating from Princeton, where he majored in American history, he stayed on to take an M.A. degree in history.

Although Rollins became a successful lawyer in New York, he and his wife collected Western Americana for forty years. During the 1920s Rollins himself began to publish books on the cowboy. As will be evident to readers of Robert Stuart's narratives in *The Discovery of the Oregon Trail,* Rollins's task as editor became a labor of love. He carefully retraced Stuart's circuitous overland route and clarified confusing references to streams, landmarks, and Indian tribes. He was particularly thorough in providing scientific names of the many hundreds of plants, trees and animals that Stuart mentioned. In the end, Rollins not only produced an exhaustive scholarly edition of Stuart's "Journal" but in a copious appendix he provided an English translation of "Travelling Memoranda," an "Account of the Tonquin Voyage," and Wilson Price Hunt's "Diary of His Overland Trip Westward to Astoria in

1811–12." Of all early accounts of western travel and exploration, Stuart's magnificent narrative is one of the best. The University of Nebraska Press is to be congratulated on reprinting Rollins's excellent edition.

One cannot resist a final word about Robert Stuart's later career. Having always been respected by Astor, in 1817 he and his fellow overland companion, the remarkable Ramsay Crooks, were made co-agents at Astor's fur post at Michilmackinac. Placed in charge of operations, Stuart oversaw some two hundred clerks and staff and perhaps as many as two thousand voyageurs. His natural ability, his love of order and efficiency, his belief in education, the temperance movement, and his devotion to the Presbyterian Church made him a respected figure both at Michilmackinac and later in Detroit, where he lived after Astor sold the American Fur Company in 1834. As a realist who dealt with situations, events, and people as he found them, Robert Stuart never questioned what role he should play in life. His innate integrity, his sense of loyalty to friends like Ramsay Crooks, his acute understanding of people, his desire to serve, and his sense of propriety qualify him as one of America's quiet but great frontier heroes.

When William Robertson Coe asked Rollins to edit Robert Stuart's "Journal," he gave him strict instructions not to be biased or partisan in his account. Even so, Rollins confessed in the preface to *The Discovery of The Oregon Trail* that he was overwhelmed by "the enthralling personalities of Robert Stuart and Ramsay Crooks, two young Scots who discovered for America her Oregon Trail, and who, despite their great adventure, had the courage to be modest." It would be difficult to find a more apt summary of Robert Stuart's character and accomplishments.

Yale University
12 December 1994

SUGGESTED ADDITIONAL READING

In the sixty years since Rollins's *Discovery of the Oregon Trail* appeared, hundreds of books and articles have been published about John Jacob Astor, Astoria, and the major participants in the Pacific Fur Company. Of these the following volumes deserve special mention.

Ross Cox, *The Columbia River*. 1831. Edited by Edgar I. Stewart and Jane R. Stewart. Reprint. (Norman: University of Oklahoma Press, 1957).

Gabriel Franchere, *Journal of a Voyage on the Northwest Coast of North America during the Years 1811, 1812, 1813, and 1814*. Edited by W. Kaye Lamb (Toronto: Champlain Society, 1969).

William H. Goetzmann, *Exploration and Empire: The Explorer and the Scientist in the Winning of the American West* (New York: Norton, 1966, 1978).

David Lavender, *The Fist in the Wilderness* (Garden City NY: Doubleday and Company, 1964).

Frederick Merk, *The Oregon Question: Essays in Anglo-American Diplomacy and Politics* (Cambridge: Harvard University Press, 1967).

James P. Ronda, *Astoria and Empire* (Lincoln: University of Nebraska Press, 1990).

Alexander Ross, *Adventures of the First Settlers on the Oregon or Columbia River, 1849*. Reprint. With an introduction by James P. Ronda (Lincoln: University of Nebraska Press, 1986).

The Discovery
of
The Oregon Trail

ROBERT STUART

From a contemporary painting

THE DISCOVERY
OF
THE OREGON TRAIL

Robert Stuart's Narratives

OF HIS OVERLAND TRIP EASTWARD FROM ASTORIA IN 1812-13. FROM THE ORIGINAL MANUSCRIPTS IN THE COLLECTION OF WILLIAM ROBERTSON COE, ESQ.

To which is added:

AN ACCOUNT OF THE *TONQUIN'S* VOYAGE AND OF EVENTS AT FORT ASTORIA [1811-12] *and* WILSON PRICE HUNT'S DIARY OF HIS OVERLAND TRIP WESTWARD TO ASTORIA IN 1811-12. Translated from *Nouvelles Annales des Voyages*, Paris, 1821

Edited by

PHILIP ASHTON ROLLINS

CHARLES SCRIBNER'S SONS

NEW YORK LONDON

1935

"...; yet I argue not
Againſt Heaven's Hand, or Will, nor bate one jot
Of Heart or Hope; but ſtill bear up, and ſteer
Right onward."

(from *Letters of State* by Mr.
John Milton, 1694, p. xlviii)

PREFACE

THE present work is the second of Mr. William Robertson Coe's publications in his projected series of printings of Western manuscripts possessed by him. The single prior publication in this series is *The Journals and Letters of Major John Owen*, edited by Seymour Dunbar and Professor Paul C. Phillips and issued at New York in 1927.

When thus making his important source material available to the student of history, Mr. Coe has demanded of his editors two things and only two things—precision in reproducing the original text and complete avoidance of controversial comment. His insistence upon the inviolability of the original text and upon the suppression of partisanship proves him a virile contributor to historical scholarship.

If perchance I have failed to comport with his interdiction of bias, my excuse is in the enthralling personalities of Robert Stuart and Ramsay Crooks, two young Scots who discovered for America her Oregon Trail and who, despite their great adventure, had the courage to be modest.

P. A. R.

154 Library Place
Princeton, New Jersey
June 10, 1935

CONTENTS

Contents

Contents

ILLUSTRATIONS

MAPS

ABBREVIATIONS USED IN FOOTNOTES WHEN CITING CERTAIN SOURCES

ABBREVIATIONS	
Abbey	California, a trip across the plains &c., by James Abbey, New Albany, Ind., 1850.
Abbott	Recollections of a California pioneer, by Carlisle S. Abbott, N.Y., 1917.
Abert	Map of the United States Territory of Oregon &c. compiled &c. under the direction of Col. J. J. Abert by Wash: Hood, 1838 and accompanying the report of Caleb Cushing, 25th congress, 3rd session, house of reps., rep. no. 101, Territory of Oregon, supplemental report, Feb. 16, 1839.
Abridgement	Abridgement of the debates of congress from 1789 to 1856, N.Y., 1857-61.
Akin	University of Oklahoma bulletin N. S. No. 172 university studies no. 9. The journal of James Akin, Jr., ed. by Edward Everett Dale, Norman, Okla., 1919.
Allen	Ten years in Oregon, travels and adventures of Doctor E. White and Lady &c., compiled by Miss A. J. Allen, Ithaca, N.Y., 1848.
Allen's Guide	Allen's guide book and map to the gold fields of Kansas &c., by O. Allen, Washington, 1859.
Ambler	The life and diary of John Floyd &c., by Charles H. Ambler, Richmond, 1918.
Am. State, Indian	American state papers, indian affairs, Washington, 1832, '34.
Angelo[A]	Idaho, a descriptive tour &c., by C. Aubrey Angelo, San Francisco, 1865.
Angelo[B]	Sketches of travel &c., by C. Aubrey Angelo, N.Y., 1866.
Annales	Annales des voyages &c., Paris, Tome XXII en 1813.
Applegate	Recollections of my boyhood, by Jesse Applegate, Roseburg, Ore., 1914.
Astoria	Astoria &c., by Washington Irving, Philadelphia, 1836.
Bagley	The acquisition and pioneering of old Oregon, by Clarence B. Bagley, Seattle, 1924.
Baillon	The natural history of plants, by H. Baillon, London, 1871-88.

Abbreviations Used in Footnotes

ABBREVIATIONS	
Baker-Astor[*A*], [*B*]	John Jacob Astor's original letter-books in Baker Library at Harvard University: [*A*] years 1813-15, [*B*] 1831-38.
Bancroft	The works of Hubert Howe Bancroft, vols. XXVII and XXVIII, San Francisco, 1884.
Bates	The life and papers of Frederick Bates, pub. by Missouri Historical Society, 1926.
Beck	A gazetteer of the states of Illinois and Missouri &c., by Lewis C. Beck, Albany, 1823.
Bennett	Journ. of James Bennett, reprinted (N.Y. 1932) from New Harmony (Indiana) Times of March 16-Aug. 3, 1906.
Benton	Thirty years' view &c., by a senator of thirty years, N.Y., 1854.
Bible[*A*]	Robert Stuart's Bible, printed in 1813 and today owned by Mrs. Homer Pierce Clark of St. Paul, Minn. This citation when accompanied by an asterisk means the mentioned entry is in Robert Stuart's handwriting.
Bible[*B*]	Mrs. Robert Stuart's Bible, printed in 1843 and today owned by Mrs. Stuart Cooper of San Francisco, Cal.
Billon	Annals of St. Louis &c. from 1804 to 1821, by Frederic L. Billon, St. Louis, 1888.
Biographical	Biographical directory of the American congress, 1774-1927 &c., Washington, 1928.
Birmingham	A journal of the Birmingham Emigrating Company &c., by Leander V. Loomis, ed. by Edgar M. Ledyard, Salt Lake City, 1928.
Blanchard	History of Illinois to accompany an historical map of the state, by Rufus Blanchard, Chicago, 1883.
Bonner	The life and adventures of James P. Beckwourth &c., by T. D. Bonner, N.Y., 1856.
Brackenridge	Views of Louisiana &c., by H. M. Brackenridge, Pittsburgh, 1814.
Bradbury[*A*]	Travels in the interior of America &c., by John Bradbury, Liverpool, 1817.
Bradbury[*B*]	*Idem*, second edition, London, 1819.
Bradford	Map of United States, copyright by T. G. Bradford, 1838.
Bronson	Reminiscences of a ranchman, by Edgar Beecher Bronson, N.Y., 1919.
Brown	Life of a pioneer, being the autobiography of James S. Brown, Salt Lake City, 1900.

Abbreviations Used in Footnotes

ABBREVIATIONS	
Brown, Gaz.	The western gazetteer &c., by Samuel R. Brown, Auburn, N.Y., 1817.
Brown, J. Robert	A journal of a trip across the plains &c., by J. Robert Brown, Columbus, 1860.
Bryant	What I saw in California &c., by Edwin Bryant, N.Y. & Phila., 1848.
Bulletin A	Bulletin no. 199, U.S. Geol. Survey, 1902.
Bulletin B	Bulletin no. 612, U.S. Geol. Survey, guidebook &c., part B, 1906.
Burpee	The search for the western sea &c., by Lawrence J. Burpee, Toronto [1908].
Burton	The city of the saints &c., by Richard F. Burton, London, 1861.
Cal. Hist. Soc. Quar.	California Historical Society Quarterly.
Caribou	U.S. Dept. of Agriculture, Forest Service, map of Caribou Nat'l Forest, Ida., Boise meridian, 1928.
Cartwright	Natural history of western wild animals &c., by David W. Cartwright &c., Toledo, 1875.
Century	The Century Dictionary and Cyclopedia, N.Y., 1911.
Chief Joseph	Chief Joseph's own story, with foreword by Donald MacRae (n.p., n.d.).
Child	Overland route to California &c., by Andrew Child, Milwaukee, 1852.
Chittenden	The American fur trade of the far west &c., by Hiram Martin Chittenden, N.Y., 1902.
Chittenden Steamboat	History of early steamboat navigation on the Missouri River &c., by Hiram Martin Chittenden, N.Y., 1903.
Clapp	A journal of travels to and from California &c., by John T. Clapp, Kalamazoo, 1851. In Everitt D. Graff's collection.
Clark	The indian sign language &c., by W. P. Clark, Philadelphia, 1885.
Clark[*A*]	History of the Willamette valley &c., by Robert Carlton Clark, Chicago, 1927.
Clarke	Old Montreal, John Clarke: his adventures, friends and family, by Adele Clarke, 1906.
Clayton[*A*]	The Latter-Day Saints' emigrant guide &c., by W. Clayton, St. Louis, 1848.

Abbreviations Used in Footnotes

ABBREVIATIONS	
Clayton[B]	William Clayton's journal &c., pub. by the Clayton Family Association, Salt Lake City, 1921.
Clyman	James Clyman &c., ed. by Charles L. Camp, San Francisco, 1928.
Coke	A ride over the Rocky Mountains &c., by The Hon. Henry J. Coke, London, 1852.
Cole	In the early days along the overland trail &c., by Gilbert L. Cole, Kansas City, 1905.
Colton[A]	Map of the United States of America, the British Provinces, Mexico, and the West Indies, showing the country from the Atlantic to the Pacific Ocean, pub. by J. H. Colton, N.Y., 1850.
Colton[B]	Colton's map of the states and territories west of the Mississippi River to the Pacific Ocean &c., pub. by J. H. Colton, N.Y., 1864.
Colton[C]	Colton's map of the states and territories west of the Mississippi River to the Pacific Ocean &c., pub. by G. W. and C. B. Colton & Co., N.Y., 1869.
Colton[D]	Nebraska and Kansas, map of; pub. by J. H. Colton & Co., N.Y., 1854.
Colton[E]	Map of the United States, the British Provinces, Mexico &c. showing the route of the U.S. mail steam packets to California and a plan of the gold region, pub. by J. H. Colton, N.Y., 1849.
Colton[F]	Map, Colton's Washington and Oregon, copyright by J. H. Colton & Co., 1859.
Colton[G]	Map of the United States of America, the British Provinces, Mexico, the West Indies and Central America, with part of New Grenada and Venezuela, pub. by J. H. Colton, N.Y., 1849.
Colton[H]	Same title as *Colton*[G], but pub. in 1854.
Colton[I]	Colton's traveler and tourist's guide-book through the western states &c., N.Y., 1855.
Colvocoresses	Four years in a government exploring expedition &c., by Lieut. Geo. M. Colvocoresses, U.S. Navy, N.Y., 1852.
Com. Bot. Mag.	Companion to the Botanical Magazine &c., London, 1835-36.
Cooke	Scenes and adventures in the army &c., by P. St. G. Cooke, Philadelphia, 1857.
Cooley	Am. commonwealths, Michigan &c., by Thomas McIntyre Cooley, Boston, 1885.

Abbreviations Used in Footnotes

ABBREVIATIONS	
Coutant	History of Wyoming &c., by C. G. Coutant, Laramie, 1899.
Cowperthwait[*A*]	Description of Oregon and California &c. with a large and accurate map of Oregon and California, pub. by Thomas, Cowperthwait & Co., Philadelphia, 1849.
Cowperthwait[*B*]	A new map of the state of California, the territories of Oregon &c., copyright by Thomas, Cowperthwait & Co., 1850.
Cowperthwait[*C*]	Geographical description of the state of Texas; also, of that part of the west coast of North America which includes Oregon, &c., pub. by Thomas, Cowperthwait & Co., Philadelphia, 1846.
Cox[*A*]	Adventures on the Columbia River &c., by Ross Cox, London, 1831.
Cox[*B*]	*Idem*, N.Y., 1832.
Coyner	The lost trappers, by David H. Coyner, Cincinnati, 1847.
Crawford	Sources of the history of Oregon, vol. I, no. 1, journal of Medorem Crawford, Eugene, 1897.
Creuzbaur	Route from the Gulf of Mexico &c., by Robert Creuzbaur, N.Y. and Austin, 1849.
Crown Maps	The Crown collection of American maps, series IV, the American transcontinental trails, ed. by Archer Butler Hulbert and pub. by the Stewart Commission on Western History.
Curley	Nebraska, its advantages, resources &c., by Edwin A. Curley, N.Y., 1875.
Cutler	A topographical description of the state of Ohio, &c., by [Jervase Cutler], Boston, 1812. Contains, at pp. 158-204, the journal of Charles Le Raye.
Dale	The Ashley-Smith explorations &c., with the original journals, ed. by Harrison Clifford Dale, Cleveland, 1918.
Dana	Geographical sketches on the western country &c., by E. Dana, Cincinnati, 1819.
Darby	The emigrant's guide to the western &c. states &c., by William Darby, N.Y., 1818.
Dawson	The Ute war &c., by T. F. Dawson and F. J. V. Skiff, Denver, 1879.
Debates	The debates and proceedings in the congress &c., 16th cong. 2nd sess., Washington, 1855.

Abbreviations Used in Footnotes

ABBREVIATIONS	
de Lacy	Map of the territory of Montana &c. drawn by W. L. de Lacy for the use of the first legislature of Montana and accompanying the volume *Stuart, Granville*[*A*], *infra.*
Delano	Life on the plains &c., by A. Delano, Auburn, 1854.
De Peyster	Personal and military history of Philip Kearny &c., by John Watts De Peyster, N.Y., 1869.
De Smet	Letters and sketches &c., by P. J. De Smet, S. J., Philadelphia, 1843.
De Smet[*A*]	Oregon missions &c., by Father P. J. De Smet, N.Y., 1847.
De Smet Letters	Life, letters and travels of Father Pierre-Jean De Smet, S. J. &c., ed. by Chittenden and Richardson, N.Y., 1905.
Disturnell	Map by J. Calvin Smith and accompanying the emigrant's guide to New Mexico, California and Oregon &c., pub. by J. Disturnell, N.Y., 1849.
Duflot	Exploration du territoire de l'Oregon &c., executée pendant les années 1840, 1841 et 1842 par Eugene Duflot de Mofras, Paris, 1844.
Dunbar	A history of travel in America &c., by Seymour Dunbar, Indianapolis (cop. 1915).
Duncan	Cassell's natural history, by F. Martin Duncan, N.Y., n.d.
Dundass	Journal of Samuel Rutherford Dundass &c., in the year 1849, Steubenville, Ohio, 1857.
Earnshaw	Across the plains in 1859, by William Earnshaw in Waterford (Wis.) Post, newspaper, 1897.
Emory	Executive document no. 7, 30th congress, 1st session, senate, notes of a military reconnaissance from Fort Leavenworth &c. to San Diego, by Bvt. Major W. H. Emory, Washington, 1848.
Ensign	Ornamental map of the United States and Mexico, copyright by Ensign and Thayer, 1848.
Ensign[*A*]	Map of the gold region of California showing the routes via Chargres &c., pub. by Ensign and Thayer, N.Y., n.d.
Exec. Doc.	Executive document no. 1, part II, 31st congress, 2d session, senate, message from the President, Washington, 1850 [contains journ. of Osborne Cross].
Fanning	Voyages to the South Seas . . . North-West coast &c., by Edmund Fanning, N.Y., 1838.
Farnham	Travels in the great western prairies &c., by Thomas J. Farnham, Ploughkeepsie [*sic*], 1843.

Abbreviations Used in Footnotes

ABBREVIATIONS	
Ferguson	The experiences of a forty-niner &c., by Charles D. Ferguson, Chico, Cal., 1924. [First edition was in 1888.]
Fitzpatrick	Nebraska place-names, by Lilian Linder Fitzpatrick, A.M., Lincoln, 1925.
Flagg	The far west &c., by [Edmund Flagg], N.Y., 1838.
Franchere[A]	Relation d'un voyage &c., par G. Franchere, Fils., Montreal, 1820.
Franchere[B]	Narrative of a voyage to the northwest coast of America &c., by Gabriel Franchere, translated and edited by Huntington, N.Y., 1854.
Franchere[C]	*Idem*, but edited with notes &c. by Reuben Gold Thwaites, Cleveland, 1904.
Frazer	On the old trails in Wyoming, a history of Wyoming for the elementary schools, grades 3-8, by Marie M. Frazer, Laramie, 1928.
Fremont	Report of the exploring expedition to the Rocky Mountains in the year 1842 and to Oregon and north California in the years 1843-44, by J. C. Fremont, Washington, 1845.
Fremont[A]	Geographical memoir upon upper California &c., by John Charles Fremont, being Misc. No. 148, 30th congress, 1st session, senate, Washington, 1848.
Frizzell	Across the plains to California in 1852, journal of Mrs. Lodisa Frizzell, edited by Victor Hugo Paltsits, N.Y., 1915.
Fuller	A history of the Pacific Northwest, by George W. Fuller, N.Y., 1931.
G. S.	Gravestone in Stuart plot, Elmwood Cemetery, Detroit, Mich.
Gass[A]	A journal &c., by Patrick Gass, Pittsburgh, 1807.
Gass[B]	*Idem*, Philadelphia, 1810.
Gebow	A vocabulary of the Snake or Shoshone dialect, by Joseph A. Gebow &c., G. S. L. City, 1859.
Gen. Register	General register of the U.S. Navy &c., Washington, 1882.
Geol.	U.S. Geological Survey map of the particular state indicated by whatever name immediately follows the word "Geol." wherever used in a footnote: as, for instance, *Geol. Idaho.*
Gibson	Recollections of a pioneer, by J. W. (Watt) Gibson, St. Joseph, Mo. [1912].
Gilbert	Exploration of western America, &c., by E. W. Gilbert, Cambridge, 1933.

Abbreviations Used in Footnotes

ABBREVIATIONS	
Gilliam	Travels over the table lands and cordilleras &c., by Albert M. Gilliam, Philadelphia, 1846.
Gove	The Utah expedition, 1857-1858, Letters of Capt. Jesse A. Gove &c., edited by Otis G. Hammond, Concord, 1928.
Greeley	An overland journey &c., by Horace Greeley, N.Y., 1860.
Greenhow	Memoir, historical &c., by Robert Greenhow, 26th congress, 1st session, senate doc. 174, Washington, 1840.
Gregg	Commerce of the prairies &c., by Josiah Gregg, N.Y., 1844.
Grinnell	Two great scouts &c., by George Bird Grinnell, Cleveland, 1928.
Grinnell[*A*]	The fighting Cheyennes, by George Bird Grinnell, N.Y., 1915.
Grinnell[*B*]	The Cheyenne indians &c., by George Bird Grinnell, New Haven, 1923.
Hamilton	Incidents and events in the life of Gurdon Saltonstall Hubbard, collected &c. by Henry E. Hamilton, Chicago, 1888.
Hastings[*A*]	The emigrants' guide to Oregon &c., by Lansford W. Hastings, Cincinnati, 1845.
Hastings[*B*]	A new history of Oregon &c., by Lansford W. Hastings, Cincinnati, 1847.
Hayden, Montana	Preliminary report of the U.S. geological survey of Montana &c., by F. V. Hayden, Washington, 1872.
Hayden, Wyoming	Preliminary report of the U.S. geological survey of Wyoming &c., by F. V. Hayden, Washington, 1872.
Hayden, Wyoming and Idaho	Twelfth annual report of the U.S. geological survey of Wyoming and Idaho, by F. V. Hayden, Washington, 1883.
Hebard	The Bozeman trail &c., by Grace Raymond Hebard and E. A. Brininstool, Cleveland, 1922.
Heitman	Historical register &c. of the U.S. army, by Francis B. Heitman, Washington, 1903.
Henry-Thomp.	New light on the early history of the greater northwest—the manuscript journals of Alexander Henry and of David Thompson, edited by Elliott Coues, N.Y., 1897.
Hewitt	Notes by the way &c., by R. H. Hewitt, Olympia, 1863.
Hines	A voyage round the world &c., by Rev. Gustavus Hines, Buffalo, 1850.
Hodge	Handbook of American indians &c., by Fred. Webb Hodge, Washington, 1907.

Abbreviations Used in Footnotes

ABBREVIATIONS	
Holditch	The emigrant's guide &c., by Robert Holditch, London, 1818.
Holt	Holt's new map of Wyoming &c., pub. by G. L. Holt, Cheyenne, 1885.
Horn	Horn's overland guide &c., by Hosea B. Horn, N.Y., 1852.
House Doc.	House document no. 45, 17th congress, 2d session, message from the President &c. relating to an establishment made at the mouth of Columbia River, Washington, 1823.
Illinois	Transactions of the Illinois State Historical Society for the year 1925, n.p., n.d.
Ingalls	Journal of a trip &c., by E. S. Ingalls, Waukegan, 1852.
Irving	The Rocky Mountains &c., by Washington Irving, Philadelphia, 1837.
Irving, John T.	Indian sketches &c., by John T. Irving, Jr., Philadelphia, 1835.
Isham	G. S. Isham's guide to California &c., N.Y., 1850.
James	Three years among the indians &c., by Gen. Thomas James, Waterloo, Ill., 1846; reprinted, with notes by Walter B. Douglas, St. Louis, 1916.
Jefferson	Map of the emigrant road &c. (in four parts), by T. H. Jefferson, N.Y., 1849.
Johnson, Harrison	Johnson's history of Nebraska, by Harrison Johnson, with accompanying map, Omaha, 1880.
Johnson & Winter	Route across the Rocky Mountains &c., by Overton Johnson and Wm. H. Winter, Lafayette, Ind., 1846.
Johnston	Experiences of a forty-niner, by Wm. G. Johnston, Pittsburgh, 1892.
journ.	Robert Stuart's manuscript journal as printed in the present work. Original in William Robertson Coe's collection. Photostatic copies in Huntington library and library of Princeton University.
Kansas	Transactions of the Kansas State Historical Society.
Keller	A trip across the plains &c., by Geo. Keller, Massillon, 1851.
Kelley	A geographical sketch &c., by Hall J. Kelley, with accompanying map, Boston, 1830.
Kelly	An excursion to California &c., by William Kelly, London, 1851.

Abbreviations Used in Footnotes

ABBREVIATIONS	
Kenderdine	A California tramp &c., by T. S. Kenderdine, Newtown, Pa., 1888.
Kingsbury	Report of the Sec. of War transmitting a report of the expedition . . . under the command of Col. Henry Dodge &c., 24th congress, 1st session, senate doc. 209.
Lander	Preliminary map of the central division Ft. Kearney, South Pass & Honey Lake wagon-road surveyed and worked under the direction of F. W. Lander &c. 1847-1858, and accompanying ex. doc. no. 108, house of reps., 35th congress, 2d session.
Langworthy	Scenery of the plains &c., by Franklin Langworthy, Ogdensburgh, 1855.
Lanman	The red book of Michigan &c., by Charles Lanman, Detroit, 1871.
Larocque Journ.	Journal de Larocque, ed. by Lawrence J. Burpee and pub. in Publication des Canadiennes, no. 3, Ottawa, 1911.
la Vérendrye	la Vérendrye, Pierre Gaultier de Varennes, Sieur de; journals and letters of &c., ed. by Lawrence J. Burpee, Toronto, 1927.
Lee and Frost	Ten years in Oregon, by D. Lee and J. H. Frost, N.Y., 1844.
Leeper	The argonauts of forty-nine &c., by David Rohrer Leeper, South Bend, Ind., 1894.
Leonard	Oregon territory &c., by H. L. W. Leonard, Cleveland, 1846.
L. & C. Hist.	History of &c. Lewis and Clark &c., by Elliott Coues, N.Y., 1893.
L. & C. Journs.	Original journals of the Lewis and Clark expedition &c., ed. by Reuben Gold Thwaites, N.Y., 1904.
Lewis and Clark	Message from the President of the United States communicating discoveries made &c., by Captains Lewis and Clark &c., Washington, 1806.
Lewis and Clark [*B*]	History of the expedition under the command of Captains Lewis and Clark &c., Philadelphia, 1814.
Light List	U.S. Dept. of Commerce, Lighthouse Service, light list &c., Pacific coast, Washington, 1929.
Linforth	Route from Liverpool to Great Salt Lake Valley &c., ed. by James Linforth, Liverpool, 1855.
Little	From Kirtland to Salt Lake City, by James A. Little, Salt Lake City, 1890.

Abbreviations Used in Footnotes

ABBREVIATIONS	
Lobenstine	Extracts from the diary of William C. Lobenstine &c., printed privately, n.p., 1920.
Long	Account of an expedition &c. under the command of Major Stephen H. Long, compiled by Edwin James, Philadelphia, 1823.
Longworth	Longworth's American almanac, New-York register and city directory for 1823-24.
Lowell	Map of Nez Perces and Salmon River gold mines &c., by Daniel W. Lowell & Co., San Francisco, 1862.
Luttig	Journal of a fur-trading expedition &c., by John C. Luttig, ed. by Stella M. Drumm, St. Louis, 1920.
Lyford	The western address directory &c., by W. G. Lyford, Baltimore, 1837.
McArthur	Oregon geographic names, by Lewis A. McArthur, Portland, 1928.
MacDonald	Ranald MacDonald, the narrative of his early life &c., ed. by William S. Lewis and Naojiro Murakami, Spokane, 1923.
Mackenzie	Voyages from Montreal on the River St. Lawrence through the continent of North America &c., by Alexander Mackenzie, London, 1801.
Macomb	Report of the exploring expedition from Santa Fé, New Mexico, to the junction of the Grand and Green Rivers &c. in 1859 under the command of Capt. J. N. Macomb, Washington, 1876.
Marcy	The prairie traveler &c., by Randolph B. Marcy, N.Y., 1859.
Masson	Simon Fraser's journal in "Les bourgeois de la Compagnie du Nord-Ouest &c", by L. R. Masson, Quebec, 1889-90.
Melish	Map of the United States &c., by John Melish, Philadelphia, 1816.
Melish[*A*]	Map United States of America, compiled &c. by John Melish, pub. by M. Carey & Son, Philadelphia, 1821.
Michigan	Michigan Pioneer & Historical collections, Lansing.
Mil. Star	The Latter-Day Saints' Millenial Star, ed. and pub. by Orson Pratt, Manchester and subsequently Liverpool, 1841-
Missouri	Missouri Historical Society Collections.
Mitchell	Map of the United States and territories &c., copyright by S. Augustus Mitchell, 1870.

Abbreviations Used in Footnotes

ABBREVIATIONS	
Mitchell[A]	Map Oregon, Upper California &c., pub. by S. Augustus Mitchell, Philadelphia, copyright by H. N. Burroughs, 1845.
Mo. Gaz.	Missouri Gazette (newspaper), issue of May 15, 1813.
Moffette	The territories of Kansas and Nebraska &c., by Joseph F. Moffette, N.Y., 1855.
Montana	Montana Historical Society Transactions.
Murphy	Rambles in north-western America &c., by John Mortimer Murphy, London, 1879.
Murray	Travels in North America, by Charles Augustus Murray, London, 1839.
Nation	The Nation, a weekly journal, &c., vol. LXV, N.Y., 1897.
Neb. Colls.	Collections of the Nebraska State Historical Society.
Neb. Hist. Mag.	Nebraska History Magazine, pub. by Nebraska State Historical Society.
Neb. Hist. Proc.	Nebraska Historical Society proceedings and collections, 2nd series.
Neb. Hist. Trans.	Transactions and reports of the Nebraska State Historical Society.
Neb. Pub.	Publications of the Nebraska State Historical Society.
Niles	The Weekly Register &c., H. Niles, editor, vol. IV, Baltimore, 1813.
North Dak.	Collections of the State Historical Society of North Dakota.
Noteware	Map of the state of Nebraska, by J. H. Noteware &c., Omaha, 1875, accompanying "Northern Nebraska &c.," by John O'Neill, Sioux City, 1875.
Nouvelles Annales	Nouvelles annales des voyages, de la géographie et de l'histoire &c., pub. par Mm. J. B. Eyriès et Malte-Brun, Paris, Libraire de Gide Fils, Tomes X et XII en 1821.
Nuttall	Journal of travels &c., by Thomas Nuttall, Philadelphia, 1821.
Official Army	Official army register of the volunteer force of the United States army for the years 1861, 62, 63, 64, 65, Washington, 1865.
Oregon	The Oregonian and indians' advocate, Boston, 1838-39.
Ore. Hist. Soc. Quar.	The quarterly of the Oregon Historical Society.
Ore. Pioneer	Transactions of the Oregon Pioneer Association, pub. at Portland, Ore.

Abbreviations Used in Footnotes

ABBREVIATIONS	
Ore. Spec.	Oregon Spectator (newspaper) pub. at Oregon City, Ore. in and after 1847.
Owen	The journals and letters of Major John Owen &c., ed. by Seymour Dunbar and Paul C. Phillips, N.Y., 1927.
Pacific Fur	Pacific Fur Co. organization agreement and collateral papers in collection of Missouri Historical Society, St. Louis, Mo. Copies of them are printed in Grace Flandrau's "Astor and the Oregon Country" (n.p., n.d.).
Pac. Tourist	The Pacific tourist &c., by Henry T. Williams, N.Y., 1876.
Palmer	Journal of travels &c., by Joel Palmer, Cincinnati, 1847.
Parker	Journal of an exploring tour &c., by Rev. Samuel Parker, Ithaca, N.Y., 1838.
Pattie	The personal narrative of James O. Pattie &c., Cincinnati, 1831.
Peck	A gazetteer of Illinois &c., by J. M. Peck, Second edition, Philadelphia, 1837.
Perrin du Lac	Voyage dans les deux Louisianes &c., by Perrin du Lac, Paris, 1805.
Pike[A]	An account of expeditions &c. during the years 1805 &c., by Major Z. M. Pike, Philadelphia, 1810.
Pike[B]	The expeditions of Zebulon Montgomery Pike &c., ed. by Elliott Coues, N.Y., 1895.
Porter	John Jacob Astor &c., by Kenneth Wiggins Porter, Cambridge, 1931.
Potter	The autobiography of Theodore Edgar Potter, [Concord, N.H.] cop. 1913.
Preuss	Topographical map of the road from Missouri to Oregon &c. in VII sections &c., compiled by Charles Preuss, 1846.
Quad.	U.S. Geological Survey's topographic map of the particular quadrangle indicated by whatever name immediately follows the word "Quad." wherever used in a footnote; as, for instance, *Quad. Gothenburg*.
Railroad Survey	Reports of explorations and surveys to ascertain the most practicable and economical route for a railroad &c., Washington, 1855, 33d congress, 2d session house of reps. ex. doc. no. 91.
Raynolds	Report on the exploration of the Yellowstone River, by Bvt. Brig. Gen. W. F. Raynolds, Washington, 1868.
Remington	Pony Tracks, by Frederic Remington, N.Y., 1895.

Abbreviations Used in Footnotes

ABBREVIATIONS	
Robertson	Oregon, our right &c., by Wyndham Robertson, Jr., Washington, 1846.
Robinson	A map of Mexico, Louisiana and the Missouri Territory &c., by John H. Robinson, M.D., engraved by H. Anderson, Philadelphia, printed and colored by John L. Narstin of Philadelphia, copyright, 1819.
Root	Journal of travels from St. Josephs to Oregon &c., by Riley Root, Galesburg, 1850.
Ross[A]	Adventures of the first settlers on the Oregon or Columbia River &c., by Alexander Ross, London, 1849.
Ross[B]	*Idem*, with notes &c. by Reuben Gold Thwaites, Cleveland, 1904.
Ross[C]	The fur-hunters of the far west &c., by Alexander Ross, London, 1855.
Russell	Journal of a trapper &c., by Osborne Russell, Boise, Ida., 1914.
Russell & Driggs	Hidden heroes of the Rockies, by Isaac K. Russell in collaboration with Howard R. Driggs, Yonkers-on-Hudson, 1923.
Sage	Scenes in the Rocky Mountains &c., by a New Englander, Philadelphia, 1846.
Sawyer	Way sketches &c., by Lorenzo Sawyer &c., with historical notes compiled &c., by Edward Eberstadt, N.Y., 1926.
Scott	History of the Oregon Country &c., by Harvey W. Scott, Cambridge, 1924.
Schmölder	Neuer praktischer wegweiser &c., von Capitain B. Schmölder &c., Mainz, 1849.
Sedgley	Overland to California in 1849, by Joseph Sedgley, Oakland, 1877.
Shepherd	Journal of travel across the plains &c., by J. S. Shepherd, Racine, 1851.
Sherman	Memoirs of Gen. W. T. Sherman, N.Y., 1890.
Shively	Route and distances to Oregon &c., by J. M. Shively, Washington, 1846.
Simpson	Executive document no. 45, 31st congress, 1st session, house of reps. letter from Sec. of War transmitting report and map of Lieut. James H. Simpson of the route from Fort Smith to Santa Fe, Feb. 18, 1850.
Smedley	Across the plains in '62, by William Smedley, n.p. [circa 1916].

Abbreviations Used in Footnotes

ABBREVIATIONS	
Smith	The travels of Jedediah Smith &c., by Maurice S. Sullivan, Santa Ana, 1934.
Smith, C. W.	Journal of a trip to California &c., by C. W. Smith, ed. by R. W. G. Vail, N.Y., n.d.
Snake Plan	U.S. Geological Survey plan and profile of Snake River, Lewiston, Idaho to Huntington, Ore. 17 sheets.
South Dak.	South Dakota historical collections &c., compiled by the State Historical Society.
Southwestern	Southwestern historical quarterly, pub. by Texas State Historical Society.
Stansbury[A]	Exploration &c. of the valley of the Great Salt Lake &c., by Howard Stansbury, special session, March, 1851, senate exec. doc. no. 3, Philadelphia, 1852.
Stansbury[B]	Separate volume of maps accompanying *Stansbury[A]*.
Steele	Across the plains in 1850 &c., by John Steele, Chicago, 1930.
Stuart, Granville[A]	Montana as it is &c., by Granville Stuart, N.Y., 1865.
Stuart, Granville[B]	Forty years on the frontier as seen in the journals and reminiscences of Granville Stuart &c., ed. by Paul C. Phillips, Cleveland, 1925.
Sumner	Map of the United States compiled from &c., pub. by H. F. Sumner, Hartford, 1839.
Symons[A]	Report of an examination of the upper Columbia River &c., by Lieut. Thomas W. Symons. 47th congress, 1st. session, senate, ex. doc. 186, Washington, 1882.
Symons[B]	Map of the Department of the Columbia projected and compiled at the engineer's office Department of the Columbia, by Lieut. Thomas W. Symons &c., pub. by office Chief of Engineers, U.S. Army, 1887.
Targhee	U.S. Dept. of Agriculture, Forest Service, map of Targhee Nat'l Forest Idaho and Wyoming, Boise and sixth principal meridians, 1925.
Tassé	Les Canadiens de l'ouest, par Joseph Tassé, Montreal, 1878.
Teton	U.S. Dept. of Agriculture, Forest Service, map of Teton Nat'l Forest Wyoming sixth principal meridian, 1928.
Thom	Map showing the routes travelled by the command of Major E. Steen, U.S. Drags. against the Snake indians in 1860, by Lieut. Joseph Dixon &c. under the direction of

Abbreviations Used in Footnotes

ABBREVIATIONS	
	Capt. G. Thom, part of senate ex. doc. no. 1, 37th congress, 2d session, Washington, 1861.
Thompson	Crossing the plains &c. in 1852. Printed from a diary &c. kept by the late Origen Thompson, Greensburg, Ind., 1896.
Thornton	Oregon and California in 1848, by J. Quinn Thornton, N.Y., 1849.
Tixier	Voyage aux prairies Osage &c., par Victor Tixier, Clermont-Ferrand, 1844.
Townsend	Narrative of a journey across the Rocky Mountains &c., by John K. Townsend, Philadelphia, 1839.
trav. mem.	Robert Stuart's travelling memoranda as included in the present work. Original in William Robertson Coe's collection. Photostatic copies in Huntington library and library of Princeton University.
Triggs	History of Cheyenne &c., by J. H. Triggs, Omaha, 1876.
Turnbull	T. Turnbull's travels from the U.S. &c., ed. by Frederic L. Paxson, Madison, 1914.
Udell	Incidents of travel to California &c., by John Udell, Jefferson, Ohio, 1856.
Union Pacific	Map of the Union Pacific Rail Road Surveys 1864, '65, '66, '67, '68 from Missouri River to Humboldt Wells, H. Lambach, del. 1689.
U. P. Folder	Union Pacific Rail Road's advertising "folder," Idaho-Utah outings.
Vinton	John Colter &c., by Stallo Vinton, N.Y., 1926.
Wadsworth	The national wagon road guide from St. Joseph &c., by W. Wadsworth, San Francisco, 1858.
War	The war of the rebellion. U.S. Govt. printing office, Washington.
Ware	The emigrant's guide to California &c., by Joseph E. Ware, St. Louis, 1849.
Warre	Sketches in North America &c., by Captain H. Warre, [London] 1848.
Washakie	U.S. Dept. of Agriculture, Forest Service, map of Washakie Nat'l Forest Wyoming sixth principal meridian, 1926.
Wash. Hist. Quar.	The Washington Historical Quarterly, pub. by Washington University State Historical Society, Seattle, Wash.
Wheeler	The frontier trail &c., by Col. Homer W. Wheeler, Los Angeles, 1923.

Abbreviations Used in Footnotes

ABBREVIATIONS	
Wheeler, Olin	The trail of Lewis and Clark, by Olin D. Wheeler, N.Y., 1904.
White	A concise view of Oregon Territory &c., by Elijah White, Washington, 1846.
Wilkes	Western America &c., by Charles Wilkes, U.S.N., Philadelphia, 1849.
Wilkes, Narr.	Narrative of the U.S. exploring expedition &c., by Charles Wilkes, Philadelphia, 1845.
Williams	Narrative of a tour &c., by Joseph Williams, Cincinnati, 1843.
Wisconsin Colls.	Report and Collections of State Historical Society of Wisconsin.
Wisconsin Procs.	Proceedings of State Historical Society of Wisconsin.
Wislizenus[*A*]	Ein ausflug nach den Felsen-Gebirgen im jahre 1839, von F. A. Wislizenus, M.D., St. Louis, 1840.
Wislizenus[*B*]	A journey to the Rocky Mountains in the year 1839, by F. A. Wislizenus, M.D., translated from the German &c. by Frederick A. Wislizenus, St. Louis, 1912.
Wistar	Autobiography of Isaac Jones Wistar &c., Philadelphia, 1914.
Wood	Journal of John Wood &c. from Cincinnati to the gold diggings in California in the spring and summer of 1850, Chillicothe, 1852.
Work	Journal of John Work &c., ed. by William S. Lewis and Paul C. Phillips, Cleveland, 1923.
Wyeth, John B.	Oregon or a short history &c., by John B. Wyeth [actual author, Benjamin Waterhouse], Cambridge, 1833.
Wyeth, Nathaniel J.	Sources of the history of Oregon, vol. I, pts. 3-6, the correspondence and journals of Capt. Nathaniel J. Wyeth &c., Eugene, Ore., 1899.
Wyld[*A*]	Map of the Oregon districts and the adjacent country, by James Wyld, London, April 10, 1845.
Wyld[*B*]	Map of the United States & the relative position of the Oregon & Texas, by James Wyld, London, n.d.
Wyld[*C*]	Map, the United States & the relative position of the Oregon & Texas, by James Wyld, London, April 9, 1845.
Wyoming	Annals of Wyoming, pub. quarterly by the State Department of History, Cheyenne, Wyo.
Wyoming Forest	U.S. Dept. of Agriculture, Forest Service, map of Wyoming Nat'l Forest Wyoming sixth principal meridian, 1925.

Abbreviations Used in Footnotes

ABBREVIATIONS	
Wyoming Landmark	First biennial report of Historical Landmark Commission of Wyoming, 1929.
Yellowstone	Map, Yellowstone National Park, Big Horn Mts., prepared in office of Chief Engineer, Mil. Div. Mo., 1881, pub. by office of Chief of Engineers, U.S.A., 1881.

In addition to the above-mentioned books, journals and monographs, the footnotes cite (by specific reference to author, title, vol. and page) the following articles and journals:

AUTHOR	TITLE	PUBLISHED IN (For following publications see "Abbreviations" in above list)
——	Battle of Blue Water	*Neb. Pub.*, IX, XX
——	Ezekiel Williams &c.	*Missouri*, IV
——	Irving's Astoria	*Nation*
Adams, Cecilia Emily McMillan	Journal of	*Ore. Pioneer*, 1904
Allis, Samuel	Forty years among the indians &c.	*Neb. Hist. Trans.*, II
Allyn, Henry	Journal of	*Ore. Pioneer*, 1921
Barrett, Jay Amos	The Poncas	*Neb. Hist. Proc.*, II
Barry, J. Neilson	Archibald Pelton	*Wash. Hist. Quar.*, XIX
——	Broughton &c	*Ore. Hist. Soc. Quar.*, XXXII
——	Fort Reed &c.	*Idem*, XXXIV
——	Madame Dorion of the Astorians	*Idem*, XXX
——	The trail of the Astorians	*Idem*, XIII
——	Astorians &c.	*Wash. Hist. Quar.*, XXIV
Biddle, Henry J.	Wishram	*Ore. Hist. Soc. Quar.*, XXVII
Biddle, Maj. Thomas	Letter by	*Am. State, Indian*, II
Bolton, Herbert E.	New light on Manuel Lisa &c.	*Southwestern*, XVII
Bradley, James H.	Journal of	*Montana*, II
Cannon, Miles	Snake River in history	*Ore. Hist. Soc. Quar.*, XX
Comstock, O. C.	Sketch of the life of Hon. Robert Stuart	*Michigan*, III
Cross, Osborne	Journal of	*Exec. Doc.*
Deland, Charles E.	The aborigines of South Dakota	*South Dak.*, III
Dewolf, Captain David	Diary of the overland trail &c. of	*Illinois*
Douglas, David	Journal of	*Ore. Hist. Soc. Quar.*, IV; *Com. Bot. Mag.*, XVI
Douglas, Walter L.	Manuel Lisa	*Missouri*, III
Drum, Gen. Richard C.	Reminiscences of the indian fight at Ash Hollow	*Neb. Colls.*, XVI
Drumm, Stella M.	More about Astorians &c.	*Ore. Hist. Soc. Quar.*, XXIV
Duffield, Rev. George	Extracts from a funeral sermon	*Michigan*, III
Elliott, T. C.	Last will and testament of John Day	*Ore. Hist. Soc. Quar.*, XVII
——	The Dalles-Celilo portage	*Idem*, XVI
——	The discovery of the source of the Columbia River	*Idem*, XXVI
——	Where is Point Vancouver	*Idem*, XVIII
——	Wilson Price Hunt &c.	*Idem*, XXXII
Gilmore, M. R.	A study in the ethnobotany of the Omaha indians	*Neb. Colls.*, XVII
Green, Maj. A. L.	The Otoe indians	*Neb. Pub.*, XXI
Green, James	Incidents of the indian outbreak of 1864	*Idem*, XIX

Abbreviations Used in Footnotes

AUTHOR	TITLE	PUBLISHED IN (For following publications see "Abbreviations" in above list)
Hall, C. L.	The Grosventre spelling of the name Bird Woman	*North Dak.*, I
Hamilton, Wm.	Letter to R. W. Furnas	*Neb. Hist. Trans.*, I
Hastings, Loren B.	Diary of	*Ore. Pioneer*, 1923
Heydenburk, Martin	Incidents in the life of Robert Stuart	*Michigan*, III
Hill, A. T.	Mr. A. T. Hill's own story	*Neb. Hist. Mag.*, X
Howay, F. W.	Captain Cornelius Sowle &c.	*Wash. Hist. Quar.*, XXIV
Howell, J. E.	Diary of	*Ore. Hist. Soc. Quar.*, I
Kern, John T.	Journal of	*Ore. Pioneer*, 1917
Lee, Jason	Journal of	*Ore. Hist. Soc. Quar.*, XVII
Lyman, H. S.	Indian names	*Idem*, I
——	Reminiscences of Louis Labonte	*Idem*, I
McArthur, Lewis A.	Location of Point Vancouver &c.	*Idem*, XXXIV
Meany, Edmond S.	Origin of Washington geographic names	*Wash. Hist. Quar.*, XIV
Merrill, Moses	Extracts from diary of	*Neb. Hist. Trans.*, IV
Morehouse, George P.	The case for Kansas	*Neb. Hist. Mag.*, X
Munday, Frank J.	Pike-Pawnee village site &c.	*Idem*, X
Nesmith, James W.	Journal of	*Ore. Hist. Soc. Quar.*, VII
Ogden, Peter Skene	Journal of	*Idem*, X, XI
Porter, Kenneth W.	Roll of overland Astorians	*Idem*, XXXIV
Pratt, Orson	Journal of	*Mil. Star*, XII
Robinson, Doane	A history of the Dakota or Sioux indians	*South Dak.*, II
Ross, Alexander	Journal of	*Ore. Hist. Soc. Quar.*, XIV
Sheldon, Addison E.	Accounts of the Pawnees by early French explorers	*Neb. Hist. Mag.*, X
——	Where the Spanish flag came down &c.	*Idem*, X
Sibley, George C.	Statement by	*Missouri*, IV
Thayer, Gen. John M.	My very first visit to the Pawnee village &c.	*Neb. Hist. Proc.*, X
Thompson, David	Journal of	*Ore. Hist. Soc. Quar.*, XV
Whitman, Mrs. Marcus	Journal of	*Ore. Pioneer*, 1891
Williams, Ezekiel	Letter by	*Missouri*, IV
Work, John	Journal of	*Ore. Hist. Soc. Quar.*, X, XIII, XIV

ROBERT STUART
From a daguerreotype

ROBERT STUART

BIOGRAPHICAL NOTE

Desiring intimate acquaintance with our guide across the Oregon Trail, we must, at the outset, turn to the British Isles instead of to America's West.

In Perthshire, Scotland, nestling into the southern fringe of the highlands is the parish of Balquhidder and its immediate neighbor, the parish of Callander.

The parish of Balquhidder contains Strathyre, otherwise known as the valley of the Balvaig; and in this valley is the *clachan* or hamlet of Ruskachan,[1] which the highway splits into Easter Ruskachan and Wester Ruskachan.[2] Commonplaceness has not characterized this region of scenic beauty, for in the kirkyard of Balquhidder rests the body of "Rob Roy." And, if Stevenson's *Kidnapped* and Scott's *Lady of the Lake* be for our present purpose allowable as history, it was in a cottage near the kirkyard that Robin Oig and Alan Breck insulted each other with the bagpipe, while in a still earlier year, Clan Alpine's fiery cross, when summoning men to arms, "glanced like lightning up Strathyre."

The clachan of Ruskachan in Robert Stuart's childhood days consisted of 13 *crofts* or small farms, and on one of these crofts in the easterly section of the clachan his parents made their home.

Robert, third of the nine children[3] of John and Mary (Buchanan) Stewart, was born February 18, 1785, in the parish of Callander[4] and was baptized the following day in the parish of Balquhidder.[5]

His father, John Stewart—otherwise known in friendly fashion as *Ian Mohr na Coille* ("Big John of the Woods")—had been baptized June 23, 1756, was schoolmaster at Strathyre and Callander, and in his turn was son of James Stewart.[6] This James, Robert Stuart's grandfather,—oftentimes styled *Seumas na Coille* ("James in the Wood")—was born about 1720-25, farmed at Tigh-na-coil, Cuilt, Balquhidder, served a while as a private soldier in the 42nd Royal Highland Regiment ("Black Watch"), and died in 1796.[7]

Robert Stuart's mother had been baptized June 6, 1756, in Balquhidder parish and was daughter of John and Mary (Ferguson) Buchanan of Ballafoil.[8]

That both of Robert Stuart's parents at the time of their marriage resided in the clachan of Ruskachan appears from the Balquhidder parish register's entry which reads:

> "1780 Aprile 15. Contracted John Stewart and Mary Buchanan, both in Ruskachan in this parish. Dues, 2 shillings Sterling."[9]

They continued to reside in the clachan till at least the midsummer of 1797, as is shown by nine further entries[10] in that same parish register: seven of these giving Ruskachan as their domicile and two—of respectively July 12, 1781, and July 22, 1797—more specifically stating it as Easter Ruskachan.[11] There would be nothing to suggest that they later changed their abode, were it not for the facts that Robert Stuart years afterward referred to them as being "of Callander"[12] and that Callander was the place where, before 1806, his father died.[13] This possible shift of residence is, however, of little importance inasmuch as the distance from Ruskachan to the kirktown of Callander was only some eight and one-half miles by a road which could not boast of entire straightness.

During Robert's minority, which was spent at his parents' home, he, according to one of his biographers, obtained a secular schooling that was thorough, and also was "educated according to the usages of the Presbyterian Church in its doctrinal belief and in a religious regard for the Sabbath, a reverence for the Sacred Scriptures as the word of God, and a respect for the ministry of that word as a divine ordinance."[14] There is tradition that part of his training was had in Paris, but this seems to be without foundation and to be inconsistent with his reputed subsequent disclaimer of sufficient command of French to permit writing a letter in that language.[15]

In 1807, when twenty-two years of age, he left Scotland, and, at the suggestion of his uncle David Stuart, who then was one of the North West Company's "agents" in Lower Canada, went to Montreal and became a clerk of the North West Company. Incidentally, during the initial twelvemonth of his employment he studied French, having as his teacher a Roman Catholic priest.[16]

He retained his clerkship until late in the spring of 1810, when he first became associated with Astor's venture; but there is rumor, apparently erroneous, that he had made a somewhat earlier defection from the North West Company and had served a while in the office of the Attorney General of Lower Canada.[17] It was probably in the latter part of July, 1810, that he journeyed from Canada to the city of New York in anticipation of his sailing thence for the Pacific coast.[18] Though at the outset of his association with Astor he not improbably was intended for a Pacific Fur Company's clerkship,[19] he became, on September 5, 1810, one of this company's partners and was allotted two participating shares.[20]

His life between September 6, 1810, when he sailed from New York,[21] and June 23, 1813, when he returned there after his overland trip,[22] is in part described by his journal and travelling memoranda (pp. 3-263) and in other part by our foreword (pp. LXXV-LXXXI). The heroics involved in those thirty-three and one-half months make the rest of his career seem relatively uneventful, but it is necessary to recite his later doings in order that there may be reached a fair estimate of the man to whom America owes much.

On July 21, 1813, at New York, he married Elizabeth Emma Sullivan,[23] who had been born there June 27, 1792,[24] the daughter of John and Mary (Palmer) Sullivan of that city,[25] and had been educated at the Moravian Seminary in Bethlehem, Pa.[26] As Stuart's helpmeet, "who was loved by her husband with a devotion beautiful to behold, until his death,"[27] she proved herself "a brave, gifted woman"[28] of spirituality, high mentality and social grace, "having as the crowning glory of her life her unselfish and supreme devotion to the good of others."[29]

Promptly after his return from the West, Stuart began shuttling between New York City and Montreal, in order—partly on his own account and partly as Astor's representative—to collect furs from traders in the northern part of the state of New York and in eastern Canada.[30] This course he pursued until 1817, possibly enlarging it on one occasion when in 1815 he seemingly considered attempting to deal at long range with indians on the lower Missouri.[31] Among numerous extant letters written during this period are the following three which set forth his general status.

JOHN JACOB ASTOR IN NEW YORK CITY TO RAMSAY CROOKS, SEPT. 14, 1814[32]

". . . I suppose you have seen or heard of some of your old companions who I am told have returned.[33] I hope to see some of them here soon, as Mr R Stuart is gone towards the lines to procure a paſsport for them to come here . . . ."

ROBERT STUART TO RAMSAY CROOKS[34]

"Brooklyn 21st. March 1815

Dear Crooks—Long ere now you must have chalked me down in your Black Buke for a most ungrateful, lazy dog, but my dear fellow you must no longer remain under that surly impression, for be it known unto you, that almost ever since you last heard from me I have been Campaigning it between this and the Canadian Lines, partly for myself and partly for an old friend of ours; the result of this peregrination &c. you shall have at full length when we meet, which I hope you will accelerate as much as circumstances may permit. I am now in the full bustle of preparation for Albany, where business calls me for a few days, therefore have only time to give you the purport of a short tete-a-tete I had with the old Cock this morning, Viz—

That he is digesting a very extensive plan for establishing all the Indian Countries within the line of demarkation between G.B. & the U.S. and the probability is that a considerable time may elapse before that object can be brought to full maturity, as he wants an exclusive grant or privelege &c. &c. he added that it would be a pity, we should in the meantime be altogether inactive, therefore as he expects a parcel of Indian goods out in the Spring it is his wish that (Lob Man) you and myself would come to some arrangement either to purchase the goods and try the S.W. on our own Acct, or take them to Mackinac and give him a certain share of the profits, (as might be agreed upon)

These are the general outlines, from which you can very easily draw your conclusions regarding his views, which I really believe are as friendly toward us all, as his own dear interest will permit, for of that you are no doubt aware, he will never loose sight until some kind friend will put his or her fingers over his eyelids.

If something like this plan would meet your ideas, it will give me much pleasure for on your judgment I can entirely rely, knowing you are perfectly conversant in every branch of that business, and there is no mortal living, I would prefer being concerned with, of this I have no doubt you are perfectly convinced. On your arrival at New York have the goodness to come to Brooklyn before you wait on the old man as I would much like to have the first confab with you. Fat McKenzie[35] is here for the third time since his arrival in the white man's country, he pesters the old Tyger's soul out to employ him again, but he dislikes him very much, sometimes says that if he enters into the business upon the meditated large scale he should like to give him a situation in some retired corner where he could do no mischief &c. &c.

I am glad that he did not propose him as one of our party as I think it would break up the concern. Keep these affairs to yourself and hasten to meet your sincere friend

ROBERT STUART

All the good folks of this family desire me to rem. them very kindly to you—I no sooner told the old Lady[36] that I expected you soon, than she began to scour her little pot, and called for the supper to be got ready for her poor Scotchman. I really think the old lady has some design upon you; and whether you are to become my father, brother or son-in-law, you will always find me yours truly

R.S.

N.B. Betsy[37] is so glad at the near prospect of your coming amongst us, that if I did not depend much on my own qualifications I assure you, it staggers my faith not a little. Magee[38] desires his best wishes to you, but is too devilish lazy to write, but promises to make up for it in chat when you meet."

JOHN JACOB ASTOR TO CHARLES GRATIOT OF ST. LOUIS, MAY 26, 1816[39]

". . . Mr Stuart & Mr Crooks engaged me Last year to Import some goods for them for the purpose of trading with Indians & & in your quater of the Cauntry."

In 1817 Stuart moved to Michilimacinac, Mich., and by agreement with Astor became co-agent with Ramsay Crooks at the local trading-post which the American Fur Company had just then acquired for the centre of its dealings on the Great Lakes and in the upper valley of the Mississippi River.[40] There Stuart had direct charge of the fur gatherers and the outdoor operations, Crooks, as his superior in rank, being the general manager of all the business in this same region.[41] When in 1822 Crooks was transferred to the general managership of the entire affairs of the American Fur Company—which had enlarged its scope by creating a so-called Western Department—and began spending less time at Michilimacinac, Stuart was elevated to the position vacated by Crooks.[42] This position he held until 1834.[43] Stuart's responsibility was considerable, since the force immediately under him "comprised about four hundred clerks and traders, together with some two thousand voyageurs."[44]

During his stay at Michilimacinac, Stuart's interest was not wholly limited to his company's commerce. From the outset he and his wife generously befriended the local missionaries.[45] For the indians' sake, he was an advocate of temperance in the use of intoxicants,[46] even though there is sure foundation for accusing him of placing large amounts of liquor in the hands of the traders.[47]

He induced Mrs. Henry Munroe Fisher to start a local boarding school at which traders' daughters were taught reading, writing, sewing and housekeeping.[48]

He served, at least in 1825, as a judge of the County Court of Michilimacinac County.[49]

Another event was his spiritual awakening in approximately 1828 or 1829; this was the result of a religious revival that was then dominating Michigan. His previously passive belief was transmuted into a cogent faith which endured until his death.[50] He and his wife became zealous members of the local Protestant church;[51] he strove for a better control of his temper,[52] his advocacy of temperance waxed more earnest,[53] and he turned himself into a rigorous observer of the Sabbath.[54]

This Sabbath homage, the strictness of which he never outgrew, was so complete as to surround his name, after his death, with a myth to the effect that, "during his journey from the Pacific to the Atlantic, he invariably rested on that sacred day, nor suffered his company to do else. And he has often been heard to say when commending the Sabbath, 'That mainly owing to that circumstance did he attribute his rapid and successful transit, in twelve months, from the mouth of the river Oregon to the city of New York.' "[55] The myth is destroyed by Stuart's own journal and travelling memoranda, which show that, of the 43 Sundays occurring between the time of his leaving Astoria and the date of his arrival in St. Louis, 23 were spent in travel, one in opening Hunt's caches, and but 19 in quiescence; and that, of these 19 Sabbaths of inactivity, 15 of them were passed in the two so-called "winter quarters," the stays at each of which Stuart thought to be required by conditions of weather and of food-supply.

His character when he was first at Michilimacinac is thus described by Gurdon Saltonstall Hubbard, a contemporary employee: "Mr. Stewart was one of those stern Scotchmen, who gave his orders abruptly and expected them obeyed to the letter, yet a man of a deal of humor and fond of fun. He had a fund of anecdotes and was excellent company. Though he often gave unnecessary orders and required everything to be done neatly and promptly, he was kind and sympathetic. He was quick tempered and wholly fearless, and the clerks knew that his commands were to be obeyed to the letter, but that if their duties were properly performed they would receive full credit and be treated with kindness and consideration."[56]

In these early days at Michilimacinac, Stuart, as a director of rough men in a business conducted on the frontier and beyond it, was occasionally compelled to use physical violence in order to maintain discipline.[57] Hubbard describes the thrashing of one voyageur,[58] while Charles C. Trowbridge (who first met Stuart in the summer of 1820 and was thenceforward his intimate friend) mentions an episode wherein Stuart seized an ebony ruler and with it floored a drunken *engagé* who came too near his desk.[59]

But, with Stuart's spiritual awakening, all this vehemence disappeared.[60] "John Agnew, a good natured, roystering ferryman, collector of the port, was much attached to Mr. and Mrs. Stuart. He watched Mr. Stuart's conduct very closely after his declared conversion, and when he saw an employé drop a package of furs into the lake, and heard Mr. Stuart tell him in a comparatively subdued tone to fish it out, instead of knocking him from the little wharf into the lake, he turned about and said 'no doubt Robert Stuart is a converted man.' "[61]

Stuart had, however, not become spineless, for it seems that in 1832, the *engagés* throughout Michigan being somewhat truculent, he wrote to Morgan L. Martin, a member of the Michigan legislature, asking for the introduction of a bill to revive the governmental whipping-post.[62]

In contrast with these accusations of severity is the following letter which appeared in a Detroit newspaper[63] after Stuart's death:

> "Mr. Editor: If you can afford me room, I shall be glad to say a few words in reference to the character of this *truly good man*, who

has recently been stricken down among us. It is gratitude which prompts the offering, and not a desire to eulogize the dead.

In the spring of 1833 I was a member of a Western College, and being in bad health, I resolved to spend my vacation in the upper country. On my way across Lake Huron, I fell in company with a son of Mr. Stuart, who was returning home to visit his parents, from an Eastern school. We arrived in Mackinaw Sabbath evening, and as I was a stranger on the Island, I determined not to go ashore. On the arrival of young Stuart, his father questioned him as to his fellow passengers, and among others he remembered the name of the invalid student. Early the next morning, I received an invitation from Mr. Stuart to dine with him that day. Accordingly I brushed up as well as I could and presented myself at his door. I was cordially received, and in half an hour's conversation he had my history, which was a sorrowful one. I had left the green mountains of Vermont several years before in perfect health, and with money sufficient to complete my education; but after three years study in a billious climate, I had broken down, and had been all winter lying sick at a public house, among strangers, until the little money I had was nearly spent. I was on my way to St. Maries, where I hoped to improve my health in which case I might return to college and to my friends; but if not, there was no alternative—I must go into the Indian country, as hundreds had done before. He said to me that I would find Mackinaw a more desirable place to rusticate in than the Sault, and as he scanned my pale and care-worn countenance, and thin and thread-bare coat, with a countenance benignant as an angels, he kindly said. 'If you will remain with us, *my table and bed shall be as free to you as David*.'[64]—My heart was too full: I could not even thank him, but left immediately, as the vessel was ready to sail. Years have passed since this little incident occurred, and he probably never thought of it again, but it touched a cord in my heart which will not cease to vibrate to all eternity; and I can say of him as his favorite bard and gifted countryman Burns said of his friend, the Earl of Glencairn, at his death:

'The bridegroom may forget the bride
Was made his wedded wife yestreen,
The monarch may forget the crown,
That on his head an hour has been,

The mother may forget the child,
That smiles so sweetly on her knee,
But I'll remember thee *Glencairn*,
And all that thou hast done for me.'

W. A. B.

DETROIT, Nov. 8th, 1848."

When in June, 1834, Stuart was notified that Astor's controlling interest in the American Fur Company's so-called Northern Department (as the Michilimacinac district was styled after 1821) had been sold to Ramsay Crooks and an Eastern syndicate, Stuart retired from the company.[65] He purchased land in Detroit, built a dwelling-house on it and moved thither with his wife, his children and his aged, beloved uncle David Stuart.[66] Incidentally, this house on Jefferson Avenue, traditionally the earliest brick house in the city, was his home till he died, and remained his widow's residence until her death.

Having thus wholly withdrawn from active participation in the fur industry, he turned to trafficking in land situated in Detroit and elsewhere in Michigan as well as in Wisconsin,[67] being associated in some of the ventures with Astor and Crooks, notably in an investment at Green Bay, Wis.[68]

But he did not content himself with mere commercialism. On November 12, 1835, he was installed as an elder of the Presbyterian Church (present-day First Presbyterian Church) of Detroit, an office he retained until his death.[69]

When in that year 1835 the Presbyterian Synod of Michigan decided to establish an institution of higher learning, it created for the purpose a board of 10 trustees, of whom Stuart was one. He was forthwith made secretary of the board. In 1839, with two other representatives of the trustees, he petitioned the legislature to charter the institution under its suggested name of Michigan College. Jealousies as to the proposed name and location and widespread opposition to fostering a privately managed college developed among citizens of the state. However, the legislature did grant a charter, but it prescribed that the name be Marshall College. Financial depression ensuing and public interest veering to the recently formed and state-controlled University of Michigan, the infant Marshall College never grew beyond its preparatory department, and, by the early part of 1842, ceased activity and began dissolution.[70]

In 1839 Stuart, as a nominee of the Whig party, was elected a director of the State Bank of Michigan,[71] and throughout the year 1840 he was state treasurer of Michigan.[72]

He served as federal superintendent of the affairs of indians in the region of Michigan from 1841 till April, 1845, when he was forced to resign in order that he might be supplanted by a man of opposite political views.[73] During his term of office he had negotiated on the government's behalf a treaty with the Chippewa tribe.[74]

In 1845 Stuart, as representative of various Eastern holders of Illinois & Michigan Canal bonds, went to Chicago on business connected with these bonds. There he became secretary of the canal company's trustees, a position he held until he died. In the spring of 1848 he had expected to resign and return to Detroit, but was persuaded to continue for prospectively another year.[75]

In the mid-autumn of 1848 he contracted a cold which doubtless was the immediate cause of his death, although by Saturday night, October 28, he seemed to have recovered. That very night, with book in hand, he sat before the fireplace in his room at the Sherman House, his hotel in Chicago. Early Sunday morning, however, his wife, hearing a gasp, attempted to rouse him, but found that already he had quietly passed beyond the horizon.[76] In his Bible[77] she later wrote: "Our head, my earthly <u>all</u> was suddenly called to his heavenly rest! on Sunday 29th October 1848 Be ye also ready—What I say unto you, I say unto all Watch! !—." A newspaper obituary said of him: "He leaveth behind him the incense of a good name."[78]

After the funeral in the Detroit Presbyterian Church on November 12, 1848,[79] he was buried in Elmwood Cemetery, Detroit, in a lot which later was to contain the graves of his widow, eight of his nine children and four of his grandchildren.

His estate, which he willed to his widow for life with remainder share and share alike *per stirpes* to his children,[80] amounted, at his death, to $78,217.93[81] and, at his widow's death, to $161,221.44.[82]

His widow died September 26, 1866, at her home in Detroit.[83]

The nine children of Robert and Elizabeth (Sullivan) Stuart and these children's descendants so far as we have ascertained were as follows:

(I) MARY ELIZABETH STUART

B. June 27, 1814 at New York City;[84] d. June 4, 1878 at Minneapolis, Minn;[85] and buried in Elmwood Cemetery, Detroit, Mich.

Md., (1st), July 18, 1834 at Michilimacinac, Mich., George Franklin Turner,[86] who, b. March 20, 1807 at Boston, Mass., was apptd. July 23, 1833 assist. surg. U.S. Army; promoted Jan. 1, 1840 to maj. surgeon;[87] and d. of yellow fever[88] Oct. 17, 1854 at Corpus Christi, Texas.[89] There were by this marriage five children:

(A) Mary Sullivan, b. Oct. 24, 1835 at Detroit, Mich.[90] and d. there March 21[91] or 25,[92] 1837.

(B) Robert Stuart, b. April 4, 1838 at St. Augustine, Fla.;[93] md. Sept. 4, 1865[94] at Madison, N. J.[95] his first cousin and step-sister, Elizabeth Emma Baker; and d. Dec. 29, 1885.[96]

(C) Kate Stuart, b. Dec. 22, 1841 at Fort Snelling in present-day Minnesota;[97] and d. of yellow fever[98] Oct. 17, 1854 at Corpus Christi, Tex.[99]

(D) George Franklin, Jr., b. Nov. 20, 1848 at Detroit, Mich.;[100] and d. July 2, 1850[101] at Morristown, N. J.[102]

(E) Elizabeth Emma Billings, b. April 8, 1853 at Fort Croghan, Tex.;[103] md. Sept. 5, 1876 Dr. Frederick Alanson Dunsmoor, U. S. A.;[104] and d. Jan. 21, 1913 at St. Paul, Minn.[105]

Her seven children were

(1) Frederick Irving, b. May 18, 1879; d. May 21, 1879.

(2) Elizabeth A. and

(3) Mary Stuart (twins), each b. Dec. 14, 1880 and each d. March 28, 1881.

(4) Marion, b. Nov. 18, 1882; and d. Feb. 17, 1884.
(5) Marjorie, b. Dec. 30, 1884; md. in 1913 W. Fred'k McCartney, and had one child, Fred'k Laton, b. Jan. 13, 1914.
(6) Elizabeth, b. Feb. 11, 1886; md. in 1910 Homer Pierce Clark and had five children as follows:
  (a) Robert Stuart, b. Oct. 31, 1917.
  (b) Thomas Kimball, b. Oct. 6, 1921.
  (c) Elizabeth Turner, b. Oct. 19, 1923.
  (d) Catherine Pierce, b. Dec. 12, 1925.
  (e) Helen Dunsmoor, b. Jan. 1, 1928.

Md., (2nd), April 18, 1856 at Detroit, Mich. William Chapman Baker[106] who, b. Jan. 27, 1809 at Natchez, Miss., d. Jan. —, 1901 at Grand Rapids, Mich. and was, at the time of the marriage, widower of her (Mary Elizabeth's) sister Kate.[107]

Her one child by this second marriage was William Chapman, Jr., who, b. Jan. 15, 1858 at Morristown, N. J.,[108] d. Aug. 22, 1887;[109] md. in 1877 Frederika M. Schneider. Their three children were
(1) William Chapman III, b. July 24, 1878; d. June 26, 1879.
(2) Robert Stuart, b. Nov. 17, 1879; d. —— — 1915; md. (1st), Elizabeth —— and, (2nd), —— ——.
(3) Looe, b. Jan. 18, 1884; md., (1st), in 1907 Charlotte Milburn and, (2nd), in —— Margaret Classy. By this second marriage there were three children as follows: Mary, b. 1919; Jeanne, b. 1919; Looe, b. 1924.

(II) DAVID STUART

B. March 12, 1816 at New York City;[110] d. on the night of Sept. 11 or early morning of Sept. 12, 1868 at Detroit, Mich,[111] and was buried there in Elmwood Cemetery.

After a schooling received partly in the East, he about 1836 became a law student in the Detroit office of Theodore Romeyn, transferring in 1838 to the office of A. D. Frazer in that same city.[112] After admission to the bar, he was in private practice in Detroit until 1849, when he was appointed prosecuting atty. of Wayne County, Mich.[113] This office being made elective, he was elected for the ensuing term.[114]

On Oct. 6, 1842, he md. Sarah Benson[115] who, the third child of John and Sarah (Lawrence) Benson of N. Y. City, was born in that city March 31, 1820[116] and d. March 23, 1895[117] at Detroit.

As a Democrat, Stuart was elected representative from 1st dist. of Mich. in 33rd U. S. Cong. (Mar. 4, 1853-Mar. 3, 1855).[118] A candidate for re-election to the 34th Cong., he was defeated by the wave of Republicanism which then was sweeping over Mich.[119] Forthwith he moved to Chicago, Ill., where he resumed the active practice of law.[120]

At the outbreak of the Civil War he espoused the Northern cause.[121] Commissioned lieut. col. 42nd Ill. inf. July 22, 1861; col. 55th Ill. inf. Oct. 31, 1861, he was stationed during the autumn of 1861 at Benton Barracks, Mo. In March 1862 he as colonel commanded the 2nd brigade of Sherman's division at the Battle of Shiloh, where he was wounded. In the subsequent advance from Memphis to Arkansas Post he commanded the 4th brigade of Sherman's division; and, at Vicksburg on Nov. 28, 1862 when Brig. Gen. Morgan L. Smith was wounded, he took command of the 2nd division of the 13th corps. He subsequently commanded the 5th division of that corps. Having been frequently mentioned for gallantry in action, he was nominated Nov. 29, 1862 brig. gen. U. S. vols.; but, the U. S. Senate failing to confirm the appointment before adjourning on March 11, 1863, he on April 4, 1863 was relieved from his divisional command; and, having the previous day resigned his commission as col., he was out of the army. The order relieving him (issued by Assist. Adj. Gen. John A. Rawlins by command of Maj. Gen. U. S. Grant), after reciting the Senate's negation, stated: "In thus relieving Brigadier General Stuart from duty, the general commanding deems it but justice to a brave, intelligent, and patriotic officer to express his deep regret at the loss to the country of his valuable services in the field, where, by meritorious action, he won the right to the position the favor of the President had conferred."[122] Gen. W. T. Sherman later wrote concerning Stuart: "I esteemed him very highly, and was actually mortified that the service should thus be deprived of so excellent and gallant an officer."[123]

After retiring from the army Stuart practised law in New Orleans, La., until, his health impaired, he returned to Detroit in vain hope that change of climate would prove beneficial.[124]

Following his death, the Detroit Bar Assn. held a commemorative meeting on Sept. 12, 1868 and adopted a resolution highly eulogizing him.[125]

His six children were

(A) Robert, b. June 23, 1843 at Detroit;[126] d. Apr. 22, 1854.[127]

(B) Marion, b. May 29, 1845 at Detroit;[128] md. there Dec. 25, 1867 Lieut. Com. (later Com.) Edward Terry, U. S. N.[129] (b. Jan. 24, 1839; d. June 1, 1882); and d. childless Aug. 2, 1906.[130]

(C) John, b. Jan. 4, 1847 at Detroit;[131] d. May 7, 1901 at Jacksonvilla, Fla.[132] He m. in 1876 Louise Foote who, dau. of John T. Foote of Morristown, N. J., was b. Feb. 7, 1850 and d. at Jacksonville, Fla., June 16, 1902. Their two children were

(1) Ellen Foote, b. July 28, 1877;

md. (1st), Oct. 17, 1899, Lieut. (later Rear Adm'l) Victor Blue (b. Dec. 6, 1865; d. Jan. 22, 1928.) Their two children were

(a) John Stuart, b. Apr. 29, 1902.

(b) Victor, Jr., b. Dec. 25, 1913 and now lieut. U. S. N.

md. (2nd), in 1930 Rear Adm'l (Ret.) Frederick Brewster Bassett, U. S. N.

(2) Marion Louise, b. July 6, 1879; md. in 1913 Dr. Charles Edward Terry.

(D) Maynard, b. Jan. 29, 1850; d. Apr. 4, 1850.[133]

(E) Sarah Lawrence, b. May 23, 1851 at Detroit;[134] d. Sept. 23, 1881.[135] She md. Oct. 3, 1871 Lieut. Com. (later Rear Adm'l) Philip Henry Cooper, U. S. N.[136] (b. Aug. 5, 1844; d. Dec. 29, 1912). Their two children were

(1) Stuart, b. Apr. 17, 1873; d. Oct. 8, 1924; was in U. S. Army; md. in 1898 Elizabeth McDougall. Their three children were

(a) Stuart, d. in infancy.

(b) Elizabeth, d. in infancy.

(c) Elizabeth, b. Feb. 6, 1911; md. in 1931 Fred'k A. Zitkowski.

(2) Philip Benson, b. Oct. 16, 1877; md. in 1899 Eleanor May Burnham (b. Apr. 4, 1878). Their five children were

(a) Eleanor Burnham, b. Mar. 7, 1900; md. in 1922 C. Gilmore McKinney, U. S. N. (b. Jan. 28, 1898). Their two children were Charles G. (b. July 14, 1923) and Jane (b. Aug. 26, 1926).

(b) Philip H., b. Mar. 7, 1900.

(c) Sarah Lawrence, b. July 14, 1901; md. in 1922 Francis E. Fairman, U. S. N. (b. Oct. 15, 1899).

Their three children were Francis E. Jr. (b. May 30, 1923), Philip Benson (b. Sept. 11, 1924) and Sarah Lawrence (b. Nov. 3, 1926).

(d) William Woodbury, b. Oct. 5, 1904; md. in 1925 Virginia Howard Milner (b. June 24, 1905). Their one child was Virginia Howard (b. Dec. 23, 1927).

(e) Robert Stuart, b. Jan. 23, 1909, and being the person whose intelligent, tireless and endearing efforts have gathered most of the data in this genealogical survey of Robert Stuart's descendants.

(F) Lefferts Brevoort, b. May 9, 1859, at Chicago, Ill.,[137] d. Feb. 1, 1865.[138]

(III) KATE STUART

B. July 20 or 21, 1820 at Michilimacinac, Mich.;[139] d. Oct. 4, 1853[140] at Morristown, N. J.[141]

Md. June 23, 1842 at Detroit, Mich., the William Chapman Baker[142] hereinbefore described under caption of her sister, Mary Elizabeth Stuart. Their six children were

(A) Mary Stuart, b. April 14, 1843 at New Orleans, La.;[143] md. Sept 19, 1867 William Newton Ladue.[144] Their seven children were

(1) William Baker, b. Nov. 26, 1868 in Mich.; cadet U. S. A. 1890; addit. 2nd lieut. engineers June 12, 1894; 2nd lieut. Jan. 6, 1896; 1st lieut. July 5, 1898; capt. Apr. 13, 1903; md. in 1898 Evelyn Knight. Their two children were

(a) Louise, b. Apr. 16, 1899; md. in 1930 Lieut. Gordon Hall, U. S. M. C.

(b) Laurence, U. S. A., b. June 14, 1903.

(2) Louise Angell, b. Sept. 2, 1870 at Morristown, N. J.; d. Sept 7, 1871 at Detroit, Mich.

(3) Kate Stuart, b. Oct. 19, ——; md. in 1909 Arthur C. Crombie.

(4) Laurence, b. Sept. 8, 1874 at Detroit, Mich.; d. Aug. 3, 1875.

(5) George Franklin, b. Aug. 26, 1877 at Detroit, Mich.; md. in 1908 Maud Crombie.

(6) Mary Stuart, b. June 30, 1879 at Detroit, Mich.; d. July 9, 1880.

(7) Robert Stuart, b. Nov. 4, 1883 at Salem, Ore.; md. in 1913 Kathleen Seymour Cram. Their two children were Mary Elizabeth (b. Jan. 10, 1914) and Robert Stuart (b. July 9, 1918).

(B) Elizabeth Emma, b. Nov. 9, 1845 at New Orleans, La.;[145] md. Sept. 4, 1865,[146] at Madison, N. J., her first cousin and step-brother Robert Stuart Turner (for whom see *ante*) and d. July 23, 1923.

(C) Sarah Morris, b. Nov. 24, 1847 at Chicago, Ill.;[147] d. Feb. 15, 1851.[148]

(D) Eliza Wardell, b. Aug. 8, 1849 at Skaneateles, N. Y.;[149] d. July 26, 1897.[150]

(E) Looe, b. July 29, 1851 at Morristown, N. J.;[151] md. in 1887 Elizabeth Saunders. Their two children were, (1) William Chapman, b. Apr. 3, 1891 and md. Julia Read; and (2), Alice, b. ———.

(F) Kate Stuart, b. Sept. 26, 1853 at Morristown, N. J.;[152] d. Feb. 21, 1878 at Minneapolis, Minn.; md. Sept. 5, 1876 at Minneapolis, W. E. Burwell. Their one child was Kate, who, b. Feb. 1, 1878, md. in 1909 Horace Lowry, and had two children: Thomas (b. Jan. 13, 1910) and Goodrich (b. in 1912).

(IV) JOHN STUART

B. March 6, 1822 at Michilimacinac, Mich.;[153] apptd. June 21, 1839 acting midshipman, U. S. N.; warranted March 30, 1841; passed midshipman July 2, 1845; master Oct. 15, 1853. Prior to his promotion to master he was, on April 19, 1853, detached from his ship, U. S. S. Columbia, and granted sick leave: a leave which, because of his illness (tuberculosis),[154] was presently modified into waiting orders.[155] On quitting his ship, he went to his mother's home in Detroit, Mich., where he remained until his death[156] on Oct. 27, 1853.[157] Buried in Elmwood Cemetery, Detroit. His funeral at Detroit on Oct. 29, 1853 was, so a contemporary local paper states, attended by the Grayson Light Guards in full uniform.[158]

On May 15, 1850 he md. Lavinia Field.[159] Their one child, Fanny

Ella, was b. Feb. 1, 1852 at Port Richmond, Staten Island, N. Y.,[160] and md., (1st), —— Hurt and (2nd), J. Howard Bridge; and d. —— ——.[161]

(V) ROBERT STUART, JR.

B. Oct. 8, 1825[162] at New York City;[163] apptd. Oct. 19, 1841 acting midshipman, U. S. N.; warranted Apr. 20, 1843; passed midshipman Oct. 10, 1847; master Sept. 14, 1855; lieut. Sept. 15, 1855. On Apr. 13, 1857, while serving on U. S. S. Dale, he resigned from the navy; his resignation being accepted three days later.[164]

After the outbreak of the Civil War he entered the U. S. Army. On June 10, 1863 he, as 2nd lieut. of the 2nd N. Y. cavalry, was commended for gallantry in an engagement the previous day at Brandy Station, Va.[165] On July 30, 1863, when acting as officer of the day of the 2nd cavalry brigade of Gen. Gregg's division, he was drowned in the Warrenton River in Virginia.[166]

On Aug. 3, 1848 he md. Ellen Cairns,[167] who d. in 1893. Their three children were

- (A) Virginia, b. June 6, 1849 at Erie, Pa.;[168] md. in 1881 Rev. Alexander Mackay-Smith (later Protestant Episcopal Bishop of Pennsylvania). Their three children were
  - (1) Helen Stuart, b. Sept. 27, 1882; md. Charles L. Marlatt.
  - (2) Virginia Grace, b. June 26, 1884; md. in 1921 Karl Boy-ed.
  - (3) Gladys Alden, b. Oct. 11, 1886; md. in 1916 William Bell Watkins.
- (B) William Cairns, b. Oct. 22, 1850 at Detroit, Mich.;[169] d. in 1911. He md. in 1879 Margaret I. Hartwell. Their four children were
  - (1) William Cairns, Jr., b. Sept. 24, 1883.
  - (2) Ellen, b. June 10, 1888.
  - (3) Clarence, b. in 1889.
  - (4) Margaret, b. —— ——.
- (C) Robert, b. Apr. 8, 1853 at Spezzia, Italy;[170] d. in 1903.
  Md., (1st), in 1877 Evelyn Marks, and,
  (2nd), in 1885 Emma Carradine. The one child of this second marriage was Robert, Jr. (b. May 18, 1887).

(VI) MARION STUART

B. May 18, 1828 at Michilimacinac, Mich.; d. Aug. 3, 1835 at Detroit, Mich.[171]

(VII) WILLIAM MAYNARD STUART

B. Apr. 14, 1830 at Michilimacinac, Mich.; d. Apr. 25, 1836 at Detroit, Mich.[172]

(VIII) CELIA STUART

B. June 3, 1832 at Michilimacinac, Mich.; d. March 18, 1836 at Detroit, Mich.[173]

(IX) WILLIAM MAYNARD STUART

(The second of this name)

B. June 2, 1837 at Detroit, Mich.; d. Aug. 10, 1838 at presumably Detroit.[174]

Notes to Biographical Note

1 Locally pronounced "Rūsgan."

2 See current ordnance map of the region in question; this map being one of the series published from time to time by the Ordnance Survey of Great Britain.

3 *I.e.*, *James*, baptized July 12, 1781; *John*, baptized June 13, 1783; *Robert*, baptized February 20, 1785; *David*, baptized August 30, 1787; *James*, baptized April 19, 1789; *Janet*, baptized August 10, 1791; *Alexander*, baptized March 3, 1793; *Mary*, baptized May 24, 1795; and *Kathrine*, baptized July 22, 1797; for all of which see Balquhidder parish register, now in the General Register House at Edinburgh, Scotland. Incidentally, each member of the entire clan seems to have reserved the privilege of spelling the name as either "Stuart" or "Stewart."

4 Under the captions of Births in *Bible* [*A*] is the following entry in Robert Stuart's handwriting: "Robert Stuart, at Callander Perth Shire, Scotland, on 19th Feby 1785—."

5 The parish register described in note 3 contains an entry: "1785 February 20. John Stewart and Mary Buchanan his wife in Ruskachan, had a child baptised called *Robert*."

6 All this information was furnished us by Mrs. Margaret Haig Stuart, wife of Alexander Stuart, Esq., who, a grandson of Robert Stuart's brother Alexander, is an advocate in Edinburgh and lately was General Superintendent of the Local Government Board.

7 All this information we obtained from Mrs. Margaret Haig Stuart. She adds that this James Stewart ("James in the Wood"), who about 1748 married Katharine Stewart, was a son of James and Janet (Ferguson) Stewart and a grandson of Alexander Stewart.

8 All this information we received from Mrs. Margaret Haig Stuart. She adds that Mary (Ferguson) Buchanan, baptized February 6, 1726, was a daughter of Donald and Janet (Stewart) Ferguson.

9 This register is now in the General Register House at Edinburgh, Scotland.

10 These nine entries relate to the baptisms mentioned in note 3.

11 See note 3 for the style of each of the nine entries.

12 Under the caption of Marriages in *Bible* [*A*] is the following entry in Robert Stuart's handwriting: "Robert Stuart (son of John Stuart & Mary Buchanan of Callander, Perth Shire Scotland, to Elizabeth Emma Sullivan daughter of John Sullivan of Irland & Mary Palmer of New York, on 21 July 1813—."

13 This information as to the place and approximate date of death we obtained from Mrs. Margaret Haig Stuart.

14 *Michigan*, III, pp. 57, 61. For various statements concerning Stuart, see *idem.*, I, p. 425, III, pp. 52-65, IV, p. 85, VI, p. 348, IX, pp. 257, 258, XI, pp. 193, 196, XII, pp. 643, 644, XIV, p. 416, XXI, p. 596, XXVI, pp. 285, 295, 296, XXVII, pp. 566, 574, 598, 600, XXVIII, pp. 190, 191, XXX, pp. 531-549, 578, XXXVI, p. 507, XXXVII, pp. 236-238; as also printed copy of address which, on the subject of Robert Stuart, was delivered by W. M. Ferry in November, 1876 at Grand Haven.

15 According to *Wisconsin Colls.*, XIV, p. 40, Elizabeth Thérèse Baird, who knew Robert Stuart at Michilimacinac, states that he was educated in Paris. However, *Wisconsin Colls.*, XX, pp. 128, 129, prints a letter dated at Michilimacinac, Mich., October 28, 1819 and which, though unsigned, its editor attributes to Stuart's authorship. This letter contains the following phrasing: "as I do Not Write French Sufficiently Well to Give your oncles the Mess[rs] Grignons My Sentiments on the above Subject, you will Much oblige Me, by Making them acquainted with what I have here Stated."

16 *Michigan*, III, pp. 57, 61. This study of French seems not to have been thorough enough to invalidate the disclaimer described in note 15 *ante*.

17 Although *Michigan*, III, p. 61, states that Stuart thus served in the Attorney General's office, Monsieur F. J. Audet, as Chief of the Information of the Canadian Public Archives at Ottawa, and Monsieur Pierre-Georges Roy, as Archiviste de la Province de Quebec, each report that, despite careful search, they have been unable to find any document disclosing such service. Monsieur Roy adds in effect that, though "Nous avons, aux Archives Provinciales, un index assez complet de tous les départements du Gouvernement, de 1797 à 1840, et dans aucun de ces index je ne trouve de références relatives à Monsieur Stuart," the absence of Stuart's name does not prove that he may not possibly have been "un des petits employés du département du Procureur général. Ces employés étaient payés à la journée, ce qui fait que nous ne voyons pas leur nom dans les Comptes Publics du temps."

18 *Franchere* [*A*], pp. 11, 13, [*B*], pp. 23, 25.

19 *Ross* [*A*], p. 8.

20 *Pacific Fur*, organization agreement.

21 *Franchere* [*A*], p. 19, [*B*], p. 32; *Ross* [*A*], p. 13.

22 On July 7, 1813 John Jacob Astor wrote from New York City to John Dorr and stated, among other things: "Mr. Stuart arrived here 14 days ago . . . ." *Baker-Astor* [*A*], p. 9.

23 See note 12 for Bible entry made by Robert Stuart. In addition to this entry in *Bible* [*A*], there is in *Bible* [*B*] under the caption of Marriages the following entry in the handwriting of Robert Stuart's wife: "Robert Stuart (Son of John Stuart & Mary Buchanan) of Perthshire Scotland—to Elizabeth Emma Sullivan—Daughter of John Sullivan & Mary Palmer of N York—On 21st July 21st 1813—."

Contrary to the proof of Stuart's marriage to Elizabeth Emma Sullivan, some of his posthumous biographers (see, for instance, *Michigan*, III, pp. 54, 58) have arbitrarily created a "Miss Catherine Sullivan" and have had Stuart not only secretly marry her before his sailing in 1810, but also delay the marriage's announcement until after his return from the Pacific coast. This erroneous statement developed probably from some garbled account of the elopement of his sister-in-law, Ellen Sullivan, with Acting-Lieutenant James Sidney Coxe, U. S. N., an elopement which occurred immediately before Coxe's departing in 1815 upon a voyage. This suggested explanation we have direct from Mrs. Alexander Mackay-Smith, who, a granddaughter of Robert Stuart, conversed in her childhood with both his widow and the widow of James Sidney Coxe.

24 Under the caption of Births there is in *Bible* [*B*] the following entry in the handwriting of Robert Stuart's wife: "Elizabeth E. Sullivan 27th June 1792 at New York—" and in *Bible* [*A*] the following entry in the handwriting of Robert Stuart: "Elizabeth E. Sullivan at New York 27th June 1792—."

25 See notes 12, 23.

26 Miss Sullivan's attending this institution (present-day Moravian Seminary and College for Women) is established by a letter which, under date of August 13, 1931, the institution's president wrote Mr. Robert Stuart Cooper. See also obituary of her in September 29, 1866 of *Detroit Tribune* (newspaper), p. 1, column 2.

27 *Michigan*, III, p. 54.

28 *Idem*, III, p. 54.

29 Quoted from obituary mentioned in note 26.

30 *Porter*, pp. 266, 687-689, 692, 693, 700, 701, 706, 707. See also *Baker-Astor* [*A*] at the hereinafter cited pages, which contain copies of letters written by John Jacob Astor in 1813 to Charles Gratiot on June 23 (p. 9), to John Dorr on July 7 (p. 14), to George Ehninger on November 10 (pp. 100, 101); in 1814 to Ramsay Crooks on September 14 (pp. 281, 282), to Robert Stuart on September 6 (p. 275), October 8 (p. 307), October 25 (p. 333), October 29 (p. 344), November 2 (pp. 347, 348), November 11 (pp. 349, 350), November 17 (p. 353); and in 1815 to Robert Stuart on January 6 (p. 424), January 18 (p. 435), February 2 (pp. 452, 453), February 6 (pp. 460, 461), February 17 (p. 476): these letters relating to various of Stuart's movements.

31 John Jacob Astor's letter of May 26, 1816 to Charles Gratiot, which letter is quoted in our text, p. XL.

32 *Baker-Astor* [*A*], pp. 281-282.

33 Doubtless meaning David Stuart, Gabriel Franchere, John Clarke, Donald McKenzie and various other former Astorians who, leaving Fort George (Astoria) in the "Grand Brigade" of April 4, 1814, travelled overland in Canada and so reached the East. *Franchere* [*A*], pp. 206 *et seq.*, [*B*], pp. 263 *et seq.*; *Henry-Thomp.*, pp. 865, 871, 874, 875.

34 Reprinted from *Wisconsin Colls.*, XIX, pp. 369-372.

35 Doubtless meaning Donald McKenzie, a former Astorian partner who, as a member of Hunt's party, had journeyed overland to Astoria and had later been a member of the Grand Brigade mentioned in note 33. *Astoria*, I, pp. 43, 132, 213, 263, II, pp. 27, 30, 74-77, 110, 200-206, 213-215, 253; *Henry-Thomp.*, pp. 44, 500, 752, 760, 761, 767, 783-785, 788, 843, 844, 854, 865, 866, 871; *Franchere* [*A*], pp. 9, 206 *et seq.*, [*B*], pp. 20, 263 *et seq.*, 368.

36 Doubtless meaning Stuart's mother-in-law.

37 Doubtless meaning Stuart's wife.

38 *I.e.*, Magee Sullivan, brother of Stuart's wife. He is mentioned in his father's will dated May 18, 1807 and probated June 5, 1807 in New York County Surrogate's Court.

39 Bernard P. Bogy Collection in library of Missouri Historical Society, letter reprinted in *Porter*, pp. 1143, 1144.

40 *Wisconsin Procs.*, XXXVI, p. 83; *Wisconsin Colls.*, II, pp. 107, 108, XX, pp. 17-31; *Porter*, pp. 700, 709-718, 734-743, 750, 754-759, 762, 765, 771, 772, 777, 779-812, 815, 820, 822, 829, 832, 833, 837, 843-846, 849, 855, 858-865, 873, 1172, 1178, 1179.

41 *Wisconsin Colls.*, XIX, pp. 52, 53; *Michigan*, VI, p. 347, XI, pp. 189, 193, 195, XVIII, pp. 330, 646.

42 *Wisconsin Colls.*, XIX, p. 371, f.n.; *Chittenden*, p. 909.

43 *Porter*, p. 779; *Michigan*, III, p. 60.

44 *Hamilton*, p. 21.

45 *Michigan*, III, pp. 56, 58; W. M. Ferry's address mentioned in note 14 *ante*.

46 *Michigan*, III, p. 63.

47 *Porter*, pp. 758, 797, 799-812, 843, 844; *Michigan*, XXXVII, pp. 236-238.

48 *Wisconsin Colls.*, XIV, pp. 22, 23.

49 *Michigan*, XII, pp. 643, 644. Present-day files of Macinac County, Michigan contain his signature as a judge in 1825.

50 *Michigan*, III, pp. 59, 63, XXVIII, pp. 190, 191; W. M. Ferry's address mentioned in note 14 *ante*.

51 *Michigan*, III, p. 64, IV, p. 85, XXVIII, p. 191; W. M. Ferry's address mentioned in note 14 *ante*.

52 *Michigan*, III, p. 54.

53 *Idem*, III, p. 59.

54 *Idem*, III, pp. 59, 60; W. M. Ferry's address mentioned in note 14 *ante*.

55 *Michigan*, III, p. 61.

56 *Hamilton*, p. 69.

57 *Idem*, pp. 69-73; *Michigan*, III, p. 54.

58 *Hamilton*, pp. 69, 70.

59 *Michigan*, III, p. 54. An *engagé* was a trapper or canoeman who contracted to work for a definite term.

60 *Idem*, III, p. 54.

61 *Idem*, III, pp. 54, 55.

62 *Wisconsin Procs.*, XLVII, p. 126.

63 *Detroit Daily Advertiser*, issue of November 10, 1848, p. 2, column 1.

64 Probably meaning Stuart's son David.

65 *Porter*, p. 779; *Michigan*, III, p. 54.

66 *Michigan*, III, p. 54.

67 *Idem*, III, p. 56, XI, p. 196. See also the two inventories made of his testamentary estate and filed on respectively February 19, 1849, November 13, 1866: as also final account filed June 27, 1868 and commissioners' report which in a partition proceeding was filed April 1, 1867: all in Wayne County, Michigan probate court (file No. 1529).

68 *Porter*, p. 863; "Map of the Town of Astor—John Jacob Astor, Ramsay Crooks & Robert Stuart Proprietors—Survey by A. G. Ellis District Surveyor," &c., 1835; *Baker-Astor* [*B*], pp. 275-277.

69 Records of First Presbyterian Church of Detroit.

70 *Michigan*, XXX, pp. 531-549.

71 *Idem*, III, p. 55. For banking conditions in Michigan, see *Cooley*, pp. 264-278.

72 *Lanman*, p. 509; *Michigan*, III, p. 60.

73 *Michigan*, III, p. 55, VI, p. 348, XIV, p. 416, XXVII, pp. 598, 600.

74 *Idem*, XXVI, pp. 285, 295, 296, XXVII, p. 566.

75 Obituary in *Detroit Daily Advertiser* (newspaper), November 2, 1848, p. 3, column 2; see also *Michigan*, III, p. 55.

76 All this information given us by his granddaughter, Mrs. Alexander Mackay-Smith. See also *Michigan*, III, p. 60.

77 *Bible* [*A*].

78 Obituary mentioned in note 75.

79 *Detroit Daily Advertiser*, November 11, 1848, p. 3. The steamer *Baltic* carried his body from Chicago to Detroit, according to *Detroit Free Press* of November 1, 1848.

80 Will dated June 4, 1847, probated at Detroit, November 13, 1848 (Wayne County, Michigan probate court's file No. 1529). In this will Stuart described himself as "of Chicago in the State of Illinois."

81 His testamentary assets are itemized in the inventories and final account mentioned in note 67. These show that he owned at his death his dwelling-house in Detroit ($14,280.00), other realty in Detroit ($11,170.00), realty in Michigan outside of Detroit ($15,430.52), realty in Wisconsin ($2,707.50), household furniture ($1,350.00), mortgages, rents accrued and amounts receivable under contracts for realty sales ($19,321.22), cash ($3,677.26), corporate securities ($4,065.00), promissory notes and debts of individuals ($6,068.32), balance of salary as Secretary of Illinois and Michigan canal trustees ($148.11).

82 Second of the two inventories mentioned in notes 67 and 81.

83 *Bible* [*A*]; *G. S.* Her funeral occurred October 1, 1866 at her home, 396

Jefferson Avenue, according to *Detroit Advertiser and Tribune* of that same date.

By her will (dated January 31, 1859) and its three codicils (the first dated May 21, 1860, the other two each dated October 29, 1862)—all probated October 31, 1866 at Detroit—she disposed of an estate which was separate from that of her deceased husband and which consisted of bonds and stock ($16,710.79), cash ($163.80), undivided one-third interest in four parcels of New York City realty ($18,666.67). See her estate's inventory filed November 3, 1866 in Wayne County, Michigan probate court (file No. 5249).

84 *Bible* [*A*],* [*B*]; *G. S.*

85 *Bible* [*A*]; *G. S. Bible* [*B*] erroneously states 1873.

86 *Bible* [*A*],* [*B*].

87 *Heitman*, I, p. 974.

88 *Bible* [*B*].

89 *Bible* [*A*], [*B*]; *G. S.*

90 *Bible* [*A*].*

91 *Bible* [*A*].*

92 *Bible* [*B*].

93 *Bible* [*A*].

94 *Bible* [*A*].

95 Information supplied us by Mrs. Homer Pierce Clark, a descendant of Robert's sister Mary Elizabeth.

96 Information supplied us by Robert Stuart Cooper.

97 *Bible* [*A*].

98 *Bible* [*B*].

99 *Bible* [*A*], [*B*]; *G. S.*

100 *Bible* [*A*].

101 *Bible* [*A*], [*B*].

102 *Bible* [*B*].

103 *Bible* [*A*].

104 *Bible* [*A*].

105 This date as also all our subsequent statements about her descendants we obtained from Robert Stuart Cooper.

106 *Bible* [*A*], [*B*].

107 This information furnished by Mrs. William Newton Ladue, daughter of Mary Elizabeth's sister Kate.

108 *Bible* [*A*].

109 This date as also all our subsequent statements about his marriage and his descendants we obtained from Robert Stuart Cooper.

110 *Bible* [*A*],* *G. S.*, and *Biographical*, p. 1583, each date birth as March 12, 1816, while *Bible* [*B*] dates it as March 6 in that year. As for place of birth, *Bibles* [*A*]* and [*B*] each give New York, while *Biographical*, p. 1583, gives Brooklyn, N. Y.

111 The *Detroit Free Press* of September 13, 1868 contains a formal notice

of death: "Died: In this city, Friday, 11th inst. . . ." The *Detroit Post* of Monday September 14, 1868, states: " . . . died at his family residence, No. 396 Jefferson avenue, in this city, at a late hour on Friday night . . . ;" while the *Detroit Free Press* of that same September 14, states: " . . . died at his house on Friday evening." These two newspapers, in thus giving the death date as September 11, agree with the record of the judicial proceeding (file No. 5750) instituted in the Wayne County, Mich. probate court for purpose of settling his estate, he having died intestate. Nevertheless, both *Bible* [*A*] and *G. S.* each give the death date as September 12.

112 *Detroit Free Press* and *Detroit Post*, each of September 14, 1868.

113 *Idem.*

114 *Idem.*

115 *Bible* [*A*],* [*B*].

116 Information obtained by Robert Stuart Cooper from Benson family Bible.

117 *G. S.*

118 *Biographical*, p. 1583.

119 *Idem; Detroit Post* of September 14, 1868.

120 *Biographical*, p. 1583; *Detroit Post* and *Detroit Free Press*, each of September 14, 1868.

121 For his military record, see numerous mentions of him in *War*, series I, Vol. X, pt. I; Vol. XVII, pts. I, II; Vol. XXIV, pts. I-III; Vol. LII, pt. II; series II, Vol. III. See also *Sherman*, I, pp. 247, 254, 258, 266, 269, 307, 318, 320, 325, 326, 334, 341, 342, 439, 449; *Heitman*, I, p. 933.

122 *War*, series I, Vol. LII, pt. II, p. 346.

123 *Sherman*, I, pp. 341, 342.

124 *Detroit Post; Detroit Free Press*, each of September 14, 1868.

125 *Idem.*

126 *Bible* [*A*].

127 *Bible* [*A*], [*B*]; *G. S.*

128 *Bible* [*A*].

129 *Idem.*

130 These data obtained by Robert Stuart Cooper.

131 *Bible* [*A*].

132 This date, as also all our subsequent statements about him, his wife and their descendants, we obtained from Robert Stuart Cooper.

133 *G. S.*

134 *Bible* [*A*].

135 This date supplied us by Robert Stuart Cooper.

136 *Bible* [*A*]. All our subsequent statements about her descendants we derived from Robert Stuart Cooper.

137 *Bible* [*A*].

138 *Idem; G. S.*

139 Though *Bibles* [*A*]* and [*B*] agree as to the place of birth, *Bible* [*A*]* gives the date as July 21, *Bible* [*B*] as July 20.

140 *Bible* [*A*], [*B*].

141 *Detroit Advertiser and Tribune* of October 11, 1853.

142 *Bible* [*A*],* [*B*].

143 *Bible* [*A*].

144 *Idem.* All our subsequent statements about her descendants we derived from Robert Stuart Cooper.

145 *Bible* [*A*].

146 *Idem.* The remainder of our statements about her we derived from Robert Stuart Cooper.

147 *Bible* [*A*].

148 February 15, according to *Bible* [*A*]; February 18, according to *Bible* [*B*].

149 *Bible* [*A*].

150 These data furnished us by Robert Stuart Cooper.

151 *Bible* [*A*]. All our subsequent statements about him, his wife and descendants we derived from Robert Stuart Cooper.

152 *Bible* [*A*]. All our subsequent statements about her, her husband and her descendants were obtained from Robert Stuart Cooper.

153 *Bible* [*A*],* [*B*].

154 *Detroit Daily Advertiser*, October 30, 1853.

155 The data as to his naval service were furnished by the Office of Naval Records and Library of U. S. Navy Dept., Washington. See also *Gen. Register*, p. 690.

156 See note 154.

157 *Bible* [*A*], [*B*]; *G. S.*

158 See note 154.

159 *Bible* [*A*], [*B*].

160 *Bible* [*A*].

161 These data concerning her marriage we obtained from Robert Stuart Cooper.

162 *Bible* [*A*],* [*B*].

163 New York, according to *Bible* [*A*];* Brooklyn, according to *Bible* [*B*].

164 The data as to his naval service were furnished by the office mentioned in note 155. See also *Gen. Register*, p. 690.

165 *War*, series I, Vol. XXVII, pt. I, pp. 996, 997.

166 *Bible* [*B*], which mentions place of death, gives date as July 30; as also does Robert Stuart Cooper relying on a Warrenton, Va. newspaper of July 31, 1863. But *G. S.* gives date as July 31. *Official Army*, pt. II, p. 312, incorrectly states that he died September 22, 1863.

167 *Bible* [*A*], [*B*].

168 *Bible* [*A*]. All our subsequent statements about her, her husband and descendants were derived from her.

169 *Bible* [*A*]. All our subsequent statements about him, his wife and descendants were derived from Mrs. Alexander Mackay-Smith.

170 *Bible* [*A*]. All our subsequent statements about him, his wives and descendants were derived from Mrs. Alexander Mackay-Smith.

171 *Bible* [*A*],* [*B*]; *G. S.*

172 *Bible* [*A*],* [*B*]; *G. S.*

173 *Bible* [*A*],* [*B*].

174 *Bible* [*A*],* [*B*]; *G. S. Bible* [*B*], however, gives an additional birthdate, October 24, 1835, for a "William Maynard Stuart Born at Detroit." This may represent merely an error by the enterer; for, though the entries in *Bible* [*A*]—which was printed in 1813—were presumably contemporaneous, the early ones in *Bible* [*B*]—which was printed in 1843—must have represented transcriptions.

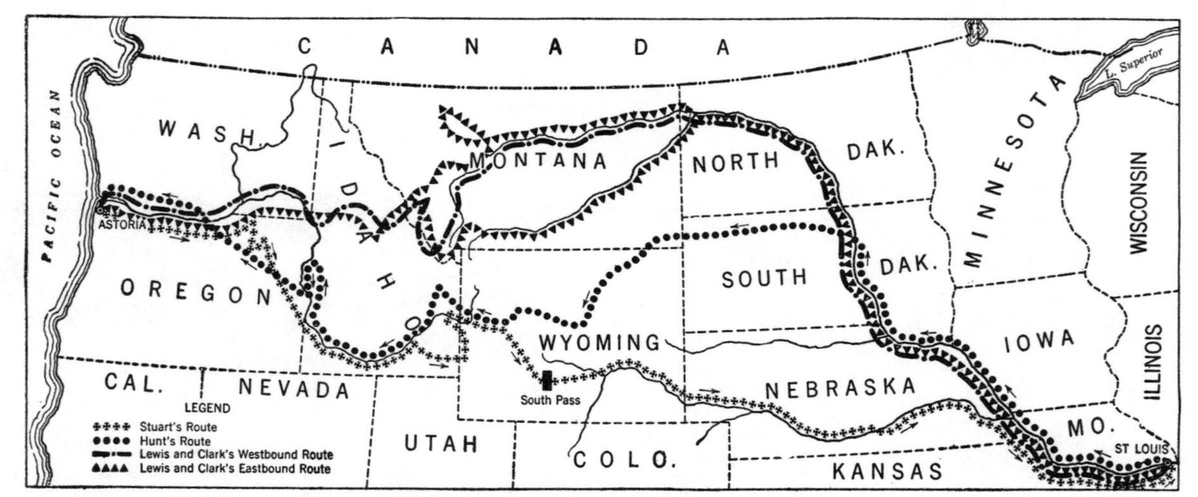

Routes of Stuart, of Hunt and of Lewis and Clark.

Foreword

The topic of this volume is the discovery of the road to Oregon. Lewis and Clark had proved in 1804-1806 that the United States' inchoate Far-Northwestern empire could be reached by transcontinental travel within the nation's own domain, but their line of march, though the logical one for an initial exploration, lacked the directness which prospective commerce needed.

In 1810-1812, Wilson Price Hunt, Astoria-bound with his comrades, essaying a somewhat more southerly latitude for the middle section of his journey and so avoiding the Lewis and Clark trace save at its eastern and western ends, struggled across country to the mouth of the Columbia River. Much of Hunt's course, however, was unprofitably devious and was prohibitive to all except the sturdiest of folk.

Shortly afterwards, Robert Stuart with a few companions started eastward from the mouth of this same Columbia and pushed overland to St. Louis, Mo. Leaving his fellow wayfarers there, he proceeded to New York. A circumstantial description of his trip from its outset till the arrival at St. Louis fills the two documents of his journal and of its revised transcript—both manuscripts wholly in his handwriting. The journal, before its entries abruptly and unexplainedly cease, continues his itinerary as far as the Green River in Kentucky.

The journal, on its opening page, he entitled: "Journal of a voyage acroſs/The Continent of North America/ from Astoria/ The Pacific Fur Companys principal Establishment/ on the Columbia/To the City of New York/ kept by/ Robert Stuart." To the revised transcript he gave no caption; but, because Washington Irving styled it "travelling memoranda of Mr. Stuart,"[1] this apt designation promises to be permanent.

Though the journal has never heretofore been printed, a large part of the travelling memoranda, rather inaccurately translated from the original English into French, was issued at Paris in the year 1821.[2]

Discovery of the Oregon Trail

Compared with all other overland diaries of the United States thus far published, Stuart's productions seem to be outranked only by the chronicles emanating from the expedition of Lewis and Clark, and to be fully as fraught with historical worth as is the French redaction[3] of Wilson Price Hunt's day-by-day account of his own caravan's westward trek.

Because the travelling memoranda were extensively tapped and freely paraphrased by Irving for inclusion in his *Astoria*,[4] Stuart's narratives, through their explicitness, provide supplement and mild correction to various statements in Irving's precious book. Thanks to Stuart's pen, we at last know in accurate detail the entire route of the so-called Returning Astorians. Also we learn, with equal exactness though with less minutiæ, some of the hitherto speculative portions of the still earlier route pursued by the Overland Astorians when they were plodding westward under the leadership of Hunt. Incidentally, "Spanish river mountain,"[5] Clappine's Rapid,[6] Hunt's caches,[7] and the Caldron Linn[8]—all of which Irving's artistry has enshrined in literature—are no longer geographically homeless, since Stuart has firmly pinned them to the map. And we now sense, with fair certitude, the path that Miller, Robinson, Hoback and Reznor followed during the period of vagrancy[9] which ended with their rescue by Stuart and his people.

In addition to this clarifying of *Astoria*, we are accorded a bit of evidence concerning part of the route of Ezekiel Williams's men.[10] We are told the western and eastern limits of the bisons' range in Stuart's day. Finally, as regards indians, not only are we given important information as to the distribution of sundry tribes, but also history is relieved of two ethnic and hitherto puzzling misnomers, for Stuart has clearly identified the "Sciatogas" of Irving's *Astoria*[11] and the "Blackarms" of *Missouri Gazette*, Niles' *Register*, Brackenridge's *Views* and Bradbury's *Travels*[12] as, respectively, Cayuses and Utes.

On their journey, Stuart and his companions used first the

westernmost fragment of the trace common to Lewis and Clark and to Hunt; next they clung to a westerly section of the independent trail of Hunt, then traversed a thitherto unknown area; next they utilized a second bit of Hunt's independent trail, and thereafter, veering southward of Hunt's path, plunged across an uncharted wilderness, into the South Pass and through the Sweetwater country of present-day Wyoming, arriving thus on the fur traders' then incipient highway of the Platte River; following it, they reached St. Louis.

They had found a continuous lane which, as later shorn of a few aberrances and consecrated by the trudging feet of countless pioneers, became known as the Oregon Trail.

That the arrival at St. Louis excited local interest—"quite a sensation," *Astoria* says—may be presumed, it being well-nigh unthinkable that the fur traders there, ever avid for information relating to their business, would have spared Stuart's party from prompt and exhaustive interrogation. This presumption is strengthened by the length and vigor of the article which the local newspaper (*Missouri Gazette*) published relative to their journey. This newspaper, a weekly, contained in its issue of May 8, 1813, a terse news-item stating the fact of the arrival, and in its issue of the following May 15 printed an interview which, under the heading of "American Enterprize," sketchily described, among other things, the overland trip, and then continued:

> "By information received from thefe gentlemen, it appears that a journey acrofs the continent of N. America, might be performed with a waggon, there being no obftruction in the whole route that any perfon would dare to call a mountain in addition to its being much the moft direct and short one to go from this place to the mouth of the Columbia river. Any future party who may undertake this journey, and are tolerably acquainted with the different places, where it would be neceffary to lay up a fmall ftock of provifions would not be impeded, as in all probability they would not meet with an indian to interrupt their progrefs; altho on the other route more north there are almost infurmountable barriers."

But interest was more than local. The *Missouri Gazette's* news-item of May 8 was forthwith reprinted or noted in at least the *National Intelligencer*[13] of Washington, D. C., Niles' *Weekly Register*[13] of Baltimore, Md., the Boston (Mass.) *Independent Chronicle*,[14] and three New York City papers—the *Herald*,[15] the *Commercial Advertiser*,[16] and the *Gazette and General Advertiser*.[17] The published interview of May 15 not only reappeared straightway in the columns of the above-mentioned papers of Washington, Baltimore, and New York,[18] but also was reproduced in *Annales des Voyages*[19] issued at Paris in 1813, in Brackenridge's book[20] issued at Pittsburgh in 1814, and in Bradbury's book[21] issued at Liverpool in 1817.

It is true that none of these advices contained information which could lead their readers to and along the newly travelled road; but the information was available, inasmuch as Stuart, soon after his journey's completion, furnished James Madison, then President of the United States, with a description of the entire route. Proof of this rests in a letter which John Jacob Astor wrote on October 18, 1813, to Thomas Jefferson, and in the course of which he remarked:

> "you may have Seen by the publick papers the arrivl of Mr Stuart & others from Columbia the former gentleman had resited there 15 months & had During that time explord a considerable part of the country he keep a journal & of his voyage across the country which he Left with the President should you feel a Desire to read it I am Sure the President will Send it to you."[22]

How and when Stuart regained his journal does not appear.

Early in the winter of 1820-1821, a trifle more than seven years after Stuart had thus acquainted the United States Government with the geographic details of his overland path, Ramsay Crooks, one of his travel-mates on that path, and Russell Farnham, another ex-Astorian, betook themselves to Washington, D. C. There they supplied much pertinent information to Thomas H. Benton, later a senator from Missouri, and to John Floyd, a representative from Virginia,[23]—two persons specially interested in the subject of Oregon. A result of Crooks's and Farnham's instruction was the formal report made, January 25, 1821, by Mr. Floyd as chairman of the committee which the House of Representatives had appointed "to inquire into the situation of the settlements upon the Pacific Ocean and the expediency of occupying the Columbia River."[24] While this report had much to say in didactic style about the importance of the fur trade during several centuries and the undeveloped possibilities of the Pacific coast, it furnished no practical advice as to how any one might reach Oregon. Though the report evoked speeches and debate within the House of Representatives in December, 1822, and December, 1824, and within the Senate in February and March, 1825, far-distant Oregon was apparently regarded as almost a chimera and the various overland routes received no mention beyond a broad statement that southward of Lewis and Clark's trace there lay other and more convenient paths which doubtless would permit the use of wagons and that one of these paths followed Wind River to its headwaters.[25] Nevertheless, it is not an unfair assumption that Crooks and Farnham provided data concerning Stuart's new-found trail, and that a portion of their message may have been remembered by at least a few of the congressional men and thus may have passed informally to various constituents. This assumption is the more justifiable because of Benton's statement that "public attention was awakened."[26]

In the year of Floyd's report, 1821, there were published at Paris the two volumes of *Nouvelles Annales* which, through the instrumentality of John Jacob Astor and the United States Minister to France, contained the French versions of Stuart's travelling memoranda, and of Wilson Price Hunt's overland diary, as well as an account both of the *Tonquin's* voyage and of events at Fort Astoria in 1811-1812.[27] The selection of France as the place of publication may have been on the initiative of Astor, who then was visiting Paris. And yet it very possibly originated with Frenchmen, for France at the time had an insatiate curiosity as to geographic exploration—witness, for example, *Annales des Voyages* (with its reprint of "American Enterprize") and *Nouvelles Annales*, which together ultimately filled 212 printed volumes.

For more than two decades after Stuart had completed his traverse from the Columbia River to St. Louis, his path had no generally accepted title, though it thereafter acquired the designation, "Oregon Trail." When, in a still later period, migration to California began, several map-makers renamed, as "California Trail" and as "Overland Trail," the part of the Oregon Trail lying eastward of the western fringes of the South Pass. But change of name did not mean change of route. And so it was by skirting the Platte River and by advancing through the Sweetwater region and the South Pass—thus virtually along the easterly half of Stuart's trace—that most of the overland "Forty-niners" and their Argonaut followers in succeeding years toiled westward toward the "diggings" of California.

These statements do not pretend that the seekers for California's gold or for homes in Oregon marched on the exact line of Stuart's footprints. On the contrary, they recognize that, after the trail was fully developed by the covered-wagon folk—a development which, however, never outgrew a state of flux—, it was not, throughout much of its length, a narrow, definite highway, but was a zone several miles in width and along which the wagon tracks meandered, crossing and recrossing each other as do threads in a loosely made skein which has been dropped upon the floor. In addition to this reticulation within the zone, the trail gradually acquired short-cuts and detours. Some of these collateral routes—notably those in present-day Idaho, eastern Nebraska and eastern Kansas—had a scale and a quantity of use at least equal to those possessed by the paralleled sections of the parent trail. While the short-cuts were originated obviously to lessen distance, the detours were devised by persons who, as incidents in their journey, had variously set out to search for new areas of forage and fuel, to hunt for less rutted surface, to avoid floods, to seek water-holes as substitutes for unexpectedly dried springs, to outmarch covertly a rival train, to gratify exploratory adventuresomeness, to escape from indians, or to evade rumored cholera on the route ahead. Additional and not infrequent causes for detours were bewilderment as to orientation and actual insanity from the unaccustomed stress of frontier travel.

However, at irregular intervals in the trail's length, topography compelled the local ends of the scattered tracks to converge and to run for a while in a single lane; these lanes in some stretches had a width of six rods, in other stretches were no wider than a wagon, and here and there were so deeply gouged by wheels, hoofs, and human feet as to resemble railway cuttings and to be as much as seventy inches deep. The convergency was thus enforced by mountain-passes and ravines, by valleys with puckering ends, by fords or ferries across deep rivers, and by the locations of both water-holes and grasslands in desert areas. The errant paths were also pulled together by the revictualling stations at Fort Boise, Fort Hall (with its successive sites), Fort Bridger and Fort Laramie.

There was excuse for variance between the line of Stuart's footprints and that of the covered-wagons' ruttings. Stuart, unhampered by any weight of luggage, could go whither he wished; and thus, for at least most of the way, he followed indian trails which tended to cling to the banks of streams, while the covered-wagon people, with their ponderous wains and their occasional herds, had to skirt the marshy soil and the eroded gullies which the stream-banks oftentimes displayed.

But, all in all, it safely may be asserted that, except for Stuart's loop from the mouth of Thomas Fork (a confluent of Bear River) to Pacific Creek, and except for a few minor differences listed in a footnote[28] to this statement, his route and that of the Oregon Trail were practically identical.

While *Coutant* (I, p. 101) acclaims Stuart as the discoverer of South Pass, there are historians who deny Stuart the credit and place it elsewhere. Further discussion of this matter of primacy will, to avoid confusing the present narrative, be deferred to later pages of this foreword. The deferment is the more willingly made because Stuart's right to honorable recognition lies, not so much in his finding of South Pass, the Sweetwater River, the Red Buttes and the upper canyon of the North Platte, as in his weaving the first three of them and the indian trails both west and east of them into an unintermitting route which in later years was to prove practicable for even such of the emigrants as were uninventive.

In order to evaluate Stuart's narratives and also to grasp the significance of the facts and people mentioned in them, we must, at the cost of perusing a very familiar story, turn for a moment to an earlier period and to the pages of other writers.

For many years prior to 1810, a powerful Canadian organization known as the North West Company had well-nigh a monopoly of the fur trade in the western half of Canada and in so much of the theretofore explored United States as adjoined that Canadian region.[29] It is true that, throughout almost two decades before this year 1810, various New England vessels, when outward bound for China in quest of tea, silks, beads and nankeens, had more or less frequently visited North America's western coast in order to barter for pelts; but this business totalled so little as to represent a mere nibbling at the local fur supply.[30] Still more anæmic was the fur trade which Russia was essaying to establish in Alaska.[31]

In 1810 John Jacob Astor, already enthusiastic over the commercial possibilities revealed by Lewis and Clark's expedition, decided to enter aggressively into the Far Western trade as conducted within at least the borders of the United States, and, to effect his purpose, he organized the so-called Pacific Fur Company.[32]

It was arranged that, of this concern's participating shares—100 in number—50 were to be owned by Astor; not to exceed an additional 12 were to be subject to his power of later appointing their holders; 35 were to be distributed among such men as he forthwith should admit to partnership; and three, until their fate was determined, should remain in the treasury.[33] It was also arranged that, for the first five years, Astor should be the partnership's sole financial sponsor.[34]

In his search for co-adventurers and for employees, Astor aimed for people who had been actively connected with his prospective rival, the North West Company.[35] His turn in this direction had one or both of the following two motives, one of them announced by him and the other by his associate, Alexander Ross. Astor declared: "I beg leave to say, that at the commencement of my undertaking it appeared to be necessary that some of the people sent to that country [the Oregon region] should be acquainted with the Indian trade, and they being very scarce in the United States, I have been under the necessity of taking some from Canada, some Candians [*sic*], and some few Scotchmen. Although they have all become citizens of the United States . . ." Ross, on the other hand, averred that Astor's incentive was belief that, if the persons procured were chiefly Britons, the undertaking would give less offense to the British nation, which already was disposed, under claim of prior discovery, to begin assertion of sovereignty over the Oregon region.[36]

The personnel of the North West Company consisted, in the main, of "agents" (which is to say, partners), of "clerks," guides, interpreters, and finally of folk who, whether as trappers, canoemen, or men-of-all-work, were interchangeably styled *engagés* and *voyageurs*.[37]

Four of the agents and ex-agents of this company, all of them harboring grievances against it, now quitted it and became partners in Astor's scheme.[38]

The North West Company's "clerks" were, in the language of one of them,

> "chiefly younger branches of respectable Scottish families, who entered the service as apprentices for seven years; for which period

> they were allowed one hundred pounds, and suitable clothing. At the expiration of their apprenticeship they were placed on yearly salaries, varying from eighty to one hundred and sixty pounds, and according to their talents were ultimately provided for as partners; some, perhaps in a year or two after the termination of their engagements; while others remained ten, twelve, or sixteen years in a state of probation. . . . Courage was an indispensable qualification, not merely for the casual encounters with the Indians, but to intimidate any competitor in trade with whom he might happen to come in collision."[39]

Among these clerks, so Irving states, were

> "several of great capacity and experience, who had served out their probationary terms, but who, either through lack of interest and influence, or a want of vacancies, had not been promoted. They were consequently much dissatisfied, and ready for any employment in which their talents and acquirements might be turned to better account."[40]

Wherefore, some of them presently joined forces with Astor's Pacific Fur Company. One of these proselytes was Robert Stuart, who, though listed at first for possibly a mere clerkship, was, on September 5, 1810, admitted to partnership and allotted two participating shares.[41]

At the formation of the Pacific Fur Company with its scheme of widespread commercial conquest, Astor had in mind, not only that the company's principal depot should be located at the mouth of the Columbia River, but also that, radiating from this depot, branch trading-posts should be installed "in every direction up the rivers and along the coast."[42]

For the erecting of this main station and some of its dependencies, two expeditions were devised, one by sea, the other by land. The seafaring group "was to carry out the people, stores, ammunition, and merchandise, requisite for establishing a fortified trading post" at the Columbia's mouth. The overland party "was to proceed up the Missouri, and across the Rocky Mountains, to the same point; exploring a line of communication across the continent, and noting the places where interior trading posts might be established."[43]

In accordance with this arrangement, the ship *Tonquin*, bearing the members of the marine section—among them, Robert Stuart—sailed from New York City in September, 1810, and, having rounded Cape Horn and touched at the Sandwich Islands, arrived, in March, 1811, at the mouth of the Columbia River.[44]

The land expedition—captained by Wilson Price Hunt—quitted St. Louis in October, 1810, boated up the Missouri River to an Aricara village some eight miles above the mouth of the present-day Grand River in South Dakota, proceeded thence on foot and horse to Henry's Fort near the site of the modern town of St. Anthony, Idaho, and at this so-called fort transferred to canoes. After reaching in these canoes a spot which today is embraced within the town limits of Milner, Idaho, the expedition was wrecked in the formidable rapids. Threatened with starvation and not knowing where to turn for immediate help, it cached the greater part of its belongings and presently subdivided into several groups which by various routes piteously trudged onward. Those who completed the journey began, in January, 1812, to straggle into Astoria, the mart which the *Tonquin's* folk had, months before, erected at the Columbia's mouth.[45]

Stuart, as passenger outbound on the *Tonquin*, at once began to encounter emergencies. Excitement began the day after the *Tonquin* left the harbor of New York; for it was then that there first appeared the feud which, throughout the rest of the voyage, was to reign between the captain and the passengers.[46]

In the course of the opening tiff, the captain, defying one of the fur-trading partners, announced that "he would blow out the brains of the first man who dared to disobey his orders on board his own ship."[47] This threat was echoed weeks later at the Falkland Islands when the craft, because of an alarming shortage of water, called there to replenish her casks. During the stop, a landing party overstayed its leave; and so the irate captain, planning to maroon the loiterers, attempted to sail. His endeavor doubtless would have been successful "but for the bold interference of Mr. R. Stuart, whose uncle was of our party, and, who, seeing that the captain, far from waiting for us, cooly continued his course," grasped a brace of pistols and "threatened to blow his brains out unless he hove to and took us on board."[48]

In the progress of the voyage, the vessel twice took fire, and three times sprang aleak.[49] Gales damaged her canvas and rigging, and also swept overboard the movables on deck.[50] Six of the ten cannon broke from their fetters and skidded about.[51]

Eventually the *Tonquin* bumped her way over the Columbia's wave-swept bar, paying there a death-toll of eight of the ship's company who had transferred to small boats for the purpose of finding a channel.[52] Stuart remained aboard the vessel, on which the struggle became at one time so severe that "Every one who could, sprang aloft, and clung for life to the rigging."[53]

As soon as the adventurers landed they began seeking a site for their establishment. Having ultimately found one in a bight beside Point George on the Columbia's south shore, they commenced, on April 12, 1811, to make the necessary clearing for the prospective buildings.[54] But so unacquainted with hewing were many of the people, and so new to immense trees were all of them, that the task progressed but slowly.[55] Meanwhile, there was the menace of indians and the consequent need of ever remaining under arms ("an axe in one hand and a gun in the other, the former for attacking the woods, the latter for defence").[56] Furthermore, because of unaccustomed climate and the character of the food, "one-half of the party, on an average, were constantly on the sick list; and on more than one occasion I have seen the whole party so reduced that scarcely one could help the other. . . ."[57]

Discontent became rife, petty feuds habitual, and courage among various of the less forceful *engagés* ebbed so far that presently some of them, in successive groups of four, six and three men, deserted, and sought flight to the "Spanish colonies"[58] in present-day California, but were recaptured.

Nearly two months of chopping and of stump-blasting bared scarcely an acre of ground, and in the interim "three of our men were killed by the natives, two more wounded by the falling of trees, and one had his hand blown off by gunpowder."[59] Nevertheless, a vegetable garden had meanwhile been planted, and one building seemingly completed, although as yet no start at fortifying had been made.[60]

Stuart was granted a respite from this labor, for, on May 2, he, with three associates, "a sufficient number of hands" and an indian guide, embarked in a canoe and proceeded up the Columbia to seek information from more distant indians, to win their favor, and also to find a supposed trading-post of whites which indian rumor had created. In the round trip of twelve days, the Cascades of the river were reached, but nothing of note befell the travellers except that they met the Spanish castaway Soto, and, during a short detour on the Cowlitz River, native warriors, inquisitive at the sight of human whiteness, disarranged the travellers' trousers and shirts in order to ascertain whether the skin on their bodies resembled that on their faces and hands.[61]

It was "soon after" this, according to *Ross* (though *Nouvelles Annales*, X, p. 23, states it was in late August or early September), that Stuart, with six men, "proceeded on an excursion to the north." Of this trip, we are told no more than that it lasted fifteen or eighteen days, that it reached latitude 47° 20′, longitude 124°, and that the travellers barely escaped attack by the indians.[62]

In July, a chief friendly to Stuart warned him of an indian plot to sack the post at Astoria and to slay its inmates. This caused the hasty erection of palisades and a bastion, but no hostilities ensued.[63]

In August, the wily, one-eyed savage,

> "old Concomly sent to *Astoria* for Mr. Stuart and me [Gabriel Franchere] to come and cure him of a swelled throat, which, he said, afflicted him sorely. As it was late in the day, we postponed till to-

> morrow going to cure the chief of the Chinooks; and it was well we did; for, the same evening, the wife of the Indian who had accompanied us in our voyage to the Falls, sent us word that Concomly was perfectly well, the pretended *tonsillitis* being only a pretext to get us in his power. This timely advice kept us at home."[64]

Early in October, the garrison found itself short of food, due to the fact that the natives on whom it had relied for supplies had retreated to distant winter quarters.[65] "It was therefore determined that Mr. R. Stuart should set out in the schooner with Mr. Mumford, for the threefold purpose, of obtaining all the provisions they could, cutting oaken staves for the use of the cooper, and trading with the Indians up the river." On October 12, they started, but "At the end of five days Mr. Mumford returned in a canoe of Indians. This man having wished to assume the command, and to order . . . the person who had engaged him to obey, had been sent back in consequence to Astoria."[66] Stuart, however, seems to have speedily accomplished his errand, and, during his short voyage, to have experienced nothing unusual beyond his cashiering of Mumford, a mild pillaging of the vessel by indians, and his playing host to some of his Astorian associates who overtook him during their pursuit of three absconding *engagés*.[67]

On December 5, having previously been told by indians of the abundance of beaver in the valley of the Willamette River, Stuart, at the head of a small party, sallied forth "to ascend that river and ascertain whether or no it would be advisable to establish a trading-post on its banks." The duration and results of the trip do not appear.[68]

Stuart's next venture was apparently his visit to the Cowlitz River, which "last winter I navigated with six men for 260 miles, partly for the purpose of diminishing the number of mouths at the Fort, and partly to explore the interior and trade with the natives—."[69]

In the latter part of March, 1812, three expeditions aggregating 17 persons left Astoria. Though bound for widely separated goals, they planned to travel in company until they should have gone many miles up the Columbia.[70]

Of the three expeditions, one, consisting of three or more men, was to proceed into present-day Idaho with a view to salvaging the articles which had been cached by Hunt's party.[71]

The second expedition, composed of the clerk John Reed and five companions, was expected to bear various despatches overland to Astor in New York, and also to succor Ramsay Crooks and John Day, two of Hunt's westbound band who as yet had failed to reach Astoria.[72]

The third expedition, headed by Robert Stuart—who, incidentally, was to be in command of all three groups until they should disunite at the focus of their several prospective bypaths—was to convey two canoe-loads of wares to the subsidiary trading-post which had been established the preceding autumn on the Okanagan River, a tributary of the Columbia in the northern part of the present-day state of Washington.[73]

And so the three expeditions, compacted for the time being into one, paddled upstream from Astoria. In April they arrived at the Dalles, where on treacherous rocks and beside dangerous rapids, the indians, without warning, fell ruthlessly upon the travellers.[74]

Stuart in his narratives gives, under date of July 20, 1812, his recollections of the attack. His recital, in comparison with those of Ross (a fellow-participant in the fight[75]) and of Franchere,[76] Cox[77] and Irving,[78] seems full and fair. Though Stuart is silent on the subject of motive, Franchere, Cox and Irving attribute the onslaught to indian cupidity for a shining metal box which, containing despatches for Astor, was strapped to the shoulders of John Reed.[79] Stuart also modestly ignores his own behavior, which is defined by Franchere[80] as that of a "self-possessed and fearless man," and by Ross[81] as "brave and prudent."

Because of the misadventure, the proposed errands to the caches and to New York were abandoned, and the three expeditions, continuing in one body, kept on to the post at the Okanagan. After a short stay there the still consolidated party, bearing the furs accumulated at the post, began its return to Astoria, where it arrived on May 11 or 12.[82] On this return journey, when they were again on the waters of the Columbia, the voyagers were hailed from the shore by two spectre-like and almost naked men who proved to be Ramsay Crooks and John Day.[83]

Next came June 29, 1812, and Stuart's final leave-taking of Astoria, for it was then that he started eastward, carrying refashioned despatches to Astor. His companions in the venture were six men, all of them veterans of Hunt's westbound overland caravan. It was expected that he would reach New York by the end of December, 1812.[84]

The story of this trip is best told in Stuart's own words in his narratives. But it will not be amiss if their first pages be prefaced with data gleaned from other sources.

His overland errand was pursuant to a resolution adopted by the partners present at a meeting held June 27, 1812, at Astoria. The resolution read:

> "Resolved, that it, being neceffary to send an Expreff to New York, and all the papers, and other things being prepared Mr. Robert Stuart is hereby instructed to have and to take charge of them, with which he is to go as directly to New York as circumstances will admit—and there to be governed by the directions of Mr. Astor as to the time of his returning to the N. W. Coast. It is also resolved that John Day, Benjamin Jones—Francois Leclerc, André Vallé accompany Mr. Stuart as far as St. Louis where he is to pay them the balances due each by means of Drafts drawn by our W. P. Hunt on John Jacob Astor on account of the Pacific Fur Company."[85]

To the squad of five men thus authorized, Ramsay Crooks and Robert McClellan forthwith attached themselves; they had relinquished their financial interests in the Astorian venture and were desirous of a prompt return to St. Louis.[86] Their consequently discrete status could in no way have changed the effect of the abovementioned resolution of June 27; and this resolution, by its phrasing, would seem to negative any suggestion that Stuart's overland party had no special leader.

Numerous other people accompanied Stuart when he thus set out from Astoria. Though he merely mentions them as being destined for the interior sections of the country, some were actually headed for the Snake River, others for the erection and stocking of a new establishment on the Spokane River; and still others for exploration of the region lying north of the then existing post on the Okanagan River.[87]

To this, Ross adds as follows: It having been ordered that "all these several parties [inclusive of Stuart's], for mutual safety, advance together as far as the forks . . . ," John Clarke, a partner, was by common consent placed in supreme command of the three expeditions so long as they should journey in company.[88]

Cox, one of the group headed for Spokane River, says:

> "We travelled in *bateaux* and light-built wooden canoes: the former had eight, and the latter six men. Our lading consisted of guns and ammunition, spears, hatchets, knives, beaver traps, copper and brass kettles, white and green blankets, blue, green, and red cloths, calicoes, beads, rings, thimbles, hawk-bells &c.; and our provisions of beef, pork, flour, rice, biscuits, tea, sugar, with a moderate quantity of rum, wine &c.: the soft and hard goods were secured in bales and boxes, and the liquids in kegs, holding on an average nine gallons: the guns were stowed in long cases. From thirty to forty of these packages and kegs were placed in each vessel, and the whole was covered by an oil-cloth or tarpaulin, to preserve them from wet. Each canoe and barge had from six to eight men rowing or paddling, independent of the passengers."[89]

Our immediate interest focuses, not on the entire personnel of this flotilla, but on the six of its people who were of Stuart's transcontinental party. These six—Crooks, McClellan, Jones, LeClairc, Vallé, and Day—accompanied Stuart when he left Astoria, though shortly afterward one of them, Day, became ill and was sent back.[90] Also our special interest attaches to four additional people—Miller,

Hoback, Reznor and Robinson—who were annexed during the progress of the eastward march,[91] even though the three of them last mentioned continued with Stuart for but some twelve days.[92]

That we may the more intimately know the men who trudged with Stuart, let us now inspect them one by one.

RAMSAY CROOKS, son of William Crooks, a shoemaker, and Margaret (Ramsay) Crooks, was born January 2, 1787, in the middle parish of Greenock, Scotland.[93]

Sailing on April 25, 1803, from Greenock for Canada with his mother, he obtained employment immediately on landing. It is conflictingly stated (1) that the earliest of this employment was (a) as junior clerk in the mercantile house of Maitland, Garden and Auldjo in Montreal, or (b) with fur traders operating from Montreal; and (2) that this earliest occupation, whatever it actually may have been, was immediately followed by (c) possibly a brief stay at Niagara, Canada, or (d) an approximately twelve months' service on Michilimacinac Island as clerk to Robert Dickson, fur-trader, or (e) service which, under a Mr. Gillespie, began in 1805 and presently took Crooks to St. Louis, Mo.[94]

In any event, Crooks eventually went to St. Louis, where, as early as the spring of 1807, he and Robert McClellan became partners in the fur trade.[95]

In the autumn of 1807, these partners, heading a trading expedition of 80 men and with an outfit furnished on shares by Silvestre Labbadie and Auguste Chouteau, started for the higher reaches of the Missouri. Having gone some distance up the river, they learned that the Sioux and Aricaras were for the moment so intensely hostile to the white man that it was unwise to continue the voyage. Accordingly, they dropped downstream to so-called Council Bluffs, a spot on the Missouri's right bank approximately 25 miles above the site of the present-day city of Omaha, and there they erected buildings and remained till the spring of 1809.[96]

In the summer of 1809, they saw the Missouri Fur Company's flotilla ascend the river and attempted to follow with about 40 men. When they reached the region of the Sioux, however, a large group of these indians, strategically posted at a bend of the river, forbade further progress and ordered the adventurers to disembark.[97]

Physical resistance being impossible, Crooks and McClellan adopted a ruse. Pretending to agree to engage in barter, they began erecting what falsely promised to become a trading-post. Most of the indians, in order to procure articles for exchange, departed for their own village some 20 miles away, leaving behind them only five warriors on guard. Forthwith Crooks and McClellan quietly dispatched a canoe-load of men upstream with orders to collect whatever furs they could and await favorable opportunity for return. As soon as this squad was thought to have passed beyond the hostile country, the partners dismantled their mimic trading-post, left their five guardians helplessly tied, and thereupon headed for their former establishment at Council Bluffs.[98] The two adventurers were wont later to assert that the miscarriage of their expedition had been due wholly to machinations of their trade competitor, Manuel Lisa of the Missouri Fur Company, and against him they harbored a bitterness which, as hereinafter described, was presently to flame.[99]

It is said that, in the spring of 1810, Crooks and McClellan made a fruitless effort to install a trading contact on the Missouri River above the Aricara villages.[100]

However, this same year 1810 saw the end of their business, both men becoming partners in Astor's recently formed Pacific Fur Company, Crooks having five, and McClellan two and one-half shares in the new enterprise.[101]

Though the new company's organizing agreement, dated June 23, 1810, recites that Crooks had "in contemplation" going with Astor's people to the Pacific coast, he seems not to have actually entered the concern until July or August when he, being at Michilimacinac and meeting there Wilson Price Hunt, joined with him in obtaining men for the prospective overland trip.[102]

About August 12, Crooks with Hunt and their recruits began a canoe trip which traversed Lake Michigan, descended the Fox, Wisconsin and Mississippi Rivers, and landed them at St. Louis in early September.[103]

Additional people having been enlisted at St. Louis, Crooks and his fellow expeditioners left there October 21, and went by boat up the Missouri River to the mouth of the Nodaway, where they established a camp in which they remained until, on April 21, 1811, they resumed their forward travel.[104]

On June 2 the expedition, having reached a spot some 30 miles downstream from the site of the present-day city of Pierre, South Dakota, was overtaken by Manuel Lisa, who, in a keelboat containing 20 picked oarsmen, had raced through rain and gales for 1100 miles.[105]

Thus Crooks and McClellan were once more face to face with their detested competitor. Lisa promptly tried to persuade Hunt's half-breed interpreter to desert, and, as a result, there commenced a quarrel into which Crooks and McClellan were eager to enter.[106] In a subsequent stage of this altercation, though Crooks seems not to have resorted to violence, Hunt challenged Lisa to a duel, and McClellan twice offered to shoot him without even this formality.[107]

A color of peace being restored, the Astorians, in distrustful company with Lisa, paddled for seven days upstream to the Aricara villages,[100] where they camped until July 18 when, quitting their boats and Lisa's party, they began their westward march.[108]

Within a very few days Crooks became too ill to ride a horse. Accordingly, he was placed on a travois and, as late as August 6, was still confined to this bumping vehicle.[109]

On October 28, nine days after taking to canoes upon the treacherous waters of Snake River, the expedition was descending the rapids below the site of the present-day dam at Milner,

Idaho. Crooks, seated in the second canoe, saw that his steersman, Antoine Clappine, was inadvertently heading for a rock. He shouted a warning, but an instant later the canoe, laden with five persons, struck the obstacle, split, and overturned. Crooks and one of his companions swam to the shore. Two others succeeded in climbing on the rock, whence they were later rescued.[110] Clappine was drowned.[111]

The expedition, immediately halting, abandoned its canoes, pitched camp, cached its surplus property and presently sent forth small squads, each committed to a specified mission.[112]

Crooks with five men started eastward on the left bank of the Snake, intending, should they not find relief sooner, to go back to Henry's Fort, regain there the horses which the expedition had left when transferring from saddle to canoe, and with these horses return to the vicinity of Milner, where a portion of the expedition was expected to remain.[113]

Three days after leaving the Milner site, however, Crooks and his party reappeared there. "A momentary joy was diffused through the camp, for they supposed succor to be at hand. It was soon dispelled. Mr. Crooks and his companions had become completely disheartened by this retrograde march through a bleak and barren country; and had found, computing from their progress and the accumulating difficulties besetting every step, that it would be impossible to reach Henry's fort, and return to the main body in the course of the winter. They had determined, therefore, to rejoin their comrades, and share their lot."[114]

On November 9, when the camp near Milner dissolved, Crooks with 19 men started downstream on the Snake's left bank. At the end of twenty-four days they had progressed to a spot a few miles below the site of the present-day town of Homestead, Ore.[115] There they found themselves on the easterly end of the Wallowa Mountains and in snow so deep as to be impassable, and accordingly, with subsistence well-nigh limited to the soles of old moccasins and to the carcass of one dog, they began to retrace their steps.[116]

Three days later, on December 6, having regained a place apparently opposite that part of the Snake known today as Kerrs Rapids and lying three-quarters of a mile north of the site of Homestead,[117] Crooks and his men were hailed from across the stream by Hunt's contingent, which had been descending the Snake's right bank.[118] Hunt at once caused a canoe to be fashioned from the skin of a horse that his men had killed the previous night. It served for carrying horsemeat to Crooks's people and, on its return trip, for ferrying Crooks and François LeClairc to Hunt's side for a conference.[119]

The canoe drifted away in the night. Next morning, Hunt's people commenced building a raft on which Crooks and LeClairc might recross the river. Finding it impossible to construct one stout enough to breast the savage current, they abandoned the attempt, and thereupon both parties, one on the right bank and one on the left, started upstream, hoping sooner or later to get succor at some indian camp.[120]

The feebleness of Crooks and LeClairc so slowed the march that Hunt's people, after remonstrating at the delay, began singly and in groups to quit the laggard line and advance at a faster pace. By evening, only Hunt and five men remained with the two invalids.[121]

The next morning, December 8, a second raft was made and on it Crooks and LeClairc several times tried to cross the Snake. When this ferriage proved impracticable, they and their six companions resumed plodding. The night was intensely cold, and during it Crooks became so ill as to be little able to travel.[122]

The available food-supply had now been reduced to three beaver skins. Accordingly Hunt, leaving two men[123] and two of the skins with Crooks and LeClairc, pressed forward with his other three men,[124] planning to overtake his seceded people and procure a horse which they were known to have.[125] On December 10, he caught up with the van of his party and soon afterward sighted an indian camp with horses grazing about it. Five of the grazing animals were seized,[126] and one of them was immediately butchered.[127] That night a mounted man carrying a supply of the newly obtained meat reached Crooks's bivouac. With the assistance of this rider's horse, Crooks and his emaciated comrades early the next morning rejoined Hunt, who had settled his party at a spot near the indian camp.[128]

Crooks on arriving found that, while food had been supplied to all the persons on Hunt's side of the river, none had been sent to the famishing contingent on the left bank. He immediately caused the construction of a skin canoe which he stocked with horsemeat. When his associates refused to provide a ferryman for the dangerous crossing, he himself attempted to navigate the craft. His strength was insufficient, but fortunately other folk presently consented to act in his stead.[129]

That evening, John Day, pitifully gaunt, was brought across the stream from the left bank in order that he might be with his old associate, Crooks. He could have found no friend more trustworthy, for Crooks, though he persuaded Hunt to hurry on, refused to desert Day. And so Crooks, Day, and one Canadian *engagé*, Jean Baptiste Dubreuil, were furnished with two live horses and part of the carcass of a slain one, and were left to their own devices.[130] The three men, for the next twenty days, were held immobile by John Day's feebleness. He was so weak that he could not rise without assistance.[131]

During the early part of this halt, indians shared their food with the refugees, who, for some undisclosed reason, seem to have lost their horses; but presently the indians, themselves becoming foodless, made their departure and left the sufferers without horse or any sustenance. Crooks dug roots, intending to cook them. But the fire had died, and for a day and night the men were too feeble to rekindle it. Meanwhile they lay in a torpor with the cheerless, if hazy, knowledge that they had nothing to eat and no water to drink. Presently two straggling indians appeared. These indians procured water, built a fire, gave food, and after two days moved on. Incidentally, they told Crooks that the roots he had collected were poisonous.[132]

The day after the two indians left, a large wolf prowled near, and with great exertion John Day shot it dead. An immediate meal was provided by the skin and by the bones pounded, mixed with roots, and made into broth. The flesh was sliced and dried for future use.[133]

Soon the derelicts were joined by André LaChapelle, François Landry and Jean Baptiste Turcotte, three cast-offs from Hunt's advancing column. At the end of the twenty days' halt, the augmented group of forlorn souls resumed the trail; but in February the newcomers, fearful of perishing from want, went their independent way. Crooks, Day and Dubreuil, faithful to each other, continued in company to follow Hunt's track in the snow.[134] Presently the track disappeared, and so the three men, during the remainder of the winter, wandered in the mountains "subsisting sometimes on horsemeat, sometimes on beavers and their skins, and a part of the time on roots."[135]

About the last of March, Dubreuil collapsed and was left with a lodge of peaceable indians; but Crooks and Day kept on. Toward the middle of April the two wayfarers reached the Columbia's left bank, and after a two days' stay with friendly natives, began to follow this bank downstream.[136]

Some 20 miles above present-day Celilo Falls, they fell in with a tribe which, after robbing them of all possessions including every shred of clothing, drove them out of camp. Painfully they started back toward the friendly natives whom they had encountered when first reaching the Columbia. After trying to eat the pounded bones of long-dead fish, they were, for four days and nights, without sustenance of any sort; but presently they chanced upon a wigwam containing both food and kindly inmates. In due time, they reached the friendly indians they were seeking. Having been provided by them with skins for raiment and with the dried flesh of a horse, they were about to leave the Columbia and head for St. Louis when they had the joy of successfully hailing the flotilla of canoes commanded by Robert Stuart and returning from the Okanagan to Astoria.[137]

Astoria was reached on May 11 or 12. On May 14, Crooks, disheartened at the prospects of the Astorian enterprise, formally relinquished his partnership and all claim to any share in the profits.[138]

On June 29, as one of Robert Stuart's overland party, he began the march that restored him to St. Louis on April 30, 1812.

Crooks's resignation from the Pacific Fur Company had severed his entire business connection with Astor, and apparently it was Astor who initiated the steps for a resumption. On June 23, 1813, the day of Robert Stuart's arrival in New York City, Astor wrote Charles Gratiot of St. Louis and, after mentioning Stuart, asked: "Can you inform me where is Mr. Crooks, Mr. Miller & Mr McClannan [McClellan], and have you understood the reason for their return. . . ."[139] The following July 19, Astor again wrote Gratiot; in this instance requesting that, if Gratiot knew the address of Crooks, he forward to him an enclosed letter from Astor.[140] In this letter for Crooks, Astor in friendly terms expressed, not only regret at Crooks's leaving the Pacific Fur Company, but also expectation that the war with England would soon end and that, on the coming of peace, Astor would re-engage in indian trade.[141] By October 8, 1813, Crooks, being then at Buffalo, N. Y., had resumed business relations with Astor. In two letters of this date, Astor referred to Crooks's supposed intention of visiting Michilimacinac if the United States troops were in possession of it, and also directed him to purchase there furs for joint account.[142]

From this time until Astor in 1817 firmly established the American Fur Company in its station at Michilimacinac, Crooks, as Astor's representative and occasional partner in various fur-trading ventures, hovered about the Great Lakes, being frequently at Buffalo, Erie, Detroit, and Michilimacinac. For the purposes of purchasing ginseng and of selling pelts to hatters, he made detours into the Ohio valley and into Kentucky.[143]

On March 17, 1817, Astor appointed Crooks and Robert Stuart as agents of the American Fur Company, Crooks to have an annual salary of $2000, an expense account, and a one-twentieth participating interest in the profits and losses.[144] Crooks was forthwith placed in command of affairs at Michilimacinac, Stuart, as his junior in rank, being in charge of the fur-gathering operations.[145] Crooks's duties kept him part of the time in New York City and much of the time in travel between various fur-trading centres. In this travel, as in that of later years, he was wont to use a canoe wherever possible and for however long a distance, going by this frail craft even from Buffalo to Michilimacinac.[146]

It was during this period that, in the winter of 1820-21, he visited Washington, D. C.,[147] and immediately afterward went to Paris for a conference with Astor.[148] The stay at Washington, though resulting in acquainting congressmen with facts about Oregon, was very possibly induced by Crooks's ardent wish that the United States Government should terminate its factory system in the indians' country.[149] It is not disclosed what relation, if any, there was between the Parisian visit and the approximately contemporary publishing of the Astorian accounts in *Nouvelles Annales*.

In 1822, on the creation of the American Fur Company's Western Department, Crooks became one of the managers of this newly formed branch. Accordingly he diminished his contact with Michilimacinac and substituted St. Louis as a focal point for his activities, continuing, however, to spend much of his time in New York City as well as in trips to the various trading-posts.[150] The New York City directories of his time list him as a householder in that city in each year from 1825 till 1859 except in the years 1827, 1828, 1838.[151]

On March 10, 1825, he married, at St. Louis, Emilie, youngest of the four daughters (Marie, Aimée, Pelagie and Emilie) of Bernard and Emilie (Labbadie) Pratte of that city.[152] By the marriage he was brought into family alliance with people dominant in the Missouri Fur Company, his mother-in-law being a daughter of Silvestre and Pelagie (Chouteau) Labbadie.[153]

When in 1834 Astor withdrew from the fur business, Crooks, heading a syndicate, purchased from him the so-called Northern Department, and, providing for a continuance of its operation under the name of American Fur Company, became its president.[154] In 1842 business reverses ended this company's existence; but Crooks remained in the fur traffic, and in 1845 he opened in New York City a commission house for dealing in pelts, a business which he conducted until his death.[155]

It is commonly though without foundation stated that he was a trustee of the Astor Library.

He died June 6, 1859, at his New York home, 14 St. Mark's Place, and was buried at Greenwood Cemetery, Brooklyn.[156]

There survived him three daughters, who had married respectively Joannes Gourd, Eugene Plunkett and Charles Noel.

Two days after his decease, the *New York Herald* in the course of an editorial said of him:

> "He seemed to die of no peculiar disease. He quietly passed from the world as one retired to sleep.
>
> His whole life, united as it was with laborious and active pursuits, was under all circumstances marked by kindness and humanity. He was emphatically an honest man."

Robert McClellan, whom Ramsay Crooks describes as "of Hagerstown, Maryland," was son of Robert, and was born about 1770 near Mercersburg, Pennsylvania.[157]

Of slight physique but muscular, with eyes dark, deep-set, and piercing, he was impetuous and reckless, and possessed a temper which sometimes was ungovernable.[158]

His earliest employment was as a "pack-horseman."[159]

Disposed for greater adventure, in 1790 he enlisted as a scout in the United States army, his initial station being at Fort Gower, a stockade in southern Ohio. Continuing as a scout, he served under Major-General "Mad Anthony" Wayne throughout the campaign against hostile indians northwest of the Ohio River, and so remained in the army until local warfare ended with the Treaty of Greenville, August 3, 1795. Meanwhile he had attained the rank of lieutenant and had been wounded, one of the injuries being from a ball which entered under his scapula and emerged at the top of his shoulder.[160]

During the four years immediately after his leaving the army, McClellan ostensibly lived with his brother at Hamilton, Ohio, but he devoted most of his time to hunting in the forest.[161]

In the summer of 1799, he went to New Orleans and there was ill for a long time from yellow fever.[162]

Later, suffering from the effects of sickness and wounds, he decided to seek a pension and betook himself to Philadelphia, where he applied to the Secretary of War. The examining surgeon reported that McClellan, though deserving compensation, was entitled to only one-third of a full pension. McClellan, greatly offended, declined at first to accept the proffered allowance, but presently, at the instance of the Quartermaster General, he acceded to the government's ruling and also took a position in the quartermaster's bureau. In 1801, he was sent to St. Louis on matters connected with the army's commissary bureau; after completing his mission, he retired from federal employ.[163]

His next venture, so far as we know, was fur trading with the indians on the Missouri River. The time of the venture's beginning is not disclosed, but it assuredly was before September 12, 1806, because on that date Lewis and Clark saw him with his outward bound crew at a camp 430 miles above the Missouri's mouth,[164] and it probably was at least as early as 1805 inasmuch as, when granting him a trading license on May 1, 1807, the granting office made note that he had been "On Missouri with Indians in amity 2 Years."[165] His fur business, which apparently was centred in Council Bluffs and Fire Prairie,[166] lasted until the autumn of 1810.

During a portion of the period (from 1807 till the spring of 1810), he had Ramsay Crooks as a partner, and shared in experiences that are recited under the caption of Ramsay Crooks in prior pages of this foreword.

After the close of the partnership, McClellan essayed to continue the business for his own account, and accordingly equipped a trading post in the vicinity of Council Bluffs.[167] Presently, during one of his absences, the Sioux besieged the post, disarmed its inmates, and stole goods worth some three thousand dollars. McClellan, on his return, confronted the robbers and demanded restitution, but was able to recover only one-sixth of the loot. Dispirited, he divided the salvage among his men, and shortly afterward he and his entire party began a retreat to St. Louis.[168]

Reaching the mouth of the Nodaway River, he found there Wilson Price Hunt's expedition encamped in winter quarters. Earlier in the year, McClellan had considered[169] joining the then prospective Astorian enterprise, and now he actively threw in his lot with it and became a partner to the extent of two and one-half shares.[170] At this time, November, 1810, he wrote from the Nodaway camp to his brother William: "Six days ago I arrived at this place from my settlement, which is two hundred miles above on the Missouri. My mare is with you at Hamilton, having two colts. I wish you to give one to brother John, the other to your son James, and the mare to your wife. If I possessed anything more except my gun at present, I would throw it into the river, or give it away, as I intend to begin the world anew tomorrow."[171]

On April 21, 1811, Hunt's expedition, including McClellan, quitted its winter quarters and resumed the westward journey. In the course of the ensuing overland trip, McClellan had the encounter with Manuel Lisa already described under the heading of Ramsay Crooks. Not satisfied with thus menacing Lisa, he later threatened to shoot the expedition's interpreter, Edward Rose, the moment suspected treachery should become a reality.[172]

When Hunt's expedition, in distress near the site of present-day

Milner, Idaho, divided itself into sections, each to pursue its individual course, McClellan with three men was despatched downstream along the Snake's right bank.[173] Presently he and his companions, chancing upon two other groups from the expedition's dispersing camp,[174] consolidated with them into a single band of eleven souls and succeeded, with severest hardship, not only in traversing mountains which a few days later became so snow-bound as to prove impassable for Hunt, but also in finding a route that led to the Columbia River and to safety.[175] Their success was made possible by the fact that McClellan's shooting of a mountain sheep had saved them from starvation.[176]

On January 10 or 18, 1812, the eleven men, all clad in "fluttering rags," reached Astoria, being the first of Hunt's overland people to arrive there.[177]

On March 1, McClellan, dissatisfied with the meagerness of his interest and having been refused "an augmentation of shares," resigned from the Pacific Fur Company and surrendered his stock.[178]

March 22 saw him start eastward as one of the five companions of John Reed. who was expected to cross the continent with messages for Astor in New York. This venture's disruption by indians gathered at the Dalles has been mentioned in earlier pages, but it is well worth while to note the credit which Stuart's narratives accord McClellan for distinguished bravery in the fight.[179] On May 11 or 12, the foiled travellers returned to Astoria, and on June 29, McClellan again started eastward, this time to accompany Robert Stuart and actually to reach St. Louis.

On May 18, 1813, less than a month after arriving at St. Louis, McClellan was imprisoned for debt, though he presently obtained release through resort to bankruptcy.[180]

The following January, with goods furnished by Risdon H. Price of St. Louis, he opened a store at Cape Girardeau, Mo., but within six months his ill health ended the business. He retired to a farm which his friend Abraham Gallatin had in St. Louis County. But he did not restrict himself to the limits of this farm, for apparently he oscillated between it and St. Louis and, in any event, was one of the citizens who aided soldiers in their defense against indians in the Fight at the Sink Hole, May 24, 1815.[181]

During his sheltering by Gallatin, he seems to have engaged in horse racing, and at the time of his death he owed Gallatin $39.25, representing thirty days' board for himself and two boys, the stabling of two horses, and the cost, not only of three bushels of oats, but also of a quart of whiskey and a dinner for the judges on the first day of the race meet. Incidentally, his estate sold his horses for $172.50 and his wearing apparel for $145.50, and found that his debts totalled $196.[182]

He died at St. Louis, November 22, 1815, after an illness of five days, and was buried on the farm of General William Clark in St. Louis County, Mo. In 1875 there was unearthed on this farm a tombstone inscribed: "To the memory of Capt. Robert McClellan. This stone is erected by a friend who knew him to be brave, honest and sincere; an intrepid warrior, whose services deserve perpetual remembrance. A. D. 1816."[183]

Benjamin Jones, whose father had emigrated from England to Virginia, was born in that state.[184] The date of his birth has not been ascertained. When sixteen years old, lured by tales of the frontier, he fled from his father's home in present-day Kanawha County, West Virginia.[185] He was in St. Louis, Mo., prior to 1802, and it is possible that at a still earlier time he had been in Kentucky, for Washington Irving refers to him as a Kentuckian. His brother Lewis, also a youthful runaway from home, arrived at St. Louis in 1802 and eventually married a granddaughter of Daniel Boone.[186]

As to the date when Benjamin Jones entered the fur trade, there seems to be as yet no evidence. We first find him on May 22, 1811, when he and his partner, Alexander Carson, having completed a two years' trapping trip in the region of the upper Missouri, were canoeing down that stream on their homeward way to St. Louis, and had reached a spot not far below the mouth of the Niobrara River. Encountering there Hunt's westbound party, they immediately joined it.[187]

During the overland journey, Jones performed two signal services. He was one of the group of hunters who discovered and reconnoitred the Cheyenne camp at which the expedition obtained many of its horses,[188] and he was one of the two men who bravely substituted for Ramsay Crooks after Crooks, having filled a canoe with horsemeat, had vainly tried to navigate it to his own starving men across Snake River.[189]

He was one of John Reed's contingent which, in March, 1812, left Astoria for New York, but which was thwarted by indians at the Dalles. In the fight, he shot a savage who was about to murder Reed.[190] On June 29, 1812, as a member of Robert Stuart's overland party, he once more set out from Astoria, and, on this trip, he reached St. Louis.

On his arrival at St. Louis, he purchased a farm lying just below the Missouri River's mouth. After cultivating it for a few years, he joined a caravan which was headed for Santa Fe and which kept him from home for the next four years. Returning to St. Louis, he moved with his family to the neighboring town of Carondelet and later to a farm on nearby Gravois Creek. He resided on this latter farm until, in June, 1835, he died of cholera.[191]

Surviving him were his widow Margaret, two daughters and two step-daughters, as also three minor sons, Ramsay Crooks Jones, Wilson Hunt Jones and William Arbuckle Jones. His will, which was dated June 2, 1835, disposed of, among other things, 54 books and 14 slaves. It also directed that his widow should "educate my minor children in a becoming manner, according to her best judgment" and that "none of the slaves bequeathed as hereinbefore mentioned, shall ever be sold, by my children or their Heirs, under any pretence whatever."[192]

François LeClairc (Le Clairc, Le Claire, and LeClerc), a

Canadian half-breed[193] and an *engagé*, was a member of Wilson Price Hunt's overland expedition. After the débâcle at the site of Milner, Idaho, and until he pushed forward with Hunt on December 12, he was of Ramsay Crooks's contingent and had the harrowing experiences described under the caption of Ramsay Crooks. Later he travelled with Robert Stuart to St. Louis and seems thereafter to have disappeared from record.

ANDRE VALLÈ (Vallée) was an *engagé*, and concerning him we find only that he was a Canadian[194] and a member of Hunt's overland party and that he subsequently accompanied Stuart to St. Louis. *Astoria*, II, p. 111, styles him "Andri Vallar."

JOHN DAY, a son of Ambrose Day of Culpeper County, Virginia, was born about 1770.[195]

It is quite probable that before moving to Missouri he had lived in Kentucky: not only does Washington Irving interchangeably style him a Virginian and a Kentuckian, but also Day had a brother Lewis, and there was a Lewis Day residing, in 1797, at Limestone (now Maysville), Ky.[196]

On March 2, 1798, John Day, being then in St. Louis, petitioned the Spanish governor to grant him 240 "arpens of land on a river south of the Missouri" for use as a "habitacion" (plantation). Either then or at some other time, Day obtained from the Spaniards a grant of 700 arpens (possibly including the abovementioned 240) on the "Waters of Point Labaddie Creek" in present-day Franklin County, Mo.[197]

Though his absence on trapping expeditions may have made farming a somewhat desultory process, by 1802 he had cultivated a large field of corn on the 700 arpens. The following year, indians wrecked the holdings of all the settlers at Point Labaddie. In 1804, Day, instead of himself tilling his land, hired one Asa Musick to do it, and, as part of the wage, allowed his own cabin to be occupied by Musick. The next twelvemonth, Day sold or mortgaged a portion of his plantation to Musick and thereupon left for the so-called Boone's Lick country, the centre of which lay about four miles from the present-day town of Franklin, Franklin County, Mo.[198]

Having discovered at or near Boone's Lick a deposit of saltpeter, in 1809 he formed with Benjamin Cooper and John Farrell a partnership for mining it.[199]

In at least some of these later years he seems, under employ by Ramsay Crooks and other traders, to have served in fur-gathering ventures on the Missouri River.[200]

In the autumn of 1810 or early part of 1811, Day entered Wilson Price Hunt's camp on the Nodaway River and was enrolled as a member of the expedition. He then, according to Washington Irving, "was about forty years of age, six feet two inches high, straight as an Indian; with an elastic step as if he trod on springs, and a handsome, open, manly countenance. It was his boast that, in his younger days, nothing could hurt or daunt him; but he had 'lived too fast,' and injured his constitution by his excesses. Still he was strong of hand, bold of heart, a prime woodman, and an almost unerring shot. He had the frank spirit of a Virginian, and the rough heroism of a pioneer of the west."[201]

During the overland journey with Hunt's caravan, Day performed three services which Irving deemed worthy of note. At the Aricara village he discovered and reported a plot in which some of the party's malcontents, bent on desertion, had stolen weapons together with a barrel of gunpowder, and were to purloin a boat and make their way to St. Louis.[202] He was one of the hunters who discovered and reconnoitred the Cheyenne camp, as already described under the caption of Benjamin Jones.[203] On the expedition's arrival at the confluence of Hoback River with the south fork of the Snake, he with two other men explored that south fork for forty-eight hours' travel below the confluence and reported it as unnavigable for canoes.[204] Thereupon the caravan resumed its weary trudge toward Henry's Fort.

The subsequent journey of Day from modern Milner's site to Astoria has been described under the caption of Ramsay Crooks. It involved such intense suffering that it may fairly be said to have been ever in the shadow of death.

Seven weeks after reaching Astoria, Day, as one of Stuart's contingent, started for St. Louis. However, he did very little more than start. Within the first four days an overtaxed physique so far rebelled that, deranged in nerves or brain, he was sent back to Astoria.[205]

Despite Irving's statement to the contrary, Day recovered, for, under date of March 20, 1814, Alexander Henry made note at Astoria: "The last of the free Americans, John Day, Carson and Canning arrived from the Willamette."[206] Shortly after this, according to Henry, "Arrangements [were] made with J. Day, Carson and other freemen, on halves for Spanish River" (Green River).[207] In all likelihood he was the "Joshua" Day who, together with David Stuart, was passenger in the seventh canoe of the "Grand Brigade" which, on April 4, 1814, left Fort George (Astoria) for the country eastward of the Rocky Mountains.[208]

Tradition is that, throughout the remainder of his life, Day was in the service of the North West Company, and frequented the upper reaches of Snake River's valley.[209]

On February 15, 1820, when encamped by a stream in one of the high valleys of Idaho's Salmon River Mountains, he, being then "infirm of body," executed a written will.[210]

On the following day he died. According to a memorandum by some of his companions, "He appeared to die the death of a good man."[211]

By his will (probated, October 28, 1836, in the Surrogate's Court of Chautauqua County, New York; the probate petitioner, Donald McKenzie, being then a resident of that county), Day not only gave to Donald McKenzie the 240 arpens of land on Point Labaddie Creek together with the one-third interest in the saltpeter mine near Boone's Lick and in that mine's accrued profits, but also gave to McKenzie's daughter Rachel "all and every my ready cash with the lawful interest arising therefrom, and lying in the hands of my former master, Mr. John Jacob Astor, Merchant of New York."[212]

Joseph Miller, asserted to have been member of a Baltimore, Md., family,[213] was born in Pennsylvania, from which latter state he was appointed in June, 1799, a cadet in the Second Regiment United States Infantry. Promoted, February 16, 1801, to a second lieutenancy in that same regiment and transferred, April 1, 1802, to the First Regiment United States Infantry, on June 21, 1805, he resigned from the army,[214] it is said because of pique at being refused a furlough.[215] Thereupon he turned to beaver trapping and to trading with the indians.[216]

Though the Pacific Fur Company's partnership articles, dated June 23, 1810, recite that Miller then had in contemplation going with Astor's people to the Pacific coast and also provide for his becoming a partner to the extent of two and one-half shares, he seems to have had no active connection with that company until the early autumn of that year, when he met Hunt at St. Louis, and there aided in the recruiting of additional men for the prospective overland expedition.[217]

As a member of this expedition, he participated on May 31, 1811, in a placating conference with belligerent indians on the bank of the Missouri River.[218]

For some time prior to the expedition's arriving, in the last week of September, at the confluence of the Hoback River with the south fork of the Snake, Miller had become increasingly discontented and irritable.[219] In addition to a possibly innate capriciousness, he was harboring dissatisfaction at the small extent of his financial interest, and he was suffering from a bodily ailment which made horseback riding extremely irksome.[220] When the mouth of Hoback River was reached, disregarding all proof of the utter impracticability of boating on the Snake's south fork, he vigorously urged that canoes be built and be substituted for horses.[221] Outvoted on this proposal, he kept on with the expeditioners until, on October 8, they had reached Henry's Fort. Arriving there, he irascibly resigned from his partnership and the company's enterprise, and thereupon announced his intention of throwing in his lot with Robinson, Hoback, Reznor and Cass, four trappers whom Hunt had just then detached from the expedition that they might do local trapping and deliver their pelts at the nearest of the fur company's prospective posts.[222]

On October 10, Miller and his four trapping companions departed under the guidance of two Snake indians.[223] Of their extensive wanderings until August 20, 1812, when Stuart's party rescued Miller and three of the four companions, there seems to be no contemporaneous record other than the account which Stuart included in his entry of that date (pp. 85, 86).

Miller, thus rescued "and his curiosity and desire of travelling thro' the Indian countries being fully satisfied,"[224] continued with Stuart's party until it arrived at St. Louis.

Concerning his subsequent life we have no information.

Edward Robinson, John Hoback (Hobaugh, Hobough, Hubbough and Hauberk) and Jacob Reznor (Rizner, Risner, Resner, Resnor and Reasoner) were Kentuckians with seemingly no differentiation in their known records other than that Robinson, who was born in approximately 1745, had been scalped in his early days and was forced always to keep a protective handkerchief atop his head.[225]

All three of them before associating themselves with the Astorians had been, from the outset or by later enlistment, members of the Missouri Fur Company's brigade which left St. Louis in 1809.[226] As such, they had journeyed up the Missouri River to the vicinity of its Three Forks, and, after being harried there by indians and by grizzly bears, with Andrew Henry and some others of the brigade they had thrust southwestward to the north fork of Snake River and, in the autumn of 1810, built upon its bank a group of cabins styled Henry's Fort.[227]

At this fort's abandonment in the spring of 1811, Robinson, Hoback and Reznor had gone eastward on a route which, save for a quite possible single divergence[228] (their seeming use of Twogwotee Pass and its approaches instead of Union Pass), was probably identical with the course along which, though in reverse direction, they later were to guide the Astorians marching westward from the Aricara village to Henry's Fort.

Reaching the Missouri River, they had started down it with firm intent to gain St. Louis.[229] Their river voyage begun, they were hailed in their two canoes on the morning of May 26 by Hunt's people, who were at breakfast on the Missouri's bank a short distance above the Niobrara River's mouth. An invitation to re-engage in trapping proved irresistible to the three adventurers, and so they relinquished thought of St. Louis and forthwith accepted employment in Hunt's brigade.[230]

Picturing to Hunt the danger from indians on the upper Missouri, they dissuaded him from his former plan of following the track of Lewis and Clark, and it was agreed that they should pilot his expedition westward along the route on which they themselves had just returned.[231]

Their accompanying the expedition as far as to Henry's Fort, where they were detached for trapping purposes, their subsequent long wandering in company with Cass and Miller, their loss of Cass and their retrieval by Stuart's party have been touched upon in former pages of this foreword.

As soon as they were rescued and had been supplied with new equipment, there occurred a recrudescence of the indomitable spirit that had made them re-enter the wilds when, fifteen months before, they first met Hunt's Astorians. Now, rather than proceed with Stuart to St. Louis, they preferred to wait until the arrival of John Reed, obtain from him further gear, and later begin a two years' independent quest for furs.[232]

On Reed's advent, they procured the furnishings they required and then set forth on a search for pelts.[233] They continued this search until the end of September, 1813; then, having shortly before been robbed by indians, they joined Reed's trapping band, Robinson and Hoback going to a cabin which Reed erected at or near the mouth of present-day Boise River, Reznor stationing himself at a camp some five days' travel from it.[234]

In January, 1814, indians attacked both cabin and camp, and slew, among others, Reed and our three friends.[235] In the words of Irving, "We cannot but feel some sympathy with that persevering trio of Kentuckians, Robinson, Reznor and Hoback; who twice turned back when on their way homeward, and lingered in the wilderness to perish by the hands of savages."[236]

Such were the companions of Stuart on his journey.

He and six of these companions were doubtless the first whites to traverse or even to espy South Pass. This is an assumption based as follows:

It seems well established that prior to the Stuart party's entering the pass on October 21, 1812, no Canadians,[237] French,[238] or Spaniards[239] had approached it; and thus the only white invaders of its general neighborhood had been (1st) the trappers of one of Manuel Lisa's two firms[240] and (2d) the westbound Astorians commanded by Wilson Price Hunt.

Accordingly, it is necessary to trace the movements of these Lisan trappers and these westbound Astorians if we would learn whether or not any of them preceded the Stuart party into the pass.

Lisa's first firm despatched from St. Louis, in the spring of 1807, an expedition[241] consisting ultimately of 44 men, inclusive of Lisa, John Colter,[242] Jean Baptiste Champlain, *fils*, and —— Porteau (*alias* Poitras). The expedition, having boated to the Big Horn River's mouth, erected there in November, 1807, a trading-post that in the spring of 1808 was made into a stronghold and styled Fort Raymond—[243] later interchangeably mentioned as Fort Manuel and as Manuel's Fort.[244] Lisa left a garrison at this fort when in the summer of 1808 he and some of his people returned to St. Louis.[245]

Subsequent to these events, Lisa's second firm, the so-called Missouri Fur Company,[246] sent from St. Louis in June, 1809, a large brigade[247] which included in its membership Lisa, Pierre Menard, Andrew Henry, Archibald Pelton and, either from the outset or as a later acquisition, Edward Robinson, John Hoback, Jacob Reznor and possibly Ezekiel Williams.[248] The brigade ascended the Missouri River as far as the Gros Ventres' (Minitaris') uppermost village,[249] in the vicinity of which it built a blockhouse.[250] From this blockhouse sallied two parties, one of which in February, 1810, reached Fort Raymond and, finding the garrison of 1808 to be yet in occupancy, merged with it.[251] The other and larger party—about 32 men in all—[252] with Pierre Menard and Andrew Henry in command and with John Colter as guide,[253] moved westerly past the Three Forks of the Missouri, and in April, 1810, began the erection of a fortified camp at a site which, lying in the gore between the Jefferson and Madison Rivers, was approximately two miles above these rivers' confluence.[254]

Of these outpost groups, the first to demand our attention is the Fort Raymond garrison, which, being stationed some 275 miles northeastward of South Pass, would be irrelevant to our present thesis were it not for the facts, (a) that from this garrison John Colter began his epic march of 1807, (b) that this garrison included Ezekiel Williams, Jean Baptiste Champlain, *fils*, —— Porteau and their future co-wanderers, and (c) that these thus included folk have been committed by *Coyner* (pp. 86 *et seq.*) to travelling—in 1810-12—amid a geographic maze which, until resolved, might seem possibly to embrace the pass. If Colter's route of 1807 as delineated on the maps of William Clark[255] and of John H. Robinson[256] was his actual one, he always kept in a latitude considerably northward of that of South Pass.[257] Also it is perhaps significant that Colter seems to have made no mention of either this pass or its neighborhood during his half-day's conversation (May 18, 1811) with Hunt's expeditioners outbound for Astoria.[258] As for *Coyner's* geographical victims—Ezekiel Williams and his fellow itinerants—, their path, as we know from the published letters of Williams[259] and of Lisa[260] and from other sources,[260] did not involve South Pass.[261]

Our investigation requires that we now shift our thought to the already mentioned fortified camp which, in April, 1810, Menard, Henry, and their men had begun building between the Jefferson and Madison Rivers. Nine days after the commencement of the camp's erection the Atsina indians killed five of the personnel[262] and inaugurated a series of attacks so frequent and so fierce that presently John Colter and two of the trappers, believing the place untenable, retreated to Fort Raymond.[263] The Atsinas' slaughter of three more of the party in May[264] and the viciousness of the assaults by grizzly bears[265] soon caused the camp to be evacuated.[266] Some of its people, under the captaincy of Menard, retraced the route by which they had come,[267] and the rest of them ("the greater part of the company," according to *James*, p. 83) advanced with Henry up the Madison River, across the continental divide, and down the north fork of Snake River to a spot near the site of the modern town of St. Anthony, Idaho.[268] At this spot they reared the cabins which collectively became known as Henry's Fort.[269] Among the persons with Henry in this venture were Robinson, Hoback, and Reznor, and possibly also Pelton,[270] though Pelton, demented by his experiences during the Atsinas' warfare, may already have begun the aimless, piteous, and uncharted wandering which held him for many months amid the Shoshone indians and eventually carried him to the vicinity of the Columbia River and to his rescue by Astorians.[271]

Henry's Fort was, in its turn, abandoned in the spring of 1811.[272] Upon its desertion, the garrison split into three groups which severally disposed themselves as follows:

Henry led some of the men in retrocession along the trail which had brought them thither, and so attained the Aricara villages in present-day South Dakota.[273] To this group, Pelton, if ever a resident of Henry's Fort, was doubtless attached until his daft vagabondage began. The second group—limited, so far as appears, to Robinson, Hoback and Reznor—went eastward by a path described under the caption of these three men's names. The third group, seeking the Spanish settlements, descended, so the record states, the "Rio del Norte"[274] (present-day Rio Grande), and was quite possibly the "party of hunters south of the Yellowstone" who "were taken prisoners by the Spaniards and carried into Santa Fe,"[275] although these prisoners may have consisted of the detachment which, as mentioned in footnote 261, withdrew from Ezekiel Williams's troop and started westerly from the regions of the Arkansas River and of the South Platte River's upper waters. A mere glance at maps, whether topographic or of old trails,[276] gives assurance that this third group which arrived on an upper stretch of the "Rio del Norte" made no penetration toward South Pass, but kept west of it when travelling southward in its latitude. Accordingly, the route of none of the refugees from Henry's Fort, other than possibly the unpurposed route of Pelton, seems to have touched South Pass. As for Pelton, is it probable that his shelterers, the Shoshone indians, would have taken him into the pass and thus into the domain of their dreaded foe, the Absarokas?

What of the westbound Astorians? When crossing the continental divide, they traversed Union Pass, but they later detached four men[277] at the Hoback River's mouth, another five men[278] at Henry's Fort, and still later released another four men[279] in eastern Oregon. That none of these detached and released folk attained South Pass is a conclusion to which the reasoning in the subjoined footnote[280] ostensibly leads.

In ending here our discussion of South Pass, we call attention to a letter which is reprinted in a footnote[281] and which, written by Ramsay Crooks, relates to the Stuart party's traversing of that pass. Inasmuch as Stuart's journal and travelling memoranda indubitably establish the fact and date of the traversal, the Crooks letter is needless for evidential purpose. Nevertheless, the identity of its author requires that it be included in our record.

The topics next to be considered are the production, the format, and the provenance of the Stuart manuscripts, which, written wholly in ink, occupy two ordinary white-paged blankbooks—the journal using one of these books, the travelling memoranda the other. These books, save for extent of wear, are identical in appearance, each of them having had originally 86 leaves 20.9 by 17 cms. in size, and being bound in original checkered brown paper boards with black linen back—the journal's binding, however, being protected by a paper covering, folded and pasted.

It is manifest that, with few exceptions, the entries in the journal were made contemporaneously with the events they describe, inasmuch as the 117½ pages immediately following the title page are solidly filled with items which, covering a period of eight months and containing intricate notations of route and distance, possess an accuracy such as denies suggestion of their having been the creatures of memory. This presumption of synchrony is corroborated by the aspect of both the ink and the penmanship. The ink, instead of being—as in the travelling memoranda's instance—of a single color (black) and a single depth of shade, appears on this page as densely black, on that page as merely blackish, and on still other pages as markedly tinged with brown, the inconstancy of tint being due to the fact that Stuart during the progress of his march was compelled from time to time to infuse new supplies of writing fluid, the ingredients consisting of saps and berry-juices thickened occasionally with drops of his own blood. The evidence relative to these pigmental needs and sources we received from Mrs. Alexander Mackay-Smith, who was told it by her grandmother, Stuart's widow. The journal's penmanship not only lacks the uniformity pervading the handwriting in the travelling memoranda and in numerous examined letters of Stuart, but also exhibits, throughout various entries, constrained strokes which intimate the writing hand to have been hindered by a comfortless posture of the writer's body. With assertive contrast, the easy, uninterrupted flow of the chirography in the travelling memoranda and in the examined letters tacitly links their creation to the use of a table or desk.

Concerning the date of Stuart's producing the travelling memoranda we have no knowledge except that it necessarily was subsequent to the period of his overland trip and prior to the time of the narrative's rendition into French for purpose of publication by *Nouvelles Annales* in 1821. Nor do we know why he prepared this narrative—whether as merely a report to Astor or as material deliberately intended for publishment. However, we may rest assured that the text as printed in *Nouvelles Annales* originated, not from any manuscript which Stuart had written in French, but instead from some other person's redacted translation of Stuart's travelling memoranda. For this assurance, there is valid foundation. On the one hand, Stuart in 1819 seems to have disclaimed sufficient fluency in the Gallic language to warrant his using it for the phrasing of even a mere business letter;[282] on the other hand, the French text in *Nouvelles Annales*, when compared with the English text in the travelling memoranda, is shown to have ineptly converted various of Stuart's creeks and hills into rivers and mountains, and not only to have stressed matters which Stuart seemingly thought routinary, but also to have omitted all reference to other matters which evidently he deemed important.

Incidentally, such a comparison also will prepare the reader for gauging the extent of dependableness in the version which *Nouvelles Annales* gives of Wilson Price Hunt's diary, both French translations showing by their stylistic mannerisms that they were made by the same person. Not improbably a perusal of this latter version will create surmise that the Hunt diary, in its rendering into French, has been so compacted as to omit many important details. But, until the time—if ever—that the original diary appears, scholars will have no closer approach to it than through the French version.

So far as appears, Stuart made no duplicate draft of either of his narratives. The journal remained in the keeping of certain of his lineal descendants in successive generations until it diverted to Frederick S. Dellenbaugh, from whom it passed direct to its present owner, William Robertson Coe. Incidentally, Mr. Dellenbaugh, when in possession of it, caused several typescript copies to be made, and one of them was given to the New York Public Library. The travelling memoranda—acquired by Mr. Coe at a sale held May 13, 1930, at the American Art Association-Anderson Galleries, Inc. in New York City—was announced by representatives of that trustworthy auction-mart to have been found in a cupboard which was in Washington Irving's home at the time of his death, and ever since its discovery to have been held by Irving's relatives.[283] Not improbably Irving obtained it in 1834 or 1835 when, as a prerequisite to his writing *Astoria*, he was seeking "journals," "letters," "documents" and "business papers" connected with Astor's Western venture.[284] Concerning the travelling memoranda's lodgement prior to Irving's tenure, there seems to be no written history other than a notation which, endorsed on the manuscript, is possibly a souvenir of the contact with Paris, for it reads, *Retour de l'embouchure de la Columbia/jusqua au Miſsouri/par/ & six personnes*, and is not in the handwriting of either Irving or Stuart.

Between Stuart's travelling memoranda and his journal there are certain discrepancies. Though severally indicated by their appurtenant footnotes, they are set forth in the following tabulation, which, in connection with each subject, gives two figures that respectively show (1) the number of instances in which both journal and travelling memoranda mention the subject and (2) the number of instances in which the travelling memoranda and journal disagree as regards it.

Compass bearing,	292	14	Number of persons	88	8
Mileage travelled	355	60	Number of objects	41	12
Width of streams &c.	202	40	Number of animals	65	9

Of the travelling memoranda's divergencies in stating compass bearings, only one is corrective; the other 13 are erroneous. Although these 13, because dealing exclusively with initial letters instead of with words—for example, with "S." as the contraction for "South"—, may possibly be dismissable as representing mere slips of the pen, and although a corresponding excuse may perchance attach to such of the other above tabulated aberrances as contain Arabic numerals, there are among these latter aberrances a few that refuse so facile a disposal. The travelling memoranda's mutation of the journal's "10 miles" into "17"[285] is readily understandable; but how are we to construe its action when, essaying to copy the journal's description of "six" Snake indians in "four" huts, it transliterates words into Arabic digits and produces "130" Snake indians in "40" huts?[286] It is perhaps a legitimate assumption that Stuart, while paraphrasing his journal into his travelling memoranda, was so preoccupied with the composing of the added matter as sometimes to lapse into unthinking parrotry when transcribing entries which smacked of mere routine.

Much of the travelling memoranda's entries, save for very numerous dissimilarities in punctuation and capitalization[287] and save for occasional differences in the spelling or choice of commonplace words and in the sequence of phrases, is a mere repetition of the corresponding entries in the journal. Accordingly, to our printing of the journal we have not added a printing of the travelling memoranda as an entire and separate entity. But, by bracketed italicized interpolations in the journal and by footnotes, we have duplicated all the supplemental matter which the travelling memoranda offer; also, by further footnotes, we have specified all the other textual divergencies except the many trivial ones listed above. Thus, in our printing, the Roman type not only carries the journal's complete text but also, in conjunction with the bracketed italics and the footnotes, gives the travelling memoranda's entire text in a form which is variant from the original in merely the inconsequential details we have just described.[288]

Foreword

The journal's text as printed in the present work is, except in the particulars hereinafter mentioned, a precise copy of the original, and thus reproduces Stuart's wording, spelling, punctuation and paragraphing. A like exactness attaches to whatever portions of the travelling memoranda we have put into print. Therefore, the occasional verbal oddities—such as "decending," "vegitation," "vigerous," "seperated," "perpetrrate," "villans," "charater," "granate," "effet" (for "effect"), "ludicerous" (for "ludicrous"), "foilage" (for "foliage")—, the few repetitive and uncompleted words, and the omission of punctuation from the ends of many sentences should not be scored as compositors' errata.

Reference has been made to excepted particulars. They are as follows:

I. Both journal and travelling memoranda, though not divided or captioned by Stuart, have arbitrarily been divided into chapters and supplied with chapter headings.

II. Though Stuart did not paginate the journal, the present editor has made bold to number its pages, and, when doing so, has ignored all that Stuart left blank.[289]

III. Three of the journal's postscripts have been moved from their normal positions in Stuart's addenda to places beside the original entries which these postscripts were designed to amend. Incidentally, this transposal compels the use of parallel columns on such of our pages as contain these particular original entries.[290]

IV. Stuart's interlineations have, without footnote comment save in a few instances, been inserted in such portions of the normal lines of the printed texts as are indicated by his carets. The texts as printed are those which Stuart made definitive by various emendations of his original phrasings—these revisions, though scant in the travelling memoranda, being numerous in parts of the journal. Except where the amendments deal with relatively unimportant matters—such as, for example, substitution of "were" for "was"—, the deleted words are reproduced in our footnotes. And in a single instance an elided word, in another instance an elided phrase, have been restored to the text—footnotes giving warning of these restorations.

V. In the travelling memoranda's manuscript there is, at the bottom of every page other than p. 24, a catchword, and there are in the left-hand margins (a) opposite each day's entry with a few exceptions, numerals stating the day's mileage, and (b) at the bottom of page 1 and at both top and bottom of each subsequent page, numerals stating the total mileage theretofore journeyed. Because of the format of our printed pages we have not reproduced either the catchwords or the numerals.

VI. Also omitted from our printing are two diagrams[291] which appear in the journal's manuscript. The first of these diagrams, because of its context, possibly represents the crude beginning of a sketch outlining an indian's fishnet; but it equally well resembles the vagrant pencillings one makes when absent-minded. The second of the omitted diagrams[292] is in the form of a gridironed chart patently intended for meteorological statistics, which were, however, never entered. The captions atop the columns of this chart read severally as follows: "Time of Observ^{ton}," "Thermometer," "Sky," "Wind," "Latitude," "Long," "Variation," "Barometer," "Remarks."

The present work, though containing a list of cited publications, proffers no bibliography relating to the Oregon Trail. This hiatus, a purposed one, is due to an assumption that a proper bibliography of that trail must necessarily include several hundred additional titles which, though of much importance, do not throw light on Stuart's march. With like aim to avoid redundancy and with a view to the reader's convenience, various manuscripts are withheld from mention in the printed list, which restricts itself to publications already made and to other readily accessible sources.

Nor does the present work display illustrations picturing the terrain which Stuart crossed. It had been planned that photographs should be made of every spot saliently connected with his journey. But forthwith the camera found itself confronted by highways, railroads, houses, fences, bridges, motor-cars, telegraph wires and signboards. While a few spots—notably the site of the first of the "winter quarters"—remain unsullied, most of them have been victimized by civilization's progress. Near the scene of the attempted cannibalism is now an advertisement of the merits of a restaurant. Where Stuart dejectedly struggled up South Pass we modern motorists learn that there is dance music in a not far distant roof-garden. And where Stuart and his companions, standing in Nebraskan snow, anxiously debated whether to press forward we of today confidently rely upon a large sign which proclaims that road maps and detailed information as to routes are obtainable at the office of the local chamber of commerce. Stuart and his comrades toiled through 1800 miles of majestic loneliness, fatiguing miles, if you please, but not monotonous. Monotony did not invade the West until the excitement of entire solitude was dashed by the rumble of the covered-wagon and by the reduction of unpopulated empires into the humdrum of mere neighborhoods. Rather than destroy the mental picture which imagination can conjure, we have foregone the camera's portrayal of present-day reality.

As for maps, we urge that the reader who seeks geographic detail with entire accuracy consult such productions of the United States Geological Survey as our footnotes cite, these productions being furnished by the Survey's office upon request and at an infinitesimal charge. In order to effect gentle coercion in this regard and also to avoid the errors which topographic charts of our own creation would doubtless contain, the maps bound into the present work are of extreme simplicity.

To escape verbosity, the footnotes, when designating location, refrain from specifying latitude and longitude save in instances where the cited maps fail to disclose a salient landmark either at the described spot or in its neighborhood.

Such portions of *Nouvelles Annales* as are translated in this work will be found in Appendix A (pp. 267-308 *infra*). This relegation to later pages, though shifting Hunt's diary—or rather a translation of the French redaction of it—from its normal position in chronologic sequence, nevertheless spares the reader from facing, at the very outset, the relatively unimportant *An account of events at Fort Astoria during more than a year (from 1811 to 1812)*.

In translating into English the French edition of the Hunt diary, we have

> (1) allotted to some of the French words in various paragraphs, not their customary English meaning, but instead the significance suggested either by the corresponding paragraphs of *Astoria*[293] or by the actual character of the described terrain,
>
> (2) transposed a few clauses so that their statements might become consonant with the local topography, and
>
> (3) indicated by letters instead of numerals the French footnotes.

Incidentally, the French text's loose use of quotation marks, though irritating—and these marks, for some undisclosed reason, appear in only the first few pages—, has been faithfully repeated in our translation, though a few additional such marks have arbitrarily been inserted by us.

Gratitude demands a listing of the people who have materially contributed to the preparation of this present volume.

My wife's well-considered counsel as to the marshalling of data and the scheme of phrasing has, from the outset of my labors, very frequently been sought and as often followed.

And when immersed in details I lost perspective as to methods of presentation, Professor Thomas Jefferson Wertenbaker of Princeton University and his colleagues generously came to my rescue with scholarly suggestions that have resulted in the format adopted for our printing.

In the matter of the trail's course there are various persons requiring mention. To Messrs. Samuel Thompson, Roy Raley, Fay LeGrow, Nesmith Ankeny and Harold Warner, all of Pendleton, Ore., and to Mr. Albert Hunter of LaGrande in that same state I am very deeply indebted for their thoughtful analyses concerning the twists and turns of Stuart's route from Walla Walla River to the Snake River. Mr. Joseph S. Harvey of Twin Falls, Idaho, has my thanks for his trustworthy pilotage in the region of Hunt's caches. Nor do I forget my obligation to Messrs. George Hiram Voorhees and Ralph William Hopkins, who throughout two days at Mr. Hopkins's law office in Pinedale, Wyo., ungrudgingly not only gave me the benefit of their wise judgment and their intimate knowledge of Wyoming's trails, but also checked and rechecked Stuart's Wyoming itinerary as outlined in our footnotes. Mr. John Gilman of Boulder, Colo., was a particularly helpful adviser at South Pass and in its vicinity. To man after man along the trace I owe many bits of local data. County surveyors, sheriffs, ranchmen, cowboys, road-menders, mail-carriers, and forest-rangers interestedly pored over a copy of Stuart's journal and over topographic maps and lent their best mentality to a charting of Stuart's course through their several neighborhoods. But, in this connection, outstanding in my recollection is my dear friend, Mr. John Pedrick Richmond of Staten Island, New York, who in his motor-car drove me from LaGrande, Ore., eastward into Nebraska. The expertness of his driving made possible such detours as allowed, for much of the distance, a following exactly in Stuart's course and thus incidentally permitted precise ascertainment of the few isolated sections that had later to be examined either afoot or on horseback. Mr. Richmond's untiring willingness to depart from roads, to hunt for the country's old-time residents and to interview these folk rendered him an invaluable companion in the quest for accuracy.

Judge Stephen Callaghan and Clarence B. Smith, Esq., each of the New York bar, were the first to furnish precise information concerning Stuart's descendants, their friendly efforts being later supplemented by the work of the United States Navy Department, of Mrs. Alexander Mackay-Smith, of Mrs. William Newton Ladue, and, beyond all, of Stuart's great-great-grandson, Robert Stuart Cooper.

Messrs. Kenneth Wiggins Porter and Howard Corning, each of Harvard University's Graduate School of Business Administration, were most graceful in their courtesy when, for my convenience, they assembled all such of the university's Astor manuscripts as could be of use to me.

Honorable J. A. Hudon, Acting Deputy Attorney General of Quebec; Monsieur F. J. Audet, Chief of the Information of the Public Archives of Canada; and Monsieur Pierre-Georges Roy, Archiviste de la Province de Quebec, were notable for their culture and amiability when searching their records for Stuart data. Our warm thanks go also to the Public Libraries of Detroit, Boston, and New York, for in these libraries numerous files of newspapers were carefully scanned by members of the staffs.

Though Professors R. R. Huestis and Louis F. Henderson of the University of Oregon are specifically thanked in a footnote to the journal, those thanks are restated here.

Inasmuch as Miss Stella M. Drumm of the Missouri Historical Society and her assistant, Miss Bernie Watson, supplied me with the foreword's quotations from *The Missouri Gazette* and from the Pacific Fur Company's minutes, the reader may rest assured that the quotations are accurate in every respect.

Mr. Edward Eberstadt of New York City has insisted that he should be omitted from our list of academic creditors. Nevertheless, the importance of his contribution demands that his insistence be ignored. So wide is his knowledge of Western history and so opposed is he to prejudice, that repeatedly he has been consulted as to the phrasing of statements intended for insertion in the foreword and footnotes, and his advice and suggestive criticisms have been put to great advantage.

Next to be mentioned is Miss Hilda F. Kortheuer, who for six years has, as my secretary, uncomplainingly slaved in the preparation of this volume. But for her patience in copying and almost endless recopying of notes, but for her quick intelligence in suggesting textual changes, these pages would have much less clarity than they now possess.

This pleasurable task of acknowledgment being accomplished, the foreword ends, and the reader is left free to travel overland with Robert Stuart, an artist in narration, a vancourier from the incipient empire of the Western United States.

P. A. R.

Notes to Foreword

1 *Astoria*, I, p. 110, II, p. 164.

2 *Nouvelles Annales*, X, pp. 88-119, XII, pp. 21-113.

3 *Idem*, X, pp. 31-88, translated at pp. 281-308 *infra*. Although this French redaction gives many details omitted from the recital in *Astoria*, a complete account must necessarily await the discovery and verbatim publishing of Hunt's original diary.

4 See *Astoria*, I, pp. 107, 110, II, pp. 79-83, 85, 88-91, 95-102, 111-184, as also additional data underived from Stuart's writings and inserted in *Astoria*, II, pp. 113, 117, 124, 134-136, 139-141, 143. For erroneous dates in *Astoria* see *Nation*, pp. 499-501.

5 *Astoria*, II, p. 153.

6 *Idem*, II, p. 23.

7 *Idem*, II, pp. 28-30.

8 *Idem*, II, p. 24.

9 For the details of their wandering, see Stuart's entry of August 20 (pp. 85, 86).

10 See Stuart's reference to Champlain's death (entry of October 18, pp. 161, 254), as also notes 260, 261.

11 *Astoria*, II, p. 62.

12 *Mo. Gaz.; Niles*, p. 265; *Brackenridge*, p. 297; *Bradbury* [*A*], p. 223, [*B*], p. 231.

13 Issue of June 19, 1813, for both *National Intelligencer* and Niles' *Weekly Register*.

14 Issue of June 21, 1813.

15 Issue of June 16, 1813.

16 Issue of June 14, 1813.

17 Issue of June 23, 1813.

18 *National Intelligencer*, June 22, 1813; *New York Herald*, June 26, 1813; *Commercial Advertiser*, June 23, 1813; New York *Gazette and General Advertiser*, June 24, 1813; Niles' *Weekly Register*, June 26, 1813.

19 *Annales des Voyages* &c., XXII, pp. 274-291. Text in French.

20 *Views of Louisiana &c.*, by H. M. Brackenridge, Pittsburgh, 1814.

21 *Travels in the Interior of America &c.*, by John Bradbury, Liverpool, 1817.

22 *Porter*, pp. 541-543, reprints the entire letter and states its locus to be Ms., Library of Congress, Thomas Jefferson Papers, Vol. CXCIX, August 6-November 11, 1813.

23 *Benton*, I, p. 13; *Abridgement*, VIII, p. 207.

24 *Abridgement*, VII, pp. 50, 74-80; *Debates*, p. 946.

25 *Abridgement*, VII, pp. 392-406, VIII, pp. 202-214; *Debates*, pp. 945-959.

26 *Benton*, I, p. 13.

27 These French versions in *Nouvelles Annales*, X, pp. 5-119, XII, pp. 21-113, which in part are translated at pp. 267-308 *infra*, contain at X, pp. 5-6 (translated at p. 267 *infra*), the following statement: "Nous devons a I'obligeance de S. Exc. M. Gallatin, ministre plénipotentiaire des Etats-Unis en France, et de M. J. J. Astor, négociant de New-York, la communication de ces manuscrits intéressans pour la géographie."

Accompanying these versions is a map (reproduced facing p. 270 *infra*) which delineates the routes of Stuart and of Hunt, with approximate accuracy except as regards Stuart's path from the Walla Walla River's mouth to the Grande Ronde Valley.

28 This note, for purposes of brevity, will use present-day geographic names as though they and all the entities they represent existed in Stuart's time. For convenience's sake in comparing the routes of Stuart and of the Oregon Trail, it will consider that trail in terms of from west to east, even though the denser travel was in the reverse direction. And finally, its stated distances will be in the scale of air-line measurement.

On this basis, the divergencies between Stuart's route and that of the Oregon Trail (hereinafter styled "O.T.") may be summarized as follows:

I. For the stretch beginning at a spot one and one-half miles west of Pendleton, Ore. (at which spot Stuart first encountered the main stem of the O.T.) and ending at the Fort Boise crossing (on the Snake's left bank opposite the mouth of Boise River), the divergencies were:

(1) In the stretch beginning one mile east of Pendleton and ending at LaGrande in the Grande Ronde Valley, Stuart kept west of the O.T.'s main stem, which ran *via* Cayuse, Emigrant Spring and Meacham (*Crown Maps*, III, Nos. 46-48), though some pioneers did go *via* Hilgard (*Idem*, No. 46) and thus did use at least a portion of Stuart's route.

(2) In passing from Grande Ronde Valley's south end to Baker Valley's north end, Stuart used Pyles Canyon, while the O.T. used Ladds Canyon, which paralleled Pyles Canyon and lay immediately west of it (*Idem*, Nos. 44, 45). Maximum divergence of some three miles.

(3) In going southward through level Baker Valley, Stuart clung to its west side, the O.T. using its centre (*Idem*, Nos. 42-44). Maximum divergence of six miles.

(4) In crossing the narrow watershed between Baker Valley's south extremity and Alder Creek's headwaters, Stuart and the O.T. threaded different coulees (*Idem*, No. 42). Maximum divergence of some five miles.

(5) In descending Burnt River's steep and narrow valley (*Idem*, Nos. 39, 40), though Stuart crossed the stream but twice, some pioneers

crossed it as many as eight times (*Diary J. E. Howell* in *Ore. Hist. Soc. Quar.*, I, p. 150). Maximum divergence of only a few hundred feet. (6) From Olds Ferry to the Fort Boise crossing, though many persons used Stuart's route, which held close to the Snake's left bank, the main O.T. ran southerly to Vale and thence southeasterly down East Cow Hollow to the Fort Boise crossing (*Crown Maps*, III, Nos. 37-39). Maximum divergence of 14 miles.

II. For the stretch beginning at Fort Boise crossing and ending at mouth of Portneuf River, the O.T. displayed two mutually independent stems; the older of which (hereinafter arbitrarily styled "south stem") continued along the Snake's left or southerly bank, while the other and newer stem (hereinafter arbitrarily designated as "north stem") confined itself to the Snake's right or northerly bank and to the area north of it. It is with only the south stem that Stuart's path needs comparison.

The routes of Stuart and of the south stem were identical except that, between Murphy and Grandview as well as between Glenns Ferry and Upper Salmon Falls and also between the mouths of Deep Creek and Desert Creek, Stuart kept nearer the Snake's left edge than did the south stem (*Idem*, Nos. 17, 28, 29). Maximum divergence of two miles in the first instance, six miles in the second instance, and three miles in the third instance. Incidentally, it should be noted that, between Desert Creek and Murtaugh, the south stem possessed twin routes separated from each other by a maximum divergence of seven miles (*Idem*, Nos. 24-27); Stuart's trace being identical with that one of these two routes which was furthest from the Snake's bank.

Though the north stem had no relationship with Stuart's trace, it is necessary now to describe it, for otherwise our previous broad statement concerning it might be misleading. This north stem, after reaching the Snake's right bank at Fort Boise crossing, made (*via* Parma and the vicinities of Caldwell, Boise, Mayfield and Mountain Home) an inland short-cut to Glenns Ferry on the Snake's right bank; and thence, in varying distances from that bank, pursued a crescentic easterly route which, though continuing to the Snake River's ferry at Ferry Butte, situated a short distance above Portneuf River's mouth, offered (at Glenns Ferry, Upper Salmon Falls, Lewis Ferry, Shoshone Falls, Starrh's Ferry, Heyburn and elsewhere) opportunity for the traveller to quit this north stem and, by crossing the Snake, to gain the O.T.'s south stem (*Idem*, Nos. 7, 26, 27, 30-37; *Symons* [*B*]). Travel on the north stem was dense west of Upper Salmon Falls and particularly dense west of Glenns Ferry. But throughout the north stem's stretch east of Heyburn, because of the extreme aridity of much of it, the journeyers were so few and so well-nigh limited to purely local wayfaring as possibly to deny that stretch all right to call itself an integral part of the O.T.

III. From mouth of Portneuf River to Alexander, the O.T. subdivided itself into a multiplicity of routes (*Crown Maps*, III, Nos. 11-16). Stuart's path would have been identical with one of the less used of these routes if, on the 13-mile stretch between Inkom and the Portneuf River's bend immediately south of McCammon, he had not made a detour up Marsh Creek; this being a detour seemingly unemployed by any of the pioneers. Maximum divergence of three miles.

IV. From Alexander to mouth of Thomas Fork (a confluent of Bear River), the O.T. displayed but a single route, which, passing through Wardboro and though proceeding as far southeast as to Pegram, emitted *en route* at Sheep Creek's mouth [eight miles southeast of Wardboro] a short-cut running directly east from Bear River to the mouth of Thomas Fork (*Idem*, Nos. 8-11). Stuart's path and the O.T.'s route from Alexander to as far as the Bear River's bend immediately southeast of Wardboro were identical: although we should keep in mind that, whereas Stuart travelled along the level prairie and immediately beside the water's edge, the pioneers, for avoidance of marshy soil, customarily restricted their wagons to the terrace which, skirting this prairie, avoided the river by a distance varying from a half-mile to two and one-half miles. It was at the above-mentioned bend near Wardboro that Stuart began his short-cut to the mouth of Thomas Fork; and accordingly there was a maximum divergence of three miles between his short-cut and the corresponding one which, as already mentioned, the O.T. emitted at the mouth of Sheep Creek.

V. From mouth of Thomas Fork to Pacific Creek (at western portal of South Pass)—a distance of 167 miles by O.T. (*Horn*, pp. 29-36; *Crown Maps*, III, No. 8, II, Nos. 23-31)—Stuart's path and the O.T.'s route were wholly unrelated except that Stuart, when descending Green River's valley, crossed, though he did not follow, the route of the O.T.'s so-called Sublett (more properly Sublette) Cut Off.

VI. From Pacific Creek to summit of South Pass, Stuart's path and the O.T.'s route seem to have been identical; except that, shortly before reaching the summit, Stuart swerved to his right and thus went south of, instead of between, the two small hills which popularly have been supposed to mark the summit of the pass.

VII. From summit of South Pass to Muddy Creek's confluence with Sweetwater River—a distance of 89 miles by O.T. (*Horn*, pp. 24-28; *Crown Maps*, II, Nos. 18-23)—, Stuart's path and the O.T.'s route were wholly unrelated and did not use the same terrain.

VIII. From Muddy Creek's confluence with Sweetwater River to Alcova (*Crown Maps*, II, Nos. 17, 18), Stuart's path veered some five or six miles south of the more southerly of the two local stems of the O.T. (this being the only one of the two stems to touch Alcova); and thus, unlike that southerly stem, encountered the North Platte River at a spot some miles above, instead of at, Alcova.

IX. From Alcova to Casper (*Idem*, II, Nos. 16, 17), Stuart's path was identical with one stem of the O.T.; the two principal stems of which were on the opposite side of the North Platte.

X. From Casper to Douglas (*Idem*, II, Nos. 13-16), Stuart's path and the earliest route of the O.T. were identical, though the O.T.'s route did not everywhere cling as closely to the North Platte's bank. A later route of the O.T. was, in some places, eight miles inland from that bank.

XI. From Douglas to Fort Laramie (*Idem*, II, Nos. 11-13), Stuart's path, which clung to the North Platte's left bank, lay across the river from the O.T.'s route, which here skirted the right bank.

XII. From Fort Laramie to spot where, three miles above Plum Creek's confluence with Platte River, Stuart crossed from left to right bank of Platte, his path was identical with that one of the O.T.'s two local stems which was interchangeably known as the Mormon Road, Mormon Trail, Northern Trail or North Bank Trail (*Crown Maps*, II, Nos. 2-11, I, Nos. 30-32), though Stuart doubtless adhered more closely to the river's edge than later travellers usually did. Incidentally, throughout all this stretch, the Mormon Road was paralleled by the O.T.'s other stem, which ran along the North Platte's and Platte's right banks (*Idem*, II, Nos. 2-11, I, Nos. 30-32).

XIII. For the stretch beginning at the spot where Stuart reached the right bank of the Platte and ending at Dogtown some nine miles east of the longitude of Kearney (*Idem*, I, Nos. 26-30), Stuart's path and the O.T.'s stem on that bank of the Platte were identical, save that Stuart clung more closely to the water's edge than the trail ordinarily did. Though at Dogtown this south-bank stem of the O.T. left the Platte and headed southeasterly toward St. Joseph, Atchison, Westport and Independence, it projected easterly a sub-stem which, commonly known as Nebraska City-Fort Kearney Road, ran close to the Platte's right bank until, in far eastern Nebraska, it swung southeasterly to its terminus (*Idem*, I, Nos. 17, 43-45). Stuart's path eastward from Dogtown was virtually identical with this road's course as far as to where the road, as above stated, swung southeasterly.

Before Stuart travelled so much of his route as began at the spot one and one-half miles west of Pendleton ("I" *ante*) and ended at the mouth of Portneuf River ("II" *ante*) Wilson Price Hunt had journeyed it, though in reverse direction—*i.e.*, from east to west. However, for the easternmost portion of the way Hunt had canoed down Snake River and thus, in that region, had not used the trails which Stuart later found. Prior to the time that Stuart made his traverse from the mouth of Portneuf River to Alexander ("III" *ante*) Joseph Miller with Robinson, Hoback and Reznor had effected a somewhat similar crossing, though also in reverse direction (Stuart's entry of September 7, p. 128). But from Alexander to the lower reaches of Platte River no white, so far as appears, had anywhere preceded Stuart and his wayworn comrades.

29 *Ross* [*A*], pp. 3-6; *Cox* [*A*], I, pp. XII-XVIII, [*B*], pp. VII-IX.

30 *Ross* [*A*], p. 4; *Astoria*, I, pp. 32, 33.

31 *Ross* [*A*], p. 4; *Astoria*, I, p. 33.

32 *Ross* [*A*], p. 7; *Astoria*, I, pp. 42, 43; *Pacific Fur*, organization agreement.

33 *Ross* [*A*], pp. 7, 8; *Astoria*, I, pp. 43, 44; *Pacific Fur*, organization agreement.

34 *Ross* [*A*], p. 8; *Astoria*, I, p. 44; *Pacific Fur*, organization agreement. Astor, in his letter of January 4, 1823, to John Quincy Adams, Secretary of State, asserted: "I preferred to have it appear as the business of a company, rather than that of an individual, and several of the gentlemen engaged, Mr. Hunt, Mr. Crooks, Mr. McKay, McDougall, Stuart, &c. were in effect to be interested as partners in the undertaking, so far as respected any profit which might arise; but the means were furnished by me, and the property was solely mine, and I sustained the loss, which, though considerable, I do not regret; because, had it not been for the unfortunate occurrence just stated [*i.e.*, McDougall's selling to the North West Company all of Astoria's assets for far less than their value], I should have been, as I believe, most richly rewarded. . . ." *House Doc.*, p. 13.

35 *Ross* [*A*], pp. 6, 7; *Cox*, [*A*], I, pp. XVII, XVIII, [*B*], p. IX; *Astoria*, I, pp. 41-43.

36 *House Doc.*, p. 15; *Ross* [*A*], p. 6. Astor's declaration (contained in his letter of February, 1813, to James Monroe, Secretary of State) that "all" the Canadians and Scots in his Pacific Fur Company had "become citizens of the United States" is more widely inclusive than *Astoria's* statement (I, p. 51), which seemingly limits the newly acquired citizenship to the *voyageurs*.

37 *Astoria*, I, p. 20; *Cox*, [*A*], I, p. XIV, [*B*], p. VIII.

38 *Ross* [*A*], p. 7; *Franchere* [*A*], p. 9, [*B*], pp. 20, 21.

39 *Cox* [*A*], I, pp. XII, XIII, [*B*], pp. VII, VIII.

40 *Astoria*, I, p. 43. See also *Ross* [*A*], pp. 6, 7.

41 *Ross* [*A*], p. 8; *Pacific Fur*, organization agreement. Incidentally, this agreement shows that Robert Stuart's shares were two of the five shares theretofore held by his uncle, David Stuart.

42 *Astoria*, I, pp. 38, 42.

43 *Astoria*, I, p. 45.

44 *Ross* [*A*]; *Franchere* [*A*], [*B*]; *Astoria*.

45 *Bradbury* [*A*], pp. 9-174, 222-233; *Brackenridge* [*A*], pp. 238-261; *Astoria; Nouvelles Annales*, X, pp. 31-88, translated at pp. 281-308 *infra*.

46 *Ross* [*A*], pp. 14, 15, 20, 26, 29, 31, 41, 42, 53, 68; *Franchere* [*A*], pp. 32, 33, [*B*], pp. 47-49; *Astoria*, I, pp. 55-60, 64, 65, 80-82.

47 *Ross* [*A*], p. 15.

48 *Ross* [*A*], pp. 20, 22-25; *Franchere* [*A*], pp. 28-33, [*B*], pp. 36, 43-49; *Astoria*, I, pp. 61-64.

49 *Ross* [*A*], pp. 16-20, 53.

50 *Ross* [*A*], pp. 19, 25, 54.

51 *Ross* [*A*], pp. 19, 20; *Franchere* [*A*], p. 24, [*B*], p. 38; *Astoria*, I, p. 45.

52 *Ross* [*A*], pp. 54-66; *Franchere* [*A*], pp. 64-75, [*B*], pp. 86-98; *Astoria*, I, pp. 82-88.

53 *Ross* [*A*], p. 61.

54 *Ross* [*A*], pp. 69-71; *Franchere* [*A*], pp. 77, 78, [*B*], pp. 101-103; *Astoria*, I, p. 96.

55 *Ross* [*A*], pp. 72-74; *Astoria*, I, pp. 97, 101.

56 *Ross* [*A*], p. 71.

57 *Ross* [*A*], pp. 74, 75.

58 *Ross* [*A*], pp. 75, 76; *Franchere* [*A*], pp. 100-105, [*B*], pp. 132-139; *Nouvelles Annales*, X, p. 26, translated at p. 277 *infra*.

59 *Ross* [*A*], p. 74.

60 *Ross* [*A*], pp. 80, 81; *Franchere* [*A*], p. 98, [*B*], p. 129; *Astoria*, I, p. 125.

61 *Ross* [*A*], p. 78; *Franchere* [*A*], pp. 79-87, [*B*], pp. 104-115.

62 *Ross* [*A*], pp. 79, 80; *Nouvelles Annales*, X, p. 23, translated at p. 276 *infra*.

63 *Franchere* [*A*], pp. 93, 94, [*B*], p. 123; *Astoria*, I, pp. 113, 114.

64 *Franchere* [*A*], p. 97, [*B*], pp. 127, 128.

65 *Franchere* [*A*], p. 100, [*B*], p. 131; *Astoria*, I, p. 129.

66 *Franchere* [*A*], p. 100, [*B*], pp. 131, 132.

67 *Franchere* [*A*], pp. 100-106, [*B*], pp. 132-141.

68 *Franchere* [*A*], p. 107, [*B*], p. 142.

69 Stuart's entry of July 2 (p. 30).

70 The date of leaving was March 22, according to *Ross* [*A*], pp. 184, 185; *Nouvelles Annales*, X, p. 28, translated at p. 278 *infra; Astoria*, II, pp. 93, 94. It was March 30, according to *Franchere* [*A*], p. 115, [*B*], pp. 151-153.

71 *Ross* [*A*], p. 184; *Franchere* [*A*], p. 115, [*B*], pp. 152, 153; *Astoria*, II, p. 93.

72 *Ross* [*A*], p. 184; *Franchere* [*A*], p. 115, [*B*], pp. 151, 152; *Astoria*, II, p. 94.

73 *Ross* [*A*], pp. 143, 184; *Franchere* [*A*], p. 115, [*B*], p. 152; *Astoria*, II, p. 93.

74 *Ross* [*A*], pp. 185, 186; *Cox* [*A*], I, pp. 105-108, [*B*], pp. 67, 68; *Franchere* [*A*], pp. 117-120, [*B*], pp. 155-159; *Astoria*, II, pp. 95-104.

75 *Ross* [*A*], pp. 185, 186.

76 *Franchere* [*A*], pp. 117-120, [*B*], pp. 155-159.

77 *Cox* [*A*], I, pp. 105-108, [*B*], pp. 67, 68.

78 *Astoria*, II, pp. 95-104.

79 *Franchere* [*A*], p. 118, [*B*], p. 156; *Cox* [*A*], p. 107, [*B*], p. 67; *Astoria*, II, pp. 95, 96, 98.

80 *Franchere* [*B*], p. 157.

81 *Ross* [*A*], p. 186.

82 May 11, according to *Cox* [*A*], I, p. 105, [*B*], p. 67; *Franchere* [*A*], p. 117, [*B*], p. 155; *Nouvelles Annales*, X, p. 30, translated at p. 279 *infra*. May 12, according to *Ross* [*A*], p. 193.

83 *Ross* [*A*], pp. 187-192; *Franchere* [*A*], pp. 119, 120, [*B*], pp. 158, 159; *Cox* [*A*], I, pp. 108, 109, [*B*], p. 68; *Bradbury* [*A*], pp. 232, 233; *Brackenridge*, p. 302.

84 *Henry-Thomp.*, p. 886.

85 *Pacific Fur*, the resolution being signed by Hunt, McKenzie, McDougall, Clarke, David Stuart and Robert Stuart. See also *Ross* [*A*], pp. 194, 195; Stella M. Drumm's *More About Astorians* in *Ore. Hist. Soc. Quar.*, XXIV, p. 335, f.n.

86 *Pacific Fur; Ross* [*A*], p. 199; *Franchere* [*A*], pp. 120, 121, [*B*], p. 160; *Astoria*, II, p. 111.

87 *Franchere* [*A*], p. 121, [*B*], p. 160; *Ross* [*A*], pp. 194, 195; *Astoria*, II, p. 110.

88 *Ross* [*A*], p. 195.

89 *Cox* [*A*], I, pp. 118, 119, [*B*], pp. 72, 73.

90 Stuart's entries of July 1-3 (pp. 28-33).

91 Stuart's entry of August 20 (pp. 85, 86).

92 Stuart's entries of August 30 and September 1 (pp. 113, 114).

93 The parish register of Greenock (Middle) contains entry as follows: "Ramsay, lawful daughter to William Crooks, Shoemaker and Margaret Ramsay, born 2nd and baptized 7th January 1787." The parish clerk's error in recording Ramsay Crooks as a "daughter" was quite possibly due to the fact that "Ramsay" had long been a commonly used first name for Scots females.

94 See *Wisconsin Colls.*, IV, pp. 95-102, XIX, p. 347, f.n.; *Chittenden*, p. 381.

95 *Chittenden*, p. 160; *Bates*, II, p. 31; *James*, p. 273.

96 *Chittenden*, pp. 160, 950; *James*, p. 262; *Bradbury* [*A*], p. 50; *Brackenridge*, p. 227.

97 *Chittenden*, pp. 160, 161.

98 *Idem*, pp. 160, 161.

99 *Idem*, pp. 161, 162.

100 *Idem*, p. 162. These Aricara villages (two in number, adjacent to each other and somewhat peripatetic) were, at the time of Hunt's visit in 1811, located on both sides of the mouth of a small stream (probably present-day Elk Creek *alias* Cottonwood Creek) which emptied through the Missouri's right bank at a spot approximately eight miles above the mouth of present-day Grand River in Corson County, South Dakota. *Brackenridge*, pp. 267, 268; *Bradbury* [*A*], pp. 109, 116; *Luttig*, p. 67, f.n.; *Geol. South Dakota.*

101 *Chittenden*, p. 162.

102 *Astoria*, I, p. 138.

103 *Idem*, I, p. 140.

104 *Idem*, I, pp. 143-147, 164; *Bradbury* [*A*], p. 46.

105 *Brackenridge*, pp. 200-238.

106 *Brackenridge*, pp. 241, 242; *Bradbury* [*A*], pp. 99, 100, 103; *Astoria*, I, pp. 205, 206.

107 *Bradbury* [*A*], pp. 103, 111; *Astoria*, I, pp. 205, 206, 210.

108 *Astoria*, I, pp. 204, 207-214, 234.

109 *Idem*, I, pp. 237, 242.

110 *Idem*, II, pp. 18, 23; *Nouvelles Annales*, X, p. 54, translated at p. 292 *infra*.

111 *Astoria*, II, p. 23; *Nouvelles Annales*, X, p. 54, translated at p. 292 *infra*.

112 *Astoria*, II, pp. 23-31; *Nouvelles Annales*, X, pp. 54-57, translated at pp. 292, 293 *infra*.

113 *Astoria*, II, pp. 27, 30; *Nouvelles Annales*, X, p. 56, translated at p. 293 *infra*.

114 *Astoria*, II, p. 30; *Nouvelles Annales*, X, p. 56, translated at p. 293 *infra*.

115 *Astoria*, II, pp. 34-47; *Nouvelles Annales*, X, pp. 58-66, translated at pp. 293-298 *infra*. See also note 215 on p. 323 *infra*.

116 *Astoria*, II, p. 45; *Nouvelles Annales*, X, p. 66, translated at p. 298 *infra; Brackenridge*, p. 301; *Bradbury* [*A*], pp. 229-230; *Mo. Gaz.; Niles*, p. 266.

117 *Astoria*, II, p. 44; *Bradbury* [*A*], p. 230; *Brackenridge*, p. 301. See also note 211 on p. 323 *infra*.

118 *Nouvelles Annales*, X, pp. 57-66, translated at pp. 293-298 *infra*; *Astoria*, II, pp. 32-45.

119 *Astoria*, II, pp. 44, 45; *Brackenridge*, p. 301; *Bradbury* [*A*], p. 230; *Nouvelles Annales*, X, p. 66, translated at pp. 297, 298 *infra*.

120 *Astoria*, II, p. 47.

121 *Astoria*, II, pp. 47, 48.

122 *Astoria*, II, pp. 48, 49; *Nouvelles Annales*, X, pp. 67, 68, translated at pp. 298, 299 *infra*.

123 *Astoria*, II, p. 49 says "two" men, while *Nouvelles Annales*, X, p. 68 (translated at p. 299 *infra*) says "three" men.

124 *Astoria*, II, p. 49 says "three" men, while *Nouvelles Annales*, X, p. 68 (translated at p. 299 *infra*) says "two" men.

125 *Astoria*, II, pp. 48, 49; *Nouvelles Annales*, X, p. 68, translated at p. 299 *infra*.

126 Seized, according to *Astoria*, II, p. 51; but purchased, according to *Nouvelles Annales*, X, p. 68, translated at p. 299 *infra*. That "seized" is accurate appears from note 224 on p. 324 *infra*.

127 *Astoria*, II, p. 51; *Nouvelles Annales*, X, pp. 68, 69, translated at p. 299 *infra*.

128 *Astoria*, II, p. 51.

129 *Idem*, II, pp. 51, 52.

130 *Idem*, II, pp. 53, 54; *Nouvelles Annales*, X, p. 69, translated at p. 299 *infra*.

131 *Ross* [*A*], p. 188; *Astoria*, II, p. 102.

132 *Ross* [*A*], pp. 187, 188.

133 *Idem*, pp. 188, 189.

134 *Idem*, p. 189; *Bradbury* [*A*], p. 232; *Astoria*, II, p. 102.

135 *Astoria*, II, pp. 102, 103.

136 *Idem*, II, p. 103; *Ross* [*A*], p. 189; *Mo. Gaz.; Niles*, p. 267. Dubreuil eventually retraced his way to a Shoshone indian camp on present-day Idaho's Boise River, and at or near this camp was rescued by John Reed in the summer of 1812. For these and further details, see note 123 on pp. 178, 179 *infra*.

137 *Astoria*, II, pp. 103, 104; *Bradbury* [*A*], pp. 232, 233; *Ross* [*A*], pp. 190-192.

138 *Astoria*, II, p. 111; *Ross* [*A*], p. 199; *Pacific Fur; Porter*, p. 205.

139 *Baker-Astor* [*A*], I, p. 9.

140 *Idem*, I, p. 27.

141 *Idem*, I, p. 27.

142 *Idem*, I, pp. 66, 67; *Porter*, p. 267.

143 *Porter*, pp. 267-273, 276, 287, 288, 543-545, 565, 577, 686-700; *Baker-Astor* [*A*], I, pp. 68, 69, 87, 91, 107, 108, 137, 138, 180, 187, 191, 202, 218, 219, 229, 281, 282, 389, 390, 395, 410, 411, 426, 427, 443, 447, 454, 471, 472, 506; transcripts in collections of both Missouri Hist. Soc. and Detroit Public Library (Burton Collection) and made from following original letters in possession of Mrs. Richard Hoguet: Crooks to Astor, dated Buffalo, October 21, 31, November 17, December 17, 1813; Erie, January 15, February 10, March 3, 1814; Pittsburgh, April 10, 14, 17, 1814; Detroit, May 8, 19, June 19, 26, July 3, August 21, 1814; Pittsburgh, November 29, December 20, 27, 1814, January 23, 1815; Lexington, February 26, 1815; Pittsburgh, April 17, 1815: Astor to Crooks, who was addressed at Buffalo, October 28, November 15, December 18, 1813; Erie, February 14, 1814; Detroit, February 25, March 5, 1814; Pittsburgh, April 5, 9, 1814; Erie, April 20, 29, 1814; Pittsburgh, May 18, 19, 1814; Detroit, May 26, June 6, July 2, September 14, 1814; Pittsburgh, December 10, 14, 1814, January 25, 29, 1815; Lexington, February 2, 14, 1815; Pittsburgh, April 5, 1815. See also *Wisconsin Colls.*, XIX, pp. 352-354, 360-364, 369-372, 427, 428, XX, pp. 17-31.

144 *Wisconsin Colls.*, XIX, p. 451; *Porter*, p. 700.

145 *Wisconsin Colls.*, XIX, pp. 52, 53, XX, pp. 17-31, 52, 53, 55; *Michigan*, I, p. 383, VI, p. 347, XI, pp. 189, 193, 195, XVIII, pp. 330, 646, XXVIII, p. 526.

146 *Wisconsin Colls.*, IV, pp. 95-102; *Chittenden*, pp. 381, 382; *Michigan*, I, p. 383.

147 *Benton*, I, p. 13; *Ambler*, pp. 53, 54.

148 *Porter*, pp. 1101, 1131, f.n. 48.

149 *Benton*, I, p. 13; *Ambler*, pp. 53, 54; *Chittenden*, p. 15; *Wisconsin Colls.*, XX, p. 240, f.n.

150 *Michigan*, I, p. 383, VI, p. 347, XI, pp. 189, 193, 195, XVIII, pp. 330, 644, XXVII, p. 526; *Wisconsin Colls.*, II, pp. 101, 108, XX, p. 283.

151 (1) *Longworth;* (2) John Doggett's New York Directories for the years 1842-1859.

152 *Chittenden*, p. 382.

153 *Billon*, pp. 179, 181.

154 *Wisconsin Colls.*, IV, p. 99; *Chittenden*, p. 364; *Michigan*, VI, p. 347.

155 *Wisconsin Colls.*, IV, pp. 99, 100; *Michigan*, VI, p. 347.

156 Death notices in *New York Herald*, *New York Tribune* and *New York Times*, all of both June 7 and 8, 1859; *Trow's New York City Directory* published May 1, 1859.

157 P. CXXXVI *infra;* Stella M. Drumm's *More About Astorians* in *Ore. Hist. Soc. Quar.*, XXIV, p. 345.

158 *Idem*, p. 345; *Astoria*, I, p. 146.

159 Stella M. Drumm, *op. cit.*, p. 345.

160 *Idem*, pp. 345, 346.

161 *Idem*, p. 346.

162 *Idem*, p. 346.

163 *Idem*, p. 346.

164 *Idem*, pp. 346, 347; *L. & C. Journs.*, V, p. 373.

165 *Bates*, I, p. 202.

166 *Bates*, II, pp. 31, 33; *Chittenden*, pp. 160, 950; *Brackenridge*, p. 227. Council Bluffs and Fire Prairie were each on the Missouri's right bank, Council Bluffs being approximately 25 miles above the site of present-day city of Omaha, and Fire Prairie being midway between the mouths of the Platte and the Missouri. See p. LXXXII *ante* and note 56 on p. 245 *infra*.

167 Stella M. Drumm, *op. cit.*, pp. 347, 348.

168 *Idem*, pp. 347, 348.

169 *Pacific Fur*, organization agreement.

170 *Pacific Fur*, organization agreement.

171 Stella M. Drumm, *op. cit.*, p. 348.

172 *Astoria*, I, p. 269.

173 *Idem*, II, p. 27; *Nouvelles Annales*, X, p. 56, translated at p. 293 *infra*.

174 *Franchere* [*B*], p. 148.

175 Stuart's entry of August 12 (p. 80); *Astoria*, II, pp. 27, 74-77; *Mo. Gaz.; Niles*, p. 266; *Ross* [*A*], pp. 181, 182. These citations, considered in the light of the topography, (1) show that the route clung more or less closely to the Snake's right bank as far at least as to the northerly end of the main portion of the Seven Devils Mountains, and (2) suggest—if Stuart's "Mulpat" was strictly used and thus designated present-day Little Salmon River rather than present-day Salmon River (formerly styled "North Fork of Lewis River") into which it emptied—that thence, turning inland, the route reached Little Salmon River, descended it to its confluence with Salmon River and, from there, descending Salmon River either to the vertex of its hairpin turn in latitude 46° or to the mouth of present-day Deer Creek, struck northwesterly to

present-day Clearwater River, from the mouth of which last-mentioned stream, it is said, McClellan's party canoed down Snake River to its junction with the Columbia and thence to Astoria. However, if Stuart's "Mulpat" designated Salmon River instead of Little Salmon River, the route, instead of turning inland at the Seven Devils Mountains, doubtless continued to descend the Snake's right bank. For differentiation between "Mulpat" (*alias* "Mulpah") and "North Fork of Lewis River," see *L. & C. Hist.*, p. 1255; *Robinson; Wyld* [*A*]; *Kelley*, p. 38 and accompanying map; *Cowperthwait* [*C*], accompanying map. See also note 65 on p. 94 *infra*.

176 *Astoria*, II, p. 76.

177 *Ross* [*A*], p. 182 dates this arrival as January 10; *Franchere* [*A*], pp. 109, 114, [*B*], pp. 144, 150 dating it as January 18.

178 Stella M. Drumm, *op. cit.*, p. 335, f.n.

179 Stuart's entry of July 20 (pp. 54-60).

180 Stella M. Drumm, *op. cit.*, p. 350.

181 *Idem*, p. 350.

182 *Idem*, pp. 350, 351.

183 *Idem*, p. 351.

184 *Idem*, p. 358.

185 *Idem*, p. 358.

186 *Idem*, p. 358; *Astoria*, II, p. 52.

187 *Astoria*, I, p. 182; *Bradbury* [*A*], p. 72.

188 *Astoria*, II, p. 238.

189 *Idem*, II, p. 52.

190 *Idem*, II, p. 99.

191 Stella M. Drumm, *op. cit.*, pp. 358, 359.

192 *Idem*, pp. 359, 360.

193 *Ore. Hist. Soc. Quar.*, XVII, p. 51.

194 *Idem*, XVII, p. 51.

195 Stella M. Drumm, *op. cit.*, p. 353; *Astoria*, I, pp. 146, 147.

196 *Astoria*, I, pp. 146, 259; Stella M. Drumm, *op. cit.*, p. 353.

197 Stella M. Drumm, *op. cit.*, p. 353.

198 *Idem*, p. 354.

199 *Idem*, p. 354.

200 *Astoria*, I, p. 146.

201 *Idem*, I, pp. 146, 147.

202 *Idem*, I, p. 234. For site of Aricara villages see note 100 *ante*.

203 *Astoria*, I, p. 238.

204 *Idem*, II, p. 10.

205 Stuart's entries of July 1-3 (pp. 28-31).

206 *Astoria*, II, p. 113; *Henry-Thomp.*, pp. 856, 857.

207 *Henry-Thomp.*, p. 861.

208 *Idem*, p. 875.

209 Stella M. Drumm, *op. cit.*, p. 355.

210 The place of John Day's death was in present-day Day's Defile, a high valley which, heading in central Idaho's Salmon River Mountains, debouched on the lava beds to the north of the Three Buttes and contained a stream heretofore styled Day's River but, because of its sinking to subterranean channels, more recently mapped as Little Lost River. See T. C. Elliott's *Last Will and Testament of John Day* in *Ore. Hist. Soc. Quar.*, XVII, pp. 375-377; *Journ. John Work* in *Ore. Hist. Soc. Quar.*, XIII, p. 369; *Journ. Alexander Ross* in *Ore. Hist. Soc. Quar.*, XIV, p. 380.

211 Stella M. Drumm, *op. cit.*, p. 356.

212 T. C. Elliott, *op. cit.*, pp. 376-379.

213 *Astoria*, I, p. 143; *Ore. Hist. Soc. Quar.*, XVII, p. 51.

214 *Heitman*, I, p. 711.

215 *Astoria*, I, p. 143.

216 *Idem*, I, p. 143.

217 *Idem*, I, p. 143.

218 *Bradbury* [*A*], p. 86; *Astoria*, I, p. 195.

219 *Astoria*, II, p. 12.

220 *Idem*, II, p. 12.

221 *Idem*, II, p. 12.

222 *Idem*, II, pp. 14, 15.

223 *Idem*, II, p. 16; *Nouvelles Annales*, X, p. 49, translated at p. 290 *infra*.

224 Stuart's entry of August 20 (pp. 85, 86).

225 *Astoria*, I, pp. 188, 189; *Bradbury* [*A*], pp. 77, 78.

226 Walter L. Douglas's *Manuel Lisa* in *Missouri*, III, pp. 259-264; *James*, p. 11.

227 *James*, pp. 31, 45-47, 53, 54, 66, 74-82; Walter L. Douglas, *op. cit.*, p. 264; *Chittenden*, pp. 140-145, 895-896. For the supposedly exact site of this Fort, see note 16 on p. 169 *infra*.

228 This quite possible divergence involved, not only (1) the pass by which they when eastward bound entered the valley of the Wind River, but also (2) the trail connecting the westerly end of the pass with the south fork of Snake River. While Wilson Price Hunt's diary indubitably establishes that his westbound expedition, on leaving the Wind River valley, used present-day Union Pass, traversed Green River's valley and reached the south fork of Snake River by descending Hoback River (*Nouvelles Annales*, X, pp. 42-45, translated at pp. 286-288 *infra*), that same diary contains a statement which with its context strongly suggests that Hunt's guides, Robinson, Hoback and Reznor, when earlier travelling eastward from Snake River's south fork to the Wind River, had kept well north of the Hoback River and the Green River's watershed and had employed present-day Twogwotee Pass, not Union Pass, as their portal to the valley of the Wind River. This statement (*Nouvelles Annales*, X, p. 46, translated on p. 288 *infra*), which was penned after Hunt's traversal of

Union Pass, was to the effect: "We should have continued at that time to follow Wind River and to cross one of the mountains because we would have reached the headwaters of this river [south fork of Snake River]; but lack of provisions forced us to make for the banks of Spanish River" [Green River].

For persons travelling from the upper stretch of Snake River's south fork to Twogwotee Pass, the normal route was the trail which, starting at the confluence of present-day Buffalo Fork with Snake River's south fork, ascended Buffalo Fork to the mouth of present-day Blackrock Creek, and thence ascended this creek to its headwaters lying at the westerly end of the pass. *Yellowstone; Quad. Mt. Leidy.*

229 *Bradbury* [*A*], p. 77; *Astoria*, I, p. 188.

230 *Bradbury* [*A*], p. 77; *Astoria*, I, pp. 188, 189.

231 *Astoria*, I, pp. 189, 190; *Bradbury* [*A*], p. 79; *Mo. Gaz.; Niles*, p. 265.

232 Stuart's entry of August 30 (p. 113).

233 *Ross* [*A*], p. 277; *Astoria*, II, pp. 196, 197, 254. Reed's party, on his arrival, included, among other people, seven persons he recently had rescued, three of these seven being men whom Hunt, when passing the mouth of Hoback River, had detached there for purpose of local trapping, and four being men who had straggled from Hunt's column when it entered Oregon. *Astoria*, II, pp. 194-196.

234 *Astoria*, II, pp. 196, 197, 254; *Ross* [*A*], pp. 277-282; *Chittenden*, p. 225; *Henry-Thomp.*, pp. 886-887, f.n.; *Journ. Alexander Ross* in *Ore. Hist. Soc. Quar.*, XIV, p. 384. But see note 38 on pp. 67-69 *infra*, as also J. Neilson Barry's *Madame Dorion of the Astorians* in *Ore. Hist. Soc. Quar.*, XXX, p. 273.

235 *Astoria*, II, pp. 254-257; *Franchere* [*A*], p. 216, [*B*], p. 275; *Ross* [*A*], pp. 277-282; *Chittenden*, p. 225.

236 *Astoria*, II, pp. 256, 257.

237 The Canadians' salient thrusts toward South Pass had been those made by the two la Vérendryes (Louis-Joseph and François), by François Larocque and by Charles Le Raye. That none of these four intrepid folk reached its vicinity appears from *la Vérendrye*, *Larocque Journ.* and *Cutler*.

238 The French, pushing out from Louisiana, are recorded as having ascended the Platte River, as having entered the present-day state of Colorado, and as having attained Santa Fe; but there seems to be no record or tradition of their being near South Pass.

239 Relics discovered in Wyoming have been attributed by some historians to the Spaniards, by other historians to the American miners of the years shortly after 1850. There is apparently no trustworthy proof that the Spaniards were ever in Wyoming; and also *Robinson* indicates a trail as leading from the Southwest to a spot a short distance inland from the easterly shore of "Laguna de Timpanogos" (seemingly, in this instance, present-day Salt Lake), and legends this spot as "The most Northern point discovered by the Spaniards in the In-

terior Latitude 41° 12′ Long. 115° 30 W." For the variant identity of "Timpanogos" on early maps, see *Dale*, pp. 102, f.n.; 153, f.n.; 154, f.n.; 193, f.n.

240 See Walter L. Douglas's *Manuel Lisa* in *Missouri*, III, pp. 233-268, 367-406.

241 See *Idem*, pp. 233-268, 367-406.

242 Colter's enlistment occurred at the mouth of the Platte River. *Brackenridge*, p. 90. See also *James*, p. 57.

243 Walter L. Douglas, *op. cit.*, pp. 255, 256; *Brackenridge*, p. 91.

244 Walter L. Douglas, *op. cit.*, p. 369; *James*, pp. 40, 45.

245 Walter L. Douglas, *op. cit.*, p. 257.

246 The company's formal title was St. Louis Missouri Fur Company, but it commonly was known as Missouri Fur Company.

247 Walter L. Douglas, *op. cit.*, pp. 259-264; *James*, p. 11.

248 *James;* Walter L. Douglas, *op. cit.*, pp. 259, 260. Quite possibly Williams reached the upper Missouri in advance of the expedition. See, in *Missouri*, IV, p. 202, his statement that his meeting with Champlain occurred on those upper waters.

249 *James*, p. 31.

250 This blockhouse was on the Missouri River's right bank at a spot in present-day McLean County, North Dakota, and some 10 or 12 miles above the confluence of present-day Knife River. *Chittenden*, p. 957; *James*, p. 32, f.n. For description of it and its subsidiary cabins see *Bradbury* [*A*], p. 143.

251 *James*, pp. 45, 46; *Missouri*, III, p. 264.

252 *James*, p. 47.

253 Colter, who acted as guide, joined the party when at the Gros Ventres' (Minitaris') uppermost village. *Idem*, pp. 35, 49.

254 *Chittenden*, pp. 141-144; *James*, pp. 53, 54, 66; *Journ. James H. Bradley* in *Montana*, II, pp. 148, 149.

255 A map of Lewis and Clark's track across the western portion, etc., reproduced in *Lewis and Clark* [*B*]; *L. & C. Hist.*, IV, pocket; *Vinton*, facing p. 44.

256 See p. XXVIII.

257 See any reliable map, as also *Dale*, pp. 27-29, 35, f.n.; *Vinton*, pp. 18, 45-70. The "Southern Pass" shown on the maps of Clark, of *Melish* and of *Robinson* ran from the headwaters of Madison River to the headwaters of north fork (*alias* Henry's fork) of Snake River, was traversed by Andrew Henry in 1810-1811 (see p. CV *ante*), and should not be confused with "South Pass."

258 *Bradbury* [*A*], pp. 17-21; *Astoria*, I, pp. 154-160.

259 Dated August 7, 1816; published September 14, 1816, in *The Missouri Gazette*, and reprinted in *Missouri*, IV, pp. 202-208. See also *Missouri*, IV, pp. 194-201.

260 Manuel Lisa's letter of September 8, 1812, addressed to "los Españoles del Nuevo Mexico" is printed in Herbert E. Bolton's *New Light on Manuel Lisa*

and the Spanish Fur Trade in *Southwestern*, XVII, pp. 63-66. Stuart's entry of October 18 (p. 161), by fixing the year of Champlain's death, parallels George C. Sibley's statement made November 20, 1813 (*Missouri*, IV, pp. 194-208); and thereby one is able confidently to rectify, as to years, the post-dated chronology in Ezekiel Williams's published letter (note 259 *ante*). See also *Dale*, p. 36, f.n.

261 The Williams party's path is readily identifiable even though there be some chronologic haziness concerning the movements on it. It seems that in August, 1810, Williams, Champlain, Porteau and 17 or 20 other men quitted Fort Raymond, and, keeping east of the main chain of the Rocky Mountains, journeyed southward to the present-day Arkansas River, in the vicinity of which they trapped in scattered bands during the ensuing autumn. (*Missouri*, IV, p. 202.) At least some of them having later made a trip to Lisa's Fort Mandan (on the Missouri River) for purpose of obtaining new equipment, they all reassembled in June, 1811, upon upper waters of what Williams termed the Platte but what his context suggests was the South Platte. See notes 259, 260 *ante*.

Thereupon agreeing to subdivide, all except 10 of them crossed the Rocky Mountains (*Missouri*, IV, p. 203)—because of the latitude using presumably a Coloradan or New Mexican pass (for trails through which, see *Macomb*, accompanying map; *Emory*, accompanying map; *Simpson; Creuzbaur*, map No. 1) —while the excepted 10 (Williams, Champlain, Porteau and seven companions), still staying eastward of those mountains, returned to the Arkansas River and pushed into the region south of it. (*Missouri*, IV, p. 203.) After reaching there, four of these seven companions started westward toward the Spanish settlements (*Idem*, p. 203); and the other three of them, who had failed thus to migrate, were killed by local indians in October or early November (*Idem*, p. 203.)

Williams remained with Champlain and Porteau during the winter of 1811-1812 at an Arapahoe camp in the Arkansas River's vicinage; but, in March 1812, he left them at this camp and headed for Boone's Lick, Mo., where he arrived the following September. (*Idem*, p. 204.) During the time he was making the journey, indians—whether of the sheltering camp or another—slew Champlain (Stuart's entry of October 18, p. 161) and apparently Porteau also. (*Missouri*, IV, pp. 205, 206.)

Incidentally, this Williams party which thus had so thoroughly disintegrated was doubtless the one for whose benefit Manuel Lisa sent, September 7, 1812, from Fort Manuel a squad "Pour serché les Chasseurs qui etet sur la Rre. des Espagnols et Arapaos" (Arkansas River). (*Missouri*, III, p. 370, IV, pp. 196, 197.)

Assuredly none of the Williams party had made contact with South Pass.

262 *James*, pp. 74, 75.

263 *Idem*, pp. 65, 66. Colter continued to St. Louis, where he arrived in May according to *Bradbury* [*A*], p. 17.

264 *James*, pp. 80, 81.
265 *Idem*, pp. 75-79, 81, 82.
266 *Idem*, pp. 83-89.
267 *Idem*, pp. 83-89; *Brackenridge*, p. 93.
268 *James*, p. 83; *Brackenridge*, p. 93.
269 See note 227.
270 *James*, p. 83, f.n., names Henry, Robinson, Hoback, Reznor (Reasoner), Pelton, Michael E. Immel, John Dougherty, William Weir and Nicholas Glineau as forming all or part of this group at Henry's Fort. However, there is vague tradition that Pelton faded from the group just before reaching the site of the fort.
271 *Cox* [*A*], I, pp. 91, 92, [*B*], pp. 61, 62; *Franchere* [*A*], p. 113, [*B*], pp. 149, 150; *Nouvelles Annales*, X, p. 29, translated at p. 279 *infra*.
272 *James*, p. 83; *Astoria*, II, p. 13.
273 *Missouri*, III, p. 268; *Astoria*, II, p. 13. For site of Aricara villages, see note 100 *ante*.
274 Letter of Major Thomas Biddle in *Am. State, Indian*, II, p. 201.
275 *Am. State, Indian*, II, p. 451.
276 See *Macomb*, accompanying map; *Robinson*.
277 *Astoria*, II, pp. 195, 196.
278 *Idem*, II, pp. 14-16.
279 *Idem*, II, pp. 194, 195.
280 The four men detached—for purpose of local trapping—at Hoback River's mouth were heading, in the spring of 1812, with their peltry-laden horses for the Missouri when they were attacked by Absarokas. One of them (Pierre Detayé) was killed, while the other three (Louis St. Michel, Alexander Carson and Pierre Delaunay) escaped and made their way on foot to present-day Idaho's Boise River, in the vicinity of which they were presently rescued by John Reed, who eventually took them to Astoria (*Astoria*, II, pp. 194-197). No tradition of a possible geographical discovery is, so far as appears, linked with any of their names.

Of the five men (Edward Robinson, John Hoback, Jacob Reznor, Martin H. Cass and Joseph Miller) detached at Henry's Fort, none, if it was a trustworthy story that the survivors of them told Stuart (see entry of August 20, pp. 85, 86), saw South Pass prior to the time that Miller in company with Stuart entered it in October, 1812.

Of the four men released in eastern Oregon, one [Jean Baptiste Dubreuil] is known to have been almost stationary before he was retrieved and escorted to Astoria (*Astoria*, II, p. 195); while the other three (André LaChapelle, François Landry and Jean Baptiste Turcotte), before arriving at Astoria, made a long detour which took them, not to the vicinage of South Pass, but to the region of the Three Forks of the Missouri, where they had a disastrous encounter with Atsina indians (*Ross* [*A*], pp. 218, 277-282).

Foreword

281 This letter and its preamble, as printed in *The Detroit Free Press*' issue of July 1, 1856, read as follows:

COL. FREMONT AND THE "SOUTH PASS"—

LETTER FROM RAMSAY CROOKS

The subjoined letter from RAMSAY CROOKS, known throughout the West as one of the earliest traders and explorers of the regions beyond the Rocky Mountains, and sole survivor of the little band which first crossed those mountains by the way of the "South Pass," has been handed to us by our fellow citizen ANTHONY DUDGEON, Esq., to whom it is addressed, and whose permission we have to publish it. Mr. CROOKS quite dissipates the halo of glory sought to be woven around Col. FREMONT's brow as the alleged discoverer of the "South Pass," and plucks the stolen plume with which his supporters have adorned him. Mr. CROOKS has been a whig all his life, but it is plain that he does not regard the exploits of which Col. FREMONT is the real hero, more than those which have been wrongfully attributed to him, as qualifications for the Presidency; and these exploits were the sole producing causes of his nomination.

NEW YORK, June 26th, 1856.

MY DEAR SIR: Just as I was about closing my letter to you of yesterday's date, I received the *Detroit Free Press* of 21st instant, containing a laudation of Col. JOHN C. FREMONT taken from the *Detroit Advertiser* of the previous day, and which (if it had been true) is not, in my humble opinion, a *very* important item in making up the essentials of such a man as *should* become the President of this glorious confederacy. I however presume it is intended to exhibit him as endowed with uncommon intrepidity and daring in exploring so wild a region surrounded by savages and grizzly bears; thereby proving great firmness of character, so very desirable, but unfortunately so very rare, in the head of a great nation. But even if the Colonel *had* discovered the "South Pass," *it* does not show any more fitness for the exalted station he covets than the numerous beaver hunters and traders who passed and repassed through that noted place full twenty years before Col. FREMONT had attained a legal right to vote, and were fully his equals in enterprise, energy, and indomitable perseverance, with this somewhat important difference, that he was backed by the United States Treasury, while other explorers had to rely on their own resources.

The *perils* of the "South Pass," therefore, confer on the Colonel no greater claim to distinction than the trapper is entitled to, and his party must be pressed very hard when they have to drag in a circumstance so very unimportant as who discovered the "South Pass."

Although the *Free Press* conclusively proves that the Colonel *could not* be the discoverer of the "South Pass," the details are not accurate, and in order that history (if it ever gets there) may be correctly vindicated, I will tell you how it was.

Mr. David Stuart sailed from this port in 1810 for Columbia River, on board the ship "Tonquin," with a number of Mr. Astor's associates in the "Pacific Fur Company," and after the breaking up of the company in 1814, he returned through the North West Company's territories to Montreal, far to the north of the "South Pass," which he never saw.

In 1811 the overland party of Mr. Astor's expedition, under the command of Mr. Wilson P. Hunt, of Trenton, New Jersey, although numbering sixty well armed men, found the Indians so very troublesome in the country of the Yellow Stone River that the party of seven persons who left Astoria towards the end of June, 1812, considering it dangerous to pass again by the route of 1811, turned towards the south-east as soon as they had crossed the main chain of the Rocky Mountains, and after several days' journey came through the celebrated "South Pass," in the month of November, 1812. Pursuing from thence an easterly course, they fell upon the River Platte of the Missouri, where they passed the winter, and reached St. Louis in April, 1813.

The seven persons forming the party were Robert McClelland, of Hagerstown, Maryland, who with the celebrated Captain Wells was Captain of spies under General Wayne in his famous Indian campaign, Joseph Miller, of Baltimore, for several years an officer in the United States army, Robert Stuart, a citizen of Detroit, Benjamin Jones, of Missouri, who acted as huntsman to the party, Francois Le Claire, a half-breed, and Andie Vallee, a Canadian voyageur, and Ramsay Crooks, who is the only survivor of this small band of adventurers.

I am very sincerely yours,

Ramsay Crooks.

Anthony Dudgeon, Esq., Detroit, Michigan.

282 See note 15 on p. lv.

283 Sales catalogue (sale No. 3850) of American Art Association—Anderson Galleries, Inc., pp. 31, 32.

284 *Astoria*, I, p. 5.

285 See entry of October 29 (p. 187).

286 See entry of October 18 (p. 160).

287 These dissimilarities occur in all the trav. mem.'s entries. The July 1 entry, for example, shows 39 in punctuation and 24 in capitalization.

288 The single exception to this method of presenting trav. mem.'s text

is in the entry of October 22d (p. 164). Here the wordings of trav. mem. and of journ. are so widely variant that, though still using the distinction of Roman type and of italics, we have placed the two texts in parallel columns—the journ.'s text (without any interpolation from trav. mem.) being in the left-hand column, the trav. mem.'s entire text in the right-hand one.

289 Of the 172 pages (all unnumbered) in the journal's manuscript, p. 1 used by Stuart as a title page contains merely the entitlement mentioned on p. LXV *ante;* while p. 2 displays only a few arithmetical sums and disjointed words so unimportant as not to be included in our printing. Pp. 3-126, except for a short blank on p. 120 and two short blanks on p. 121, are solidly written and in our printing are numbered [1]-[124]. Pp. 127, 128 are torn out, their former presence being evidenced by a stub devoid of writing. Pp. 129, 130 (in our printing numbered [125], [126]) are solidly written. Pp. 131-148, 150, 155, 156, 158-167, 169 are blank. P. 149, only one-half of which contains writing, corresponds to p. [127] in our printing, while pp. 151-154 (pp. [128]-[131] in our printing) are solidly written. P. 157 contains only the meteorological chart described on p. CXII *ante*, while p. 168 (p. [132] in our printing) contains writing. Pp. 170-172 (in our printing [135]-[133]) are solidly written. This reversed order of the last mentioned three pages is caused by the fact that Stuart, when beginning his three-page description of his trip eastward from St. Louis, turned his book upside down and thereby transmuted the actual bottom of p. 172 into the top of the description's initial page. Accordingly, pp. [133], [134], [135] in our printing severally represent inverted pp. 172, 171, 170 of the manuscript.

290 An undated postscript on Stuart's pp. [123]-[125], he designed to amend the journ.'s original entry of October 13 on his p. [77]—our pp. 155, 156; and this postscript he rephrased in trav. mem.'s entry for that date. Two other postscripts (respectively dated October 14 and 15) on his p. [131] he designed to amend the journ.'s corresponding original entries on his pp. [77], [78]—pp. 158, 159; and this October 15 postscript he rephrased in trav. mem.'s entry for that date. Of our parallel columns on pp. 158, 159 the left-hand one contains the text of only the journ.'s original entries, while the right-hand one gives the texts both of the journ.'s postscripts and of the trav. mem.

291 On manuscript's p. [122], which in our printing is Stuart's p. [120]. See note 289.

292 On manuscript's p. [157]. See note 289.

293 This adaptation to *Astoria* is on the theory that Irving, in his authorship, had access to the original text of Hunt's diary.

Discovery of the Oregon Trail

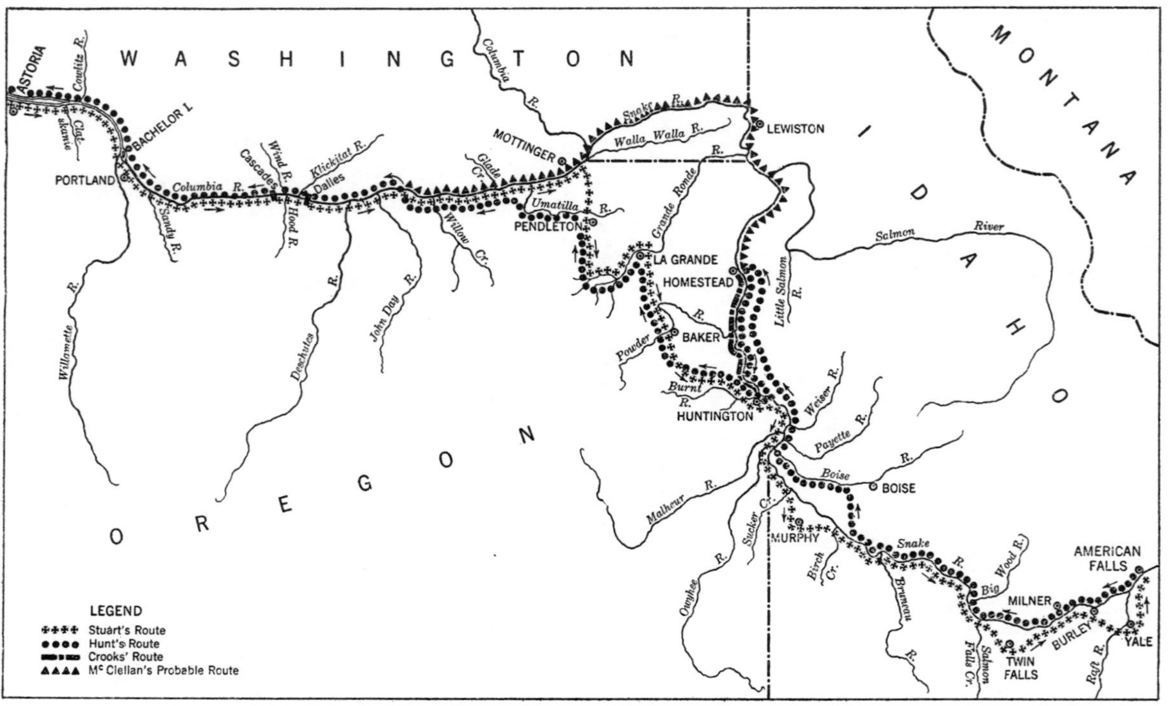

Routes of Stuart and of Hunt in Oregon and western Idaho

CHAPTER I

JUNE 29, 1812

By Canoe up the Columbia River from Astoria to Tongue Point

Departure from Astoria · Astoria Described · Local Indians, Flora and Fauna

[*Editor's Note.*—The bracketed italicized interpolations in the text of this and subsequent chapters are from the travelling memoranda]

[1] In the afternoon of Monday the 29th[1] day of June 1812 we sailed from Astoria under a Salute of Cannon from the Fort[2] Mr. Hunt the Agent[3] Mr McDougall[4] Mr Ehninger[5] and Captain Sowles[6] of the Company's ship Beaver[7] accompanied us as far as Tongue Point,[8] where we found two Barges and Ten Canoes,[9] which had set out from the Establishment this morning, destined for the interior parts[10] of the Country above the Forks[11] of the Columbia— Mefsrs. Mackenzie,[12] [*D.*] Stuart[13] and Clarke[14] had charge of the [*two*] Boats[15] and nine Canoes, with seven Clerks, 32 Canadians and 12 Sandwich Islanders[16] under them— the other contained R. McClellan,[17] R Crooks,[18] John Day,[19] Benjamin Jones,[20] André Vallé,[21] François Leclairc[22] [*engagés*] and myself[23] with the necefsaries for the prosecution of this voyage— It being late and some preparation necefsary we agreed to pafs the night here,[24] which is 4 miles from Astoria & 19 from Cape Disappointment—[25] The[26] Columbia is about seven[27] miles wide at the Fort, crossing from Point George[28] to that of the Chinooks,[29] but both above & below, it is nearly twice as much— [*It*[30] *would be in vain to attempt giving a description of our establishment in its present*

unfinished state, I will therefore content myself by observing that it is delightfully situated on the Southeast extremity of point George, which is a commanding as well as in every other respect a commodious station, having an excellent harbour within fifty yards of the shore for vessels not exceeding two hundred Tons.— Our present Fortification in place of being 120 square yards in extent, as was at first projected, is only about 75 feet by 80, it is well stockaded with pickets 17 feet long and 18 inches diameter, having two strong Bastions, at opposite angles, so as to rake two sides each, inside are a framed store two stories high, 60 feet by 30, with good cellars and a powder magazine.— a dwelling house, one story high & 60 feet by 25.— a Blacksmiths shop, and a large shade for carpenters, coopers &c., the ensuing winter about 20 Men are to be employed in extending the Fortification, and 30 are now engaged in preparing a frame for a dwelling house, to be two stories high & 60 by 30 feet, which with another Store and Kitchen shall be the principal additions made to the present buildings.—] Fort Clatsop[31] (now in ruins) [, *the residence of Capts. Lewis & Clark while in this country*,] is at the distance of 7 miles in about a south west direction [*it was very disagreeably situated, being surrounded with swamps and quagmires, but the immense number of Elk*[32] *& wild Fowl which resort thither in winter for feed more than compensates for that inconvenience.*—]— The[33] Clatsops[34] and Chinooks are the only Tribes in the immediate vicinity, the former can bring 214 and the latter 280 fighting men to the field—

About 40 miles to the n.w. along the Coast[35] live the Chi-hee-lash[36] 234 men and about the same distance [2] to the Southward[37] are the Callemex[38] in number 200— these four nations generally come directly to the Establishment with what Furs &c. they have to trade, which for the most part consist in Sea Otter,[39] Beaver[40] River otter,[41] [*Bear Skins*,] Drefsed Elk skins [, *Muskrats*,[42]] Roots[43] and Salmon,[44] but the Chinooks are more especially the intermediate Traders between the Whites[45] and the more inland Tribes particularly those to the northward—[46] A few Deer[47] and some Black Bear[48] are found in the neighbourhood [*of our establishment*], but Elk seems to be almost the only animal which may be called an inhabitant of the country near the Coast, and untill the underwood ceases to grow, will very probably remain so, the country is likewise so very broken and heavily timbered, that it is seldom poſsible to distinguish an object more than 40 Yards,[49] which when added to an impenetrable undergrowth,[50] affords such a secure retreat that the utmost efforts of the Hunter are seldom crowned with succeſs, besides from the middle of Octr. to the middle March no man in the woods can poſsibly keep his arms in order, on account of the unceasing rains which fall during these 5 months— [*The whole tract of Country along the coast is remarkably rugged and mountainous, and in my opinion, the clouds collected on these mountains, uniting with those which come off the ocean, must occasion this succeſsion of heavy rains which is frequently accompanied by tremendous Thunder & lightning,*] the remainder of the year (if an almost total want of the decending fluid may so be termed), poſseſsing the best [*and most agreeable*] weather in the world— [*The dews are abundant throughout this whole country in the spring, summer, and Autumnal nights, and in a great measure supply the want of rain during those seasons, altho' the atmosphere is then loaded with humidity, its wholesomeneſs is not in the least injured thereby, for both natives and whites sleep in the open air with perfect security— Fogs are very common along and in the vicinity of the coast, especially in the spring, and Autumn, however these continue generally but a few hours in the morning, and as they consist only of watery particles, are not like ours, prejudicial to the health of the inhabitants or (from appearances) to vegitation— The S. & S.East winds usually bring rain, and the North to S.West a clear sky, these serve as infalliable indications, to the aborigines who thereby presume to prognosticate the state of the weather.— From the coast to the neighbourhood of the cordilleras, or Rocky mountains, the quantity of snow that falls in the Winter is very trifling, it usually melts while falling, and it is uncommon to have it remain on the ground more than 2 or 3 days, except on the highest summits of the mountains which are constantly covered with snow & are distinguishable at a great distance by their whiteneſs, which occasions their forming a very singular & pleasing appearance.—*

The mild temperature which this tract of country almost always enjoys must depend in a great measure upon the succeſsion of winds from the Pacific ocean, which extend from Latitude 20° to at least 50° North, their effect is equally agreeable in summer for they cool the air so much that in the shade no one is ever incommoded with perspiration: and the dreſs of the inhabitants is the same in summer as in Winter.—

The difference in the vegitation of the maratime and interior countries depends leſs upon the inequality of the climate than that of their respective soils; that upon the coast is generally poor ground, of a brown colour inclining to red, it is brittle, and in some parts clayey and mingled with gravel— In the interior, or rather in the vallies of the rocky mountains, the soil is generally of a blackish colour, but in some places yellow, and frequently mixed with marll; and marine substances in a state of decomposition, this quality of the soil is continued to a considerable depth, as is discernable in the ravines and beds of rivers.— The vegitation in these vallies is much more vigerous and exuberant than near the coast.— The principal trees, that came within the compaſs of my perambulations, are the hemlock,[51] *spruce,*[52] *white*[53] *and red*[54] *Cedar, (all of which grow to an enormous size) and incredible as it may appear we found some of them 7-9 fathoms in circumference and 250 to 300 feet long, there are likewise white Oak,*[55] *White and swamp Ash,*[56] *Cottonwood,*[57] *Willow*[58] *and a few Walnut.—*[59] *Of aromatic shrubs, and other undergrowth, there is an endleſs variety, as also of Berries, such as Gooseberries,*[60] *Strawberries,*[61] *Raspberries (of two kinds, red*[62] *and yellow,*[63] *and very large having an exceeding fine flavour) Whortleberries,*[64] *Cranberries,*[65] *Juniperberries,*[66] *serviceberries,*[67] *Blue or Blacberries,*[68] *Currants,*[69] *Sloes,*[70] *Wild and choke cherries*[71] *&c: &c:— Climbing plants or creepers are found in great abundance in all the thickets, among others is a species of vine*[72] *that deserves to be noticed; its flowers, each of which is composed of six petals or leaves, about 3 inches in length, are of the most beautiful crimson, spotted within, with white; its leaves are disposed by threes, of a handsome green and an oval shape, this plant climbs upon the trees like the ivy, but without attaching itself to them, when it reaches the top of a tree it descends from it perpendicularly and as it continues to grow, extends from tree to tree untill at length it exhibits some re-*

semblance to the rigging of a ship, it is much tougher and more flexible than Willow, and can be procured from 50 to 100 fathoms in length; the indians manufacture baskets of it, which are of so close a texture as to hold water, and are employed for many domestic purposes.— The principal quadrupids I have seen, are the Moose Deer,[32] *or Elk,*[32] *the Stag,*[47] *the fallow Deer,*[47] *Hart,*[47] *black and grizzly Bear,*[73] *antelope,*[74] *Ibex,*[75] *Beaver,*[40] *Sea*[39] *and River*[41] *Otter, Muskrats,*[42] *Foxes,*[76] *Wolves,*[77] *a few Panthers,*[78] *&c. &c.— Horses*[79] *and Dogs*[80] *are the only domestic animals in possession of the natives.—*

The country abounds with an infinity of both aquatic and land Birds, particularly the Swan,[81] *Wild Goose,*[82] *Brant,*[83] *Ducks*[84] *of almost every description, Pelicans,*[85] *Herons,*[86] *Gulls,*[87] *Snipe,*[88] *Curlews,*[89] *Eagles,*[90] *Vultures,*[91] *Crows,*[92] *Ravens,*[93] *Magpies,*[94] *Woodpeckers,*[95] *Wild Pigeons,*[96] *Partridges,*[97] *Grouce,*[98] *Pheasant,*[99] *and a very numerous collection of singing Birds.—*

The Rivers are remarkably well stocked with Salmon,[44] *Sturgeon,*[100] *Trout,*[101] *Chub,*[102] *Conger,*[103] *and a variety of fresh water smelt*[104] *which are excellent of their kind.—*

There are very few Reptiles in the country and the only dangerously venemous ones are the Rattle-Snake,[105] *and a kind of Serpent which is striped with black, yellow, and white, sometimes mixed with brown,*[106] *the largest I have seen of either, did not exceed 4 feet in length, in the swamps a great many Snakes may be found, but are all harmlefs,*[107] *there are also, Frogs,*[108] *Toads,*[109] *Land Turtles,*[110] *and a kind of Lizard, which lives usually under ground in the plains, their length exclusive of the tail, is nine or ten inches, and three inches in circumference, the head is triangular, covered with small square scales, the upper part of the body is covered with small scales, green, yellow, black and blue; the feet have each five toes furnished with strong nails; the tail is round, and of the same length and colour as the body.—*[111]]

Fish,[112] Roots and what few animals they can kill [3] is alike the only diet [*sole dependence for sustenance*] of the White and Red man— The coast near the mouth of the River produces a few Sea Otter and some scattering Beaver, which the natives both from inexperience & indolence seem as yet little inclined to reduce in number— Few Salmon are caught before the latter end of May but from that to the middle of August they can be got in tolerable plenty [*and are by far the finest fish I ever beheld,*[113] *they are mostly caught in shallow water by seines*[114] *made of nettles.*—]— but till the ensuing May nothing but Sturgeon Dogtooth Salmon[44] and Uthulhuns[104] or Smelts can be procured from the waters, and them in such small quantities that no real dependence can be placed on them for the support of any number of men— [*from August untill December is the season for Dog-tooth Salmon, a very inferior species of that fish, and so named by us from their having a double row of teeth exceedingly sharp and at least half an inch long, they are generally killed with the Spear, in small rivulets, smoked and laid by as store for the dreary months of January and February, after which Sturgeon and Uth-le-chan may be taken in great numbers, the former sometimes by the Spear, but more generally by the hook and line; and the latter by the Scoop Net.— The Uthlechan is about six inches long and somewhat similar to our smelt, is a very delicious little fish, and so fat as to burn like*[115] *a candle, and are often used for that purpose by the natives.—*

The[116] *Religion or rather enthusiastic superstition of these people, I had not sufficient opportunity or knowledge of their language to investigate fully, and notwithstanding my making the strictest enquiries, all I could collect was, that they represent the supreme being as an immense Bird, inhabiting the Sun, (called by them Uth-lath-Gla-gla, being a benevolent spirit, and omnipotent.— to him they attribute the creation, and suppose him capable of aſsuming any shape or appearance at pleasure, but upon extraordinary occurances, he is believed to take the likeneſs aforesaid, occasionally ranging through the aerial regions, and in his wrath, hurling down Thunder & lightning upon us guilty mortals; to him they offer annual sacrifices of their first Salmon, Venison, &c. &c.— A particular being is ascribed to the fire, of whom they are in perpetual dread, and constantly offer sacrifices, supposing him equally poſsessed of the power of good and evil: they are very desirous of being patronised by this Gentleman, for it is he alone who has the power of interceding with their winged protector, and procure them all de-*

sirable things, such as male children, a plentiful fishery, abundance of game, with comforts and riches of every description.—

When any of their chief personages is supposed to be on his death bed, or any way in imminent danger of his life, all the Literati of the Nation are immediately convened, the High Priest and Physician, or medecine Man, brings and consults each his deity (i.e. the benevolent or spirit of the air and that of the Fire,) which are made of wood and ingeniously carved, with a number of Beaver's teeth, Bear and Eagles claws, suspended from them, they are capriciously formed in shape of a Horse, Bear, Deer, Beaver, Swan, Fish &c.: Those Idols with their poſseſsions are placed in a remote corner of the Lodge, for the purpose of consultation, but should they not agree regarding the patients malady, the owners, who are mostly always competitors for fame, power, and influence, beat them violently against each other, untill a tooth or claw falls of one, which is always taken as a full proof of his confutation, consequently the advice and prescriptions of the other are implicitly attended to; should the sick person recover, a sacrifice is immediately made to the revered deity, and his adherent is liberally rewarded, but should he on the contrary make his exit, no offering or compensation is given, and the failure is entirely attributed to the displeasure of the offended deity.— A day or two after his death, a few of the nearest relatives carry off the corpse, which, with his most valuable moveables, they deposit in a canoe prepared for the purpose, and neatly covered with handsome matts made of straw, they then lay it on a scaffold, or suspend it between two trees, in a retired part of the woods; all the deceased's well wishers cut of their hair in token of grief, and for several days neither eat or drink but mope about the village, howling and lamenting the departed; when the season of mourning is over (which generally lasts about one month) a division of the slaves and other property takes place agreeably to the defunct's request on his death bed.—

Their manner of courtship and marriage is somewhat singular; when a fair one has the good fortune to kindle a flame in the bosom of a hero, he watches for a private conference, and if favorably received, repairs soon after to her Father's lodge with a considerable present, which he carelessly throws down at the old Gentleman's feet, then his intention is disclosed, generally by a friend he prefers on this important occasion, the Sire then enquires whether the proposal is agreeable to his daughter, and on being answered in the affirmative, demands so many slaves, Horses, Canoes &c. according to her beauty and accomplishments, and promises a certain return on her going into house-keeping; preliminaries thus settled, the remainder of the day is devoted to festivity and mirth,— at a late hour the party breaks up, and all retire to rest, except the lover, who steals to her Ladyship's couch where he remains untill morning, when if they are satisfied with each other's company, the match is finally settled; but should either be inclined to retract, they are at liberty so to do, as the present the lover had made his intended Father-in-law, is thought a full equivalent for this breach in the maid's virtue or reputation.— Both sexes seem incapable of forming any tender attachment, the women are very inconstant to their husbands, and the worst of disorders is deeply rooted among them, having been first introduced by some of our country-men, probably from the Sandwich Islands, where it has been known, time immemorial, the effects however are not so destructive as might be expected.—

Poligamy is not only allowed, but considered honorable, and the greater number of wives a man can maintain, the more power & influence has he in the Nation.— The first Wife is always respected as the real and legitimate one by all the others, who are called secondary wives, she has the management of all domestic concerns, and regulates the interior of the house; the husband has sometimes much to do to keep harmony among so many women, who are not a little inclined to jealousy, the usual manner is, each night at supper, to make known his choice of her who is to have the honor of sharing his bed, by directing her to prepare it.—

The chieftanship is not hereditary, but he who exceeds in the number of his wives, male children and Slaves is elected.—

Their system of criminal jurisprudence, in a particular manner, is very imperfect: the offences that are deemed deserving of capital punishments, are treachery, intentional homicide, and the robbing of any valuable article, neverthelefs those found guilty of homicide can most generally screen themselves from punishment by a composition with the relatives of the murdered.— but should the afsafsin be inclined to make no reparation or concefsion, the injured family often assume the right of pursuing and punishing him, or some of his kindred, considering themselves under the most sacred obligations of supporting, even by force, the rights of their relations—

Husbands and Fathers are not subject to any punishment for killing their wives or children, as they are declared by their laws to be natural masters of their lives:— but most generally the power of deciding controversies and of punishing offences is entrusted to the chiefs—they being considered by the lower order as omnicient and having an indisputable right to those privileges, however it cannot be supposed that a rugged proprietor of the forest or Rocks, unprincipled and unenlightened, can be a nice resolver of entangled claims, or very exact in proportioning punishments to offences, but generally, the more he indulges his own will, the more he holds his subjects in dependence, therefore innocence and forbearance, without the favor of the Chief, confer no security, and crimes however atrocious, involve no danger when the judge is resolute to acquit.—

Their Arms are principally Bows and Arrows, Iron and bone Bludgeons, with a few muskets which they are extremely fond of, and so much is their effect dreaded by the surrounding tribes (who have few or none) that a dozen on either side are sufficient to decide their most obstinate conflicts— When a quarrel arises between two tribes, a day and place are appointed where the affair is settled in a pitched battle, *which is their universal mode of warfare; they generally prefer the banks of a rivulet for the field of action, and post the adverse parties on either side of the stream; the number of killed and wounded never exceed half a dozen, and should an equal number of each party fall, the war is ended, but otherwise the conquerors must make an equivalent compensation in slaves &c., else hostilities are renewed on a future day; they seldom make prisoners, but when this is the case, they are always well treated and never reduced to slavery, these poor creatures are procured from the interior Tribes, who are much more ferocious, but fortunately like the most of savage Nations, their military power is an undiciplined rabble, unfit to contend with 1/5 their number of Whites: They like the others seldom shed much blood in their engagements, and sometimes battles are fought which last 2 or 3 days, yet altho' 5 or 600 men may be engaged on each side, and the conflict terminated in a complete rout, the whole loss is seldom more than 12 or 15 killed and wounded,— predatory excursions are the favorite war like exploits of these people, consequently many such plundering parties are formed who make frequent incursions on their enemies, and sometimes upon their friendly neighbours, they seldom exceed 50 or 60 in number, but when fortunate enough to fall on a small band, they maſsacre all the men, and carry away the women and children as slaves; the rest of their plunder is carried off on horses, each man being provided with two or three of these animals on all such expeditions.—*

There[117] *is perhaps no race of people in the world, (for that they are of the same origin I have little doubt) who can exhibit a greater variety, with regard to size and appearance, than those of the tract we traversed.— The affluent (as they may be termed) whose good fortune has placed them among the Buffalo plains on the east side of the mountains, are generally from 5 feet 8 to 6 feet 2 inches in stature, well proportioned, extremely strong and active.— while*[118] *the indigent inhabitants of the western side are in general below the middle size, indolent, and of a very unhealthy complexion, evidently stunted by the badneſs of their food and the want of proper clothing, it is however very uncommon to find a crooked or deformed person among them, not from their pursuing, as some have maintained, the cruel custom of destroying such unfortunate children, but in my belief, because they leave to nature the care of forming them, without obstructing her operations, by the improper application of bandages, stays, corsets &c. &c.—*

They have very round faces, with small animated eyes, a broad flat nose, a handsome mouth, even and white teeth, well shaped legs and small flat feet.— In their infancy the crown and forehead are flatened by means of a small piece of board, shaped and tied on for that purpose, this in their opinion is a great acquisition to personal beauty, consequently whoever has the broadest and flatest head is esteemed by far the handsomest person.— They have scarce any beard, and it is seldom the smallest hair is to be discerned on their faces, from the care they take to pluck out the little that appears, they esteem it very uncooth and impolite to have a beard, calling the whites by way of reproach, the long beards; the same attention is paid to removing it from their bodies where its growth is more abundant, that of their head is thick and black, but rather coarse; they allow it to grow to a great length, sometimes wearing it pleated and sometimes fancifully wound round the head in tresses: of this they are as proud & careful as they are averse to beards, nor could a greater affront be offered them than to cut it off.— Those[119] *whose lot it is to inhabit the interior country depend chiefly on hunting, consequently lead a roving life through the plains, without any stationary habitation, whereas*[120] *those who live near the sea subsist I may say entirely on Fish, and dwell in large scattering villages on the banks of the principal water courses: their lodges are constructed of cedar boards, a little sunk in the ground, and leaning against strong poles set erect, (with cross spars) which serve likewise as a support to the roof; those dwellings are generally large enough for the accommodation of 3 or 4 families, have a door in the gable end, made of a square piece of board, or framed seal skin, a fire place (or places) in the middle, & a hole over it, in the roof of the house which serves at once for the discharge of the smoke and the admission of light— the sides are partitioned off for sitting and sleeping places, and covered with neat grass mats: the principal houses have a small apartment attached to them, which serves as a vapor bath, to prepare which stones must be heated and placed in a large hole dug in the middle of the bath, or sweating house, where the heat may be increased to any degree by the steam of the water which is poured on them.—*

They pass a great portion of their lives in revelry and amusement, music, dancing and play form their customary diversions, as to the first it scarcely deserves the name, both from the defficiency of their instruments; and their manner of singing has something in it harsh & disagreeable to the ear, their songs being almost all extempore, on any triffeling object that strikes the imagination; they have several kinds of dancing, some of which are lively, pleasing, and possess some variety, the women are rarely permitted to dance with the men, but form their companies apart, and dance to the sound of the same instrument and song.—

Their games are numerous and for the most part ingenious, and they sometimes indulge in play to very great excess, indeed there have been instances of their losing everything they possessed in the world, even their Women, Children and Lodges.— They are notorious thieves, and he who is so dexterous as on all occasions to elude detection is much applauded, acquires great celebrity and popularity, but the wretch who is unfortunate enough to be discovered is severely punished, and sometimes loses an ear &c., which is thought so disgraceful as to reduce him to a level with the women; and disqualifies him ever after from becoming a warrior; some whose family have much influence may be indulged with the privilege of being mogsan[121] *carrier to a war party.—*

Their[122] *general mode of hunting Elk and Deer is with the Bow and Arrow, very few poſseſsing or knowing the use of Fire Arms; they frequently go in large parties, surround the game while grazing in a favorable place, such as a small prairie or meadow environed by Wood; they plant themselves in the different avenues, or paths leading to this spot, then set in their dogs, which throws the affrighted animals in such confusion as to scatter in every direction, thereby giving the most or all a chance of exercising their skill, for let the consternation of these poor creatures be ever so great, they can only escape by those leading paths,— some of the best warriors shoot an arrow with such force as to send it thro' an Elk or Buffalo*[123] *at the distance of 15 or 20 paces,*[124]*— On*[125] *certain occasions they use darts, which are adapted with the greatest judgement to the different objects of the chase; for Animals, a single barbed point; for Birds, they have them with three points of light bone, spread and barbed; for Seals & Sea Otter, they use a false point, inserted in a socket at the end of the dart which parts on the least effort of the animal to dive, remaining in its body: a string of considerable length is fastened to this barbed point and twisted round the wooden part of the dart; this serves as a float to direct them to the animal, which having the stick to drag after it, soon tires, and becomes an easy prey; (it however requires skill to humour it, perhaps equal to our angling.— The boards used in throwing these darts are very judiciously fixed, in semblance of a gutter, which enables the Natives to cast them with great exactneſs to a considerable distance.—*

Their Canoes for the most part are made of cedar, and altho' poſseſsed of no other instrument than a small chisel, it would be in vain for any White, (with every tool he could wish) to set up a competition with them in this art; if perfect symmetry, smoothneſs and proportion constitute beauty, they surpaſs anything I ever beheld: I have seen some of them as transparent as oiled paper, thro' which you could trace every formation of the inside: and the natives of this river & its vicinity are the most expert paddle men any of us had ever seen; two or three of these fellows, in a small canoe, can with perfect security navigate in the most boisterous weather, for no sooner does their canoe fill or upset, than they spring into the water, (more like amphibious animals than human beings,) right and empty her, when with the greatest composure, they again get in and proceed.— The men never wear any other garment than a small robe made of Deer, or Musk-rat skins, thrown loosely over the shoulders; and the women have no other addition than a fringe of cedar bark, tied round the waist, and reaching about two inches below the knees.— There are no two tribes who speak the same tongue, but most generally, each nation understands the tongue of the nearest neighbours, on either side, so that each horde may be said to comprehend three different languages.—

They poſseſs their present lands and situation from time immemorial.— They are never troubled with epidemic, or contagious diseases, except the small-pox, which, from nation to nation, has found its way acroſs the rocky mountains, and sometimes its effects are so calamitous as to carry off three fourths of those who have the misfortune to be attacked therewith.— Their method of life neither secures them perpetual health, nor exposes them to any particular diseases; it is generally supposed that life is longer in places where there are few opportunities of luxury, but I found few or no instances among them, of extraordinary longivety, an Indian grows old over his smoked salmon just like a citizen at a turtle feast: instances of long life are often related here, which (it appears to me) those who hear them are more willing to credit than to examine.—

They informed us that Capt. Gray[126] *of the Ship Columbia, from Boston, was the first white who entered the river; on the veſsels first appearance in the offing, they were very much surprised & alarmed, but after her entering and anchoring in the river, they were all seized with such consternation as to abandon their village, leaving only a few old people who could not follow, some imagined that the ship must be some overgrown monster, come to devour them, while others supposed her to be a floating island, inhabited by cannibals, sent by the great spirit to destroy them, and ravage their country &c. &c. however a Boats crew soon went ashore, who by their mild behaviour, and distributing a few trinkets, succeeded in assuring the old people, of their friendly intentions, which they soon found means to communicate to the fugitives, thus a friendly intercourse was immediately entered into, which has never since been interrupted.—]*

Notes to Chapter I

1 *Ross* [*A*], p. 195, *Cox* [*A*], I, p. 118, [*B*], p. 72, and *Nouvelles Annales*, X, p. 31, agree with Stuart as to this date; but *Franchere* [*A*], p. 121, gives "le 31 Juin au soir," and *Franchere* [*B*], p. 161, states "30th of June, in the afternoon."

2 The Astorians' establishment, for description of which see later in this same day's entry, as also *Ross* [*A*], pp. 69 *et seq.*, *Franchere* [*A*], pp. 94, 98, [*B*], pp. 123, 124, 129, and *Cox* [*A*], I, pp. 110, 111, [*B*], pp. 68, 69.

3 Wilson Price Hunt, a partner and also "agent" or general manager. So detailed and charming is the tribute paid him by Irving's *Astoria* that there remains for us only to add in preface and in supplement a few bald statements of biographical detail. Described by Ramsay Crooks as "of Trenton, New Jersey" (p. CXXXVI *ante*), he was son of John P. and Margaret (Guild) Hunt of Hopewell, N. J., and was born at Asbury, N. J., on, it is said, March 20, 1783. In 1804 he went to St. Louis, where until 1809 he was in a merchandising business in partnership with a John Hankinson. In 1817, having returned from his Astorian adventure, he purchased several thousand acres on Gravois Creek near St. Louis and began to farm them. At least in 1837 he advertised himself as a dealer in furs and peltries with office at the northwest corner of Front and Chestnut Streets in St. Louis. He was postmaster of St. Louis, 1822-40. On April 20, 1836, he married Anne (Lucas) Hunt, widow of his cousin Theodore Hunt, and, childless, died at St. Louis on April 13, 1842. His widow died April 12, 1879. Of him, his Astorian associate, Alexander Ross, wrote: ". . . Mr. Hunt was a conscientious and upright man—a friend to all, and beloved as well as respected by all." *Billon*, pp. 193, 194; *Ross* [*A*], p. 276; *Chittenden*, p. 907; *Lyford*, p. 421; T. C. Elliott's *Wilson Price Hunt, &c.*, in *Ore. Hist. Soc. Quar.*, XXXII, pp. 130-134.

4 Duncan McDougall, who was a partner with local authority second to only that of Wilson Price Hunt and had arrived at Astoria on the ship *Tonquin*. *Astoria; Pacific Fur; Franchere* [*A*], pp. 9, 16, [*B*], pp. 20, 29, 368; *Henry-Thomp.*, pp. 759-762, 765, 774, 775, 779, 851-854, 861-865, 868, 889-894, 899-906.

5 George Ehninger, a son of John Jacob Astor's sister Catherine. He was born in New York City in 1792 and as a clerk arrived at Astoria on the ship *Beaver*. After the ending of the Astorian venture he married Eliza, daughter of John Whetten, and conducted a fur store in New York City. *Porter*, pp. 200, 1030; *Cox* [*A*], I, p. 1, [*B*], p. 25; *Franchere* [*A*], p. 116, [*B*], p. 155; *Longworth*, p. 166.

6 Cornelius Sowle, a native of Rhode Island (F. W. Howay's *Captain Cornelius Sowle* in *Wash. Hist. Quar.*, XXIV, pp. 243-249; *Porter*, p. 199). Though

his surname was actually "Sowle" (*Baker-Astor* [*A*], pp. 103, 111, 131, 133, 167, 182; *Ross* [*A*], p. 239; *Astoria*, II, p. 106), Stuart's journ.—as also *Cox* [*A*], I, p. 1, [*B*], p. 25, and *Franchere* [*A*], p. 117, [*B*], p. 155—call him "Sowles," while Stuart's trav. mem. mentions him as "Soule."

7 Sailed from New York October 17, 1811, and reached Astoria May 10, 1812. *Cox* [*A*], I, pp. 1, 105, [*B*], pp. 25, 67; *Porter*, pp. 200, 201. See also *Astoria*, II, pp. 107-109.

8 This rocky peninsula, situated four miles east of the Astorians' establishment and projecting northeasterly from the Columbia's left bank, had in 1792 received from Lieutenant Broughton the aptly descriptive name of Tongue Point. Lewis and Clark later restyled it Point William in honor of Clark, but the Astorians subsequently restored its appellation of Tongue Point, which designation it still bears. *Chart* No. 6151; *L. & C. Hist.*, p. 722; *Franchere* [*A*], p. 165, [*B*], pp. 104, 220, 221; *Ross* [*A*], p. 103; *Cox* [*A*], I, pp. 109, 110, [*B*], pp. 68, 69.

9 For Stuart's description of these canoes, see pp. 35, 36.

10 See p. LXXXI.

11 Confluence of Snake and Columbia Rivers.

12 "McKenzie" in trav. mem. He was Donald McKenzie, for whose biography see note 35 on p. LVII.

13 David Stuart, the journalist's uncle and an Astorian partner, who had arrived at Astoria in the ship *Tonquin*. He was born in Scotland—on December 22, 1765, according to *G. S.;* on December 19, 1766, according to the Mrs. Margaret Haig Stuart mentioned in note 6 on p. LIV. "Our dear old Uncle David Stuart" died at Detroit, Mich., "Oct. 18, 1853," according to *Bible* [*B*] entry in Mrs. Robert Stuart's handwriting. For this amiable and much respected man, see *Astoria; Franchere* [*A*], [*B*]; *Ross* [*A*]; *Henry-Thomp.*, pp. 760, 767, 781-787, 790-794, 807, 810, 844, 845, 848, 854-856, 863, 865, 875, 886.

14 John Clarke, who had arrived at Astoria on the ship *Beaver* and four days later, on Astor's nomination, become a partner. Clarke is reputed to have been born in 1781 at Montreal (*Astoria*, II, p. 106, terms him, however, " a native of the United States"), to have been distantly related to Astor, and to have been in the service of the North West Company from 1804 till 1810. It is also said that, after Astoria's collapse, he joined the Hudson's Bay Company. *Porter*, pp. 200, 201 (citing *Clarke*, pp. 9, 11, 15, 16), 578; *Pacific Fur; Astoria; Cox* [*A*], I, p. 1, [*B*], p. 25; *Franchere* [*A*], p. 116, [*B*], p. 155; *Henry-Thomp.*, pp. 759, 761, 764, 766, 767, 770, 774, 779, 783, 784, 787, 788, 854-857, 865, 872, 874, 899.

15 Seemingly identical with the "two Barges" already mentioned by Stuart.

16 Doubtless some of those imported in the *Tonquin* and *Beaver*, which ships, when calling at the Sandwich Islands, had taken aboard natives for service in the Astorian enterprise. *Astoria*, I, pp. 78, 107; *Cox* [*A*], I, pp. 64, 65, [*B*], pp. 50, 51; *Franchere* [*A*], pp. 62, 63, [*B*], p. 84; *Henry-Thomp.*, p. 756, f.n.

17 Robert McClellan. See pp. XCI-XCV for biographical note concerning him.

18 Ramsay Crooks. See pp. LXXXII-XCI for biographical note concerning him.

19 For biographical note concerning him, see pp. XCVII-C.

20 For biographical note concerning him, see pp. XCV, XCVI.

21 "Andre Vallee" in trav. mem., which uniformly uses the spelling "Vallée" instead of, as throughout the journ., "Vallé." For biographical note concerning him, see p. XCVII.

22 "Francois Leclerc" in trav. mem. For biographical data concerning him, see p. XCVI. Though Stuart in both journ. and trav. mem. ordinarily spells the name as "Leclairc," he in one instance in the journ. styles it as "LeClairc" and in one instance in the trav. mem. uses the form "LeClerc."

23 If the roster as here stated by Stuart be enlarged by inclusion of the Clatsop interpreter—who is subsequently mentioned by Stuart as being added to the party— it would total 62 persons and thus agree with *Franchere* [*A*], p. 121, [*B*], p. 161 and with *Ross* [*A*], p. 195; but *Cox* [*A*], I, p. 118, [*B*], p. 72, by increasing the number of clerks, Canadians and Sandwich Islanders, creates a total of 90. The trustworthiness of Cox's figures is clouded by the fact that, with patent error, he rates Stuart's overland party exclusive of John Day as consisting of 11 men instead of the actual 6 (*Cox* [*A*], I, p. 114, [*B*], p. 83). This and subsequent criticisms of Cox in our footnotes should not suggest that we question the accuracy of any of his statements except such as relate to the size of the party and also to certain dates and distances.

24 Tongue Point. Inasmuch as *Cox* [*A*], I, pp. 120, 121, [*B*], p. 73, places the camp six miles east of Tongue Point, it is possible that the entire expedition did not camp at a single spot.

25 This cape on north side of Columbia's mouth received its name from the English navigator John Meares (1756?-1809), who, by the name, registered his inability to locate the river which the Spaniard, Bruno Hecata, had suggested as existing. *Scott*, I, pp. 126, 150.

26 In the journ.'s manuscript Stuart made the following two interlineations. Above the word "The" he placed "2d" and above the word "Fort" at the commencement of the next sentence he placed "1st"—all this suggesting possibly intention ultimately to transpose the sentences, which he thus transposed in the trav. mem.

27 "is six miles wide" in trav. mem.

28 The western extremity of the Astorian peninsula. Vancouver's expedition named it Point George in honor of the British King, George III; but at the present day it is termed Smith Point because a Samuel C. Smith, after settlers began flocking to Oregon, acquired a donation land claim which included the point. *McArthur*, p. 327; *Chart* No. 6151.

29 On the opposite or right bank of the Columbia.

30 *Cf.* journ.'s postscript, p. 252 (paragraph 1, 2)—of all of which, save for

a few inconsequential differences, a portion of this description is a duplicate.

31 Lewis and Clark's winter quarters, which were situated "about 200 yards" west of the left bank of the Netul (now termed Lewis and Clark) River and three miles above its mouth. *L. & C. Hist.*, pp. 727, 728.

32 Save in possibly one instance the term "elk" wherever used by Stuart unquestionably denotes the wapiti, *Cervus canadensis;* a more specific nomenclature designating, as *Cervus canadensis occidentalis* (*Ham. Smith*), the wapiti of the Pacific slope and, as *Cervus canadensis canadensis* (*Erxleben*), the wapiti both of the Rocky Mountains and of the country east of those mountains. The one possible exception to this generalization concerning Stuart's use of "elk" lurks in "Moose Deer, or Elk" (trav. mem., p. 7). That the "Elk" there made synonymous with "Moose Deer" was a wapiti and not a moose, *Alces americanus americanus* (*Jardine*), is suggested by sportsmen's nomenclature (see *Duncan*, p. 361); but it nevertheless should not be forgotten that *Colvocorresses*, pp. 279, 283, when mentioning the killing of an "elk" in the Columbian region, illustrates the event with a picture of a moose.

33 When shifting this sentence from journ. into trav. mem. Stuart not only transposed the names of the two tribes (thereby automatically altering his statement as to these tribes' respective sizes) but also reduced "280" to "180."

34 For description of this tribe and of all other tribes hereinafter mentioned by Stuart and for his variant spellings of tribal names, see pp. 331-364.

35 Seacoast.

36 "çhi-hee-leesh" in trav. mem.

37 On the seacoast.

38 "callemax" in trav. mem.

39 *Latax lutris. L. & C. Hist.*, pp. 852, 853.

40 *Castor canadensis*, the beaver common to all North America.

41 *Lutra canadensis pacifica* (*Rhoads*).

42 *Fiber zibethicus osoyoosensis* (*Lord*).

43 Edible roots, for the most used of which, the wappattoo (ouapatou), see entry of July 1, p. 30. According to Lewis and Clark, eight varieties of roots were eaten by the local indians—a thistle, *Cnidus edulis;* a fern, *Pteris aquilina;* a horsetail, *Equiætum telmateia;* a licorice, *Glycyrrhiza lepidota;* a cat-tail, *Typha latifolia*, it being the common cat-o'-nine-tail; the wappattoo, *Sagittaria variabilis*, it being the common arrowhead; and two others, each small, one of them possibly *Iris tenax*, the other of them not identified. For detailed description of these various roots and of their culinary treatment by indians, including an occasional seasoning with whale oil, see *L. & C. Hist.*, pp. 821-824, 929. H. S. Lyman's *Indian Names* in *Ore. Hist. Soc. Quar.*, I, p. 325, mentions four additional edible roots: camas, foxtail tuber, blue lupine, and wild tulip or brown lily, while *Thornton*, I, pp. 353, 356 adds yet more.

44 The salmon in the Columbia River, as everywhere else on the Pacific coast, are of a single genus, *Oncorhynchus*, subdivided into five species: (a), king-

salmon or quinnat, *O. tschawytscha* otherwise known as *O. quinnat*, which, commonly considered the most palatable of all the species and averaging over 20 pounds in weight, has occasionally attained 100 pounds; (b), blue-backed or sock-eye salmon, *O. nerka*, second in present-day commercial value; (c), silver salmon, *O. kisutch;* (d), dog salmon or dog-toothed salmon, *O. keta;* (e), humpbacked salmon, *O. gorbuscha:* the fish in each of these last four species weighing but from 3 to 6 or 8 pounds apiece. *L. & C. Hist.*, pp. 891, 892.

45 Seafaring folk who, hailing principally from Boston and Salem, Mass., had for years been accustomed to triangular voyages in which they laded their ships with trading goods beloved by indians, exchanged these goods for furs among the savages on the Pacific coast, bartered these furs for tea, nankeens, and silk in China, and then with their precious oriental cargo returned to their home port.

46 Because of differences in the character of the fauna, the northward country provided more furs than did the southward country.

47 "Deer and a few Bear" in trav. mem. Stuart, in both journ. and trav. mem., frequently mentioned "deer," "fallow deer," and "black-tailed deer." To this listing he added, in trav. mem. (p. 7), the terms "stag" and "hart," doing so as a possible result of his boyhood training which had taught him that, in old-world nomenclature, these latter terms meant male deer which respectively were in their fifth year (stag) and older than five years (hart). Stuart could have encountered during his Columbian stay and his eastward journey but three species of deer: (1), the so-called Virginia deer or American red deer —existing in several specialized varieties, of which the first encounterable by him was the so-called Oregon white-tailed deer or Douglas white-tailed deer, *Odocoileus leucurus* (*Dougl.*), and the one encounterable by him when eastward of the Columbia was *Odocoileus virginianus macrourus*, otherwise styled *O. americanus macrourus*—; (2), Columbian black-tailed deer, *Odocoileus columbianus;* and, (3), mule deer, *Odocoileus hemionus hemionus* (*Raf.*), often popularly but ineptly termed Rocky Mountain black-tail (*L. & C. Hist.*, pp. 842-845). Stuart's "deer" of the lower Columbia country doubtless included all three of the above species, while his "deer" of the country eastward of the Columbia could have been of only the first and third species. His "black-tail deer," because of the places of his encountering them, were unquestionably mule deer. For the same reason and also because the Virginia deer were greatly outnumbered by the mule deer in the regions he traversed, his "fallow deer" were probably mule deer, unless it be that he differentiated on the basis of size rather than of coloration and anatomy, and thus gave to the relatively small Virginia deer the name of "fallow."

48 *Ursus americanus* (*Pallas*), the black bear common to all North America.

49 "100 yards" in trav. mem.

50 For like statement, see *L. & C. Hist.*, pp. 834-839; *L. & C. Journs.*, IV, pp. 60, 61, 64.

51 Hemlock-spruce or American fir, *Tsuga mertensiana* (*Carr.*) otherwise

termed *Tsuga heterophylla (Raf.)*. *L. & C. Journs.*, IV, pp. 43–45; *L. & C. Hist.*, pp. 830, 1022.

52 *Picea sitchensis*. *L. & C. Journs.*, IV, p. 41; *L. & C. Hist.*, p. 829.

53 *Abies grandis*, the great white fir of the Pacific coast. *L. & C. Journs.*, IV, pp. 45, 48; *L. & C. Hist.*, p. 831.

54 Douglas fir, *Pseudotsuga taxifolia*. *L. & C. Journs.*, IV, p. 47; *L. & C. Hist.*, p. 831.

55 *Quercus garryana*. *L. & C. Journs.*, III, p. 197.

56 Stuart's "white ash" was *Fraxinus oregona (Nutt.)*. His "swamp ash" was probably the broad-leaved maple, *Acer macrophyllum*, which Lewis and Clark said "resembles ash except the leaf." *L. & C. Journs.*, III, pp. 174, 197, IV, p. 201; *L. & C. Hist.*, pp. 908, 911.

57 The Pacific coast's cottonwood was *Populus trichocarpa*. (*L. & C. Journs.*, III, p. 197; *L. & C. Hist.*, p. 911). Stuart, when but a short distance inland, encountered two other varieties as follows:

(1) *Populus angustifolia*, the so-called bitter cottonwood. To indicate this particular type, frontiersmen were wont to prefix "cottonwood" with one of the following interchangeable terms: bitter, bitter-leaf, long-leaf, narrow-leaf.

(2) *Populus angulata*, which these same frontiersmen adjectived interchangeably as sweet, sweet-bark, round-leaf, wide-leaf, or broad-leaf. This "sweet" variety's bark was a customary and excellent food for horses. *Dale*, pp. 125, 130, 136, 137; *L. & C. Journs.*, VI, pp. 145, 146; *Chittenden*, pp. 799, 800; *Smith*, p. 10; journ., p. 193 *infra*.

58 Three varieties: *Salix lasiandra var. caudata (Sudw.); Salix amygdaloides (And.); Salix exigua (Nutt.)*. Incidentally, the latter two were the varieties prevalent on Snake River. *L. & C. Journs.*, III, p. 111.

59 Doctor Louis F. Henderson advises us that no walnut is indigenous to the region in question; and that Stuart's "walnut," if not the local white ash—*Fraxinus oregona (Nutt.)*, having leaves somewhat resembling those of the walnut—, was possibly the sumac, *Rhus glabra*, which, with leaves of this same walnut-like appearance, is found in the Dalles' vicinity, but never attains a height exceeding 10 feet.

60 *Ribes divaricatum (Dougl.)*. *L. & C. Journs.*, IV, p. 201.

61 *Fragaria chilensis*.

62 So-called Western raspberry, *Rubus leucodermis (Dougl.)*.

63 Salmon-berry, *Rubus spectabilis (Pursh.)*.

64 Western blueberry, *Vaccinium occidentale (Gray)*.

65 *Vaccinium oxycoccos intermedium (Gray)*. *L. & C. Journs.*, IV, p. 19.

66 Doctor Louis F. Henderson advises us that juniper, *Junipereus occidentalis*, although common on the headwaters of the Columbia and Snake Rivers, is absent from the lower Columbia. He suggests that yew, *Taxus brevifolia*, prevalent in this last-mentioned region, may despite the color of its berries—coral-red instead of juniper-blue—have been Stuart's "juniper."

67 Also commonly termed shadberry, *Amelanchier alnifolia.*

68 Probably *Rubus macropetalus (Dougl.). L. & C. Journs.*, IV, pp. 60, 61, 64; *L. & C. Hist.*, p. 835.

69 In two varieties: red, *Ribes sanguineum* (*Pursh.*); and yellow, *Ribes aureum* (*Pursh.*).

70 Doctor Louis F. Henderson advises us that, though the region has no actual sloe, it does have a bush, *Viburnum ellipticum* (*Hook*), which the local folk commonly term "sloe."

71 Respectively, (1), *Prunus emarginata* (*Dougl.*) or *Padus serotina* (*Ehrh.*) and, (2), *Prunus demissa* (*Nutt.*) or *Padus virginiana* (*L.*). *L. & C. Journs.*, IV, p. 274.

72 Doctor Louis F. Henderson advises us that, while no vine such as Stuart described exists in the Columbian valley, the description may perhaps represent Stuart's composite memory of three separate plants which, common in the lower stretches of that valley, are as follows: (1) poison ivy, *Rhus diversiloba* (*T. & G.*), which, although having leaves—as Stuart said—"disposed by threes" and although ascending 30 to 50 feet upon the trees, nevertheless adheres closely to the tree trunks and thus never simulates the ship's "rigging" that Stuart mentioned; (2) honeysuckle, *Lonicera ciliosa* (*Parr*), which, often 10 to 16 and occasionally 20 feet in length and having clusters of handsome red or "crimson" flowers, is wont to string itself from shrub to shrub; (3) trillium, *Trillium sessile*, which never more than 12 to 16 inches high has flowers composed of three sepals and three petals.

For density of vine entanglements in Stuart's day, see *L. & C. Journs.*, IV, pp. 60, 61, 64, 256; *L. & C. Hist.*, pp. 837, 838.

73 Stuart could have encountered but two species of bear: (1), black bear, *Ursus americanus* (*Pallas*); and, (2), grizzly bear, *Ursus horribilis* (*Ord*), which last-mentioned animal he interchangeably termed grizzly bear and white bear. Although the black bear was the prevalent type in the Columbian region, and although Lewis and Clark failed to record the presence there of any grizzly, the latter beast did exist in at least the present-day Willamette River's valley. *Journ. David Douglas* in *Ore. Hist. Soc. Quar.*, IV, pp. 79, 80 and *Com. Bot. Mag.*, XVI, p. 126; H. S. Lyman's *Reminiscences* of *Louis Labonte* in *Ore. Hist. Soc. Quar.*, I, pp. 172, 173.

Stuart's occasional use of the term "white bear" as a synonym for "grizzly" was in accord with the then contemporary habit of numerous Westerners (see, for example, *L. & C. Hist.*, p. 288); the French-speaking trappers, however, interchangeably styling the beast either as *ours blanc* or as *ours gris*. Any of these designations referred patently—as presumably do the modern forms, "silver-tipped grizzly" and "silver-tip"—to the adult brute's grizzled appearance caused by the interspersal of white and white-tipped hairs amid an otherwise dark coat. However, Coues (*L. & C. Hist.*, p. 842) queries as to whether the correct prænomen is possibly *grisly* (in the sense of frightful), as it was by this spelling that various writers were accustomed to mention the majestic beast.

74 Prong-horned antelope, *Antilocapra americana americana* (*Ord.*).

75 So-called big-horn or Rocky Mountain sheep, *Ovis canadensis canadensis; Ovis cervina*—possibly that particular variety styled *Ovis cervina californiana* (*Dougl.*).

76 That variety of red fox, *Vulpes fulvus*, which is more specifically styled *Vulpes cascadensis* (*Merriam*). *L. & C. Hist.*, pp. 848, 849.

77 Two types, namely: (1), gray wolf or timber wolf, *Canis nubilus* (*Say*), and, (2), those two varieties of coyote or prairie wolf, *Canis latrans*, which are more specifically styled mountain coyote of Oregon and Rocky Mountains, *Canis lestes* (*Merriam*), and Nebraskan or plains coyote, *Canis nebracensis nebracensis* (*Merriam*).

78 Stuart's "panthers" might have been either, (1), that variety of puma (*alias* cougar or mountain lion), *Felis concolor*, which is more particularly styled *Felis oregonensis oregonensis* (*Raf.*), or, (2), the Columbian lynx, *Lynx rufus fasciatus*.
Lewis and Clark used "panther" as a synonym for lynx. *L. & C. Journs.*, IV, pp. 86, 113–115.

79 Described in *L. & C. Journs.*, IV, pp. 73, 74.

80 Described in *L. & C. Journs.*, IV, pp. 78, 79.

81 Two varieties: whistling swan, *Cygnus columbianus;* and trumpeter swan, *Cygnus buccinator*. *L. & C. Journs.*, IV, p. 148; *L. & C. Hist.*, pp. 885, 886, 915.

82 At least four varieties: (1), Canada goose, *Bernicla canadensis occidentalis* otherwise termed *Branta canadensis canadensis;* (2), a sub-variety of Canada goose, *i.e.*, Hutchins goose, *Bernicla hutchinsi* also styled *Branta canadensis hutchinsi;* (3), white-fronted goose, *Anser albifrons gambeli;* and, (4), snow goose, *Chen hyperboreus hyperboreus*. *L. & C. Hist.*, pp. 882–885.

83 *Bernicla branta*. *L. & C. Hist.*, pp. 884, 885.

84 Lewis and Clark noted, as present in the Columbian country, seven varieties as follows: duckinmallard, *Anas boscas;* canvasback, *Marila valisineria;* red-headed fishing duck or red-breasted merganser, *Mergus serrator;* blue-winged teal, *Querquedula discors;* ring-necked scaup duck, *Marila collaris;* black duck or American coot, *Fulica americana;* and a black and white duck, *Charitonetta albeola*, which last-mentioned bird was akin to the butterduck of the Atlantic coast. *L. & C. Hist.*, pp. 886-890.

85 Two varieties: white, *Pelecanus erythrorhynchos;* and California brown, *P. californicus*.

86 Great blue heron, *Ardea herodias herodias*.

87 *Larus argentatus*, *L. glaucescens* and *L. occidentalis*. *L. & C. Hist.*, pp. 880, 881; *L. & C. Journs.*, IV, pp. 139, 140.

88 Two varieties: (1), *Gallinago wilsoni* or *G. delicata;* and, (2), *Tringoides macularius*. *L. & C. Hist.*, p. 877.

89 Long-billed curlew, *Numenius americanus* or *N. longirostris*.

90 Golden eagle, *Aquila chrysætus;* and white-headed or bald eagle, *Haliæetus leucocephalus*.

91 *Gymnogyps californianus. L. & C. Hist.*, pp. 872, 873.

92 In addition to that variety which is closely allied to the common black crow, *Corvus americanus*, and is specifically known as Northwestern crow, *Corvus caurinus*, there possibly were included two other birds, each of light color but of crow-like caws and habits: *i.e.*, Oregon jay, *Perisoreus obscurus*, and Clarke's crow or nut-cracker, *Nucifraga columbiana.*

93 *Corvus corax sinuatus.*

94 *Pica pica hudsonica.*

95 At least four varieties: *Ceophlœus pileatus*, *Colaptes mexicanus*, *Sphyropicus ruber* and *Dryobates villosus harrisi. L. & C. Journs.*, IV, p. 132.

96 Band-tailed pigeon, *Columba fasciata;* and the mourning dove, *Zenaidura macroura marginella* or *Z. macroura carolinensis.*

97 Probably the so-called California mountain quail or mountain partridge, *Oreortyx picta. L. & C. Journs.*, IV, pp. 250-253.

98 Probably in the two varieties noted by Lewis and Clark and today known respectively as Columbian sharp-tailed grouse, *Pedioecetes phasianellus columbianus*, and sage grouse, *Centrocercus urophasianus. L. & C. Hist.*, pp. 867, 868.

99 Undoubtedly grouse and consisting of probably three varieties: (A), the two noted by Lewis and Clark as "pheasants"—*i.e.*, [a], Sabine's, Oregon or red-ruffed grouse, *Bonasa umbellus fuscus;* and, [b], Franklin grouse or the fool hen, *Canachites franklini; Dendragapus franklini*—and, (B), that sub-variety of dusky grouse, *Dendragapus obscurus*, which locally is now often termed sooty grouse. *L. & C. Hist.*, pp. 870-872.

100 *Acipenser transmontanus*, which had quite commonly a length of 7 feet and in occasional instances of from 10 to 15 feet. Because of its size, profusion and edibility, it was deemed of very great importance. See entry of July 1 and its postscript, pp. 30, 253; *L. & C. Hist.*, pp. 716, 732, 791, 896, 953; *Henry-Thomp.*, pp. 752, 753.

101 Probably, (1), steelhead trout, *Salmo gairdneri;* and, (2), black-spotted or cut-throat trout, *Salmo clarkii. L. & C. Journs.*, IV, p. 167.

102 *Mylochilus caurinus. L. & C. Journs.*, IV, p. 326.

103 Doctor R. R. Huestis advises us, (1), that the conger eel, though existing in southern California, is unknown to the Oregon country; (2), that the lamprey, *Eutosphenus tridentatus tridentatus tridentatus*, is very common in the Columbia and Willamette Rivers.

104 This fish (which Stuart elsewhere in his narratives interchangeably termed "uthulhun," "uthlecan" and "uthlechan") was identical with the "othlecan," "olthen," "uthlecan" or "eulachon" of other diarists (p. 308 *infra; L. & C. Hist.*, p. 895; *Franchere* [*A*], p. 179, [*B*], p. 238; *Ross* [*A*], pp. 94, 95) and was in fact the eulachon, *Thaleichthys pacificus*, otherwise known as the candlefish; this last name being derived from its extreme fattiness which caused it, when lighted, to burn like an oiled wick. It was a small salmonoid related to and resembling the caplin, *Mallotus villosus*, of Newfoundland, Labrador, and

Greenland. Unknown to science until discovered by Lewis and Clark, it was by them erroneously rated as an anchovy; whereas Stuart, in his entries of June 29 (p. 7) and July 1 (pp. 30, 253), was nearer to accuracy when he termed it either a smelt or "kind of Smelt." *L. & C. Hist.*, p. 895; *Henry-Thomp.*, pp. 786, 787; *L. & C. Journs.*, IV, pp. 102, 103, 107-109, 123.

105 Two varieties: *Crotalus oregonus* (*Holbrook*)—also known as *Crotalus lucifer*—existing on the lower Columbia, and *Crotalus confluentus* farther inland.

106 King snake, *Ophibolus getulus*, a non-venomous constrictor of superb courage, great strength, and lightning-like speed. Its death-dealing aggressiveness toward other snakes, inclusive of the rattlesnake, may well have suggested to Stuart that it was venomous. The Columbia's basin had but one poisonous snake, the rattlesnake.

107 These were gartersnakes, *Eutænia sirtalis;* for the vast number of which in the locality, see *L. & C. Hist.*, p. 898; *L. & C. Journs.*, IV, pp. 211, 216.

108 Two varieties: *Rana pretiosa* and *Hyla regilla. L. & C. Journs.*, V, p. 87; *L. & C. Hist.*, pp. 915, 1018.

109 *Bufo columbiensis.*

110 Possibly the ellachick, *Chelopus marmoratus.*

111 Doctor R. R. Huestis advises us that the local reptiles most nearly commensurate with Stuart's description are, (1), alligator lizard, *Cerrhonotus principis*, 12 inches long and yellowish-red in color; and, (2), fence lizard, *Sceloporus graciosus*, five to six inches long and having some blue in its coloration.

112 The remainder of this day's original entry in journ. was rephrased and supplemented in journ.'s postscript, p. 252, this postscript being later incorporated in the trav. mem.

113 Because of Stuart's reference to superior quality, doubtless meaning the king-salmon, which was then—as it yet is—first in importance in the Columbia's fishing. See note 44.

114 "long Seines" in journ.'s postscript, p. 253.

115 "as bright as" in journ.'s postscript, p. 253.

116 Stuart's account from this point to the end of the chapter relates to exclusively the indians of the lower Columbia River except where (as indicated by notes 117, 119, 122) he has interjected three short allusions to more easterly tribes.

117 See end of note 116.

118 Here resumes description of indians of lower Columbia River.

119 See end of note 116.

120 Here resumes description of indians of lower Columbia River.

121 *I.e.*, moccasin.

122 This account of the hunting methods of certain indians (whom *Astoria*, II, p. 64 identifies as Sciatogas) appears in a slightly variant form in the journ.'s postscript, p. 253.

123 This mention of buffalo strongly suggests that the described indians were not dwellers on the lower Columbia.

124 "12 or 15 paces" in journ.'s postscript, p. 253, which adds: "& they seldom shoot at any thing farther than 30 yards."

125 From here to the end of this day's entry the description is restricted to indians of the lower Columbia River.

126 Robert Gray (1755-1806) of Boston, Mass., captain of the trading-ship *Columbia*, discovered the river, May 11, 1792, ascended it for approximately 25 miles, and, before putting to sea on May 20, bestowed on the stream his vessel's name. Upon this well-conducted discovery and exploration, upon the explorations by Lewis and Clark, and upon the settlement and explorations subsequently made by the Astorians, the United States Government successfully relied when eventually disputing with Great Britain as to sovereignty over the Oregon region.

CHAPTER II

JUNE 30 · JULY 13, 1812

By Canoe Up the Columbia from Tongue Point to Mouth of Klickitat River

[SEE MAP FACING PAGE 3]

Winship's Attempted Settlement · Cowlitz and Willamette Rivers, Their Characteristics, Peoples and Exploration · John Day's Illness · Surmount Columbia's Cascades · Indian Thievery · Astorians' Canoes

Tuesday 30th — At the dawn of day every man was at his post & the Canoes loaded soon after— a few minutes only were spent in mutual wishes of health and prosperity between the Gentlemen who accompanied us,[1] and those of our Party, when we embarked and proceeded acrofs Shallow Bay[2]— at 2 P M pafsed the Cathlamat village[3] containing 94 warriors, and on the opposite side[4] of the River, the Waak-i-cums of 66, these last and the Chinooks were originally the same but on account of a dispute, (about two generations back) between the then Chief & his Brother, the latter seperated himself from the nation and settled where they at present live— His descendants [4] out of respect to his memory call themselves after his name having come about 15 miles we stopped on a small rising ground[5] for the night on the south side— the natives brought Salmon & a few [*Beaver*] skins to trade

Wednesday, 1st July 1812 — We embarked soon after daylight appeared, and experienced a greater degree of rapidity in the current than we had any idea of, the River has fallen very considerably but not as yet sufficiently to admit of our encamping in the bottoms,[6] indeed from Hill to Hill the country has no very different appearance from an immense Swamp,— our days marches are therefore very irregular, being compelled either to stop (often) at an early hour or sleep in our boats, without the pofsibility of finding a sufficiency of Land whereon to kindle a fire for culinary purposes[7]

about 2 hours before sunset we reached the establishment made by Captain Winship[8] of Boston in the Spring of 1810— It is situate on a beautifull high bank on the South side[9] & enchantingly diversified with white oaks,[10] Ash[11] & Cotton wood[12] [*and Alder*][13] but of rather a dimunitive size— here he intended leaving a Mr. Washington[14] with a party of men, but whether with the view of making a permanent settlement or merely for trading with the Indians untill his return from the coast, the natives were unable to tell, the water however rose so high as to inundate a house he had already constructed, when a dispute [5] arose between him and the Hellwits,[15] by his putting several of them in Irons on the supposition that they were of the Chee-hee-lash[16] nation, who had some time previous cut off a Schooner belonging to the Rufsian establishment of New Archangel,[17] by the Governor of which place he was employed[18] to secure any of the Banditti who perpetrated this horrid act—

The Hellwits made formidable preparations by engaging auxilliaries &c. for the release of their relations by force, which coming to the Captain's knowledge, as well as the error he had committed, the Captives were released, every person embarked, and left the Columbia without lofs of time[19]— Between the hour we stopped here, and dusk, evident symptoms of mental derangement made their appearance in John Day one of my Hunters who for a day or two previous seemed as if restlefs and unwell but now uttered the most incoherent absurd and unconnected sentences— several spoke to him, but little satisfaction was obtained, and he went to bed gloomy and churlish— 3 miles below this spot, live the Hellwits[20] a nation of about 200 men, their lands produce a good many

Beaver, and Wapatos[21] in abundance— this root is considerably smaller but in every respect other bears a strong resemblance to our Potatoe; they are found in marshes, and require great labour in extraction[22]

Here[23] are the best and almost only Fisheries of Uthulhuns[24] and Sturgeon— the former they take in immense numbers by the operation of the Scoopnett from the middle of March till the middle of April,[25] and the latter [*principally*] by the hook and line during the [6] Spring and Fall Seasons— the Uthulhuns are a kind of Smelt, and when dried for preservation, are much similar to Smoked Herrings— the general length of the Sturgeon is seven feet, but some are only five and others nine[26]— this neighbourhood is also by far the greatest place of resort in the Spring and Autumn for Swans,[27] Geese[28] & Ducks,[29] for the procuring of which we had a Clerk and some men stationed at the Hellwits village,[30] who combining that with the fishery procured us a plentiful subsistance during the last Season— our distance today is 22 miles

Thursday 2nd At an early hour we sett off again with a fair wind and at 10 A.M reached the Cow-lit-sick[31] a river 200 yards wide which last winter I navigated with six men for 260 miles,[32] partly for the purpose of diminishing the number of mouths at the Fort,[33] and partly to explore the interior and trade with the natives— For the first 50 miles the face of the country evinces your being still in the vicinity of the Great River,[34] but from thence to the extreme of my discovery beautiful high Prairies make their appearance occasionally, interſpersed with a few Oaks [,*Walnut*,] & pines[35] &c and are the feeding grounds of a great many Elk [,*Bear*] & Deer— this River[36] takes its rise in Mount Ranier,[37] at a small distance from the Straits of Juan de Fuca,[38] runs Southardly, is very rapid, and navigable only 190 miles [7] Beaver are tolerably plenty, & of a good quality, but from my being able to barter only 260 skins among the Le Cow-lit-sick[39] nation of 250 men am led to believe them totally ignorant of the mode of taking them

The Indians[40] are peaceably inclined [*and not so thievishly disposed as those on the coast*], but their demeanor [*is*] somewhat haughty and insolent— By sunsett we got to Puget's (or Gafs's[41] Deer) Island[42] where we encamped it is considerably elevated, but overflows in great freshes otherwise it would be an excellent place for a permanent settlement during the night[43] John Day's disorder became very alarming, and several times he attempted getting possession of some of our arms, with the intention of committing suicide, but finding all his attempts fruitless, he at length feigned great remorse, & appeared to be quite sensible of the enormity of the crime he intended to perpetrrate, this [*change*] entirely lulled our suspicions, which enabled him (a little before daylight) to get possession of a pair of loaded pistols, both of which he put to his head & fired, but fortunately too high to take effect, he was instantly Secured & placed under a guard, in one of the boats [*where I intend to keep him untill we can determin what may be most advisable to be done with him*]— today's march was 25 miles[44]—

Friday 3rd — By daybreak we were again in the Boats— our route was along the Island and south shore[45] to the mouth[46] of the first channel[47] of that large [*and beautiful*] Stream called by the Indians Wallamat,[48] by Lewis and Clarke Multinamah[49] and by Mr. Donald Mackenzie[50] who lately[51] explored it for 500 miles Mackay's River,[52] we then crofsed to Cathlapootle Island[53] where finding that John Day's insanity amounted to real madnefs I agreed with some Indians of the Cathlapootle nation for a few articles to carry him back to the Fort,[54] as he had become not only an entirely uselefs member of the expedition, but likewise kept us continually in alarm, for his own safety & that of some individuals against whom he had evidently some evil design— it was also the opinion of all the Gentlemen that it would be highly imprudent to suffer him to proceed any farther for in a moment when not sufficiently watched he might em-[8] broil us with the natives, who on all occasions he reviled by the appellations Rascal, Robber &c &c

&c— he was completely disarmed before embarking with the Chief, who I knew well, and have every confidence in his carrying him down in safety.

This first branch[55] of the Wallamat is 200 yards wide & at its entrance live the Cathlakamaſs about 120 strong & directly opposite the Cathlapootle's of 180— on Long Island[56] Immediately above are the Cathlanamencimens,[57] once a very powerfull tribe, but now reduced by the Small Pox to [*about*] 60 Men— the upper end of the Island (which is ten miles long) is inhabited by the Math-la-nobs, about 80 strong,[58] who with the other tribes are poſsest of a few[59] Beaver and Dreſsed Elk Skins— the main body of Mackays River,[60] which here joins the Columbia in a northardly direction is 500 yards from bank to bank at the distance of 45 miles above the junction it is contracted to about 100 yards [*in width*] where the waters rush over a perpendicular ledge of smooth rock 30 feet high[61]— it soon after expands to about the same Width as below the Falls and continues so for a great distance till paſsing a number of tributary streams,[62] it becomes perceptibly reduced in size, when Mr. Mackenzie[63] was obliged to relinquish his enterprise on account of some sickneſs among his men— the current is unbroken by Rapids and descends with great [9] velocity— the country nearly to the Falls[64] resembles that on the main River,[65] but from then upward, it is delightful beyond expreſsion, the bottoms are composed of an excellent soil thinly covered with Cottonwood [*black Walnut,*[66] *Birch,*[67] *Hazel*[68]] & Alder & White Oaks, Ash, and the adjoining Hills are gently undulating, with a sufficiency of Pines to give variety to the most beautifull Landscapes in nature — The bottoms are inhabited by innumerable herds of Elk, and the Uplands are equally overstocked by Deer[69] and Bear[70]— Few or no Fish are found in its waters above, & the Salmon [*& Sturgeon*] ascend no farther than the foot of the Falls,[71] this want is however well compensated for, by the incredible numbers of Beaver who inhabit its banks which exceeds (from all accounts) any thing yet discovered on [*either side of*] the Continent of America,— the first nation above the Falls are the Cathlapoo-yays,[72] supposed to be 300 strong— a little farther up on an Easterly Branch[73] live the Cath-lath-las[74] of 80 men, and along the River as far as Mr McK[75] went natives are very numerous and go by the name of Shoshonas[76] they have neither Horses nor canoes [, *when they want to crofs the river they prepare a large bundle of reeds on which they throw themselves and sweam acrofs*] and their clothing is principally Beaver [*and Deer skins, they have no villages or stationary habitations, but live in temporary huts along the river banks— Mr. McKenzie says that their behaviour to him was respectful and obliging in the extreme.—*] the general course [*of the river*] is from about SSE to NNW— on a rising ground opposite the mouth we encamped[77] for the night having come 23 miles [*against an exceeding rapid current.—*]

23[78]
25
22
15
18 103

[10] Saturday 4th At the distance of 8 Miles from last nights station, is Vancouvers Point,[79] as beautiful a piece of scenery as any the Columbia affords— It is composed of an enchanting meadow near the river bank, while the rear is a ridge of considerable elevation, moderately wooded with a variety of Trees of the Pine species— [*in the middle of the meadow stands a pond*[80] *of pure limpid water well stocked with Fish of different kinds, and in Spring and Autumn the surface is covered with wild fowl,—*] 23 miles higher Quicksand River[81] enters on the South side— It is[82] about 80 yards wide—a rapid stream its length is unknown to the Whites, but from Indian information it is of considerable extent & contains a good many Beaver, Elk & Deer— In the main river[83] opposite this, is a ledge, called the Seal Rocks[84] (visible only in a moderate stage of the water, and) frequented by numbers of these animals[85] as a resting place— a little lower down a small Creek[86] comes in on the north

side, is of no note except for its being the asylum of a few animals whose skins are valuable— [*about*] 2 miles above quicksand on an open spot— north side we pitched our Tents for the night[87]— the total distance today was 33 miles

Sunday 5th Nothing worthy of remark occurred during the days journey. We sailed the greater part and at 4 P.M. having come 23 miles stopped on an Island[88] 5 miles below the Great Rapids[89] in order to prepare everything for the Portage— about 12 miles below this place on the South side[90] is a [*very extensive*] Bluff with two small cascades[91] of at least 150 feet high— the face of the precipice is a smooth rock to where these Falls project from the [11] hill, but from thence to the top, it is very curiously intersected by ravilins which give it strong resemblance to antique Towers & fortifications the Country thro' which we have passed today is of a very uninviting aspect, barren, rugged & mountainous, with the exception [*of*] a few small bottoms, the resort of a good many Elk & Bear

Monday 6th— We sett out early with the hopes of being able to paſs the Rapids[92] before night, but after proceeding about 2 miles[93] had to encamped[94] in consequence of strong appearances of rain,—

Tuesday 7th Rain fell for the greater part of yesterday afternoon, as soon as it ceased every mans arms were put in the best of order, and their Catridge boxes replenished— This was a measure of precaution only, for although all the natives below aſsured us of the certain hostility of those who reside in this neighbourhood still our determination was to avoid everything like altercation, and to punish only where they were the willfull aggreſsors— the party was accordingly divided in two brigades[95] the one to guard the Heights[96] immediately overlooking the River, to prevent surprise and protect those who were employed in dragging up the Canoes or carrying the Goods along the margin of the Rapids[97]— but few Indians came near us all day, and every thing went on although not fast, yet in the greatest safety & good order till having ascended about 3 miles the large Canoe of Mr David Stuart on paſsing between 2 large rocks,[98] unfortunately touched the outer one, wheeled round, and before sufficient aſsiſtance could reach her, filled and upset, although it was afforded with the greatest promptneſs and alacrity a part of the Packages floated off, but the greatest part sunk not far below the remainder were picked up by light canoes dispatched for the purpose— on the supposition that [12] some of the articles must have been caught by the residents of Strawberry Island,[99] I instantly embarked in a large Canoe with 5 men and our Interpreters,[100] and had the good fortune to recover several small packages[101] with part of a Bale which had been taken up and was already divided among the Captors— I returned at sunset, and in croſsing through a rapid,[102] the water which appeared as if boiling gushed in at both sides of the Canoe at such a rate as to create real alarm for our safety,— a few strokes of our Paddles luckily extricated us from the danger, and we soon after reached the shore[103]— Had the Canoe filled, it would have upset in a moment, and no doubt can exist but every soul should have perished, as we were a great way from the foot of the rapids,[104] the current like that of a Mill Sluice, and so rough that the Ocean agitated by a tempest would be but a faint comparison—

Wednesday 8th The Canoe which upset yesterday, was very much damaged, and unfit to proceed without being thoroughly repaired— In the meantime I sett out as before with the hopes of getting the remainder of the Bale of Merchandize, as I was given to understand it was at no great distance— after inceſsant paddling in different directions for a long time we discovered their recepticle in a hut situated in a Deep Ravine[105] nearly opposite our camp,[106] and there recovered some of the packages[107] I expected, with the greatest part of another— the Canoe [13] was in Sufficient order by night to hazard its being put again in the water, though still too crazy to risk anything like a load in it— The Canoe is the same as those made use of by the North West Company on this side of the Rocky Mountains, it is composed of Cedar boards ¼ of an Inch thick, its only support within are [*a few*] braces or Knees of the same material ⅜ of an inch to which the boards are sewed with sturgeon twine, and the space which is caulked in boats is here filled up with Gum— Thus you have a veſsell to answer the purpose of a Birch Canoe[108] so far as regards facility of transportation, but in every other respect so much its inferior, that an attempt at comparison cannot with justice be made— even in strength the latter is far superior, for the Bark[109] will bend and give way to a preſsure without material injury, which would split the Cedar one and send her to the bottom.

Such canoes are very excellent in Shallow water, long and bad Portages, and may do tolerably in small and insignificant Rapids, but nothing short of strong and well built Boats do I think fit to face the Granite Rocks of the Falls[110] & Grand Rapids[111] of Columbia River— indeed I have no hesitation in saying that a Schenectady Boat[112] constructed of wood properly seasoned, would in the same situation of Mr Stuarts Canoe have escaped with little or no damage— we remained in the same Camp

[14] Thursday 9th We renewed our daily toil at an early hour, & after great exertion & labour encamped[113] late in the afternoon, about a mile and a quarter farther on

Friday 10th All hands were employed by the dawn of day & we got along without much interruption 1¼ miles,[114] but a Bluff point of Rocks projecting far into the Rapid, obliged us to make a Portage of about 500 paces to a small Bay above, where we stopped for the night[115]—

Saturday 11th Those who were unnecefsary in navigating the Boats went by land as a Gaurd, and by breakfast time all were aſsembled at the low water Portage[116]— in coming up this morning two of Mr Clarkes Canoes filled but nothing was lost— From this place the Goods were carried half a mile, & the Boats got on by water where the whole were again loaded and taken up the remaining Rapids without diminishing their cargoes except at 2 small points where for greater safety a part of the Packages were landed— from last nights resting place to the Head of the Rapids is about 3 miles, [*& which we paſsed about 2 P.M. finding it rather early to halt*] we continued on & encamped[117] 2 miles above the Grand Rapids—

In low water by making a portage of 2 miles you paſs all the bad part of these Cascades, and may jump the remainder without much risk, but in high water it is one continued Rapid from what is commonly the begining of the Portage to some distance below Strawberry Island—a distance of [*nearly*] 6 miles[118]—

Sunday 12th The goods which got wet by Mr. Clarke's Canoe filling were this morning put out to dry. one of our young gentlemen[119] went back to the Rapids for the Chiefs, with whom he returned in a short time,[120] when a counsel was held after which they were presented with some Tobacco [&c] and were told at same time that it was [15] given on account of their peaceable and decorous behaviour & that so long as they continued the same kind of conduct, they would always be sure of experiencing a reciprocal friendship in the whites— the goods were dry by the middle of the afternoon when we proceeded 5 miles and encamped on the northern side[121]—

Here our Clatsop interpreter,[122] meeting with 2 Indians from above expreſsed a wish to return to the Rapids[123] to procure the aſsiſstance of a friend without whom he could not interprete precisely[124] the language of the natives at the Falls[125]— his request was [*reluctantly*] granted and he sett off with a promise to rejoin us next day—

Monday 13th Went on with a fine Breeze all day, and stopped for the night about 12 miles below the Falls[126]— paſsed 2 [*considerable*]

Creeks on the North[127] and 1 on the South side,[128] in two[129] of which according to Indian information Beaver is tolerably plenty [*this tract of country is very barren and hilly, well wooded, and stocked with a good many Bear and Deer,— came in all*] 25 miles

Notes to Chapter II

1 Seemingly Hunt, McDougall, Ehninger, and Sowles (entry of June 29, p. 3). By the term "Gentlemen" Stuart here implies what he later (entry of August 27, p. 111) somewhat affirmatively asserts: a social distinction between two groups, the first composed of partners and clerks; the second, of engagés and other subordinates.

2 Situated immediately to the eastward of Tongue Point and today known as Cathlamet Bay, it was a wide, shallow, sand-bar bestrewn indentation in the Columbia's left bank. It should not be confused with that other bay which, lying opposite it and biting into the Columbia's right bank, was by Lewis and Clark called Shallow Bay and is today known as Gray's Bay. *Chart* No. 6151; *McArthur*, p. 64; *L. & C. Hist.*, pp. 703, 720.

3 "Cath-lamet" in trav. mem. This village, situated in approximately longitude 123° 35′ 12″, lay on the Columbia's left bank at the mouth of present-day Warren Creek. *Chart* No. 6152; *L. & C. Hist.*, pp. 705, 721; *McArthur*, p. 65.

4 Right bank.

5 Doubtless present-day Aldrich Point, which, on Columbia's left bank and in approximately longitude 123° 30′ 48″, projects slightly into the stream and also rises a little above the adjacent flats. During pioneer times it was called Cathlamet Point in recognition of the Cathlamet indians, but it later obtained its name of Aldrich Point in honor of a Mr. R. E. Aldrich who for a while lived on the point and maintained there a small mercantile establishment (*Chart* No. 6152; *McArthur*, p. 5). The "small bottom" on which *Cox*, p. 74, places the camp was the flat which, adjoining Aldrich Point, was earlier called Fanny's Bottom. It had thus been named for Clark's youngest sister, Frances. *L. & C. Hist.*, p. 909, f.n.

6 The river was receding from the climax of the freshet which, occurring in June of every year, was caused by snows melting on the mountains. *Wilkes, Narr.*, IV, pp. 336, 337; *Oregon*, I, p. 271.

7 This statement as to inconvenience in travel must have been based to a large extent on remembrance of earlier journeys through this neighborhood because, on the present trip, Stuart had been travelling for only two days.

This statement by Stuart is virtually identical in both journ. and trav. mem. but in trav. mem.'s manuscript he interlined "2d" above the word "either" and "1st" above "compelled," evidently suggesting a transposition.

8 Nathan Winship, master of the ship *Albatross*, for whom and his attempted settlement, see *Bancroft*, XXVII, pp. 306, 308, 309, 317, 319, 321, 323-325, XXVIII, pp. 130-134; *Scott*, I, pp. 165, 286, III, p. 339; *L. & C. Journs.*, III, pp. 305-307, IV, p. 178; *L. & C. Hist.*, p. 1263; *Henry-Thomp.*, pp. 795, 828.

9 This "high bank" was seemingly the point which, thrusting from the Columbia's left bank at a spot immediately below the lower end of present-day Crims Island and in longitude approximately 123° 10′ 36″, projected a short distance into the stream. This projection (designated in bygone years as Oak Point and now shown without name on *Geol. Oregon* and *Chart* No. 6152) should not be confused with the one which, known today as Oak Point, lies opposite it and is thus on the Columbia's right bank in the present-day state of Washington. *Chart* No. 6152; *L. & C. Hist.*, p. 909; *Geol. Oregon; Geol. Washington.*

10 See note 55 on p. 22.

11 See note 56 on p. 22.

12 See note 57 on p. 22.

13 *Alnus rubra* or *A. rhombifolia. L. & C. Hist.*, pp. 698, 724, 749, 833, 911. *Alnus oregana (Nutt.). L. & C. Journs.*, IV, p. 55.

14 *L. & C. Journs.*, III, pp. 305-307, IV, p. 187, without disclosing Washington's first name, mention him as habitually a trading visitant at the Columbia's mouth.

15 Throughout this day's entry, "Hellwits" in journ.; "Chil-wits" in trav. mem.

16 "Chee-hee-lish" in trav. mem.

17 "New Archangle" in trav. mem., but today known as Sitka, Alaska.

18 For description of the Russian establishment and its relations with indians and with Americans, see *Bancroft*, XXVII, pp. 345, 353, 373, 374, 522, XXVIII, pp. 197, 644, 650.

19 The references cited in note 8 are silent as to Winship's arrest of indians; and offer, as the sole reason for his discontinuing the attempt at colonization, the alleged facts that the remonstrant savages, all of whom lived westward of the Winship site, objected to the erection of any trading post which, being east of their home territory, would deprive them of their accustomed profits received through the purchasing of peltry from inland indians and the subsequent reselling to such white traders as occasionally visited the Columbia's mouth.

20 This Hellwit village, the "great Whill Wetz" village of Alexander Ross, was on Columbia's left bank at or near mouth of present-day Clatskanie River. *Geol. Oregon; Chart* No. 6152; *Ross* [*A*], p. 104, [*B*], p. 117, f.n.; *Franchere* [*C*], p. 261, f.n.; *Henry-Thomp.*, p. 794.

21 See note 43 on p. 20.

22 See *L. & C. Hist.*, p. 929; *L. & C. Journs.*, IV, pp. 7-10, 217, 218.

23 This entry was rephrased by Stuart in journ's postscript, p. 253.

24 "Uthlechans" in trav. mem.

25 "till the beginning of May" in trav. mem.

26 Trav. mem. varies this by stating: "their most common length is about six feet, but some are only four, while others arrive at the enormous length of nine to ten." Also see note 100 on p. 25.

27 See note 81 on p. 24.

28 See note 82 on p. 24.

29 See note 84 on p. 24.

30 See note 20 for site of village.

31 "Cow-lit-sic" in trav. mem. This, the "Coweliske" and "Coweliskee" of Lewis and Clark, the "Kowlitch" of Henry, the "Cowelitz" of Warre, the "Cowilitz ou Kaoulis" of Duflot, is today called Cowlitz River. It emptied through the right bank of the Columbia in present-day Cowlitz County, Washington. *Chart* No. 6153; *Geol. Washington; L. & C. Hist.*, pp. 698, 910, 1250, 1263; *Henry-Thomp.*, p. 839; *Warre*, p. 3; *Duflot*, carte 18 in accompanying atlas.

32 This figure is inconsistent with the "190 miles" mentioned later in this same day's entry in both journ. and trav. mem. Because both of Stuart's figures far exceed the actual one for the length of the main stream, it is not improbable that his stated mileage included also round trips on the numerous confluents of that stream.

33 The establishment at Astoria.

34 Columbia.

35 Of the pine proper, Stuart doubtless saw specimens of the white pine of the Pacific, *Pinus lambertiana;* but it is possible that he included in his category of pines various of the firs and spruces common in this part of Oregon and described in *L. & C. Hist.*, pp. 829-833.

36 Cowlitz River.

37 The river originated on the southerly slope of Mt. Rainier (altitude 14,408 or, as sometimes stated, 14,526 feet), but much water entered from tributaries rising on the northerly slopes of Mt. Adams (altitude 12,307 feet) and the northerly and westerly slopes of Mt. St. Helens (altitude 9671 feet). Though United States Government maps now designate Mt. Rainier by this selfsame name, many people still use its original indian entitlement, Tacoma (sometimes spelled Tahoma). The name Rainier was originally given the mountain, May 8, 1792, by George Vancouver in honor of Rear-Admiral Peter Rainier of the British Navy. *McArthur*, p. 292.

38 Straits lying immediately south of Vancouver Island and separating it from the present-day state of Washington's Olympic Peninsula.

39 "Le-cow-lit-sic" in trav. mem.

40 "These people" in trav. mem.

41 Patrick Gass of the Lewis and Clark expedition.

42 Not the island known today as Puget Island but instead one which, farther up the river and called "Elallah" or "Elalah" by early local indians, was by Gass and by Lewis and Clark termed Deer Island, which name it still bears on United States Government maps and charts. It was described by Clark as being "an extensive low Island Seperated from the Lar[d] side [Columbia's left bank] by a narrow channel," and was characterized by Ross Cox as being a "fine meadow island." This island, five miles long and with a maximum width of one and one-half miles, had its lower end (where Stuart camped) in ap-

proximately longitude 122° 51′ 25″, latitude 45° 59′ 0″. *Chart* No. 6153; *Geol. Oregon; L. & C. Journs.*, III, p. 201, IV, pp. 207, 212; *L. & C. Hist.*, pp. 696, 911-913, 932, 1263; *Cox* [*A*], I, p. 122, [*B*], p. 74.

43 "evening" in trav. mem.

44 From this date (July 2) till July 27 the chronology in Ross Cox's account (*Cox* [*A*], I, pp. 122-144, [*B*], pp. 74-83) is erroneous, for which see notes 94 and 121 *infra*, as also notes 1, 63, and 79 on pp. 64, 71, 73.

45 Thus sailing the length of that "narrow channel" which, mentioned in note 42, is now officially designated as Deer Island Slough. *Chart* No. 6153.

46 Situated near site of present-day town of St. Helens, Ore. *Geol. Oregon; Chart* No. 6154.

47 Now officially designated as Multnomah Channel (*Chart* No. 6154), and being the more westerly of the two channels of the mouth of present-day Willamette River.

48 This, the largest river entirely within the present-day state of Oregon, emptied through the Columbia's left bank and is today known by the generally accepted name of Willamette; but in bygone days it was variously called Wallamette, Wallamet, Wallammet, Wallamat, Wallamut, Wallamitt, Willamet, Wallamt, Wilarmet, Wahlahmath, Walla Matta, Wallama, Wullamette, Multnomah, Mulknoma, &c. *McArthur*, pp. 388, 389; *L. & C. Hist.*, pp. 691, 692, 919; *Smith*, pp. 112, 121.

49 "Multnomah" in trav. mem. Stuart does not disclose how he obtained his information concerning Lewis and Clark, but such of his associates as had been members of Hunt's party had doubtless possessed, before leaving St. Louis, ample opportunity to confer with Clark. Whether or not they embraced the opportunity does not appear, but it does appear that Hunt had access to a map by Clark (see *Nouvelles Annales*, X, p. 76, translated at p. 303 *infra*) and that, soon after leaving St. Louis, Hunt's people consulted John Colter, who had accompanied Lewis and Clark to the Pacific coast. *Bradbury* [*A*], pp. 17-20.

50 "McKenzie" in trav. mem. For his identity see note 35 on p. LVII.

51 In April, 1812, according to *Franchere* [*A*], p. 115, [*B*], p. 153; March 31-May 11, according to *Nouvelles Annales*, X, pp. 28, 30, translated at pp. 278, 279 *infra*.

52 "McKay's River" in trav. mem., named for probably either Alexander McKay (an Astorian partner) or his son Thomas (an Astorian clerk), both of whom had arrived at Astoria in the *Tonquin* (*Franchere* [*A*], pp. 16, 17, [*B*], pp. 29, 30; *Ross* [*A*]; *Townsend*, p. 82; *White*, p. 101). This Alexander McKay had, as a North West Company clerk, been a member of Alexander Mackenzie's overland party which, in 1793, reached the Pacific; but, despite *Astoria*, I, p. 43; *Ross* [*A*], p. 7, [*B*], p. 38, he seemingly had not accompanied Mackenzie on the expedition of 1789 to the Arctic. After the *Tonquin's* arrival at the Columbia River, he remained on the ship and was killed at the time of her destruction.

Tassé, I, p. xxv; *Henry-Thomp.*, pp. 580, 777, 797; *Mackenzie*, pp. 1-113, 151, 155 *et seq.*

53 The crossing, one and one-fourth miles in length, took Stuart from left side of Columbia River to lower or northern end of Cathlapootle (today known as Bachelor) Island, the Quathlahpotle Island of Lewis and Clark. This island was approximately three miles long with a maximum breadth of one and one-fourth miles, and was separated from the Columbia's right bank by a narrow channel which today is known as Bachelor Island Slough. *Chart* No. 6154; *L. & C. Hist.*, pp. 696, 914, 916.

54 The establishment at Astoria.

55 Present-day Multnomah Channel, for which see note 47.

56 This, the Columbia River's largest island (approximately 12 miles long with a maximum width of 4 miles), was the "Wappatoo Island" of Lewis and Clark, the "Wapto Island" of Franchere, the "Multnomah Island" of Wilkes, the "Wyeth Island" or "Wyeth's Island" and "Willamette [in all its variant spellings] Island" of several early cartographers. It is today called Sauvie Island in misspelled recognition of a Jean Baptiste Sauve who, in the pioneer settlers' time, was an employé at the Hudson's Bay Company's dairy farm then located on this island. *Chart* No. 6154; *Geol. Oregon; L. & C. Hist.*, pp. 914, 916; *McArthur*, p. 311.

57 "Cathlanaminimins" in trav. mem.

58 "Mathlanobes, 130 strong" in trav. mem.

59 "a good many Beaver" in trav. mem.

60 Willamette River, see note 48.

61 Present-day Willamette Falls at the site of Oregon City, Clackamas County, Ore.

62 In the stretch of river between the sites of the present-day cities of Oregon City and Eugene there were, in addition to lesser tributaries, twelve of sufficient importance to be named on the average modern map, six of them entering from the east and six from the west. *Geol. Oregon.*

63 "McKenzie" in trav. mem.

64 "country near the falls" in trav. mem.

65 Columbia.

66 See note 59 on p. 22.

67 *Betula fontinalis* (*Sargent*), if Stuart was accurate in his mention of birch; but probably a more commonly seen tree, the aspen (popularly styled "quaking aspen" or, in frontiersmen's vernacular, "quakin' ass"), *Populus tremuloides*, which, in its architecture, coloration and scenic assertiveness, much resembles the birch tree of the Atlantic coast. *L. & C. Journs.*, IV, p. 342.

68 *Corylus californica* (*Dc.*). *L. & C. Journs.*, III, p. 148.

69 See *L. & C. Hist.*, pp. 715, 843, 844.

70 See note 73 on p. 23 for varieties of bear.

71 "The salmon do not ascend these falls, the rocks being too high and the

drop too steep." *Henry-Thomp.*, p. 811. "To this place, and no farther, the salmon ascend." *Ross* [*A*], p. 235.

72 "Cath-la-poo-yaas" in trav. mem.

73 Query: if not present-day Molalla River, was it not present-day Pudding River? See *Geol. Oregon.* Molalla River is named for the Molele (*alias* Molale, Mollale, Molalah, Molayless, Moolalle, &c.) indians, a tribe which, of Waiilatpuan stock, once dwelt on this stream and in its neighborhood (*L. & C. Hist.*, p. 1038; *McArthur*, p. 231). According to *McArthur*, pp. 289, 290, Pudding River (earlier termed *Housuchachuck* and *Anchiyoke* by the local indians), which flows into Molalla River immediately above the latter stream's confluence with the Willamette, derives its modern name from the French word *boudin*, and does so for the following reason. Prior to January 23, 1814, some hungry French-Canadians, hunting on this watercourse, shot a number of wapiti. Indian women, attracted by the sound of firing, salvaged gore from the slain beasts and concocted a blood pudding which they gave to these Canadians. The recipients of the dish were so pleased that they forthwith dubbed the stream *Riviere au Boudin.*

74 "Cath-lack-las" in trav. mem.

75 "McKenzie" in trav. mem.

76 "Shoo-shoo-nays" in trav. mem.

77 On Columbia's right bank and opposite the more easterly of the two channels of Willamette River's mouth. *Chart* Nos. 6154, 6155; *Geol. Oregon; Geol. Washington.*

78 These figures seem to represent, in inverse order, the days' mileages since leaving Astoria; and, if so, the final figure "18" should have been "4."

79 Site of present-day city of Vancouver, Wash., but not the spot which, farther upstream, Broughton earlier had named Point Vancouver. See note 87.

80 Present-day Lake Vancouver. *L. & C. Journs.*, IV, p. 219; *L. & C. Hist.*, p. 917.

81 So named by Lewis and Clark, but today known as Sandy River. Rising on Mt. Hood's westerly slopes, it emptied through Columbia's left bank. *L. & C. Journs.*, III, p. 192; *L. & C. Hist.*, p. 690; *Henry-Thomp.*, p. 798; *Robinson; Chart* No. 6146; *Geol. Oregon.*

82 In the journ.'s manuscript are Stuart's following two interlineations: the term "2[d]" above these words "It is," and the term "1st" above the words "a rapid stream" at the beginning of the next sentence, evidently suggesting a transposition, which he actually made in trav. mem.

83 Columbia.

84 For corroborative description see *Henry-Thomp.*, pp. 798, 810. The ledge (see *Chart* No. 6146) is now surmounted by a light for navigators' benefit and is by modern cartographers variously termed Washougal Island, Washougal Rock and Washougal Light. *Light List.*

85 Harbor seals, *Phoca vitulina.*

86 This stream, the "Seal river" of Lewis and Clark, the "Washough-ally" of Ross, and today called Washougal River, emptied through Columbia's right bank in longitude 122° 24′. Its present-day name is said to be an indian word meaning "rushing water." *Chart* No. 6146; *Geol. Washington; L. & C. Hist.*, p. 690; *L. & C. Journs.*, IV, pp. 425, 426; Edmond S. Meany's *Origin of Washington Geographic Names* in *Wash. Hist. Quar.*, XIV, p. 138.

87 Camped on Columbia's right bank at a spot approximately one mile west of present-day Vancouver Point: a projection which, indicated on *Chart* No. 6146 as being in longitude 122° 19′ 30,″ was seemingly referred to by David Thompson as Point Vancouver; though subsequently it for many years was known as Cottonwood Point. What Broughton, prior to all these times, had named Point Vancouver was apparently, not this particular projection, but instead a neighboring sand-bar. *Henry-Thomp.*, p. 798; *Scott*, I, p. 151, II, pp. 165, 174; L. A. McArthur's *Location of Point Vancouver* in *Ore. Hist. Soc. Quar.*, XXXIV, pp. 31-38; T. C. Elliott's *Where is Point Vancouver?* in *Ore. Hist. Soc. Quar.*, XVIII, pp. 73-82; J. Neilson Barry's *Broughton &c.* in *Ore. Hist. Soc. Quar.*, XXXII, pp. 301-312.

88 Either present-day Hamilton Island (the "Strawberry Island" of Lewis and Clark, so named by them because of the quantity of strawberries found on it) or one of the small islands (two existing today though possibly three in Stuart's time) which lay immediately below Hamilton Island's lower end. *Quad. Mount Hood and vicinity; L. & C. Hist.*, pp. 687, 688; *L. & C. Journs.*, III, pp. 188, 189; *Henry-Thomp.*, p. 801.

89 Present-day Upper Cascades, for which see note 92.

90 Columbia's left bank.

91 From the crest of this "bluff" within a frontage of 8.3 miles, there descended actually seven falls, with heights and present-day names as follows: Latourell (249 feet), Bridal Veil (not visible except in flood), Mist or Widow's Tears (a tiny, evanescent affair), Wahkeena (some 400 feet), Multnomah (620 feet), Oneonta (in a gorge and not viewable from the Columbia), and Horsetail (221 feet). Stuart's failure to notice more than two of these falls may have been owing to their poor visibility because of the rain which his next day's entry records, or it may have been due to screening by trees. Incidentally, this was his fifth trip in front of the tier. David Thompson on his way upstream in 1811 made a like note of but two falls and gave their respective heights as 120 and 40 feet. Concerning both men's marked underestimate of height, we should keep in mind that, as they canoed on the river, the lower sections of all the falls were hidden from them by an intervening ridge. (*Journ. David Thompson* in *Ore. Hist. Soc. Quar.*, XV, p. 110; *Quad. Mount Hood and vicinity.*) Hunt also noticed these falls (p. 307 *infra.*).

92 Present-day Lower Cascades. Stuart was now nearing the foot of the four and one-half mile stretch (measured in terms of length of channel and not of sinuous bank to which Stuart's mileages apply) of rioting, rock-strewn water

that marked the Columbia's passage across the axis of the Cascade Mountains. Though this spumey stretch is today commonly considered an entirety and, as such, termed the Cascades, many folk, particularly pioneers, have been wont to divide the stretch into Upper Cascades and Lower Cascades—a severance which comports with conveniently recognized sections of the river. The Columbia, at the head of the Upper Cascades [the "great Shute" (*alias* "Great Shoot") of Lewis and Clark], abruptly made a right-angled bend, constricted to one-sixth of its former width and began its downhill rush with a descent of approximately 20 feet in the first 400 yards of the course. This wild river-stretch together with an additional but less savage rapid at its foot (the two aggregating 1 mile in length) formed the Upper Cascades. The succeeding 3½ miles represented the Lower Cascades and yielded a further drop of approximately 20 feet. The total drop for the entire 4½ miles was 45 feet during freshet periods and 36 when the water was low. *L. & C. Hist.*, pp. 681, 686, 938, 940, 941; *L. & C. Journs.*, III, pp. 179-185; *Quad. Mount Hood and vicinity; Wilkes*, p. 51; *Farnham*, p. 167; *Johnson & Winter*, pp. 36, 37; *Townsend*, pp. 164-167; *Henry-Thomp.*, pp. 799 *et seq.*

93 *Ross* [*A*], p. 195, states that somewhere in this vicinity indians "shot a few arrows at the canoes as they passed." *Cox* [*A*], I, pp. 125, 126, [*B*], p. 75, adds that at night the camp was "thrown into a state of frightful confusion" through the accidental discharge of a gun which so wounded the clerk Francis B. Pillet that he was unable to walk for a month. Not only the failure of both Stuart and Ross to mention this episode of the gun and the wounding, but also the description in *Ross* [*A*], p. 195, suggest that the episode occurred probably during some other trip in which Cox had participated.

94 That the camp was on present-day Hamilton Island near its upper end is inferable from the following day's entry in journ. and trav. mem. and from *Cox* [*A*], I, pp. 122, 123, [*B*], pp. 74, 75. *Cox* [*A*], I, p. 122, [*B*], p. 74, dates this encamping as July 4; and thus not only disagrees with Stuart's date of July 6, but also implies that the expedition had spent no more than two days in paddling the 84 miles from Deer Island to the foot of the Cascades although it previously had consumed, so Cox and Stuart agree, four days in negotiating the 71 miles from Astoria to Deer Island. Also, as appears in note 121 *infra*, Cox unduly shortens the time devoted to portaging the Cascades.

95 Cox, having exaggerated the party's initial membership to 90 and though failing to deduct for the loss of John Day, states that the division was into three watches, each of 5 officers and 25 men. *Cox* [*A*], I, pp. 118, 123, [*B*], pp. 72, 74, 75.

Cox [*A*], I, p. 123, [*B*], p. 74, states: "Each man was provided with a musket, and forty rounds of ball-cartridge, with pouch, belts, &c.; and over his clothes he wore leathern armour; this was a kind of shirt made out of the skin of the elk, which reached from the neck to the knees. It was perfectly arrow-proof; and at eighty or ninety yards impenetrable by a musket bullet. Besides the muskets, numbers had daggers, short swords, and pistols; and, when armed *cap-à-pié*, we presented a formidable appearance."

96 The heights near the river rose 500 to 1000 feet above it while those a short way inland ascended for approximately a further 2300 feet. *Quad. Mount Hood and vicinity.*

97 Along the right bank of the river-stretch which, being a portion of the Lower Cascades, consisted of the rapids that began at the foot of present-day Bradford Island ("Brant Island" of Lewis and Clark) and ended at the head of Hamilton Island. *Quad. Mount Hood and vicinity; L. & C. Hist.*, IV, map of Great Shoot.

98 Impossible to identify now.

99 Hamilton Island, lying at the foot of the rapid which caused the accident. See notes 88, 97.

100 "interpreter" in trav. mem. In the journ.'s manuscript, the word "two" which originally preceded "Interpreter" was deleted by Stuart; and, in its place, he inserted the word "our." But he did not delete a pen stroke which, at the end of "Interpreter," seems to have been a flourish, though it may have been a letter "s." As later appears (entries of July 12, 17, pp. 37, 53), Stuart at the time had but one interpreter, a Clatsop indian.

101 In the journ.'s manuscript the phrase "several small packages" (this same phrase in trav. mem.) was inserted by Stuart in place of an earlier but deleted wording which read: "a Box of Soap, several other things."

102 A stretch of the rapid described in note 97.

103 Doubtless right bank.

104 *I.e.*, were above the foot of the rapids.

105 Almost surely the ravine which, now known as Tanner Creek Canyon, debouched through the Columbia's left bank at the site of present-day town of Bonneville, Ore. If not that ravine, it was the one which, known today as Eagle Creek Canyon, debouched through the Columbia's left bank 1.3 miles east of Tanner Creek Canyon. *Quad. Mount Hood and vicinity.*

106 Located at approximately the site of present-day town of Cascades, Skamania County, Wash., and thus at the head of the rapid described in note 97.

107 "package" in trav. mem.

108 "bark canoe" in trav. mem. This type of undecked canoe, used by all such Eastern indians as lived in forested areas, consisted of a light and widely spaced framework of strong wood over which was laid a "skin" made of wide strips (a single strip if one large enough were obtainable) of birch bark approximately one-eighth of an inch thick, sewn into place with deer sinews and caulked with pitch. Canoes of this sort were confined to a particular section of the East, because in solely that section grew the tree known interchangeably as white birch, paper birch or canoe birch, *Betula papyrifera* (*Marsh*), this being the only tree with bark sufficiently tough, pliable and waterproof.

109 Birch bark.

110 Celilo Falls and the Dalles; for description of which see note 1 on p. 64.

111 Identical with the "Great Rapids" in entry of July 5 (p. 34) and today known as Upper Cascades.

112 Commonly so called because of a specialized type of boat prevalent on the Mohawk River, to which river the village of Schenectady, N. Y., was contiguous. " . . . their length about 30 feet and the width 8 feet & pointed bow and stern, flat bottom and rowing six ores only the Skenackeity form." *L. & C. Journs.*, V, p. 390. See also *Dunbar*, I, p. 282.

113 On Columbia's right bank nearly opposite head of Bradford Island, and thus part way up the rapid which began above that island and continued till past the island's head; all as indicated on *Quad. Mount Hood and vicinity.* See also *L. & C. Hist.*, IV, map of Great Shoot.

114 Incorrectly "1½ miles" in trav. mem.

115 Camp was on Columbia's right bank at seemingly the site of the indians' ancient village mentioned by Lewis and Clark and thus in longitude approximately 121° 55′ 4.″ *Quad. Mount Hood and vicinity; L. & C. Hist.*, pp. 681, 682, 942 and Vol. IV, map of Great Shoot; *L. & C. Journs.*, III, pp. 173, 175, 178.

116 Assembled at downstream end of the portage which, situated on Columbia's right bank, is indicated in *L. & C. Hist.*, IV, map of Great Shoot. Stuart, by ascending this portage, reached a spot which, immediately above the head of the Upper Cascades, was due west from present-day town of Cascade Locks, Ore. *Geol. Oregon; Quad. Mount Hood and vicinity.*

117 Stuart fails to disclose on which side of the Columbia he camped; but his stated mileage locates this camp, if on the right bank, as having been at approximately the mouth of present-day Rock Creek (flowing past the westerly outskirts of present-day town of Stevenson, Skamania County, Wash.) and, if on the left bank, as having been on a mud flat opposite that site (*Quad. Mount Hood and vicinity*). The mud flat's undesirability as a camping place suggests, particularly in light of *Cox* [*A*], I, pp. 123-126, [*B*], pp. 74, 75, that the camp was on Columbia's right bank.

118 The remainder of trav. mem.'s entry for this July 11 is restricted to a description of the local fisheries and is a duplicate of so much of the journ.'s July 14 entry on pp. 51, 52 as is covered by note 4 on p. 65.

119 This phrase, "one of our young gentlemen," inserted by Stuart in lieu of the journ.'s previously written and then deleted words, "Mr Matthews," refers to the clerk William W. Matthews, a New Yorker, who had come to Astoria in the ship *Tonquin* and who, when the British later acquired Astoria, entered employ of the North West Company. *Franchere* [*A*], p. 17, [*B*], p. 30; *Henry-Thomp.*, pp. 760, 783, 787, 810-815, 820, 827-830, 834, 838-840, 844, 849, 851, 867, 868, 877, 878, 888, 892, 893, 903.

120 "returned about 11 A.M." in trav. mem.

121 Stuart's wording identifies the camp's site as having been on the Co-

lumbia's right bank at such a distance above the head of the Cascades as to place it at the mouth of the present-day Wind River. *Cox* [*A*], I, p. 128, [*B*], p. 76, gives this same location and specifically mentions the stream. See *Geol. Washington* and *Quad. Mount Hood and vicinity.*

However, *Cox* [*A*], I, pp. 122-129, [*B*], pp. 74-76, dates the camping as July 6; and thus not only disagrees with Stuart's date of July 12 but also, in variance with Stuart's detailed account of six days' labor, implies that less than two days were spent by the expedition in portaging the Cascades.

Wind River was the "Cruzatte's River" of Lewis and Clark, so named by them in honor of Peter Cruzatte, a member of their expedition. *L. & C. Hist.*, p. 679.

122 See note 100 for there being but one interpreter.

123 The Cascades.

124 As regards local indian tribes' inability to understand each other's language, see *L. & C. Hist.*, p. 672.

125 If strictly speaking, meant present-day Celilo Falls; though, as used here by Stuart, seems to have included not only the falls but also the so-called Dalles (a series of rapids) below them.

126 The context and stated mileage show that by the word "Falls" as here used Stuart meant not the Celilo Falls, but the downstream end of the so-called Dalles. Accordingly, we may confidently assign the site of the night's camp, if on right bank, to approximately the mouth of present-day Klickitat River (the "Cataract river" of Lewis and Clark) and, if on left bank, to approximately mouth of present-day Brown's Creek. *Geol. Washington; Geol. Oregon; L. & C. Hist.*, p. 676; *L. & C. Journs.*, III, p. 169.

127 The ones noted by Stuart were, because of their size, doubtless present-day Little White Salmon River and, east of it, present-day White Salmon River. The other and much lesser streams (such as present-day Collins Creek, Dog Creek and Major's Creek) might well have escaped the eye of a canoeist on the Columbia. White Salmon River (the "Canoe Creek" of Lewis and Clark, so named by them because of the numerous indians fishing from canoes in the stream. *L. & C. Hist.*, p. 677; *L. & C. Journs.*, III, p. 171) was thus termed, so Edmond S. Meany states, for one of two reasons: either the presence of white salmon-trout or the fact that, each autumn, there entered the stream vast schools of salmon so sick that not only their flesh had blanched but also the numerous sores on their skins, through possible attack by a fungus, had whitened as well. Edmond S. Meany's *Origin of Washington Geograbhic Names* in *Wash. Hist. Quar.*, XIV, pp. 211, 212.

128 Doubtless present-day Hood River, this because of its superior size. The Columbia's numerous other local confluents from the south—such as present-day Gorton, Lindsey, Warm, Starvation, Viento, and Mosier Creeks—were trivial in comparison. Hood River, on its discovery by Lewis and Clark, received from them the name Labeasche in honor of Francis Labieche (*alias*

Labeasche, Labuche, Labuish), a member of their expedition (*L. & C. Hist.*, p. 677; *L. & C. Journs.*, I, pp. 12, 30, III, p. 171). In place of this name, there was substituted in covered-wagon days the name Dog River—not through any mistranslation of *La biche* (the French term for female deer), but because some starving emigrants had eaten a dog beside the stream. Presently local residents, objecting to the homeliness of this latter name, changed it to Hood River, because of the stream's rising on Mt. Hood. *McArthur*, p. 165.

129 Doubtless White Salmon River and Hood River, this because of their size and characteristics.

CHAPTER III

JULY 14 · JULY 30, 1812

By Canoe up the Columbia from Klickitat River to Mouth of Walla Walla River

[SEE MAP FACING PAGE 3]

Ascend Dalles · Local Indians · Astorians' Fight with Natives in Preceding Spring · Capture of Indians Who Had Robbed Crooks and Day Arrive at Walla Walla's Mouth · Local Indians · Horses Obtained

Tuesday 14th This day at Noon we arrived at the commencement of the long Narrows,[1] discharged all our Arms, cleaned and reloaded them. Here our Clatsop came up with us accompanied by two Indians from below, which was very agreeable to us all as it was in paſsing these Rapids that we expected the Savages would make the attempt were they in the least desirous of measuring their prowess with ours in which case the having an Interpreter was of the first Importance, we paſsed several inferior Ripples and encamped 2 hours before sunsett on the South Side[2] [*which is by far the best & shortest portage*]— at this place the whole company were divided into three equal parts, to stand guard—19 from Dusk till 11 P M.—19 from that till 1 A M and the other 19 from 1 to daylight[3]— and this precaution is to be continued until [*we*] are above all the Falls and [*bad*] Rapids—

[16] The[4] Indians at these Rapids are composed of the Cathlakahikits[5] & Cathlathlallas each mustering about 150 Warriors are

saucy, impudent Rascals, will steal when they can, & pillage whenever a weak party falls into their clutches— Here is one of the first rate Salmon fisheries on the river they erect stages or scaffolds to project some distance from the bank, by binding two long but slender trees together with strong withes, next tying a stout piece of wood acrofs the two former from 4 to 6 feet below where they are bound together— thus arranged this preparation is set erect in the water, when the ends of two Slabs Several Inches thick and from 20 to 40 feet long are laid on the crofs piece of the two uprights, so as to reach 6 or 8 feet beyond them, with the other end resting on the rocks along the waters edge— at the farther extremity are a few thin boards from Slab to Slab on which the Fisherman stands on plying his Scoopnett, on the end of this erection which rests on the shore are placed huge stones not only to be a counterpoise to the weight and exertions of the actor but also to give it sufficient solidity to resist the action of the current— The places chosen are always a point where the water is strongest, and if pofsible a mafs of rock near[6] the projection between which and the shore the Salmon are sure to pafs, to avoid the greater body of the current— the [17] Scoopnett used here is made fast to a [*large*] Hoop to which a very long handle is attached the fisherman pushes this to the depth of several feet perpendicularly in the water allowing it to decend with the flood untill it encounters the Salmon who struggling to go upwards, Keep the nett always distended and is pulled up with such ease that Boys are often employed, who succeed equally with the most robust Men— the Fish come this far by the middle of May, but the two following months are the prime of the season— during this time the operator hardly ever dips his nett without taking one and sometimes two Salmon, so that I call it speaking within bounds when I say that an experienced hand would by afsuidity catch at least 500 daily—

Wednesday 15th We went on but slowly as the men had to make two trips with the Canoes on account of their numbers being reduced by a guard of 20 men, kept on the bank for the same purpose as at the lower Rapids,[7]— a good many Indians kept about us all day, but were not suffered to come near the Baggage nor the men at work— at one place today the Packages were carried 200 paces, and unremitting exertions only enabled to get to this station[8] which is only 1½ miles from that of last night—

Thursday 16th The Goods were this morning transported by land 500 yds to a large village[9] where we breakfasted they were again embarked for 250 when a Portage of 880 paces succeeded, [*which brought us*] to the upper end of the Indian Camp— Here everything was [18] put in the Canoes, and towed along the Rocks for a mile to a fine sand Beach[10] where we stopped for the night— while in the vicinity of the Town, the natives came about us in great numbers but few were armed They [*upon the whole*] behaved very much to our satisfaction in consequence of which a present of Tobacco was given to the chief.[11]

Friday 17th The first Watch had scarcely taken their stations last night when two Indians from below came running towards our Camp— The word "To Arms" was immediately given and every man was at his Post in an instant— the natives came up much out of breath, and nearly petrified with horror, related how a War party of Shoshonays[12] had attacked one of their Canoes late in the afternoon and killed 4 men & 2 women

Our Clatsop[13] was absent at this time, but he soon after arrived and corroborated the statement we had just heard

Not however placing too much confidence in the report, we hauled up the Boats & Canoes, of which and the Packages a good Breastwork was made on three Sides, with the River in our rear

The night past without molestation, and we began at the dawn to make a Portage[14] of the remaining narrows[15] as it was utterly impracticable to do any thing by water— the Goods and veſsells were first carried 200 yds from our Camp, where a Guard of ten men was posted as soon as the first Parcel was laid down and the other Watch of ten remained untill all was taken away [19] from our last nights station— In this way we paſsed the whole Carrying Place, never at any time being more than 300 paces, between the resting places, by which means 10 persons well armed were constantly on the lookout at each end while the others were perpetually going and coming so that in case of an attack at least 20 [*men*] would be on the spot, and the whole could join in the course of two minutes

We reached the upper extremity by 4 P.M. and after making a present of Tobacco to the Chiefs of two villages we past today on this side,[16] and the like to the Sachem of a strong tribe on the North side[17] who rendered us the honor of a formal visit went on about 1½ miles where on account of a heavy Gale we encamped for the night[18]

Sunday 19th Yesterday the wind continued too strong for us to move, and today we got only within [*about*] half a mile of the Falls[19] when Mr Clarkes Boat proved too leaky to proceed. Consequently we had to encamp for the night in order to have her repaired,

Monday 20th We started with the dawn & got within 140 yds of the upper end of the Falls without diminishing our cargoes, when by carrying the Goods that distance, we got up our Craft by water—[20] The Long Narrows Falls and the space between are inhabited by the Chipanekikekiks[21] 100 Cathlaskos, 150—Ilthakyemam-its[22] 100 & Hellwits[23] 200 Strong— the three first have villages and live here constantly, but the last reside a little inland[24] and come in summer to fish— all mix promiscuously at this season, and the choice of stations is guided [*entirely*] by whim & caprice, or the attractions which one fishing place may poſseſs over another, besides most of the Indians from near the Forks[25] of Columbia [20] aſsemble here to procure wherewith to paſs the winter in greater comfort, than the resources of their own country affords, so that when added to the residents of this quarter, 700 men might be collected in two hours— the quantity of Salmon destroyed here if put in figures would exceed the bounds of probability, so I must refer the imagination to its own resources for the number, which may be calculated in the ratio of what was mentioned at the Grand Rapids,[26] as the produce of an expert Scooper in one day; from this some idea may be formed of the incredible shoals of Salmon which annually ascend the Columbia and its waters—

Last spring[27] In the prosecution of a voyage to Mr. [*David*] Stuarts [*establishment*][28] with 16 men[29] I got to the Portage[30] of the long narrows early in the month of April, where[31] the Cathlaskos not only behaved impudently, but carried off two Bales of Goods with some other articles which were intrusted to their care to be by them transported on horses to the upper end of the Carrying Place & our Canoes being too heavy for the number of men, we were constantly compelled to employ these Villains to carry them — this they executed well, but while five men were watching them, they maliciously threw large stones on one, which damaged it considerably, at the same [21] time pillaging what Knives, Handkfs &c. they could lay their hands on— being dusk before we succeeded in getting all together, it was impofsible [*at such a late hour*] to better our [*forlorn*] situation before morning, so we pafsed the night under arms without one of us closing an eye, and when day was yet scarcely visible in the East, every thing was embarked, and we gladly bid adieu to this abominable den of robbers— Elated I suppose with the succefs of yesterday,[32] we were this day[33] escorted by the whole tribe who by the time we reached the Falls[19] had augmented their numbers to upwards of 400 armed principally with Bows & Arrows, and where these were deficient War Clubs, Battle Axes &c were substituted. Surrounded with this host they requested permifsion to make the Portage for us, which I declined by saying that it was now too late, but that if they behaved well, I would accept their offer in the morning, and in the meantime engaged them to take up the Canoes, a service they executed with fidelity but were no sooner recompensed for their trouble, than they manifested an intention to destroy them, notwithstanding the presence of ten[34] [*exceedingly*] well armed men whom I had dispatched as a Gaurd, and were only at last prevented by the interference of an old man, who seemed to be a considerable Personage among them— With the exception of thirty[35] the whole of this hostile band, croſsed to the north side,[36] soon after the termination of the hoary gentlemans lecture, which I suppose only tended to diſsuade them for the present, and to watch an oppy to [22] strike a more decisive blow— Well aware that their proffered aſsiſstance was not for the best of purposes, I determined to defeat if poſsible their infernal machinations, and, at 1 A M by the aid of Moonlight began the transportation of the Goods with the hopes of getting all over before the dawn— Two loads were only remaining at daybreak, when those spies who had remained to watch our motions perceived what had been going on & thinking themselves too weak for an attack gave the alarm to those on the opposite side,[37] who to about the number of 130 embarked without loſs of time [*in several large canoes*]— I immediately sent the people to the lower end for another load, with orders to Mr Reed[38] to keep what men he thought neceſsary with him as I supposed the gentry from the other side were not croſsing with any good intention, He [*very imprudently*] refused retaining any [*of them*] saying he would with Mr Robert McClellan[39] take care of what little remained— No sooner did the Canoes touch the shore than their cargoes leaped on the Rocks and without [*the least*] hesitation made directly for the Goods beginning an indiscriminate pillage, which the two Gentlemen vainly attempted to oppose. Mr.[40] McClellan soon perceiving how unavailing any exertions of human strength would be retired with his Arms calling to Mr Reed to do the same, and "they would give it to them while plundering" the latter was however already wrestling with an Savage who had hold of his Gun, when another running [23] up to the muzzle of the formers arms, threw a Buffalo Robe over his head,— Mr McClellan jumped back in a moment disengaged himself from the Skin, had just time enough to draw up his Piece, when the Villain made a lunge at him with his Knife & received the contents of his Rifle in the Breast, which laid him lifeleſs on the spot— Mr Reed was still scuffling for his Gun, and Mr. McC. attempted in vain to get off the cap and shoot the Scoundrel who held it, in the instant that another Rascal made a blow at him with an Axe handle, which by Springing over a Canoe, he avoided but the stroke fell on Mr Reeds head a little below the ear and deprived him of his senses— a small pocket Pistol was all the reserve Mr Mc C had, which he discharged instantaniously at the fellow who finished Mr R and saw him fall apparently as dead as the first— Among Indians unaccustomed to Fire Arms one would have supposed that seeing two of their Comrades fall, the rest would have sought safety in flight, but far different was their conduct; they continued to preſs forward for what little yet remained inflicted five wounds with a Tomahawk on Mr. R Head and Mr McC only hopes depended on the effect of his empty gun— this he presented and rushed at them, on which they gave ground, and he had a load in his piece in a moment, & he was still unharmed, but as before, running directly at the main body, raised the Indian Yell, which soon produced a partial retreat and immediately after a general flight— He followed them some distance and gave up the pursuit on account of seeing a party of savages coming from above— On his return to the Field of Action, the Pistol shot [24] Indian was miſsing, but Mr. Reed and the other lay weltering in their blood— He examined the former, (who yet gave some faint sign of existence, but supposed them to be his last struggles), and found in his pocket a well loaded Pistol, which taking, he sett out to encounter those whom he saw coming from above— there was but three, and they avoided the Path in which Mr McClellan was walking, by going a considerable way to one side— Having heard the report of a Gun a short time before the people with their loads came to the upper end, I was suspicious of the cause, and as soon as enough arrived to take care of the Goods, sent Mr Farnham[41] to see what was the matter, who met Mr Mc. C on the road and they returned together

Our Canoes were leaky and the oars were still at the lower end —some Hands began caulking and Mr McC with four others returned for what was left— During his absence the dead Indian was carried off & Mr. Reed recovering from the wounds he had received but weak from the loſs of Blood was wandering about on the Rocks, not knowing whither he went; he was accordingly aſsiſsted in getting to the upper end where he soon after fainted and in this situation was embarked and we continued our voyage up the South shore—[42] news of this affair no sooner reached the Cathlasko village, than [*two horses were killed, and the blood, in its crude state, was drank by the warriors in order to give them additional courage, and intrepidity, this ceremony, with their dead dance and war song finished, they to the number of*] 120 men[43] clothed with their garments and [*furnished with*] every other accoutrement for War, mounted their Horses and followed us panting for revenge, we however fortunately discovered them some distance above the Shoshone River[44] croſsing to the side[45] by which we were ascending, and when near the place found them posted among [25] cut[46] Rocks close along which we must unavoidly paſs— Finding they had the advantage of the grounds we stopped about 400 yds below, discharged and reloaded our arms, made a fire and Mr Mc[47] dreſsed Mr. Reeds head, on which were five gashes of the Tomahawk, of about 2 Inches in length each— this done we lashed the Canoes together, went[48] to a rock[49] at a small distance from the shore, (from which we could retreat with facility in the event of being too hard pushed) and there awaited the onsett— not long after the War Chief with 3 others[50] came to us in a Canoe; [*and after a long preamble,*] said we had killed[51] 2 of his nation, that their relatives, incensed had compelled him to take the command of the Party against his will but that they were come purposely to fight, determined on having satisfaction in some shape or other; and proposed as the only means of appeasing their fury that we should deliver up Mr. Reed (who he observed was already dead)[52] to the friends of the savages who fell, to be by them cut in pieces— this would (he said) completely obliterate their present animosity, and that the greatest harmony would prevail for the future— Our answer was NO, the man you wounded is our Brother and you must destroy [*all of*] us before you get him— We are prepared and ready for your Warriors, bring them on and we will teach you a more serious lefson than you learned this morning— this they [*some time*] considered of & [*after mature deliberation*] The businefs was soon after compromised for 3 Blankets[53] to cover the dead, and some Tobacco to fill the Calumet of Peace, on condition they should [26] immediately crofs River and leave our pafsage free, which was Soon complied with [*they recrofsed to the north side*] and we saw no more of them

Mr Reed is certainly indebted to Mr. McClellan for his life, as without the invincible & succefsfull bravery with which he resisted at least 30 determined Villains, he must have fallen a sacrifice, and endangered the safety of the whole Party— And here I most willingly acknowledge that through all this trying situation, I received the most prompt afsifstance, and was much aided by that advice which Mr McClellans long intercourse & residence among Indians enabled him to give—[54]

The Country which at the Fort[55] was an impenetrable Wildernefs began at the Grand Rapids[56] gradually to diminish in the quantity of Timber—small Prairie Knobs[57] occasionally chequered the Landscape, and by the time we reached the foot of the long narrows[58] the Woods were at a considerable distance behind us— From the Sea to the Rapids[56] the Forests continue of nearly the same charater, but a little farther up, the Pines become stinted and intermixed with scrubby Oaks, which latter Tree gains an almost total ascendency as you approach the upper extremity of this wooded Track, apparently opposite Mount Hood—[59] This Mountain is entirely detached from any other, and when we consider the great height [27] of the River Hills (which in a civilized soil would be thought nearly impaſsable from their magnitude, and above which this gigantic maſs appears as a Steeple overlooking the lowest Houses of a City) it will easily be imagined that it is not a Hillock of the common order— At present the trees are discernible about halfway up the aclivity, the tops of others in a higher region begin to emerge from the Snow, but the Summit never knows a change of Seasons—

Here the Bluffs come close to the River on both sides, along that of the North[60] we pursued our course, croſsed to the Island[61] opposite the Shoshone River[62] and encamped[63] some distance above— This River has a considerable Cascade near its entrance and is about 200 yards wide— Nothing else is known of it except its being thickly inhabited by the Shoshone[64] nation— Here and all along the River from the Sea to the Forks the word "Shoshone" signifies an Inhabitant of the interior[65] to distinguish them from those of the main River called Fish Indians—[*about two days march up this stream it is well wooded, & its banks are the asylum of a great many Bear, Deer and Beaver.*—]

Tuesday 21st. At an early hour we continued our route along the south side and at breakfast time recognized two of the villans who robbed Meſsrs Crooks and Day[66] when on their way from St. L.[67] to Astoria, they having been left behind by the rest of the party last Spring in consequence of their having become so debilitated by long privations & fatigue as not to be capable of keeping pace with them— they were immediately seized, bound hand & foot, and put in the Canoes, [*we*] telling the Bystanders that so soon as the property pillaged was [28] restored they should be set at liberty— Expreſses were by them sent off in different directions and before night they arrived with the 2 Rifles, but the smaller articles they found impoſsible to recover— their bands were then loosened[68] and they departed with evident symptoms of terror little expecting to get off with so much clemency— A small River[69] adds its tributary Waves about 2 Miles below where we encamp[70] tonight,— It is about 60 yds wide at its mouth and ifsues from among high Hills entirely destitute of Timber as is also its banks, and the Soil is nothing but Sand [*today we*] were obliged to unload twice[71] [*in consequence of bad rapids*] & came in all 18 miles—

Wednesday 22nd Had a strong fair wind all day which enabled us to sail 40 miles[72] the Country is without a stick of wood, and the soil an entire desert of sand even on the tops of the Bluffs—

Thursday 23rd Light Breezes [*of southy wind*] prevailed the greatest part of the day— the Hills have now receded and the Columbia Plains commence, with a similar quality of Land to that pafsed yesterday— the length of todays march was 30 miles

Friday 24 —We reached the Umatulla River,[73] before night, opposite which we encamped[74] having come 20 miles—[75]

This stream takes[76] its rise in the mountains[77] which bound the Columbia Plains to South East & is 80 yds at its mouth & is well stocked with the Furr'd race—[78]

[29] Saturday 25th This day we found intolerably hot, and after coming 15 miles stopped at an Indian Village[79] where traded 4 horses having in the course of our [*todays*] journey procured 5 others—[80] Here we got some Lamper Eels,[81] which with a Kind of Chub[82] seem peculiar to these waters above the Falls—[83] Stayed here the 26th

Monday 27 — We 2 more Horses were traded this morning and continuing on 15 Miles Farther pafsed the Walla Walla River,[84] about 2 Miles above which we met a number of Indians and encamped[85] for the night—which is about 50 yds[86] wide, takes its source with the Umattulla,[87] and poſseſses a good many Beaver [*& Otter, and Deer in great numbers frequent its vicinity:*]

On this stream [*near the entrance*] and its neighbourhood live the nation from whom it derives its name— they are good Indians, about 200 in number, but as yet entirely ignorant of the modes & destitute of the means to ensnare the furred inhabitants of their lands

The Natives of this quarter have but a scanty subsistence when compared to those of the Falls, as their country poſseſses very few fishing places and them being none of the best, they are consequently obliged to content themselves with [*a little venison and*] Roots the greater part of the year & these require great labour in [*hunting and*] extraction; so that a fellow who considers it a hardship to be industrious soon makes [*the best of*] his way to the Falls, where he can indulge his sloth without fear of starvation

By[88] such worthleſs Dogs are these noted Fishing Places peopled, which like our great cities may with propriety be called the School of Villainy or the Head Quarters of vitiated principles

[30] Tuesday 28th Late last night a great many Indians accompanied by a few Squaws of the Walla Wallas, danced for a long time round a fire made for the purpose at one end of our Camp this was to welcome us into their Country and their behaviour evinced how much they were pleased at our paſsing the night among them—[89]

From this band I procured What was wanting[90] to complete the 12[91] Horses neceſsary for my voyage for all of which with their appendages I gave Merchandize to the amount of $179.82 but had I been in possession of the proper articles they should not have Cost more than half the Value In the afternoon we Crossed the Columbia and encamped on the opposite[92] side at the mouth of the Creek[93] to which place I was escorted by Meſsrs McKenzie[94] Stuart[95] & Clarke[96] and their people, except [*a detachment of those belonging to*] the latter who dispatched his Canoes to the entrance of Lewis' River,[97] there to trade what Horses were requisite to continue his inland expedition—

Thursday 30th Mr Clarke left us this morning with a strong westerly wind, and it was evening before our [*pack-*] saddles and packages were ready, although we made the best use of the time both yesterday and today—

Notes to Chapter III

1 The lower end—termed "the commencement" by Stuart because he was travelling upstream—of the fast water below that stretch of the Dalles which is called by him "the long Narrows" and which is today styled Five Mile Rapids. Although Stuart and Cox agree that two days were consumed in journeying hither from the mouth of Wind River, Stuart dates the arrival as noon on July 14; Cox as the evening of July 8. *Cox* [*A*], I, pp. 128, 129, [*B*], p. 76.

Stuart was now to ascend the superbly cruel river-stretch which, beginning at the crest of Celilo Falls and extending downstream for approximately 14 sinuous miles, had an aggregate drop of 62½ feet in mean high water of freshet periods, and 81½ when the water was low. This river-stretch below the Falls is known in its entirety as "The Dalles," but to various of its sections (for which see notes 2, 7, 10, 15, 18, 19) special names have commonly been given—the more recent ones being in terms of miles and thereby disclosing their distances above the site of the present-day town of Dalles, Ore. (colloquially known also as "The Dalles").

That the word Dalles had, prior to April 12, 1814, become already established as the title for at least such portion of the river as is today known as Five Mile Rapids appears from *Franchere* [*A*], p. 207, [*B*], p. 264.

Concerning the derivation of this earlier name, DeSmet states: "Dalle is an old French word, meaning a trough, and the name is given by the Canadian voyageurs to all contracted running waters, hemmed in by walls of rocks" (*DeSmet* [*A*], p. 214). For another phrasing of this, see *DeSmet*, pp. 384, 385. In this same trend of thought, T. C. Elliott avers the place-name to be a "corruption of the French words 'd'aller' meaning TO GO." T. C. Elliott's *The Dalles-Celilo Portage* in *Ore. Hist. Soc. Quar.*, XVI, p. 135.

However, the French word *dalles* meant also flagstones, both in general and also of the type employed for lining gutters; and many historians have ascribed the Oregonian place-name to this second source, instead of to the one offered by DeSmet, as above set forth. See, for instance, *L. & C. Hist.*, pp. 954, 955. And, in this second source-meaning, the name was a befitting one because of the myriad columnar basaltic rocks through which the Columbia here tore its way.

2 On left bank at apparently foot of present-day Five Mile Rapids (the "Long Narrows" of Lewis and Clark; the "Dalles," "Long Dalles," "Great Dalles," and "Big Dalles" of other diarists). *L. & C. Hist.*, p. 669; *L. & C. Journs.*, VIII, map 32, part 1.

Stuart, in order to reach this camp-site, had first ascended three miles of swift river which was accented here and there by rocks upstanding from its bed. Having thus arrived at the foot of present-day Three Mile Rapids—a short affair—he had surmounted them, as well as the one and one-half miles of river lying above their head; and so had found himself at the lower end of present-day Big Eddy. Immediately above the upper end of this eddy was the foot of Five Mile Rapids and the site of the camp.

3 Making a total of 57 on guard duty. The entire company, because of the loss of John Day, now contained 61 men inclusive of both the Clatsop interpreter and also the 4 partners, namely McKenzie, Clarke, David Stuart, and Robert Stuart. To reconcile this figure of 61 with Stuart's implied aggregate of 57, we must assume that some of the party—probably the interpreter and possibly three of the partners—were excused from sentry service.

4 The remainder of this July 14 entry in the journ. is, except for the differences stated in notes 5 and 6, duplicated by a portion of the trav. mem.'s entry for July 11, which last-mentioned entry, however, places the scene of action, not at the lower end of Long Dalles, but farther downstream, *i.e.*, at The Cascades. Possibly this shift of scene was due to inadvertence when transcribing from journ. to trav. mem., or it may be that Stuart, intent on describing the Columbia's two most salient fisheries, thought that because their importance and method of fishing were alike they could be treated as a single entity. Neither the productiveness nor the prevailing method of fishing at these two places was characteristic of other parts of the Columbia. The productiveness was due to the fact that salmon, when ascending a river, are wont to congregate at the foot of the falls and rapids. See *L. & C. Hist.*, pp. 665 *et seq.*; *Journ. Mrs. Marcus Whitman* in *Ore. Pioneer, 19th annual reunion*, 1891, pp. 61, 62. See also note 118 on p. 48 *ante*.

5 "Cath-lak-a-heekits" in trav. mem.

6 "a little outside" in trav. mem.

7 Stuart had spent this day in ascending the Five Mile Rapids, which, one and one-half miles long and having a pitch of 10 feet per mile, murderously ran for their entire length in a trough with vertical basaltic walls varying from 125 to 300 feet apart.

8 This camp at approximately the upper end of Five Mile Rapids was undoubtedly on the Columbia's left bank, because a crossing of the stream in this vicinity would have been very difficult, and Stuart's July 17 entry reveals him as being still on the left bank.

9 Query: was this the village raided at this time by Donald McKenzie for purpose of regaining a gun stolen in the preceding April, all as described by *Ross* [*A*], pp. 196-198? Seemingly the village was a temporary one; see *L. & C. Hist.*, p. 660.

10 On Columbia's left bank and apparently near lower end of present-day Ten Mile Rapids (the "Short Narrows" of Lewis and Clark; the "Short Dalles," "Little Dalles," and "Petite Dalles" of other journalists). This day, Stuart, on leaving his camp near the upper end of Five Mile Rapids, had ascended a river-stretch approximately 1800 feet in length and down which the water poured at

a gradient of 11 feet per mile. At the head of this stretch he had begun his ascent of a less boisterous three and one-fifth miles of river which led to the foot of the Ten Mile Rapids.

11 "Chiefs" in trav. mem.

12 "Shooshonies" in trav. mem. That these particular "Shoshonays" were not necessarily of the actual Shoshone nation appears from a statement in the entry of July 20 (p. 60).

13 See note 100 on p. 47 for fact that this man was the sole indian interpreter.

14 Along left bank.

15 Ten Mile Rapids—one-half mile long, having a pitch of 7⅓ feet per mile at low water, and ragingly confined between high vertical basaltic walls approximately 200 feet apart.

16 Left bank.

17 Right bank.

18 On left bank and approximately one mile above upper end of Ten Mile Rapids and two miles below the foot of Celilo Falls.

19 Celilo Falls (the "Great Falls" of Lewis and Clark), 47 feet high in times of low water, though during vernal freshets the huge volume of the current so much submerged these falls that they appeared as little more than a pronounced descending curve in the onrushing flood.

As to why and when the falls obtained their name Celilo there is question. *Angelo* [*A*], p. 39, and [*B*], p. 46, spelling the word as "Celilo" and "Celillo," relate that the source was a bit of indian jargon which, meaning a "floating sand-cloud," was applicable because of the dense scuds of sand that constantly wafted through the air on windy days. T. C. Elliott, at p. 135 of his *The Dalles-Celilo Portage* in *Ore. Hist. Soc. Quar.*, XVI, quotes and repudiates an alleged derivation from a corrupted form of the French *Cela l'eau;* and suggests, as possible derivations, undesignated indian words severally meaning, in order of preference, (1), tumbling waters, (2), shifting sands, (3), an indian chief's name.

For description of the falls as well as of the Dalles (which latter term was often loosely used as inclusive of both falls and the 14 miles of swift river below them) see *L. & C. Hist.*, pp. 658-669, 954-955; *L. & C. Journs.*, III, pp. 146-159; *Wheeler, Olin*, II, p. 149; Henry J. Biddle's *Wishram* in *Ore. Hist. Soc. Quar.*, XXVII, map facing p. 115; *Wilkes*, p. 51; *Farnham*, pp. 158, 159; *Johnson & Winter*, pp. 34, 35; *Wyeth, Nathaniel J.*, pp. 174, 175; *Applegate*, pp. 51, 52; *DeSmet*, pp. 384-387; *McArthur*, p. 349.

20 Thus had arrived at top of Celilo Falls.

21 "Cheepan-chick-chicks" in trav. mem.

22 "Ilth-kye-mamits" in trav. mem.

23 "Chelwits" in trav. mem.

24 *I.e.*, inland from the ocean. See entry of July 1 (p. 29).

25 Confluence of Snake River with Columbia.

26 See note 4.

27 Left Astoria on March 22, 1812 (*Ross* [*A*], p. 184; *Astoria*, II, p. 94); on March 30, 1812 (*Franchere* [*A*], p. 115, [*B*], p. 151). Stuart's reminiscent account, beginning here, continues for six of his pages.

28 David Stuart's outpost on present-day Okanagan River.

29 "2 Clerks and 14 Men" in trav. mem. It had been arranged that all 16 men should travel with Stuart as far as to the mouth of present-day Walla Walla River, where some of them should quit him and head thence in part for Hunt's caches and in other part for New York, and only the remainder should continue with him to the Okanagan. See pp. LXXVIII, LXXIX.

As to the size of the prospective New York party, there is no uncertainty—*Ross* [*A*], pp. 184, 185, and *Astoria*, II, pp. 93-95, agreeing on a membership of five (Reed, McClellan and three men) and *Franchere* [*B*] not stating the number. But as to the size of the cache party, there is a conflict. While *Franchere* [*A*], p. 115, [*B*], pp. 151-153, specifies for it a total of three (Farnham, McGillis and a guide), *Astoria*, II, p. 93, allots it not only these two clerks and their guide, but also eight additional men, and thereby attempts to send Stuart from the Walla Walla to the Okanagan without a single associate to aid him in the management of what *Franchere* [*B*], p. 152, terms "two canoe-loads of goods."

30 That the portage was along left bank appears from Stuart's subsequent mention (p. 56) of indians leaving the portage and crossing to Columbia's "north side."

31 In substitution for the passage beginning here and ending with the phrase "their hands on," trav. mem. states: "but being too few in number to transport the Canoes and Goods acrofs the carrying place, I was necefsitated to employ the Cathlascos for that purpose, and dispatched M[r] John Reed with 5 men well armed, to guard the first load, but no sooner had they got fairly out of sight than their disposition to plunder became evident, and notwithstanding the men's utmost exertions, the villans carried off two bales of merchandise, with several small articles; and seeing that even this did not provoke the long beards to any hostile measure, they at length became so audacious as to pillage the poor fellows, even of their knives and pocket handkerchiefs; word was soon brought me of these proceedings, and I made all possible expedition to join them (at the Indian village)."

32 This "yesterday," because included in the reminiscent account, related not to the then current month of July, but to the preceding April.

33 Also in the preceding April.

34 "8" in trav. mem.

35 "about 50" in trav. mem.

36 Right bank.

37 Right bank.

38 John Reed, "a rough, warm-hearted, brave old Irishman" (*Cox* [*A*], I, p. 282, [*B*], p. 138), was a clerk of the Pacific Fur Company and had been a

member of Hunt's overland expedition. Immediately after that expedition had been wrecked at "Caldron Linn," Reed, with three men (two of whom presently returned to "Caldron Linn"), had been dispatched by Hunt down Snake River's right bank for purpose of exploration and seeking aid. Falling in with the contingents under Robert McClellan and Donald McKenzie, which had also pushed forward from "Caldron Linn," Reed and his remaining man continued with them to Astoria, where they arrived on January 18, 1812.

On March 22, 1812, Reed began the journey which is now being reminiscently described by Stuart. It was expected to take him from Astoria to New York City; but, because thwarted by indians at the Dalles, it carried him only to the Okanagan River and thence back to Astoria.

On June 29, 1812, he again set out from Astoria, his intent this time being to assist McKenzie in establishing a post at the mouth of the Boise River, and later, not only to salvage the contents of Hunt's caches and transport them to this new post, but also to rescue various Astorians who had dropped from Hunt's column when it was marching west. During his trip to the caches he encountered eight of these wanderers [Jean Baptiste Dubreuil (for whom see note 136 on p. cxxvii as also note 123 on pp. 178, 179), André LaChapelle, François Landry, Jean Baptiste Turcotte (for which three see note 49 on p. 121, as also note 123 on pp. 178, 179), Louis St. Michel, Alexander Carson, Pierre Delaunay (for which three see note 123 on pp. 178, 179), and Edward Robinson] and led all of them, except Robinson, to McKenzie's post. McKenzie, on hearing of the war with Great Britain, cached his goods and with Reed and their men hastened to Astoria, where all arrived on January 15, 1813.

On the following February 2, Reed with McKenzie and others left Astoria upon various missions. These missions were (1) to warn the outlying posts that, because of the war, Astoria was to be abandoned (2) to salvage both the furs already gathered and also the supplies, inclusive of such as had been cached by McKenzie, and (3) to procure horses for the overland journey which was expected to follow the prospective evacuation of Astoria. Reed's part in this expedition took him to the posts of John Clarke and of David Stuart. He seems to have arrived back at Astoria in June, 1813, though *Franchere* [*A*], pp. 126, 127, [*B*], p. 168, states that on March 20 Reed returned from the Willamette River, whither he had conducted some of the engagés in order to obtain better subsistence than that which Astoria could provide.

On July 5, 1813 (*Cox* [*A*], I, p. 212, [*B*], p. 110, erroneously states October 29), Reed, at the head of a small party of hunters and trappers, left Astoria under orders to "pass the winter in the Snake country, collect the stragglers still wandering through that quarter, and at a certain point await the arrival of the main body, and join it on its way across."

The people in this party were stationed, at first, on the Snake's left bank; but, presently crossing this stream, they located themselves, in part, at a cabin which Reed erected at seemingly the mouth of Boise River, and, in other part, at a camp some four or five days' travel from this cabin. In January, 1814, indians attacked both cabin and camp and killed Reed and all of his personnel save only the wife and children of Pierre Dorion. *Ross* [*A*], pp. 217-226, 246, 266, 276-282; *Franchere* [*A*], pp. 126-127, 214-217, [*B*], pp. 168, 273-276; *Astoria*, I, p. 164, II, pp. 10, 26, 30, 31, 46, 74-77, 94-101, 104, 193-197, 203, 206, 254-256; *Cox* [*A*], I, pp. 277-283, [*B*], pp. 136-138; *Henry-Thomp*., pp. 760, 761, 784, 844, 883, 886, 887; Stuart's entry for September 1, (p. 114); J. Neilson Barry's *Fort Reed and Fort Boise* in *Ore. Hist. Soc. Quar*., XXXIV, pp. 60-67.

39 See p. XCI-XCV for McClellan's biography.

40 In substitution for the passage beginning here and ending with "south shore" on p. 58, trav. mem. states: "Hearing the war yell on their first arrival I well knew my presence would be necefsary, and with 8 brave fellows arrived to their assistance at this critical moment, when we found Mr. Reed weltering in his blood, having received five Tomahawk wounds on the head.— notwithstanding our sudden appearance with presented arms not one of them seemed in the least alarmed, nor did they make any disposition to attack us untill I called to the fellow who was mauling Mr. Reed to desist, or he should be shot instantly, this seemed to rouse them all, and some began to advance upon us in a very menacing manner; finding matters had gone this far, and that further forbearance would avail nothing, I formed the men, showing a front two deep, and ordered the most advanced to shoot down the brave (who still continued beating Mr. Reed) this was executed in a twinkling, when we gave a cheer and charged, which so disconcerted our afsailants as to produce an instant and universal flight.— Mr. Reed /who by this time was lying senselefs on the ground,/ we carried to the canoes, which were found too leaky to be put in the water, and the oars were still at the lower end of the portage, this unavoidable detention created much alarm among some of the men, particularly two young fellows who became so terrified as literally to faint away; the moment they recovered their senses, I ordered them to be deprived of their arms, their under clothes taken off and a piece of cloth tied round the waist, in imitation of a squaw, then stowed them away among the goods in one of the canoes, this ludicerous affair, in spite of the perilous situation we were placed in, excited considerable mirth, and seemed to reafsure a few who were rather in a state of wavering between fear & determination:

"The Indians having all crofsed to the other side, induced me to send some men for the oars, while the others were employed in caulking &c. our water craft, which were shortly got ready, when we embarked, and continued our voyage up the south side.—"

41 Russel Farnham, Astorian clerk who had arrived at Astoria in the ship *Tonquin*. In 1814, upon consummation of McDougall's improvident sale of Astoria to the North West Company, Farnham was deputed to deliver to Mr. Astor in New York the original records as also bills of exchange drawn on Montreal for a total of $42,281.50—these bills of exchange, in conjunction with

a draft for $1,483.24 and an assumption of $14,090.17½ alleged indebtedness, representing the net proceeds of the sale. Because the War of 1812 was still in progress, it was thought unwise for Farnham to traverse the United States and risk capture by invading British soldiers. Accordingly, quitting Astoria April 2, 1814, he crossed the Pacific Ocean, walked the breadth of Siberia and of at least eastern Europe, sailed in October, 1816, from Copenhagen for Baltimore, and successfully concluded his mission. Stella M. Drumm's *More About Astorians* in *Ore. Hist. Soc. Quar.*, XXIV, pp. 338-344; *House Doc.*, pp. 12, 16-63 and schedule attached to p. 65; *Henry-Thomp.*, pp. 767, 787, 788, 828, 830, 851, 864, 886, 899.

42 Left bank.

43 "450 men" in trav. mem.

44 "Shooshonie river" in trav. mem., "Chochoni River" of Hunt (p. 305 *infra*). This stream, present-day Deschutes River, empties through Columbia's left bank. The local indians, according to Lewis and Clark, called it "Towornehiooks," "Towarnahiooks," "Towannahiooks," or "Towannahhiooks,"—"meaning the River on which the Snake Indians live" (*L. & C. Journs.*, III, pp. 147-149, IV, pp. 280, 313, 336, 364, 366, VI, p. 66). Coues, in *L. & C. Hist.*, p. 657, varied these spellings into "Towarnehiooks," "Towannehooks" and "To-war-na-he-ooks." Hunt gives the indian name as "Tou-et-Ka" (p. 305 *infra*). Lewis and Clark for a short while styled the stream "Clark's River" in honor of Clark, but soon reverted to the indian names mentioned above (*L. & C. Journs.*, IV, pp. 313-315, 363, 364). It was the "Falls River" and "River of the Falls" of Peter Skene Ogden in 1825, the "river aux Rapide" of Nathaniel J. Wyeth, the "Falls or Shutes" River of Wilkes, the "river De Shoots" of Hines, the "Deschuttes" of Hewitt, the "Riviere des Chutes" of other early travellers, the "Shutes River" of Geo. L. Curry in 1847 (*Journ. Peter Skene Ogden* in *Ore. Hist. Soc. Quar.*, X, pp. 338, 340; *Wyeth, Nathaniel J.*, p. 183; *Wilkes, Narr.*, map of Oregon in accompanying atlas; *Hines*, p. 160; *Hewitt*, p. 52; *McArthur*, p. 106; *Ore. Spec.*, II, No. 16, p. 2, col. 1). For additional variant spellings, see *Symons* [*A*], p. 131. The tradition that its names Falls and Deschutes implied either the stream's nearness to the Dalles of the Columbia or else the stream's having prominent falls is discussed in *McArthur*, pp. 105, 106.

45 Crossing to Columbia's left bank, but whether in canoes or on swimming horses is not disclosed. That it was possible to cross thus on horses is shown by *Journ. John Work* in *Ore. Hist. Soc. Quar.*, X, p. 304.

46 Western colloquialism meaning extremely steep through erosion. For further description of this locality, see *Fremont*, pp. 185, 186.

47 McClellan.

48 "made fast" in trav. mem.

49 See *L. & C. Journs.*, III, pp. 146, 147.

50 "with three of his principal warriors" in trav. mem.

51 "killed one and wounded another" in trav. mem.

52 "already on the verge of the grave" in trav. mem.

53 "a blanket" in trav. mem.

54 This last paragraph beginning "M[r] Reed" was omitted from trav. mem. Here ends the reminiscent account begun in journ., p. 55. See note 27.

55 Establishment at Astoria.

56 The Cascades, thus identified by Stuart's mention of the diminishing quantity of timber.

57 Western colloquialism for isolated, abrupt hills. *Fremont*, p. 161.

58 Five Mile Rapids.

59 Mt. Hood, a majestic, snow-covered peak, altitude 11,225 feet, was discovered, October 29, 1792, by Lieutenant William Robert Broughton, and by him named in honor of Baron, later Viscount, [Samuel] Hood. *McArthur*, pp. 237-239.

60 Canoed along right bank.

61 One of the islands which, lying in the Columbia River and screening the mouth of Deschutes River (*Geol. Oregon*), are described in *L. & C. Journs.*, III, pp. 146, 147; *Fremont*, p. 186; *Cox* [*A*], I, p. 137, [*B*], p. 80; *L. & C. Hist.*, p. 657.

62 "Shooshonie" in trav. mem. See note 44 for this stream, the Deschutes River.

63 That the camp was on Columbia's left bank appears from (a) the immediate context; (b) the next day's entry of "continued our route along the south side," and (c) Ross's statement: "encamped for the night near the spot where Mr. Crooks and John Day had been robbed on their forlorn adventures down the river" (*Ross* [*A*], p. 198). However, *Cox* [*A*], p. 137, [*B*], p. 80, states: "We encamped on the north side opposite the island."

64 "Shooshonie" in trav. mem.

65 *Ross* [*A*], p. 117, makes a like distinction.

66 For this robbery of Ramsay Crooks and John Day, see p. LXXXVIII. When this day's entry was copied from journ. into trav. mem., Stuart incorrectly transposed the phrase "last Spring" from a position immediately after "the party" to one immediately before "when on their way," and thereby created an erroneous statement as to the time of the robbery.

67 In the journ.'s manuscript Stuart, having originally written "down," deleted it; and, in its stead, interlined "St. L."—but in trav. mem. "St. Louis" was written in full.

68 In conflict with this, *Ross* [*A*], p. 198, states: "but after keeping him a prisoner for two days, he was set at liberty."

69 This stream, present-day John Day River, emptying through Columbia's left bank, was styled "Le Page River" by Lewis and Clark, who "gave it the name of Lepage's river from Lepage one of our company"; *i.e.*, John Baptiste Le Page (*alias* Lepage, La Page and Lapage), a French-Canadian who, in November, 1804, at Ft. Mandan, enlisted in Lewis and Clark's expedition

(*L. & C. Journs.*, I, pp. 12, 216, 284, III, p. 144, VI, p. 66; *L. & C. Hist.*, pp. 255, 655). Subsequently the river's name was changed to "John Day" in honor of the Astorian John Day. Peter Skene Ogden, on November 29, 1825, recorded: "We reached John Day's River." *Journ. Peter Skene Ogden* in *Ore. Hist. Soc. Quar.*, X, p. 337.

70 This camp on Columbia's left bank was at the vertex of the river's northerly bend. *Geol. Oregon.*

71 Because of encountering, first, present-day Hellgate Rapid (the "Fishtack Rapid" of Lewis and Clark) and, second, the rapids immediately above and below the spot where the Columbia received the waters of John Day River. *L. & C. Hist.*, pp. 657, 658, 1262; *L. & C. Journs.*, III, pp. 143, 144, VI, p. 66.

72 Incorrectly "45 miles" in trav. mem. The sites of Stuart's camps on this and the following day are unidentifiable save as hereinafter set forth. If *Cox* [*A*], I, p. 142, [*B*], p. 82, be trustworthy, these sites were quite possibly on the Columbia's right bank. Stuart's stated mileages for July 22-24 aggregate 90, whereas Lewis and Clark give, for the same course, a total of 83 (*L. & C. Hist.*, pp. 649, 650, 1261, 1262). A prorating of the daily mileages as stated by Stuart, if read in conjunction with the above-cited pages of *L. & C. Hist.*, would place his two camp sites as follows: July 22, approximately at mouth of present-day Willow Creek, a confluent emptying through Columbia's left bank; July 23, at a spot approximately three miles northeast of mouth of present-day Glade Creek, a confluent emptying through Columbia's right bank. *Geol. Oregon; Geol. Washington; Quad. Arlington; Quad. Blalock Island.*

73 "Umatalla" in trav. mem. This stream, present-day Umatilla River, was the "Youmalolam" of Lewis and Clark and of Hall J. Kelley, the "Euotalla" of Hunt, the "Umatallow" and "You-ma-talla" of Ross, the "Umatallow" of Wyndham Robertson, Jr., and of Abert, the "Yourmatalla" of Rector, the "Ottillah" and "Utalla" of Nathaniel J. Wyeth, the "Utalle" of John Work, the "Utalla, or Emmitilly" of Townsend, the "Utilla" of Hines and of Clyman, the "Unadilla" of Medorem Crawford, the "Umatalla" of Greenhow, the "Umatilah" and "U-mah-ti-lah" of Fremont, the "Um-a-til-a" of Lee and Frost, the "Umatilla" of Hastings and of Leonard (*L. & C. Journs.*, IV, p. 336; *L. & C. Hist.*, p. 970; *Kelley*, p. 37; p. 303 *infra; Ross* [*A*], pp. 125, 130, [*C*], I, p. 186; *Robertson*, map; *Abert; Railroad Survey*, XI, map facing p. 23; *Wyeth, Nathaniel J.*, pp. 173, 232; *Work*, p. 74; *Townsend*, pp. 152, 245; *Hines*, p. 163; *Clyman*, pp. 105, 106; *Crawford*, p. 21; *Greenhow*, p. 19; *Fremont*, p. 179; *Fremont* [*A*], accompanying map; *Lee and Frost*, p. 123; *Hastings* [*A*], [*B*], p. 29; *Leonard*, p. 48). For additional early variant spellings, see *L. & C. Hist.*, p. 970; *McArthur*, p. 364; *Symons* [*A*], p. 132. The name, an indian one, is said to mean "water rippling over sand." *McArthur*, p. 364.

74 Camped on Columbia's right bank.

75 Incorrectly "26 miles" in trav. mem.

76 In the journ.'s manuscript, not only is "2[d]" interlined above this word

"takes" and also "1st" interlined above the "is," the fifteenth word following it; but also the "&" immediately preceding that "is" seems to have been inserted after the original writing had been completed. The transposition of clauses suggested by the above inserted numerals was made by Stuart in the trav. mem.

77 Present-day Blue Mountains, which, lying in southeastern Washington and northeastern Oregon, were described without name by Lewis and Clark (*L. & C. Journs.*, III, pp. 116, 117, 122, 125, IV, pp. 336, 338; *L. & C. Hist.*, pp. 642, 975, 978, 982, 983). David Thompson referred to them on July 8, 1811, as the "Shawpatin Mountains," but a month later he noted: "Beginning of course see the Blue Mountains"; this latter being possibly the earliest known mention of the mountains by their present-day name (*Journ. David Thompson* in *Ore. Hist. Soc. Quar.*, XV, pp. 56, 121). "From their colour the Canadians called this chain Les Montagnes Bleues," according to *Cox* [*A*], I, p. 146, [*B*], p. 84; and likewise *Hines*, p. 223, writes of " . . . that range which, from its azure-like appearance, has been called the 'Blue Mountains'."

78 "with Beaver" in trav. mem.

79 This village (where Stuart camped on the 25th and 26th), if on the Columbia's right bank, was at approximately the site of the present-day town of Mottinger, Benton County, Wash. And the village doubtless was on the right bank because Stuart, having camped on that bank on the 24th, was also to camp on it on the 27th (see note 85; as also *Geol. Washington; Cox* [*A*], I, p. 139, [*B*], pp. 81, 82; *L. & C. Journs.*, VIII, map 31, pt. II). However, with palpable error, *Cox* [*A*], I, p. 139, [*B*], p. 81, dates the arrival at this village as July 14; and thus, not only disagrees with Stuart's date of July 25, but also implies that the expedition spent merely one day, instead of Stuart's seven days, in travelling hither from the vicinity of the island which, near the mouth of Deschutes River, was 116 miles away. As a result and also because Cox agrees with Stuart that the date of reaching their camp at the Walla Walla's mouth was July 28, Cox latently requires the expedition to consume 14 days, instead of Stuart's 2 days, in paddling the 19 miles between the indian village and that camp. *Cox* [*A*], I, pp. 139-144, [*B*], pp. 81-83.

80 One or more of these nine horses may have been killed and eaten. See *Cox* [*A*], I, pp. 139-142, [*B*], pp. 81, 82.

81 See note 103 on p. 25 for ichthyologic identity of these lampreys.

82 *Mylochilus caurinus*. *L. & C. Hist.*, p. 970; *L. & C. Journs.*, IV, pp. 326, 327.

83 Celilo Falls.

84 This stream, present-day Walla Walla River, emptying through Columbia's left bank, was the "Wallah lahlah," "Wallah Wollah," "Wollah Wollah," "Wallow Wallow," "Wallah Waller," "Wallah Wallah," "Woller Woller," &c., of Lewis and Clark, the "Oualla-Oualla" of Hunt, the "Wille Wah" of Robinson, the "Wallhalla" of Gilliam, the "Walahwalah" of Fremont (*L. & C. Journs.*, IV, pp. 323-349, VI, p. 115; *L. & C. Hist.*, p. 969; p. 303 *infra;*

Robinson; Gilliam, map of Oregon, &c., opposite p. 371; *Fremont*, p. 183). For additional variant spellings of the name—which, of indian origin, meant "small, rapid stream"—see *McArthur*, p. 373; *L. & C. Hist.*, p. 969.

85 On Columbia's right bank, Stuart crossing to the left bank on the following day.

86 "60 yards" in trav. mem.

87 "Umatalla" in trav. mem. The headwaters of the two streams rose in the same general locality.

88 In copying this sentence into trav. mem. Stuart omitted the phrase "the School of Villainy or" and thereby left the sentence in the form quoted in *Astoria*, I, p. 110.

89 A like dance had been given for Lewis and Clark when they camped here on April 28, 1806. *L. & C. Hist.*, pp. 972-974; *L. & C. Journs.*, IV, pp. 331-334.

90 "procured 4 more horses" in trav. mem.

91 "15" in trav. mem.; *Mo. Gaz.; Niles*, p. 265; *Bradbury* [*A*], p. 223, [*B*], p. 236; *Brackenridge*, p. 297. But *Cox* [*A*], I, p. 144, [*B*], p. 83 and *Astoria*, II, p. 117, state "twenty." Eleven horses had previously been acquired, though one or more of these may have been killed and eaten. See entries for July 25 and 27, as also *Cox* [*A*], I, pp. 139-142, [*B*], pp. 81, 82. *Astoria*, II, p. 117, adds a description of a horse which Stuart is said to have purchased for his own use, and at p. 124 asserts that Stuart intended to take this animal to New York and to present it to Astor.

92 Crossed from right to left bank and thus to the mouth of Walla Walla River, which Stuart had passed on July 27 though he did not then halt there. Although *Cox* [*A*], I, p. 144, [*B*], pp. 82, 83, agrees with Stuart that the date of this camping at the mouth of the Walla Walla was July 28, *Ross* [*A*], p. 199, gives July 29.

93 "the Walla-Walla" in trav. mem. Stuart's camp at its mouth was on its right bank because he states that, two days later, he crossed to the left bank.

94 Donald McKenzie journeying toward his then as yet unbuilt post on Snake River at the mouth of Boise River. *Henry-Thomp.*, pp. 760, 761; *Ross* [*A*], p. 194 and map. See also note 138 on pp. 99, 100 *infra*.

95 David Stuart bound for present-day Okanagan River. *Ross* [*A*], p. 194.

96 John Clarke heading for present-day Spokane River. *Ross* [*A*], p. 194.

97 Lowermost reach of present-day Snake River.

CHAPTER IV

JULY 31 · AUG. 20, 1812

On Horseback from Walla Walla River to Mouth of Vinson Wash

[SEE MAP FACING PAGE 3]

Leave Mouth of Walla Walla · Site of Present-Day Pendleton · Grande Ronde River · Hot Lake · Burnt River · Along Left Bank of Snake River · Hunt's Route · Tidings of Wandering Whites · Meet Indian Who Had Guided Hunt Over Teton Pass · He Tells of South Pass · Steals Stuart's Horse · Arrival at Mouth of Vinson Wash · Find Robinson, Hoback, Reznor and Miller.

Friday 31st We had breakfasted and were with everything[1] acrofs[2] the Walla Walla River by 9 A.M.[3] where bidding [*probably a last*] adieu to our friends,[4] we soon after ascended the Hills,[5] and steered a SSE course— the day was hot in the extreme, with just wind [31] enough to raise the sand on the Knobs[6] sufficiently to produce an almost suffocating effect— We travelled on without making any thing like a halt till sunsett, over Hills for the most part of moderate height whose composition was of Sand and brittle clay in nearly equal proportions, without the least appearance of having experienced any share of the dews of heaven since the time of Noahs Flood—[7] Toward dusk the Ravines became lefs deep, [*and the country gently undulating*,] but the shallow drains[8] still bent their way to the Columbia— Already had a fine young dog (our only companion of the kind) given up for want of water, and Le Clairc[9] to preserve respiration drank his own Urine,[10] when despairing of finding a brook, we began to talk of stopping for the night— Searching a little farther on, for an eligible situation we discovered by the faint remains of daylight, at a great distance ahead something like a wood,[11] in the vicinity of which we were confident of getting a supply of that element we so much wanted—

A pace of the speedy Kind took place of our common one and at a late hour we reached the Umattulla[12] near a Ripple, which the Horses (I suppose) hearing, rushed forward to immediately, drank immoderately and went to the other side,[13] where a Gravel Beach being the first dry spot near, we took up our quarters[14] on it for the night, having come this day at least 45 miles—

[32] Saturday 1st August 1812— In consequence of our long & laborious ride yesterday the Sun had gained considerable strength, before any one seemed inclined to quit his rocky couch, and it was nearly 8 oClock before we set out— The River[15] is here about 60 yds wide, full of small rapids, but too shallow to afford an asylum for [*any of*] the Finny Race— the Bottoms are from 3 to 600[16] paces broad, well covered with Cottonwood poſseſs [*a good*] many Swamps & Ponds in which reside a great multitude of Beaver—

We continued up this stream 3 miles,[17] when pursuing the same course as yesterday[18] over a level Plain[19] we at the end of 20 more got on another Fork,[20] wooded in the similar manner, but except in holes totally destitute of water and encamped on the north side[21]

Sunday 2nd Before sunrise our Horses were loaded and we proceeded 5 Miles up the Fork in an Easterly direction,[22] to where it divides into 2 branches—[23] then took that from the South for 6 Miles to its final separation into small brooks;[24] thence 6 more up the Mountain still going towards the midday Sun,[25] then taking a dividing ridge,[26] we went SE 8 more and halted at 4 P.M. on a Branch[27] of the Glaise River[28]

These mountains[29] are the South East boundary of the Columbian Plains and divide the waters of the main River[30] from those of Lewis's[31] in this quarter—

[33] Monday 3d. The Sun appeared with unusual splendor in the East, just as we had regained our tract— The road was over very high Hills[32] intersected by deep ravines[33] for 4 Miles due E. thence decending into the short drains of the Branch[34] where we lay last night— We next made 9 SSE to a considerable Fork[35] of the Glaise[36] then following that 3 more between Rocks and Bluffs encamped at 1 P.M. opposite a Creek[37] coming in from the South which rather exceeds in magnitude the one we descended—

Tuesday 4th— Not long after daylight we continued down the Creek[38] till 9 A.M. when finding a deep Hole with some Salmon in it, we halted 4 hours and Speared seven— Proceeded on again at 1 P.M. through a most enchanting tract (for a few miles) where the gloomy heavy timbered Mountains subside into beautifull Hills, chequered with delightfull pasture ground, which when added to the [*numerous*] Rivulets murmuring over their gravely serpentine beds toward the glade below, afford a scene truly romantic and such as is seldom to be met with in these regions [*of solitude and gloom*]— We soon after entered on a similar road to that of this morning & stopped at sunsett on the left bank—[39] 20 miles[40] was the extent of this days march two branches[41] came in on each side of the Creek, which is extremely crooked altho' the general course is about North East—

Wednesday 5th The sun had made his appearance above the Cliffs when we left our last nights station— the road was rugged in the extreme and the proximity of the Mountains obliged us frequently to crofs the River, a businefs our Horses are [34] by no means fond of

We went on but slowly and at the end of 12 Miles[42] extricated ourselves from among Rocks & Precipices[43] to enter the Big Flat,[44]

where (on account of having broke several saddles) we encamped on the right bank about 1 Mile below the narrows,[45] in the evening shot a Salmon[46] an a Beaver—

Thursday 6th The men were busily employed yesterday afternoon and [*all*] today making & mending Saddles, which are at last completed, & will enable us to sett out early in the morning

Friday 7th It was 6 A.M. before our Horses were collected & loaded— our route lay along the mountains[47] on the South side of Big Flat, for 11 Miles, then winding to the East for 9 more came to a Gap,[48] out of which ifsued a small Branch[49] where we encamped for the night— about seven miles from this place to the Westward,[50] and close to the Hills is a Sulphur Lake[51] 300 yards in circumference, fed by a Spring in the S.E. corner which appeared nearly 10 feet square, and as greatly agitated as if boiling— at a short distance the vapour was excefsively noisome, and for 500 Paces[52] round, the olfactory nerves were sensibly affected thereby— It is much frequented by Elk which animal is tolerably plenty in the adjacent mountains and it would appear from their numerous Horns, strewed every where round the margin of the Pond, that they visit it mostly in the Spring[53] of the Year— Continuing[54] a few [35] miles farther through the Plain a large Creek[55] comes from the S.E. and nearly opposite its mouth another[56] from the West, both of which join the Glaise River[57] a little way above its reentrance into the Narrows,[58] where it is upwards of a hundred yards wide—

This Flat[59] is at least 60 Miles in circumference, in but few places swampy, of an excellent soil and almost a dead level with the Glaise and its 2 Branches just mentioned meandering in every direction through it— the banks of these streams are high and muddy, covered in particular Spots with dwarf Cottonwood, & the residue in a large and thick growth of Willows which afford an inexhaustible stock of Food for the incredible multitudes of the Furred race who reside in their bosoms, but the S.E. Fork[60] excells both the others in the number of its inhabitants of the Otter Tribe.

a few Deer and Racoons[61] are the only animals you may add to the Elk, Beaver & otter as being natives of this Tract

The River[57] at the extremity[62] of this Prairie is very deep, but it there enters a range of mountains[63] much superior in size to those through which we decended along its border

—It falls into the Snake or Kimooenem[64] River about 30 miles above its junction with the Pasheecone,[65] and is called by the aborigines at its mouth Kooskooske[66]

[36] Saturday 8th Sett out late and continued up the branch[67] for 8 Miles E.S.E.[68] then 6 S.S.E.[69] to the Westerly bend of a large Creek[70] but whether it is the S.E. Fork[71] of the Glaise or a tributary stream of Kimooenem am unable to say— Having gone 9 Miles up this through a high Prairie & crofsed 2 considerable branches,[72] proceeding out of the mountains[73] which bound this Plain[74] to the South, encamped[75] on the bank of the River some time before sunsett

Sunday 9th Our course today was about South through the Prairie and along the same Stream as yesterday 20 miles[76] to where it ifsues from the Mountains which are the highest in this quarter and run from E.S.E. to W.N.W.—[77] at its entrance[78] into this Pile it is about 20 yards wide, the banks are everywhere [*very*] well supplied with Willows, and a good many Beaver, but the soil is very indifferent—

Monday 10th This days march was in all 24 Miles[79] 14 of which were in a S.E. direction up a small branch[80] and over the dividing ridge[81] which is composed of low sandy Hills to a Fork[82] of Wood Pile Creek[83] then 10[84] down that E.S.E.—[85] when near the height of Land[86] we saw no lefs than 19 Antelopes[87] a sight so uncommon in this country that we in some measure for a considerable time doubted the evidence of our senses We tried all possible means to get a shot at some of them, but they were so exceedingly shy as to avoid our every endeavour at an [*near*] approach— This animal is already too well described by several naturalists for me to attempt any addition on that head—

[37] Tuesday 11th Continued down the Branch[88] 4 Miles, which leaving,[89] were in 4 more on the main body of the Creek[90] which we followed for 6 m[91] where the bottoms became large & of a gravelly soil,[92] with a great many Cottonwood and Willow[93] 3 miles through the Hills was the next part of our tract to a small Northerly Rivulet,[94] 1½[95] along that to the River again, and then 4½ to a bend where we crofsed and encamped[96], having come in all 23 Miles[97] S.E.

Wednesday 12th In The first part of this mornings march the Hills came very close to the Creek[98] on both sides, which made the road [*very*] Stoney & bad[99]

The stream[98] is still about 30 yds wide, abundantly furnished with Willows, and contains some Beaver—[100] Having followed it 15 Miles[101] S.E. came to an Indian Fishing Place where the Creek[98] making a short turn[102] to the north, we quitted[103] it & in 5 Miles[104] reached the Snake River, proceeding up which 3 more brought us to our station for the night[105]

This River is here about 400 yards in breadth, has [*high*] sandy banks little or no Willow & a rapid current— It is the main branch of the right hand Fork of Lewis's River, called by Lewis & Clarke Kimooenem, by some Indians Ki-eye-nim[106] by the Snakes Biopaw[107] and by the generality of Whites the Snake River[108]

Immediately below this it enters the Mountains,[109] which become gradually higher to the end of 150 miles where the whole body of the River does not exceed 40 yards in [38] width and is confined between Precipices of astonishing height, Cascades &

Rapids succeed each other almost without intermiſsion, and it will give a tolerable idea of its appearance were you to suppose the River to have once flowed subterraneously through these mountains, and that in proceſs of time, immense bodies of Rock were detached occasionally from the ceiling till at length the surface of the Heights decended into the Gulph and forms at present the bed of this tumultuous water course.

Mountain here appears as if piled on Mountain and after ascending inceſsantly for half a day, you seem as if no nearer the attainment of the object in view than at the outset—

From the accounts of Meſs^rs Mackenzie & Mc Clellan[110] this kind of country continues for near 300 miles by the meanders of the River which is very crooked— their tract last winter[111] was as near the bank as poſsible, but were often compelled to leave it by the intervention of impervious maſses of Rocks— they were in all 12 persons, took 21 days [*constant travelling*] to the Mulpat River[112] and subsisted during that time [39] on an allowance by no means proportionate to the bodily labour they daily underwent— [*being no more than two Ibex and 5 Beaver; the skins of which they preserved and subsisted on for the last 5 days; the best, and indeed only method of dreſsing those skins is, first to singe them well, after which, they must be boiled for several hours, then cut into small pieces so as to be fit for bolting or gulping, which is a well known practice among the York shire Men in feeding on fat pork—*] Meſs^rs Hunt & Crooks with 39 men[113] Subsequently attempted a paſsage[114] through these narrows in December, but the snow was too deep and the Country being entirely destitute of Game, they were compelled to relinquish their undertaking after the former having penetrated 120 miles and the latter /with 18 men /[115] 30 farther

They returned, and ascending Wood Pile[116] Creek, went to the Umatulla[117] by the route we have now come[118] where they found the Sciatogas,[119] [*and got relief*] This Nation [*is about 250 strong, and possess that tract of country, bounded on the Southeast by the Big flat,*[120] *on the North*[121] *by Lewis' river, on the West*[122] *by the Columbia, and on the south*[123] *by the Walamat, comprising an extenı of nearly 100 miles square, intersected by many handsome streams, which are well stocked with those animals we have come so far in quest of.— but untill now, the natives having had little inducement to diminish their numbers, they remained in undisturbed possession of their native soil.—*

This tribe as well as the Flatheads (who are reputed to be excellent Indians, about 1,800 warriors and inhabit that tract of country situate between Lewis' River and the northwest branch, or main Columbia, bounded in the rear by the rocky mountains,) own immense numbers of horses, a great proportion of which run wild in these boundlefs plains; and are often the red and white man's only dependance for food— These two nations are lefs thievish, and much more cleanly, than any of their neighbours; but they are of a haughty and imperious disposition, very impatient of insult, and revengeful in the extreme; however by proper treatment, they might be rendered the best and most useful division on this side the mountains.—]

Thursday 13th Continued up the South Side of the River in an E.S.E direction 18 miles[124] and encamped[125] an Indian came to our Camp [*late in the evening*] with the grateful tidings of two white men being with his people [*about*] a days march above

Friday 14th The River makes a turn at almost right angles,— We went in 20 miles to a Creek[126] 50 yards wide with numerous Willows & Beaver [*along its banks*], crofsed it and at the end of 6 more S.S.E. stopped[127] for the night— The Bottoms during this days march were [*very*] extensive, covered principally with Saltwood[128] except near the River where there are some willows [*but*] in high water[129] they overflow so much as to render them a perfect Swamp,

The Hills are low, of a sandy Soil and like the high bottoms, the same shrub predominates—

[40] Saturday 15th Proceeding on due South we struck the

bends[130] of the River from time to time, till having come 15 Miles[131] we found a Creek[132] 70 yards wide in everything resembling the one[133] paſsed yesterday, where we found 10 lodges of Shoshonies [*or Snakes*]— These people giving us to understand that some whites were on the other side of the River we encamped[134] in the neighbourhood of their huts, and dispatched an Indian in quest of the men we had heard of, supposing them to be either those left by Mr Crooks in the winter[135] or the Hunters who remained in the Rocky Mountains last Fall[136]—

Opposite[137] our present station a large River[138] comes in from the East, is well Timbered, contains many Beaver, and is the most renowned Fishing place in this Country It is consequently the resort of the majority of the Snakes,[139] where immense[140] numbers of Salmon are taken, forming after the [*esculent*] Roots,[141] the principal article of food which the natives of this Barren Tract poſseſs—

28 miles below is another large Creek,[142] and 16 still lower down is Wisers River,[143] a Stream 60 yards wide; well stocked with small wood & Beaver, in which it strikingly resembles the former [41] course[144] Last night the musquitoes aſsailed us in innumerable hosts, and completely deprived our eyelids of their usual functions, even after the dew had fallen those infernal Pests Still continued their music to our no small annoyance

Sunday 16th Finding our information regarding the people[145] incorrect, we croſsed the Creek[146] early in the morning and sometime after were overtaken by the Indian who[147] guided the Party over the Mad River Mountain last Fall—[148] He said that he parted ten nights ago with 3 of our Hunters, who had caught a great many Beaver, but that the Absarokas [/*Crow Indians*/] had discovered the place where this hunt was conſealed and carried off every thing—

That the others had lost their Horses & were stripped by the same nation with whom they at present were— the three whom he lately saw were on their way down, had only a horse each, & but one Gun[149] among the them their names he said are Alexis, Michel & Makan[150]

Hearing that there is a shorter trace[151] to the South [42] than that by which Mr Hunt had traversed the R Mountains,[152] and learning that this Indian was perfectly acquainted with the route, I without loſs of time offered him a Pistol a Blanket of Blue Cloth —an Axe—a Knife—an awl—a Fathom [*of blue*] Beads a looking Glaſs and a little Powder & Ball if he would guide us from this to the other side,[153] which he immediately accepted, saying that the Salmon were not as good as La Vache ([*which signifies*] Buffaloes) and returned to the Wooded River[154] for his arms &c promising to rejoin us tomorrow [*morning*]— We went 10 miles South[155] and 10 more[156] turning gradually to North East where we encamped—[157]

Monday 17th The Flies & musquitoes tormented our Horses greatly over night which caused them to ramble to a considerable distance which made it late before they were collected and loaded— about 4 miles from camp we met our Guide who had croſsed the River yesterday evening and slept some distance above, went 5 more where the Indian said the nearest road was acroſs the Hills, but as it would take nearly a day to reach [43] the River again advised our encamping[158] having come no more than 9 miles in about an east course

Tuesday 18th We arose with the dawn but our Guide was miſsing and on collecting our Horses found the Indians and mine were gone—[159] From his former good conduct we had not the least suspicion that he should attempt committing an act of this nature, but following the tracts for some time,[160] were convinced of his being the perpetrator, as they made towards the water a few miles above our Camp, and croſsed to the opposite side—

the margin of the stream 12 miles South East to the first perpendicular Bluffs on this side — these coming too near the waters edge to afford a passage for our horses we went up a Ravine 6 miles due South, then ascending the hills and steering S.E. over a level Plain in 8 more struck a Bend of the River where we took up our Encampment —

Concluding from our lesson of yesterday morning that no dependence could be placed in the Indians, notwithstanding their uniform good behaviour, and the praises lavished on them for rectitude and integrity & conduct by all the Whites who have travelled through the Country they inhabit, We determined to keep a constant guard during the remainder of this voyage — the night to be divided into three watches, & one person to stand at a time — In the vicinity of our Camp is a Lodge of Shoshonees so miserably poor — that they could not furnish us even with a fish —

Thursday 20th. we went East by South 12 miles across the Bends when going to drink we found John Hoback fishing and in an instant Mr Miller Edward Robinson & Jacob Regnor who had been similarly employed came out of the Willows & joined us — They had on leaving the Party at Henrys Fort last Fall, gone 200 miles South, where they made that season's hunt on a River which must discharge itself into the Ocean to the southward of the Columbia — From thence they steered

A PAGE OF STUART'S JOURNAL

We went 20 Miles[161] south East, over the same kind of ground as we have paſsed for the last four days—[162]

Wednesday 19th The exceſsive heat that has prevailed since we left Wood Pile Creek[163] is very much diminished and the [*suffocating*] Sultry nights have become agreeably cool, in consequence of which our Musquitoe Serenades are so irregular that it is only now & then we hear the song of some solitary Warbler— The cause of this decrease in our nocturnal Tormentors is owing to the nearly total disappearance of the River Bottoms, for the Hills are in the neighbourhood, and the declivities serve as its banks—[164] Our relief from such torment, has not been of long duration, for another nearly allied in blood to the former, aſsails us vigorously[165] in innumerable hordes for the greater part of the day— so that the Sand Flies[166] these Champions of light may verily be paired with the Imps of Darkneſs— our route today was mostly along [44] the margin of the stream[167] 12 Miles South East to the first perpendicular Bluffs[168] on this side— these coming too near the waters edge to afford a paſsage for our Horses we went up a Drain[169] 6 miles due South—[170] then ascending the Hills and steering S.E over a level Plain in 18 more struck a Bend of the River where we took up our lodgings—[171]

Concluding from our leſson of yesterday morning that no dependance could be placed in the Indians, notwithstanding their uniform good behaviour, and the praises lavished on them for rectitude and integrity of conduct by all the Whites[172] who have travelled through this Country they inhabit; We determined to keep a constant Guard during the remainder of this voyage— the night to be divided into three Watches, & one person to stand at a time— In the vicinity of our Camp is a Lodge of Shoshonies so miserably poor that they could not furnish us even with a fish—

Thursday 20th went East by South 12 Miles acroſs two Bends[173] where going to drink we found John Hobough[174] fishing and in an instant Mr Miller Edward Robinson & Jacob Reznor who had been similarly employed came out of the Willows & joined us— They had on leaving the Party at Henry's Fort last Fall, gone 200 Miles[175] South, where they made that season's Hunt on a River[176] which must discharge itself into the Ocean to the Southard of the Columbia— From thence they steered [45] 200 more[177] due East where they found about Sixty lodges of Arapahays [*who are an out law'd band of the Arapahoes*], who robbed them [*of several horses as well as the greater part of their clothing &c.*]— they then left them & continued their journey 50 miles,[178] where they wintered, and early in the Spring were overtaken by the same Rascals, [*who then*] robbed [*them*] of all[179] their Horses & almost every thing else— They [*with half of the ammunition left*] purchased of them two of their own Horses and after travelling about 950 miles in which they suffered greatly by Hunger, thirst & fatigue, met us [*almost in a state of nature*] without even a single animal to carry their Baggage— Caſs[180] one of their party, having villainously left them with one of the Horses [*while*] on [*the head waters of*] the Big Horn,[181] and the other was stolen by some[182] Indians on this side of the Rocky Mountains— For the greater part of their route, scarcely either quadruped or Bird came within reach of their Guns, and the Inhabitants of the Waters were their only means [*of*] subsistence during this long and tedious journey— they say that all the [*southern*] water courses they have visited are abundantly stocked with Beaver of the largest size & best quality they have ever seen[183] [*particularly in the vicinage of the mountains— All*[184] *the unknown Indians they became acquainted with, during their perambulation in that quarter, are a southern band of Snakes,*[185] *the Arapahays, who may probably muster 350 warriors—*[186] *the Arapahoes, 2,700,*[187] *and the Black Arms,*[188] *about 3,000 strong, the two latter nations are generally at enmity with each other, but are very friendly to the whites, and poſsess the best beaver country on this side the mountains— particularly the latter, whose territories extend to the neighbourhood of the spainards—*

After[189] *regaling our half famished friends with the best our small pittance of luxuries could afford; we proceeded along the banks of the river, for 3 miles,*[190] *to a good fishing and grazing place, where we took up our lodgings for the night—*[174]]

Notes to Chapter IV

1 "with our horses &c." in trav. mem.

2 Crossed from right to left bank.

3 "7 A.M." in trav. mem.

4 Though *Ross* [*A*], p. 199, and Stuart agree on July 31 as the date of departure, *Cox* [*A*], I, p. 144, [*B*], p. 83, gives it as July 30.

5 The hills in this immediate locality rose from 700 to 1400 feet above the plain. *Quad. Wallula.*

6 Western colloquialism for isolated, abrupt hills.

7 For a like description of this arid section, see *Fremont*, pp. 182, 183.

8 The heads of a series of canyons now respectively known as Missouri Gulch, Despain Gulch and Stage Gulch. Earlier in the day Stuart had crossed successively a series of canyons, *i.e.*, present-day Juniper Canyon and the several branches of present-day Cold Springs Canyon. *Geol. Oregon; Quad. Umatilla; McArthur*, p. 106.

9 "Leclairc" in trav. mem.

10 Various engagés had done likewise in the course of Hunt's march. *Astoria*, II, p. 38; *Nouvelles Annales*, X, p. 61, translated at p. 295 *infra*.

11 Trees fringing the Umatilla River's stretch, which, beginning at present westerly boundary of city of Pendleton, extended approximately two miles downstream and, because unscreened by high bluffs such as flanked the river elsewhere in this neighborhood, was observable from the northward. The natural avenue which Stuart was descending would lead him direct to the Umatilla's right bank at a spot one and one-half miles below Pendleton's present westerly city limits. Down this avenue and to that same spot ran an indian trail from the Walla Walla River, as also did in subsequent years the Oregon Trail's spur from Waiilatpu.

12 "Umatalla" in trav. mem.

13 To left bank.

14 Camp was on left bank opposite the point of initial contact described in note 11.

15 Umatilla.

16 "4 to 600" in trav. mem.

17 Through the swampy lands mentioned in Stuart's preceding paragraph and which, as later drained, lie in part within the present-day city limits of Pendleton. The end of Stuart's "3 miles" placed him on the bank of the Umatilla at a spot which was approximately on what is now the western boundary line of the Umatilla Indian Reservation and one mile east from the city limits of Pendleton. Here the bench south of the river was lower and the slope of the

hills less steep than at any other place encountered since reaching the Umatilla; and accordingly he here quitted the river and resumed his southing.

18 Approximately South-Southeast.

19 Known today as the Tutuilla Flats. It is a plain gradually ascending toward the south and at its southerly end the hills break away in deep canyons that drain toward the westerly flowing stretch of present-day McKay Creek. For the word Tutuilla, *McArthur*, pp. 361, 362, offers, with a warning, two possible derivations—an indian word of undetermined meaning or, instead, a white child's prattling invention perpetuated through the sentiment of elders.

20 McKay Creek (named for Doctor William McKay, son of the Astorian clerk, Thomas McKay; see *McArthur*, p. 219), which, rising southeasterly of Pendleton and flowing first northwesterly, next westerly, and again northwesterly, empties through the left bank of the Umatilla at a spot some two miles west of Pendleton (*Geol. Oregon*). Incidentally, *Symons* [*B*] designates as McKay's Creek only that portion of the stream which lies above the confluence of its own north and south forks, and applies the name Stewart Creek to all of the stream below these forks.

21 Camped on right bank of McKay Creek at apparently mouth of so-called Sumac Gulch, one of the canyons descending from Tutuilla Flats (see note 19) and having its mouth some three and one-half miles below the junction of the north and south forks of McKay Creek. Throughout the length of this gulch there has run until at least very recently an indian trail of patently great age. The terrain is such that it is well-nigh certain that Stuart reached McKay Creek by descending Sumac Gulch.

22 Ascending McKay Creek's westerly flowing stretch described in note 20. *Geol. Oregon.*

23 McKay Creek's north and south forks, which met at site of present-day town of McKay. *Geol. Oregon.*

24 Stuart, ascending the south fork of McKay Creek, encountered three small tributaries: the first two (present-day Seven Mile Creek and Wood Hollow Creek) emptying through left bank of the south fork of McKay Creek, and the third (present-day Rail Creek) emptying through its right bank at a spot immediately above Wood Hollow Creek's mouth. See *Geol. Oregon* for some of these details.

25 Stuart, after reaching the confluence (described in note 24) of Wood Hollow Creek with south fork of McKay Creek, doubtless pursued an indian trail which—today ancient, still visible and in places worn to a depth of three feet—ascended from that confluence to the summit of the ridge at the eastward. Approximately six miles of travel along this ridge would put him atop his "dividing ridge" and at a spot near what is now known as Box Spring.

26 The ridge described in note 25 and now topped by an old road which, known as Rocky Ridge Road, leads southeasterly from the town of Pilot Rock to the Grande Ronde River.

27 Present-day McCoy (*alias* Ensign) Creek, though some of the few people now dwelling in its vicinity style it "Meadow Brook" despite the fact that the name "Meadow Creek" is borne by another and nearby stream. McCoy Creek was, as described in note 28, a confluent of present-day Starkey Creek, which, in its turn, was a confluent of Grande Ronde River (*Geol. Oregon*). Stuart's camp was at head of McCoy Creek at a spot near what is today known as the McKenzie Sheep Corrals.

28 Present-day Grande Ronde River. It was the "Willewah" of Lewis and Clark—whose entire knowledge of its name and existence was derived from the indians—the "Grande Rond" of Lowell, of Sage and of Thom, the "Grande Rond" of Colton, the "Grande Ronde" of Mitchell (*L. & C. Journs.*, III, p. 104; VI, p. 115; *L. & C. Hist.*, p. 1255; *Lowell*, accompanying map; *Sage*, accompanying map; *Thom; Colton* [*F*]; *Mitchell*). For variant spellings of the name, see *McArthur*, pp. 146, 147.

Because *Glaise*, the journ.'s appellation for the stream, was the French word for "clay" (trav. mem. in this and all its subsequent mentionings, uses *glaize*, which is the Canadian habitants' spelling), it is interesting to find that Peter Skene Ogden, on September 14, 1827, made note: "Reached Clay River or River de Grande Ronde." However, Washington Irving, in his *The Rocky Mountains*, wrote of "the Fourche de glace or Ice river, sometimes called the Grand Rond." Did not Irving, when examining his source material (*i. e.*, Captain Bonneville's manuscript narrative), misread a possible *glaise* into *glace?* (*Journ. Peter Skene Ogden* in *Ore. Hist. Soc. Quar.*, XI, p. 361; *Irving*, II, p. 195.)

In order that Stuart's geographical allusions in various of his subsequent entries may be clearly understood, it is necessary to consider certain details. Southwest of and parallel with McCoy Creek, mentioned in note 27, was a larger stream, present-day Starkey (*alias* Meadow) Creek [the name Starkey, according to *McArthur*, p. 335, in honor of a pioneer homesteader, Fred Starkey], which, after flowing southeasterly, turned northeasterly, received the waters of McCoy Creek and, within the next one and one-half miles, not only acquired the waters of a northern confluent (present-day Dark Canyon Creek), but also arrived at the junction with yet another watercourse, this last one coming from the south. Incidentally, this last-mentioned stream from the south, styled in bygone days Marion Creek, has recently been thought by some cartographers to be the uppermost reach of the main stem of the Grande Ronde River; and accordingly, on various maps, it bears this river's name. From the above described junction of Starkey Creek and erstwhile Marion Creek, the thus composite stream (today for its entire subsequent length styled Grande Ronde River; but, in earlier times, continuing as "Starkey Creek" for so much of its course as lay above the confluence with present-day Catherine Creek) flowed by serpentine route to the site of Stuart's camp of August 4, receiving, on the way, the waters of one northern confluent (present-day Spring Creek) and of four southern confluents (present-day Beaver, Jordan, Whiskey and Rock

Creeks). *Geol. Oregon; Symons* [*B*]. After passing the site of Stuart's camp, the stream maintained its meandering until it emptied into the Snake.

29 Blue Mountains.

30 Columbia.

31 An early name for the lowermost reach of Snake River.

32 Their summits varying from 750 to 1,000 feet above the mean level of the neighboring valleys.

33 Not canyons with vertical walls, but instead narrow valleys between very steep hillsides.

34 Stuart thus had left the bank of McCoy Creek; but, by traversing the "very high Hills," he had taken a short-cut across the bases of some of the bends of that sinuous creek and presently was to regain its bank at a spot further downstream.

35 This still was McCoy Creek, Stuart's seeming failure to recognize its identity being due possibly to its sinuosity and to its increase in size since he had quitted its bank further upstream.

36 Grande Ronde River.

37 Starkey (*alias* Meadow) Creek, for which see note 28. Camp was on left bank of McCoy Creek at the spot where this creek flowed into Starkey Creek (*Geol. Oregon*). Any thought that the camp (which Stuart states was at a confluence) was one and one-half miles further along Stuart's route and thus at the junction of Starkey Creek with the Grande Ronde is negatived by his subsequent comment to which note 41 relates.

38 The route "down the Creek" was along the left bank of Starkey Creek for one and one-half miles to where the creek joined the Grande Ronde, and thence was along the left bank of that river.

39 Camp was seemingly on left bank of the Grande Ronde at the mouth of present-day Five Points Creek, and thus one-half mile south of the site of town of Hilgard. *Geol. Oregon.*

40 In the journ.'s manuscript Stuart made the following two interlineations: the term "2nd" above this figure "20," and the term "1st" above the word "two" at the beginning of the next sentence—all this suggesting possible intention ultimately to transpose the sentences, which he thus transposed in the trav. mem.

41 Though Stuart makes note of both the branches which entered from the north—*i.e.*, present-day Dark Canyon and Spring Creeks—he records but two of the four confluents from the south, which confluents he had met in the following sequence: Beaver, Jordan, Whiskey (these latter two perhaps considered by him too insignificant to warrant mention) and Rock Creeks (*Geol. Oregon*). The fact that he noted two confluents, and not merely one, as coming from the north assures, as stated in note 37, that his camp of August 3d had been at the confluence of McCoy Creek with Starkey Creek rather than at the subsequent junction of Starkey Creek and Grande Ronde River.

42 Actually about nine miles. Stuart here was descending a valley which,

for most of its length, was very narrow and was girt by steep slopes of from 500 to 700 feet in height. There were widenings at only three or four places; that at the mouth of Rock Creek being some 175 yards across, and another still lower on the course spanning approximately one-half mile.

43 Here the hills ended and the Grande Ronde River flowed into the large, quasi-circular plain known today as Grande Ronde Valley.

44 Grande Ronde Valley.

45 This defile through which the Grande Ronde River made its exit from the hills is today locally termed The Narrows. Camp was on right bank of the river and within, or very close to, the present-day limits of the city of LaGrande.

46 "two Salmon" in trav. mem.

47 Foothills of Blue Mountains. Stuart's thus clinging to the toes of the foothills was doubtless because of the marshiness which unquestionably then prevailed in portions of the valley.

48 The narrow, rocky, northern portal of a valley which, coming from the southward and today styled Pyles Canyon (named for James M. Pyle, a pioneer settler in the vicinity), debouched into the southerly end of Grande Ronde Valley at a spot one and one-half miles south from site of present-day town of Union (*Quad. Telocaset; McArthur*, p. 290). Though thus termed a canyon, this valley, save at its above described northern portal, lacked vertical sides; and, for Stuart, was in the main merely a gently ascending passage between treeless rounded hills rising 700 to 2200 feet above the valley's floor (*Quad. Telocaset*). The present-day tracks of the Oregon Railway and Navigation Company here follow Stuart's route; but the Oregon Trail of covered-wagon days ran, not through Pyles Canyon, but through a valley which, immediately to its westward, is now styled Ladds Canyon. *Quad. Telocaset; McArthur*, p. 191; *Crown Maps*, III, Nos. 44, 45.

49 Now generally known as Pyles (*alias* Pyle) Creek, though many local folk term it interchangeably Canyon Creek or Clover Creek. A mere rivulet, it originated near the site of present-day town of Telocaset and flowed through the length of Pyles Canyon (*Quad. Telocaset; Geol. Oregon*). Camp was at Pyles Canyon's northern portal described in note 48.

50 Actually northwestward. *Quad. Telocaset.*

51 This, known at the present time as Hot Lake and having a daily flow of 2,500,000 gallons at 208° Fahrenheit, was at a spot immediately beside the site of the present-day tracks of the Oregon Railway and Navigation Company; and, save for the presence of sanitarium buildings and for the absence of wapiti horns, is today as Stuart described it. *Geol. Oregon; Quad. Telocaset.*

52 "half a mile" in trav. mem.

53 The antler-shedding season for wapiti in eastern Oregon.

54 The paragraph here beginning relates wholly to characteristics of the Grande Ronde River, and not to any route which Stuart had taken or intended to take.

55 Present-day Mill Creek, for which see note 57.

56 Present-day Catherine Creek.

57 Grande Ronde. This river, having issued from the "narrows" mentioned in the entry for August 5 (p. 78), meandered easterly and southeasterly to the easterly side of the Grande Ronde Valley. It then turned northward; and, a short distance downstream from this turn, received the combined waters of Mill Creek (coming from the southeast) and of Catherine Creek (at its very mouth coming from the west, but earlier in its roundabout course having almost boxed the compass), which two creeks, having met head-on and coalesced a short distance inland, flowed through a single channel to their above-mentioned confluence with the Grande Ronde (*Quad. Telocaset; Geol. Oregon*). The thus augmented river continued its course northward, picking up here and there additional feeders; and, entering the hills at the northerly end of the Grande Ronde Valley, passed through them on its way toward its confluence with the Snake.

58 Not the "narrows" mentioned in the entry for August 5 (p. 78), but instead those near site of present-day town of Elgin. *Geol. Oregon.*

59 Present-day Grande Ronde Valley, the "Grande Ronde or Great Circle" of *Cowperthwait* [*A*], p. 29; the "Big Flat" of many a diarist. For varied spellings of its name, see *McArthur*, pp. 146, 147.

60 Catherine Creek, for which see note 57.

61 *Procyon lotor*, if Stuart restricted himself to the true raccoon. He may, however, have also included in his classification the so-called Oregon ring-tailed cat, otherwise known as the bassarisk or cacomistle, *Bassariscus astutus oregonus* (*Rhoads*).

62 Northerly end of Grande Ronde Valley.

63 The river there flowed between the foothills of Blue Mountains and those of Wallowa Mountains.

64 "Kimooenem" in each of its three mentionings in journ., pp. 79, 80; but successively "Kimooenin," "Kinooenin" and "Kimoo-inem" in the corresponding positions in trav. mem. Lewis and Clark seemingly restricted their name of "Ki-moo-e-nem" to so much of Snake River as was above the mouth of present-day Clearwater River (*L. & C. Journs.*, III, pp. 101, 103, 105; VII, pp. 174, 175, 181; *L. & C. Hist.*, pp. 596, 597, 620, 621, 635, 637; *Wilkes, Narr.*, map of Oregon in accompanying atlas). For some of Snake River's various other and transitory names, such as "Lewis," "Lewis Fork," "Shoshone," "Saptin," "Sahaptin," "Nez Perce," "Chopunnish," see *Symons* [*A*], p. 131; *McArthur*, pp. 328, 329. According to *Stuart, Granville* [*A*], pp. 40, 88, the Snake indians' name for the stream was *Po-ho-gwa*, meaning "Sagebrush River," and was given because the upper and larger part of its immense valley was a sagebrush plain. However, it should be remembered that indians were not so much disposed to bestow a single name on a stream in its entirety as they were to allot particular names to the several salient portions of it.

65 "Pacheecum" in trav. mem. Present-day Salmon River, to which Lewis and Clark referred as "Pawnashtee" and "Tommanamah." *Geol. Idaho; L. & C. Hist.*, p. 1255.

66 "Koos-kooskee" in trav. mem. This indian name, meaning "much water," indians of the Columbian region attached to the lower reaches of various large streams; but historians have, for convenience's sake, been wont to follow Lewis and Clark's lead in restricting it to present-day Clearwater River. *Geol. Idaho; L. & C. Hist.*, pp. 596, 597.

67 Pyles Creek, for which see note 49.

68 Thus approximately to the spot indicated on modern maps as the railway station for the nearby town of Telocaset. Incidentally, this upland town was known as Antelope Stage Station in the bygone period of horse-drawn vehicles; but, on the advent of the railway, the name was changed to the Nez Perce indians' word *Telocaset* (properly though not usually pronounced Taulekarset), meaning "a thing at the top." Stuart, immediately after crossing here a low watershed, commenced an easy descent through a somewhat hilly but quite open country. *Quad. Telocaset; Geol. Oregon; McArthur*, p. 346.

69 Seemingly should have read S.S.W.

70 Present-day Powder River, which Stuart first encountered at seemingly a spot which on the left bank was approximately three miles downstream from site of modern town of North Powder (*Geol. Oregon; Quad. Telocaset*). Though Peter Skene Ogden on August 24, 1827, mentioned the watercourse by its present name, Joseph Williams in 1841 referred to it as "Gunpowder River" (*Journ. Peter Skene Ogden* in *Ore. Hist. Soc. Quar.*, XI, p. 361; *Williams*, p. 17). Powder River, according to *McArthur*, p. 285, derived its name from *polallie illahe*, Chinook jargon meaning "powdered or sandy soil."

71 Catherine Creek, which is described in note 57.

72 In addition to his "2 considerable branches" (Wolf Creek and North Powder River), Stuart crossed two other and much smaller streams (present-day Jimmy Creek and Hot Creek). *Geol. Oregon; Quad. Telocaset; Quad. Baker City.*

73 Blue Mountains, for which see note 77 on p. 73.

74 Present-day Baker Valley, named for Edward Dickinson Baker, United States senator from Oregon in 1860 and later major-general, United States Army; killed at battle of Balls Bluff, Virginia, October 21, 1861. *McArthur*, p. 16; *Heitman*, I, p. 183.

75 Camped on left bank of Powder River at approximately mouth of present-day Muddy Creek and thus two miles due north from site of present-day town of Haines. This stretch of river above its junction with North Powder River is oftentimes locally styled South Powder River. *Quad. Baker City; Geol. Oregon.*

76 Incorrectly "26 miles" in trav. mem. Stuart camped at a spot which, on the outskirts of the modern city of Baker (formerly Baker City), was at the outer end of the small, flaring mouth of the valley of Powder (*alias* South Powder)

River; the camp, because of the topography, being doubtless on the river's left bank. *Quad. Baker City; Geol. Oregon.*

77 Incorrectly "N.N.W." in trav. mem.

78 Assuredly "entrance into" means "exit from."

79 Incorrectly "27 miles" in trav. mem.

80 Up present-day Sutton Creek to its headwaters; Stuart thus ascending a treeless, gently sloping valley which lay between low hills. *Quad. Baker City; Geol. Oregon.*

81 A wide, high, rolling and treeless prairie; Stuart crossing it seemingly through the coulee situated approximately two and one-half miles southwest from present-day town of Pleasant Valley. *Quad. Baker City.*

82 Present-day Alder Creek. *Quad. Baker City;* indicated, without naming, on *Geol. Oregon.*

83 This stream, present-day Burnt River, is termed "Wood Pile Creek" in both journ. and trav. mem., "Woodpile Creek" in *Astoria,* II, p. 122; but is styled "Woodville Creek" in at least one later edition of *Astoria.* It was the "Burnt River" of Peter Skene Ogden in 1826, his "River Brule" in 1827, the "Burnt river" of John Work in 1830 and 1832, the "Brule" of Townsend and of Nathaniel J. Wyeth in 1834, the "Brule or Burnt River" of Johnson and Winter, the "Burntwood creek" of Osborne Cross, and earlier was the "Walshlemo" and "Walshlem" River of Lewis and Clark, whose knowledge of its name and existence was limited to information obtained from indians. It appears as "Wash-le-mo" on Wyld's map. (*Journ. Peter Skene Ogden in Ore. Hist. Soc. Quar.,* X, pp. 352, 356, XI, p. 361; *Work,* p. 169; *Wyeth, Nathaniel J.,* p. 230; *Townsend,* p. 143; *Johnson and Winter,* pp. 32, 115, 116; *Exec. Doc.,* pp. 209, 210, 216; *L. & C. Hist.,* p. 1254, ed. note; *Wyld* [*A*].)

For tradition that the name Burnt River was derived from either charred timber on the river's bank or from cauterized appearance of rocks at the river's mouth, see *McArthur,* p. 44. See also *Root,* p. 30.

84 Incorrectly "13" in trav. mem.

85 Stuart, having descended Alder Creek for ten miles, camped on it approximately at site of present-day town of Unity. *Quad. Baker City.*

86 See note 81.

87 From the locality and numerousness, these doubtless were prong-horned antelope, *Antilocapra americana,* and not mountain goats, *Oreamnos montanus montanus* (*Ord*). The two animals, however, were by many travelers interchangeably termed antelope and goat (*L. & C. Hist.,* p. 109). In 1826 Peter Skene Ogden's party killed in this immediate vicinity "4 sheep (Ibex)," which beasts, because of the term "Ibex," were doubtless mountain sheep, otherwise known as "big-horns," *Ovis canadensis canadensis; Ovis cervina.* See *Journ. Peter Skene Ogden* in *Ore. Hist. Soc. Quar.,* X, p. 352.

88 Alder Creek, for which see note 82.

89 Stuart left Alder Creek at not improbably the place where, emerging

from the hills, it swerves easterly toward its nearby confluence with present-day Lawrence (*alias* Pritchard) Creek, and thereupon he began a short-cut which took him either to the right bank of Lawrence Creek or else to the left bank of Burnt River at a spot a slight distance above where this river receives the waters of Lawrence Creek. *Quad. Pine; Geol. Oregon.*

90 Burnt River; though, as suggested in note 89, Stuart may have come to it, not directly, but by way of Lawrence Creek.

91 Incorrectly "about 8" in trav. mem.

92 "sandy soil, in some places mixed with large brown gravel" in trav. mem.

93 Stuart was here descending the large flat valley in which today is the town of Durkee. *Quad. Pine; Geol. Oregon.*

94 This compulsory and steep detour was one of the salient and most vociferously berated sections of the Oregon Trail in covered-wagon days. For Stuart, its details were as follows. Travelling southeasterly on the left bank of Burnt River and arriving at present-day Swayze Creek, he found himself confronted on his side of the river by present-day Gold Hill, which, with its summit 1550 feet above the river, rose so abruptly from the water's edge as to preclude any passing along that edge. Thereupon, by ascending Swayze Creek to its headwaters, he reached the saddle situated at Gold Hill's northeast corner. After crossing this saddle, he veered southeastward and then southward; and, encountering the headwaters of a small southerly flowing drain one mile west from present-day Sisley Creek, he descended this drain to its confluence with Burnt River at a spot approximately one mile upstream from site of present-day town of Weatherby. *Quad. Pine; Geol. Oregon.*

The Oregon Trail, when making this detour, followed the small drain for but a short distance; and, thence cutting across to Sisley Creek, descended that stream to Burnt River. *Quad. Pine; Crown Maps*, III, No. 41.

95 Incorrectly "3½" in trav. mem.

96 Camped in a small flat which, on the right bank of Burnt River, lay approximately midway between mouths of present-day Sisley and Dixie Creeks. *Geol. Oregon.*

97 Incorrectly "27" in trav. mem.

98 Burnt River.

99 See *Fremont*, pp. 176, 177.

100 "many Beaver" in trav. mem.

101 Incorrectly "17" in trav. mem.

102 At site of present-day town of Huntington, Ore.

103 Stuart, travelling southward from here, soon came to a saddle between two hills. He approached and crossed it along a route later adopted by the Oregon Trail. Thence, continuing southward, he descended a long and somewhat steep slope which led him directly to the Snake's left bank at a river-curve later known to many covered-wagon folk as Farewell Bend (*Crown Maps*, III, No. 39; *Thompson*, p. 84; *Fremont*, p. 176). For concurrence with Stuart's

subsequent description of his route from this spot to present-day American Falls, see *Journ. John T. Kern* in *Ore. Pioneer, 42nd annual reunion*, 1917, pp. 174-179.

104 Incorrectly "7" in trav. mem.

105 This camp, in view of the stated distance, the topography and the comparative absence of herbage elsewhere in the neighborhood, was doubtless on the grassy flat included in a small point projecting from the left bank of the river.

106 "Ka-eye-nem" in trav. mem.

107 "Byo-paa" in trav. mem.

108 See note 64 for nomenclature.

109 Some nine miles below Stuart's camp, the Snake began its spumey journey between rocky walls which presently, becoming on the left a part of Oregon's Wallowa Mountains and on the right a part of Idaho's aptly named Seven Devils, made a defile that was in places 3000 feet deep and that everywhere was floored with all the requisites for the torturing of water. Although at site of present-day town of Pittsburg Landing, 121 miles below Stuart's camp, the Snake had passed beyond the Seven Devils and had meanwhile roistered through 112 rapids, its struggle was not finished. In the next 75½ miles, *i.e.*, between sites of Pittsburg Landing and present-day city of Lewiston, Idaho, were 24 additional rapids. Then followed 101 miles of somewhat milder strait-jacketing before the Snake emerged into the plain; and in these 101 miles were 22 rapids. Fifty-three miles beyond the emergence the Snake, after writhing across a final series of 13 rapids, poured itself into the Columbia River. *Snake Plan; Quad. Pine; L. & C. Hist.*, pp. 625-635; *Geol. Washington.*

110 This journey by Donald McKenzie and Robert McClellan is described in *Astoria*, II, pp. 27, 74-77. For route, see note 175 on p. CXXVIII *ante*. That their party aggregated 11—and not 12 as stated by Stuart—appears from p. XCIV and note 184 on p. 320.

111 "last fall" in trav. mem.

112 "Mulpat River," when strictly used, meant present-day Little Salmon River, a northward flowing confluent of Salmon River (*Geol. Idaho*). It was the "Mulpah River" of Lewis and Clark (*L. & C. Hist.*, p. 1255), of *Robinson*, of *Wyld* [*A*] and of *Kelley*, p. 38 and accompanying map. See however note 175 on p. CXXVIII *ante*.

113 Actually were 38 men, 1 woman and 2 children. *Nouvelles Annales*, X, p. 58, translated at p. 293 *infra*.

114 For account of this attempt, see *Nouvelles Annales*, X, pp. 58-71, translated at pp. 293-301 *infra;* and see also *Astoria*, II, p. 32 *et seq.*

115 Actually were 19 men. *Nouvelles Annales*, X, p. 58, translated at p. 293 *infra.*

116 Burnt River, for which see note 83.

117 "Umatalla" in trav. mem.

118 This establishes the identity of so much of Hunt's route from the Snake to the Umatilla as is not defined by *Nouvelles Annales*, X, pp. 71-74, translated at pp. 300-302 *infra*.

119 In the journ.'s manuscript this word "Sciatogas" ("Scyatogas" in trav. mem.) was originally followed by the phrase "and got relief"; but Stuart deleted the phrase and, by writing the words "This Nation," began a sentence which he did not complete. However, in the corresponding entry in trav. mem. he revived the deleted phrase and also completed the sentence.

120 Grande Ronde Valley.

121 Error—Stuart should have written "East."

122 Error—Stuart should have written "North."

123 Error—Stuart should have written "West."

124 Incorrectly "19" in trav. mem.

125 Camped on left bank of the Snake at the spot where, opposite site of present-day city of Weiser, Idaho, the river began an approximately right-angled bend toward the south. See following day's entry, as also *Quad. Weiser; Geol. Oregon; Geol. Idaho.*

126 This stream, present-day Malheur River, emptying through the Snake's left bank, was the "Shecomshink," "She-com-shenk," "She-cam-skink" of Lewis and Clark (whose knowledge of the stream's name and existence was limited to information obtained from indians) and was also the "river Mathon" of John Work, the "Riviere aux Malheurs" of Fremont, the "Malore" of Joel Palmer, the "Malure" of James Clyman, the "Malair" of John Owen, the "Malheur" of Origen Thompson, and the "Mallair" of Shively. It was interchangeably referred to by Peter Skene Ogden in his journal as "Malheur" and "unfortunate river"; and furthermore, under date of February 14, 1826, he noted: "We encamped on River au Malheur (unfortunate river) so called on account of goods and furs here discovered and stolen by the natives." James Wyld displays not only a "She-com-shent River" but also a "Malheur," and erroneously causes the latter of these two streams to flow into his "Walsh-le-mo River" or, in other words, into Burnt River, for which last mentioned stream see note 83. *L. & C. Hist.*, p. 1254, ed. note; *Work*, pp. 168, 174; *Fremont*, p. 174; *Palmer*, p. 50; *Clyman*, p. 101; *Owen*, I, pp. 37, 38; *Thompson*, p. 82; *Shively*, p. 10; *Journ. Peter Skene Ogden* in *Ore. Hist. Soc. Quar.*, X, pp. 353, 354; *Wyld* [*A*].

127 Camped on left bank of the Snake at site of present-day town of Malheur Junction (*Geol. Oregon*). Stuart's entire day's travel had been along a plain. *Quad. Weiser; Quad. Nampa.*

128 In the journ.'s manuscript Stuart originally wrote "Sage," later deleted it and substituted "Saltwood." It is "salt wood" in trav. mem. Stuart's "Saltwood" was not improbably *Purshia tridentata*, which, in 1842, Fremont observed in this locality. *Fremont*, pp. 170, 171, 314. See also *Baillon*, I, p. 370.

129 "in the spring season" in trav. mem.

130 Travelling along a sagebrush plain situated on Snake's left bank and

but slightly higher than the surface of the river, which here was extremely sinuous. However, Stuart was not closely following the zigzags of the river's bank but instead was cutting across the bases of the various bends. *Quad. Nampa; Quad. Mitchell Butte; Geol. Oregon.*

131 Incorrectly "25" in trav. mem.

132 This stream, known today as Owyhee River (*Owyhee* being an early spelling of *Hawaii*), was the "Timmoonumlarwas," "Timmooenum-larwas," "Tim-moo-e-num" and "Tim-mo-a-men" of Lewis and Clark, whose knowledge of the stream's name and existence was limited to information obtained from indians. It was the "Tim-mo-a-men" of James Wyld. Peter Skene Ogden, who in his journal interchangeably used for this stream the terms "Owyhee" and "Sandwich Island," noted under date of February 18, 1826: ". . . we reached Sandwich Island River, so called, owing to 2 of them murdered by Snake Indians in 1819." James Clyman designated it as the "great Woile." *L. & C. Hist.*, p. 1254, ed. note; *Wyld [A]; Journ. Peter Skene Ogden* in *Ore. Hist. Soc. Quar.*, X, pp. 353, 363, XI, p. 361; *Clyman*, p. 125.

133 Malheur River, for which see note 126.

134 Camped on left bank of Owyhee River at its mouth. Both banks of the Owyhee rose here but a few feet higher than the water's surface.

135 Jean Baptiste Dubreuil, André LaChapelle, François Landry and Jean Baptiste Turcotte, for whom see p. LXXXVIII, as also note 49 on p. 121.

136 Hunt had left one detachment at the mouth of Hoback River, another at Henry's Fort. For the names of the men detached see p. CI and note 123 on pp. 178, 179.

137 On the opposite or right bank of the Snake.

138 This stream, present-day Boise River, was the "Copcoppakark," "Copcoppahark," "Cop-cop-hah-ark," "Cop-pop-pah-ash" of Lewis and Clark, whose knowledge of the stream's name and existence was limited to information obtained from indians. It was, for a time after Lewis and Clark's day, called "Riviere du Bois," "Riviere Boisee," "Wooded River" and occasionally, because of John Reed's death on or near it, "Reeds [or, with equal frequency, "Reid's"] River." Alexander Ross, under date of May 10, 1824, noted: "Reid's River . . . on which a post was begun by Mr. Mackenzie in 1819. I might say begun by Mr. Reid in 1813." Peter Skene Ogden, in his journal under date of February 18, 1826, stated: "on the north side opposite this fork is Reed's River, who was also with all his party, to the number of 11, murdered by the Snakes and their establishment destroyed." It apparently was the "Lake River" of *Wyld [B]*, *[C]* and of *Bradford*. In Nathaniel J. Wyeth's journal, it appears interchangeably as "Woody River," "Big Wood," and "Reeds otherwise called Big Woody," while in the journal of John Work it is "Read's River." Thomas J. Farnham referred to it as "Boisais River." *L. & C. Hist.*, p. 1254, ed. note; *Journ. Alexander Ross* in *Ore. Hist. Soc. Quar.*, XIV, p. 380; *Journ. Peter Skene Ogden* in *Ore. Hist. Soc. Quar.*, X, p. 353; *Wyeth, Nathaniel J.*, pp. 229, 230;

Work, pp. 152, 154, 162; *Farnham*, p. 139; *Abert; Colton* [*E*]; *Wilkes*, *Narr.*, map of Oregon in accompanying atlas. See also *Fremont*, pp. 172, 173; J. Neilson Barry's *Fort Reed and Fort Boise* in *Ore. Hist. Soc. Quar.*, XXXIV, pp. 60-67.

In conflict with some of the above-quoted references to Reid's River are (1) *Henry-Thomp.*, p. 761, f.n., wherein Coues makes Reid's River identical with present-day Payette River, and (2) Peter Skene Ogden's journal wherein, at *Ore. Hist. Soc. Quar.*, X, p. 357, Ogden states "destroyed Mr. Reid and party, on Sandwich Islands," *i.e.*, on Owyhee River, for which see note 132.

139 Snake indians.

140 "incredible" in trav. mem.

141 See note 43 on p. 20 for edible roots.

142 This stream, present-day Payette River, was named for François Payette, who is said to have arrived at Astoria on the ship *Beaver*, to have been an engagé with McKenzie on the Snake River in 1818, and later to have been commandant at Fort Boise. It was the "Pagette [*sic*] or middle river" of Alexander Ross, the "Payette's River" of John Work, the "Shuxpellalima or Payette River" of Abert. It also was the "Shushpellanimmo," "Shurk-pal-ha-nim-mo" and "Shush-pel-la-mine-mo" of Lewis and Clark, whose knowledge of the stream's name and existence was limited to information obtained from indians. *Journ. James W. Nesmith* in *Ore. Hist. Soc. Quar.*, VII, p. 352; *Ross* [*C*], II, p. 98; *Journ. John Work* in *Ore. Hist. Soc. Quar.*, XIII, p. 366; *Abert; L. & C. Hist.*, p. 1254, ed. note; J. Neilson Barry's *Astorians &c.* in *Wash. Hist. Quar.*, XXIV, pp. 292–296.

143 This stream, coming from the northeast and today styled Weiser River, emptied through the Snake's right bank. It was the "river Wuzer" of Alexander Ross, the "Wazer's River" of Peter Skene Ogden in 1827, the "Wazer" and "Waser" River of John Work, the "Wagner or Waze River" of Abert in 1838. It also was the "Nemo" River of Lewis and Clark, whose knowledge of the stream's name and existence was limited to information obtained from indians. *Ross* [*C*], II, pp. 98, 99; *Journ. Peter Skene Ogden* in *Ore. Hist. Soc. Quar.*, VII, p. 362; *Journ. John Work* in *Ore. Hist. Soc. Quar.*, XIII, p. 366; *Work*, pp. 166, 167; *Abert; L. & C. Hist.*, p. 1254.

One tradition has the river named for a Peter Wiser, who, as appears in *L. & C. Journs.*, I, p. 13, was a private in the Lewis and Clark expedition. A second tradition that it was named for a Jacob Wayer or Wager, a North West Company trapper with Mackenzie in 1818 (all as reservedly stated in *Work*, f.n. 323 on p. 166), is seemingly contradicted by the fact that Stuart's above styling of the river as "Wisers" occurred in 1812.

144 In the journ.'s manuscript the phrase "called the Middle River between Wiser and the Wooded River" originally followed this word "course," but was deleted by Stuart. That this Middle River and Wooded River were respectively Payette River and Boise River appears from notes 142 and 138.

145 Patently the white people mentioned in entry of August 15 (p. 83).

146 Crossed Owyhee River to its right bank.

147 That this indian was a Shoshone appears from *Nouvelles Annales*, X, pp. 47, 48 (translated at pp. 288, 289 *infra*). In the journ.'s manuscript the phrase "proved to be the person who" was originally written by Stuart after the word "who" and before the word "guided," but was deleted by him.

148 This obviously refers to the guiding of Hunt's party in the autumn of 1811 westward over present-day Teton Pass, which, lying close to the present-day Idaho-Wyoming boundary, was presently to be crossed, October 7, 1812, by Stuart's party.

149 "Rifle" in trav. mem.

150 "Mackaio" in trav. mem. For the seven men (Louis St. Michel, Alexander Carson, Pierre Delaunay, Jean Baptiste Dubreuil, André LaChapelle, François Landry and Jean Baptiste Turcotte) who, formerly of Hunt's party, were possibly now in Stuart's vicinity, see note 123 on pp. 178 ,179 and note 49 on p. 121. Query: could the indian's "Alexis" have been Alexander Carson, his "Michel" have been Louis St. Michel? But what was the significance of the indian's "Makan" or "Mackaio"? It bore no tonal relationship either to the name of any of the seven men or to the name of any of the other four of Hunt's men (Miller, Robinson, Hoback and Reznor) whom Stuart was to encounter four days later as described in entry of August 20 (p. 86). Could the indian have heard his erstwhile white companions mention either Donald McKenzie or Alexander McKay, each of Astorian connection, and have thought the name to have been that of the mentioner?

151 This "trace" which the indian said was "shorter" and more southerly than the one the Hunt party had followed across the mountains meant undoubtedly South Pass, inasmuch as the indian knew exactly what route the party had taken. That he had such knowledge appears from the fact that before guiding Hunt's people over the Teton Pass (in Teton Range) he—according to *Nouvelles Annales*, X, pp. 47, 48, translated at pp. 288, 289 *infra*—had followed them across Union Pass (in Wind River Range and north of South Pass).

152 "rocky mountains" in trav. mem. Beyond any reasonable doubt, Hunt's route, as outlined by *Nouvelles Annales*, X, pp. 42, 43 (translated at pp. 286, 287 *infra*) and by *Astoria*, I, pp. 279, 280, and as stated in terms of present-day names, was as follows:

Having traversed the Big Horn Range and subsequently encountered Wind River, he ascended this river as far as to the mouth of the DuNoir River. From this latter spot he entered the Wind River Mountains, crossed them *via* Union Pass, and thence descended into the valley of the Green River.

That this was his actual route is established by the following facts:

Astoria tells us that he quitted Wind River at its "forks"; while *Nouvelles Annales* adds that, when leaving Wind River and entering the mountains, he travelled southwesterly to a pass which took him direct into Green River's valley. Keeping in mind these cited statements, let us now examine the terrain and especially the three passes available to him—*i.e.*, the Union, the Sheridan and the Twogwotee.

The "forks" mentioned by *Astoria* must have been either, (a), the confluence of Horse Creek with Wind River—this being at site of town of Dubois (altitude 6909 feet)—or, (b), the spot (altitude 7242 feet) where, 10 miles farther up Wind River, this latter stream received the waters of DuNoir River; all as indicated on *Teton*, *Washakie* and *Quad. Younts Peak.*

Union Pass (altitude 9210 feet)—for naming and character of the pass see *Raynolds*, p. 88—lay west of the Horse Creek confluence and southwest of the DuNoir confluence, and led direct into the valley of Green River. Sheridan Pass (altitude 9200 feet) was west of the DuNoir confluence and led, not into the Green River valley, but direct to the valley of Gros Ventre River (a confluent of Snake River); the two valleys being separated from each other by a high divide. Twogwotee (*alias* Togwote) Pass (altitude 9658 feet) was northwest of the DuNoir confluence and led, not into the Green River valley, but direct to the valley of Buffalo Fork, a confluent of Snake River and separated from Green River's valley by two high divides. *Teton; Washakie; Yellowstone; Quads. Younts Peak, Fremont Peak, Mt. Leidy* and *Gros Ventre.*

Accordingly, Sheridan Pass and Twogwotee Pass, because not southwest of the DuNoir confluence and because not leading direct into the Green River's valley (all as required by *Nouvelles Annales* and *Astoria*), are eliminated from our reckoning and we are left with the confident realization that Hunt used Union Pass, and had approached it from the mouth of the DuNoir River.

Hunt's route from Green River's valley to Teton Basin on the Rocky Mountains' extreme westerly side was, except in two slight particulars, doubtless identical with that which subsequently and in reverse direction was followed by Stuart as detailed in his entries of October 2-12 (pp. 152-155). The two excepted particulars relate to, (1), Hunt's ascending present-day Beaver Creek from its mouth to the confluence of its north and middle forks and thence ascending this north fork (present-day North Beaver Creek) to its headwaters, whereas Stuart, on encountering these headwaters of the north fork, made a short-cut easterly to Green River; and, (2), Hunt's following Hoback River to its mouth, while Stuart encountered this river at a spot approximately two miles above its mouth.

153 From Pacific slope to Atlantic slope. The willingness of Stuart's party not to retrace Hunt's trail is thus explained by Ramsay Crooks (p. CXXXVI *ante*): ". . . considering it dangerous to pass again by the route of 1811, turned towards the south-east as soon as they had crossed the main chain [Teton Range] of the Rocky Mountains. . . ."

154 Boise River, for which see note 138.

155 Along left bank of Snake to foot of river-bend situated four miles south of site of present-day town of Adrian. *Quad. Mitchell Butte; Geol. Oregon.*

156 Incorrectly "19 more" in trav. mem.

157 Having continued along the plain on Snake's left bank, camped on that bank at approximately mouth of present-day Sucker Creek, the "Succor Creek" of *Symons* [*B*]. See also *Quad. Mitchell Butte; Quad. Nampa; Geol. Oregon; Geol. Idaho.*

158 In the journ.'s manuscript, the phrase "and we took his advice" originally followed the word "encamping" but was later deleted by Stuart. Camp was on Snake's left bank at seemingly the foot of the river-bend situated approximately two miles east-southeast of present-day town of Clatonia. *Geol. Idaho; Quad. Nampa.*

159 *Astoria*, II, p. 124 adds an account of an indian's admiring Stuart's horse and claiming to have been its owner when the Walla Wallas stole it. See also note 91 on p. 74 *ante*.

160 "distance" in trav. mem.

161 Incorrectly "26" in trav. mem.

162 Camped on Snake's left bank at approximately a spot which, situated in longitude 116° 40′, was later known as Bernard Ferry. *Quad. Silver City.*

163 Burnt River.

164 See *Quad. Silver City.*

165 "most unmercifully" in trav. mem.

166 Midges, *Similium nocivum*. "Gnats here trouble us much . . ." according to *Wyeth, Nathaniel J.*, p. 169.

167 Snake River.

168 Immediately east of site of present-day town of Guffey. *Quad. Silver City; Geol. Idaho.*

169 Present-day Rabbit Creek. *Quad. Silver City; Geol. Idaho; Symons* [*B*].

170 Thus to site of present-day town of Murphy. *Quad. Silver City; Geol. Idaho.*

171 Camped on left bank of the Snake at the bend situated two miles west by north from mouth of present-day Castle Creek. *Quad. Bisuka; Geol. Idaho.*

172 Seemingly these whites must have been limited to members of Hunt's earlier and westbound party of Astorians.

173 Stuart cut across the bases of (1) the bend containing Castle Buttes, and (2) the bend lying three miles southeast of it (*Quad. Bisuka*). This placed him on the Snake's left bank at the mouth of a northeasterly flowing drain which (indicated, without naming, on *Quad. Bisuka* and *Geol. Idaho* as the next stream southeast from Birch Creek) is today known locally as Vinson Wash.

174 "Hobough" wherever mentioned in journ.; "Hoback" wherever mentioned in trav. mem. Concerning the meeting with Hoback and his comrades, note 11 on p. 257 offers data not contained in journ.'s original entry though included in trav. mem. These data allow us to determine the night's camp to have been at a spot that, on Snake's left bank, was approximately one and one-half miles northwest of site of present-day town of Grandview. *Geol. Idaho.*

175 This distance would have taken them as far south as to the extreme southern portion of Idaho or the northernmost portion of Utah. Their subsequent assertion (in this same day's entry) to the effect that pushing eastward from their most southerly point they ultimately had arrived among Southern Arapahoe indians (for whose territory see pp. 333, 334) and seemingly also Ute indians (for whose territory see p. 363) substantiates their stated mileage.

176 This "River" unquestionably was the southerly flowing stretch of present-day Bear River in Idaho, although present-day Green River in Wyoming also ran southward. Bear River, an extremely serpentine watercourse, having entered the southeasterly corner of Idaho and thence flowed north and northwesterly to the northerly end of present-day Bear River Range of mountains, made there a hairpin westward turn and thence ran southerly to its outlet at Salt Lake (*Caribou; Geol. Idaho; Hayden, Montana,* pp. 151, 152). That the scene of the men's autumn hunt was this stretch below the turn, and was not Green River, may confidently be deduced from (1) the men's mention of their travel having been south—not southeasterly—to the stream on which they hunted, (2) their implication of this stream's flow as southward, (3) Miller's recognition of Bear River when later he encountered it with Stuart (September 9 entry, p. 129) and his subsequent mystification when, beginning to ascend it above the vertex of the turn, he found it to be flowing north instead of south (September 13 entry, p. 131), and (4) Miller's futile effort, after leaving Bear River, to find a southward flowing stream (September 13-16 entries, pp. 131-133).

177 This distance would have taken them across the lower valley of Green River and to the longitude of Wyoming's Sierra Madre Mountains.

178 This distance, if added to the 200 miles involved in note 175, would have taken them as far eastward as the meridian of Wyoming's Medicine Bow Mountains. If the men's account as to southward and eastward mileages be approximately correct and their assertion of having been among Utes and Southern Arapahoes be trustworthy, they, while as yet westward of the meridian of South Pass, went southward to a latitude much south of that of the Pass; and, then turning, trudged eastward either in extreme southern Wyoming or in northern Colorado. This eastward course would not have carried them through any pass or over any highland, because in its latitude there was a wide hiatus in the continuity of the Rocky Mountains. Though high peaks rose both north and south of this break, the break itself was a plain which—incidentally, today traversed by the main line of the Union Pacific Railway—extended uninterruptedly from the level lands west of the Rockies to the level lands east of them. However, the surface aridity of much of this plain prevented, until the advent of the railway, any crossing by horse-drawn vehicles. The railway brought tank-cars and afterwards settlers who dug wells. Meanwhile South Pass to the north and Bridger Pass to the south offered the emigrant his only serviceable routes.

Not only is the men's recital inconsistent with the thought that they might have visited South Pass; but also, as evidenced later in the entries of October 20-23 (pp. 162-165), Miller, when ultimately accompanying Stuart through the Pass, appears not to have recognized any part of it or of its approaches.

In *Hidden Heroes of the Rockies* (a book which, so its introduction states, was written for boys and girls), the authors, for the seeming purpose of interesting youthful readers, have inserted various bits of alleged conversations. In one of these ostensible chats, Hoback, Reznor, Robinson, and Miller are made to inform Stuart, on a date prior to his reaching South Pass, that they themselves had already discovered and traversed it. These printed colloquies are presumably fictional because, (1), no portion of any of them is contained in the source material cited in the book and, (2), their principal statements are, as hereinbefore shown, refuted by Stuart's journ. and trav. mem. *Russell & Driggs*, pp. 33, 34, 37, 38, 42, 44, 48, 49, 56-59, 62, 63. The above-described fictional talks present themselves in summarized form in the subsequently published *Frazer*, p. 93.

179 "robbed them of the remainder of" in trav. mem.

180 Martin H. Cass. *Astoria*, II, p. 129, mentions and deprecates rumor that his companions had eaten him.

181 An enigma here as to the identity of this watercourse. Not only does the text locate the incident's scene as on the headwaters of the Big Horn, but also, by its antithetic context ("on this side [*i.e.*, west] of the Rocky Mountains"), implies that the stream was in country either east of or amid those mountains. Also, a subsequent entry (December 11, p. 192) gives a more specific allocation of the incident to "that Fork of the Spanish river called Big Horn." But—here is the enigma—what confluent of Green River was Stuart's "Big Horn"?

Present-day Big Horn River, lying east of Green River, could not have been involved because it was physically unconnected with Green River. It rose immediately eastward of the continental divide in west-central Wyoming and flowed northward to its confluence with the Yellowstone River in present-day Montana. Incidentally in this connection, it should not be forgotten that during early years present-day Arkansas River, flowing eastward from the Rocky Mountains, shared with above-mentioned Green River the distinction of being termed "Spanish River."

182 "the snake" in trav. mem.

183 See note 11 on p. 257.

184 See note 11 on p. 257 for these data's deletion from journ.'s postscript.

185 Probably either Bannocks or else Shoshones proper, for both of whom see pp. 355-359.

186 "300 strong" in journ.'s deleted postscript contained in note 11 on p. 257.

187 "2,500" in journ.'s deleted postscript contained in note 11 on p. 257.

188 That these probably were Utes appears from Stuart's description of

their home's locus, their friendliness to the white man, and their enmity toward the Arapahoes. See p. 363.

189 See note 11 on p. 257 for this paragraph's deletion from journ.'s postscript.

190 "about 3 miles" in journ.'s deleted postscript contained in note 11 on p. 257.

CHAPTER V

AUG. 21 · SEPT. 5, 1812

On Horseback from Vinson Wash to American Falls

[SEE MAP FACING PAGE 3]

Barter for Horses · Salmon Falls · Indian Fishery · "Caldron Linn" · Hunt's Caches · Equip Hoback, Reznor and Robinson · They Remain to Trap, But Miller Continues with Stuart · Camp Above American Falls

Friday 21st We this day cut off the turns of [*the*] River[1] as usual & at the end of 16 miles, East, found 30 lodges of Shoshonies[2] encamped on the banks of Rocky Bluff Creek,[3] who having some Horses, we took up our quarters[4] at a small distance below hoping to get a few as we are much in want of these animals in[5] consequence of Mr Miller & the 3 hunters determination to accompany us to St. Louis— They brought and traded a good many Salmon for awls &c but seem by no means fond of parting with any of their Horses this Creek is 20 yds wide, ifsues from among Hills which give its name & the banks are without [46] a Twig— it runs from S.S.E. to N.N.W.[6]— The few Salmon it contain are far better than we had any right to expect [*from the shallownefs of its water*]— at this advanced season

Saturday 22nd Strong were the inducements we held out for a few Horses, but they withstood [*all*] our temptations, saying they had not a sufficiency for themselves, consequently we were obliged to content ourselves by exchanging two that were worn out for a couple of [*vigorous and*] fresh ones

We crofsed the Creek[7] at a late hour and ascending the Bluff our road was due East over a Barren Plain for 12 Miles[8] where again striking the River we went 4 Miles S.E. mostly along its banks to the next narrows— then leaving them to our left in 6 more East reached a Bend of the Main Stream[9] where we encamped[10]— pafsed a few Huts of wretched Indians

Sunday 23rd Our route lay along the River bank all day—partly on the sides of the Hills which came close to the stream, and were very stoney, but mostly through Salt Wood Barrens and low sandy plains— Scarce & bad indeed is the fodder of our Cattle,[11] what little we can procure being generally the rankest Grafs & coarse Weeds— a few Shoshonie [*or snake*] Camps were pafsed today, who have to struggle hard for a livelihood, even though it is the prime of the fishing season in this Country— So poor are they that we seldom or never can get even a single Salmon of them. our whole march was this day 21 miles E.S. East[12]

[47] Monday 24th The Sun was an hour high ere we had taken up our line of March. continued as near the water[13] as the Bluffs would admit Cut acrofs a [*large*] Bend[14] over a Hilly road, and at the End of 12 miles East struck the River[15] again, which has much decreased in width and is full of Rapids— From hence turning gradually to [*the*] S. East the road was [*very*] rough and Stony in the extreme for 18 [*miles*] more, when finding a small patch of grafs, and the Country looking fully worse ahead we thought it most prudent to stop[16] for the night in order to let our poor[17] donkies bring up their Cargoes; Saw some Indians on the opposite side swimming after dead & wounded Salmon [*which were*] floating on the surface of the water—

Tuesday 25th We went 2 Miles East—1 S.E. to Cascade Creek[18]

which comes in on the North Side, & is 20 yds wide at the mouth, but although the banks are tolerably lined with Willows, other appearances preclude the idea of its being the afylum of any great number of the furred race— 1 Mile more same course brought us to the Salmon Falls,[19] where we found about 100 lodges [*of*] Shoshonies[20] busily occupied in Killing & drying Fish—

The perpendicular pitch is on the north side upwards of 18 feet,[21] but towards the South it might more properly be called a series of Cascades.[22]

The Fish begin to jump soon after sunrise when the Indians in great numbers with their spears swim in, to near the centre of the Falls, where some placing themselves on Rocks & others to their middle [48] in Water, darts on all sides afsail the Salmon, who struggling to ascend, and perhaps exhausted with repeated efforts, become an easy prey— With the greatest facility prodigious quantities are slaughtered daily and it must have been from this place that the dead & wounded came which we saw picked up by the starving wretches below; am completely at a lofs to conceive why these [*poor*] creatures do not prefer mingling with their own nation at this immense fishing place (where a few hours exertion would produce more than a months labour in their own way); rather than depend on the uncertainty of a Fish ascending close along shore or catching a part of what few make their escape wounded From these Falls—

Their spears are a small straight piece of Elks Horn, out of which the pith is dug, deep enough to receive the end of a very long willow pole & on the point an artificial beard is made fast by a preparation of Twine and Gum

this point of Horn is about seven inches long and from a little below where the Pole enters a strong string of the same length is attached, which is fastened in a like manner to the handle so that when the Spearsman makes a sure blow the wicker [49] catches, pulls off the point and leaves the salmon struggling with the string through his body While the spear is on one side & the handle on the other— The string is an excellent & necefsary invention for were they to depend on the Spear without it so slender is their construction that I have no doubt but it would require at least six to make & mend these instruments in sufficient quantities for the use of one Spearer—

Mr. Miller says that he[23] stopped here on his[23] way down— it was in the afternoon, by far the best spearing time, when to his utter astonishment the Indians in a few hours killed some thousands of fish, and one Salmon in particular leaped in the presence of himself & others from the commencement of the foam at the foot of the pitch clear over all the Cascade which must in my opinion have been upwards of 30 feet

Having soon traded what we wanted, our road was up the River 3 miles South—[24] 1 due West[25] up the Hills 5 S.W.[26] on the Highlands, 4 East to the water[27] at some [*considerable*] rapids[28] then S.E. 5 miles acrofs the uplands[29] to the mouth of Muddy River[30] where we stopped[31] for the night

Wednesday 26th Muddy Creek[30] is 20 yds wide, the banks tolerably covered with Willow, and comes from among barren Hills in the South West

Crofsed it early and went 5 miles S E[32] to the main [50] Stream,[33] then along that 13 more East to where the Iron bound Bluffs put in very near on both sides— at this [*place*] the road ascending the aclivity and not Knowing when we would reach water, [*we*] thought it most advisable, though early, to pafs the night here—[34] Two Indians their Squaws & one child came from below with 5 Horses, they said their road was the same as ours and wished to travel in Company in expectation of which they tarried with us all night—

Thursday 27th [*Jones*] Caught a Beaver this morning and I traded a Horse from the Indians

As the property hid by Mr Hunt last fall when he abandoned

19561

93

Friday 28th — We ascended the bluffs early, and following the trace, in 9 miles S.E. crossed
(23) precipice Creek, up which we continued 14 more, and encamped — The banks of this stream, at, and some distance above its discharge, are almost 200 feet perpendicular, but as you progress upwards they gradually diminish in heighth, and recede from each other, till small willow bottoms of from 20 to 50 yards wide, occasionally vary the eternal rocky sameness of the river sides —

Saturday 29th — The Indian path going by far too much to the South, for our purpose, we on leaving Camp, steered E. by S. for 30 miles, over what is (in this Country) called a prairie, but Forest of worm wood is more properly its name — we again struck the main River at the Caldron Linn, where one of the unfortunate Canoes was lodged among the rocks, but although we wished on several accounts to see in what state she was, the Bluffs
979 intimated, that to gratify our wish, we must risk

A PAGE OF STUART'S TRAVELLING MEMORANDA

the Canoes is only about 50 miles from our present station, and knowing that all would go, did these fellows discover the place, I therefore thought it best to remain here today which will be of infinite advantage to our horse[35] as they are much in want of rest and the grafs is very good; by this days march the savages will be too far off, for us to fear being seen by them while taking out [*&c*] of the Cache what articles belong to the gentlemen & Canadians along with me

[51] Friday 28th We ascended the Bluffs[36] early, and following the Trace in nine miles S.E. crofsed Precipice Creek,[37] up which we continued 14 more and encamped—[38]

The banks of this stream at & for some distance above its discharge are almost 300 feet perpendicular. But as you progrefs upward they gradually diminish in height and recede from each other till small willow Bottoms of from 20 to 50 yards wide occasionally vary the eternal rocky samenefs of the river sides[39]

Saturday 29th The Indian path going by far too much to the south for our purpose, we on leaving Camp steered E by S. for 20 miles over what is (in this Country) called a Prairie, but Forest of Wormwood[40] is more properly its name; we again struck the main River[41] at the Caldron Linn,[42] where one of the unfortunate Canoes[43] was lodged among the Rocks, but although we wished on several accounts to see in what state she was, the Bluffs intimated that to gratify our wish we must risk our necks, so we of course declined it—

Continuing on same course for 12 more,[44] occasionally in sight of the water and where [*it was*] hid from the eye the Ear could with facility conduct us to it—

Being now in the neighbourhood of the Caches[45] and finding good grafs we unloaded and took up our quarters [52] Anxious to know in what state the property was, I proceeded in company with others,[46] to the spot soon after stopping, [*where to our astonishment*] we found six[47] of them open and except a few Books which lay scattered by[48] the wind in every direction, the whole of the contents had vanished— From appearances they must have been taken up some time in the Summer, and the Wolves were undoubtedly the beginers— these attracted no doubt by the skins they contained, had Paths beat everywhere round, which there is reason to believe was what directed the Indians to the Place—[49] We had some Thunder and a heavy gust of rain this afternoon, which is the first [*storm*] worthy of notice we have experienced since we left the Walawala[50]

Of all the Canoes left[51] here by the Party last Fall, only three remain & those too much shattered to[52] be good for any thing— 30 Miles below our present station is a fall[53] of between 40 & 50 feet,[54] from whence to this spot, the River banks on both sides are [*nothing but*] cut[55] Bluffs of a Rock & giving some[56] indications of Iron, at least 300 feet perpendicular, there is in some places a Beach under these Cliffs, but seldom of any extent and entirely[57] composed of immense mafses of Rocks which have from time to time been hurled from the adjacent Precipices— But for the greater part [53] nothing that walks the earth could pofsibly pafs between [*them*], & the water, which in such places is never more than 40 yds[58] wide, rushing with irresistable force over a bed of such Rocks as makes the spray fly equal to the surf of the Ocean, breaking [*violently*] on a lee Shore, In particular spots the stream expands to the breadth of an hundred yards,[59] but its general width for the 30 miles in question is from 35 to 40,[60] and in one place, at the Caldron Linn the whole body of the River is confined between 2 ledges of Rock somewhat lefs than 40 feet[61] apart & Here indeed its terrific appearance beggars all description— Hecate's caldron was never half so agitated when vomiting even the most diabolical spells, as is this Linn[62] in a low stage of [*the*] water[63] & its bearing in idea such a proximity of resemblance to that or something more infernal, I think well authorizes it to retain the [*new*] name it has, more particularly as the tout ensemble of these 30 miles has been baptised the Devils Scuttle Hole—[64]

1 Mile above is Clappins [*Rapid*], a very long & bad Rapid, where a man of that name was drownded [*last fall, in the partie's descent*], when Mr Crook's Canoe split filled and upsett—[65]

[*Here as I have already partially observed, the party were obliged /from the badneſs of the navigation/ to abandon their Canoes, and travel on foot to the Falls of Columbia, a distance of 790 Miles; from thence they proceeded to Astoria by water, having with much difficulty procured conveyance from the Natives*—]

[54] Sunday 30th Having nothing to eat I dispatched Jones & Reznor up the river to try what either their guns or Traps could produce, and proceeded to open the remaining 3 Caches, where we found a few Dry Goods Traps & Ammunition, out of which I furnished Robinson, Reznor & Hobough[66] as far as lay in my power with every thing neceſsary for a two years hunt, which they are to make on this River below Henry's Fort as they preferred that, to returning in their present ragged condition to civilized society— [*Mr. Millers curiosity and desire of travelling thro' the Indian countries being fully satisfied he has determined on accompanying us*—] Meſsrs Miller[67] & McClellan fished the greater part of the day and caught 13 Trout, which with some[68] Rice made our [*frugal and not over plenteous*] suppers— the Chub has entirely disappeared, and a very excellent species of Trout[69] supplies their place, a change we are by no means sorry for, as the former is by far the most worthleſs of all the Finny race—

Monday 31st Some traps were set [*last night*], but furnished nothing for that very desirable operation, the wagging of the jaws Every person was busily employed all day mending Saddles &c, and in the evening we closed the Caches, having taken [*out what belonged to the people, with*] a few small articles neceſsary for this expedition, and put in a part of what merchandize[70] [55] I brought from the Columbia,[71] being convinced they were a superfluity which only served to increase our Baggage—

The Books [*and papers*] were also [*carefully*] collected, & put into a Hole[72] and covered snugly up—

Tuesday 1st September 1812—

Having written two Letters for Mr Reed[73] I stuck one on a Pole near the place of deposit, and gave the other to Mr Robinson, in order to insure if poſsible some mark of our being here in safety, as also of the destruction of the property— about 20 days after we parted at the entrance of the Walawala[74] River he[75] was to set out from Lewis' Fork for the expreſs purpose of finding these Hunters,[76] if poſsible, and to carry down whatever was put in the ground at this place last Fall— If nothing happens he must be here before long and as these men are still in great want of many neceſsaries, they will wait his arrival, which is very desirable as the only Canoe fit for a person to risk himself in is on this side,[77] and it would be impoſsible to succeed in Rafting the River it being [*so*] full of Rapids— at a late hour we left our Camp [*and*] carried the Hunters things up the River [*about*] six miles where [56] they say Beaver enough can be procured to support them some time— about six farther [*on*] we found Jones & Reznor with only 2 Beaver, one of which we took & leaving the latter to return to his Companions the former mounted his Horse & we (once more seven in number) continued on for 3 miles and croſsing a small Creek,[78] encamped on its bank— todays course was East 15 Miles— saw a number of Antelopes—which were [*so*] exceedingly wild [*as not to allow our approach within a mile*]—

Wednesday 2nd We departed from our station [*at an*] early [*hour*]— The Bluffs & Hills have [*at length*] receded to a great distance on the North, & those of this side are also some miles from the River

the Banks are thickly clothed with Willows & mostly low the

highest not exceeding 30 feet, and along both, great numbers of Beaver have their houses

The whole face of the Country appears level before us, a sight we have scarcely been indulged with even in miniature since we left the Columbia Plains; than which these seem far more ex-[57] tensive and like them the Sage, Wormwood & Saltwood[79] (these abominable and detested Shrubs) cover a parched Soil of Sand, dust & gravel— Leaving the River[80] a few miles from last nights camp, we followed a small tract in about an E S E[81] direction to the Hills, which we found poſseſsed of a good many Cedars [*& pines*] in different places, and the Indian lodge trace paſsing along the foot, we kept it, till supposing ourselves 20 miles farther in our journey; we stopped [*for the night*] on a small Branch[82] of excellent water—

Thursday 3rd Last night and till 10 A.M. the weather was disagreeably cool— We set out early and pursuing the Indian route for 23 miles E S E struck a Creek[83] 30 feet wide with many Willows and some Beaver

Here we found a few[84] Shoshonies from whom we procured a Dog, a little dried Salmon and an excellent sort of Cake made of [*pulverized roots, and*] Service Berries[85] with the disagreeable information of our having left the right tract some distance back, to regain which we must go down the Creek[86]— Taking their advice we continued along the right bank for five miles in nearly a north direction, and encamped[87] having come today 28 miles—

[58] Friday 4th— Last night We made a hearty supper on the dogs carcase & between the evening & this mornings pastime caught a sufficiency of trout for Breakfast [*which we found delicious, they being fried with the dogs fat and a little Flour we had still preserved—*]

Leaving the Creek[88] to the left we soon found & followed the Lodge Trace for 14 Miles E.S.E. to Trout Run—[89] here unloading our Horses we plied our Fishing rods for two hours with indifferent succefs— [*then*] resumed our journey and after sunset stopped on a low point on the banks of the main River,[90] which we kept in sight, all this afternoon & is from Trout Run 16 Miles[91] N.N E —

Saturday 5th Caught a small Beaver last night & at a late hour continued our journey over a pretty level tract along a very Rapid part of the River for 12 Miles N by E when reaching Portage Falls[92] we again tried our lines & drew out a few Trout— These Falls are about 25 feet high[93] on the West side, but are little else than a series of Cascades on the East—[94] The whole body of the Stream is here scarcely sixty yds[95] wide, but immediately above expands to the breadth of half a mile, with little or no current & the banks sufficiently covered with Willows to afford a plentifull supply of food for the incredible numbers of furred animals who inhabit its [59] borders— The country pafsed since yesterday morning has improved greatly— the Sage and its detested relations gradually decrease, and the soil though parched, produces fodder in abundance for our Cattle— at the end of 3 miles due North, above the Falls we took up our nights quarters[96] close to the River—

Notes to Chapter V

1 Snake River.

2 "Snakes" in trav. mem.

3 Known today as Bruneau River, a name which, used in this same form by John Work on May 19, 1831 (*Journ. John Work* in *Ore. Hist. Soc. Quar.*, XIV, p. 297), is traditionally a modification of an alleged earlier form, *Brun Eau*, meaning "brown water" (*Scott*, III, p. 303). It was the "Bruneau River" of *Abert* and the "Middle River" of *Colton* [*F*].

4 Camped on the flat on left bank of Bruneau River near its mouth.

5 "in consequence of Mr Miller & the 3 hunters determination to accompany" in journ.; "since the late augmentation of our number, they having all determined on accompanying" in trav. mem.

6 Plainly "N.N.W." in journ., but in trav. mem. Stuart failed to complete the second "N."

7 Bruneau River.

8 These 12 miles represented a short-cut across the base of an extensive bend of Snake River, this bend running well to the north. *Geol. Idaho.*

9 Snake River; Stuart encountering it at the spot where, due south from the mouth of present-day Rattlesnake Creek (a confluent emptying through Snake's right bank), the Snake began the bend mentioned in note 8.

10 Camped at a spot which, on Snake's left bank, was at the river's bend southwest of site of present-day town of Reverse. *Geol. Idaho.*

The remainder of this entry—"pafsed a few Huts," &c.—Stuart did not reproduce in trav. mem.

11 "horses" in trav. mem.

12 Camped approximately at mouth of present-day Dead Man· Creek, a stream which *Geol. Idaho* indicates (without naming) as flowing through Snake's left bank at a spot two and one-half miles southwest of town of Glenn's Ferry.

13 "river" in trav. mem.

14 Made a short-cut across the base of the far-northward swinging bend which lay immediately south of site of present-day town of King Hill. *Geol. Idaho.*

15 "stream" in trav. mem.

16 Camped on left bank of Snake at a spot shown by next day's entry to have been three miles below where present-day Big Wood River emptied through Snake's right bank. *Geol. Idaho.*

17 "jaded steeds bring up their leeway" in trav. mem.

18 Though this stream for its entire length is today popularly known by interchangeable names of Big Wood River, Wood River and Malad (or Malade) River, some modern cartographers apply (1) the name Big Wood River to

only so much of it as extends from its source to its confluence with Little Wood River and (2) the name Malad (or Malade) River to the united stream below this confluence. It owes the name Malad, so Alexander Ross states, to the following circumstances which occurred in 1824 (Peter Skene Ogden gives the date as 1819): Thirty-seven members of Ross's party when camped on this river having been made ill by eating the flesh of locally trapped beaver, "we supposed these animals must have lived on some root of a poisonous quality, which, although not strong enough to destroy them, yet was sufficiently deleterious to injure us: from this it was I named this stream Riviere aux Malades." It was the "River Malade" and "Sickly River" of Peter Skene Ogden in 1826, the "Sickly River" of John Work in 1830, his "Sukly River" in 1832, the "Sickly River" of Wilkes in 1841. *Ross* [*C*], pp. 75, 82, 114-116; *Journ. Peter Skene Ogden* in *Ore. Hist. Soc. Quar.*, XIII, p. 366; *Wilkes, Narr.*, map of Oregon in accompanying atlas; *Work*, p. 145; *Bulletin A*, p. 28.

19 Present-day Lower Salmon Falls (*Geol. Idaho*). They were the "Big Salmon Falls" of Osborne Cross in *Exec. Doc.*, p. 198, the "Fishing Falls" of *Colton* [*A*], [*B*], [*C*], [*F*], [*G*] and of *Disturnell*. See also *Bulletin A*, p. 28.

20 "snakes" in trav. mem.

21 Originally written "20 feet" in journ., the "20" later changed to "18"; "20" in trav. mem.

22 For a like description see *Fremont*, p. 169.

23 "they . . . their" in trav. mem.

24 Along the narrow strip of low land skirting Snake's left side and extending inland from the water's edge to a range of high flat-topped hills which, as Stuart advanced, he found to be pinching toward the river.

25 By thus tortuously ascending both a side and the inner end of an alcove which led directly inland from the Snake and was eroded deeply into the hills mentioned in note 24, Stuart placed himself on a plateau high above the river's surface and thereby was able to avoid swamps bordering the river and to begin the course mentioned in note 26.

26 These five and the succeeding four miles took Stuart around the rectangular bend lying south of Lower Salmon Falls. *Geol. Idaho.*

27 Snake River.

28 These, present-day Upper Salmon Falls, were the "Grand Rapids" of *Smedley*, p. 43, the "Little Salmon Falls" of Osborne Cross in *Exec. Doc.*, p. 196. See also *Geol. Idaho.*

29 A short cut across the base of the Snake's bend lying southeast from Upper Salmon Falls. *Geol. Idaho.*

30 "muddy creek" in trav. mem. This stream, present-day Salmon Falls Creek of *Geol. Idaho*, is the "Salmon River" of many of the now living folk and was the "Falls River" of Abert, the "Clarks River" of Wilkes, of Mitchell, of Cowperthwait, of Wyld and of Ensign. *Abert; Wilkes, Narr.*, accompanying Map of the Oregon; *Mitchell* [*A*]; *Cowperthwait* [*A*], [*B*]; *Wyld* [*B*], [*C*]; *Ensign* [*A*].

31 Camped on left bank of Salmon Falls Creek at the confluence of this creek with Snake River, and thus on a small, flat alluvial plain which is today, as it doubtless was in Stuart's time, thickly covered with willows ten feet or more in height. Whether or not these willows barred Stuart's view downstream along the Snake, his journ. and trav. mem. fail to note the many cascades which, representing the outlets of subterranean watercourses, theatrically gushed from openings part-way up the Snake's right-hand canyon wall: one of these cascades, or rather jets, being described in *Fremont*, pp. 167, 168. See also *Journ. Osborne Cross* in *Exec. Doc.*, p. 197.

32 A short cut across the base of the Snake's bend lying between the mouths of Salmon Falls Creek and present-day Deep Creek. *Geol. Idaho.*

33 Snake River, Stuart thus re-encountering it at the mouth of Deep Creek. *Geol. Idaho.*

34 This camp, as shown by the context and by the entry of two days later, was in the bottom of Snake River's canyon at the mouth of present-day Desert Creek (locally termed Cedar Draw), a deeply canyoned stream emptying through Snake's left bank.

35 "horses" in trav. mem.

36 This ascent to the Snake's canyon rim lying some 400 or more feet above the level of his camp was, because of the precipitous terrain, unquestionably made on a trail which led from the Snake's waterside and up the Desert Creek mentioned in note 34. This trail, existing today, was doubtless already old in Stuart's time.

Stuart, when atop the canyon's rim, was on a fairly level plain.

37 Present-day Rock Creek (see *Geol. Idaho*), a canyoned confluent of the Snake. It was the "Rock Creek" of *Palmer*, p. 45 and *Fremont*, p. 167 and was the "Rock River" of *Abert.*

Stuart's place of crossing Rock Creek may, because of his stated mileage and compass bearing, be confidently fixed as one or the other of two locations which respectively were some two and one-half and three and one-half miles above the creek's mouth. The extreme ruggedness of the terrain precluded the possibility of horsemen crossing elsewhere on the creek's lower stretches. *Geol. Idaho; Crown Maps*, III, No. 25.

38 This camp, which was at or near the spot where Fremont camped in 1842 (*Fremont*, p. 167), was on Rock Creek and approximately five miles due southeast from site of present-day city of Twin Falls. *Geol. Idaho.*

39 For parallel description, see *Fremont*, p. 167; *Palmer*, p. 45; *Thompson*, p. 75; *Smedley*, pp. 38, 39.

40 *Artemisia tridentata.* See *Bulletin B*, p. 125.

41 This spot at which Stuart regained the Snake was—as shown by (*a*) his stated mileage, (*b*) his stated compass bearing as corrected for compass error, and (*c*) his narratives' contexts—unquestionably within the limits of the modern town of Murtaugh and on such portion of the Snake canyon's left rim as

lay above the maelstrom at the confluence of present-day Dry Creek with Snake River.

Dry Creek (the "Dry Branch" of *Palmer*, p. 45, the "Cut-Rock Creek" of *Journ. Cecilia Emily McMillen Adams* in *Ore. Pioneer, 32nd annual reunion*, 1904, p. 310) crossed the plain where Stuart was, thence slid tortuously downward through a narrow break in the Snake's tall canyon wall, and so joined the Snake's berserk waters which Stuart graphically describes in later paragraphs of this day's entry. *Geol. Idaho.*

42 The description which Stuart's later paragraphs in this day's entry accord Caldron Linn is so keen and accurate that there remains for us only to sketch the geologic formation which caused the spot to be terrible and superb.

Immediately above the linn the Snake River, with its current's forcefulness increased by an abrupt converging of its canyon walls, plunged over Dry Creek Falls. At the foot of these falls, turning sharply to the left, it dashed into a whirlpool that had no outlet other than a vertical slit which, except for the flare at its top, was hardly more than 40 feet in width. Through this slit roared the entire river, titanic in its possession of melted snows from a thousand mountains. The whirlpool and its awesome portals were Caldron Linn.

Below the linn the canyon walls resumed their accustomed distance from each other.

Stuart seems to use the name Caldron Linn as though it had already been established. If so, it disproves the theory sometimes advanced, that the name was created by Stuart and not, as stated in *Astoria*, II, p. 24, by Hunt's party.

43 See *Astoria*, II, pp. 23, 26 for description of this wreckage.

44 Travelling on the left rim of Snake River's canyon to a spot which, as shown by Stuart's subsequent reference to its being one mile below "Clappins Rapid" (p. 113), was approximately two and one-fourth miles downstream from the present-day dam at Milner. *Geol. Idaho.*

45 Made by Hunt's party. *Astoria*, II, pp. 28-30; *Nouvelles Annales*, X, pp. 55-57 (translated at pp. 292, 293 *infra*).

These caches (for method of making caches see *Marcy*, pp. 162-164; *Chittenden*, pp. 41, 42) were on the Snake's left bank as indicated by the map accompanying *Nouvelles Annales* (facing p. 270 *infra*), and not on its right bank as indicated by the map accompanying *Astoria*. As appears in a later portion of this August 29 entry and also in the next day's entry, Stuart was on the left bank and, when going to the caches, did not cross the river. Also, as appears in the September 1 entry as well as in the citations *infra*, John Reed, heading for the caches and coming from McKenzie's post on the Boise River, was presently to appear on the Snake's right bank and would need to cross the Snake and thus to its left bank before he could reach the caches. *Astoria*, II, pp. 142, 257, 261-267; *Henry-Thomp.*, p. 761; *Cox* [*A*], I, p. 147; [*B*], pp. 83, 84; *Ross* [*A*], pp. 194, 214, 215.

46 "with Mefs.rs Crooks & McClellan" in trav. mem.

47 There were nine in all, as is disclosed by the next day's entry. This agrees with *Astoria*, II, p. 30; but *Nouvelles Annales*, X, pp. 55-57 (translated at pp. 292, 293 *infra*), suggest that yet another cache was made at seemingly the site of present-day town of Burley, Idaho. See note 187 on pp. 320, 321 for conflicting statements regarding the caches.

48 In journ.'s manuscript a figure "2" is interlined above this word "by" and a figure "1" above the word "in," which is the third word following, all this doubtless with view to future transposition of clauses. This transposition was made in trav. mem.

49 The caches had been robbed by indians led thither by André LaChapelle, François Landry and Jean Baptiste Turcotte, three members of Hunt's overland party who on reaching eastern Oregon had become so fatigued and discouraged that they withdrew from Hunt's advancing column and returned to western Idaho, where they spent the winter in a camp of Shoshones. Early in the spring of 1812, having overtaxed the camp's charity and desiring reinstatement in the indians' good graces, they nefariously conducted their benefactors to the caches. A pilfery of the contents was so elating that the whole crew felt constrained to attempt a raid among the bison in the Atsinas' territory at the headwaters of the Missouri River. This foray was opposed by the Atsinas in characteristic manner; and, it having cost some of the Shoshones their lives and all of the invaders their entire property, the chastened adventurers returned to the encampment from which they had originally set out. See entry of October 18 (p. 161); as also *Astoria*, II, pp. 194, 195 and note 123 on pp. 178, 179 *infra*.

50 "Walla-Walla" in trav. mem.

51 Nine canoes, according to *Astoria*, II, pp. 18, 19, 23, 26.

52 "to be fit for actual service" in trav. mem.

53 Present-day Augur (*alias* Pillar) Falls situated in Snake River, a short distance above confluence of the Rock Creek described in note 37. *Geol. Idaho.*

Upstream from Augur Falls, and thus between it and Stuart's present camp, were not only Dry Creek Falls (for which see note 42), but also two other cataracts of the Snake: (1) present-day Shoshone Falls (by a few early folk styled Canadian Falls), which, with its width of approximately 900 feet and its well-nigh vertical drop of 212 feet, was situated some three and one-half miles northeast of site of the modern town of Twin Falls; and (2) present-day Twin Falls (erstwhile known as Little Shoshone Falls), which, a single cataract bifurcated by a rock upon its crest and having a drop of 182 feet, was approximately due north from site of present-day town of Kimberly. *Geol. Idaho; Journ. Osborne Cross* in *Exec. Doc.*, p. 196; *Pac. Tourist*, pp. 168-170; *Bulletin A*, p. 28; *Century*, p. 928.

Because Stuart's route from Rock Creek to Dry Creek had kept him far inland from the Snake River he had had no opportunity to view either Shoshone or Twin Falls, but the fact that local awesomeness was not restricted to these major falls appears from his later context. Also John Mortimer Murphy, a visitor there in after years, commented: "Glancing up the stream, we could see that its sinuous course for half a mile was one mass of screaming rapids and small cataracts. . . ." *Murphy*, p. 183.

Though Hunt, on November 10, 1811, skirted both Shoshone and Twin Falls, his diary (p. 294 *infra*) fails to mention them. Because travelling upon the canyon's rim, he could, if he glimpsed them at all, have seen no more than their crests for each of these cataracts plunged into a ravine gouged deeply into the canyon's floor.

54 Incorrectly "50 to 60" in trav. mem.

55 Western colloquialism meaning extremely steep through erosion.

56 "strong" in trav. mem.

57 "principally" in trav. mem.

58 Incorrectly, "60 feet wide" in trav. mem.

59 Incorrectly, "50 yards" in trav. mem.

60 Incorrectly, "30 to 35" in trav. mem.

61 Incorrectly, "30 feet" in trav. mem. For description of Caldron Linn see note 42 and *Palmer*, p. 45.

62 "vortex" in trav. mem.

63 During freshets, though there was terrifying power in the current, the maelstrom-forming rocks were too deeply submerged to allow much visible evidence of their devilish capability.

64 See *Astoria*, II, p. 31. Almost all of this erstwhile fury and scenic grandeur has now disappeared. Today, because of dams across the Snake at both Milner and the crest of Shoshone Falls, and because of irrigating and power canals emerging from behind these barriers, Clappine's Rapid and Caldron Linn hold a mere trickle of water, while Shoshone Falls is fluidless, though Twin Falls, thanks to seepage from subterranean (and hence undammable) streams above it, manages still to continue a brave exhibit.

65 For the shattering of Crooks's canoe and the resultant drowning of Antoine Clappine, see *Astoria*, II, p. 23 and *Nouvelles Annales*, p. 54 (translated at p. 292 *infra*). These two accounts—especially *Nouvelles Annales*' allusion to "the entrance of a canyon"—strongly suggest that the rock which caused the catastrophe was the shaft that, approximately one and one-fourth miles below the present-day Milner dam, rises from the river bed at the centre of a bowl scoured into the Snake's left bank at the spot where the river veers sharply to the right. In the days before man-made dams and canals diverted the water, this bowl caught the full violence of the stream in its steeply descending rush and, because of the abruptness of the right-hand turn, contained a particularly vicious whirlpool. It was doubtless in this whirlpool that Clappine, "one of the most valuable of the voyageurs," met his death.

66 "Hoback" in trav. mem.

67 "Crooks" in trav. mem.

68 "a little" in trav. mem.

69 *Salmo clarkii.* The fishermen this day were Crooks and McClellan according to trav. mem.

70 Probably trading goods, for character of which see Ross Cox's description on p. LXXXI *ante*.

71 "from Astoria" in trav. mem.

72 "into one of the old receptacles" in trav. mem.

73 John Reed, who, as appears in the text and also in note 45, was scheduled to attend at the caches.

74 "Walla Walla" in trav. mem.

75 John Reed.

76 Robinson, Reznor and Hoback.

77 *I.e.*, on left bank. See note 45. Stuart's statement implies that it would be necessary for Robinson and his fellows to wait by the canoe (which was on this left bank) in order that they might use it in ferrying Reed from the right bank to the left.

78 This camp was seemingly at a spot which, within the municipal limits of modern Burley, Idaho (see *Geol. Idaho*), was on the right bank of a now abandoned channel of present-day Goose Creek (the "Elance River" of *Abert*, the "Goose River" of *Fremont*, p. 166) and immediately above this channel's confluence with Snake River. Though this channel is today deeply covered with alluvial soil, the fact of its existence was disclosed in July, 1929, through the digging of a trench a hundred or so yards west of the Burley end of the bridge across Snake River.

79 By these three terms Stuart doubtless meant the three locally prevalent plants which, as stated in his same order, have for many years been designated by Westerners as sagebrush, *Artemisia tridentata;* rabbit-brush, *Bigelovia graveolens* or *Chrysothamnus nauseosus;* and greasewood, *Sarcobatus vermiculatus*. See *Bulletin B*, p. 125 as also note 128 on p. 98 *ante*. The journ.'s "(these abominable and detested Shrubs)" is omitted in trav. mem.

80 Quitted Snake River at a spot which, due south from site of present-day town of Heyburn, was at northwestern end of the river's large southerly bend. *Geol. Idaho*.

81 Stuart, here commencing a short-cut, went diagonally inland from the Snake and traversed (1st) flat lands, (2d) a rolling plain with high buttes at its inland edge, (3d) a flat upland, and (4th) a series of low, rounded hills.

Later in his sentence, as also in subsequent parts of his narratives, Stuart mentions "lodge trace"; thereby meaning an indian trail scarified by the dragging ends of wigwam poles which were attached like wagon-shafts to the horses' sides. Ordinarily a lodge trace denoted peaceable indians, because war parties rarely encumbered themselves with tentage.

82 "brook" in trav. mem. This small stream (not improbably the one indicated, without naming, on *Abert*) is today seemingly merged in the inter-

locking series of channels and canals which, thanks to engineers, now grace the environs of Goose Creek and of its easterly neighbor, Marsh Creek. Stuart's camp accordingly was at a spot approximately eight and one-half miles due south from site of present-day town of Rupert. *Geol. Idaho.*

83 This stream, present-day Marsh Creek as indicated on *Geol. Idaho*, was the "Swamp Creek" of *Fremont*, p. 166, the "Marshy creek" of *Thompson*, p. 73, the "Bullrush Creek" of *Journ. Cecilia Emily McMillen Adams* in *Ore. Pioneer, 32nd annual reunion*, 1904, p. 309, and the "Charles River" of *Abert*. Apparently the spot where Stuart "struck" it was at its forks situated three miles northeast from site of present-day town of Albion. *Geol. Idaho.*

84 "5 lodges of" in trav. mem.

85 *Amelanchier alnifolia*, of which indians gathered and dried large supplies for winter use (*Stuart, Granville* [*A*], p. 86). For one method of preparing these berries for food, see *L. & C. Journs.*, III, p. 16; *L. & C. Hist.*, p. 419.

86 Marsh Creek.

87 Camped on right bank of Marsh Creek at a spot approximately three miles west by south from site of present-day town of Cotterel. *Geol. Idaho.*

88 Marsh Creek.

89 Present-day Raft River, which empties through the Snake's left bank. Stuart seemingly first encountered it at approximately the site of present-day town of Yale (*Geol. Idaho; Crown Maps*, III, No. 20). It was at Raft River in the days of the gold rush that many California-bound emigrants diverted from the Oregon Trail.

Having been mentioned as "Raft River" by Peter Skene Ogden in 1826, Jason Lee in 1834 called it by this same name and added: "received its name from the circumstance that some of the Traders were obliged to make a raft to cross it in high water." It was the "Raft River" of Abert in 1838, the "Casu River" and "Ocassia" of Nathaniel J. Wyeth in 1832, the "Cozzu (or Raft river)" of Osborne Russell in 1838, the "Raft river (Riviere aux Cajeux)" of Fremont in 1843, the "Cassia Creek" of Joel Palmer in 1845, the "Casus Creek" of Lobenstine, the "Decassure Creek" of Marcy, and the "Ogden's River" of Osborne Cross in 1849 (*Journ. Peter Skene Ogden* in *Ore. Hist. Soc. Quar.*, X, p. 357; *Abert; Wyeth, Nathaniel J.*, p. 163; *Russell*, p. 72; *Fremont*, p. 166; *Palmer*, p. 44; *Lobenstine*, p. 48; *Marcy*, p. 282; *Journ. Osborne Cross* in *Exec. Doc.*, p. 194; *Journ. Jason Lee* in *Ore. Hist. Soc. Quar.*, XVII, pp. 243, 244).

A westerly confluent of Raft River is today styled Cassia Creek. *Geol. Idaho.*

90 Snake. Camp was on its left bank approximately at the mouth of present-day Rock Creek. This creek (not to be confused with the Rock Creek described in note 37) was the stream to which, on September 26, 1843, Fremont "gave the name of Fall Creek." It was the "Fall River" of Ware, the "Fall Creek" of Symons, of Stansbury and of Colton, and was probably identical with both the "Bench Creek" of Akin and the "Levy creek, or Beaver-dam creek, as it is sometimes termed" of Joel Palmer. *Geol. Idaho; Fremont*, p. 165; *Preuss*, Sec. VI;

Ware, accompanying map; *Stansbury* [*B*]; *Colton* [*B*], [*C*]; *Akin*, p. 21; *Palmer*, p. 44.

91 Fremont, when following this same route, reckoned the distance as seventeen and one-half miles. *Fremont*, pp. 164, 165.

92 Present-day American Falls: so named, according to Joel Palmer, because a party of American trappers, when canoeing, had been swept over the cataract; all but one of them being killed. *Geol. Idaho*; *Palmer*, p. 44.

93 Incorrectly "about 35 feet" in trav. mem.

94 For a like description, see *Smedley*, p. 36; *Fremont*, p. 164 and plate facing it. See also *Bulletin A*, p. 28.

95 Incorrectly "60 feet" in trav. mem.

96 Camped on left bank of Snake River at a spot which, three miles above American Falls, is now covered by the lake created by the present-day dam at those falls.

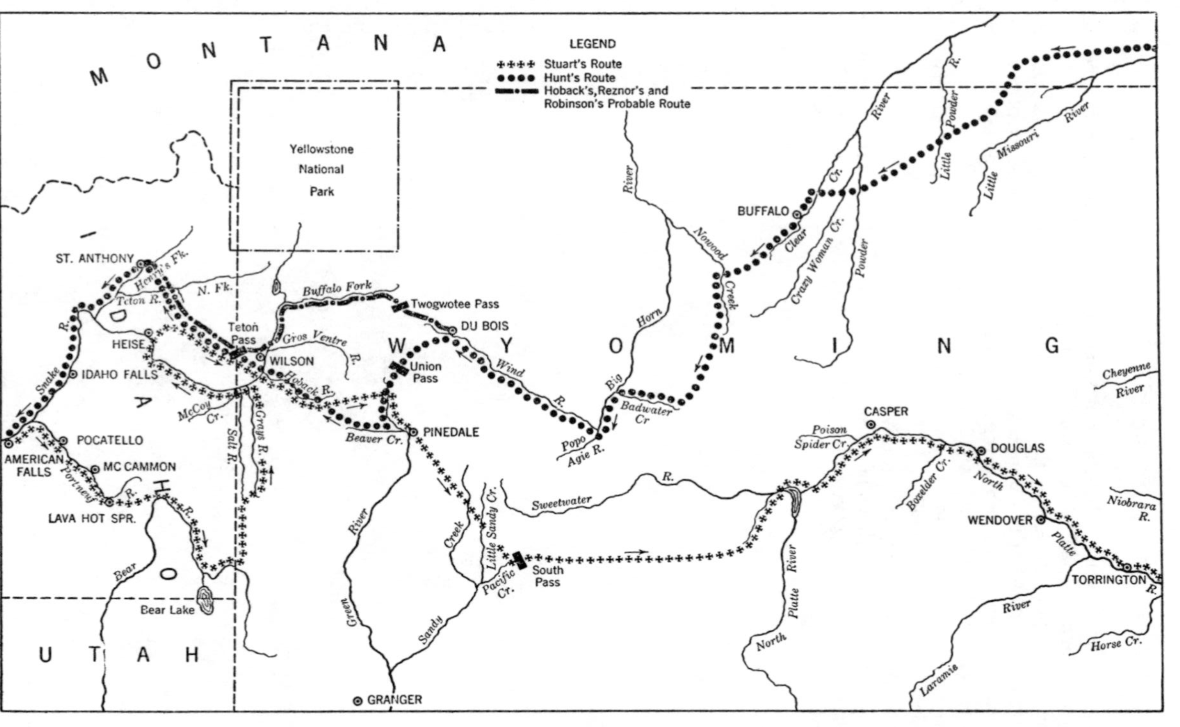

Routes of Stuart and of Hunt in eastern Idaho and in Wyoming.

CHAPTER VI

SEPT. 6 · SEPT. 29, 1812

On Horseback from American Falls to McCoy Creek and Thence by Raft and on Foot to Moody Creek

Ascend Portneuf River and Marsh Creek · Ascend Bear River · Absarokan Visitors · Thomas Fork and Spring Creek · Descend Salt River and Greys River · Uncertain as to Whereabouts · Resolve to Head for Teton Pass · Reach South Fork of Snake River · Begin Its Descent · Indians at McCoy Creek Steal All Horses · Continue on Foot and Later by Raft Down South Fork of Snake River · Thence on Foot to Moody Creek

Sunday 6th. Our course was E.N.E. today 23 miles on the top of a tolerably level ridge with a channel of the river meandering along its base— The main body[1] is a great way off and appears thickly cloathed with Willows, over which we often discover the top foilage of Trees, supposed to be Cottonwood, [*and as*] far as the eye can reach [*heavy*] Timbered Bottoms seem of such magnitude as to hide every vestige of undergrowth

Two families of Indians[2] came and encamped close by us[3] this evening from whom we got some dried Salmon and a Horse, for which I was obliged to give a great price

Monday 7th. The Indian notwithstanding the extra[*va*]gant price I gave for his Horse regretted his bargain brought back the Goods and requested permission [*to*] retain him— this I would not have afsented to, but considering the great distance we had to travel through this Country, and the facility of stealing these creatures, I thought it best to save at least the articles I had given him, rather than run [60] the risk— 2 Miles E.N.E. brought us to Falls Creek, so called from its numerous Cascades—[4] it is from 20 to 50 yards[5] wide, has good banks, some Willow, & Beaver

This being the Water course which guided Mr Miller to the Snake River[6] & having determined [/*by very urgent persuasions*/] on taking his tract as leſs circuitous [*and more out of the* *walks* *of the Blackfoot Indians*, /*who are very numerous, and inimical to the whites*,/] than that by Henrys Fort,[7] we [*soon after leaving camp*,] parted with the Indians [*and*] followed up the left bank for 25 Miles S.E. & encamped[8] a mile above the discharge of a small Branch[9] coming in from the West

Tuesday 8th We went 10 Miles E.S.E. to the Forks,[10] when learning that the main or most easterly one,[11] was very rocky & a bad road, we took the other[12] & followed it 5 miles S.S.W.— 2 South — & 11 S W to where we stopped for the night.[13] Hoping by this route to fall in once more with the Lodge Trace which [*Mr Miller supposes*] we had left to our right 6 Miles below Portage Falls—[14] The Bottoms for the first 10 Miles were very narrow, but the remainder up this Fork are large & poſseſs a good soil, except in some few places where they are low and swampy— Along the Hills are a few Serviceberry bushes but the [*prime of their*] season of their fruit is past, and[15] few or no Cherries remain on the twigs, though there is plenty of different kinds,

Wednesday 9th On our arrival last evening I sent Benjamin Jones up the Creek to endeavour if poſsible to find the Indian road, who after walking a considerable distance[16] [61] returned without discovering any thing of it, and he says further that the tract we had followed all day bent still more to the west

This proving of course totally unfit for our purpose, we this morning croſsed the Creek,[17] went due East 3 Miles over stony hills,[18] when reaching the main Fork[19] we followed along the left bank for 7 more and found a Camp, & large road; which we took for the one in question— Mr. Miller having [*as he supposes*] come by a route more to the north[20] and knowing nothing of this spot, we thought it most advisable to continue up the Creek[21] more particularly as it lay directly in our course

3 miles above the Indian Camp a Branch[22] came in from the South, up which a great part of the road[23] went, and 3 farther on, the water[24] again subdivided—[25] the main body[26] ran [*about*] N & S. with a continuation of its Cascades, but the small one,[27] which the majority of the trails followed came from the E

We crofsed[28] the latter and although to us an unknown route, trusted the tract, which in 4 Miles brought us to where the branch turned all at once round to S.W.—

Here ascending,[29] we pafsed through a Gap[30] in the mountains[31] on the left; which soon brought us to the opposite decent and discovered an extensive Plain[32] lying before us— through this we steered due East and in 18 Miles [62] struck a River[33] running through an apparently level Country in about a South direction, which Mr. Miller at once pronounced the Stream where he had made his last Falls hunt,—[34] This River is 100 yards wide, and is here confined between a high rocky Bluff bank and a [*high*] Hill partially covered with Trees of the Pine species, but at present appears no more the asylum of the ingenious Beaver, than do the bleak summits of the Cordilleras;— The prairies being here burnt smooth, we were obliged (though now dusk[35]) to proceed 2 Miles farther[36] ere we could find grass enough to satisfy our hungry Horses for the night; having come in all this day 42 miles nearly East—

[*In the large plain we passed thro', there is considerable fresh sign oj Buffalo, which we are in hopes of overtaking in a few days—*]

Thursday 10th Leaving our station early we travelled 10 miles E.S.E.[37] and 5 S.E.[38] where finding an excellent grafsy Bottom we stopped[39] for [*the*] night, in order to recruit the strength of our Cattle,[40] who are a good deal jaded by a few of our last days journeys— a plain lodge trace is our guide, which follows up the right bank of this stream, and shall be our [*only*] dependence untill we reach that part Mr Miller explored

We saw a number of Goats[41] on our march, but have as yet waged an unsuccefsfull war against them

[63] Friday 11th We went 6 miles S.W.[42] 2 E.S.E. 2 South[43] and 15 S.S.E. to our encampment on a small Branch[44] ifsuing from the Pine covered mountains[45] on our left which have in the course of todays journey furnished numberlefs Rills and many Runs[46] equal to this where we now are— The River meanders in almost every direction with a gentle current, but the margin is woefully deficient in all Kinds of small growth, what little there formerly was having been totally destroyed by the Beaver, neverthelefs a few of these animals still remain, and their principal susbistence are roots and herbs—

a few Antelopes and a good many Geese are the only creatures we get a shot at, a couple of the latter I was fortunate enough to arrest during this days march and an enormously large black Bear pafsed in the vicinity of our Camp last evening, but although we made every exertion were unable to do him any injury— Our succefs is bad in the extreme among the land inhabitants, and our almost only resource for food is the produce of our fishing rods from day to day which is poor Trout and a species of Sucker which is fat & really excellent, called by Virginians the Stone-toater[47]

Saturday 12th Immediately on leaving our last nights station the country opened very much to the South,[48] the mountains receded to a great distance and a beautiful low Plain occupied the intervening [64] space— 8 Miles E.S.E. and 6 S.E. brought us to the Forks[49] of the River, where the banks were well supplied with a middling growth of Cottonwood— The south Branch[50] being considered out of our course, we went along the other[51] 8 [*miles*] East & 1 N.E.[52] making in all 23 miles— When we returned from drawing our Suppers from the water, a number of Indians of the Absaroka or Crow nation were at our Camp— they behaved decently, and some returned to their Camp to bring us Buffaloe meat [&c.]—

Sunday 13th Knowing the adroitneſs of these fellows in stealing Horses we doubled our Watches, a precaution by no means unneceſsary, for having by midnight augmented their numbers to 21 they conducted themselves in such a manner as made it requisite for all of us to keep guard the remainder of the night— at daybreak I traded what little Meat they had with a few pieces of Buffaloe skin, which done, they insisted on selling us Horses, and demanded Gun Powder [*in return*]— this I refused but they would absolutely exchange some, and at length I acceded in one instance— Their behaviour was insolent in the extreme and indicated an evident intention to steal if not to rob—[53] we kept close poſseſsion of our arms, but notwithstanding our vigilance they stole a Bag containing the greater part of our Kitchen furniture— To prevent an open rupture we gave them abou twenty loads [65] of Powder and left them[54] happy at getting off on no worse terms

Going 10 Miles East over hills[55] to where a large Fork[56] came in from the North, we found smokes on several of the highest mountains in different directions, which concluding to be signals[57] for the purpose of collecting a reinforcement of these Rascals to pursue and attack us, as we could easily discover that a want of strength and not of will was the only thing which prevented them doing us all poſsible harm this morning, we thought it best to vary our former course not only the better to keep out of their way, but from the information of Mr Miller, would much sooner reach the part of the Country with which he was acquainted; we left the main stream[58] and after following up the right bank of the

Fork[59] for 15 miles due north encamped on a small Branch[60] having come this day 25 miles

Monday 14th We unexpectedly paſsed the night in quietneſs and soon after sunrise continued up the Fork[61] 3 miles, then ascending the Mountains on our right[62] steered a little to the W. of N. for 18 more, when we found a considerable Branch[63] running due north on which we stopped for the night.[64]

Three Snake Indians came to us in the evening, who on hearing that the Absarokas were at no great distance left us immediately in apparent consternation—

[66] Tuesday 15th Soon after sunrise we were again on horseback croſsed the Branch[65] and continued on for 12 miles N.N.E. to a low ridge,[66] which paſsing over we found another stream[67] and went north 15 more to where it cut through the mountains,[68] here ascending 3 miles E.N.E. brought us to our nights lodgings on the last Watercourse—[69] Saw in the course of the day a multitude of Antelopes, but were unsucceſsfull in procuring meat

Wednesday 16th Our course was 2 miles E.N.E. & 4 N.E.[70] to a large stream[71] running towards the north, which croſsing we found a deep Indian Path and followed it for 19 more due north and encamped[72] on the Bank of the river, which runs with great rapidity over a stony and gravely Bed—[73] On striking this watercourse we easily discovered how far we had failed in attaining the object in view; for, from all we had learned concerning Millers River we ought to have struck it hereabouts, whereas the one we are on runs quite a contrary course and must be a Branch of the Snake River— Having thus lost the intended track by which we proposed croſsing the Rocky Mountains knowing it must be to the South, and the great probability of falling in again with the Crows, the large Band of whom did we meet, our Horses would undoubtedly be sacrificed, [*the*] other property forcibly taken from us, and our lives perhaps endangered we at once concluded that our best, safest and most certain way would be to follow this River down, and paſs the first spur[74] of mountains by the route of the Party[75] who came acroſs the Continent last year [67] Saw a [*Black*] Bear and a great many Antelopes, but could not approach either

Thursday 17th Leaving our Camp late we kept at some distance from the right bank of the River[76] for 11 miles N.[77] on account of swampy ground,[78] next 9 N.N.W.[79] when the Path winding to the East we followed it till seeing two streams iſsuing from the mountains, examined and found the most Southerly[80] a watercourse of considerable magnitude, and the other[81] much greater which from the opinion of those of last Fall's Party must be Mad River— Here sending Jones to see if a paſsage was practicable in that direction, we turned our faces to the West, and at the end of 3 miles took up our nights quarters[82] [*in a low point*] among some small Cottonwoods— Killed[83] a buck Antelope today which was in fine order, and proved an agreeable addition to our stock of provisions, now become very low—

Friday 18th Our [*poor*] horses having good employment for their jaws, it was late before we left Camp, when proceeding 1½ miles West croſsed the Fork[84] we have followed these two days; as Jones brought accounts of the impoſsibility of paſsing where he went[85]

This Fork joined the main body[86] a little below, where the velocity of the current[87] became incredible and ran so close to the mountains as to compell us to ascend several inferior rises[88] along an abominable road, caused by the fallen Timber and Rocks— 14½ miles N.W. brought us to where we stopped[89] for the night, the latter part of the way being through Beaver Ponds & quagmires, where our progreſs was slow indeed, which has been the case the greater part of this days journey— On the Watercourses of every size and description, which we have seen since we left the Crows, the Beaver have by their Dams inundated all the low grounds, and are in abundance [68] wherever there is a poſsibility of their finding a place to live in & a few Willows for their sustenance— The Indians attempt[90] on many of the small Branches to dig them out, but from all appearance they do not succeed to any extent, no doubt from the want of the neceſsary implements & a little practicle knowledge

Saturday 19th We[91] were all up soon after the dawn and I had just reached the river bank, when I heard the Indian yell raised in the vicinity of our Camp, and the cry "To Arms" "There's Indians echoed by all of our Party— We had just time to snatch our arms when two[92] Indians at full gallop paſsed 300 yards to one side of our station driving off [*by their yells*] every horse we had [*notwithstanding their being tethered & hobbled*], towards them we rushed, and got [*almost*] within shot of the nearest when repeated yells in the direction from which they came, made us desist from the pursuit in order to defend ourselves and Baggage; for there being only two Indians[93] after the Horses, we very readily imagined that the main body were in reserve to attack our rear did we follow the foremost, or to plunder the Camp if opportunity offered— At the rate the Horses were going all attempts to rejoin them was unavailing, and had we pursued farther every thing else would have been lost to a certainty, which would undoubtedly have made our situation if possible far more deplorable than it really is— The savages whose yells made us return to the Baggage paſsed soon after at full speed in the others tracks and we could not discover that the whole party amounted to more than 20, which had we known [69] only three minutes sooner, a few Horses might [*probably*] have been saved & a scalp or two fallen into our hands— From a few words we heard, they were beyond all doubt of the Absaroka[94] nation and I believe the Band we met on Millers River[95]

[*This*[96] *method of stealing horses is deserving of being more minutely described; one of the party rode past our camp and placed himself on a con-*

spicuous knob in the direction they wanted to run them off; when the others (who were hidden behind our camp) seeing him prepared, rose the warwhoop, or Yell, (which is the most horribly discordant howling imaginable, being in imitation of the different beasts of prey, at this diabolical noise the animals naturally rose their heads to see what the matter was— at that instant he who had placed himself in advance, put spurs to his steed, and ours seeing him gallop off in apparent fright, started all in the same direction, as if a legion of infernals were in pursuit of them.— In this manner a dozen or two of those fellows have sometimes succeeded in running off every horse belonging to war parties, of perhaps 5 or 600 men; for once those creatures take fright, nothing short of broken necks can stop their progreſs—]

On the whole it was one of the most [*daring and*] intrepid actions I ever heard of among Indians, and convinced me how determined they were on having our Horses, for which they would unquestionably have followed us any distance, and nothing but seeing us prepared and ready to defend ourselves prevented their attacking us where we first saw them— We have been busy all day making preparations to set out in the morning on foot down the River, along the Plains of which below Henry's Fort, we have hopes of meeting with some of the Snakes, from whom if we can procure a couple of Horses, we shall continue our former determination and if poſsible reach the Cheyenne River before the Winter sets in, but should we fail in this, our Winter quarters will probably be somewhere on the Spanish River—[97] We have just food enough for one meal, and rely with confidence on the inscrutable ways of Providence to send in our road wherewith to subsist on from day to day—

Sunday 20th [*Last night*] Jones set our old Beaver Trap (the only one we have) and caught a middle sized Beaver— It was 10 A.M. before we were ready to depart, when collecting every article we could not carry committed to the flames whatever would consume, and the remainder [70] we threw into the River— [*resolved*[98] *to prevent the villans benefiting more by us—for two of the same band were (by Jones) seen this morning sculking near our camp, in order no doubt to observe where we should deposit what part of our effects we could not carry—]* We went on for 10 Miles N.W.[99] when finding a good fishing place we stopped[100] for the night and Forty Trout were taken by dusk— We took with [*us*] only what we considered absolutely necefsary but we find our Bundles very heavy as the road is by no means a dead level

Monday 21st. We set out early and going along the River found a Beaver in our Trap, which taking we [*cut up, in order that each might carry his share—*] at the end of 8 miles N.W. [*we*] stopped[101] for the purpose of making Rafts to crofs the River as Wood appears scarce below us, and it is not fordable— Forty[102] trout were again caught today, but they are poor and very indifferent food— [*and were it not for the little meat we occasionally fall in with, I really think they would not even support life—*]

Tuesday 22nd. The Rafts were ready and we embarked on them at 10 A.M. three on [*the*] one and four on the other, after going through some very strong & rough water, found them safe & steady which instead of crofsing induced us to continue on for 20 Miles N.W. when we encamped[103] on a beautiful low point— [*In the evening going to set the Trap,*] Jones killed a Fallow Deer and a Wolverine[104] [*which is the more fortunate, as we can carry the meat on our rafts—*], pulled our boats[105] out of the water to let them dry—

Wednesday 23d. In addition to the produce of Jones's hunt yesterday Vallé caught a large Beaver in the Trap and shot another which [*was so fat that it*] unfortunately sank [*before he could get to the spot*]— We embarked late and went 10 miles N.W. 2 N. 1 N.E. 6 N.W. 1 N. 1 N.E. which brought us to our nights station[106] early, as we nearly upset our Raft[107] a little way above and wet all our things—[108] the River is very rapid & full of Beaver [*we might have shot several in the course of the day, but thought it a pity, as we have meat enough for the present*]— 21 miles

[71] Thursday 24th It was late before everything was dry and shipped— 4 miles NW brought us to a part of the River where the mountains on the right and cut[109] Bluffs on the left made us apprehensive of Rapids impaſsable for our craft being at no great distance— We [*therefore*] stopped and on examination found the water good except in one place where to preserve our bundles from getting wet we unloaded & made a short portage— 2 miles[110] farther on we came to a little Island where were some Elk, one of which on being wounded took to the stream & drifted a mile before we overtook and hauled it ashore, where on account of strong appearances of bad weather we stopped for the night—[111] the last 3 miles were [*in*] about [*a*] N.E. [*direction*]—

Friday 25th On skining the Elk a Ball and an Arrow point were found in its body, which to all appearance, must have been in it about a week— this leads us to believe that the Blackfeet were here not long since, and were the persons who wounded it— The meat proved very good and we remained here all day drying it— Rain, Hail and at last, Snow fell in the course of the evening and night[112] and the day has menaced us with a repetition notwithstanding which the quantity that decended has much diminished, and the weather is by no means cold—

Saturday 26th Rain fell during the greater part of the night— at a late hour we embarked everything and at the end of 1 mile N N W put ashore on the left bank for the purpose of completing the drying of our Elk and adding some logs to our Rafts as the additional weight of meat sinks them too deep to proceed with safety—

Sunday 27th Our Rafts were ready before sunset and we sett off this morning early— our course was 1 mile W N W — 1 W — 2 N W 2 W — 2 N N W — ½ W N W — 2 N W — 2 W — 1½ N W — ¼ W — 2 W N W — 1 N W — 1¼ N N W — 2 N W — 2 N N W — ½ W N W — 1½ N N W — ½ N W — 1 W N W — 1 N W — ¼ W N W — ¼ N N W — ¼ N W — ½ N — ¼ N N W — ¼ W N W — 1½ N W — ¼ W N W — ¼ N W — ¼ W — ¼ N W making in all 31¼ miles[113] when having advanced considerably into the low Plain on the left and the mountains on the right being now reduced to moderate sized Hills, we stopped on the left bank for the night[114] intending to crofs the River in the morning and proceed on foot—

[72] Monday 28th We remained in the same Camp all [*this*] day making Mogasins & other preparations for our journey— Before sunset our meat about 20 lb each was divided and every thing else in readinefs to crofs the River early and proceed by the foot of the mountains[115] which bound the Plain to the south of Henry's Fort— Mad River[116] is generally a very rapid stream from One to 200 yards wide, winds about among the mountains in every direction, which are of great magnitude on the East, but deserve no other name than Hills on the West—[117] Its bed is gravel and the banks for the most part are of the same material, occasionally indeed a thin soil covers this but is partial even in the same Bottom— The body of the Mountains and Hills is a hard black Rock, the former produce great numbers of the Pine species and some red Cedars, but the latter are little else than Barrens with a growth of short stinted grafs— Immense quantities of Beaver inhabit Mad River and its tributary streams, and wherever the soil is in the least propitious a great abundance of small Cottonwoods and Willow are every where to be found for their support

Though this watercourse runs with incredible velocity, it is (so far as I can judge from information and observation) entirely free from either Fall, Cascade or bad Rapid & is generally confined in one body untill it here extricates itself from the mountains and divides into innumerable channels, making Islands without number, all covered with some kind of Wood and equally the asylum of Beaver in multitudes—

Tuesday 29th Crofsed[118] the River early and after traversing a considerable Bottom of Cottonwood Hawthorn[119] and Willow ascended the upper bank and went 15 Miles N E over very rough ground, where we encamped on a small Branch[120] in the Hills, very much fatigued—

saw three Antelopes but thought it imprudent to shoot at them fearing the Black feet may be in the vicinity & well aware that if discovered by them inevitable destruction must be our lot

Notes to Chapter VI

1 Stuart, having followed the left bank of the Snake and arrived at the mouth of present-day Portneuf River, ascended the left bank of this latter stream which, for the moment, he seemingly thought to be one of the channels of Snake River. *Geol. Idaho.*

2 "shoshonies" in trav. mem.

3 The camp, as appears from the context and particularly from the subsequent day's entry, was on the left bank of Portneuf River at a spot two miles below the mouth of present-day Ross Fork (named for the fur trader, Alexander Ross). *Geol. Idaho.*

4 This brought Stuart to the spot which, on Portneuf River's left bank, was opposite the mouth of Ross Fork (*Geol. Idaho*). Stuart's "Falls Creek" was accordingly so much of Portneuf River as lay above this confluence.

Portneuf River, the "Portniff creek" of *Shively*, p. 9, has possessed individuality through the fact that prehistoric flows of lava so washboarded much of its bed as later to produce a long series of quiet pools separated by cascades varying from one inch to four feet in height. *Chittenden*, p. 479.

For the derivation of the name, there are the following two conflicting traditions. Nathaniel J. Wyeth, in 1832, wrote that it is "called Portneuf from a man killed near it" and Scott, repeating this tradition, adds that this man, a French-Canadian trapper serving under Peter Skene Ogden, was murdered by indians in 1825. However, Scott, in his same comment *ante*, gives the other tradition that the name came from two French words which, respectively meaning "gate" and "nine," referred to the many lava obstructions in the river's bed. *Wyeth, Nathaniel, J.*, p. 162; *Scott*, III, p. 293. See also *Chittenden*, p. 785.

5 "20 to 50 yards" in journ.; "40 to 50 yards" in trav. mem. Either measure is sufficiently accurate according as the measurer includes or excludes various narrow stretches.

6 Doubtless meaning that Miller, Hoback, Reznor, and Robinson had descended northerly flowing Portneuf River when recently returning from their hunting trip in areas which, in part, adjoined present-day Bear River and, in other part, lay eastward of its lower stretch. See notes 175-178 on pp. 104, 105.

7 Stuart's immediate goal being that part of Green River's valley which adjoins South Pass—this Pass being the "shorter trace to the South" reported to him by the indian on Aug. 16 (p. 84) — he now decided, after "very urgent persuasions," that, instead of taking in reverse Hunt's trail from Green River to Snake River (*i.e.*, from Green River, *via* Hoback River and Teton Pass, to Henry's Fort on north fork of Snake River), he would travel in reverse the

westerly portion of Miller's route mentioned in note 6 and which, leading *via* Bear River to Green River, would be shorter and also free from the menace of the Atsinas.

Stuart had at hand serviceable data on which to base his decision inasmuch as, in addition to the information received from the indian, (1) all of his companions—inclusive of Miller—,when previously travelling westward with Hunt, had crossed Green River's valley in a latitude north of South Pass (*Nouvelles Annales*, X, pp. 43, 44, translated at pp. 286, 287 *infra; Astoria*, I, pp. 271 *et seq*) and (2) Miller also, when later hunting with Hoback, Reznor, and Robinson, had twice traversed it (*i.e.*, from west to east and subsequently returning from east to west) in a latitude south of that Pass (notes 175-178 on pp. 104, 105). Accordingly, Stuart knew the geographic relation which (a) Bear River's valley bore to that of Green River, and (b) Green River's valley bore, not only to South Pass, but also to Union Pass—this latter pass, lying north of South Pass, having already been penetrated by all of his companions when westward bound with Hunt.

That Stuart's plan of pursuing the Bear River route toward Green River and South Pass was a definite one appears from the following phrasings (the underscorings are ours) in his entries of

Sept. 9, when on Portneuf River, "we thought it most advisable to continue up the Creek [Portneuf River] more particularly as it lay directly in our course" (p. 129).

Sept. 10, when on Bear River, "a plain lodge trace is our guide, which follows up the right bank of this stream and shall be our only dependence untill we reach that part Mr Miller explored" (p. 130).

Sept. 12, when on Bear River, "The south Branch [Bear Lake's outlet into Bear River] being considered out of our course, we went along the other" (Bear River) (p. 131).

Sept. 13, when on Bear River at mouth of Thomas Fork, "we thought it best to vary our former course not only the better to keep out of their [Absarokan indians'] way, but from the information of Mr Miller, would much sooner reach the part of the Country with which he was acquainted" (p. 131).

Sept. 16, when, after leaving Bear River, had reached Greys River, a northward flowing stream, "On striking this watercourse we easily discovered how far we had failed in attaining the object in view; for, from all we had learned concerning Millers River [Bear River] we ought to have struck it hereabouts, whereas the one we are on runs quite a contrary course and must be a Branch of the Snake River— Having thus lost the intended track by which we proposed crofsing the Rocky Mountains knowing it must be to the South . . . we at once concluded that our best, safest and most certain way would be" to regain Hunt's trail east of Henry's Fort and follow it eastward to Green River (pp. 132, 133).

The reason for Miller's misapprehension concerning Bear River after it had been reached is stated in note 176 on p. 104.

There naturally arises the question as to why Stuart, on first arriving on that river—at the vertex of its turn described in note 176 on p. 104,—elected to ascend the stream rather than descend it as Miller had previously done when on his autumn hunt. The text suggests, though it does not assert, an answer. The arrival was at dusk; and also the grass had been so burned that Stuart, to obtain forage for his horses, was forced to travel upstream to the spot where the turn commenced (entry of Sept 9, p. 129). The next day disclosed a well-defined indian trail leading in the desired southward direction although upstream, and this trail Stuart followed (p. 130). As a matter of fact, the stretch of Bear River along which he travelled was better for his purpose than would have been the southern flowing stretch which Miller vainly sought, and Stuart's actual route became afterward part of the Oregon Trail.

8 On left bank of Portneuf River.

9 Present-day Mink Creek, which, flowing rapidly downward from its sources in the neighboring hills and emptying through the Portneuf's left bank, is, on *Geol. Idaho*, indicated but not named as the first stream debouching southeast of the site of present-day city of Pocatello.

10 Confluence of present-day Marsh Creek with Portneuf River. *Geol. Idaho*.

11 Portneuf River.

12 Marsh Creek.

13 Camped on left bank of Marsh Creek at a spot due west from Portneuf River's right-angled bend which lay southeasterly of site of present-day city of McCammon, Idaho. *Geol. Idaho.*

14 American Falls.

15 In substitution for journ.'s phrasing: "and few or no Cherries remain on the twigs, though there is plenty of different kinds," trav. mem. states: "however wild cherries of various kinds are to be had in the greatest perfection & abundance." The journ.'s "cherries" quite possibly meant "service berries." The trav. mem.'s "wild cherries" doubtless included chokecherries, *Prunus demissa*. See *L. & C. Hist.*, p. 420, as also *Fremont*, pp. 34, 47, 140.

16 In journ.'s manuscript, Stuart, having first written the phrase "number of miles," deleted it and in its stead inserted the words "considerable distance."

17 Marsh Creek. Crossed to its right bank.

18 Stuart, immediately after fording Marsh Creek, traversed the watershed lying between it and Portneuf River. *Geol. Idaho.*

19 Portneuf River, encountering it at the bend described in note 13. *Geol. Idaho.*

20 Because of the references which journ. and trav. mem. make to Miller's

vague knowledge of his route, it would appear that Stuart had become conscious of Miller's geographic unreliability.

We suggest that, if Miller lacked innate sense of orientation, he may have been confused by the detour up Marsh Creek's valley and by what, to an uncritical observer, might well seem this valley's miniature similarity to Portneuf's valley.

21 Portneuf River, Stuart travelling on its left bank.

22 Present-day Dempsey Creek. *Geol. Idaho.*

23 "traces" in trav. mem.

24 Portneuf River.

25 Confluence of present-day Fish Creek with Portneuf River, this being at site of present-day town of Lava Hot Springs. *Geol. Idaho.*

26 Portneuf River.

27 Fish Creek.

28 To Fish Creek's left bank, and then along it.

29 Stuart thus quitting the floor of the basin in which Fish Creek here flowed.

30 The northerly one of two low gaps running from west to east, the present-day highway traversing the southerly one.

31 High hills forming the watershed between the valleys of Fish Creek and Bear River.

32 The wide valley of Bear River.

33 Bear River, for description of which see note 176 on p. 104. Stuart's initial contact with the river, being at the vertex of the turn described in that note, was at a spot directly across the stream from present-day Soda Point, the pine-covered hill of Stuart's text, the "Sheep Rock" of covered-wagon days, and thus was on or near the site of present-day town of Alexander, *alias* Alexandria and earlier known as Morristown (*Caribou; Geol. Idaho; Fremont*, p. 135 and map opposite it; *Hayden, Wyoming and Idaho*, I, map following p. 269). Bear River is styled "Millers R." on map accompanying *Nouvelles Annales* and reproduced facing p. 270 *infra.*

34 See note 176 on p. 104.

35 "dark" in trav. mem.

36 These two miles, in light of next day's entry, were travelled upstream and on the right bank. Camped on right bank of Bear River at approximately the spot which, on westerly outskirts of site of present-day town of Soda Springs, was where the river began the turn described in note 176 on p. 104.

37 Upstream on right bank of Bear River, which here was flowing northwesterly. The end of Stuart's "10 miles" placed him at approximately the spot where, one mile east by north from site of present-day town of Rose, the Bear River made a right-angled turn from north to west. *Caribou; Geol. Idaho.*

38 Upstream on Bear River's right bank.

39 Camped on right bank of Bear River at a spot approximately one mile

northwest from mouth of present-day Ninemile Creek. *Caribou; Quad. Slug Creek.*

40 "horses" in trav. mem.

41 Possibly *Oreamnos montanus montanus* (*Ord*)—now popularly termed mountain goat or white goat,—but more probably prong-horned antelope, *Antilocapra americana;* this last, not only because of the locality but also because, as appears in note 61 on p. 172, Stuart was seemingly not immune from the earliest Westerners' habit of mentioning antelope as goats.

42 Should have been "S.E." as it is in trav. mem.; this, because "S.W." would have put Stuart into the river. The end of these six miles placed him at approximately the river-bend which, in longitude 111° 24′ 40″, was immediately south from site of U. S. Government's present-day triangulation station as indicated on *Caribou* and *Quad. Slug Creek.*

43 Stuart's completion of these last four miles had taken him around the bend mentioned in note 42, and had placed him in the vicinity of a stream which, sometimes termed Big Spring Creek, is indicated, without naming, on *Caribou* and *Quad. Montpelier* as debouching into Bear River at a spot one-half mile northwest from the most northerly of the mouths of present-day Twin (*alias* Georgetown) Creek.

44 Present-day Montpelier Creek. *Caribou; Quad. Montpelier; Geol. Idaho.*

45 Present-day Preuss Range. *Quad. Montpelier.*

46 Fifteen creeks and drains in addition to those mentioned in notes 39, 43, 44 are indicated on *Caribou*, *Quad. Slug Creek* and *Quad. Montpelier* (see also *Hayden, Montana*, pp. 155, 156; *Horn*, pp. 36-38; *Crown Maps*, III, No. 10, f.n.). Present-day Aspen Range furnished the creeks and drains which were crossed by Stuart in the morning; while its southeast continuation, Preuss Range, provided those which he crossed in the afternoon. *Caribou; Quad. Slug Creek; Quad. Montpelier.*

47 The "poor Trout" owed their mediocrity, it would seem, to the fact that they were caught at the close of the spawning season.

The "Sucker" was a catostomoid fish, *Catostomus* or *Hypentelium nigricans*, known also, in popular parlance, as stone-roller, stone-lugger, sucker, hog-sucker and hog-molly.

48 See *Quad. Montpelier.*

49 Apparently confluence of present-day Bear Lake Outlet with Bear River. But, from the hereinafter cited maps, it appears that since Stuart's time, (1) this confluence has moved southward through swamp and alluvial soil, and (2) Bear River below this confluence and as far south as the latitude of present-day town of Dingle has not only shifted the major portion of its waters to a channel skirting the easterly upland, but also well-nigh abandoned the channel which, passing west through the site of town of Dingle and then turning northwestward, was doubtless the one that Stuart followed. *Quad. Montpelier; Preuss*, sec. V; *Fremont*, accompanying large map, as also map facing p. 133.

50 Bear Lake Outlet.

51 Bear River.

52 Camped at approximately the spot which, on Bear River's right bank, was at the vertex of the river's northerly hairpin turn situated immediately southeast of site of present-day town of Wardboro and two miles east by north from site of town of Dingle. *Geol. Idaho; Quad. Montpelier.*

53 *Astoria*, II, pp. 134, 136 adds an account of Stuart's successfully resisting a mild assault alleged to have been made on him by the indians' chief.

54 "& departed," in trav. mem.

55 Across (1st) the watershed between Stuart's camp and present-day Sheep Creek, and (2nd) the watershed between Sheep Creek and present-day Thomas Fork (*Quad. Montpelier*). Though Stuart at the end of his "10 Miles" was only 169 miles from Pacific Springs on the westerly end of South Pass (*Horn*, pp. 29-36) and though he theretofore had been heading for that pass and had been following quite closely the route later adopted by the Oregon Trail, he, for the reasons given in the text, now began a northerly detour which, on the basis of his stated mileages, added 417½ miles to the distance he had to travel before reaching Pacific Springs. Nevertheless, on September 16 and again on September 17, he tried to push eastward from the course to which his detour had committed him. See entries of these two days (pp. 132, 133).

56 Thomas Fork (which *Chittenden*, p. 478, implies should properly be Thompson Fork, as originally so named for one of Ashley's trappers), Stuart first encountering it at seemingly its confluence with Bear River (*Geol. Idaho; Quad. Montpelier*). At this confluence, approximately eight and one-fourth air-line miles east by south from site of Stuart's camp on September 12, Bear River began a great hairpin turn which, carrying far to the southward, skirted the combined mass of the two watersheds mentioned in note 55. At the turn's north-westerly end the river swung into its other and smaller turn described in note 52.

57 See *Marcy*, pp. 226-229, for smoke signalling.

58 Bear River at mouth of Thomas Fork.

59 Thomas Fork, Stuart travelling upstream on its right bank.

60 Seemingly the rivulet which, immediately south of and approximately parallel with present-day Preuss Creek, emptied (approximately in latitude 42° 22′ 30″, longitude 111° 4′ 25″) through right bank of Thomas Fork's most westerly fork—all as indicated on *Quad. Montpelier.*

61 Apparently right fork of Thomas Fork. *Quad. Montpelier.*

62 The southerly end of present-day Gannett Hills, Stuart first encountering those hills at entrance of Thomas Fork Canyon where they rose eventually to some 850 feet above the valley. Stuart's "ascending the Mountains" signified probably no more than his climbing a short way up the face of the hills and then travelling along it, thus avoiding the mire which here and there marked the valley's floor. *Quad. Montpelier.*

63 Probably present-day Spring Creek, a northwardly flowing tributary of

present-day Crow Creek, which latter stream was a confluent of the watercourse now known as Salt River. *Caribou; Wyoming Forest; Quad. Crow Creek; Quad. Afton.*

64 Seemingly camp was on Spring Creek's right bank approximately in latitude 42° 31′ 22″, longitude 111° 0′ 30″.

65 Crossed apparently that one of the confluents of Spring Creek which emptied through the creek's right bank at a spot one and one-half miles southeast from the peak known today as The Pinnacle. *Caribou; Quad. Crow Creek.*

66 Query: should this not have been E.N.E.? If so, Stuart crossed the Gannett Hills and later encountered Salt River at approximately a spot which, two and one-fourth miles south of mouth of present-day Fish Creek, was in latitude 42° 30′ 38″, longitude 110° 52′ 47″.

67 Salt River, which stream, according to Granville Stuart, was interchangeably called by Snake indians (1) *To-sa car-nel* (meaning "white lodges" and so named because of the presence of some small white buttes near the river) and (2) *O-na-bit-a pah* (meaning "salt water" and so named because of the existence of saline springs and ledges of rock salt near the stream's banks). *Stuart, Granville* [*A*], pp. 40, 85, 86.

68 Query: should not Stuart have stated his mileage as five instead of as fifteen? If so, the place at which the river "cut through the mountains" was where, two and one-half miles south by east from site of present-day town of Smoot, Salt River, escaping from constriction by the Gannett Hills on the west and Salt River Range of mountains on the east, entered the southerly end of present-day Star Valley. True, Salt River again cut through the mountains at a spot which, some 20 miles further on its course and in latitude 42° 50′ 38″, is today termed The Narrows. But this latter spot was not commensurate with Stuart's mileages and compass bearings as stated in his entries for subsequent days. *Quad. Afton; Caribou; Wyoming Forest.*

69 Apparently travelled across the base of the southerly hairpin turn made by Salt River in the region southeast from site of town of Smoot; and, thus regaining Salt River, camped on its southwesterly flowing stretch above the commencement of the hairpin turn.

70 It would seem that Stuart's route at this point was approximately that known today as Sheep Trail. This trail, as indicated on *Quad. Afton* and *Wyoming Forest*, runs northeasterly till eastward of Mt. Wagner, turns northward through Sheep Pass and then descends Spring Creek to its confluence with Greys River, a northwardly flowing tributary of south fork of Snake River.

71 Greys River (*Caribou; Wyoming Forest; Quad. Afton; Geol. Wyoming*). Some maps (as, for instance, *Holt; Yellowstone;* and map following p. 270 in *Hayden, Wyoming* and *Idaho*) style it "John Days River."

72 Camped on right bank of Greys River at approximately a spot which, in latitude 42° 50′, was one mile below mouth of present-day Elk Creek. *Quad. Afton.*

73 This comment identifies the stream as Greys River in contradistinction

from Salt River with the latter's sluggish current above a muddy bottom. Trav. mem. states "stony and uneaven bed."

74 Present-day Teton Range and its southward continuation into present-day Snake (*alias* Snake River) Range.

75 Hunt's westbound Astorians.

76 Greys River.

77 To seemingly the vicinity of the abrupt westerly bend which, in approximate latitude 42° 57′ 35″, the river made at the confluence of present-day Deadman Creek. *Quad. Afton; Wyoming Forest.*

78 Present-day Greys Meadow. *Quad. Afton; Wyoming Forest.*

79 Stuart's route thus swerved at the beginning of these nine miles because both river and valley here deflected toward the northwest. *Wyoming Forest; Geol. Wyoming.*

80 Present-day Little Greys River. *Wyoming Forest; Teton; Caribou; Targhee; Geol. Wyoming.*

81 This "other" watercourse was the "Mad River" of Hunt's overland party (*Astoria*, I, p. 285) and was all that portion of Snake River which *Targhee, Wyoming Forest* and other present-day maps designate as south fork of Snake River. These maps designate as north fork of Snake River the stream which, in bygone days, was known as Henry's fork of Snake River. Astoria's phrase, "had received the name of Mad River" (*Astoria*, I, p. 285, and see also *Nouvelles Annales*, X, p. 46, translated at p. 288 *infra*), suggests that possibly the name had been bestowed prior to the arrival of Hunt's party, and, if so, by Andrew Henry's men.

82 Camped, according to context, at a spot which, approximately in latitude 43° 8′ 40″, longitude 110° 50′, was on the small plain lying immediately north of the northwesterly end of present-day Middle Range, a chain of hills skirting Greys River on the east. *Wyoming Forest.*

83 "We at last succeeded in killing" in trav. mem.

84 Greys River.

85 This reliance on Jones's report, though possibly denoting error in Stuart's judgment, negatives any accusation to the effect that Stuart's "absurd northern detour" was due to his being so thoroughly "lost" as to have "forgotten that the sun rises in the east." See, for instance, *Chittenden*, pp. 209, 214. A mistake in judgment? Yes and no. True, it was not more than 30 miles to where, on Hoback River, Stuart was to camp on October 9; but apparently there was no reason for him to know this fact, and the montane pocket which then encircled him granted no views of distant landmarks. Nevertheless the mere sending of Jones eastward on a reconnaissance seems to indicate that Stuart had been attempting to push direct to the Hoback River, the Green River valley, and the South Pass.

86 South fork of Snake River.

87 Of south fork of Snake River.

88 Stuart was here journeying downstream on left bank of south fork of Snake River, and thus was travelling on the toes of the foothills of present-day Caribou Mountains.

89 Camped on left bank of south fork of Snake River at approximately mouth of present-day McCoy Creek. *Targhee; Caribou; Geol. Idaho.*

90 In journ.'s manuscript are Stuart's following two interlineations: a figure "2" above this word "attempt," and a figure "1" above the word "on" which immediately follows—evidently suggesting transposition of the clauses, which were thus transposed in trav. mem.

91 See journ.'s supplemental statement in paragraph beginning on p. 253.

92 "several" in trav. mem.

93 "a few Indians" in trav. mem.

94 "Crow" in trav. mem.

95 Bear River.

96 This paragraph from trav. mem. virtually duplicates entry in journ.'s postscript, pp. 253-254.

97 The Cheyenne River, known today by this same name, lay north of the Platte River, rose in Wyoming, flowed northeasterly across the present-day state of South Dakota, and emptied into the Missouri River. Stuart's reason for selecting the Cheyenne River as his goal is not disclosed.

The "Spanish River" of Stuart's text is today called Green River.

98 This passage from trav. mem. duplicates journ.'s supplemental entry on p. 254, except that journ. states "some" of the same band.

99 Travelling downstream on left bank of south fork of Snake River.

100 On left bank of south fork of Snake River at or near mouth of present-day Big Spring Creek situated approximately in latitude 43° 15′ 39″, longitude 110° 8′ 38″. *Targhee; Caribou.*

101 On left bank of south fork of Snake River at a spot approximately opposite mouth of present-day Little Elk Creek and approximately in latitude 43° 19′ 8″, longitude 111° 9′ 25″. *Caribou; Targhee.*

102 "Forty-five Trout were the produce of Mr Millers and my fishing rods" in trav. mem. For the poor quality of the trout see note 47.

103 Approximately at or opposite mouth of present-day Fall Creek. *Caribou; Targhee; Geol. Idaho.*

104 Wolverine, *Gulo luscus*, known also as carcajou and as skunk bear.

105 "flat bottoms" in trav. mem.

106 At a spot approximately one and one-half miles south by east from mouth of present-day Gormer Canyon (*Targhee*). Stuart was now in the so-called lower canyon of south fork of Snake River. *Yellowstone.*

107 "one of our rafts" in trav. mem.

108 "Arms &c" in trav. mem.

109 Western colloquialism meaning extremely steep through erosion.

110 Incorrectly "12 miles" in trav. mem.

111 Camped approximately at or opposite mouth of present-day Bear Gulch. *Targhee.*

112 "afternoon and evening" in trav. mem. The remainder of this entry Stuart did not reproduce in trav. mem.

113 In lieu of journ.'s detailed list of courses trav. mem. states: "our course was, I believe from every point of the compafs, for 32 miles."

114 This camp on left bank of south fork of Snake River was, as shown by later context, across the river from approximate site of present-day town of Heise, Idaho, situated in latitude 43° 39′, longitude 111° 42′. *Targhee.*

115 Snake River Range.

116 See note 81.

117 The south fork of Snake River (this fork being Stuart's "Mad River"), emerging from present-day Jackson's Lake, flowed in sinuous course southwesterly between the present-day Gros Ventre Range on the east and the present-day Teton Range on the west. On reaching the southerly end of the Teton Range, the stream turned southeasterly, and, closely hugging the southeasterly edge of Snake River Range, passed between it and the westerly end of Gros Ventre Range. Thence the stream, entering its so-called upper canyon and continuing to cling closely to Snake River Range, flowed around the southerly end of that range and along its westerly side (the latter third of this westerly course through the stream's so-called lower canyon) to the range's extreme northwesterly corner. At this corner the stream poured itself northwesterly into the plain, where it was joined by the waters of the north fork, *alias* Henry's fork.

Stuart's characterization of Mad River and of the mountains was patently restricted to the locality in which he was at the moment. Consequently, his mountains "of great magnitude on the East" were those of the Snake River Range, while his "Hills on the West" were the river buttes and the foothills of the present-day Caribou Mountains.

118 Crossed to right bank of south fork of Snake River, and thus approximately to or a short distance downstream from the site of present-day town of Heise, Idaho, for which see note 114.

119 *Crataegus Piperi Britt.* See *L. & C. Journs.*, III, p. 86.

120 Present-day Moody Creek. Stuart, after traversing the most northwesterly foothills of Snake River Range, camped on this Moody Creek (a confluent of Snake River's north fork) and not improbably at or near the junction of the creek's two parent forks, present-day North Moody Creek and South Moody Creek (*Targhee; Geol. Idaho*). The map *Yellowstone* indicates an old and well-established trail running from the south fork of Snake River and crossing Moody Creek immediately above the junction of the creek's two parent forks.

CHAPTER VII

SEPT. 30 · OCT. 28, 1812

On Foot from Moody Creek to Sweetwater River

[SEE MAP FACING PAGE 127]

McClellan Leaves Party · Ascend Teton River · Cross Teton Pass · Ascend Hoback River · Begin Descent of Green River · Near Starvation · Cannibalism Proposed · Rescue McClellan · A Deserted Indian Camp · Acquire Pack Horse · Big Sandy Creek · South Pass · Take Eastward Course South of Green Mts. · Through Muddy Gap · Sweetwater River.

[73] Wednesday 30th We yesterday fell in with a large trace made by Horses apparently about a month[1] ago, but of what nation cannot as yet tell, we are however inclined to believe they were Absarokas come here probably to see whether an Establishment had been made in this neighbourhood, which from what Mr Hunt[2] told them last year they had every reason to suppose was the case— They had encamped a little higher on this Branch,[3] which their road crofsed and lay in our course for 2 miles when it seperated in every direction and we lost it— Our course was the same as yesterday and 19 miles more brought us to our nights lodgings in a deep gulley near a boiling spring[4] M^r. Crooks is a good deal indisposed[5] and [*this evening*] has a considerable[6] fever— [*A little to one side of our camp one of the Canadians /in searching for good water/ discovered several very astonishing springs of various qualities and temperatures, some of them are cold, others hot: one of the cold we found to be acidulated and impregnated*

in a small degree with iron; but the principal one in the group is very hot & sulphuric, the water is oily to the touch, and foams like soap suds; its margin is covered with a yellow efflorescence of sulphur, which affects the sense of smelling at some distance, and the volume of smoke[7] *that issues immediately from this spring may be distinguished at least two miles off.—]*

Thursday 1st. October 1812

At an early hour we ascended the Hill[8] where Mr. McClellan to whose lot it had fallen to carry the Trap, refused to be its bearer any farther, neither would he pack an equivalent in dried meat but leaving us said he could kill enough for his daily subsistence and when informed that we would crofs the mountain[9] to the right the better to avoid the Blackfeet in whose walks we now were, his answer was, that he must consult the ease of his sore feet and went on, round the mountain[10]— We reached the other side by the middle of the afternoon and found the pafsage of the mountain somewhat difficult on account [*of*] the snow which in many places was of considerable depth— Mr McClellan was seen ahead of us in the Plain[11] below as we were decending— 6 miles from its base we reached a river[12] 50 yds wide and about knee deep with abundance of Willow & Beaver— The Plain from the mountain we traversed today to that of the Pilot Knobs[13] is about 16 miles[14] in width, and the River[15] running through it falls into Henrys River halfway between his Fort and the [74] mouth of Mad River—[16] the whole of this days march was 18 miles E.S.E.—[17]

[*Mr. Crooks' indisposition increased so much this afternoon that I insisted on his taking a dose of Castor oil, which fortunately had the desired effect, but he has such a violent fever, and is withal so weak as to preclude all idea of continuing our journey untill his recovery— notwithstanding the urgent solicitations of my men, to proceed without him; very justly representing the imminent dangers we exposed ourselves to by any delay in this unknown and barren tract, among most inveterate enemies to whites, and in the midst of impervious mountains of snow, at such an advanced season, without one days provision, and no very favourable appearances of procuring an addition here, did we even venture to hunt— such a prospect I must confeſs made an impreſsion on my mind that cannot easily be described, but the thoughts of leaving a fellow creature in such a forlorn situation were too repugnant to my feelings to require long deliberation, particularly as it was probable he might get well in a few days; this hope I suggested and at length prevailed on them, tho' very reluctantly to abide the event—*

The sensations excited on this occasion, and by the view of an unknown & untravelled wilderneſs, are not such as arise in the artificial solitude of parks and gardens, for there one is apt to indulge a flattering notion of self sufficiency, as well as a placid indulgence of voluntary delusions; whereas the phantoms which haunt a desert, are want, misery, and danger, the evils of dereliction rush upon the mind; man is made unwillingly acquainted with his own weakneſs, and meditation shews him only how little he can sustain, and how little he can perform—]

Friday 2nd Jones on searching for a place to set the Trap met a White Bear,[18] which contrary to our determination he was obliged to shoot in his own defence, but only wounding him he made his escape— Mr Crooks's indisposition increased so much yesterday that he last evening took a dose of Castor Oil, which had the intended effect, [*is rather easier*] but has such a fever and [*unable to move or take any food*] is withal so weak as to preclude the idea of continuing our route untill he gets better— [*therefore*] Not knowing how long we might be compelled to remain here, however disagreeable and dangerous on account of the advanced state of the season, and the excursions of the Blackfeet Indians I sent Jones out early in quest of Game, who in about an hour[19] returned having killed five Elk— We immediately moved forward [(*supporting Mr Crooks*) *for*] 6 miles south up the Fork to where the dead animals lay and encamped[20] in the vicinity [*—the weather for some days past has been piercingly cold—*]

Sunday 4th Mr. Crooks continued both yesterday and today too weak and feverish to proceed, we had no more medicine, but had recourse to an Indian Sweat,[21] which had a good effect and we are in great hopes of moving on again tomorrow—

Monday[22] 5th By carrying Mr Crooks's things we were enabled to go on 8 miles for the most part through swamps[23] in a southerly direction, when finding some good firewood and an excellent Camp we stopped for the night—[24] Several Branches[25] ifsue from the Pilot Knob Mountain on the East, which on reaching the low grounds are dammed up by Beaver and occasion the Swamps through which we pafsed today— On our way here we Killed a White Bear which [*had 3½ Inches fat on the rump, and*] proves an agreeable addition to our stock of [*Elk*] meat

[75] Tuesday 6th We set out early and leaving the swamps[26] on our right[27] proceeded along the mountain[28] through the Plain 13 miles S S.E, where the main body of the River,[29] ifsuing from the Pilot Mountain[30] we ascended it 4 miles S E and encamped[31] where it divides into nearly equal Branches Mr [*C*][32] mends slowly and was able to carry a part of his things[33] [*for the most part of*] today—

Wednesday 7th We continued on up the right hand Fork[34] for 13 Miles S E by E to the summit[35] of the Pilot Knob Mountain on which we found little or no snow—[36] 9 Miles same course brought us to Mad River[37] and in 2 more reached the opposite bank[38] having crofsed Five channels of from 30 to 60 yards wide each and from 1½ to 3 feet[39] water a very rapid current, and in every other respect of the same character as the part where we decended on the Rafts, with the exception that the valley is here several miles wide, and some of the Bottom upwards of a mile in breadth and thickly timbered with bitter Cottonwood[40] and Pines—

Thursday 8th 6 Miles E.S.E.[41] brought us to a considerable path along the Hills[42] 6 S.S.W. was our next course down to where

Mad River enters the mountains,[43] when ascending a high Hill[44] we went 11 more S S E[45] and encamped on a small Branch[46] [*there being good sign of Beaver*—] saw a great many Antelopes very wild— Killed none[47] [*although we had not a mouthful to eat*]—

Friday 9th In 6 Miles S.E. we reached Hobacks Fork[48] a stream about 50 yds wide with a good body of water which runs to the West and joins Mad River some distance below We next proceeded up the Fork[49] 6 miles East, when killing an Antelope we encamped[50] immediately although early in the day— It was a Buck and very poor but with a Beaver which Vallé caught last night[51] it made tolerable eating— [*at least we found it so, having ate nothing since we breakfasted on a few poor Trout and a small Duck yesterday morning*—]

[76] Saturday 10th Our route was today 6 miles up the Fork[52] to Crofs Creek[53] 20 yds wide—3 to Henrys Hill[54] 2 up the small Branch,[55] where the side of a mountain having been precipitated from the main body has partly stopped the channel of the Run and made a Pond[56] upwards of an hundred yards in circumference very deep and the residence of some Beaver 3½ miles over a mountain[57] brought us again to Hobacks Fork which following for 4½ more we reached Hunters Fork[58] & encamped[59] between that and the main stream,[60] having come 19 miles nearly due East— the greater part along an abominable road occasioned by the proximity of the mountains where the track is often in places so nearly perpendicular, that mifsing a single step you would go several hundred feet into the rocky bed of the stream below—

Sunday 11th We eat the remainder of our goat meat[61] and went on at a smart pace 10 miles S.E.[62] when taking up a small Branch[63] in 9 more East found where Mr McClellan had encamped [*and supped upon the carcase of a poor wolf*] the night before, which being as near the Spanish River Mountain[64] as we could find water, and too late [*the day too far advanced*] to ascend it we stopped[65] at the same place, and went to bed without supper

Monday 12th At the dawn we continued on for 2 miles to the base of the mountain, and found the ascent steep and difficult We soon [*about noon*] reached the drains[66] of the Spanish River[67] and by the middle of the afternoon struck[68] the main body a stream about 60 yds[69] wide with no great depth of water, no timber, and but few Willows— Here we expected to find Buffaloe in abundance, but a few [*old*] Bull tracks was all [77] we had for hope, with the exception of a few Antelopes [*on the brow of the mountain*] which were so wild as to preclude all hope of getting near them— our course was E S E to the River 16 miles[70] which crofsing we followed its left bank for 9 more S W in quest of Beaver sign which we at last found [*and encamped in the vicinity*]—[71] Saw a large smoke at some distance to the South west and sent Leclairc to see what occasioned it— We had great hopes of its being Indians and [*consequently*] sat up late waiting his return in expectation of getting something to eat, but at last despairing of his coming we went to bed about 11 o'Clock[72] again supperlefs[73] but in hopes of our old trap procuring us something for breakfast

[*Editor's Note.*—For the significance of these parallel columns see p. cxi and note 290 on p. cxxxvii.]

[Journ.]

Tuesday 13th We[74] started early and met Leclairc coming up the River, the smoke was at Mr McClellans camp, who he found late in the evening Le said Mr Mc C was waiting at his camp

[Journ.'s postscript and trav. mem.]

[*Tuesday 13th*—] We[79] were up with the dawn and visited our Trap in anxious expection, but had[80] nothing in it except the forepaw of a large Beaver— which has greatly damped our

[*Journ.*]

and continuing on at the end of 9 miles from our last nights station S.W. we reached the spot,[75] and learned from him that he had been very much indisposed and lived on very little ever since he left us, and was then like ourselves without a mouthfull to eat— He soon tied up his Bundle and we all ascended the Hills[76] going nearly East, and had scarcely proceeded 2 miles[77] when to our great joy we discovered three Buffaloe Bulls and killed one, which soon made us determine on encamping, as we were hungry enough to relish a hearty meal— We skinned the animal which was poor, but we carried a large quantity to camp[78] and eat lustily

[*Journ.'s postscript and trav. mem.*]

spirits, as we do not feel in very good trim to resume of[81] journey, but there being no alternative, we started and soon after met Leclairc coming up the river with information that the smoke was occasioned by Mr. McClellan's camp getting on[82] fire while he was at some little distance fishing but without succefs he informed Leclairc that he had been very much indisposed and lived on little or nothing [*ever*] since he parted with us, that he [*was happy of our being near* (*as well he might*) *and*] would wait our arrival at his camp in hopes we should have something for him to eat, without which he could not proceed much farther— when we arrived[75] we found him lying on a parcel of straw [, *emaciated and*] worn to a perfect skeleton & hardly able to [*raise his head, or*] speak from extreme debility—[, *but our presence seemed to revive him considerably, and*] by much persuasion we prevailed on him to accompany us, but with apparent reluctance— [124] as he said it was as well for him to die there as any where else, there being no prospect of our getting any speedy relief— we carried all his things and proceeded on for 17 miles S.E.,[83] over a level barren of sand, to a small branch[78] where we encamped [*early*] on account of seeing a few antelopes in the neighbourhood—

Soon after stopping we all made an unsuccefsful attempt to procure some meat, and after dark returned to camp with heavy hearts but I must confeſs we could not [*in justice*] enter the same complaint against our stomachs—

As we were preparing for bed one of the Canadians[84] advanced towards me with his rifle in his hand, saying that as there was no appearance of our being able to procure any provisions at least untill we got to the extreme of this plain, which would take us three or 4 days, he was determined to go no farther, but that lots should be cast and one die to preserve[85] the rest, adding as a farther inducement for me to agree[86] to his proposal that I should be exempted [*in consequence of being their leader &c.*], I shuddered at the idea & used every endeavour to create an abhorrence in his mind against such an act, urging also the probability of our falling in with some animal on the morrow but, finding that every argument [125] failed [*and that he was on the point of converting some others to his purpose*] I snatched up my Rifle cocked and leveled it at him with the firm resolution to fire if he persisted, this affair so terrified him that he fell [*instantly*] upon his knees and asked the whole party's pardon, [*solemnly*] swearing he should never again suggest such a thought— after this affair was settled I[87] felt so agitated and weak that I could scarcely crawl to bed—

My thoughts began to ruminate on our hapleſs and forlorn situation with the prospects before us untill I at length became so agitated and weak that it was with difficulty I crawled to bed and after being there I for the first time in my life could not enjoy that repose my exhausted frame so much wanted

This naturally led my revery to a retrospective view of former happy days, when [*troubles,*] difficulties and distreſses were [*to me*] only things imaginary, which [*now*] convinces me how little a man who will [*rolls in affluence, and knows neither cares nor sorrows, can feel for those of others, and he undoubtedly of all people in the world, is least qualified for pious deeds—*

Let him but visit these regions of want and misery; his riches will prove an eye sore, and he will be taught the pleasure and advantage of prayer— If the advocates for the rights of man come here, they can enjoy them, for this

is the land of liberty and equality, where a man sees and feels that he is a man merely, and that he can no longer exist, than while he can himself procure the means of support.—]

[Journ.]

Wednesday 14th We[88] remained in the same Camp all day bringing up our leaway and reposing ourselves after the late fatigues— We cut up a quantity of meat to dry and intend going down this River[89] so long as it lies in our course or at least to the point of a mountain[90] we see in the East near which we expect finding the Miſsouri waters

[Journ.'s postscript]

[131] Wednesday 14th We[91] resumed our line of march a little before daylight and went on but slowly for 9 miles S.E.[92] when we came to the base of some low hills[76] which we ascended going nearly East and had scarcely proceeded 2 miles when to our great joy we discovered an old run down Buffalo Bull, which after considerable trouble we succeeded in killing about 2 P.M.— and so ravenous were our appetites that we ate part of the animal raw— then cut up the most of what was eatable and carried it to a brook[78] at some little diſtance, where we encamped being hungry enough to relish a hearty meal

[Journ.]

[78] Thursday 15th At a late hour we left our camp and in 12 miles E.S.E. over low Hills struck a bend of the River and stopped for the night—[93] We this day croſsed a large Indian trail about fifteen days old, steering nearly a N E course,

[Journ.'s postscript and trav. mem.]

Thursday 15th We[94] sat up the greater part of the night eating and barbecueing meat, I was very much alarmed at the ravenous[95] manner in which all ate, but happily none felt any serious effects therefrom, probably in consequence of my not allowing

[*Journ.*]

which we suppose made by the Absaroka nation, who from the numerous carcases of Buffaloe we find in every direction must have been hunting in this Country for a great length of time— No Buffaloe in sight, only a few Goats & them very wild

[*Journ.'s postscript and trav. mem.*]

them to eat freely before they had supped a quantity of broth—

Being[96] somewhat [*recruited and*] refreshed [*by the middle of the day,*] we at a late hour left camp, with the intention of going down this river[89] so long as it lies in our course or at least to the point of a mountain[90] we see in the east near which we expect to find the Mifsouri waters, in 12 miles E.S.E. [*over low hills, struck a bend of the river, and stopped for the night—*[93]

We this day crofsed a large Indian trail, about 15 days old, steering nearly a N.E. course, which we suppose must have been made by the Crows, who from the numerous skeletons of Buffaloe we find in every direction, must have hunted in this country the most part of the summer: We have seen only a few goats, which were exceedingly wild—]

Friday 16th. By sunrise we left the River[97] which here ran to the West of South, when pafsing over a low ridge found a Flat extending to the foot of the mountains[98] on our left with a Willow Branch[99] meandering through it which we crofsed soon after— 15 miles from last nights station we forded another stream[100] of considerable magnitude, whose banks were adorned with many Pines, near which we found an Indian Encampment of large dimensions deserted apparently about a month ago with immense numbers of Buffaloe carcases[101] [*strewed every where*] in the neighbourhood— In the centre of this camp is a Lodge 150 feet in circumference composed of [*or rather supported by*] twenty trees 12 Inches in diameter and 40 feet[102] long— ac[*r*]ofs these were branches of Pine and Willow laid so as to make a tolerable shade

At the West end, and immediately opposite the door three persons lay interred with their feet towards the East—at their head were two Branches[103] of red Cedar firmly inserted in the ground and a large Buffaloes scull painted black placed close by the root of each— This Building is circular, on many parts of it were suspended [*numerous ornaments, and among the rest*] quantities of children's [79] mogasins, and from the quantity and size of the materials must have required great labour and time in erection, from which we infer that the personages on whose account it was constructed were not of the common order— 9 miles farther on we reached another Creek[104] equal in size to the last, with a few Cottonwoods and many Willows— here we encamped[105] having come 24 miles E S E

Saturday 17th 5 miles from last nights station is a large Creek[106] and 7 farther on is another[107] with a great many Willows and a few trees of Pine and Cottonwood— It is very Shallow and like the others we have lately croſsed runs to the West of South with a considerable range of Hills[108] along its left bank

All these Creeks are tributary Streams of the Spanish River and take their rise in the ridge of mountains[109] to the East, which is the main range of the R.M.[110] stupendiously high[111] and rugged, being composed of huge maſses of a blackish coloured rock, Almost totally destitute of timber and covered in many places with snow— Our journey today was 12 Miles E S E.[112] saw a few Bulls[113] and many Antelopes but could not kill any— Our living has been and is of the meanest kind being poor Bull meat or Buck Antelope, both too bad to be eat except in cases of starvation—[114]

Sunday 18th Soon after croſsing the ridge[115] which lay before us we found the stream we encamped on last night coming from the S.E.—[116] Wading it we proceeded through a low Plain till having gone 12 Miles S.E. struck it again[117] and on ascending the opposite bank met six[118] Indians of the Snake nation— They were encamped on the Creek and by accompanying the natives 3 miles N.E.[119] we reached their Huts which were four[120] in number, made principally of Pine branches— They [80] were [*poor but*] hospitable in the extreme, and for a Pistol, a Breechclout an axe, a Knife a tin Cup two Awls and a few Beads they gave us the only Horse they had [, *the Crows in their late excursion through this country, having deprived them of these animals, as well as of a number of their Women &c.,*] & for a few trinkets we got [*some*] Buffaloe meat and leather for mogasins, an article we much want— We encamped close to the Lodges—

[*They*[121] *informed us that the crows had fallen in with two of our hunters last spring and robbed them of every thing, which the poor fellows opposed, and in the fray killed 7*[122] *savages, but were at last overpowered and maſsacred—*[123] *They also told us that two of the Canadians left by Mr. Crooks last Winter had early in the spring accompanied one of their bands to hunt Buffalo on the head waters of the Miſsouri, where they, as well as many of their people, were killed by the Blackfeet:—*[124] *It undoubtedly was those two unfortunate wretches who conducted the Indians to our Caches on the snake River—*

Last summer they said that the Arapahays fell in with Champlain,[125] *and 3 men he had hunting Beaver some distance down the Spanish River,*[126] *murdered them in the dead of the night and took poſsession of all their effects—*

When we told them the day was not far distant when we should take signal vengeance on the perpetrators of those deeds, they appeared quite elated, and offered their services in the execution, which were of course accepted, and a long smoke out of the Calumet of peace, ended the conference—

These fellows have a kind of wild Tobacco,[127] *which grows spontaneously in the plains, adjacent to the spanish River Mountains, the leaves are smaller than those of ours, and it is much more agreeable, not being nearly so violent in its effects— These mountains, which my* <u>*hungry spell*</u> *prevented me from noticing in due order, are principally composed of pumice stone, granate, Flint &c.— there is a species of clay which is very fine, and light, of an agreeable smell, and of a brown colour, spotted with yellow, diſsolves readily in the mouth, and like all those kinds of earth, adheres strongly to the tongue, the natives manufacture jars, pots, and dishes of different descriptions from it; these veſsels communicate a very pleasant smell, and flavour to the water.*

&c. that is put in them, which undoubtedly proceeds from the solution of some bituminous substance contained in the clay: there are also several kinds of metallic earths, or chalks, of various colours, such as green, Blue, yellow, Black, White and two kinds of ochre, the one pale and the other a bright red, like vermillion, these are held in high estimation by the natives and neighbouring Tribes, who use them to paint their bodies and faces, which they do in a very fanciful manner.—

Monday 19th We loaded our [*old*] Horse by sunrise with meat for six days[128] and everything except our Bedding, which we find easy loads compared to what we have carried for this some time past— 3 miles south over very rough ground brought us into the large Crow trace along which not leſs than sixty Lodges[129] must have paſsed

We followed this road 12 miles S E. by S[130] to a Creek[131] coming from the East, then, croſsing[132] went 3 E.S.E.— Here the track turned all at once to E N E up a low ridge and in 3 more Keeping that course we found the last stream again running through a considerable Flat covered with Willow— The wind blew cold from the North East with some snow which made us think of encamping and by going down the Creek one mile we found an eligible place[133]

Tuesday 20th Vallé and Leclairc killed a [*young*] Bull[134] last evening which was in [*very*] good order— Some snow fell in the night which made it after sunrise before we set out, when we pursued a S E course for 18 miles through a beautifully undulating country[135] having the main mountain[136] on the left and a considerably elevated ridge on the right

The ridge of mountains[137] which divides Wind river[138] from the Columbia and Spanish waters[139] ends here abruptly,[140] and winding to the North of East becomes the seperator of a Branch of Big Horn and [81] Cheyenne Rivers from the other water courses which add their tributary waves to the Miſsouri below the Sioux Country— On the Spanish River as far as we could see yesterday the country appeared to be almost a dead level bounded to the West by a range of (in many places) very high mountains[141] running about S.W. and on the East by the ridge[142] to the right of the country through which we pafs[*ed*] today which keeps a course about S.S.W.— We abandoned the Crow trace early in the day as it bore to the north of East, and being somewhat apprehensive of falling in with some of their spies, for according to the information received from the Shoshonies[143] they are on a River[144] at no great distance to the East and we suppose ourselves now at the source of the Spanish river waters in this quarter— Our right hand ridge becoming very low we pafsed over into a low Plain and 8 miles S S E brought us to camp on a little drain[145] in the bare Prairie, where our fuel was an indifferent growth of Sage, which proving an unsuccefsfull competitor against the peircing North Easter of this evening we were obliged to take refuge in our nests at an early hour

[*In the plain we traversed today, are several springs of clear and limpid water, which overflows the surface and becomes crystallized into a salt as white as snow—*

This valley[146] *is about 10 miles in circumference, and is entirely covered for the depth of a foot to 18 inches, with a crust of salt, which is collected by the natives who are excefsively fond of it, while those near the sea, hold it in abhorrence, and will eat nothing that has in the least been touched thereby*[147]*—*

The surrounding mountains as far as I could discover, afford no indication of mineral salt, but they must necefsarily abound with it, from the great quantities deposited by these springs—]

Wednesday 21st Mr McClellan killed some Buffaloe last evening to get a part of which we waited this morning—

The cold continued and was accompanied by Snow soon after we left the drain which compelled us to encamp at the end of 15 miles E N E on the side of a Hill[148] [*which we must inevitably traverse*] where we found a sufficiency of dry Aspen for firewood, but not a drop of water about two miles back we croſsed a large lodge trace steering a little to the right of the point of the mountain[149] in the N E which [*as well as the other trails we have lately croſsed*] we suppose made by another Band of [*the*] Absarokas[150] who may have been hunting lower down on the Spanish River than those whose road we left yesterday— saw a few Buffaloe— Vallé & Leclairc found a little bad water 1½ miles from camp & we got a drink at last

[*Editor's Note.*—For the significance of these parallel columns see note 288 on pp. CXXXVI, CXXXVII.]

[Journ.]

[82] Thursday 22nd We set out[151] by daylight and at the distance of 5 miles from camp found a small stream of water and breakfasted[152] 10 more brought us to the head drains of a watercourse[153] running East among banks and low Hills of a loose Blueish coloured earth, apparently strongly impregnated with Copperas—[154] Pursuing our course for 5 miles more along these drains[155] we at last found a little water oozing out of the earth, it was of a whiteish colour and poſseſsed a great similarity of taste to the muddy waters of the Miſsouri— Here we encamped[156] having come 20 miles E by South, over broken ground whose soil was principally sand and gravel, covered

[Trav. mem.]

[*Thursday 22d.— We set out*[151] *at day light, and ascended about 3 miles, when we found a spring of excellent water, and breakfasted,*[152] *5 more brought us to the top of the mountain,*[159] *which we call the big horn, it is in the midst of the principal chain;*[160] *in scrambling up the acclivity, and on the top, we discovered various shells,*[161] *evidently the production of the sea, and which doubtleſs must have been deposited by the waters of the deluge.*

The summit of this mountain, whose form appears to be owing to some volcanic eruption, is flat, and exhibits a plain of more than 3 miles square,[162] *in the middle is a considerable Lake,*[163] *which from every appearance was formerly the crater of a volcano; the*[164] *principal chain of these mountains is situated between*

[*Journ.*]

with but little Grafs, some Sage and a good deal of Saltwood—[157] Snow fell in the morning but by the middle of the afternoon it had totally disappeared, except on the high Mountains[158] to the north where it seemed to snow incefsantly—

[*Trav. mem.*]

four of less height that are parallel to it, these lateral chains are generally about 40 or 50 miles distant from the principal, but are connected with it, in several places, by transverse spurs, or ramifications, from these ridges many other branches extend outwardly, composed of small mountains, occasionally running in different directions—

12 miles more brought us to the base of the mountain, where we found a little water[155] *oozing out of the earth, it was of a whitish colour, and possessed a great similarity of taste to the muddy waters of the missouri—*

Here we encamped,[156] *having come 20 miles E. by south, We saw a number of Ibex, or big horn, and killed two, which we find excellent eating*—]

Friday 23rd The morning was peircing cold, but immediately after an early breakfast we continued on[165] supposing this a water of the Mifsouri, with the intention of following its banks

For a few miles it ran East, but turning gradually to S by West we left it and steered S.E. in hopes of falling in with a bend of it—ascending a Hill at the end of 23 miles[166] we saw the Creek[167] at a considerable distance running about S S.E. and the Country in every direction South of East [*is*] a Plain bounded only by the Horizon; we at once concluded to give up all idea of taking the Creek for our Guide, and to make the best of our way for a range of mountains[168] in the East about sixty miles off, near which we are in great hopes of finding another stream and have determined on wintering at the first eligible place

This Hill we call Discovery Knob, which leaving we seperated in quest of water, and were fortunate [*enough*] in finding a few puddles in the high Plain[169] about 1½ miles due north [*here we had to encamp without a single stick of firewood*]— We[170] pafsed several Knobs of the same Kind as yesterday and the soil retains a similar character—

[83] Saturday 24th The wind blew excefsively cold from the North East and our fuel being principally Buffaloe dung we decamped soon after the dawn— 22 miles[171] East by North was the length of this days journey over tolerably level ground of [*very*] indifferent quality,[172] a march truely disagreeable as we were greatly annoyed by a heavy snow which accompanied the high wind for several hours— being [*very*] late in the day, and seeing no appearance of water we [*at length*] contented ourselves with snow as a substitute and[173] encamped in the vicinity of large Wormwoods—

Sunday 25th This day was on the whole mild and pleasant— found a small Branch[174] with water a few miles from camp, [*where we breakfasted*] but after travelling 30 miles[175] East encamped[176] after dusk with but little fuel and no water— Saw a number of Buffaloe, and a [*very lofty*] range of snowy mountains[177] in the south running East and West [*—a great many Buffalo have lately travelled thro this country, and a few were seen at no great distance from us to day, but in consequence of getting the wind of us, the scampered before we could approach near enough to do execution—*

Our poor old horse is almost done out, for want of two very material necefsaries—grafs and water, the latter in particular, we have been very scantily supplied with for several days back—]

Monday 26th We went 5 miles by the dawn when having past a low Gap[178] to the right of the mountain, on a drain[179] running E.S.E. we found water and halted a couple of hours— After breakfasting at this spot we renewed our march for 5 more[180] where seeing the channel of this stream turn due south without a drop of water running over its sandy bed, we quitted it without hesitation and steered E.N.E. for a wooded ravine[181] in another mountain, at a small distance from the base of which, we discovered to our great joy a Creek[182] with muddy banks and a great abundance of Willow, running with a considerable body of water N N W where we stopped for the night[183] having come today 10 miles[184] E.S.E. and 13 E.N.E.—

Tuesday 27th Jones caught a Beaver last night and early this morning two Bulls [*that straggled near camp*] were put to death on account of which and feeling ourselves as well as our Horse pretty much fatigued we remained in [*the*] same Camp all day—

[84] Wednesday 28th Making an early start we followed the right bank of the Creek[185] 10 miles N N W when turning abruptly to N E by E it broke through[186] a range of Hills[187] into a handsome Plain,[188] where meandering still more to the north we steered E.N.E. and stopped for the night on its bank[189] at the end of 12 miles—[190] Here the Creek which at last nights camp was scarcely eight feet wide,[191] had increased to the breadth of twenty yards, which accumilation of water, excepting two little rivulets[192] from the South West, joined the Branch[193] we decended about three miles above this, from nearly a north direction

Notes to Chapter VII

1 "about 3 weeks" in trav. mem.

2 See *Nouvelles Annales*, X, p. 50 (translated at p. 290 *infra*); *Astoria*, II, p. 18.

3 Moody Creek, or at least one of its two forks described in note 120 on p. 149.

4 Known now as Pincock Hot Springs (a tourist resort) and situated on present-day Canyon Creek, a confluent of the stream which, though for many years called Pierre's River, is styled Teton River on recent maps. *Targhee; Yellowstone; U. P. Folder*, p. 38; *Geol. Idaho*.

Within a few miles of this spot Hunt's party camped on Oct. 7, 1811; for which see *Astoria*, II, p. 13; *Nouvelles Annales*, X, pp. 48, 49, translated at p. 289 *infra*.

Pierre's River, as also Pierre's Hole mentioned in note 11, was, after Stuart's time, named by or for one Pierre (the "Vieux Pierre" and "Old Pierre" of Alexander Ross), an Iroquois indian who, in 1824, while scouting for Alexander Ross's Snake River expedition, entered this country. *Journ. Alex. Ross* in *Ore. Hist. Soc. Quar.*, XIV, pp. 370, 371, 375, 382, 385; *Ross* [*C*], II, pp. 128, 129; *Coutant*, p. 134.

5 "has been somewhat indisposed for two days" in trav. mem.

6 "a very alarming" in trav. mem.

7 *I.e.*, steam. This spot was within the area of thermal waters centering about present-day Yellowstone National Park.

8 This "Hill" east of present-day Canyon Creek was one of the northwesterly toes of the Snake River Range.

9 Merely a continuation of one of the northwesterly toes of the Snake River Range. *Astoria*, II, p. 149, adds that Stuart, when crossing his "mountain," saw snowy peaks, "from two of which smoke ascended in considerable volumes, apparently from craters, in a state of eruption." This "smoke," if not consisting of fleecy clouds, may well have been steam rising from thermal waters on the edge of present-day Yellowstone National Park.

10 "base" in trav. mem. McClellan was familiar with the locality because he had previously traversed it with Hunt's party.

11 The valley which, now known as Teton Basin (*Targhee; Yellowstone; Chittenden*, pp. 657, 747, 784; *Wyeth, John B.*, pp. 36 *et seq.*), was until recently styled Pierre's Hole. It pushed its way southerly between the Teton Range on the east and the Snake River Range on the west. In old-time Western parlance the word "hole" indicated a large, flat, and usually circular or quasi-circular valley surrounded by high mountains. *Chittenden*, pp. 743 *et seq.*

12 South fork of present-day Teton River, for which river see note 4. This fork, after flowing northerly through Teton Basin and receiving *en route* numerous confluents from both east and west, joined with the so-called north fork of Teton River, abruptly turned westward and eventually emptied into the north fork (*alias* Henry's fork) of the Snake.

13 "to the pilot knobs" in trav. mem. The "Pilot Knobs" were the Teton Range. The Snake indians' name for these mountains was, according to Granville Stuart, *Tee Win-at* signifying "the pinnacles." The dominant portions of them, which Hunt named Pilot Knobs (*Astoria*, I, p. 280), were by French voyageurs dubbed *Trois Tetons*, meaning three female breasts. *Stuart, Granville* [*A*], pp. 44, 95.

14 Incorrectly "19 miles" in trav. mem.

15 Teton River.

16 Stuart's statement in effect that the mouth of Teton River (Pierre's River) was midway between Henry's Fort and the confluence of the north and south forks of Snake River assures that Henry's Fort was in the vicinity of the site of present-day town of St. Anthony, Ida. (*Geol. Idaho; Targhee; Yellowstone*). Stuart's "halfway," if strictly construed in terms of mileage, would place the fort at a spot approximately one and one-half miles east (*i.e.*, upstream) from this town's site. But if we grant "halfway" a more tolerant construction, we may safely rely on Miles Cannon's conclusion as to the fort's location. In his *Snake River in History* in *Ore. Hist. Soc. Quar.*, XX, p. 7, he places the fort in a small valley which, some 20 acres in size, was "two miles below the present town of St. Anthony and on the left bank of the river."

17 Camped on Teton River approximately at mouth of present-day Packsaddle Creek, a confluent from the southwest. *Targhee; Yellowstone.*

18 Grizzly bear.

19 "about two hours" in trav. mem.

20 Camped on Teton River approximately at mouth of present-day Bear Creek, a confluent from the east. *Targhee; Yellowstone.*

21 The "Indian Sweat" was obtained by building a "wickyup," a small dome-shaped erection of withes, covering it with skins or blankets, placing inside of it red-hot stones, and thereupon pouring water onto these stones, whereat the structure became filled with steam. The patient, stripped naked, lay sweltering beside these stones. *L. & C. Hist.*, p. 626.

22 Incorrectly "Saturday" in trav. mem.

23 See *Yellowstone.*

24 Camped on Teton River approximately at mouth of present-day Teton Creek, a confluent from the east. *Targhee; Yellowstone.*

25 Stuart had thus far seen present-day Leigh, Bear and Teton Creeks and next day was to encounter present-day Darby and Fox Creeks, all coming from the Teton Range. *Geol. Idaho; Targhee; Yellowstone.*

26 See *Yellowstone.*

27 Thus keeping somewhat inland from the right bank of Teton River's south fork.

28 Along the lowest level of the ground eventually rising into the foothills of the Teton Range.

29 Present-day Trail Creek, it being the modern cartographer's name for the larger of the two parent branches which, by coalescing, formed Teton River. See *Targhee; Yellowstone.*

30 Issuing from the canyon on the southeast outskirts of the site of present-day town of Victor, Idaho. See *Targhee.*

31 Camped at confluence of Trail Creek and present-day Moose Creek (*Targhee; Yellowstone*). At this confluence, the valley of Trail Creek abruptly contracted, and began, with steeply slanting sides and narrow rock-strewn floor, to climb rapidly toward the summit of present-day Teton Pass.

32 Evidently Mr. Crooks.

33 "to carry his Rifle & Pistols" in trav. mem.

34 Trail Creek, which, though geographically the left fork, was actually Stuart's "right hand" fork as he stood at the confluence mentioned in note 31. *Targhee; Teton; Yellowstone.*

35 Teton Pass (altitude 8429 feet), which lay between southern end of Teton Range and northwesterly side of Snake River Range. *Targhee; Teton; Wyoming Forest; Yellowstone; Raynolds,* pp. 95, 96.

36 "about nine inches snow" in trav. mem.

37 Stuart, after crossing the summit of Teton Pass, went down the valley descending easterly from it and so encountered the south fork of the Snake (his "Mad River") at approximately a spot due east from the site of present-day town of Wilson, Wyo. *Targhee; Teton; Wyoming Forest; Geol. Wyoming.*

38 The left bank of south fork of the Snake. Stuart was now in what later was called Jackson's Hole (altitude 6213 feet); named, in or shortly after 1829, for David Jackson of the Rocky Mountain Fur Co. *Targhee; Holt; Chittenden,* pp. 261, 289.

39 "2 to 3½ feet" in trav. mem.

40 See note 57 on p. 22.

41 Incorrectly "S S E" in trav. mem.

42 Southwesterly foothills of present-day Gros Ventre Range; this mountain range thus named in recognition of its having been periodically skirted by the Atsina indians (*alias* Gros Ventre of the Prairie) when on their astonishing pilgrimages described on p. 336.

43 Here, immediately below where present-day Flat Creek (formerly Little Gros Ventre River *alias* Creek) emptied into the south fork of Snake River, the westerly toes of the Gros Ventre Range and the southeasterly toes of the Snake River Range came so close together as to leave restricted space for the river to flow between them. *Yellowstone; Holt; Targhee; Teton; Wyoming Forest.*

44 One of the most southerly of the Gros Ventre Range's foothills, which

here, keeping only a few hundred feet inland from the left bank of south fork of Snake River, skirted it through successive miles.

45 Incorrectly "E.S.E." in trav. mem.

46 Present-day Horse Creek, which emptied through left bank of the Snake's south fork. Stuart's camp on it was approximately a half-mile above its mouth (*Targhee; Teton; Wyoming Forest; Holt*). At this spot Stuart was not more than 30 miles from the mouth of Greys River, where he had been on September 18.

47 "did not succeed in killing any" in trav. mem.

48 This stream, the Hoback or Hoback's River of *Teton, Wyoming Forest, Geol. Wyoming, Holt* and *Yellowstone*, the Hoback Fork of present-day colloquial nomenclature, was, in or prior to 1812, named for the John Hoback who has frequently been mentioned in these pages. See *Astoria*, I, p. 284. Stuart first encountered it at a spot approximately two miles above its mouth. On some modern maps it is styled Fall River.

49 Hoback River.

50 Camped on right bank of Hoback River near mouth of present-day Camp Creek. *Teton; Wyoming Forest; Geol. Wyoming.*

51 "Vallée killed some distance below" in trav. mem.

52 Hoback River. Stuart, because of the topography and as revealed by his subsequent text, was travelling on the river's right bank.

53 Present-day Granite Creek, which emptied through Hoback River's right bank. *Teton; Wyoming Forest; Geol. Wyoming.*

54 Present-day Game Hill (altitude 7950 feet), which, on Hoback River's right bank, rose abruptly from the water's edge. *Teton; Wyoming Forest; Quad. Gros Ventre.*

55 Present-day Shoal Creek, which emptied through Hoback River's right bank at a spot immediately west of Game Hill. Stuart, confronted by Game Hill and being in a valley with acutely steep sides and with no floor other than a river brawling over boulders, here deserted the Hoback and, turning to his left, ascended Shoal Creek. Having thus reached the arête that extended northeasterly from Game Hill, he crossed it to the head of a shallow coulee which, carrying a stream equal ordinarily to little more than a mere strip of dampness, debouched through Hoback River's right bank at a spot upstream from Game Hill. By descending this coulee, he regained the Hoback's right bank at a site a trifle east of the mouth of present-day Cliff Creek, a confluent emptying through the Hoback's left bank. Stuart was here emerging into the wide Alpine valley in which today lies the town of Bondurant. *Teton; Wyoming Forest; Quad. Gros Ventre; Geol. Wyoming.*

56 Though this particular pond has now disappeared, there may yet be seen here and there along Shoal Creek's course unmistakable evidences of numerous bygone slides; and, some 12 miles above its mouth, there exists today a slide-made lake.

57 The arête mentioned in note 55.

58 Present-day Jack Creek, which, immediately after receiving the waters of present-day Dell Creek, emptied through Hoback River's right bank. *Teton; Wyoming Forest; Quad. Gros Ventre; Geol. Wyoming.*

59 Camped approximately at site of town of Bondurant.

60 Hoback River.

61 "our old Buck meat" in trav. mem. Doubtless meat of the antelope killed October 9.

62 Ascending Hoback River to mouth of present-day Fish (*alias* Fisherman) Creek. *Teton; Wyoming Forest; Quad. Gros Ventre; Geol. Wyoming.*

63 Fish Creek.

64 Not a mountain, but a long ridge forming the local portion of the wall which enclosed the Green River's basin. An abrupt ascent over rough ground took Stuart to the summit of this ridge where, at his place of crossing it (approximately latitude 43° 9′, longitude 110° 11′ 30″), he found himself atop the so-called rim-rock which, extending the length of the ridge, consisted of a more or less horizontal cap of lava. A descent of the gnarled quasi-vertical face of this rim-rock was followed by a scramble down the steeply sloping talus which led from the rock's foot to the floor of the Green River's valley.

65 Camp was on headwaters of Fish Creek and approximately two and one-eighth miles due west from where Stuart crossed the ridge mentioned in note 64.

66 Three most northerly forks of present-day North Beaver Creek. *Teton; Wyoming Forest; Quad. Gros Ventre; Geol. Wyoming.*

67 This stream, present-day Green River (which by confluence with Grand River forms the Colorado River), was the "Rio Verde" of the Spaniards, the "Spanish River" of other early voyageurs, and the "Colorado of the West" of Bonneville in 1837. The Snake indians who frequented it termed it, so Granville Stuart states, *Can-na-ra o-gwa*, meaning "Poor River"; this because the soil adjacent to much of its course was such as not to support either trees or grass. Nevertheless, *Gebow*, p. 10, has these same indians term it *Pe-ah-o-goie.* Fremont avers that its Absarokan name was *Seeds-ke-dee-agie*, meaning "Prairie Hen River" and applied because of the prevalence of that bird, *Tetrao urophasianus*, in the river's valley (*Railroad Survey*, XI, map facing p. 34; *Stuart, Granville* [*A*], pp. 30, 68; *Fremont*, p. 129). For variant names and their history see *Dale*, p. 156, f.n., as also ed. note in *Sawyer*, pp. 50, 51.

68 Stuart's point of initial contact with Green River was approximately at the mouth of present-day Little Twin Creek (latitude 43° 8′ 15″, longitude 110° 3′ 50″), and thus in the immediate vicinity of the site of present-day town of Kendall. *Teton; Wyoming Forest; Quad. Gros Ventre; Geol. Wyoming.*

69 Incorrectly "160 yards" in trav. mem.

70 See note 68.

71 Incorrectly "11 more" in trav. mem. Camped on left bank of Green River at a spot approximately three and one-half miles below the mouth of

present-day Spring Creek and thus approximately in latitude 43° 6′. *Teton; Wyoming Forest; Quad. Gros Ventre.*

72 "about midnight" in trav. mem.

73 If notes 74 and 79 are accurate, it was on this night (October 12) that there occurred the episode of threatened cannibalism, which, though unmentioned in journ's. original entries, is described in journ.'s postscript and trav. mem. entries for October 13. Also, *Astoria*, II, pp. 156, 157, presumably in reliance on trav. mem., gives the night as the 13th.

Stuart's abstention from contemporaneous reference to the gruesome incident was in accord, so history discloses, with the usage of diarists confronted with a like tragedy.

74 This October 13th original entry in journ., as also portions of the journ.'s October 14th and 15th original entries, were so rephrased in journ.'s postscripts and also in trav. mem. as to add important details and also to create divergencies which at first sight—but only at first sight—seem unalterably inconsistent. These divergencies are restricted to the date of obtaining the bison meat which averted the party's starvation and to the direction and extent of travel on October 13 and 14. There is no disagreement regarding the course and distance travelled and destination reached on October 15.

Incidentally, while the format of the journ.'s manuscript does not reveal just when the various postscripts were written (they all are on the rear pages—see note 289 on p. CXXXVII), it does reveal that the ones dated October 14 and 15 were made after March 15, 1813, inasmuch as these latter postscripts immediately succeed another addendum (pp. 255, 256) which, from its text, could not have been penned earlier than this specified day in March.

On comparing the rephrasings with the original entries which they purport to alter, it clearly appears that Stuart in his rephrasings somewhat confused his dates, erroneously duplicated a previous statement of mileage, and unduly increased one such mileage. More specifically, these aberrances are as follows:

Oct. 13. Although the journ.'s original entry of this date and the corresponding rephrasings agree (a) as to the identity of the spot from which Stuart began his day's march and (b) as to his going downstream from that spot to McClellan's camp (a journey of 9 miles S.W. acc. to journ.'s original entry—the rephrasings do not mention the distance), they disagree concerning the course and distance travelled after leaving McClellan's camp. The journ.'s original entry records them as "nearly East . . . . 2 miles" (thus a total of 11 miles for the day); but the rephrasings give them as "17 miles S.E.," which unquestionably represents an errant transcription of the original entry's total of 11.

That the course ("nearly East") and mileage ("2 miles") given in the journ.'s original entry are accurate appears from the facts that they,

[1] in conjunction with the course and distance for Oct. 15 (as concordantly stated in journ.'s original, journ.'s postscript and trav. mem.'s

entries, all for Oct. 15), would lead Stuart direct to present-day New Fork River's bend in approx. lat. 43° 0′ 0″, long. 110° 0′ 0″—see *Wyoming Forest; Geol. Wyoming*—, and these three entries show that on Oct. 15 he reached this bend; and,

[2] in conjunction with the course and distance for Oct. 15 and also for the morning of Oct. 16 (as concordantly stated in both journ. and trav. mem. entries for this latter day—there is no corresponding journ.'s postscript), would lead Stuart direct from New Fork River's bend to the site of present-day Pinedale, and these entries for Oct. 16 agree that on this day he reached this site (see *Wyoming Forest; Quads. Gros Ventre* and *Fremont Peak*).

Although no further proof as to the inaccuracy of the restated "17 miles S.E." is seemingly needed, we nevertheless call attention to the fact that, if Stuart had journeyed the entire "17 miles," he would have arrived approximately at present-day Soda Lake (situated eight airline miles due north of Pinedale's site), and thus could not later have attained the Pinedale site by the route which journ. and trav. mem. agree that he took thither. Moreover, the last half of the "17 miles," instead of leading Stuart, as the rephrasings state, over "a level barren of sand," would have conducted him across a terrain that was very far from level.

Oct. 14. While the journ.'s original entry of this date has Stuart remain immobile for the day, the corresponding rephrasings, by erroneously reiterating the mileage in the journ.'s original entry for Oct. 13, make him seem to trudge 11 miles. If the thus duplicating mileage in these rephrasings were added to the errant "17 miles" above mentioned, Stuart's camp on the night of this 14th would fallaciously appear to have been some 7 airline miles E.N.E. of the site of Pinedale instead of, as actually, some 27 miles W.N.W. of it.

With the aberrances thus corrected, there is complete accord among all the various texts. Wherefore it confidently may be assumed that Stuart's actual experiences on October 13 were those (a) described, under date October 13, in journ.'s original entry and in the corresponding portion of trav. mem.'s entry; (b) further described in journ.'s undated postscript for October 13 as modified by note 79; and (c) still further described, under erroneous date October 14, in journ.'s postscript and trav. mem.'s corresponding entry, each as modified by note 91.

A consolidation of these various items would produce a reading somewhat as follows:

Tuesday 13th. We were up with the dawn, and visited our Trap in anxious expectation, but found nothing in it except the forepaw of a large Beaver, which has greatly damped our spirits, as we do not feel in very good trim to resume our journey. But there being no alternative, we started early and soon after met Leclairc coming up the river with information that the smoke was at the camp of McClellan, whom he found late in the evening, and had been occasioned by the camp's getting on fire while McClellan was at some little distance fishing but without success. McClellan had informed Leclairc that he had been very much indisposed and lived on little or nothing ever since he parted with us; that he was happy of our being near (as well he might) and could wait our arrival at his camp in hopes we should have something for him to eat, without which he could not proceed much farther. Continuing on at the end of 9 miles from our last night's station S.W., we reached him. We learned from him that he was then like ourselves without a mouthfull to eat— He was lying on a parcel of straw, emaciated and worn to a perfect skeleton, hardly able to raise his head, or speak, from extreme debility, but our presence seemed to revive him considerably, and by much persuasion we prevailed on him to accompany us, but with apparent reluctance, as he said it was as well for him to die there as anywhere else, there being no prospect of our getting any speedy relief. He soon tied up his Bundle, we carried all his things and we all came to the base of some low hills which we ascended, going nearly East over a level barren of sand, and had scarcely proceeded 2 miles when to our great joy we discovered three Buffalo Bulls and, after considerable trouble, we, about 2 P.M., killed one (an old run down one), which soon made us determine on encamping. So ravenous were our appetites, that we ate part of the animal raw; then cut up the most of what was eatable and carried it to a brook at some little distance, where we encamped, being hungry enough to relish a hearty meal. We sat up the greater part of the night eating and barbecuing meat; I was very much alarmed at the ravenous manner in which all ate, but happily none felt any serious effects therefrom—probably in consequence of my not allowing them to eat freely before they had supped a quantity of broth—

75 Seemingly on Green River's left bank and approximately three miles due north from the latitude of the confluence of present-day Beaver Creek with Green River. *Teton; Wyoming Forest; Quad. Gros Ventre; Geol. Wyoming.*

76 A chain of round-topped and very low hills.

77 As discussed in note 74, this "nearly East . . . 2 miles," is erroneously restated as "17 miles S.E." in both journ.'s postscript and trav. mem.

78 The site of this camp, if two miles "nearly East" of where McClellan was encountered, was approximately in latitude 43° 1′ 40″, longitude 110° 3′ 50″, and at the head of a small drain which, flowing southeasterly, is indicated on *Wyoming Forest* and *Quad. Gros Ventre.*

79 From the beginning of this paragraph and to the end of the fifth succeeding paragraph, the text of the journ.'s postscript and of the trav. mem., though in the form of a continuous narrative relating ostensibly to a single date, actually relates, it appears, to two dates. The first paragraph is devoted to a rephrasing of the journ.'s original entry for October 13. But the next five para-

graphs are supplemental, it would seem, to the journ.'s original entry for October 12: this, for the reason that the threatened cannibalism episode must have occurred before bison meat was obtained; and the time of obtaining the meat was assuredly the afternoon of October 13.

For the errors of journ.'s postscript and of trav. mem. in their statements of the courses and distance travelled on October 13, see note 74.

80 "found" in trav. mem.

81 "our" in trav. mem.

82 "taking fire" in trav. mem.

83 That "17 miles S.E." should have been "2 miles E." appears from note 74.

84 *Astoria*, II, p. 156, states that this Canadian was Leclairc. However, it seemingly could not have been he; for, as appears in the entries of October 12, 13 (pp. 155, 156), he had already departed in his search for McClellan and did not rejoin Stuart till the next day.

85 "to save" in trav. mem.

86 "assent" in trav. mem.

87 These words "I felt so" were deleted by Stuart; but, for the sake of textual clarity, have been reinserted. Trav. mem. states "became."

88 Pursuant to note 74, it confidently may be assumed that Stuart's actual experiences on this October 14 were those (a) described in journ.'s original entry for this date and (b) further described, under erroneous date October 15, in the forepart of this latter date's entries in journ.'s postscript and in trav. mem., both as modified by notes 91, 92, 94.

A consolidation of these various entries would produce, at the cost of partial reiteration (see end of note 74), a reading approximately as follows:

> Wednesday 14th. Having sat up the greater part of last night eating and barbecuing meat—I was very much alarmed at the ravenous manner in which all ate, but happily none felt any serious effects therefrom, probably in consequence of my not allowing them to eat freely before they had supped a quantity of broth—, we remained in the same Camp all day bringing up our leaway and reposing ourselves after the late fatigues. We cut up a quantity of meat to dry and intend going down this River so long as it lies in our course or at least to the point of a mountain we see in the East near which we expect finding the Mifsouri waters.

89 Green River.

90 A peak in Wind River Range. Stuart's phrase "lies in our course" is significant in connection with South Pass.

91 This paragraph, though dated October 14, represents obviously a rephrasing of part of the journ.'s original entry for October 13, not 14—see note 74. Consequently, though it erroneously duplicates the actual mileage of October 13, it nevertheless adds to that October 13 original entry a trustworthy

statement (repeated in trav. mem.) that the night's camp was on a brook, for the location of which brook see note 78.

92 Southwest rather than Southeast, if note 91 is accurate.

93 The thus encountered bend belonged, not to Green River, but instead to present-day New Fork River, which, flowing here southeast, ultimately became a confluent of the Green. This bend, the site of Stuart's camp, was approximately in latitude 43° 0′ 0″, longitude 110° 0′ 0″. *Wyoming Forest; Geol. Wyoming.*

94 This paragraph is patently supplemental to journ.'s original entry for October 14. Pursuant to note 74, it well may be believed that Stuart's actual experiences on this October 15 were those (a) described in journ.'s October 15 original entry and (b) further described in the second half of both journ.'s postscript and trav. mem.'s October 15 entries as modified by note 96.

A consolidation of these various entries would produce, at the cost of partial reiteration (see end of note 88), a reading somewhat as follows:

> Thursday 15th. Being somewhat recruited and refreshed by the middle of the day, we, at a late hour, left camp, with the intention of going down this river so long as it lies in our course or at least to the point of a mountain we see in the East, near which we expect to find the Mifsouri waters; and in 12 miles E.S.E. over low Hills struck a bend of the River and stopped for the night. We this day crofsed a large Indian trail, about fifteen days old steering nearly a N.E. course, which we suppose made by the Absaroka nation, who, from the numerous carcases of Buffaloe we find in every direction, must have been hunting in this Country for a great length of time. No Buffaloe in sight; only a few Goats & them very wild.

95 "voracious" in trav. mem.

96 This paragraph manifestly represents a partial rephrasing of journ.'s original entry for October 15, even though it reiterates a portion of journ.'s original entry for October 14.

97 New Fork River, which Stuart crossed here and which at this spot ran actually to the east of south and not, as Stuart states, to west of south.

98 Wind River Range.

99 Present-day Willow Creek, which emptied through left bank of New Fork River. *Wyoming Forest; Geol. Wyoming.*

100 Present-day Pine Creek, which emptied through left bank of New Fork River. That the place of Stuart's crossing Pine Creek was at or very near the site of present-day town of Pinedale is conclusively established by his description of the trees. Pine Creek boasted the only grove of pines in this otherwise almost treeless section of Green River's valley floor. *Wyoming Forest; Geol. Wyoming.*

101 "bones" in trav. mem.

102 "44 feet" in trav. mem.

103 "at the head of each was a branch" in trav. mem.

104 Present-day Pole Creek, which emptied through the left bank of New Fork River.

105 Camp was at approximately the confluence of present-day Fall Creek with Pole Creek. *Wyoming Forest; Geol. Wyoming.*

106 Present-day Boulder Creek, which, some miles below its emergence from Boulder Lake, emptied through left bank of New Fork River. *Wyoming Forest; Geol. Wyoming.*

107 Present-day East Fork River (this lower stretch of its course styled "Muddy Creek" by some cartographers), which emptied through left bank of New Fork River. Stuart thus first encountered East Fork River at seemingly where it, having altered its northwesterly course, was beginning to veer southwesterly in order to effect its hairpin turn around the northern fringe of Fremont's Butte. *Wyoming Forest; Geol. Wyoming.*

108 Outlying foothills of Wind River Range.

109 Wind River Range.

110 "rocky mountains" in trav. mem.

111 Several materially exceeding 13,000 feet (*Washakie; Wyoming Forest*). ". . . a grand bed of snow-capped mountains rose before us, pile upon pile, glowing in the bright light of an August day" according to *Fremont*, p. 61. See also *Clapp*, p. 28.

112 Stuart's "E S E." should seemingly have been "S.S.E." Camped on East Fork River at point of initial contact mentioned in note 107.

113 Doubtless bison.

114 It was during the animals' mating season and accordingly the flesh of the males was apt to be tough and also unpleasant in flavor.

115 One of the long, low "rolls" which here interrupted the otherwise flatness of the plain.

116 Present-day Silver Creek, which emptied through East Fork River's left bank. *Wyoming Forest; Geol. Wyoming.*

117 East Fork River, Stuart encountering it approximately at the mouth of present-day Pocket Creek, one of its confluents from the north. *Wyoming Forest; Geol. Wyoming.*

118 "about 130 Indians" in trav. mem.

119 Probably ascending left fork of Pocket Creek. *Wyoming Forest.*

120 "40" in trav. mem.

121 This and the two succeeding paragraphs are trav. mem.'s rephrasing of the journ.'s postscript on p. 254.

122 "killed 5 of them" in journ.'s postscript, p. 254.

123 This represents the indians' garbled version of a portion of the following facts:

When, in September, 1811, Hunt's westbound Astorians reached the mouth of Hoback River, four of the party (*i.e.*, Pierre Detayé, Louis St. Michel, Alexander Carson and Pierre Delaunay) were detached for purposes of local trapping and of later taking their thus obtained furs to one of the depots which it was supposed Astor's associates would meanwhile establish. In the spring of 1812 these four men with their peltry-laden horses were heading for the Missouri when they were attacked by Crow indians with the result that Detayé was slain while his three companions, robbed of every possession, escaped and made their way on foot to a Shoshone indian camp on present-day Boise River. In this camp they found four stragglers from Hunt's party, *i.e.*, Jean Baptiste Dubreuil but newly arrived there, André LaChapelle, François Landry and Jean Baptiste Turcotte, these last three having, shortly before Dubreuil's arrival, returned from the cache-robbing expedition mentioned in note 49 on p. 121. All seven of these men were presently rescued by John Reed.

Of the seven, St. Michel (who later in the summer of 1812 was trapping on Snake River), Carson (who subsequently was a "free" trapper on Willamette River) and Dubreuil quitted the Columbian region when they embarked with the so-called Grand Brigade, which, starting in 10 canoes from Ft. George (*alias* Astoria) on April 4, 1814, steered for the country eastward of the Rocky Mountains. Carson and Dubreuil, however, eventually remigrated to western Oregon and there became farmers. Delaunay, LaChapelle, Landry and Turcotte, in the summer of 1813, returned with John Reed and other persons to the Boise region of the Snake River country and there erected, as described in note 38 on pp. 67-69, the two camps which presently were to witness the indians' massacre of LaChapelle, Reed, Giles Leclerc and Pierre Dorion, and also to see what was not the first exhibition of patient, majestic and endearing heroism on the part of this Dorion's indian wife. Turcotte and Delaunay were not involved in the massacre. Turcotte had earlier died from syphilis. Delaunay, a sullen chap, had, some months before the massacre—the reader may elect between two inconsistent tales—either wandered from camp during a fit of moroseness without leaving the slightest trace, or, while trapping, been killed by indians who treasured a scalp afterwards recognized as his. As for Landry, there are two reports: one, that he was slain in the massacre: the other that, months prior to it, he had died as the consequence of a fall from a horse.

See *Astoria*, I, pp. 182, 199, 247, 250, 251, II, pp. 10, 11, 53, 56, 57, 102, 194-197, 213, 254-256; *Henry-Thomp.*, pp. 667, 856, 857, 861, 862, 871-875, 884, 886, 887; *Franchere* [*B*], pp. 273-276; *Ross* [*A*], pp. 218, 277-282; H. S. Lyman's *Reminiscences of Louis Labonte* in *Ore. Hist. Soc. Quar.*, I, pp. 169-177.

124 For this escapade of LaChapelle, Landry and Turcotte, in which none of them despite the indians' account was killed, see note 49 on p. 121.

125 These data in trav. mem. are a restating of journ.'s postscript, p. 254. Also on protective wrapper on back cover of journal Stuart wrote "The Arapahays killed Champlain & 3 men in Summer 1812—"

Jean Baptiste Champlain, *fils*, whom Manuel Lisa in 1812 termed "mozo Honrado" (honorable young man), was a person of education and not improbably a European Frenchman. He was in St. Louis as early as 1800. He went with the Lisan brigade of 1807 from St. Louis to the mouth of the Big Horn River, whence in August, 1810, he with Ezekiel Williams and others embarked upon the journey which resulted in Champlain's murder in the spring or summer of 1812 by Arapahoe indians on or near the present-day Arkansas River. Walter L. Douglas' *Manuel Lisa* in *Missouri*, III, pp. 249, 250, 255-257; *Ezekiel Williams* &c. in *Missouri*, IV, pp. 194-208; Herbert E. Bolton's *New Light on Manuel Lisa* &c. in *Southwestern*, XVII, p. 65; *Chittenden*, pp. 652 *et seq.;* notes 260, 261 on pp. CXXXII, CXXXIII *ante;* and, for what it may be worth, *Coyner*, pp. 86 *et seq.*

126 Present-day Arkansas River, flowing eastward from the Rocky Mountains. See references cited in note 125.

127 *Nicotiana quadrivalvis.*

128 "5 days" in trav. mem. The remainder of the sentence is omitted from trav. mem.

129 "100 lodges" in trav. mem. Frontiersmen could quite accurately estimate the number of lodges by noting the marks which the dragging ends of horse-drawn lodgepoles had made upon the ground.

130 Incorrectly "S.E." in trav. mem.

131 Present-day Big Sandy Creek, Stuart's point of initial contact having been approximately one and one-half miles southeast from the site of present-day town of Big Sandy. *Wyoming Forest; Geol. Wyoming.*

132 Crossed to left bank.

133 Camped on left bank of Big Sandy Creek approximately at the forks of the creek (*Wyoming Forest; Geol. Wyoming*). That Stuart was consciously heading for South Pass appears from the journ.'s postscript: "we therefore made the best of our way for a gape disernable in the mountains in a S.E. direction." This same postscript adds in reference to Stuart's crossing of the continental divide: "we passed thro a handsome low gap—." See also note 90 *ante*, as well as note 7 on pp. 140-142.

134 Doubtless bison.

135 See *Brown*, p. 403, for parallel description.

136 Southeasterly end of Wind River Range.

137 Wind River Range.

138 So named because of the well-nigh constant breeze which, emanating from a gap between the Shoshone and Wind River ranges of mountains, blows down the river's valley. This name for the stream has extended itself to the adjacent mountain range as well.

139 Although the Wind River Range of mountains was actually the watershed between (1) the waters which, immediately east of that range, discharged into the Missouri River and (2) those which, immediately west of that range, were in the Green River's valley and thus flowed toward the Gulf of California, nevertheless the Wind River Range was not concerned with any streams which

drained into the Columbia River basin. However, immediately northwest of Wind River Range and topographically tied to it, was the Gros Ventre Range, which did divide the waters destined for the Missouri from those destined for the Columbia.

140 See *Cole*, p. 68, for parallel description.

141 Southerly end of present-day Salt River Range.

142 A long, low ridge rising not more than 50 feet above the average level of the valley's floor.

143 "snakes" in trav. mem.

144 Doubtless one of the following three streams which, by present-day names, are Wind River, Popo Agie River and Sweetwater River. *Geol. Wyoming.*

145 Present-day Dry Sandy Creek, Stuart's camp on it being approximately in latitude 42° 18′, longitude 109° 7′, and thus at a spot some 11 miles southeast by south from the site of present-day town of Elkhorn. *Geol. Wyoming.*

146 One of the numerous shallow depressions which characterize the floor of Green River's valley.

147 Concerning Stuart's "salt," his description—especially his reference to coastal indians' dislike for the commodity—shows it was that extremely bitter precipitate which is popularly known as alkali and for which see *Encyclopædia Britannica* (14th Edit.), I, p. 641. Any particular "alkali" deposit tends to disappear as soon as its creative spring or watercourse ceases to exist. Stuart's deposit can no longer be found save in widely scattered spots.

148 Incorrectly "side of a lofty mountain" in trav. mem. Stuart's camp on a hillside was approximately in latitude 42° 20′, longitude 108° 56′, and thus immediately northeast of present-day Pacific Springs and one mile due south from extreme headwaters of present-day Pacific Creek. *Holt; Geol. Wyoming.*

Stuart, now well within the constricting western entrance to South Pass, was squarely on the main route of the subsequent Oregon Trail and but a scant two miles southwesterly from the spot which, when later covered by that trail, was called by its emigrant users the Summit of South Pass. See *Horn*, p. 28.

The upland on the side of which Stuart camped was one of the group of numerous, wide-based, plateau-crowned and comparatively low hills which adjoined the abrupt southeasterly end of the Wind River Range, substituted themselves for mountains in this particular section of the continental divide, and collectively formed the South Pass. Amid various of these hills and across their plateaus and along their lower flanks ran eventually the Oregon Trail. The pass, instead of being a narrow montane corridor, was twenty-odd miles in width; but, since the beginning of emigrant days, the term "South Pass" has usually been intended to specify such portion of the pass as either was covered by or was immediately adjacent to the Oregon Trail. *Railroad Surveys*, I, Chap. II, pp. 66, 67. See also *Hayden, Wyoming*, p. 39; *Fremont*, pp. 59, 60, 128, 129; *Greeley*, pp. 191-193; *Wadsworth*, p. 97; *Horn*, p. 28; *Sawyer*, pp. 46-48; *Burton*, pp. 200-202; *Langworthy*, p. 72; *Thornton*, I, p. 139; *Ware*, p. 26; *Abbott*, p. 42;

Udell, p. 22; *Turnbull*, p. 178; *Frizzell*, p. 29; *Ferguson*, p. 34; *Delano*, pp. 114-116; *Dundass*, p. 34; *Wistar*, I, p. 93; *Allen*, p. 161; *Kelly*, I, pp. 189, 190, 195; *Gove*, pp. 63, 64; *Ingalls*, p. 26; *Kenderdine*, p. 86; *Birmingham*, pp. 51, 52; *Bryant*, pp. 132, 133; *Coke*, p. 189; *Steele*, p. 98; *De Peyster*, pp. 120, 121; *Crown Maps*, II, No. 23; *Diary &c of Captain David Dewolf* in *Illinois*, p. 202; *Gilbert*, pp. 140-150.

For discussion of identity of discoverer of South Pass, see Charles L. Camp's note in *Cal. Hist. Soc. Quar.*, IV, pp. 126-129 and in *Clyman*, pp. 38, 39. See also *Smith*, pp. [ii], 13, 162; *Gilbert*, pp. 140, 141.

149 If not present-day Limestone Mountain, then the more easterly elevation situated between present-day Twin Creek and Beaver Creek and styled Sheep Mountain. *Washakie; Holt.*

150 "Crows" in trav. mem., which omits so much of the sentence as follows "Spanish River."

151 Stuart veering southeasterly and away from the line of the then future Oregon Trail, and thus travelling southward of the two small hills (each about 60 feet high) which in covered-wagon days were frequently styled Twin Buttes, Twin Mounds, or Twin Hills. In the shallow valley between these two hills ultimately ran the main stem of the emigrant trail and also lay the emigrant's so-called Summit of South Pass. Not all of the emigrants, however, crossed at the "Summit," since some of them used the "Lander [Lander's] Cut Off," which, extending from New Fork River to the site of present-day South Pass City, lay northward of the "Summit." *Brown, J. Robert*, p. 62; *Bennett*, p. 27; *Horn*, p. 28; *Holt.*

The fact that Stuart, when crossing South Pass, detoured southward from both these routes later used by the covered-wagon emigrants (his detour continued until, well eastward of the Pass, he reached the right bank of Sweetwater River at a spot three miles below the mouth of Muddy Creek) allows speculation as to his reason, a reason which he himself does not affirmatively give. In this connection, we should remember that, although so much of this emigrants' ultimate route as ran eastward from the crest of South Pass skirted more or less closely for numerous miles the Sweetwater River's headwaters, and thereby furnished the easiest gradients for wagons and offered a maximum of water, nevertheless the westernmost end of this skirting stretch was not self-evident to a person who was unacquainted with all the characteristics of the Pass and, like Stuart, was approaching it from the westward. And Stuart had little chance of gaining foreknowledge of at least some of these characteristics because, when his indian informant told him in central Idaho (p. 84) of "a shorter trace to the South" (*i.e.*, the Pass), contracted to guide him "from this to the other side" (*i.e.*, to and through the Pass), and next day absconded, the indian very likely did not go into detail sufficient to explain the geographic relation which the Pass bore to the Sweetwater's headwaters. Consequently, Stuart's detour may have been unintentional. If, however, it were purposed, its motive might possibly be found in his expressed wish to avoid the Absarokan indians whose trail, on the day before his entering the Pass, he had discovered bearing north of east, and thus apparently trending toward the northerly edge of the Pass and so toward the Sweetwater River's headwaters. Also Stuart may have had in mind that his goal, St. Louis, lay southeastward of where he was.

Having once begun his detour, Stuart was committed to it because, until he reached Muddy Creek, he could not conveniently attain the Sweetwater River, being separated from it by successively the rugged ranges of present-day Sweetwater Mountains (otherwise known as Antelope Hills) and of present-day Green Mountains, each of which ranges paralleled that river's course.

The journ.'s and trav. mem.'s entries for October 22 agree as to place of departure, as to aggregate distance travelled and as to destination reached; but these pages of the trav. mem. contain the following misleading statements:

(1) Their initial "about 3 miles" should seemingly be, as in journ., "5 miles."

(2) Their "top of the mountain" was apparently the extensive champaign plateau which capped a large portion of South Pass.

(3) Their "principal chain" meant seemingly the continental divide, which, at South Pass, rose but little more than a thousand feet above the adjacent plain.

(4) Their "considerable Lake," if not created by mirage or a mistaken recollection as to site, was doubtless a shallow ephemeral product of torrential rain or melted snow.

(5) Their descriptions of "the principal chain" and "lateral chain" represent apparently an attempt to delineate, not South Pass, but instead the terrain of the various high mountain ranges in its neighborhood.

(6) Their "base of the mountain" was seemingly the western end of the plain lying east of the continental divide and south of the present-day Green Mountains.

Incidentally, their reference to "various shells" does not identify a particular spot because cretaceous fossils were common in this general locality.

152 The site of this halt was, it seems, approximately in latitude 42° 18′, longitude 108° 51′, and at the head of the stream which (indicated, without name, on *Geol. Wyoming* as emptying through Sweetwater River's right bank at a spot three miles east of Fish Creek's mouth) was the "Muddy Creek" of Lander and has been by various cartographers termed "Oregon Slough." *Lander; Crown Maps*, II, No. 22.

153 Headwaters of present-day Sand Creek—a sometimes almost waterless stream which flowed easterly and then southerly, to lose itself in the arid soil of the semi-desert. *Geol. Wyoming; Holt.*

154 The journ. under date of October 22 having described the terrain, trav. mem. absorbs that description into its own entry for October 23; but, under either date, the description is accurate. However, in that entry of trav.

mem., Stuart, by repeating part of the wording of the journ.'s entry for October 22, is made to say that the Sand Creek's section along which he then travelled was the "head drains" instead of, as correctly stated in journ., a lower reach.

155 Sand Creek.

156 This camp on Sand Creek was approximately in latitude 42° 16′, longitude 108° 37′, and at a spot some seven and one-half miles due south from confluence of present-day Rock Creek with Sweetwater River. *Geol. Wyoming.*

157 Greasewood, *Sarcobatus vermiculatus.*

158 Southeasterly end of Wind River Range. For a like description, see *Smith, C. W.*, p. 51; *Leeper*, pp. 39, 40.

159 A hill, not a mountain. See note 148.

160 Probably meaning continental divide. See note 151.

161 See note 151.

162 South Pass is on an elevated plain.

163 See sub-paragraph "(4)" of note 151.

164 See sub-paragraph "(5)" of note 151.

165 Immediately after this word "on," Stuart, when transcribing this sentence from journ. into trav. mem., erroneously interpolated matter paraphrased from the journ.'s entry for October 22 and reading as follows: "for 7 miles E.S.E. which brought us to the head drains of a watercourse, running east among banks, and low hills of a loose, bluish coloured earth, apparently strongly impregnated with Copperas."

166 Incorrectly "26 miles" in trav. mem. The "Hill" from which Stuart obtained his view cannot be identified today. It was merely one of the numerous sand dunes which characterize this particular area. See *Holt*, as also Stuart's later reference (in this same day's entry) to it as a "Knob."

167 Seemingly not Sand Creek but instead lower stretches of present-day Lost Creek, which, rising in the Green Mountains, flowed into a semi-desert and there disappeared either by evaporation or by seepage into a subterranean channel. *Geol. Wyoming.*

168 Present-day Seminoe Mountains, which rose approximately 1500 feet above the plain (*Hayden, Wyoming*, p. 32). These mountains were thus named by or for Basil Lajeunesse, who, a member of Fremont's expedition in 1842-44, had earlier been dubbed "Seminoe" by the Snake indians with whom he had lived during several years. Cartographers sometimes style the mountains as "Seminole." *Wyoming*, VI, p. 237; *Fremont*, pp. 9, 47, 105, 121.

169 This "Plain" ("prairie" in trav. mem.) was the bench running lengthwise of the southern side of the Sweetwater Mountains. Camp was, it seems, approximately in latitude 42° 10′, longitude 108° 16′, and at a spot some 21 miles due south from confluence of present-day Sulphur Creek with Sweetwater River. *Geol. Wyoming.*

170 This sentence is omitted from trav. mem.

171 Incorrectly "27 miles" in trav. mem.

172 Alkaline flats south of Green Mountains.

173 For the remainder of this sentence trav. mem. substitutes: "had no other fuel than Buffalo Dung." Camp was approximately in latitude 42° 16′, longitude 108° 0′, and at a spot about one mile northeast of where Lost Creek changed its course from westerly to southwesterly. *Geol. Wyoming.*

174 Lost Creek.

175 Incorrectly "32 miles" in trav. mem.

176 The camp was approximately in latitude 42° 15′, longitude 107° 41′, and apparently near the headwaters of right fork of present-day Lost Soldier Creek. This creek, rising in the Green Mountains, met the same evaporative fate as that suffered by Sand Creek and Lost Creek. *Holt; Geol. Wyoming.*

Lost Soldier Creek's name has its origin explained in a letter written May 21, 1898, by Doctor Thomas G. Maghee to Doctor C. G. Coutant, for a copy of which letter we are indebted to the unfailing courtesy of Mrs. Cyrus Beard, State Historian of Wyoming. The letter reads:

> "Mr. Tom Sun tells me that in 1880 William Daley and others selected a route from Rawlins to Lander. They were accompanied as guards by some soldiers, one of whom wandered away from camp on what is now Lost Soldier Creek and losing himself wandered east to Tom Sun's ranch. The latch string was out but the soldier removed two panes of glass and unbuttoned the hinged sash, entering the cabin in this way found victuals to satisfy his hunger and a place to sleep. From this came the name Lost Soldier. Tom Sun says a man who has not sense enough to go into a man's home by the door when it was left open would get lost anywhere."

177 Would be, according to altitude of Stuart's viewing point, either northwest portion of present-day Sierra Madre Mountains or else buttes which, northwest of that range, were, because snow-capped, exaggerated in seeming height.

178 A gap which, sometimes termed Lost Soldier Gap, was situated on south side of the Green Mountains near their easterly end.

179 Lost Soldier Creek, for which see note 176.

180 Incorrectly "9 more" in trav. mem.

181 Present-day Muddy Gap, which lay between Green Mountains and present-day Ferris Mountains; these latter mountains named, it is said, by or for the American Fur Company's clerk, Warren Angus Ferris, for whose biography see *Chittenden*, pp. 366, 395, 666-670. *Geol. Wyoming; Holt.*

182 Present-day Muddy Creek, which flowed northerly through Muddy Gap and which, at its mouth, was the "Deep ravine and creek" of Clayton, the "creek and steep ravine" of Horn, the "creek and ravine" of Andrew Child, the "deep ravine creek" of Wadsworth (*Clayton* [*A*], p. 15; *Horn*, p. 24; *Child*, p. 27; *Wadsworth*, p. 95; *Holt; Geol. Wyoming*). This Muddy Creek was not the Muddy Creek mentioned in note 152.

183 Camped at southern portal of Muddy Gap.

184 Incorrectly "14 Miles" in trav. mem.

185 Muddy Creek. See note 182.

186 Northern portal of Muddy Gap.

187 Green Mountains and Ferris Mountains, for which see note 181.

188 For similar description, see *Stansbury* [*A*], pp. 66-68.

189 Stuart, by thus veering to his right, missed the confluence of Muddy Creek with Sweetwater River; and, having arrived on the Sweetwater's right bank, camped on it three miles below Muddy Creek's mouth.

190 Incorrectly "17 miles" in trav. mem.

191 "10 feet" in trav. mem.

192 Muddy Creek had actually four confluents, all coming from the southwest, three of them emptying through Muddy Creek's left bank, and one through its right bank (*Holt*). Two of the three which emptied through the left bank were, because of the seasonal lateness of Stuart's visit, doubtless dry at the time. The one debouching through the right bank was present-day Whiskey Gap Creek, so named, according to Coutant, because in 1862 Major O'Farrell, camping there with his squadron of Eleventh Ohio Cavalry, confiscated a barrel of whiskey belonging to his men and poured it on the ground. The soldiers, discovering that the whiskey had seeped into a neighboring spring, assailed the spring with cups, canteens and buckets; all with the result that, from a numerous group of intoxicated warriors, one soldier advanced to the headquarter's tent and maudlinly reported that it was the finest spring he had ever seen and the best water he had ever tasted. *Coutant*, pp. 386, 387.

193 This was Sweetwater River itself. Stuart mistakenly assumed (1) that Muddy Creek, instead of Sweetwater River, was geographically the principal stream, and (2) that he thus was still on Muddy Creek. Incidentally, *Astoria*, II, p. 166, confused Muddy Creek with the main body of the North Platte, which, eastward of this creek, flowed parallel with it.

As for the Sweetwater—"This stream takes its name from its beautiful clear cold waters having a sweetish taste, caused by the alkali held in solution in its waters, not enough, however, to cause any apparent injurious effects" (*Stuart, Granville* [*B*], I, p. 46). It, the "Eau Sucre" of early voyageurs, the "Riviere-de-l'Eau-douce," "Eau Sucree" and "Sugar river" of Father DeSmet, was, according to him, so called from the great purity of its waters in contrast with the waters of neighboring streams; but Chittenden, in a footnote, cites Ferris as asserting the name "Eau Sucre" to be due to a sugar-laden pack mule having been lost in the stream. *DeSmet Letters*, pp. 214, 297, 1360. See also *Chittenden*, p. 471.

CHAPTER VIII

OCT. 29 · DEC. 31, 1812

On Foot from Sweetwater River to Sites of First and Second Winter Quarters

[SEE MAPS FACING PAGES 127, 209]

Devil's Gate · Upper Canyon of North Platte · Red Buttes · Erect First Winter Quarters · Indian Guests · Abandon Camp · Trudge Eastward into Nebraska · Return to Wyoming and, near Site of Present-Day Torrington, Erect Second Winter Quarters.

Thursday 29th[1] The River[2] after running 3 miles nearly south forced a paſsage[3] through a considerably high range of Rocky Cedar covered Hills into an extensive low Country[4] affording excellent pasture for the numerous herds of Buffaloe with which it abounded— We killed three Buffaloe Cows this morning, which are the first of these animals we have been able to lay our paws on, [*the hump meat is by far the most delicious I have ever tasted*] and after following the river 10 miles[5] E.N.E. we encamped[6] among a few large white Willows— To the north the Plain is bounded by low bare ridges but toward the south they are much higher,[7] very rugged and poſseſs a few Cedars—

Friday 30th Some[8] snow fell in the night and at an early hour we renewed our march along the river— In the afternoon finding that the river ran to the south we croſsed it,[9] ascended the opposite Heights and went along them[10] some distance till the hour of encamping being at hand without any prospect of getting water in the highlands, we decended a steep ravine thickly wooded with scrubby Cedars, in hopes of reaching the stream every moment, but to our surprise the way became impaſsable to our Horse [85] where being obliged to leave him, we continued on a few hundred yards and found the stream[11] reduced to one half of what it was[12] where we croſsed[13] and confined between red coloured Precipices of stone at least three hundred feet[14] high— the bed of the river was composed of huge maſses of rock and the current dashing over them appeared foamingly tumultuous—[15] [*to form somewhat of an adequate idea, let one imagine numerous streams pouring from the mountains, into one channel, struggling for expansion in a narrow paſsage, exasperated by rocks rising in their way, and at last discharging all their violence of waters by a sudden fall thro' the horrid chasm*—] The wind was cold and we took refuge[16] for the night among the Cedars, having come today 26 miles[17] E.N.E.— Light was the supper of our fourfooted Companion and not a drop of water to slaik his or our thirst, till Leclairc with considerable danger to himself succeeded in procuring us enough for a drink each—

Saturday 31st. We resumed our march at daylight but were compelled to go considerably out of our course on account of the Bluffs which extended much farther into the interior than we had any idea of.[18] We saw many Buffaloe in the high Plains and numerous flocks of Ibex or Big Horn [*and black Tail'd Deer*] in the Bluff ravines, which were for the most part composed of a loose white earth, with occasionally a few [*partial patches of*] stinted cedars along their sides [*We*[19] *came at last to a place where we could overlook the river, and saw a channel torn through red piles of rocks by which the stream is obstructed and broken, till it comes to a very steep descent of such dreadful depth that we were naturally inclined to turn aside our eyes; here it discharges its impetuous waters by a fall of at least 1000 feet,*[20] *the spray extends at least a quarter of a mile, and the noise may be plainly heard at the distance of 30 miles*[21]—]

Jones killed an excellent Buffaloe Cow and by the middle of the afternoon we at length reached the river bank below the Precipices,[22] which in consequence of the prevalent colour we call the Fiery Narrows— The distance today was NNE 12 and N.E. 8 miles—[23]

Sunday 1st November 1812

Partial showers of [*sleet and*] rain fell during the night and notwithstanding the menacing appearance of the Heavens we crofsed[24] the River early and travelled 12 miles to a Stream[25] we call Cottonwood Creek, on account of the great abundance of those trees which adorn its banks— the bed is sandy, about 40 feet wide, with but little water on its surface but from appearances a good deal must ooze unseen through [86] its subterraneous pafsages— In 6 miles[26] from this place we reached a considerable mountain[27] through which the River ran 4 miles, when the Country opening, it made a large bend to the north, to the lower end of which we went in 2 more and encamped[28] in a beautiful bottom[29] of Cottonwoods surrounded with a thick growth of the common Willow— our days journey was 24 Miles[30] N E

The bed of the River is here 150 yards wide with a [*very*] strong current of water about one third of that distance in breadth & from its northerly course we now believe it the Cheyenne,[31] though for some time we entertained strong hopes of its being Rapid Water River[32]

Saw [*a great*] many Buffaloe [*Ibex & Deer*] and a large gang of Elk [*feeding about the base of the mountain*] but did not kill any

Monday 2nd We proceeded down 6 miles when seeing that the River still bent its course to the north of East doubts were no longer entertained of our being on the Cheyenne, in consequence of which I held a general consultation when we were unanimously of opinion that by going lower down we might afsure ourselves of meeting the Indians from whom the River takes its name, in whose village there being a number of Sioux, their worthy relations on the Mifsouri would of course soon be advertised of our approach and lay in ambuscade for us along the banks of the River in the Spring— All were convinced that it was in vain to attempt prosecuting the voyage on foot at this inclement season of the year through such an extensive Prairie Country where the procuring of fuel was extremely precarious so that even admitting it to be Rapid Water River and of course free from all apprehensions of seeing the bad Sioux, all we could gain would be the very agreeable neighbourhood of the villainous and rascally Poncas,[33] therefore as it was the universal voice that we must undoubtedly winter [87] somewhere on this side of the Mifsouri, I deemed it highly imprudent to go any lower, as it would endanger our safety without the least probable benefit to the expedition; more particularly as our last nights encampment is a situation pofsefsing all the necefsary requisites, for here we have wood in abundance both for building and firewood, and the Country around is plentifully stocked with Game

Returning to camp[34] according to agreement, we have determined on pafsing the Winter here and will leave it on the opening of the navigation in one or perhaps two Buffalo-hide Canoes, till which time we entertain strong hopes of living in peace and quiet without being honoured with the intrusive visits of our savage Neighbours

Wednesday 4th Yesterday five persons went out to hunt and this evening one of them arrived with the agreeable intelligence of their having killed twelve Buffaloe[35]

Friday 6th Nine Inches[36] of snow fell yesterday and the weather has since continued so boisterous and severely cold as to freeze the river, which makes a bridge that will greatly diminish the labour of transporting our meat, now collected at the mouth of a small Branch[37] which joins the main stream 1 Mile above—

Saw some Buffaloe [*near camp*] when it was too late to attack them.

Sunday 8th The Buffaloe were in the Bottom Yesterday morning and by ten o'Clock six[38] of them belonged to us— Commenced building a hut— the weather is still disagreeably cold.

Tuesday 10th[39] We were yesterday and today busily employed in transporting our meat to camp and building the Hut all of which busineſs was finished before dusk— Our cabin is 8 feet by 18 [*wide*] with the fire in the middle after the Indian fashion, the sides are 3 feet[40] high and the whole covered with Buffaloe skins, so we have now a tolerable shelter and eighteen Black Cattle[41]

[88] Thursday 12th The weather has become so mild as to break up the river— The two Canadians went in search of game[42] yesterday for leather to make mogasins &c. and returned in the evening with eight skins of Ibex and Black tailed Deer and we this day procured twenty skins more which with a White Bear was the hunt of six persons— The mountains[43] to the South East are at the distance of two miles— the declivities[44] are thickly wooded with Firs and red Cedars shooting promiscuously out of the crevices of the Rocks but in the upper region the extensive tracts of Pitch Pine are occasionally chequered with small patches of quaking aspen— There are many Precipices and cut[45] rocky Bluffs in different parts of the mountain which afford a safe retreat to numbers[46] of Ibex while the timbered summit and ravines are the residence of many [*Bear, &*] Black tailed Deer— This range is not remarkably high but it extends to the East, South and South West as far as the eye can reach—

Thursday 10th December 1812[47] Relying with confidence on the snugneſs of our retreat which from its isolated situation we supposed sufficiently concealed to elude even the prying investigation of Indian spies, we were astonished and confounded at hearing the savage yelp early this morning in the vicinity of our Hut— Seizing our arms we rushed out when twenty three Arapohays made their appearance and after the first surprise was over [*on either side*] they advanced in a friendly manner, telling us they were on a war excursion against the Absarokas[48] who had [*some time ago*] stole a great many of their Horses, taken some of their women prisoners & were then on a River[49] six days march to the Northward where they were going in hopes of obtaining revenge— They also related that [89] in paſsing through the mountain two days ago they heard the report of firearms, and on searching found where two of our people had killed some Deer which ultimately conducted them to our Cabin, being the sixteenth days travel from their village which is on a large stream,[50] from this nearly due South[51] but joins the River[52] we are on, a great distance below

Friday 11th The behaviour of the Indians was far more regular and decent than we had any reason to expect from a War party; they threw up two breastworks of Logs where the whole excepting the Cheif and his Deputy betook themselves to rest tolerably early; these two we permitted to sleep in our hut, and one of us remained awake alternately all night— They all ate voraciously and departed peaceably about 10 A.M. carrying with them a great proportion of our best meat in which we willingly acquiesced— They begged a good deal for ammunition but a peremtory refusal soon convinced them that all demands of that nature were unavailing and they laughingly relinquished their entreaties— No sooner were we relieved from the company of our disagreeable guests than considering the dangerous situation of our residence, with the Absarokas[53] within two days ride on one side, and the villains who robbed Mr Miller and the Hunters on that Fork of the Spanish River called Big Horn[54] on the other at the distance of five and being completely satisfied that their good conduct in the present instance was merely to lull our suspicions in ideal security that they might the better return with a reinforcement and surprise us when least on our guard, we determined to abandon our Chateau of Indolence as soon as we can finish the drefsing of a sufficiency of leather for Mogasins &c. &c. that we may be [*the better*] able to withstand the severity of the weather [90] Our present intention is to extricate ourselves out of the paws of our rascally neighbours by going a very considerable distance down this River, which from a minute review of the course and distance we have come from Henry's Fort and a map given us by our [*late*] guests we now believe the Rapid Water River,[55] and if pofsible make our next Cantonment on the banks of the Mifsouri, but should we not be able to proceed so far the probability is that we shall at least by this movement be enabled to decend in Canoes more durable than those of Buffaloe Skin—

Saturday 12th We this evening finished drefsing our leather and will set out tomorrow morning— The Indians were kind enough to leave us our faithfull Quadruped, not [*probably*] for our accommodation, but because he would be more injurious than usefull at present, no doubt intending at their return to ease us forever of any further trouble on his account—

Sunday 13th Left our Hut two hours after sunrise and went 18 miles[56] East by north— The Country is [*extremely*] barren, only a few Cottonwoods to be seen along the river; but many Buffaloe rove about in the Bottoms— Snow about three Inches[57] deep—

Monday 14th Began our march early and went 22 miles[58] East over the same kind of Country as yesterday, with the snow somewhat deeper than above, [*The only food we can procure for our horse is Cottonwood bark and Willow tops*—] Saw abundance of game [*We are very much fatigued in consequence of the crust not being hard enough to bear us, and our feet are excefsively sore, which makes us begin to think of taking up our quarters in the first eligible situation, and rather than die on the march, fall valiently on the field of Mars—]*

Tuesday 15th We travelled 24 miles[59] E by S today— Fourteen from Camp we crofsed a Creek[60] ifsuing from the mountains on the right, it is nearly 20 yards wide, has a good current of water and is well timbered with bitter Cottonwoods—

The bottoms on the main stream have become extensive and produce Trees sufficiently large for Canoes— The river has a gravelly bottom, rapid current & is 80 yds[61] wide but its bed is much larger

[91] Wednesday 16th Going 17 miles[62] East we pafsed two Creeks[63] on the right near the last of which we saw a large village of Prairie Dogs[64] [*which are nothing more than ground Squirrels—*] and in 8 more S.E. cutting off a very large bend we reached our nights station[65] on the right bank of the River—

The range of mountains[66] which began above our Hut and continued at a short distance parallel with the main stream ever since has at length subsided into low Hills, but about fifty miles to the South, we see another of much greater magnitude[67]

The Snow has been upwards of a foot[68] deep here, but is a good deal reduced by the thaw which began yesterday morning and still continues— [*Very few Buffalo were seen during this days march—*]

Thursday 17th 4 miles S.S.E. from Camp we crofsed[69] the river which here ran towards the point of the high mountains,[70] in nearly a South direction— Went 6 more same course and 15 E S E[71] to the river where we encamped—[72] The margin of the Stream still continues decorated with considerable bodies of Timber, but the Cottonwoods are of a small growth, and interspersed with a good many Box Alders

Friday 18th East North East 2 miles brought us to a large Wooded

Fork[73] entering on the left in a N N E direction from whose junction the main stream ran 10 due South partly through Rocky Hills,[74] then 6 East and 1 south to camp[75] where we killed two Buffaloe, which animals are [*much wilder and*] lefs numerous than usual—

We at one time today left the river in hopes of shortening our route, but found the country so very rough that we were compelled to follow the meanders of the Stream, [*and afterwards*] as often marching on the Ice, as along its banks—

[92] Saturday 19th We followed the meanders of the river today 19 miles, the first few through a level tract and the residue partly on the Ice as yesterday— The course was various but the general one, South— Killed an Ibex and encamped at the mouth of a Creek[76] coming from the West it has a good many Willows and Cottonwood and among them one ash [*the first we have yet seen*]—

Sunday 20th In our march today which was 20 miles[77] S E we saw a great abundance of Buffaloe, Ibex and Antelopes and among the timber several Ash [*and White Oak*] Trees—

Monday 21st A very small part of this days journey of 23 miles S.E. extricated us from among the Narrows we have been in for some time, and the remainder was over a level Country—[78]

These narrows are composed of high rocky Hills with Bluffs and Precipices on each side of the river, on the declivities of which are numerous Cedars interspersed with Pitch Pines affording an asylum to great numbers of ibex and Deer— Since leaving the Hills the snow has [*almost*] entirely disappeared, and the weather has every appearance of a mild autumn— Ash increases fast and the Bottoms are thickly wooded and extensive, with the river running nearly due East below—

Tuesday 22nd Soon after leaving Camp the Country opened

greatly to [*the*] Eastward, and a well wooded stream[79] apparently of considerable magnitude came in from the South West, but whether it is the Arapohays river,[80] we cannot tell—

Abundance of Buffaloe and Antelopes [*were seen*] in this days march of 26 Miles East South East—[81]

[93] Wednesday 23rd Went 11 miles[82] same course, killed two Buffaloe and some Antelopes—[83] The Bottoms are from one to two miles wide and thickly covered with Cottonwoods some distance back from the margin of the river which now flows in several channels[84] over a bed of sand—

Thursday 24th The timber gradually diminished all day, and at the end of 27 miles same course the few trees where we encamped[85] were all we could see— the Bottoms became wider producing grafs 8 Inches high on which we saw multitudes of Buffaloe feeding this afternoon and among them a number of wild Horses—

15 miles above, a Fork[86] of large dimensions joined the main River from the South West, and[87] now runs over a Sandy bed, sometimes half a mile in width—

Friday 25th 21 miles same course brought us to camp[88] in the bare Prairie, but were fortunate in finding enough of driftwood for our [*culinary*] purpose— The Hills[89] on the south have lately approached the river, are [*remarkably rugged and*] Bluffy and pofsefs a few Cedars— Buffaloe [*very*] few in number and mostly Bulls—

Sunday 26th The [*extreme*] coldnefs of the night made us decamp early and after travelling 22 miles same course encamped[90] in a similar situation to that of last night— Pafsed a very few scattering trees today, but not a twig is to be seen to the Eastward— Game of all Kinds except some old scabby Bulls[91] has entirely vanished— The snow has been very deep in this country, is still upwards of six Inches,[92] and towards sunrise every thing appears white though none has fallen since we left our Hut

The Bottoms increase greatly in breadth, indeed the rising ground a few miles off is hardly of sufficient magnitude to merit a distinction—

[94] Sunday 27th The night was cold in the extreme, and getting up with the dawn we took into consideration that having last evening seen at least fifty miles[93] to the Eastward without any indications of Timber, [*and should there be some little driftwood about the banks of the river, the depth of snow is too great to admit of our finding it*] and deprecating [*therefore*] the wretchedneſs of our situation should we be overtaken in these boundleſs Plains by a snow storm, particularly as we have reason to expect it daily, and the Country before us such an inhospitable waste as even to be deserted by every kind of quadruped, we at once concluded, five votes to two, that our best plan was to return up the river to where we shall find Buffaloe for our support and timber for Canoes, there to await the opening of the navigation— The bed of the river is here nearly a mile[94] wide, composed of quicksand cut into innumerable channels, with very low banks & destitute of even a single twig— This being so different from the character we ever heard of the Rapid River;[95] our having southed so much of late, and its appearance coinciding exactly with that of the Great River Platte, we have strong inducements to believe that we are on the main Branch of the last mentioned stream— We accordingly retraced our steps and took up our nights lodgings[96] four miles above our camp of the 25th Instant

Monday 28th Paſsed our encampment of the 24th Instant [*about*] six miles and stopped[97] early having killed three Buffaloe— The wind blew strong from the West all day and is very cold—

[95] Tuesday 29th Several herds of Buffaloe were scattered [*all*]

over the Prairie this morning— Crofsed the main River[98] [*a little*] above the mouth of the wooded Fork,[99] the Ice was entirely gone but [*fortunately*] the water was not in any of the channels more than knee deep— The Fork is about 50 yards wide, up which we proceeded three miles[100] in hopes of finding an elegible situation, as we conceived this an excellent spot for game, but on a close examination found the Trees too insignificant for Canoes

Wednesday 30th Leaving Camp after breakfast we went up the main stream[101] 12 miles[102] to opposite the first large body of Woods where we killed four Buffaloe, and Leclairc who [*had*] crofsed the river below in quest of Canoe Trees, came to us with the agreeable tidings of his having found three— We brought in the meat, and encamped[103] among some scattering timber near the bank

Thursday 31st At an Early hour we Crofsed[104] the river, which was running thick with Ice took up our residence[105] close to the bank and by the middle of the day we had a shelter made and our meat scaffolded— Began building our Hut, one side of which we raised before dusk

Notes to Chapter VIII

1 Trav. mem. erroneously states this date as "Tuesday 29th."

2 Sweetwater.

3 This, "the Gap, or Devil's Gate, as it is sometimes called," of *Palmer*, p. 31, the "Devil's Gate" of virtually all other diarists, is well described in *Burton*, p. 186; *Stansbury* [*A*], pp. 65, 66; *Fremont*, p. 57.

4 For parallel descriptions, see *Stansbury* [*A*], pp. 64, 65; *Fremont*, pp. 56, 57.

5 Incorrectly "17 miles" in trav. mem.

6 Camped on right bank of Sweetwater at a spot approximately four miles east of Independence Rock.

Stuart's failure to comment concerning Independence Rock is readily understandable. This rock, when seen from the west, as Stuart first saw it, was of relative unimportance in the landscape, although, when viewed from however far away in the east, it stood assertively as an eye-arresting beacon. Moreover, to Stuart and his companions, presumably the earliest whites to cast eyes on it, the rock could offer none of the historical interest which in later years it acquired through intimate association with passing emigrants.

7 Ferris Mountains and Seminoe Mountains.

8 "Considerable" in trav. mem.

9 Crossed to left bank of the Sweetwater at approximately the place where that river, immediately after receiving the waters of present-day Horse Creek, abruptly swerved toward the southeast. Thereupon Stuart, quitting the Sweetwater, traversed the wedge of land which lay between it and present-day North Platte River and immediately north of their confluence.

10 For a detailed description of this route, see *Fremont*, pp. 55, 56, 72-77.

11 North Platte River. Stuart here was on the left rim of what in later years was known as Upper Canyon of the North Platte (see *Fremont*, pp. 55, 56, 72-77). Much of the canyon, except for its two rims, lies today under the waters impounded by the recently built Pathfinder Dam. *Geol. Wyoming.*

12 Narrow here because between canyon walls.

13 Stuart erred in assuming that the river beside him was the one crossed earlier in the day, *i.e.*, the Sweetwater.

14 Incorrectly "500 feet" in trav. mem.

15 "dashing over them with the most violent impetuosity" in trav. mem. For parallel description, see *Fremont*, pp. 55, 56, 72-77.

16 Camped on left rim of Upper Canyon of North Platte at a spot approximately two miles west of the meridian of present-day Canyon Creek's debouchment into present-day Pathfinder Reservoir. *Holt; Geol. Wyoming.*

17 Incorrectly "34 miles" in trav. mem.

18 See *Fremont*, pp. 55, 56 for description of terrain.

19 For a supplemental description, see *Fremont*, pp. 72-77.

20 Error in Stuart's figure. No vertical fall of any great height was in this canyon; but there was a series of awesome cataracts, the aggregate pitch of which, according to *Fremont*, p. 73, was approximately 300 feet.

21 Error in Stuart's figure. "3" would have been more nearly proper (see *Fremont*, p. 72). If a zero be deleted from Stuart's "1000" (note 20) and "30," his figures would not be amiss.

22 The spot at which Stuart reached the river and made his camp was on North Platte's left bank; and, if immediately beyond the canyon's lower portal, was approximately one-half mile east of site of the Pathfinder Dam. *Geol. Wyoming.*

23 The day's travel aggregated 20 miles in journ., and incorrectly 29 miles in trav. mem.

24 Crossed to right bank of North Platte; and, as Stuart's later text shows, travelled along this bank till December 17, although between November 4 and December 13 (on which last-mentioned date the first winter's quarters were abandoned) the North Platte was crossed at least once in quest of bison.

25 Present-day Bates Creek, which was described by Fremont as "a pretty little creek, an affluent of the right bank. It is well timbered with cottonwood. . . ." This was the "Carson's Creek" of Preuss, the "Carson Creek" of Fremont and of Stansbury (thus named in honor of "Kit" Carson), the "Poison Creek" of De Lacy. *Fremont*, p. 55 and accompanying map; *Preuss*, Section IV; *Stansbury [B]; De Lacy; Geol. Wyoming.*

26 Incorrectly "9 miles" in trav. mem.

27 Present-day Red Buttes, thus styled in 1834 by Townsend, Osborne Russell, Nathaniel J. Wyeth and Jason Lee, each of whom used the name as though it already were well established (*Townsend*, p. 66; *Russell*, p. 4; *Wyeth, Nathaniel J.*, p. 224; *Journ. Jason Lee* in *Ore. Hist. Soc. Quar.*, XVII, p. 131). For description of Red Buttes, see citations immediately above and also *Parker*, p. 70; *Fremont*, pp. 54, 55; *Stansbury [A]*, pp. 62, 63; *Johnson & Winter*, p. 19. For parallel of Stuart's subsequent description of his route from this spot to mouth of Horse Creek, see *Triggs*, pp. 41-43.

28 Camped, according to entry of November 6, on right bank of North Platte at a spot one mile below where present-day Poison Spider Creek ("Red Springs Creek" of *Stansbury [B]*) emptied through North Platte's left bank. The spot is today readily identifiable because (a) Poison Spider Creek—from the mouth of which Stuart measured his mile—is, at its mouth and for some distance inland, stoutly flanked on each side by a geologic dike and thus cannot have shifted its position since Stuart's time; and (b) there now is, on the North Platte's right bank one mile below Poison Spider Creek's mouth, a grove which patently antedates Stuart's visit inasmuch as, in 1929, a bit of exploratory digging amid the trees disclosed fragments of very old stumps and roots that clearly were in original situ and thereby furnished evidence that the local

topography had not materially altered since Stuart's day. As to when and why Poison Spider Creek obtained its name we have found no explanation.

29 "beautiful low point" in trav. mem.

30 Incorrectly "27 miles" in trav. mem.

31 Present-day Cheyenne River, for which see note 97 on p. 148.

32 This stream ("rapid River" wherever mentioned in trav. mem.) is present-day Niobrara River, which, lying between the Cheyenne and Platte Rivers and approximately paralleling them, was, in now bygone years, styled interchangeably "Riviere qui Court," "L'Eau qui Court," "Quicourre," "Quicurre," "Spreading Water" and "Running Water."

Might not the "strong hopes" of Stuart's party have been based on knowledge previously acquired by five of its men when, boating up the Missouri with Hunt, they had passed the mouths of both the Cheyenne and the Niobrara and had thus learned that the mouth of the Niobrara was some 300 miles nearer St. Louis than was the mouth of the Cheyenne?

33 "Puncas" in trav. mem.

34 See note 28 for location of camp. At the end of this day's entry as printed in *Nouvelles Annales*, XII, p. 94, there is added a statement, the author of which is undisclosed. If not Stuart, he may possibly have been Ramsay Crooks, who, as appears on p. xc *ante*, was at Paris in the year of this French version's publication. The statement, as translated, is: "Since leaving Astoria, we have come 2174 miles. A portion of this long distance was uselessly travelled because, after going south to Millers River, we returned to the north, then returned to the south, and ended by finding ourselves but a short way east of Millers River, from which the mountains separated us."

35 "32 Buffalo" in trav. mem. *Astoria*, II, pp. 170, 171, adds (1) an account of Crooks's alleged adventure with a grizzly bear and (2) a statement that Miller killed a bear of this breed.

36 "Two feet" in trav. mem.

37 Poison Spider Creek.

38 "by 10 OClock we had killed 15 of them" in trav. mem.

39 This day's entry is possibly the one which Stuart intended to supplement by the first paragraph in journ.'s postscript, p. [127]—*i.e.*, pp. 254, 255. See, however, note 1 on p. 223.

40 "six feet" in trav. mem.

41 Bison, because "eighteen" ("47" in trav. mem.) tallies with the "twelve Buffaloe" killed November 4 and the additional six "Buffaloe" which "belonged to us" on November 8.

42 "Deer" in trav. mem.

43 Present-day Casper Range; so named, though with perverted spelling, in honor of Lieutenant Caspar Collins, who, on July 26, 1865, was killed in a battle with indians near the Platte Bridge Station (*Wyoming Landmark*, p. 23). For description of the range, see *Fremont*, p. 52.

44 Erroneously "declivity" in trav. mem.

45 Western colloquialism meaning extremely steep through erosion.

46 "innumerable flocks" in trav. mem.

47 "Thursday Dec. 12" in trav. mem.; "12th Dec^{r}." in journ.'s postscript on p. 256. In the year 1812, December 10 fell actually on a Thursday.

This entry has possible supplement in a paragraph of the journ.'s postscript on p. [127]—*i.e.*, pp. 254, 255.

48 "Crows" in trav. mem.

49 Not improbably present-day Powder River, if we assume that these indians, being on the warpath, would disclose their actual plans. Stuart's recital is varied by *Astoria*, II, pp. 172-175, in so far as to (1) increase the duration of the indians' visit, (2) state that some of the visiting indians were recognized by Miller as men who previously had robbed him, and (3) add, not only ostensibly quoted conversation, but also an account of Stuart's alleged leadership in dealing with these indians.

50 Present-day South Platte River.

51 Erroneously "east" in trav. mem.

52 North Platte.

53 "Crows" in trav. mem.

54 See note 181 on p. 105 for discussion as to identity of Big Horn.

55 Niobrara River, for which see note 32.

56 Incorrectly "22 miles" in trav. mem. Camped on right bank of North Platte at a spot approximately five miles east of site of present-day city of Casper, Wyo. *Geol. Wyoming.*

57 "about 15 inches" in trav. mem.

58 Incorrectly "27 miles" in trav. mem. Camped on right bank of North Platte at approximately mouth of present-day Muddy Creek (the "Muddy Creek" of Horn, the "Turbid Creek" of Jefferson, the "Crooked Muddy Creek" of Osborne Cross, and the "Crooked, muddy creek" of Clayton). *Geol. Wyoming; Horn*, p. 20; *Jefferson*, Part II; *Exec. Doc.*, pp. 162, 163; *Clayton* [*A*], p. 13. See also *Sawyer*, p. 38.

59 Incorrectly "26 miles" in trav. mem. Camped on right bank of North Platte at a spot approximately opposite site of present-day town of Clayton. *Geol. Wyoming.*

60 Present-day Deer Creek, for description of which under that same name see *Clayton* [*A*], p. 13; *Fremont*, p. 51; *Sage*, p. 114; *Stansbury* [*A*], p. 274; *Wood*, p. 26; *Geol. Wyoming.*

61 "100 yards" in trav. mem.

62 Incorrectly "19 Miles" in trav. mem.

63 The more westerly, and thus the first to be reached, of these two confluents emptying through North Platte's right bank was present-day Boxelder Creek, so named for box-elder, the common western term for the ash-leaved

maple, *Negundo aceroides* (*L. & C. Hist.*, p. 267). This stream was the "Mikeshead creek" of Joel Palmer, the "Mikes Head Creek" of Riley Root, the "Boxwood creek" of Clyman, the "R. Boisse" of Stansbury, the "Fourche Boise" of Delano, the "Fourche Boisee" of Fremont and of Preuss, the "Fourch Bois" of Keller, the "Boisee Creek" of Jefferson, the "Fourche de Bois River" of Shepherd.

The more easterly, and thus the second to be reached, of the two confluents was present-day La Prele Creek, the "R. a la Prele" of Preuss, of Horn and of Clayton, the "A La Prele River" of Isham, the "A la Parele Creek" of Orson Pratt. Its name, unless possibly perpetuating that of some French voyageur, was due to the presence of prêle, the common scouring rush, *Euequisetum hyemale*. See *Geol. Wyoming; Palmer*, p. 137; *Root*, p. 20; *Clyman*, p. 87; *Stansbury* [*B*]; *Delano*, p. 83; *Fremont*, p. 51; *Preuss*, Section III; *Keller*, p. 16; *Jefferson*, Part II; *Shepherd*, p. 14; *Horn*, p. 19; *Clayton* [*A*], p. 13; *Isham*, p. 11; *Journ. Orson Pratt* in *Mil. Star*, XII, p. 115; *Moffette*, p. 17; *Stansbury* [*A*], p. 27.

64 Because of the locality and the reference to "large village," these creatures may well have been actual prairie dogs, *Cynomys ludovicianus ludovicianus* (*Ord*), which in 1839 Doctor Wislizenus saw in this vicinity (*Wislizenus* [*A*], p. 42; [*B*], p. 65). However, if trav. mem.'s comment, "Prairie Dogs, which are nothing more than ground Squirrels," be other than a figure of speech, the animals very likely were Kennicott ground squirrels, *Citellus armatus* (*Kennicott*) popularly known as picket pins.

65 Camped on right bank of North Platte approximately at site of present-day town of Arnold. *Geol. Wyoming*.

66 Casper Range. See note 43 for source of its name.

67 Present-day Laramie Peak in Laramie Range: each named (as were also Laramie River, Laramie Plains, Fort Laramie and the city and county of Laramie) for a French-Canadian trapper who has been recorded variously as Jacques Laramie, Larama, La Ramée, La Ramie and de la Ramé. Indians, in approximately 1821, killed him on or near the Laramie River. *Journ. Jason Lee* in *Ore. Hist. Soc. Quar.*, XVII, p. 129; *Chittenden*, p. 469; *Hebard*, I, p. 102; II, p. 233.

68 "18 inches" in trav. mem.

69 Crossed to North Platte's left bank (*i.e.*, to approximately site of present-day town of Douglas), thus avoiding the "bad-land" formation which began here on the right bank and extended for some miles downstream. Thereafter and until December 29 (except when on the river's ice during portions of December 18 and 19 and possibly except for camp of December 20) Stuart travelled exclusively on the left bank.

70 Laramie Range, which, because of its overspreading by sombre-hued trees, the early emigrants styled Black Hills (see *Horn*, p. 60; *Journ. James W. Nesmith* in *Ore. Hist. Soc. Quar.*, VII, p. 341; *Journ. Henry Allyn* in *Ore. Pioneer, 49th annual reunion, 1921*, p. 401; *Diary Loren B. Hastings* in *Ore. Pioneer, 51st*

annual reunion, 1923, p. 16)—not to be confused with the present-day Black Hills in South Dakota.

71 A short-cut across the base of the triangle formed by a bend in the river. *Geol. Wyoming.*

72 Camped on left bank of North Platte two miles above mouth of present-day Muddy Creek, sometimes termed Yellow Creek, and not to be confused with the Muddy Creek mentioned in note 58. *Geol. Wyoming.*

73 Muddy Creek.

74 This river-stretch, cutting through hills and today termed Lower Canyon of the North Platte, was accorded a long description by Joel Palmer, who styled it "Dalles of Platte." Riley Root termed it "Black Hills Gap." *Palmer*, p. 29; *Root*, p. 19. See also *Cooke*, pp. 338, 339; *Moffette*, p. 34; *Railroad Survey*, Vol. I, Chap. II, p. 68.

75 Camped on left bank of North Platte at a spot approximately one mile south-southeast of site of present-day town of Cassa and directly opposite mouth of present-day Bear Creek. *Geol. Wyoming; Quad. Hartville.*

76 Present-day Cottonwood Creek, which emptied through North Platte's right bank at site of present-day town of Wendover (*Quad. Hartville; Geol. Wyoming*). Camp was seemingly on right bank, for Stuart states "at the mouth" instead of "opposite the mouth."

77 Incorrectly "22 miles" in trav. mem. Camped on bank (probably left) of North Platte at a spot shown by next day's entry to have been a short distance upstream from where, approximately one mile north of present-day town of Guernsey, the river emerged from the lower end of its final canyon. *Quad. Hartville; Geol. Wyoming; Fremont*, p. 47.

78 Camp was, according to next day's entry, on North Platte's left bank and a short distance above where Laramie River emptied through North Platte's right bank.

79 Laramie River.

80 South Platte.

81 Camped on left bank of North Platte approximately at mouth of present-day Rawhide Creek. *Geol. Wyoming; Quad. Patrick; Jefferson*, Part II; *Horn*, p. 16.

82 Incorrectly "18 miles" in trav. mem. Camped on left bank of North Platte at a spot approximately two miles below site of present-day town of Torrington, Wyo. *Geol. Wyoming; Quad. Patrick.*

83 "3 antelope" in trav. mem.

84 Referring probably to the chain of sand-bars which today (as doubtless also in Stuart's time), beginning in longitude 104° 30′, extend to approximately two and one-half miles west of town of Torrington. *Quad. Patrick.*

85 Camped on left bank of North Platte at a spot which was, according to Stuart's reckoning in the journ.'s context, 15 miles below the mouth of present-day Horse Creek and thus, pursuant to the adjustment made in note 86, was

approximately three miles southeast from site of present-day town of Mitchell, Neb. *Geol. Nebraska; Quad. Scotts Bluff.*

86 Horse Creek. It was the "Wild Horse Creek" of Nathaniel J. Wyeth in 1832, the "Horse Creek" of Fremont and of Medorem Crawford in 1842 and seemingly of all subsequent diarists except only Dundass, who, by error patent in his context, styled it "Horse Shoe Creek." *Wyeth, Nathaniel J.*, p. 156; *Fremont*, p. 34; *Crawford*, p. 10; *Dundass*, p. 26; *Clyman*, p. 83; *Bryant*, p. 105; *Johnston*, p. 118; *Shepherd*, p. 13.

From the mouth of Horse Creek to the mouth of Rush Creek the mileage, as stated by Stuart in the journ.'s subsequent entries, totals 114, whereas, according to U. S. Geological Survey maps, it should be 87, and the journ. fails to pin itself to any intermediate landmark except for one implied reference to Scotts Bluff. Wherefore the journ.'s stated mileages for this section have been prorated by the editor on the basis of the above-mentioned ratio, but with due regard to local topography as offering or denying proper camp-sites. The fact of this prorating should be borne in mind when reading footnotes relating to the camps made December 24-28 and March 20-22.

87 Instead of "and," should not Stuart have written "which"—thus more clearly referring to the North Platte?

88 Camped on left bank of North Platte at a spot which, according to Stuart's reckoning, was 36 miles below Horse Creek's mouth. Not only a prorating of this figure in accord with note 86 but also Stuart's reference to Scotts Bluff suggest that the camp was approximately at the site of present-day town of Minatare, Neb. *Geol. Nebraska; Quad. Scotts Bluff.*

89 This portion of the "Hills" was present-day Scotts Bluff, situated near present-day town of Gering, Neb., and named by early emigrants in memory of Hiram Scott, a fur trader who, having been deserted by his companions, died of starvation either here or else at so short a distance upstream on the North Platte as to allow the waters to float the body hither (*Journ. Jason Lee* in *Ore. Hist. Soc. Quar.*, XVII, pp. 128, 129; *Bryant*, p. 104; *Johnson & Winter*, p. 18). For description of the bluff, see *Burton*, pp. 95-98; *Delano*, pp. 72, 73; *Quad. Scotts Bluff.* Though most diarists used the title "Scott's Bluff," Horn wrote: "Capital Hills . . . By some called 'Scott's Bluffs' "; while Moffette mentioned: "the Capitol," and Burton stated: "The politer guide-books call them 'Capitol Hills.' " *Horn*, p. 15; *Moffette*, p. 29; *Burton*, p. 97.

90 Camped on left bank of North Platte at a spot which, according to Stuart's reckoning, was 58 miles below the mouth of Horse Creek and thus is, by prorating, indicated to have been approximately five miles east by north from Chimney Rock and four miles west of meridian of present-day town of Camp Clarke, Neb. *Quad. Camp Clarke.*

91 Unquestionably bison, because "wild cattle" did not venture so far north from their Texan ranges, and there were not then any domestic cattle in the North Platte's valley.

92 "15 inches" in trav. mem.

93 This extensive view was obtained doubtless from the top of a hill which, northeast of camp, rose 562 feet above the plain. *Quad. Camp Clarke.*

94 "here 1½ mile" in trav. mem.

95 Present-day Niobrara. See note 32 for its description and various names.

96 The site of this camp, which was on left bank of North Platte, is determinable by Stuart's phrase "four miles above our camp of the 25th Instant." If this phrase relates to the river's course, the site was four miles upstream from the location of the December 25 camp, and thus four miles northwest from site of present-day town of Minatare, Neb. (see note 88), and the day's mileage was 26. But, if the phrase relates to Stuart's own course of travel, the site was four miles downstream from the location of the December 25 camp, thus was four miles southeast from site of Minatare, and the day's mileage was 18. At whichever spot the camp was pitched, Stuart camped there again on March 20 according to his narratives.

97 Camped on left bank of North Platte at a spot approximately two miles west of site of present-day town of Mitchell, Neb. See note 85. This day's travel was either 23 or 31 miles, accordingly as the site of the December 27 camp is determined as in note 96.

98 Crossed to right bank of North Platte.

99 Horse Creek.

100 Camped seemingly on Horse Creek three miles above its confluence with the North Platte. Both journ. and trav. mem. omit any reference to the nine miles of travel necessary between site of camp of December 28 and the mouth of Horse Creek.

101 North Platte.

102 Query: were the 12 miles measured from a camp situated three miles up Horse Creek or were they measured from the mouth of that creek?

103 This camp on right bank of North Platte, being approximately 12 miles (see note 102) above the mouth of Horse Creek, was at or near the mouth of present-day Cherry Creek, which latter creek emptied through the North Platte's right bank at a spot a short distance below where on the North Platte's left bank was the site of present-day town of Torrington, Wyo. *Geol. Wyoming; Quad. Patrick.*

104 To left bank of North Platte.

105 This camp, termed by historians "the second winter quarters," was approximately on the site of the earlier camp of December 23; see note 82. Accordingly, it was within the present-day state of Wyoming, and not, as heretofore commonly supposed, within the present-day state of Nebraska.

C H A P T E R I X

JAN. 1 · APRIL 11, 1813

On Foot from Second Winter Quarters to Site of Present-Day Edholm, Nebraska

Abortive Attempt to Canoe · Resume Travel on Foot · Follow Left Bank of North Platte and Later of Platte · Cross to Platte's Right Bank · Trudge Along It · Find Deserted Squaws · Various Indian Tribes.

Friday 1st January 1813— Was solely devoted to the gratification of our appetites, all work was suspended for the day, and we destroyed an immoderate quantity of Buffaloe Tongues [, *Puddings*,] and the choicest of the meat, making it a rule to eat the best first so that we would always have the best[1] Our stock of Virginia weed is totally exhausted, but in commemoration of the new year we cut up as a substitute and smoked Mr Millers[2] Tobacco Pouch

[96] Saturday 9th our Hut though incomplete we entered on the evening of the 2nd—[3] On the 6th finished our spacious dwelling and killed seven Buffaloe;[4] and we this day felled our Canoe Trees and found them all hollow but have chosen the two best and began working them—

Sunday 7th March 1813

The river having been open for several days and the weather promising a continuation of the thaw we dragged our Canoes to the bank and prepared them for our reception tomorrow morn-

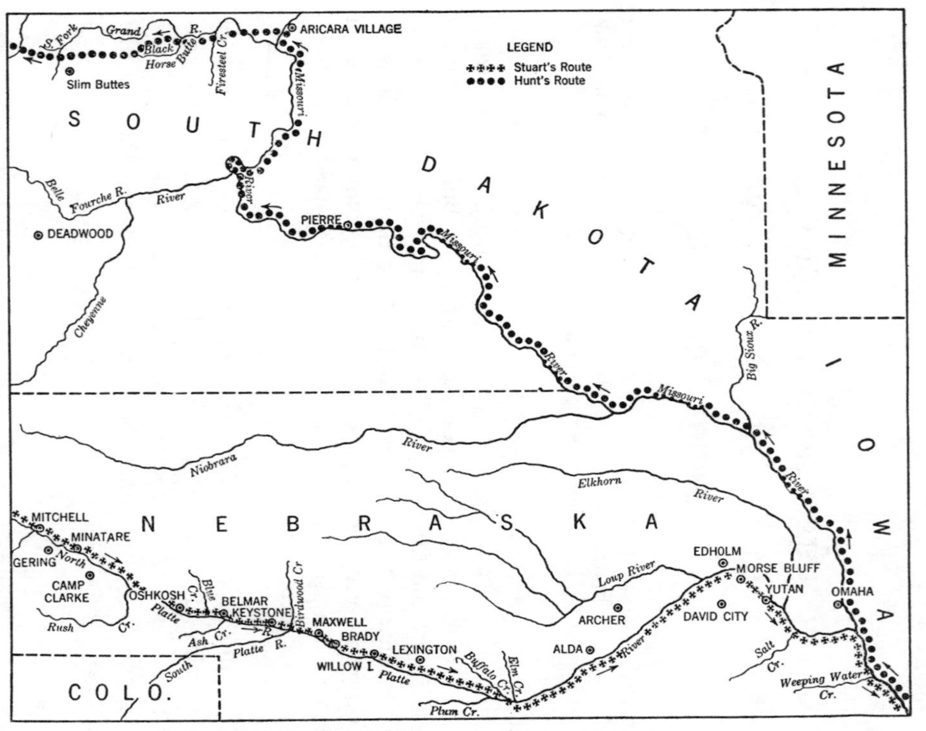

Routes of Stuart in Nebraska and of Hunt in South Dakota

ing— One wild goose made her appearance this afternoon and was killed [*for dinner*]—

Monday 8th[5] Breakfasting at an early hour we embarked but on decending a few hundred yards found the water so low that Mr McClellan and myself went by land hoping thereby that the Canadians would be able to proceed— The other Canoe being small went on tolerably; but it was with very considerable labour in wading and dragging that ours got down eight miles by the middle of the afternoon when finding an Indian Pen sufficient to screen us from the severity of the weather we stopped[6] in it, determined to wait a rise of [*the*] water

Monday 15th I sent back to our Hut for the Horse yesterday and this morning the river having risen four inches[7] we again embarked a small part of our baggage and four of us in the Canoes, while the residue was carried by [97] our quadruped—[8] To the Fork[9] we went on [*pretty*] well, but immediately below the river became much wider and so shallow that it was with great exertion we reached another Pen on the left bank, seven miles below our last station, where we found our people who had gone by land— Here we took up our lodgings[10] pretty much tired of this new mode of inland navigation, and resolved on taking our landtacks on board again, unlefs the river rises soon to such a height as will afsure us to a certainty of getting on by the common mode of paddling—

Saturday 20th It snowed with but little intermifsion during the 16 & 17th Instant, and excepting a little thaw towards noon on the 18 & 19th the weather has of late been worse than any we experienced throughout the Winter; in consequence of which and being very doubtfull whether we can in any reasonable time proceed by water, it was agreed that we should try it once more on foot; so we accordingly continued down the left bank to our encampment of the 27th December where we stopped for the night[11]

Sunday 21st We travelled till late in the afternoon and stopped about a mile above our camp of 26 December—[12] Killed a [*very fat*] goose which as well as Buffaloe have been abundant all day

[98] Monday 22nd We encamped[13] this evening twenty three miles lower than we have yet been on this River

Nothing but a boundleſs Prairie plentifully stocked with animals appears before us, and the river running East South East so shallow as[14] makes us happy at having abandoned our Canoes[14] for its bed is for the most part upwards of a mile wide and the sandbars so numerous and flat that it would require more water than we have any right to expect to have made it fit for our purposes—

Tuesday 23rd About midnight the wind which has for some time been in the East veered to [*the*] North, blew with violence and was withal so cold that our bedclothes appeared as if converted into seives for we were in the bare Prairie and our fuel what little driftwood[15] we could collect— We set out soon after daylight and stopped at the end of 23 miles[16] same course— The Hills on the opposite side of the river approached [*much*] nearer than usual this afternoon and poſseſs some timber but whether Pine or Cedar or both we cannot tell— On our side there is not a twig to be Seen, and the rising grounds seldom come within leſs than a mile[17] of the river—

[99] Wednesday 24th This days march was 23 miles[18] long, over a similar tract to that paſsed for a number of days with the agreeable variation of finding half a dozen withered Cottonwoods[19] to encamp at—[20] The Hills[21] on the South are much higher than on ours[22] and keep close to [*the*] river which making the low Prairie

in general very narrow The Buffaloe have but an indifferent range and apparently prefer the North side, where the plain is for the most part a mile wide and poſseſses excellent graſs in abundance for their support—

Thirteen miles back a Creek[23] with a very sandy bed and a good many trees on its banks, joined the main stream from the South, but was not of any depth of water— The weather continued extremely cold with the wind from the East—

Thursday 25th We remained in [*the*] same camp all day as Mr Millers feet were so much blistered as to render him totally unfit to travel, besides the wind from the Eastward was too strong and piercing cold to encourage our preſsing forward, particularly as every one was [*very*] willing to rest— Some Bulls[24] coming near our station we killed three and with their hides made a comfortable shelter—

[100] Friday 26th Our journey today was 24 miles[25] same course and Kind of Country— 13 miles from last nights Camp we croſsed a Creek[26] thirty yards wide coming from about N.N.W. [*and*] iſsuing from among sand Hills there were a few trees on its banks, and from the appearance of the water it must run through an excellent soil [*somewhat*] farther up—

3 Miles lower, another Branch[27] joined the main stream from the south, it is thickly wooded a short distance from its mouth, but with what kinds we could not well distinguish— For a considerable way above but more particularly below its junction the River Bluffs are very near and sometimes constitute its banks— they are composed principally of [*a blue lime*] stone and poſseſs many Cedars on which account we call the last mentioned Branch, Cedar Creek— saw sixty Wild Horses[28] [*, and for the last 3 days march, the Country is/I may say,/literally covered with Buffalo—*]

Saturday 27th Some distance above and below last nights station is an extensive swamp, the residence of immense numbers of Geese & Brants; a few Swans and an endlefs variety of Ducks; and during [*the latter part of*] this days march we found many[29] similar places all well stocked with Wild Fowl—

The Country on our side is little else than sand, but where the Bottoms have the least claim to goodnefs of soil they produce a considerable growth of straw, being the first we have yet seen [*since leaving the Columbia bottoms*]— Pafsed two Creeks[30] ifsuing from our sand Hills,[31] and encamped[32] opposite an Island, which on account of its timber we call Cedar Island [*on which I killed 3 swans, and a Goose, with one shot, the distance acrofs the river was 170 yards*—] having come 23 Miles[33] East by South— In walking among the straw in the neighbourhood of our camp we raised five Pheasants or as they are called in this Country Prairie Hens[34] [*this induces us to believe the Mifsouri bottoms not far distant, as these creatures have never been known to progress any great distance into the interior*—]

[101] Sunday 28th We went 23 miles[35] due East today, the greater part through low wet grounds and the residue over barren sands—

The Hills on the south have very much diminished in size and sand now appears to be the principal part of their composition— on our side they are with the exception of a few spots wholly of that material, but the Bottoms are again of a superior quality and produce grafs in abundance for the multitudes of Buffaloe we see feeding on them

The Country is still without Timber, and as far as we can see is almost destitute of even a Hill— The River is generally from three quarters to a mile wide but is for the most part too shallow to float even an empty Canoe

Monday 29th Our course was 12 miles East by North, then

paſsing over a range of sand Hills whose base was washed by the River we in 3 more[36] East croſsed a stream[37] one hundred yards wide running over a bed of quicksand but very far from being deep—[38] Here the Hills on both sides especially those on the south receded to a greater distance than they have yet done [*since we left the head waters of the river*] and by the time we reached Camp[39] at the end of 10 miles more same course, they were at least seventeen miles[40] apart— On collecting fuel from among the driftwood we found a number of pieces cut by an axe close to the ground, but whether they were chopped[41] in this manner on account of their being too wet or too hard frozen to be extracted by the application of the hand alone, we cannot tell, so are at a loſs to say at what season or who the people were who left those vestiges On the other side there is every appearance of a large [102] Stream[42] having broken through the Hills, but [*we*] have not yet seen the entrance; however it poſseſses a few trees and Buffaloe without number— Before us the Country somewhat resembles the Ocean with a Promontory[43] projecting from the north, for on the south the view is bounded by the horizon alone

There is yet no timber, but a small growth of Willows all along the main shore, and on almost every Island gives us great hopes of finding at no very distant day trees of such size and number as will put an end to the dreary sameneſs of the Prairie wastes— The weather [*at length*] has not only become [*very*] mild, but is towards noon if any thing too hot to be agreeable [*particularly*] to a person[44] with a [*heavy*] budget on his back—

Tuesday 30th 8 miles East brought us to an Indian encampment[45] of considerable magnitude, and in the course of the day we paſsed two others[46] which from all appearance were occupied last Fall by people who seem to have valued the animals they killed, for we found numerous marks of their having stretched skins, all the Buffaloe skulls had the brains taken out, the dung lying in heaps contrary to the custom of Wolves convinced us that even the paunches had been preserved and at the last Camp we found a number of the Cobs of Indian Corn—[47] from all of which we suppose those signs were made by the Panees or Ottos more particularly as in the afternoon we reached [103] an Island[48] with large timber[49] on its banks, which answering [*to*] the description of one[50] we have heard of as being some distance above the Loup Fork[51] of the Platte, we are willing to believe ourselves there— One mile above the Island the large stream[52] from the south joined the main River,[53] but as we could not get opposite its entrance on account of swamps,[54] I have only the account of our people, who when hunting saw it from the Hills and say that it is at least as large as the one we decended

The Hills[55] on the south come close to the River immediately below its mouth, and from thence downwards as far as the eye can reach we see large bodies of Timber all along their base, which seem to keep close in the vicinity of the other channel of the River while on our side they are about one mile[56] distant— We travelled 20 miles[57] East by south when being opposite the first woods on our Island[58] we encamped,[59] having come 28 miles[60] today through Bottoms of rich Land producing straw six feet high, and four miles above our present station watered by a Creek[61] twenty yards wide, [*about*] knee deep, its banks [*well*] lined with Willow and poſseſsing a few[62] Beaver— Prickly Pears,[63] Antelopes and Wild Horses[64] have entirely disappeared within the last three days, but our dearly beloved friends the Buffaloe still remain to comfort our solitary wanderings, and five Fallow Deer ran acroſs our path [*some distance above*] in the course of the day

[104] Thursday 1st April 1813— Having killed a Buffaloe[65] and both ourselves and Horse [*being*] a good deal inclined to rest, we did not leave our camp yesterday

At an early hour we set out this morning and travelled 19 miles[66] East 6 East by south and 3 south East to a low point where we encamped[67] without any other fuel than small dry Willows and Buffaloe dung neither of which were very abundant— Our route was through the low [*bare*] Prairie all day but following the Indian trace we traversed only one swamp though from the quantity of wild Fowl there must have been many in the neighbourhood— The Island[68] has as yet abounded with Timber, but not a single tree decorates the main shore— The southern Hills have become much higher and [*very*] steep, with many wooded ravines, but on our side they still retain their former insignificance— We had considerable of both thunder and lightning before sunset which made us put up our little Tent, but only a small shower fell during the whole of the night— [*In the evening we*] saw a number of Fallow Deer[69]

Friday 2nd A short distance below camp we paſsed the end of the Island,[70] so [*that*] if this is the Grand Isle[71] of the river Platte instead of its being ninety miles long and thirty broad,[72] it does not exceed thirty two in length and ten in width—[73] in other respects it however agrees with our information for the banks are well lined with Timber as is also the southern main shore, but ours is still woefully deficient in that article

We followed the trace 15 miles E.S.E. and 7[74] S.E. by East, when the atmosphere indicating bad weather we stopped[75] for the night in a [*large*] thicket of Willows, but before we could erect our shelter it began to rain heavily and continued so till midnight— The Hills on this side became gradually lower till within the last six miles when they disappeared entirely and a range of greater elevation[76] about twelve miles off have aſsumed their place

Saturday 3rd Our days march[77] was 25 miles S E by East & 1 East south East[78] along the Indian path which suddenly vanished a short distance back, so we are as formerly obliged to take the River [105] for our guide— There was no Timber of [*any*] consequence on either side yesterday or today, what little we see are small Cottonwoods and are almost wholly on the numerous Islands with which the river abounds; its bed is upwards of a mile[79] wide and of course very shallow

Early this forenoon we discovered about ten miles to our left a few scattering trees which gradually increased in number till opposite our encampment where they were augmented to a considerable stripe of woods about six miles off with the range of Hills[80] we first saw yesterday running parallel in the vicinity— That some watercourse[81] is near us on the north we have not the least doubt but knowing of no other than the Loup Fork[82] and thinking ourselves not so far advanced we are at a loſs what to make of it— We neverthelefs hope for the best and shall not be sorry to find it what we dare hardly expect— Saw four animals on the other side of the river which we believe were Buffaloe but on ours we have not seen any for the last two days & very little old vestiges—

Sunday 4th After travelling 8 miles E.S.E. we croſsed[83] the river where it was divided into ten channels with a bed of such quicksand that it was difficult for our Horse to get over though the water was in no place more than two feet deep— Soon after reaching the southern bank we found the Indian path, which following for 3 miles[84] we paſsed a Creek[85] twenty yards wide with some Willows and where it iſsued from the Hills about four miles above a few trees [*of the Pine species*]— several other little guts ran acroſs our way but we suppose them the drains of swamps— The Hills on this side have dwindled to almost nothing and those of the other which are beyond the stripe of woods we saw yesterday and continued to see all this day have also lost something of their height,[86] but the Fork[87] has not yet added its waters to the main stream [106] About a mile back we found a straw Hut in an old Indian encampment inhabited by three squaws who appeared very much terrified on our approach but after a little time gave us to understand they were Panees, but although we spoke to them in the language of their neighbours the Ottos and gave them some dried meat with other demonstrations of our friendship, yet they continued much agitated and told us nothing we could comprehend except that there were white people in the country at no great distance— The total of this days journey was 8 miles[88] S E by E. 13[89] E.S.E and 6 East by South—[90]

Monday 5th We came 25 miles[91] East by south along the Indian trace which on leaving camp consisted of three roads,[92] but from the middle of the day till we stopped[93] they increased to ten, all running parallel— The watercourse[94] we saw [*the*] wood on for two days past joined the main stream ten miles back, but it is impoſsible for us to say how large or what it was — Below its mouth began a considerable body of large Timber, which runs down as far as we can see and the Hills of that side appear about the same place to have either turned off abruptly to the left, or resumed their former character and become a part of the Plain— Killed three geese and two Swans, and in the craws of the latter found several of the identical root dug by the natives of the Columbia below the Falls of that River and called by them Wapatoes[95]

Tuesday 6th 26 miles East was the length of this days walk.[96] The body of Timber has increased greatly and extends too far to the north for the eye to tell what is its width we are neverthelefs obliged to wade a narrow channel[97] to procure fuel as well as food for our Horse; for the graſs on the main is totally consumed [*by fire*] and all the woods are on an Island[98] which from every appearance must be what we have so long looked for, "the Big Island"[99] [, *if so we are now about 140 miles from the mouth of the Platte—*]

[107] There are no Hills to be seen on the other side, and for these [*last*] two days [*march*] those on this [*side*] have been extremely low and never come within half a league[100] of the river— The Timber now consists of Cottonwood, Elm, Box Alder[101] [*Ash*]

and White Willow, with an almost impenetrable undergrowth of Arrow Wood,[102] Common and Red Willow [&c]; but all this induces but few of the furred race to inhabit the banks— Found[103] today some of the roots called by the Ottos "Toe"[104] & the Canadians Pomme de Terre— they are but seldom of larger dimensions than a hens egg with a rough warty brown skin, are never more than six inches deep in the earth and when boiled resemble very much in taste the "Sweet Potatoe"— Saw some Fallow Deer, and of late Kurlews[105] and oldfield Larks[106] are most the only birds except wild Fowl[107] that we see

Wednesday 7th Soon after leaving camp it began to rain [*very*] hard which continued at intervals all day— at the end of 16 miles[108] East finding good feed for our Pony who is extremely weak and jaded we stopped on a small Island[109] for the night—

A number of little Islands are scattered promiscuously along the channel,[110] they poſseſs a few Beaver and some Wood, but it is for the most part small, while that on the Big one[111] is very large and of too great [*an*] extent for the eye to measure it— On our side there is seldom a twig, but [*we*] have again found the unburnt Prairie— the Hills after coming close to the river this morning immediately receded and are now at about the same distance as formerly—[112] Andre Vallé killed a Fallow Deer, which is the first we have been able to lay our claws on— it is very poor, but as our [*stock of*] dried meat [*/which we have been keeping in reserve/*] is getting [*very*] low we are glad of the addition to our stock

Thursday 8th 9 miles East north East 9 North East by East and 4 East north East[113] brought us to our nights lodgings[114] in a more extensively wooded Bottom than we have met with since we left our winter quarters— The Hills came close to the river in the early part of the day and have since continued [108] in the vicinity— they are low, but much broken and poſseſs a good soil producing a short kind of graſs[115] which our Horse is very fond of and is apparently in his estimation nearly equal to rushes, now found in great plenty on the Islands—

The Grand Ile[116] terminated two miles back, so according to our ideas it is 72 miles long and if we may calculate its width in the same ratio, it will be [*about*] 24 broad— It has throughout poſseſsed great bodies of Timber affording shelter and subsistence to a good many Deer, some Elk and a few Beaver— Ever since we lost sight of the Buffaloe their dung and other sign of last winter, and also Indian encampments of same time have been seen every where, from which we are confident a number of the Panee nation must have wintered on the Platte, and from the snow being yet visible on the last Hills we saw on the north, that season must have been [*very*] severe, else the Buffaloe would not have come so low, which from all we can now discover is very uncommon— These Indians travelled towards the south early in the Spring when these animals no doubt left the Woods, so the three women we found in one of their camps must have been sick and abandoned [*there*] to their fate at that season by their savage relatives—

Every appearance of Savage and Buffaloe is at an end all the freshest roads seemed to croſs the Big Island[117] which we suppose the route to their present Towns on the Loup Fork; so we have now to rely on an indistinct path, formerly very extensive, but not travelled for some years, which in the end we hope will lead us to the old Panee Village[118] near the mouth of the above Fork [109] The river is about the same breadth as formerly, much broken by innumerable Islands in which the most of the Timber generally is— Jones killed a Deer close to camp—

Friday 9th Our journey today was 6 Miles East north East 14 East by north and 4 East north East[119] when a heavy gust of rain obliged us to encamp on a small Island—[120] The Hills on this side continue[121] as yesterday, but nothing can be seen on the other (when the Islands permit) but a smooth burnt prairie—

The Indian path has become scarcely decernable and in many places not a vestige remains, however as the uplands is always close[121] to the river we find it good walking as the grafs on them is for the most part very short— a vast difference from the Bottoms where it is generally five feet high

Saturday 10th The road was still visible and along it we travelled 12 miles E.N.E. 9 East by north and 13 East[122] to our nights station on an Island[123] as usual— The opposite shore seems equally destitute of Timber with this, and the Hills of either side [/*if I may be allowed a Bull*/] are also Prairie. indeed it is extraordinary though no lefs true that while the mainland pofsefses but few trees and sometimes not even a Willow; yet there is scarcely an Island of however diminutive dimensions but is for the most part wholly covered with wood—

It is hardly pofsible to guefs at the width of the river as we but seldom see the whole at once, on account of the numerous Islands which are scattered from shore to shore, but so far as we can judge it is[124] much about what it has been for a week past—

We saw a number of Fallow Deer (the only kind to be seen) one of whom Jones took the life of— The weather is occasionally so hot as to be truly disagreeable—

[110] Sunday 11th 8 miles from Camp an Indian of the Otto nation overtook us,[125] with whom two of our people[126] returned to their station for the purpose of [*getting news and*] ascertaining exactly where we are

7 miles farther on the Loup Fork[127] entered from the north It is upwards of 200 yards wide, a clear rapid stream, with about three feet[128] water to follow the channel to the Paducas Fork[129] a distance of 99 miles— 45 miles from the mouth is Beaver Creek[130] ten paces wide— 30 higher is Willow River[131] forty five yards broad— 12 more brings you to Cornfield Creek,[132] thirty feet[133] between the banks where now stands the grand Panee village of

about nine hundred warriors under the Sachemship of Ku-taw-row or Long Hair—[134] 1 league farther on the Paneemaha Village (of 450[135] fighting men) stands on the margin of a Branch[136] in size the same as that of the village below, Ash-ay-Koy-pay-rou[137] or the Cheifs Knife[138] is their head— 9 miles higher the Paducas Fork 80 yards wide joins the main stream and 18 more takes you to that of Pommes de Terre[139] equal in size to with the last; from whence it is at least 450 miles by the meander of the river to its source in several Lakes of considerable extent[140] situated in a beautifull [*high*] Plain— The main stream above the mouth of the Pommes de Terre is apparently but little diminished in size and the Timber which everywhere below decorates its borders gradually becomes lefs thick[141] and at its final seperation into small Branches wood is to be found only in patches—

All the tributary streams enumerated above join the main river from the north,[142] all are considerably wooded and pofsefs a good many of the furred animals whose skins are precious, besides their wooded recefses shelter some Deer and a few Elk—[143] The Paneemahas or Loups for the most part rove from their Town to the extremities of the Fork which bears their name, but [111] the Big Village[144] crofsing the Loup Fork and intervening plain pafs the River Platte and following it to near the end of the timbered tract below Ringing Water River[145] progrefs southward to the branches[146] of the Kanzes River,[147] where generally they make their Buffaloe hunt— some times indeed they penetrate even to the frontier villages of New Mexico, but we cannot say that their range pafses the northern Forks of the above stream

These Indians come to their towns[148] early in April, plant their Corn, Pumpkins and Beans towards the end of May, stay till it is a certain height, when hoeing it, they then abandon it to the benign care of the Allseeing Providence and return to the plains to pursue the humpbacked race—[149] In August they again revisit their village and after gathering in the harvest depositing safely and secretly[150] in excavations made for the purpose in the earth they once more leave their homes for their favorite pursuit of the Buffaloe at which they employ themselves till the following April—

The grand Panees make annually about one hundred and twenty[151] packs[152] of Buffaloe [*robes*] and twelve[153] of Beaver and the Loups[154] eighty[155] of the former and five[156] of the latter this may be considered as the average, but in a good year they kill have[157] as much more—

We came on 6 miles to where the grand Panee village[158] stood on an elevated bank of the Platte [*about*] four years ago and 7 more[159] brought us to camp[160] at a large point of woods where we killed a Turkey,[161] the first we have seen

The total distance today was 28 miles[162] in nearly a due East direction—

Notes to Chapter IX

1 This day's entry is possibly the one which Stuart intended to supplement by the first paragraph in journ.'s postscript, p. [127]—*i.e.*, pp. 254, 255. See, however, note 39 on p. 201.

2 "M^{r} McClellan's" in trav. mem. This sentence in journ. is supplemented by second paragraph in journ.'s postscript, p. [127]—*i.e.*, p. 255.

3 This date is restated as "3^{d} Jany." in journ.'s postscript, p. [130]—*i.e.*, p. 256.

4 "17 Buffalo" in trav. mem.

5 The date of departure is, with seeming error, restated as "7th March" in journ.'s postscript, p. [130]—*i.e.*, p. 256.

6 Camped on bank of North Platte at a spot four miles above the mouth of Horse Creek. This spot, if the creek has not changed its course since Stuart's time (and it seems not to have done so materially, if at all), was approximately one and one-quarter miles west of present-day boundary-line between states of Wyoming and Nebraska. Stuart does not disclose whether his camp was on the right or left bank.

7 "5 or 6 inches" in trav. mem.

8 "our good old Rozinante" in trav. mem.

9 Horse Creek.

10 This camp on left bank of North Platte and three miles below mouth of Horse Creek was approximately at the spot now covered by the north end of the bridge which, crossing the North Platte, is south of site of present-day town of Morrill, Neb. There are, and doubtless were in Stuart's time, three sand-bars in the river here. *Quad. Scotts Bluff; Geol. Nebraska.*

Stuart's route from this spot to where, on April 4, he forded the Platte was virtually identical with the subsequent so-called Mormon Trail. For description of this Mormon Trail, see *Mil. Star*, XII, pp. 49, 50, 65-68, 81-83, 97, 98; *Clayton* [*B*], pp. 131-189; *Crown Maps*, I, 30-32, II, 1-9.

11 See note 96 on p. 206 for site of camp of December 27.

Stuart's abortive undertaking to canoe on the North Platte has been sharply criticized by various writers who perhaps were not familiar with the general aspect of the stream. Though in many stretches this river is ordinarily very shallow, its broad waters in numerous other stretches are so turgid as to have drowned countless cattle. Its appearance, which deceived Stuart, deluded also sundry other fur traders in the two and a half decades after his attempt, and thus history records not a few endeavors at its navigation. See, for instance, *Chittenden*, p. 771; *Gilbert*, pp. 54, 55.

12 See note 90 on p. 205 for site of camp of December 26.

13 Camped on left bank of North Platte at a spot which, according to Stuart's reckoning, was 81 miles below the mouth of Horse Creek and which, by prorating, is shown to have been seven miles southeast of site of present-day town of Northport. *Geol. Nebraska; Quad. Camp Clarke.*

14 In lieu of this phrase "as makes us happy at having abandoned our Canoes" trav. mem. substitutes: "that we are now convinced of the impoſsibility of getting along in Canoes."

15 "little dry Buffalo dung" in trav. mem. For dried buffalo dung (the *bois de vache* of the French-speaking trappers, the "buffalo chips" of the later American pioneer) as fuel, see *Marcy*, pp. 155, 156; *Wadsworth*, pp. 66, 67.

16 Incorrectly "26 miles" in trav. mem. Camp, as shown by following day's entry, was on North Platte's left bank at a spot approximately two miles due west from present-day boundary line between the counties of Morrill and Garden, Neb. *Geol. Nebraska; Quad. Browns Creek.*

17 "3 miles" in trav. mem.

18 Incorrectly "29 miles" in trav. mem.

19 Because withered, they provided ready firewood.

20 Camped on left bank of North Platte approximately at site of present-day city of Oshkosh, Garden County, Neb. *Geol. Nebraska; Quad. Chappell.*

21 See *Quad. Sidney; Quad. Chappell.*

22 "our side" in trav. mem.

23 This stream, present-day Rush Creek, was the "Ruth Creek" of Noteware, the "Smith's Fork" of Fremont and seemingly the "Spring Creek" of Joel Palmer. *Geol. Nebraska; Noteware; Fremont*, accompanying map; *Palmer*, p. 24.

24 See note 91 on p. 205 for identity as bison.

25 Incorrectly "27 miles" in trav. mem. Camped on left bank of North Platte at a spot approximately three miles west of site of present-day town of Belmar, Keith County, Neb. *Geol. Nebraska; Quad Chappell; Quad. Ogalalla.*

26 This stream, present-day Blue Creek, but also known locally as Blue River and Blue Water Creek, was the "Black River" of Long, of Bradford, of Schmolder, of Sumner and of Ensign, the "Blue Water Creek" of general map accompanying *Railroad Survey*, Vol. XI. It was the "Castle River" of Horn, the "Castle Creek" and "Castle River" of William Clayton. *Geol. Nebraska; Quad. Chappell; Long*, western section of accompanying map; *Bradford; Schmolder*, map opposite p. 1; *Sumner; Ensign; Horn*, p. 14; *Clayton* [*B*], p. 368.

Upon the upper reaches of this stream was fought, September 3, 1855, the Battle of Blue Water (more commonly termed Battle of Ash Hollow) between General W. S. Harney's troops and some 700 Sioux (Brulé, Ogalalla and Minneconjou) and Northern Cheyennes. *Neb. Colls.*, XVI, pp. 143-164; *Neb. Pub.*, XX, pp. 278-282.

27 Present-day Ash Creek, on which was fought, in 1835, a fierce battle between Pawnees and Sioux. Its valley, "the Coulée des Frênes" of Fremont,

has since his day been known as Ash Hollow, owing this name "to a few scattering ash trees in the dry ravine" (*Fremont*, p. 23; *Bryant*, p. 97; *Sage*, pp. 49, 50; *Little*, p. 87; *Geol. Nebraska; Quad. Chappell*). Through Ash Hollow ultimately ran the perhaps most commonly used link between the Oregon Trail's two easterly stems, one of which followed the Platte's north bank and the other the south bank.

28 "65 wild horses" in trav. mem.

29 "several" in trav. mem.

30 Actually crossed three; though one of them, present-day Sand Creek, was doubtless dry and so escaped comment. The other two, present-day Otter and Lornegan Creeks, each indicated on *Quad. Ogalalla*, were respectively the "Horn's Creek" and "Camp Creek" of *Horn*, p. 13.

31 "ifsuing from the sandy bluffs to the N.E." in trav. mem.

32 Camped on left bank of North Platte at a spot approximately opposite the island lying off present-day Cedar Point and thus some three miles west of site of town of Keystone, Keith County, Neb. *Quad. Ogalalla; Geol. Nebraska.*

33 Incorrectly "29 miles" in trav. mem.

34 Pinnated grouse, *Tympanuchus americanus.*

35 Incorrectly "27 miles" in trav. mem. Camped on left bank of North Platte at a spot approximately three miles west from present-day boundary line between Nebraskan counties of Keith and Lincoln. *Geol. Nebraska; Quad. Paxton.*

36 Incorrectly "9 more" in trav. mem.

37 This, present-day Birdwood Creek, was the "Plover Creek" of Sage, the "North Bluff Creek" of Horn, of Linforth and of Clayton, the "Spring Creek" of Curley; and was the stream which, from its mouth as far upstream as to its forks, Harrison Johnson termed "Tepe Creek," styling only the easterly fork "Braidwood Creek." According to Lilian Linder Fitzpatrick, the name Birdwood is either a parallelism or literal translation of *Zintka-chan wakpala*, the Dakota indians' title for this same stream, each so given because the birdwood or indigo shrub, *Amorpha fruticosa*, was common along its banks. *Geol. Nebraska; Quad. Paxton; Sage*, p. 150 and accompanying map; *Horn*, p. 12; *Linforth*, p. 90; *Clayton* [*B*], p. 368; *Curley*, map VII opposite p. 304; *Johnson, Harrison*, accompanying map; *Fitzpatrick*, pp. 94, 95.

38 "quicksand, and about waist deep" in trav. mem.

39 Camped on left bank of North Platte at a spot which, approximately in longitude 100° 53′, lay some seven miles northwest from site of present-day city of North Platte. *Quad. North Platte; Geol. Nebraska.*

40 Incorrectly "27 miles" in trav. mem.

41 This clause was rephrased in journ.'s postscript, p. [132]—*i.e.*, p. 256.

42 Present-day South Platte.

43 Either a distant bank of cloud or else a mirage characteristic of the Platte Valley. See *Potter*, p. 42. In ordinary conditions of light there is in this

neighborhood no appearance of special prominence among the northerly hills, which vary from 200 to 475 feet in height above the river. *Quad. North Platte.*

44 "poor Devil" in trav. mem.

45 On left side of North Platte River but probably inland from its littoral swamp and situated approximately due north of site of present-day city of North Platte. *Quad. North Platte.*

46 See *Sage*, p. 150.

47 Maize; for indians' cultivation of which, see *Chittenden*, p. 807.

48 Present-day Brady Island, so styled prior to 1843 in memory of a man surnamed Brady. About 1841 he was murdered on or near the island by one of his companions who presently made atonement through his own appalling death, all as described in *Sage*, pp. 43-45; *Fremont*, p. 21. The head of this island lay approximately one mile below the confluence of North Platte and South Platte Rivers.

49 "Brady's Island is well wooded" according to *Fremont*, p. 21.

50 Doubtless present-day Grand Island, which, lying much further eastward in the Platte, was not to be encountered by Stuart until April 6.

51 For Stuart's description of Loup Fork, see entry of April 11 (pp. 220, 221).

52 South Platte.

53 North Platte.

54 See *Earnshaw*, 5th installment.

55 A low ridge with irregular crest. *Quad. North Platte.*

56 Incorrectly "3 miles" in trav. mem.

57 Incorrectly "26 miles" in trav. mem.

58 Brady Island.

59 This camp on Platte's left bank was, according to the later context, approximately at the site of present-day town of Maxwell, Lincoln County, Neb. *Geol. Nebraska; Quad. North Platte.*

60 Incorrectly "33 miles" in trav. mem.

61 Present-day Pawnee Creek, which, being the outlet of a swamp and emptying through the Platte's left bank at a spot approximately midway between the sites of present-day towns of Gannet and Maxwell, has in recent years atrophied as a result of engineers' partial draining of the swamp. *Quad. North Platte.*

62 "numerous" in trav. mem.

63 *Opuntia polyacantha.* See *Frizzell*, p. 24; *Thompson*, p. 42; *Cartwright*, p. 191; *Thornton*, I, pp. 66, 69.

64 Wild horses habitually ranged in large numbers this far to the north, though wild cattle not at all. However, the horses, obedient to conditions of weather and herbage, might temporarily desert any particular locality.

65 "2 Buffalo" in trav. mem.

66 Incorrectly "25 miles" in trav. mem.

67 Camped on left bank of Platte at a spot a short distance west of the meridian of the easterly end of Brady Island.

68 Brady Island.

69 "a few fallow Deer, & 17 Elk" in trav. mem.

70 Brady Island.

71 Grand Island, for which see note 50.

72 These exaggerated measurements for Grand Island were obviously based on hearsay as Stuart had never previously been in this region. See entry of April 8 (p. 219) for Stuart's subsequent modification of these measurements and also note 116 for the actual dimensions.

73 The actual dimensions of Brady Island were doubtless in Stuart's day, as they are now, approximately 18 miles in length and one mile in maximum width. The Platte, imprisoned in heavy sand, has not, within historic times, seemed disposed to alter permanently its banks or islands. *Quad. North Platte; Quad. Gothenburg; Fremont*, pp. 19, 20.

74 Incorrectly "12" in trav. mem.

75 Camped on left bank of Platte at a spot approximately due south of site of present-day town of Willow Island. *Geol. Nebraska; Quad. Gothenburg.*

76 Though low hills existed here, it is quite possible that what Stuart saw was a mirage. *Quad. Lexington; Potter*, p. 42.

77 Camped on left bank of Platte at a spot approximately due south of site of present-day town of Lexington, Neb. *Quad. Lexington; Geol. Nebraska.*

78 "East south East" in journ.; and incorrectly "East" in trav. mem. *Quad. Lexington.*

79 Incorrectly "2 miles" in trav. mem.

80 Low ridges. *Quad. Lexington.*

81 Present-day Spring Creek and Buffalo Creek, paralleling each other, flowing southeasterly and emptying through Platte's left bank. *Quad. Lexington; Geol. Nebraska.*

82 Not till eight days later did Stuart pass Loup Fork's mouth; see entry of April 11 (p. 220).

83 To Platte's right bank at a spot approximately coincident with the north end of present-day boundary line between Gosper and Phelps Counties, Neb.

Nouvelles Annales, XII, pp. 104, 105 paraphrases the beginning of this day's entry by a wording translatable as follows: "For two days we had seen on our side neither bison nor traces of them. Consequently, on the 4th, we crossed the river at a spot where it was divided into ten channels." For possible source of *Nouvelles Annales*' added data see note 34 on p. 201 *ante.*

84 Incorrectly "9 miles" in trav. mem.

85 Present-day Plum Creek. Though Stuart does not here mention this stream by name, he, in his entries of April 11 and 18 (pp. 221, 237), reminiscently refers to it as "Ringing Water" River, a designation previously used

for it by Lewis and Clark, whose knowledge of its name and existence was hearsay. It was the "Plumb Creek" of Stansbury, of Clyman and of O. Allen, the "Plum Creek" of Sawyer and of Gibson, and seemingly was the "Deer Creek" of Robinson, the "Falling Creek" of Pike. A half-mile west of its mouth, indians, on August 6, 1864, perpetrated the so-called Plum Creek Massacre of whites. *L. & C. Journs.*, VI, p. 41; *L. & C. Hist.*, accompanying map entitled "A Map of part of the continent of North America . . . Compiled . . . by M. Lewis"; *Geol. Nebraska; Quad. Lexington; Stansbury* [*B*]; *Clyman*, p. 232; *Allen's Guide*, p. 63; *Sawyer*, p. 31; *Gibson*, pp. 22, 70; *Robinson; Pike*, accompanying map entitled "The First Part of Captn Pike's Chart of Internal Part of Louisiana"; *Neb. Pub.*, XIX, pp. 1-5; *Neb. Hist. Mag.*, XIV, pp. 182-184.

86 Amounting here to no more than a very slight rise in the distant portion of the plain (see *Quad. Lexington*); but Stuart may have been deceived by clouds, by sunshine on remote trees, or by a mirage.

87 See note 81 for identity of the "fork."

88 Incorrectly "11 miles" in trav. mem.

89 The journ.'s figure "13" (originally entered as "15") is nearer to accuracy than is the trav. mem.'s "15."

90 The camp was on the Platte's right bank at a spot approximately due south from site of present-day town of Elm Creek. *Quad. Kearney; Geol. Nebraska.*

In fixing the approximate sites of this and later camps to and including that of April 10, the present editor has taken into consideration the fact that from the mouth of Plum Creek (which Stuart crossed on April 4) to the mouth of Loup River (which he passed on April 11) the mileage, as stated in journ., totals 178; whereas, according to U. S. Geological Survey maps, it should be 140. Accordingly, Stuart's daily mileages have been arbitrarily lessened in accord with this same ratio, though with due regard to having each asserted campsite comportable with the topography as described by Stuart.

91 Incorrectly "29 miles" in trav. mem.

92 "paths" in trav. mem.

93 Camp was on Platte's right bank and, as indicated by Stuart's description of the receding hills, was at a spot approximately one and one-half miles west of site of present-day town of Newark. *Quad. Wood River; Geol. Nebraska.*

94 Present-day Buffalo Creek; but Stuart was 17 miles, instead of his stated ten, east of its mouth. Possibly he had thought one of the Platte's northerly channels to be a continuation of Buffalo Creek.

95 See note 43 on p. 20 for identity of this edible root.

96 Camped, as shown by later context, either on Platte's right bank or on closely adjacent present-day Elm Island; in either case at a spot approximately five miles due east from present-day boundary line between the counties of Buffalo and Hall, Neb. *Quad. Wood River; Geol. Nebraska.*

97 Platte's south channel, a very narrow affair. *Quad. Wood River.*

98 Elm Island.

99 "Grand Isle" in trav. mem.

100 "within 4 or 5 miles" in trav. mem.

101 Meaning "box-elder," for which see note 63 on pp. 202, 203.

102 Probably either dogwood, *Cornus asperifolia*, or Osage orange, *Toxylon pomiferum* (*Raf.*)—each of which was employed by indians for arrow shafts—; but may have been that other popularly termed arrow wood, *Viburnum dentatum* or *V. molle*, the bark of which was used by indians for smoking in their pipes. M. R. Gilmore's *A Study in the Ethnobotany of the Omaha Indians* in *Neb. Colls.*, XVII, pp. 346, 349; *L. & C. Journs.*, III, pp. 219, 220, VI, pp. 140, 153; *L. & C. Hist.*, p. 139.

103 In lieu of journ.'s phrase "Found today some of the roots," trav. mem. substitutes: "since leaving the Columbian plains we have found few or no esculent roots, untill this afternoon, when we fell in with a large field of the root."

104 Bradbury, when on the Missouri River, made note: "I observed in the broken banks of this island, a number of tuberous roots, which the Canadians call *pommes de terre*. They are eaten by them, and also by the Indians, and have much of the consistence and taste of the Jerusalem artichoke; they are the roots of *Glycine apios*." See *Bradbury* [*A*], p. 14.

M. R. Gilmore's article cited in note 102 *ante* states that *Psoralea esculenta*, which was ordinarily the size of a hen's egg, was the "pomme blanche" and "pomme de prairie" of the French voyageurs, that *Apios apios* was these voyageurs' "pomme de terre," and that other bulbs, tubers and roots eaten by indians in this vicinity were *Helianthus tuberosa*, *Allium spp.* and *Sagittaria latifolia*. *Neb. Colls.*, XVII, pp. 325, 351.

For "pomme blanche," see also *Sage*, p. 107; *Wislizenus* [*A*], p. 39, [*B*], p. 61; *Murray*, I, p. 265.

105 Long-billed curlew, *Numenius longirostris*, *N. americanus*.

106 The prairie lark, *Sturnella neglecta;* but closely resembling the true Oldfield lark, *S. magna*. *L. & C. Hist.*, p. 876.

107 "water Fowl" in trav. mem. If Stuart's "wild Fowl" were land birds, they not improbably were sharp-tailed grouse, *Pediœcetes phasianellus campestris*, and also the bird interchangeably known as pinnated grouse or prairie chicken, *Tympanuchus americanus*.

108 Incorrectly "23 miles" in trav. mem.

109 This island, evidently in Platte's south channel, lay approximately due south from site of present-day town of Alda, Hall County, Neb. *Geol. Nebraska; Quad. Grand Island.*

110 South channel.

111 Grand Island.

112 "as for some days back" in trav. mem.

113 "4 East north East" in journ., and incorrectly "11 N.E" in trav. mem.

114 Camped on Platte's right bank at a spot approximately due south

from site of present-day town of Archer, Merrick County, Neb. *Geol. Nebraska; Quad. St. Paul.*

115 Inasmuch as *Bulletin B*, p. 13, states that Nebraska has more than 200 native grasses of which 150 are valuable for forage, it seems futile to attempt present-day identification of the "short kind of graſs" beloved by Stuart's weary horse.

116 Grand Island. Its reputed length and breadth have, since time immemorial, varied in accord, not only with temporary changes of depth in the Platte's water (the shallower the river, the larger the island), but also with the observer's judgment as to which, if any, of neighboring sand-bars should be considered a part of the island. Kingsbury, in 1835, accorded it a length of "about sixty miles," Fremont later conceded it a length of 52 miles and an average breadth of one and three-quarter miles, Shepherd granted it 45 miles of length, Thornton "about fifty-two." Moffette figured it as 60 miles long by from three to four in width, Curley as "some sixty miles long by five or six broad at the widest point," while *Bulletin B*, p. 24, officially makes the length "about 42 miles." Though Stuart's earlier exaggeration of the island's width had been based on hearsay (see note 72), his continued exaggeration was very possibly due to his mistaken assumption that trees and uplands north of the river's left bank were situated on the island. Kingsbury found the island to be so heavily timbered as to hide "the opposite bank of the river entirely from our view." See *Kingsbury*, p. 13; *Fremont*, p. 78; *Shepherd*, p. 9; *Thornton*, I, p. 67; *Moffette*, pp. 31, 32; *Curley*, p. 265.

117 Grand Island.

118 Situated on the Platte's right bank at a spot approximately due north from site of present-day David City, Butler County, Neb. *Robinson; L. & C. Hist.*, accompanying map entitled "Map of part of the Continent of North America . . . Compiled . . . by M. Lewis"; *L. & C. Journs.*, VI, p. 41; *Neb. Pub.*, XX, p. 3.

119 "14 East by north and 4 East north East" in journ.; and incorrectly "17 E by N. and 4 N.E by E." in trav. mem.

120 Not improbably present-day Baker Island lying immediately east of present-day easterly boundary line of Merrick County, Neb. *Quad. Stromsburg.*

121 See *Quad. Stromsburg.*

122 Stuart turned eastward on reaching a spot approximately due southeast of site of present-day town of Silver Creek. *Quad. Stromsburg; Geol. Nebraska.*

123 This camp was approximately due south from site of present-day town of Duncan, Platte County, Neb.; and the island on which it was situated was doubtless the large one which *Quad. David City* indicates, without naming, as being in that exact locality.

124 In lieu of the remainder of this sentence trav. mem. substitutes: "is about 2 to 3 miles which has been the case for the last three or four days—."

125 Approximately at mouth of present-day Clear Creek. *Quad. David City; Geol. Nebraska.*

126 These two people, according to entry for following day (p. 233), were Crooks and Vallé.

127 This stream, today termed Loup River but in bygone days known more commonly as Loup Fork, was the "R. des Loups" of Perrin du Lac and the "Woolf river" of Lewis and Clark. *Perrin du Lac*, map; *L. & C. Journs.*, VI, p. 39.

Stuart in his description of the river does not, except for his mentioning the mouth, deal with any locality he had traversed or even seen. Instead, digressing for the moment from his narrative of travel, he attempts, on the faith of hearsay information, to describe the entire Loup River and its principal tributaries. Though his recital is very inaccurate as to mileages, it is nevertheless possible to identify the streams he mentions and to state their present-day names as in notes 129-132, 136, 139.

128 "about 5 feet" in trav. mem.

129 This stream ("Padcau Fork" in trav. mem.) is North Loup River. Incidentally, North Platte River and South Platte River were each also styled as Paduca (or Paduca's) Fork on various early maps.

130 Beaver Creek.

131 Cedar River.

132 Either Horse Creek or less probably its neighbor, Cottonwood Creek.

133 "20 yards" in trav. mem.

134 Long styles him "Tar-ra-re-ca-wa-o or Long-hair." *Long*, I, p. 160.

135 "650" in trav. mem.

136 Either Spring Creek or less probably (and only if Cottonwood Creek has been allocated as in note 132) its neighbor, Rock Creek.

137 "Ash-ay-Koy-pay-row" in trav. mem.

138 Long styles him "Knife Chief." *Long*, I, p. 162.

139 So much of Middle Loup River as lay above its confluence with South Loup River.

140 In modern nomenclature: Moon Lake (less than three miles long), still smaller Brush Lake and Dismal River's tiny pond.

141 "plenty" in trav. mem.

142 Incorrectly "south" in trav. mem.

143 "innumerable Deer and Elk with a few Bear" in trav. mem.

144 Meaning inhabitants of Big Village.

145 Plum Creek, for which see note 85.

146 "banks" in trav. mem.

147 Present-day Kansas River, for which see note 50 on p. 245.

148 "Town" in trav. mem.

149 Patently bison.

150 "securely" in trav. mem.

151 "150" in trav. mem.

152 A pack of furs was a standardized unit in the fur trade, and, weighing about 100 pounds, contained 10 pelts, if bison (pelts of bison being usually termed robes); 14 pelts, if bear; 60, if land otter; 80, if beaver; 80, if raccoon; 120, if fox; 600, if muskrat. See *Chittenden*, I, p. 40.

153 "20" in trav. mem.

154 Pawnee Loup indians.

155 "100" in trav. mem.

156 "12" in trav. mem.

157 "will have as many more" in trav. mem.

158 See note 118 for site of this village.

159 Incorrectly "17 more" in trav. mem.

160 On Platte's right bank approximately at site of present-day town of Edholm, Butler County, Neb.

161 Wild turkey, *Meleagris gallopavo*.

162 Incorrectly "38 miles" in trav. mem.

CHAPTER X

APRIL 12 · APRIL 30, 1813

On Foot to Oto Village and Thence by Canoe to St. Louis

Meet Dorouin and Roi · Indian Lodges · Build Canoe · Embark in It · Obtain Another Canoe · Fort Osage · Reach St. Louis · Characteristics of Missouri River and of Settlements on It.

[112] Monday 12th Early in the morning Mr Crooks and Vallé overtook us— they had walked till long after sunset but the night being [*too*] dark to discover us they slept at a little distance from us

They went back with the Indian six miles where the[*y*] found two families of Ottos from whom they learnt that Mr Francois Dorouin[1] was [*the trader*] at their village; that he had sent some people to trade with the Panees and Mahas and that [*for a year past,*] the Americans and English were at loggerheads—[2] as to the distance to their town they said we would not sleep more than two nights—

7 miles[3] from camp we paſsed a Creek[4] where a village of Panees formerly lived— next we followed the road along the foot of the Hills for 8 more[5] when ascending the ridge it began to rain heavily which compelled us to make for a point of woods on the Platte where we stopped[6] for the night having come in all 20 Miles[7] East South East—[8]

Tuesday 13th 4 miles nearly south brought us to the trace which paſsed in the vicinity of a Branch[9] of the Saline River[10] over a

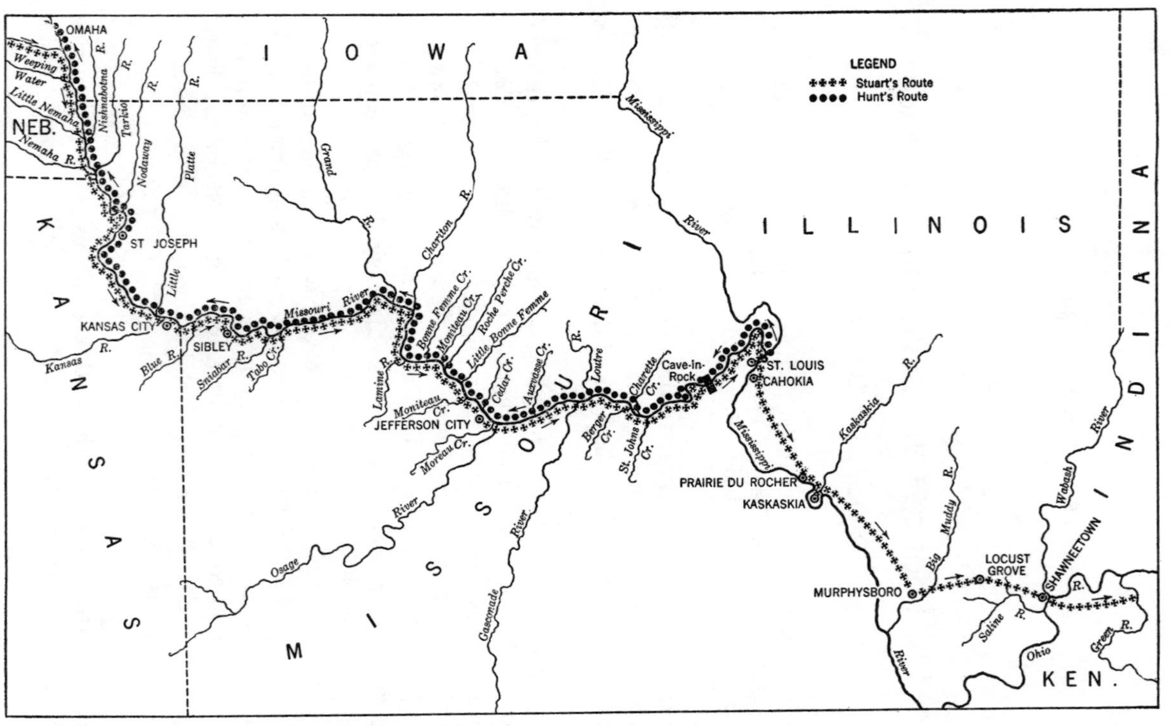

Routes of Stuart and of Hunt in Missouri and of Stuart in Illinois and Kentucky

high plain 18 miles;[11] then ascending a ridge of considerable elevation[12] we in 6 more reached the Otto Village standing on a Hill about four hundred paces from the right bank of the Platte[13]

The river is three quarters of a mile wide with some Islands which as well as the opposite shore are thickly covered with Cottonwood and a few other kinds of wood [*Ash*, *Oak*, *Hickory &c*]— The day was extremely cold for the season and in the course of it[14] several showers of [*sleet and*] Hail fell

We found here Mr [*F.*] Dorouin and Mr. Baptiste Roi[15] who after a voyage of six weeks from Saint Louis, reached this place three days ago— The winter was on the Mifsouri severe beyond any seen in this country, for the last twenty years, the snow was [*4½ deep*] two feet deeper than usual; and all out-of-doors work could not be accomplished without the afsistance of snowshoes— [113] The disagreeable intelligence of a war between America and Great Britain was here confirmed, but in such a confused manner was it related that we could comprehend but little

Our horse we gave Mr Dorouin, who in return is to get us a skin Canoe and provisions sufficient to take us to Fort Osage, where if we find no conveyance to St Louis we will no doubt get the proper means of constructing a Wooden Horse,[16] which the people here are totally destitute of—

Wednesday 14th Some snow fell in the course of the night and so cold was the day that nothing could be done towards making our Canoe other than putting the hides in the River to soak— The Ottos and Mifsouris are of equal force & jointly can bring 200[17] fighting men into the field— they have resided together for a number of years and by marriage have become so intermixed that we may at this day justly call them the same people; more particularly as their habits, manners, customs and pursuits are exactly the same— Many lodges are about to be constructed but the village consists at present of only thirty containing from two to four families [*each*], all are much of a size and built in the following manner, being every way the same as those of the Panees, except that the latter are much larger—

From a pole stuck in that spot of ground intended for the centre of the fabric, a cord upwards of thirty[18] feet long is extended, which carrying round the extremity is marked every ten feet by the insertion of a small stick in the earth making an area of at least 100 feet in circumference— Forked poles eight feet high and four inches in diameter are next put firmly in the ground taking the place of the pegs [&] marking the extreme of the circle— acroſs these are laid straight pieces of wood of the [114] same size and others considerably smaller, having one end in the earth are leaned against the last— Six large strong Forks are then set up, halfway between the extremes and centre; 12 feet high on which powerfull beams are placed as before; serving as a support to 120 poles running from the first elevation to the middle where a hole two feet wide is left to emit the smoke

Willows are laid acroſs the last Poles everywhere with a good covering of straw firmly attached thereto, & one foot of earth being tramped down hard over all completes the mansion, excepting the entrance, from whence runs out an erection of similar materials seven feet high, six wide and ten[19] long The door is generally an Elk or Buffaloe hide— The floor is 1½ feet lower than the earth outside, and for the fireplace the ground in the centre of the Building is scraped away so as to make it the lowest place in the lodge, & from near it, a Pole surpaſsing in height any put in the roof, is put out at the chimney where are suspended their Medecine Bags and War Budgets[20] carefully concealed in innumerable wrappers [*which effectually protects them*] from the influence of the weather—

Friday 16th Our Canoe was finished last evening and consisted of five Elk & Buffaloe hides sewed together with strong sinews, drawn over and made fast to a frame composed of Poles and Willows 20 feet long 4 Wide and 1½ deep, making a veſsell somewhat shaped like a Boat, very steady and by the aid of a little mud[21] on the seams, remarkably tight— In this we embarked [115] at an early hour and drifted ten miles when the wind becoming too high, we encamped[22] and began making oars an absolutely necessary part of our equipment, [*and*] not to be procured at the Indian Village— 2 miles back we passed the Elk Horn River[23] coming from the north, the water is [*exceedingly*] black, the current strong, its banks well covered with Willow Cottonwood &c. and it possesses a good many Beaver [*& otter*]—

Sunday 18th We completed our set of oars yesterday morning but the wind continued too high to try them

4 miles from camp we passed the Saline[24] a considerable stream coming from the south and in 31 more reached the Missouri—[25] The Platte from the Otto Village to its discharge keeps about its former course and is in every respect much the same as we found it all the way from Ringing Water;[26] with this exception that the Hills possess a beautifull growth of Oaks and the other Timber is not as formerly confined to the Islands alone—

Thursday 22nd On the 19th we came upwards of 60 miles[27] and passed a creek called Weeping Water—[28] the next day on account of bad weather we travelled only 27[29] and saw little Neemaha[30] & Nish-na-ba-ta-nay[31] Rivers— yesterday brought us to the Black Snake Hills[32] 63 from last nights camp,[33] having seen today[34] Big & little Taw-go-you-Wolf Creek[35] and Nowdoway River,[36] but the march of today was only about 20 miles long[37] as we were compelled by a strong head wind to put ashore by ten o'Clock and we passed the remainder of the day making a new frame for our Canoe, as the one we had was become unfit for the purpose for which it was originally intended— We killed some Deer & Turkeys today—[38]

[116] Saturday 24th Yesterday we were off early, and at the end of 68 miles encamped at a wintering place[39] of last season,

where we found two [*old wooden*] Canoes and took poſseſsion of the largest one— Having travelled 55 miles we in the afternoon of this day[40] reached Fort Osage[41] and learnt to our satisfaction the melancholy truth of war being waged since June last between the United States and Great Britain

This Fortification was built by a Company of regulars under the command of Captain Clemson[42] in the Fall of 1808 and has reduced the turbulent Kanzes to a proper sense of the true relation in which Indians stand with their civilized neighbours— there is a United States Factory[43] here for all tribes who chuse to come for the purposes of trade, but more particularly for the Osages who resided in the environs some time ago, but at present have their villages[44] on the Osage River[45]

In this days[46] journey we paſsed the little River Platte,[47] Blue Water,[48] the Cabin de Paille[49] and the Kanzes River[50] called after the Indians of that name who live on it about Eighty leagues from the mouth a band of Panees also reside on a Fork of it,— they are upwards of 600 in number, occupied some years ago the same town with the grand Panees on the Platte, and on account of their revolt from their chief[51] have since been known by the name of Republicans, which title is also given to that branch[52] of the Kanzes river where their village stands

Monday 26th In consequence of bad weather we remained the whole of yesterday at Fort Osage [*and were very hospitably entertained by Lieut. Brounson*[53]*/who commands in the absence of Major Climson/*] and procured [*he furnished us very generously with*] a sufficiency oı Pork & flour [*&c.*] to carry us to St Louis—

This days journey was 70 miles[54] and we paſsed in the course of it Eber's[55] and Fiery Prairie[56] Creeks and Tabeaus River[57] as also a place called the old little Osage village,[58] where the tribes[59] of that name resided a great many years ago

[117] Friday 30th April 1813— Setting out early on the 27th

we paſsed Grand Charaton,[60] and Lamine[61] Rivers [, *a distance of 75 miles*]—[62] during the following day we saw the discharges of Big[63] & little[64] Bonne Femme, Big[65] & little[66] Manitoes, Bear,[67] Split Rock[68] Moreau[69] and Cedar[70] Creeks also the Osage River[71] [—*68 miles*—]— Yesterday we came to the Cave in Rock[72] [*a distance of 78 miles*], leaving behind us the two Muddy Creeks,[73] those called Loutre,[74] Charette,[75] Shepherds[76] and Woods[77] not forgetting that fine stream the Gasconade,[78] and this day [*after descending 35 miles*][79] a little before sunset we reached the Town of Saint Louis all in the most perfect health after a voyage of ten months from Astoria during which time we[80] had the peculiar good fortune to have suffered in one instance only by want of provisions— Immediately on entering the Miſsouri at the mouth of the River Platte we found both the main land and Islands thickly covered with Timber of but few kinds, but as we progreſsed the variety became greater till at its junction with the Miſsiſsippi we could enumerate Cottonwood—Sycamore—[81]Ash —[82] Hackberry—[83] Walnut—[84] Hickory—[85] Box Alder—[86] Mulberry—[87] Elm[88] and Oak[89] besides the smaller growth of Dogwood[90] and Papa[91] and an endleſs variety of underwood— Game is not in the greatest abundance in the vicinity of the Platte but from a little distance below to near the mouth of the Miſsouri Elk—Deer, Black Bear Racoons, Wild Cats[92] and Turkeys are to be found in the greatest plenty on the land, while the Rivers furnish a considerable number of Beaver & Otter [, *with a variety of excellent Fish*[93]]

[*The soil is wonderfully fertile, but its fertility is not equal throughout the country, principally owing to the many rugged hills with which it is interspersed, these altho' not susceptible of any Agricultural improvement, still afford excellent pasture*—]

The christian Settlements extend 198 miles up the Miſsouri made principally by emigrants from Kentucky who (if it had not been for the present war) would have advanced much farther, but at present content themselves within the fortifications they have constructed on account of the Indians and raise a bare sufficiency for the subsistence of their families—

The Ottos and Mifsouris on the Platte make annually [118] about 150[94] packs of skins, of which it is common to find 35[95] of Beaver— The Republican Panees generally bring out the same quantity and kind as their relations the Big village[96] of the Platte— In the village of 350 Kanzes is yearly to be found about 150[97] Packs, among which there is from twelve to twenty[98] of Beaver— The Osages are said to be upwards of a 1000[99] warriors, and can produce on an average five hundred Packs, but the quantity of precious skins[100] is not so great in proportion as at the Ottos & Mifsouris—

The Mifsouri from where we struck it, to its discharge is [*upwards of*] 600 miles in length, from ¼ to a mile wide—a rapid current—the water intolerably muddy, and every bend of it pretty well supplied with Sawyers and Planters[101] occasioned by the falling in of the banks, which carrying the trees along with them, the roots become immoveably fixed in the bed of the river and form an object of considerable risk to persons unaccustomed to such a navigation—

[*The distance from St. Louis to N. York*	1345 *miles*
add distance from Astoria to St. Louis	3768[102]
Total Distance from Astoria to N. York	5113 *miles*]

Notes to Chapter X

1 "Doruin" in trav. mem.; "Dornin" in *Astoria*, II, p. 183; "Derouen" and "Deroin" in fur license lists of 1807, 1811 (*Bates*, I, p. 202; II, p. 201); "Derouin" in St. Louis tax list of probably 1805. (*Missouri*, III, p. 190.)

2 "at war" in trav. mem.

3 Incorrectly "17 miles" in trav. mem.

4 Present-day Skull Creek, which Stuart crossed approximately at site of town of Linwood, all as indicated by his reference to "foot of the Hills" and by *Quad. Wahoo.*

5 Stuart's route for these eight miles is now occupied by the roadbed of Chicago & Northwestern Railway. *Quad. Wahoo; Geol. Nebraska.*

6 Camp was on Platte's right bank at a spot approximately two miles east of site of present-day town of Morse Bluff. *Quad. Wahoo; Geol. Nebraska.*

7 Incorrectly "31 miles" in trav. mem.

8 "East South East" should have been "East North East." *Quad. David City; Quad. Wahoo; Geol. Nebraska.*

9 Present-day Sand Creek.

10 This stream, now known as Salt Creek, emptied through the Platte's right bank. It was the "Saline River" of *Kingsbury*, p. 3; *Melish* [*A*]; *Cowperthwait* [*A*]; *Wyld* [*B*], [*C*]; *Colton* [*A*], [*D*], [*H*]; the "Saline Creek" of *Stansbury* [*B*] and *Union Pacific;* the "Salt Creek" of map "[*B*]" accompanying *Kingsbury* and of general map accompanying *Railroad Survey*, Vol. XI.

11 Incorrectly "23 miles" in trav. mem. Stuart had here been making a southeasterly short-cut across the base of a bend in the Platte. *Quad. Wahoo; Quad. Fremont.*

12 200 feet above the river's level. *Quad. Fremont.*

13 The village was situated approximately one and one-half miles southeast from site of present-day town of Yutan (named for an Oto chief, Yutan, *alias* Jutan and Ietan; for whom see *Fitzpatrick*, p. 128, and *Kingsbury*, pp. 3, 4). *Quad. Fremont; Geol. Nebraska.*

14 "in the afternoon" in trav. mem.

15 "Mr Roi" in trav. mem. Doubtless Jean Baptiste Antoine Roy, who, a son of Antoine and Felicité (Vasquez) Roy, was born August 13, 1794, at St. Louis. *James*, p. 162, f.n. See also *Astoria*, II, p. 183.

16 "constructing a Canoe" in trav. mem.

17 "300" in trav. mem.

18 "40" in trav. mem.

19 "15" in trav. mem.

20 Packets containing amulets and military trophies.

21 *Astoria*, II, p. 183, styles it "unctuous mud."

22 Camped on bank of Platte at a spot two miles below the mouth of Elkhorn River.

23 Present-day Elkhorn River, the "R. Corne de Cerf" of Perrin du Lac, which Lewis and Clark termed variously "Corne des Cerfe or hart's horn river," "Elk River" and "Corne de charf or Elk Horn River." *Perrin du Lac*, accompanying map; *L. & C. Journs.*, I, pp. 87, 90, VI, p. 40.

24 See note 10 for description and various names of this stream.

25 Camped seemingly at mouth of Platte, for which see following day's entry.

26 Plum Creek, for which see note 85 on pp. 227, 228.

27 Incorrectly "came 65 miles" in trav. mem.

Camp was apparently at, or across the Missouri River from, Bald-Pated Prairie. This prairie was so named by Lewis and Clark because of bare-topped hills in the vicinity, and was seemingly the "Cote grand Brule" of Luttig. Lying on the Missouri River's right bank and opposite the northwesterly corner of the present-day state of Missouri, it was estimated by Lewis and Clark, who camped on it, to be 61 miles below the mouth of the Platte. *L. & C. Journs.*, I, pp. 81, 82, V, p. 380, VI, pp. 5, 38, 58; *L. & C. Hist.*, pp. 47, 1206, 1258; *Luttig*, p. 42.

28 This stream, termed by early French voyageurs "L'Eau qui pleure," was the "Crys Creek" of Floyd, the "Crying Water" of Whitehouse, the "Water-which-cries, or the Weeping stream" of Gass, and appears on present-day maps as Weeping Water Creek.

Lilian Linder Fitzpatrick asserts this latter name to be a misnomer derived as follows: The Oto and Omaha indians' title for the creek was *Nigahoe*—from *ni*, "water," and *gahoe*, "swishing"—the syllable *ho* having the sound of an English guttural letter "h." Because these same indians had also a word *hoage* (meaning "weeping"), white men, confused by similarity in sounds, erroneously assumed that the indians' term for the creek was *Nihoage*, and so produced the mistranslation "Weeping Water."

The creek emptied through the Missouri's right bank. Lewis and Clark estimated its mouth to be 32 miles below that of the Platte. *Gass* [*A*], p. 23; [*B*], p. 23; *L. & C. Journs.*, I, p. 85, VI, pp. 38, 58, VII, pp. 19, 43; *L. & C. Hist.*, pp. 50, 1258; *Fitzpatrick*, p. 33.

29 Camped a short distance below mouth of present-day Nishnabotna River, for which see note 31.

30 "little neemahaa" in trav. mem. This watercourse, the "Petit Nimakas" of Perrin du Lac, the "little Mohaugh" of Whitehouse, the "Nemahaw" of Floyd, the "Ne-ma-har" and "Ne-me-har" of Lewis and Clark, the "little Mahonir" of Luttig, the "Little Namaha" of Delano, the "Little Nemashaw" of map "[A]" accompanying *Kingsbury*, and now called Little Nemaha River, was a small stream which, in present-day Nemaha County, Neb., emptied through the Missouri's right bank. Its mouth was, according to Lewis and Clark,

23 miles below Bald-Pated Prairie and 84 below the mouth of the Platte. *Perrin du Lac*, map; *L. & C. Journs.*, I, pp. 79, 80, VI, pp. 38, 57, 58, VII, pp. 18, 42; *L. &. C. Hist.*, pp. 46, 1258; *Luttig*, p. 41; *Delano*, pp. 35, 42. For additional variant spellings, see *L. &. C. Hist.*, p. 43.

31 This stream, the "Neesh-nah-ba-to-na Creek" or "Nish-nah-ba-to-na River" of Lewis and Clark, the "Neeshba Creek" of Floyd, the "Nishnay Baton River" of Whitehouse, the "Wash-ba-to-nan river" of Patrick Gass, the "Nichinibatone" of Perrin du Lac, the "Ichinipokine" of Luttig, is today interchangeably known as Nishnabotna or Nishnabotona River. For additional variant early spellings, see *L. & C. Hist.*, p. 43. Its confluence with the Missouri River was in the extreme northwesterly part of the present-day state of Missouri, and was reckoned by Lewis and Clark to be eight miles below the mouth of Little Nemaha River. *L. & C. Journs.*, I, pp. 79, 82, VI, pp. 37, 38, 42, 57, 58, VII, pp. 18, 42; *Gass* [*A*], p. 22; [*B*], p. 22; *Perrin du Lac*, map; *Luttig*, p. 41; *L. & C. Hist.*, pp. 45, 1258.

32 The so-called Black Snake Hills embracing the site of present-day city of St. Joseph, Mo. (*Chittenden*, III, p. 949). Stuart's camp on April 21st must, from his stated mileage, have been approximately five miles north of that site.

33 Apparently Stuart meant his camp of April 20th and not that of April 21st.

34 This word "today" should have been "yesterday" because, as appears in note 35, the mouths of his listed watercourses lay above the Black Snake Hills and consequently must have been passed on the 21st and not on the 22nd.

35 "big and little Taw-go-you, woolf Creek" in trav. mem.—three streams today respectively known as Tarkio and Little Tarkio Rivers and Wolf Creek.

As for the two Tarkio rivers, they were two boggy and interlacing streams which, at least in Lewis and Clark's day, seeped at various places through the Missouri's left bank but had their principal outlets (possibly a combined and single outlet) at a spot three miles below the mouth of the Nishnabotna. They together constituted the "Tarkio Creek" of Lewis and Clark, the "Big Tarkuo River" and "Tarcio Creek" of Floyd, the "Tarkia Creek" of Whitehouse, the "Tarico Creek" of Patrick Gass. *L. & C. Hist.*, pp. 42, 44, 1248; *L. & C. Journs.*, I, pp. 74, 77, VI, pp. 37, 57, VII, pp. 17, 42; *Gass* [*A*], p. 21, [*B*], p. 21.

Wolf Creek (the "Loup River" or "Woolf River" of Lewis and Clark, the "Riviere du Loup" of early French maps) emptied through the Missouri's right bank at a spot reckoned by Lewis and Clark to have its mouth 30 miles below that of their Tarkio Creeks. *L. & C. Journs.*, I, pp. 72, 73, VI, p. 37; *L. & C. Hist.*, pp. 42, 1207, 1258; *Gass* [*A*], p. 21, [*B*], p. 21.

36 This stream, known today as Nodaway River, was the "Nadawa," "Nordaway," "Nodaway," "Nadiway" of Lewis and Clark, the "Nan doughe" of Whitehouse, the "Nodowa" of Brackenridge, the "Nadowa" of Gass, the "Nadawa" of Floyd, the "Madavvay" of Perrin du Lac, and the "Naduet" of Bradbury. For additional variant spellings see *L. & C. Hist.*, p. 41. The

month of the Nodaway, reckoned by Lewis and Clark to be 150 miles below the mouth of the Platte, was the site of the winter's camp of Hunt's westbound Astorians. *L. & C. Journs.*, I, pp. 70, 71, 78, 92, 93, 101, V, p. 382, VI, pp. 4, 57, VII, pp. 16, 41, 189, 190; *L. & C. Hist.*, pp. 41, 1258; *Gass* [*A*], p. 21, [*B*], p. 21; *Brackenridge*, pp. 222, 223; *Bradbury* [*A*], p. 44; *Perrin du Lac*, map; *Astoria*, I, pp. 146 *et seq.*

37 Camped at approximately the lower and westernmost end of the extensive and S-shaped river bend in the immediate vicinity of site of present-day city of St. Joseph, Mo. Thus Stuart's 20 miles of travel from his camp of April 21st had been largely consumed by his following the river's sinuosities.

38 In lieu of this sentence trav. mem. states: "I sent out two hunters, who soon returned with two Deer and 4 Turkeys."

39 A wintering place of either fur traders or much less probably indians. It was approximately at or across the Missouri from the site of present-day city of Leavenworth, Kansas.

40 April 24th.

41 Located on what Lewis and Clark termed Fort Point, it was six miles below the mouth of present-day Little Blue River and stood near the site of what is now the town of Sibley, Mo. (*Chittenden*, pp. 12, 948; *L. & C. Journs.*, I, p. 56; *L. & C. Hist.*, pp. 30, 1257; *Bradbury* [*A*], pp. 35-37). For description and history of the fort, see Stella M. Drumm's note in *Luttig*, pp. 33, 34.

42 Eli B. Clemson (erroneously "Climson" in trav. mem.), who, born in Pennsylvania, was appointed, March 3, 1799, Second Lieutenant in First Regiment of Infantry; First Lieutenant, April 30, 1800; Captain, March 4, 1807; Major, January 20, 1813; Lieutenant-Colonel of Sixteenth Regiment of Infantry, March 9, 1814; honorably discharged, June 15, 1815 (*Heitman*, I, p. 309). For his biography, see Stella M. Drumm's note in *Luttig*, pp. 145, 146.

43 Governmental trading post. See *Chittenden*, p. 12.

44 "village" in trav. mem.

45 Called today by this same name, it flowed from the southwest into the Missouri a little below the site of present-day Jefferson City, Mo. *Chittenden*, p. 722.

46 April 24th.

47 Now known as Platte or Little Platte River, it was called by the fur traders "Petite Riviere Platte." It emptied through the Missouri's left bank and its mouth was, in Lewis and Clark's day, 251 miles below that of the Platte. *L. & C. Journs.*, I, p. 62, VI, p. 57, VII, p. 14; *L. & C. Hist.*, pp. 35, 1258.

48 Now known interchangeably as Blue River and Big Blue River. Its mouth on the Missouri's right bank was, according to Lewis and Clark's reckoning, 269 miles below the mouth of the Platte. *L. & C. Journs.*, I, pp. 58, 59, VI, pp. 35, 57; *L. & C. Hist.*, p. 1257.

49 Present-day Little Blue River, emptying through the Missouri's right bank at a spot which was, according to the reckoning of Lewis and Clark,

288 miles below the mouth of the Platte. It was the "Hay Cabbin Creek" of Lewis and Clark (so named "from Camps of Straw built on it"), the "Hay Creek" of Floyd, the "Straw Hill River" of Whitehouse. *L. & C. Journs.*, I, p. 57, VI, pp. 35, 57, VII, pp. 13, 38; *L. & C. Hist.*, pp. 31, 1209, 1257.

50 This stream of erstwhile numerous variations in spelling—sometimes termed the Kaw, called "Cansas" by Luttig, but now known as Kansas River —emptied through the Missouri's right bank. Its mouth Lewis and Clark reckoned to be 260 miles below the mouth of the Platte. *Luttig*, p. 36; *L. & C. Journs.*, VI, pp. 4, 35, 39, 57; *L. & C. Hist.*, pp. 33, 516, 517.

51 "from the others" in trav. mem.

52 Present-day Republican River, named for the Republican Pawnees, for whom see p. 351.

53 John Brownson, who, born in Vermont, was appointed, June 29, 1804, Ensign in First Regiment of United States Infantry; Second Lieutenant, January 31, 1807; First Lieutenant, December 8, 1808; Captain, January 31, 1814; and was honorably discharged, June 15, 1815. *Heitman*, I, p. 255.

54 Camped at approximately the site of Lewis and Clark's "antient village of the Missouri Nation," which lay four miles below the mouth of present-day Grand River and thus, according to Lewis and Clark's reckoning, 364 miles below the mouth of the Platte. *L. & C. Journs.*, I, pp. 49, 50, VI, pp. 34, 57; *L. & C. Hist.*, pp. 22-24, 1257.

55 This stream, now known as Sniabar Creek, emptied through the Missouri's right bank at a spot computed by Lewis and Clark to be 312 miles below the mouth of the Platte. Coues, on p. 29 of his *L. & C. Hist.*, traces as follows the alphabetic struggles of the stream's name: Called by Gass "Du Beau or Du Bois;" by Lewis interchangeably "Bau-beaux," "Eubert" and "Euebaux;" by Pike "Eabeace"; by Clark "Eue-bert"; by Biddle "Hubert"; and by Brackenridge "Ibars": it seems to have appeared on some maps as the "Chenal aux Herberts"—*chenal* being the French word for "slough," and the "Herberts" representing presumably the name of some early voyageur. The "Chenal aux Herberts" presently was perverted into "Chneij au Barre" as used by Long and into the more common form of "Chenia aux Barre," and thereafter assumed the present-day style of "Sniabar" or, as frequently spelled, "Snibar." *Long*, p. 102; *Gass* [*A*], p. 18, [*B*], p. 18; *L. & C. Hist.*, pp. 29, 1257; *L. & C. Journs.*, I, p. 54, VI, pp. 35, 57, VII, p. 12.

56 This stream, today interchangeably known as Fire-prairie Creek or Fire Creek, was the "Riviere du Feu" of Perrin du Lac, the "fire Prairie Creek" of Luttig. It flowed through an area which Luttig termed "Prairie du foe." The names of creek and area were derived from the fact that some indians were burned to death by a sudden blazing of dry grass in the meadows at the creek's source. The creek emptied through the right bank of the Missouri at a spot which, according to Lewis and Clark's reckoning, was exactly midway between the mouths of the Platte and Missouri Rivers—300 miles from each of

them. *Perrin du Lac*, map; *Luttig*, p. 33; *Gass* [*A*], p. 18, [*B*], p. 18; *L. & C. Hist.*, pp. 30, 1257; *L. & C. Journs.*, I, p. 55, VI, p. 57, VII, p. 12; *Long*, p. 102.

57 This stream, the "tabor Creek" of Floyd, the "Tabo" or "Tabbo Creek" of Gass and of Lewis and Clark, the "Tabeau Creek" of Long, and now known as Tabo Creek, was named for one Tabeau, a voyageur. It emptied through the Missouri's right bank at a spot which Lewis and Clark figured as 271½ miles above the mouth of the Missouri. *Gass* [*A*], p. 18, [*B*], p. 18; *L. & C. Journs.*, I, pp. 52-57, VII, pp. 12, 36; *L. & C. Hist.*, pp. 27, 28; *Long*, p. 102.

58 This village, according to Lewis and Clark's reckoning, was 256 miles above the mouth of the Missouri. *L. & C. Hist.*, p. 1257; *L. & C. Journs.*, I, p. 49.

59 "tribe" in trav. mem.

60 Present-day Chariton River. It was the "Sharriton Carta" [*i.e.*, *Charretins écartés*] of Lewis and Clark, the "Charlotte" of Gass, the "Grand Charleton" of Perrin du Lac. Flowing southerly, it emptied through the left bank of the Missouri at a spot which, in the southerly tip of present-day Chariton County, Mo., was, according to Lewis and Clark's reckoning, 220 miles above the Missouri's mouth (*L. & C. Hist.*, pp. 19, 516, 1257; *L. & C. Journs.*, I, p. 57, VII, p. 13; *Perrin du Lac*, map; *Gass* [*A*], p. 16, [*B*], p. 16). For numerous early variant spellings of the river's name and particularly for Coues's query as to whether it might not have originally been Charlatan in verbal pairing with the neighboring Gasconade River, see *L. & C. Hist.*, p. 19.

61 This river, known at the present day by this same designation, was, so Lewis and Clark stated, named for lead mines in its vicinity. It was the "Riviere a la Mine" of Renaudiere in 1723 and of Perrin du Lac in 1805, the "Mine River" of Gass and of Lewis and Clark, though D'Anville in 1752 termed it "Riviere au Vermilion." Flowing northeasterly, it emptied through the right bank of the Missouri at a spot which, a few miles west from the site of present-day town of Boonville, Cooper County, Mo., was estimated by Lewis and Clark to be 200 miles above the Missouri's mouth. As clearly appears from Stuart's entry for April 28th, his camp on the night of April 27th was between the mouth of Lamine River and the mouth of Bonne Femme Creek. *Gass* [*A*], p. 16, [*B*], p. 16; *L. & C. Hist.*, pp. 17, 18, 1257; *L. & C. Journs.*, I, p. 43, VI, pp. 34, 57; *Perrin du Lac*, map.

62 Actually about 43 miles. See note 61.

63 Present-day Bonne Femme Creek, emptying through the Missouri's left bank. It was the "Good-woman's River" of Lewis and Clark, the "Riviere Bonne femme" of Perrin du Lac, and the "Big Good Woman's creek" of Gass. Its mouth, at which Lewis and Clark camped on June 7, 1804, was reckoned by them to be 191 miles above the mouth of the Missouri. *L. & C. Hist.*, pp. 17, 1257; *L. & C. Journs.*, VI, p. 33, VII, p. 34; *Perrin du Lac*, map; *Gass* [*A*], p. 16, [*B*], p. 16.

64 Present-day Little Bonne Femme Creek, emptying through the left

bank of the Missouri near site of the present-day town of Wilton, Boone County, Mo. Its mouth, according to Lewis and Clark's reckoning, was 155 miles above the mouth of the Missouri. *L. & C. Hist.*, p. 15; *L. & C. Journs.*, I, p. 40, VI, pp. 32, 33, VII, pp. 8, 34.

65 This stream, present-day Moniteau Creek, was the "Manitou River" of Lewis, the "Grand Manitou" of Clark, the "Riviere grand Manithou" of Perrin du Lac, the "Manitoo of Brackenridge, the "Big Manito creek" of Long, and "the river of the Big Devil" of Floyd and of Gass. It emptied through the left bank of the Missouri at a spot which, in the southeasterly corner of present-day Howard County, Mo., was, according to the reckoning of Lewis and Clark, 182 miles above the mouth of the Missouri. *Gass* [*A*], p. 16, [*B*], p. 16; *Long*, p. 88; *L. & C. Hist.*, pp. 17, 1257; *L. & C. Journs.*, I, pp. 42, 43, VI, pp. 33, 57, VII, pp. 8, 34; *Perrin du Lac*, map.

66 Present-day Moniteau Creek, emptying through right bank of the Missouri. It was the "Little Manitou Creek" of Lewis and Clark, the "Riviere au Diable" of D'Anville, the "Petit Manitou" of Perrin du Lac, the "Maniteau" of Nicollet, the "Manitoo" of Brackenridge. According to Lewis and Clark's reckoning, its mouth was 162 miles above that of the Missouri. *L. & C. Journs.*, I, p. 40; *L. & C. Hist.*, pp. 15, 1257; *Perrin du Lac*, map.

67 This stream, present-day Louris Creek, the "Bear Creek" of Long and of Gass, the "R. à l'ours" of Perrin du Lac, emptied through the Missouri's right bank. According to Lewis and Clark's reckoning, its mouth was three miles below that of the Osage River and 130 miles above the mouth of the Missouri. *L. & C. Hist.*, p. 11; *L. & C. Journs.*, I, p. 37, VII, p. 7; *Gass* [*A*], p. 15, [*B*], p. 15; *Perrin du Lac*, map.

Stuart's camp on the night of April 28 was, from his text, patently between the mouths of Louris Creek and of the Little Auxvasse mentioned in note 73.

68 This stream, the "Split rock Creek" of Lewis and Clark, was stated by them to have been thus named because of an adjacent "projecting rock with a hole thro: a point of the rock." It was earlier termed "Roche Pierce" (*alias* "Percee" and "a Pierce") and is now known as Roche Perche Creek. Its mouth, which was on the Missouri's left bank, was reckoned by Lewis and Clark to be 170 miles above the mouth of the Missouri and was adjacent to the site of present-day town of Providence, Boone County, Mo. *L. & C. Hist.*, pp. 16, 1257; *L. & C. Journs.*, I, pp. 41, 42, VI, pp. 33, 57; *Long*, p. 87; *Brackenridge*, pp. 210, 265.

69 Present-day Moreau Creek. It was the "Murow [*alias* "Murrow"] Creek" of Lewis and Clark, the "Marrow Creek" of Brackenridge and of Gass, the "Moreau's Creek" of Long, the "Riviere a Morou" of Perrin du Lac. Its mouth, which was on the Missouri's right bank at a spot a short distance east of site of present-day Jefferson City, Mo., was reckoned by Lewis and Clark to be 138 miles above the mouth of the Missouri. Coues suggests that *Moreau* as applied to the stream might mean either "nose-bag" or "black horse."

L. & C. Hist., pp. 14, 1257; *L. & C. Journs.*, I, p. 38, VI, pp. 32, 33, 56; *Brackenridge*, p. 265; *Gass* [*A*], p. 15, [*B*], p. 15; *Long*, p. 86; *Perrin du Lac*, map.

70 Present-day Cedar Creek, the "Riviere de Cedre" of Perrin du Lac, the "Cedar Creek" of Brackenridge, the "Cedar [*alias* "Seeder"] Creek" of Lewis and Clark. It emptied through the left bank of the Missouri at a spot which, in present-day Callaway County, Mo., was computed by Lewis and Clark to be 145 miles above the mouth of the Missouri. *L. & C. Hist.*, pp. 14, 1257; *L. & C. Journs.*, I, p. 39, VI, pp. 31, 32, 57; *Brackenridge*, p. 265; *Perrin du Lac*, map.

71 Present-day Osage River, the "Rivière des grands Os, ou Osages" of Perrin du Lac, the "Osarge," "Osarges," "Osage," "Osages" and "Grand Osage" of Lewis and Clark. It forms the present-day boundary line between Cole and Osage Counties, Mo. Its mouth, which was on the Missouri's right bank, was, according to Lewis and Clark's reckoning, 133 miles above the mouth of the Missouri. *Perrin du Lac*, p. 198 and map; *L. & C. Journs.*, I, pp. 37, 38, 49, 137, V, p. 389, VI, pp. 3, 31, 32, 56, VII, pp. 7, 33, 189, 190; *L. & C. Hist.*, pp. 10-12, 1257; *Long*, p. 85.

72 This spot at which seemingly Stuart camped on the night of April 29th was, in his time, more commonly known as the Tavern or the Tavern Rock (*alias* Rocks): so named, as Brackenridge asserts, "from the circumstances of a cave in one of them affording a stopping place for voyageurs . . ." The cave, a large one, was decorated with indian pictographs. The "rock" was part of the precipitous bluff which, between 200 and 300 feet high, rose from the Missouri's right bank in the extreme northeasterly corner of present-day Franklin County, Mo., and, according to Lewis and Clark's reckoning, was 47 miles above the mouth of the Missouri. *L. & C. Journs.*, I, p. 27, VI, p. 56, VII, pp. 5, 31; *L. & C. Hist.*, pp. 7, 8; *Brackenridge*, p. 203; *Bradbury* [*A*], p. 14; *Gass* [*A*], p. 13, [*B*], p. 13.

73 Present-day Auxvasse Creek and Little Auxvasse Creek, each emptying through the Missouri's left bank in present-day Callaway County, Mo. Auxvasse Creek was the "R. a la Vase" of Perrin du Lac, the "Au Vase" of Long, the "Big Miry" and "Big Muddy" of Lewis and Clark; while the Little Auxvasse was the "R. petite Vase" of Perrin du Lac, the "Little Mirey" and "Little Muddy" of Lewis and Clark. The mouths of these streams, according to Lewis and Clark's reckoning, were respectively distant as follows from the mouth of the Missouri: Little Auxvasse, 118 miles; Auxvasse, 115 miles. *L. & C. Journs.*, I, pp. 36, 37, VI, pp. 7, 33; *L. & C. Hist.*, pp. 10, 1257; *Gass* [*A*], p. 15, [*B*], p. 15; *Perrin du Lac*, map; *Long*, p. 80.

74 Present-day Loutre River. It was the "Loutre Creek" of Long, the "R. a la Loutre" of Perrin du Lac, the "Otter Creek" of Patrick Gass and of Lewis and Clark, and emptied through the Missouri's left bank in present-day Montgomery County, Mo. *L. & C. Hist.*, p. 9; *Long*, pp. 76, 79; *Gass* [*A*], p. 14, [*B*], p. 14; *Perrin du Lac*, map; *L. & C. Journs.*, I, p. 34, VII, pp. 6, 32.

75 Present-day Charette Creek. It was the "Chaurette Creek" and "River a Chouritte" of Lewis and Clark, the "R. Charrette" of Perrin du Lac, the "Charette" of Brackenridge and of Bradbury, and emptied through the left bank of the Missouri in present-day Warren County, Mo. Its mouth, according to the reckoning of Lewis and Clark, was 68 miles above the mouth of the Missouri. In the neighboring village of La Charette died the famous Daniel Boone. *L. & C. Journs.*, I, p. 28, VI, pp. 30, 56; *Perrin du Lac*, map; *Brackenridge*, p. 205; *Bradbury* [*A*], p. 16; *L. & C. Hist.*, pp. 8, 1257.

76 Present-day Berger Creek, emptying through the Missouri's right bank in the northwest corner of Franklin County, Mo. It was the "Shepperds [*alias* "Shepherds"] Creek" of Lewis and Clark, the "Burgois Creek" of Luttig in 1812. Coues, in *Pike* [*B*] at p. 365, states that he had been informed that *Berger*, instead of being a French word meaning "shepherd," was a personal name, probably that of a German pioneer, Caspar Burger, the founder of a colony in the vicinity. This stream's mouth, according to Lewis and Clark's reckoning, was 83 miles above the mouth of the Missouri. *L. & C. Hist.*, pp. 9, 1257; *L. & C. Journs.*, I, p. 29, VI, p. 56; *Brackenridge*, p. 265; *Luttig*, p. 29.

77 This, present-day St. Johns Creek, the "Riviere du Bois" of Perrin du Lac, the "Wood River" of Patrick Gass and of Lewis and Clark, emptied through the Missouri's right bank in present-day Franklin County, Mo. Its mouth, according to Lewis and Clark's reckoning, was 59 miles above the mouth of the Missouri. *L. & C. Hist.*, p. 8; *L. & C. Journs.*, I, pp. 28, 29, VII, p. 5; *Gass* [*A*], p. 13; [*B*], p. 13; *Perrin du Lac*, map.

78 This stream, known today as Gasconade River, though at times spelled Gaskenade, was the "Gasconade," "Gasconnade," "Gasnage" of Lewis and Clark, the "Gasganade" of Floyd and of Whitehouse, the "Gaskenade" of Gass, the "Gasconade" of Brackenridge, Bradbury, Long and Perrin du Lac. Meriwether Lewis stated that "at its entrance it is 157 yards wide, but is much narrower a little distance up, and is not navigable [hence the name gasconade]." Emptying through the right bank of the Missouri River in present-day Gasconade County, Mo., its mouth was, according to the reckoning of Lewis and Clark, 100 miles above the mouth of the Missouri. *L. & C. Journs.*, I, pp. 34, 35, VI, pp. 3, 30, 56, VII, pp. 6, 32, 189, 190; *L. & C. Hist.*, pp. 9, 1257; *Gass* [*A*], p. 14, [*B*], p. 14; *Bradbury* [*A*], p. 21; *Long*, p. 79; *Brackenridge*, p. 207; *Perrin du Lac*, map.

79 Actually 53 miles. See note 72.

80 For the remainder of this sentence trav. mem. substitutes "we underwent many dangers, hardships, & fatigues, in short I may say, all the privations human nature is capable of."

81 *Platanus occidentalis.*

82 *Fraxinus americana.*

83 *Celtis occidentalis.*

84 *Juglans cinerea* and *J. nigra.*

85 *Carya alba.*

86 See note 63 on pp. 202, 203 for identity of this tree.

87 *Morus rubra.*

88 *Ulmus americana.*

89 See *L. & C. Journs.*, VI, p. 140.

90 *Cornus sericea.*

91 The papaw *alias* pawpaw, *Asimina triloba.*

92 *Lynx rufus.*

93 First in importance—this, because of its quantity—was the catfish family, *Nematognathi*, in three varieties: *i.e.*, "blue cat," *Ictulurus furcatus;* "channel cat," *I. punctatus;* and the one known interchangeably as "bullhead" or "horned-pout," *Ameiurus nebulosus.*

Among other fish were the bass in three varieties, *Pomoxis sparoides*, *Micropterus salmoides*, and *M. dolomieu;* the white sucker, *Catostomus commersoni;* the pike, *Esox lucius;* the red-horse, *Moxostoma aureolum;* the buffalo-fish, *Ictiobus cyprinella;* and the paddle-fish, *Polyodon spathula.*

94 "250" in trav. mem.

95 "40" in trav. mem.

96 See note 118 on p. 230 for site of this village.

97 "200" in trav. mem.

98 "from 20 to 30" in trav. mem.

99 "1500" in trav. mem.

100 "precious skins" in journ.; "Beaver" in trav. mem.

101 Sawyers bobbed in the current at the river's surface, while planters were immobile. Sawyers were the more dreaded inasmuch as one of them might emerge suddenly from temporary concealment and, rising under a boat, upset it. *Bradbury* [*A*], pp. 194, 195; *Chittenden Steamboat*, pp. 80, 81.

102 That this figure should have been 3704¾ appears from the following table:

Stuart's Stated Mileages

	Acc. to journ.	*Acc. to trav. mem.*[a]
By canoe from Astoria to mouth of the Walla Walla.	370	381[b]
On horseback from mouth of the Walla Walla to Bear River camp of Sept. 12, where Absarokas were first encountered.	909	952

[a]The figures in this column are taken from the left-hand margin of trav. mem. In this margin Stuart attempted to insert (1) opposite each day's entry the mileage for that particular day, and (2) at both the top and bottom of each page the total mileage since leaving Astoria.

[b]Excludes excess of three miles in trav. mem.'s marginal figure "6" in entry for July 7.

[c]Excludes excess of two miles in trav. mem.'s marginal figure "18" in entry for August 3; and also (1) includes 36 miles omitted from margin in trav. mem.'s entry for August 19 and (2) allows for deficiency of two miles in trav. mem.'s marginal figure "26" in entry for September 8.

On horseback from Bear River camp to mouth of Greys River.	125½	125½
On horseback from mouth of Greys River to where, at McCoy Creek's confluence with south fork of the Snake, horses were stolen by Absarokas.	14½	14½
On foot from McCoy Creek's mouth to where rafts were built.	18	18
By raft down south fork of the Snake to opposite site of Heise, Ida.	80¼	91
On foot from site of Heise, Ida., to near mouth of Hoback River.	140	140
On foot from near mouth of the Hoback to Pacific Springs.	208	227
On foot from Pacific Springs to second winter quarters—including the 12 miles of reconnoitring east of site of first winter quarters and also the 140 miles of reconnoitring east of site of second winter quarters.	601½	676½[d]
By canoe for some of the party and on foot for others from second winter quarters to site of bridge at Morrill, Neb.	15	15[e]
On foot from site of Morrill Bridge to Oto village.	573	669[f]
By canoe from Oto village to mouth of Platte.	45	45
By canoe from mouth of Platte to St. Louis.	605[h]	610[g]
	3704¾	3964½

[d]Excludes excess of seven miles in trav. mem.'s marginal figure "29" in entry for December 26: and also includes (1) 15 miles omitted from margin in trav. mem.'s entry for October 21; (2) one-half mile omitted in trav. mem.'s marginal addition in entry for October 23; (3) six miles representing retracement of course on November 2 and omitted from margin in trav. mem.'s entry for that date; (4) 19 miles omitted from margin in trav. mem.'s entry for December 19; (5) aggregate of 49 miles omitted from margin in trav. mem's entries for December 27 and 28; (6) three miles omitted from margin in trav. mem.'s entry for December 29; (7) 12 miles omitted from margin in trav. mem.'s entry for December 30; (8) nine miles representing distance from camp of December 28 to mouth of Horse Creek and neither specified in trav. mem.'s text nor entered on margin in trav. mem.'s entry for December 29.

[e]Omitted from margin in trav. mem.'s entries for March 8-15.

[f](1) Includes 55 miles omitted from margin in trav. mem.'s entries for March 20 and 21; (2) allows for one mile omitted in trav. mem.'s marginal addition in entry for March 29.

[g]Excludes excess of 32 miles in trav. mem.'s marginal figure in entry for April 27 (see note 62); and also includes 18 miles omitted from margin in trav. mem.'s entry for April 30 (see note 79).

[h]The journ., in connection with descent of Missouri River, gives the successive mileages no further than mouth of Platte to "antient village of Missouri nation," an aggregate of 363 miles. Because the journ.'s figures for these particular mileages exceed by only one mile the corresponding figures of Lewis and Clark (*L. & C. Hist.*, pp.1257, 1258), the present editor has, for the distance from that "antient village" to St. Louis, used Lewis and Clark's figure, 242.

However, all this statement as to distances is of merely academic interest in view of note 28 on pp. CXIX-CXXIII.

CHAPTER XI

Postscripts to Various Entries in Journal

Astoria · Various Kinds of Fish · Indian Tribes · Some of Journal's Statements Rephrased and Supplemented · Summary of Portion of Journey.

[*Editor's Note.*—These postscripts possibly should be regarded as primarily representing, not addenda to the journal's original entries, but instead a preliminary phrasing of part of the travelling memoranda, into which most of these postscripts in more or less modified form were ultimately incorporated.]

[119] it[1] would be in vain to attempt a description of our Establishment in its present unfinished state— suffice it therefore to say that it is Commanding & Commodiously situated on the S.E. extremity of Pt George, having the very desirable advantage of an excellent harbour within 50 yards of shore for vessels not exceeding 200 Tons

I will therefore content myself by noticing that in place of 120 square yd which is the projected extent of our fortification we have only a square of about 75 feet which is well stockaded with pickets 17 feet long and 18 inches diameter, with two strong Bastions at opposite Angles, so as to rake two sides each of the Fortification

[120] Altho'[2] Their sole dependence for sustenance is upon Fish, Roots[3] & what few animals they Can Kill— few Salmon[4] are Caught before the latter end of May but from that to the middle of August they can be got in great plenty, & are by far the finest fish I ever beheld— they are mostly caught in shallow water by

long Seines, made of Nettles[5] from Augᵗ till Decʳ is the Season for Dogtooth Salmon,[4] a very inferior Species of that Fish, & so named by us in consequence of their having a double row of teeth at least ½ Inch long & exceedingly Sharp— they are generally Killed with the spear in small Rivulets—smoked—laid by for the [*dreary*] months of Jany. & Feby.— Feby, Commences the Sturgeon fishery—when Sturgeon[6] & Uthlechan[7] may be taken in great numbers, the former sometimes by the spear,[8] but more generally by hook & line, and the latter by the Scoop Net— the Uthlechan is about Six inches long & somewhat similar to our Smelt, is a very delicious little fish & so fat that they burn as bright as[9] a candle & are often used for that same purpose by the Natives

[121] Their[10] general mode of hunting is with the Bow and arrow, very few possessing, or knowing the use of fire arms— They frequently go in large parties— surround the game while grazing in a favorable place, such as a small prairie or meadow environed by wood, they plant themselves in the different avenues or paths leading to this spot, then set in their dogs, which throws the poor creatures in such confusion as to scatter in every direction, thereby giving the most or all a considerable chance of exercising their skill for let the Consternation of these animals be ever so great they Can only escape by those leading paths— Some of the best warriors shoot [122] an arrow with such force as to send it thro' an Elk or Buffalo at the distance of 12 or 15 paces & they seldom shoot at any thing farther than 30 yards[11]

This[12] method of stealing horses is deserving of being more minutely described, One of the party rode past our camp & placed himself on a conspicuous knob, in the direction they wanted to run off the Horses— when the others (who were then hidden behind our Camp) seeing him prepared— rose the war hoop or yell, (which is the most horribly discordant howling imaginable being in imitation of the different beasts of prey) at this diabolical noise the animals naturally rose their heads to see what the matter was— at that instant he who had planted himself in advance, put spurs to his horse & ours seeing him gallop off in apparent fright started all in his track as if [123] a host of the infernals were in pursuit of them in this manner a Dozin or two of those fellows have sometimes succeeded in running off every Horse belonging to war parties of perhaps 5 or 600 men— for once those creatures take a fright nothing short of broken necks can stop their progrefs—

resolved[13] to prevent the villains benefitting more by us for some of the same band were (by Jones) seen this morning sculking near our Camp in order no doubt to observe where we should deposit what part of our effects we could not carry

[*Editor's Note.*—Stuart's next entry beginning on this p. [123] and continuing to the end of the third paragraph on p. [125] has, in its entirety, been shifted by us to pp. 155–157.]

They[14] informed us that the Crows had fallen in with two of our hunters, and robbed them of every thing, which the poor fellows resented and killed 5 of them, but were at last overpowered and mafsacred— They also told us that two of those left by Mr. Crooks last winter had early in the Spring accompanied one of their bands to hunt on the head waters of the Mifsouri, where they as well as many of their people were killed by the Blackfeet— We have little doubt but it was those two unfortunate wretches who conducted the Indians to the Caches on the Snake River— Last Summer The Arapahays fell in with Champlain & 3 men he had hunting Beaver some distance [126] down the Spanish river, murdered them at night and took possefsion of all their effects—

When we informed them that the day was not far off when we should take signal vengeance on the perpetrators of these deeds they appeared quite elated and offered their Services in the execution, which were of course accepted, and a long smoke out of the Calumet of peace ended the conference—

[127] I[15] was the only person in Company who carried a shirt

except that on their back, therefore, it may be supposed, it was soon destroyed by wearing and the repeated washings it required, but delicacy forbids a disertation on the subject— it would have been truly ludicerous to have witnefsed one of our washing parties— The prime object was to make a very strong lye or ley of wood ashes of which we had a great abundance, into which the Flannel was plunged and concocted for a couple of hours, under and arden wish of putting an end to certain vagrants of a particular genera with which most of Indian voyagers are well acquainted— during the boiling the votaries of cleanlinefs cloaked in a blanket or Buffalo robe, watched the ebullitions of the kettle; this operation over the shirts were borne to the house where each washed his own, and walked about untill it dried, almost in a state of nature—

No[16] conception can hardly be formed of the force habit has on the human race— one who uses Tobacco is as little able to abstain from that enjoyment as I would be, if compelled to refrain from my usual meals

[128] (Contrary[17] to our first determination) and in days arrived at the Plains below Henrys Fort a distance of miles— the banks are well timbered & stocked with Beaver Elk & Bear— here we were obliged to leave the River & steering an East S.E. Course got on the head branches of the Spanish river which is miles from Mad River & that over the most rugged & barren Country I ever beheld— in short we have in this tract Suffered every hardship & privation I believe human nature Capable of— here we intended to pass the dead of winter, should game be plenty, but to our astonishment there was not a single Buffalo in the whole of that Country; our sensation on the occasion may easily be conceived. thus situated at such a season, & knowing ourselves to be 17 or 18.000 miles from the nearest Settlement. however this was not time for indesision & delay— we therefore made the best of our way for a gape[18] [129] disernable in the mountains in a S.E. direction, and after a hard tramp of

miles in days, got on the east side of all the Rocky Mountains, which on either Side of us were stupendiously high— but we passed thro a handsome low gap—[19] and on 1st November[20] put into winter quarters, about 106 miles down the R. Platte, which takes its rise in the big horn Mountain[21] & adjacent Plains— here we found plenty of Buffalo, Beaver, Bear Elk, Deer & Ibex and Antelope— and Considered ourselves perfectly secure of having no farther trouble from Indians, but on 12th Decr.[22] a War party of Arapahays, in going against the Crows, happened to discover our retreat & altho' we got them off at that time without proceeding to extremities, we were apprehensive of their return, & that probably with a reinforcement— we therefore Concluded to decamp & altho the snow was deep, travelled miles down the River, where we [130] found an eligible situation & on 3d Jany.[23] 1813 found ourselves once more in a snug hut, where we remained in peace & plenty untill 7th March[24] during our stay here we made two Canoes expecting to get down by water in the Spring freshes but to our great mortification the river did not rise more than 3 inches— & that oozing thro' the sand, in such a manner as at places to show 2 feet water while at others the bed was entirely dry— this want of rise in the water was probably owing to the very mild winter we have experienced— from the Source of the river to this place the Country is a perfect plain (the soil sandy, but producting tolerable grass) Covered with Buffalo & wild horses, one of which we Caught & tamed— finding that it was absolutely impossible to get along by water—we prepared our horse & started at an early hour— having travelled untill late in the evg. we encamped near

[*Editor's Note.*—Stuart's next two entries occupying the whole of his p. [131] have in their entirety been shifted by us to pp. 158, 159.]

[132] but[25] either they were chopped in this manner

Notes to Chapter XI

1 This and the next paragraph, with inconsequential changes, Stuart incorporated in trav. mem.'s entry for June 29 (pp. 3, 4).

2 This paragraph, with minor changes, Stuart incorporated in trav. mem.'s entry for June 29 (pp. 7, 8).

3 See note 43 on p. 20 for edible roots.

4 See note 44 on pp. 20, 21 for varieties of salmon.

5 According to *Henry-Thomp.*, p. 753, "Salmon are taken in seines about 50 feet long, made with twine of domestic manufacture; the materials used are nettles procured from the natives above."

6 See note 100 on p. 25 for description of sturgeon.

7 See note 104 on p. 25 for description of candlefish.

8 For sturgeon the natives used also a dragnet in the form of a bag with a small bunch of feathers tied to its lower end. *Henry-Thomp.*, p. 754.

9 "burn like a candle" in trav. mem., p. 8.

10 This entire paragraph in slightly modified form Stuart incorporated in trav. mem.'s entry for June 29 (p. 14). *Astoria*, II, p. 64, allocates it, with elaboration of details, to the so-called Sciatogas, *i.e.*, to the Cayuses or to the Umatillas.

11 Immediately after this paragraph Stuart wrote and subsequently deleted two additional paragraphs reading as follows:

> "after regaling our new found friends who were almost famished with the best our small stock luxuries could afford, we proceeded on for about 3 miles, to a good fishing and grazing place where we took up our abode for the night."
>
> "The unknown Indians they became acquainted with during their perambulations in that quarter are a southern band of the Snakes, the Arapahays about 300 strong, the Arapahoes 2,500 and the black arms a very numerous nation, who inhabit that whole tract of Country from thence to the neighbourhood of the Spaniards, they are very friendly to whites and poſsess a great many furs—".

These paragraphs in slightly modified form (see notes 185-188 on pp. 105, 106) were incorporated by Stuart in his trav. mem.'s entry for August 20 (pp. 86, 87).

12 This paragraph, with minor changes, Stuart incorporated in trav. mem.'s entry for September 19 (pp. 134, 135).

13 This paragraph, with minor changes, Stuart incorporated in trav. mem.'s entry for September 20 (pp. 135, 136).

14 This and the next paragraph, with minor changes (see notes 122-126 on pp. 178-180), Stuart incorporated in trav. mem.'s entry for October 18 (p. 161).

15 This paragraph correlates with either entry for December 10 (pp. 191, 192) or entry for January 1 (p. 207).

16 This paragraph correlates with entry for January 1 (p. 207).

17 This entry ending with "late in the evg. we encamped near" represents an uncompleted and not wholly accurate attempt to summarise the narratives' prior account of that section of the trip which commenced west of Henry's Fort (p. 132) and ended at the leaving of the so-called second winter quarters (p. 209).

18 The later context and the earlier entries in the narratives indisputably show this "gape" to have been South Pass.

19 South Pass, for description of which see note 148 on pp. 181, 182.

20 This date should have been 8th-10th November. See entries for these latter dates on p. 191.

21 A geographical error based doubtless on hearsay. North and South Plattes both rise in Colorado.

22 See note 47 on p. 202 for error in the date, which should have read December 10.

23 See note 3 on p. 223 for probable error of one day in the date.

24 See note 5 on p. 223 for seeming error of one day in the date.

25 This fragmentary entry correlates with the narratives' entry for March 29 (p. 213).

CHAPTER XII

MAY 16 · MAY 24, 1813

On Horseback from St. Louis Across Illinois to Green River in Kentucky

[SEE MAP FACING PAGE 235]

Cahokia · Prairie du Rocher · Kaskaskia · Shawneetown and Its Inhabitants · Green River

[133] 1 Delegate to Congress[1]

Left St. Louis[2] on Sunday 16th May slept at Cahokia[3] a wretched village of about 50 dwellings principally French— 4 miles M 17th Started early and travelled through a very rich but Swampy Country, arrived at Prairie du Rocher[4] in the evening where we stopped for the night 45 Miles— this as well as Cahokia is in the Illonois[5] Territory, have no School, or any publick buildings offices &c Send one delegate[6] to Congress— the Village about 70 dwellings— French T 18th Got to Kaskaskia[7] early in the forenoon where we remained all day in order to get our Horses

Shod— this is 15 Miles from P. du Rocher and about equals it in insignificance— W 19th Started at dawn in Company with the Courier Slept at Coxes[8] 42 Miles Country very thinly inhabited altho' pleasantly Situated and rich Soil— Thursday 20th Slept at Jordan's Station[9] a distance of 43 Miles, here a Man was killed & another wounded a few days ago by the Indians, those in the Fort 12 in number allowed him to be Scalped within 100 yds of the Block House— the Indians make their descents frequently on the Frontiers in this vicinity which has occasioned the desertion of the [134] whole tract between here & Coxes— big Muddy[10] is about 80 yds Wide & frequently overflows its banks in such a manner as to prevent this road being travelled, here we found an abandoned farm with all the Cattle Poultry, Furniture &c. about the Door, the owner left it 10 days ago altho' furnished with a guard of 6 Rangers— Friday 21st Slept at the Saline[11] a distance of 29 Miles this tract is also abandoned with the exception of one Block house about half way, which is kept for the Safety of the Mail, the Country is very productive & handsomely situated all around the this place they generally make 10,000 Bushels of Salt for meat— Saturday 22d— There fell a good deal of rain last night which has rendered the road very disagreeable travelling got to Shaunian Town[12] about midday this Village is Situate on the West bank of the Ohio a Situation extremely disagreeable & unhealthy on account of the overflowing of the River which Swept off a considerable part of the houses, fences & a great proportion of the Cattle in the Spring— the inhabitants are a set of the most wretched and ragamuffian looking animals I have yet met with— indeed the accomodation all along between here & St Louis is horrible— Crossed the [135] River[13] & Slept at Judge Lethains 6 Miles from the Ohio the greater part of this is a Swamp (to the horse's belly)— Sunday 23d here I remained all day on Account of indisposition being extremely feverish for Several days— Monday 24th went to Green River[14] 35 Miles very muddy & uneaven road miserable fare— green

River is a very muddy Stream about 120 y[ds] wide fertile Country but thinly inhabited

[15]Stage hire to Philadelphia........................	$ 8 —
D° " ...Baltimore..........................	16 —
Expences at Philadelphia..........................	8.13½
Baltimore....................................	9.94
	37½
	42.54
Yours rspecy	13.25
To Washington	$29.25

At D°	2.50	Duncan
......	2.25	
....	1.12½	
	1.—	

Stage hire to Philad

Notes to Chapter XII

1 This entry, "1 Delegate to Congress" (patently a mere preliminary notation) is duplicated in the paragraph immediately following it.

2 Stuart here crossed the Mississippi River.

3 This town, situated near the Mississippi River in present-day St. Clair County, Ill., was originally settled by the Caoquia (*alias* Cahokia or Kahokia) indians (a tribe of the Illinois confederation, see *L. & C. Hist.*, I, p. xxx); was, in the seventeenth century, colonized by the French ex-companions of La Salle; and, still retaining its name Cahokia, exists at the present time. *Long*, I, p. 50; *Flagg*, II, pp. 226-229; *Dana*, p. 150; *Darby*, p. 213; *Brown, Gaz.*, p. 27; *Peck*, pp. 168, 169; *Beck*, pp. 94-96; *Blanchard*, p. 27; *Geol. Illinois.*

4 This town, an early French settlement and existing without change of name to the present time, lay south of Cahokia and near the Mississippi River in present-day Randolph County, Ill. According to *Flagg*, II, p. 179, the town owes its name to its location beneath "the battlement of the cliffs." *Long*, I, p. 50; *Flagg*, pp. 177-182; *Dana*, p. 154; *Brown, Gaz.*, p. 27; *Peck*, p. 276; *Beck*, pp. 149, 150.

5 Stuart wrote originally, and then deleted, the words "Isle aux"; inserting in their stead "Illonois." His first intent seems to have been to use an old-time occasional spelling, *Isle aux nois*, a form misleadingly suggesting French origin for the name. The actual derivation of Illinois was from the self-imposed entitlement of a local confederacy of indians, their *illini*, "a man," being retained; while their plural ending, *uk*, was changed by the French to the Gallic *ois*. See *Century*, XI, p. 525.

6 The single congressional representative whom the federal government, in 1812, authorized from the then Illinois territory. *Blanchard*, p. 119.

7 This town, still bearing the same name and now situated in Randolph County, Ill., was, at the opening of the eighteenth century, moved to its present location from an earlier site on the Illinois River. In Stuart's day this new and present site was inland from the Mississippi River, though it now, because of the river's shifting, is on an island. Originally settled by the Kaskaskia indians [a tribe of the Illinois confederation, see *L. & C. Hist.*, I, p. xxx], it was colonized by the French at the same time as was Cahokia. *Darby*, p. 213; *Brown, Gaz.*, p. 27; *Flagg*, II, pp. 137-143, 150-158; *Long*, I, p. 50; *Peck*, p. 232; *Beck*, pp. 120-122; *Blanchard*, p. 27; *Dana*, p. 154.

8 Seemingly at Cox's Prairie, which was approximately six miles west by north from site of present-day city of Murphysboro, Jackson County, Ill. *Peck*, p. 185; *Blanchard*, accompanying map; *Geol. Illinois.*

9 Frank Jordan Fort, erected in 1810, approximately at the site of present-day town of Locust Grove, Franklin County, Ill. *Blanchard*, accompanying map.

10 Present-day Big Muddy River, a confluent of the Mississippi. It was the "river Au Vau" of Dana, the "Vasseux river" of Darby, the "Auvase Cr." of Pike. *Dana*, p. 149; *Darby*, p. 157; *Pike* [*A*], map entitled "The First Part &c. of Louisiana."

11 United States Saline, locally better known as The Saline. It was situated on present-day Saline River at where is now the easterly boundary line of Saline County, Ill., and was a salt-producing establishment purchased by the federal government in 1803. *Long*, I, p. 33; *Blanchard*, accompanying map; *Holditch*, p. 83; *Beck*, p. 153.

12 Present-day Shawneetown in Gallatin County, Ill. It was originally a Shawnee indian village. *Colton* [*I*], p. 39; *Dana*, p. 155; *Nuttall*, p. 40; *Beck*, pp. 155, 156; *Peck*, pp. 290, 291; *Brown, Gaz.*, pp. 27, 28.

13 Ohio River. By thus crossing it, Stuart entered the state of Kentucky.

14 This river, known today by the same name, flowed northwardly into the Ohio River. It now forms the eastern boundaries of the Kentuckian counties of Webster and Henderson.

15 Concerning Stuart's course from the Green River to New York City, no evidence has been found beyond this memorandum relating to stage hire and to expenses. However, because he had clung to a well-travelled route while going from St. Louis to the Green River (see *Darby*, pp. 157, 158), it is quite possible that he held to the eastward continuation of this route throughout the remainder of his journey.

If he did so, he would have gone, *via* the Kentuckian towns of Petersburg, Frankfort and Paris, to Chillicothe, Ohio, and thence, by way of Zanesville, Ohio, Wheeling, W. Va., and Alexandria, Pa., to Washington, Pa. At this last-mentioned place, he would have an election of proceeding either

(A) to Pittsburgh and thence, via Philadelphia, to (a) New York City or (b) Baltimore and Washington, D. C., or

(B) to Cumberland and thence, by way of Hagerstown and Frederick, to Washington, D. C., and so to New York City. *Darby*, p. 158.

In any event, the date of his arrival in New York City was approximately June 23, 1813, as appears from a copy of a letter written July 7, 1813, by John Jacob Astor in New York City to John Dorr and stating, among other things: "Mr. Stuart arrived here 14 days ago and the account he gives is satisfactory." *Baker-Astor* [*A*], p. 9.

APPENDIX A

TRANSLATIONS FROM
NOUVELLES ANNALES DES VOYAGES
DE LA GÉOGRAPHIE ET DE L'HISTOIRE
[X, pp. 5-88, Paris, 1821]

AN ACCOUNT OF THE *TONQUIN'S* VOYAGE
AND OF EVENTS AT FORT ASTORIA IN 1811-12

WILSON PRICE HUNT'S DIARY
OF HIS OVERLAND TRIP WESTWARD TO
ASTORIA IN 1811-12

A SEA VOYAGE FROM NEW YORK TO THE COLUMBIA'S MOUTH

An account of events at Fort Astoria during more than a year

(1811-1812)

AND

A JOURNEY FROM SAINT LOUIS TO FORT ASTORIA

Translations and extracts from the manuscript diaries kept by the travellers, in English (a)

THE Columbia, a river of North America, has its mouth on the northwesterly coast of the continent in 46° 19′ north and 126° 14′ 15″ [6] west of Paris. It was discovered, May 7, 1792, by Captain Robert Gray, commanding the ship *Columbia*. Finding himself six miles from land, he saw an opening which seemed to be a harbor. He immediately launched a boat to seek an anchorage. None was found; but, the ship having approached the coast there was discovered from the masthead a passage in the middle of a sand-bar. It was not till the 11th that the *Columbia*, having bested the currents and passed the sand-banks and having cleared the breakers, entered a great river of fresh

(a) We owe to the courtesy of His Excellency, Mr. Gallatin, [6] U. S. Minister Plenipotentiary in France, and of Mr. J. J. Astor, New York merchant, the contribution of these interesting manuscripts relating to geography.

water. Captain Gray anchored there. Afterwards he went up the river for fifteen miles, where its bed so much narrowed that it was almost impossible to navigate. Accordingly, Captain Gray thought that he had not followed the proper channel for further ascent. Having ceased his manœuvres and made an examination of the region, he named the river Columbia; the point to the north of the entrance, Cape Hancock; and that to the south, Adams Point. Later he successfully recrossed the bar, and put to sea on the 20th.

During his entire stay in the Columbia's waters, the ship had been surrounded by canoes of Tchinouk indians.

[7] The details into which we enter seem necessary, because various geographical books have wrongly credited some English navigators with the discovery of this river. Those that we offer are taken from an authentic extract from the log or journal of Captain Gray. Moreover, a consideration of the names he gave suffices to convince one that they could have been imposed by only an American navigator: that of Columbus has frequently been used by the citizens of the United States since the time of their independence; those of Hancock and of Adams recall two founders of American freedom. Also there are found in Vancouver's voyage some very valuable references to the Columbia's discovery. This English captain, to whom geography is so deeply indebted for his reconnaissance of the northwest coast of North America, met, April 29, 1792, near the entrance of Juan de Fuca in 48° 24′ north, Captain Gray, who advised him of his discovery: but, at that time, had not yet entered the river; he had merely found its mouth. He added that, for nine days, the force of the current which issued from there and the strength of the return current had prevented him from entering. Vancouver later continued his voyage to the north, and Gray made sail toward [8] the south (b). Vancouver, having ended his first cruise to the north, returned south; and, on October 19, found himself opposite Cape Disappointment, "which," says he, "forms the northerly point of the entrance of the river called the Columbia by Mr. Gray" (c). He wished to enter the river in the wake of the *Chatham*, his consort; the adverse wind, the fogs and the force of the reflex current offered an obstacle to the execution of his plan; he was constrained to abandon it, being persuaded that Mr. Broughton (d), who commanded the

(b) *Vancouver's Voyage*, French translation, Vol. I, p. 252, quarto.
(c) *Ibid.*, p. 473.
(d) This is the same man who made a voyage of discovery in the northern part of the great ocean and explored, after Lapérouse, the Gulf of Tartary. This voyage has been translated into French.—Paris, Dentu, 1807, 2 vols. octavo, by the undersigned.

Chatham, would neglect nothing in exploring the navigable portion of the Columbia, and in acqúiring, as regards the interior of the country, all the information that it was possible to gather. Broughton, in fact, ascended the river for 84 miles from the mouth; and he took possession of it in the name of the King of Great Britain, because he believed that no subject of any other civilized power had entered there before him (e). But Captain Gray was [9] the first in date as concerns the right of possession, and the treaties have confirmed the claims of the United States.

Vancouver also reconnoitred a haven discovered by Gray to the north of the Columbia and named *Gray's Harbor* (f).

Mackenzie, to whom we are indebted for important discoveries in the western part of North America, has erred in indicating on his map the Columbia's mouth as being that of the Tacoutché Tessé,[1] the course of which he had followed for a long time and which he had quitted in the midst of the mountains. This river empties into the sea near 50° north: and, between its mouth and that of the Columbia, the great Ocean receives near 48° the waters of another river, the Caledonia,[2] a name which proves that knowledge of it is owed to some navigators from Great Britain, natives of Scotland. But, if Mackenzie was deceived as to the course of the Columbia, he had accurately judged the advantages that this stream offers to commerce. "Whatever road one follows," says he, "on leaving the shores of the Atlantic Ocean, one must join the Columbia in order to reach the great Pacific Ocean; this river is the line [10] of communication which Nature has traced between the two seas, as it is the only one navigable in the entire extent of the coast examined with so much care by Vancouver; its banks offer also the first level country which one finds on the coast south of Cook's Inlet and consequently the most northerly spot where one can establish a colony suitable for the abode of a civilized people" (g).

These wise observations have not passed unnoticed by the citizens of the United States of North America; and, the Columbia's mouth being included within the limits of the Union which extends from 42° to 49° north parallel, they naturally planned to found an establishment on this river. Already Captains Lewis and Clark had in 1805 erected at its mouth a fort in which to pass the winter, but it was entirely aban-

(e) Vol. II, p. 64.

(f) Map No. 6 in the atlas of *Vancouver's Voyage* gives a plan of the Columbia's mouth and of Gray's Harbor.

(g) *Voyages through the continent of North America.*—London, 1802, 2 vols. octavo, Vol. II, p. 309; French translation, Vol. III, p. 350, 3 vols. octavo.—Paris, Dentu.

doned at their departure. In lieu of it, Fort Astoria, constructed on the left bank of the Columbia's mouth, has existed since 1811, and promises to become the principal town of a colony. It owes its name to Mr. J. J. Astor, merchant of New York, and director of the company which was formed in that city for fur-trading on the Pacific Ocean.

[11] In 1810, Mr. Astor sent the ship *Tonquin* with a cargo to go trading for pelts at the Columbia's mouth. This vessel carried also a number of mechanics and hunters, chiefly Canadians, who were expected to stay at the establishment which would be formed. On the other hand, five of the company's partners went from New York by land. Having arrived at Saint Louis on the Mississippi at the mouth of the Missouri, they assembled their party composed of some sixty people, and travelled westerly as far as the Columbia's mouth. The American newspapers gave at the time an epitome of this journey, as well as of the one which was undertaken later by some of the partners in returning from the Columbia to Saint Louis (h). These epitomes, the last of which is very terse, have been translated in the *Annales des Voyages* (i); but, as the original diaries contain many interesting particulars, we have thought that a more extensive extract, especially of a *Journey from the mouth of the Columbia to Saint Louis*, would please the readers of *Nouvelles Annales;* and we have added a map drafted from data furnished by the travellers.

[12] On September 6, 1810, the ship *Tonquin*, commanded by Captain Jonathan Thorn, sailed from New York. In addition to her crew of twenty-one[3] men, she carried four of the company's partners, Messrs. A. Mackay, Duncan McDougall, D. Stuart and R. Stuart; ten[4] clerks; and seventeen[5] mechanics of various trades, laborers and hunters. The names of most of them proved their French origin.

On December 25th, she doubled Cape Horn with a favoring wind; the weather was pleasant enough, but cold.

On February 11,[6] 1811, she anchored in the bay of Karacacoa in the island of Ovaïhy. She afterwards went to Vahou and took aboard there, with their consent, seventeen[7] islanders who were to serve either as sailors or as mechanics.

On March 22, the *Tonquin* arrived off the Columbia's mouth. The bad weather prevented her from crossing the bar before the 25th. There had been lost, on the 22nd, through the violence of the waves, a boat manned by an officer, a sailor and three Canadians.[8] On the 24th, an-

(h) *National Intelligencer* of Washington, June, 1813.
(i) Vol. XXII, p. 274.

GRAND OCÉAN MER DU SUD OU OCÉAN PACIFIQUE
NOUVELLE HANOVRE
M É X I Q U E
Partie inconnue
Entrée de Juan de Fuca
Cap Flattery
Emb. de la Columbia
Nootka
C. Perpetua
C. Blanc
C. Mendocin
Port St François
Ind. Pieds Noirs
Ind. du Sang

The map as published in *Nouvelles Annales* measures 24.5 by 40.

other boat had also capsized; and, of five men, three—one of them a Sandwich Islander—had also perished.[9] [13] These two accidents were caused by the captain's obstinacy.

On the 28th, they disembarked the animals, which consisted of a ram, a ewe, three male goats, one she-goat, four boars and ten sows.[10] Later there was selected on the river's south bank a site on which to erect a fort. The ground was so covered with half-rotted stumps, fallen large trees and thick underbrush that there was great trouble in clearing it. However, the carpenters busied themselves with cutting and shaping the wood necessary for the construction of the lodgings, the storehouses and a boat. At the same time, the soil was dug up in order to sow corn, potherbs and vegetables, and to plant potatoes.

On June 2nd,[11] the *Tonquin*, after landing the part of her cargo intended for the establishment, went to trade for pelts further north along the coast. Mr. Mackay embarked as supercargo attached to the captain. The fate of this ship was sad. Toward the middle of July, one was confusedly informed by indians that the crew had been massacred. One had no faith in these reports; but, on the afternoon of August 11,[12] a Tchinouk came to the American office and gave some details which it was no longer possible to doubt. He had them from other indians recently arrived from the country of the Niouetians. Accord-[14]ing to their story, the cause of the catastrophe should be blamed on Captain Thorn. The Niouetians having come aboard to barter, he had been unwilling to give them more than two woolen blankets for a sea-otter's pelt. The indians were very discontent with this; and a chief spoke insolently to the captain, who struck the indian's face with an otter-skin. The chief, stung with rage, sent all his people to the shore. The next day, the *Tonquin*, setting sail for Noutka, was followed by some sixteen canoe-loads of Niouetians, who went immediately in search of the chief of Noutka, to ask him to join them. He ended by consenting; and, on the following day, they came alongside the ship with some furs, which they sold at the rate of an otter-skin for two blankets and two knives, and seemed quite satisfied. The traffic proceeded rapidly. Their number increased every moment. At a given signal, four of them fell upon Captain Thorn and a fifth stabbed him in the neck. Some others wished to throw themselves on Mr. Mackay, but he retreated to the forecastle where, with his dagger, he killed three of these madmen. However, they finished by overpowering him, and he received on his head a blow from a club which felled him. Meanwhile, each of the crew had been attacked by two indians and slain, with the exception of four sailors who descended to the powder magazine, lit a fire there and [15] ended their lives in a heroic manner by exploding the ship with some hundred savages who were on board (j).

The Americans at the office perceived that the Tchinouks, their neighbors, had known for some time all the details of this sad affair. "Concomby, their chief, had strictly enjoined against speaking of it under pretext of not grieving us"; says the narrator Mr. McDougall, "but we had good reasons to believe that the friendship he professed for us was merely feigned: indeed his conduct for some time and various suspicious happenings made us think that his sole purpose in not telling us this news had been to inspire us with a false sense of security so that, in not keeping us on our guard, we could be the more easily attacked when the opportunity presented itself. I am convinced that, since the *Tonquin's* departure, they had only waited for a favorable moment. Consequently, I required all my men to drill, and I took care that the arms were kept in good condition."

Moreover, the indians gave bits of news which were not always to be verified. On the 30th of April, one [16] of them arrived from the rapids of the Columbia. He announced that he had seen a company of thirty whites[13] who were erecting some houses, etc., near the second rapids. We supposed that these whites, according to the description he gave of them, were some representatives of the English North West Company; and accordingly we despatched a party to gather information in that regard, and to take measures in case there should be reason to fear opposition to forming the establishment. The party was commanded by Messrs. Mackay and D. Stuart. On their return, May 15th, they reported that they had gone as far as to the grand rapids, where they had encountered some indians who live ordinarily near the *Monts Rocailleux* (Rocky Mountains). These folk, just as had those who reside in the vicinity of the grand rapids, assured the Americans that no white man had appeared in the neighborhood; but they had learned from some indians who had come from beyond the mountains that a party of whites[13] like those whom they had seen with Captains Lewis and Clark was on its way to the Columbia. The Americans supposed that these were some people belonging to their own company because it was improbable that any others would dream of establishing themselves on this river.

(j) This account differs in some quite unessential details from that in *Annales des Voyages,* Vol. XXII, p. 287.

Appendix A

At[14] another time, it was June 14th, Kemakiah, [17] chief of the Clatsops, informed the Americans that two indians who had come from very far in the interior were at the Cathlamets' village;[15] and he added, concerning the purposes of their journey, a long story, not a word of which was understood. Next day, the two indians—one of them a man and the other a woman—arrived in a canoe with seven other natives, most of them Clatsops. He delivered a letter which was addressed to Mr. Stuart at Fort Estekakamac. Mr. McDougall opened it. It was dated from Fort Flathead, April 5th. Neither its contents nor the questions put to the indian could throw any light on the reason for his journey. But it was quickly noticed that this stranger spoke the language of the Knistenaus, which raised a suspicion that he was a half-breed of the nations of the northwest and a spy of the company of the same name. A few days later, the stranger incurred the enmity of the Tchinouks. They threatened to kill him; and the poor devil earnestly wished to take himself off, but all the indians of the neighborhood had designs on him. "We made every effort to reassure him," says Mr. McDougall, "although we were thoroughly convinced that his fears were well founded. If we had not taken him under our protection the instant he arrived, he would have been victim of their dread that he would give them the smallpox. He had had the imprudence to boast of possessing [18] the power to do it. The chiefs of the Tchinouks and the Clatsops frequently came begging that we surrender him to them, as well as his squaw, for the purpose of making them slaves, or that we ourselves keep them as such. We pretended to consent to this latter part, well knowing that, if these unfortunates were once in their power, their death was inevitable. Fear rendered this Indian more communicative concerning the inhabitants and products of the interior, and especially the distance from the North West Company's establishment to the grand rapids of the Columbia. We learned, to our great surprise, that they were not further than some fourteen days' travel on horseback. The various reports he made us relative to the upper part of the river, the favorable manner in which he portrayed the numerous tribes scattered along its banks, finally the fear lest he escape and thus cause us to lose the opportunity of acquiring accurate knowledge about the country, inasmuch as three of us understood his language, decided us after mature deliberation to send Mr. D. Stuart with eight men to the shores of the Ouahnadihi[16] or Djaaggama-Nibi, as the Indian termed it. It would be necessary to form a small establishment there, if the inhabitants' character and the country's appearance were inviting, and to hire the Indian to remain with them, or preferably to return to the fort, because the knowledge [19] which he would glean of the country would render him very useful at another time. Mr. D. Stuart set out on July 22.[17] His small party departed in three bark canoes, which carried also an assortment of merchandise. They started in company with Mr. Thompson, agent of the North West Company of Canada. He had arrived on the 15th in a canoe of cedar bark manned by eight men. He had crossed the Rocky Mountains in the previous December and January."

The 11th of August,[18] the day on which they learned of the *Tonquin's* disaster, several indians came to the fort; they had amongst them a Tchinouk who, a few days earlier, had arrived from the south. "He told us that nearly a year previously," adds Mr. McDougall, "he had gone to the north in a ship from Boston; but that, on the return, the weather was so bad that the captain did not dare to enter the river, and set out for Canton. He sold there his cargo and returned to America, where he took up trading with the Spanish colonies. On that coast he met some other American ships. The captain of one of them enticed the Tchinouk and the Niouetians from the ship on which they were, and set sail for the Columbia. But scarcely had he left the Spanish establishments, when a violent snow-storm arose. During the night the ship went on the rocks and was broken to pieces, all the [20] whites perished. The Tchinouk and the other indians, putting themselves in a boat, successfully reached the shore, which was deserted. They followed it for several days without being able to procure either food or fire. At last they encountered some huts, the inhabitants of which offered them something to eat. The travellers refused because of fear of being poisoned, and preferred to sustain themselves with shellfish and frogs. Also the natives of that place gave a scarcely better welcome. After a two days' rest, the travellers resumed their journey. At the end of some days, the country became less arid. They found it more populated, but the inhabitants seemed fierce and ill-disposed toward the strangers. They attacked the poor travellers, killed seven of them, and kept the other four in slavery. Finally Dhaickouan, one of the chiefs of the Clemaks,[19] having some fifteen days previously come into that region to trade, ransomed them. The Tchinouk gave some singular details concerning the coast he had traversed. He told, among other things, of the mouth of a great river which he had had much difficulty in crossing."

The Tchinouks and the Clatsops, from the very outset, came daily to visit the Americans. Very frequently they brought pelts, rarely in large quantity. They had at their homes salmon in abundance, [21] but a superstitious idea prevented them from supplying the Americans with a sufficient amount. They believed that, if this fish were cut crosswise and if it were boiled, no more would return to the river.[20] They insisted therefore that its preparation and cooking be left to them. Seeing that they brought so little of it, we supposed at first that they had formed the plan of starving the establishment; and we were agreeably surprised when we had learned the actual motive for their conduct.

But, as we have already seen, the Tchinouks, despite their protestations of friendship, gave room for doubting their sincerity. "We knew," says the narrator, "that they had had the plan of attacking us after the departure of the ship. An accident came to our rescue. While playing ball, Gassagass, Concomby's[21] son, dangerously wounded a chief of the Ichitchilichs.[22] The Tchinouks, apprehending that this misfortune might drag them into a war with that tribe in case the wound should be fatal, showed us more than usual good will. Some even came to caution us that the Ichitchilichs, assembled in a neighboring bay[23] for sturgeon fishing, had evil designs against us. Besides, we knew that in reality some fifty canoes were expected from the north, and as many from the south; this coinci-[22]dence of warning made us think that there had been formed a general project for attacking us. The sole method of being able to resist so large a number of men was for us strongly to fortify ourselves, which we did as well as our means permitted.

"Two days later, some Tchinouks coming to see us were displeased at the defensive preparations which they perceived. We needed stakes for our palisades; we went to cut some; the indians also furnished us some. Kamakiah, chief of the Clatsops, and Concomby and his son brought us some. We made believe to Concomby that we intended them for building a house for the blacksmith, because the thought of helping us to enclose ourselves with a fence was distasteful to him.

"Toward the end of August, some Ichitchilichs came to us and brought us some beaver and some sturgeon. We asked them why their tribe did not fetch us products of the chase and of the fishery, instead of sending them to us by the Tchinouks. They replied that these latter had warned them not to come into our presence because we were incensed at them by reason of their conduct toward some other Americans[24] who previously had come to trade on this coast, and conse-[23]quently they did not care to put themselves in our power. We convinced them of the falsity of this report, which the Tchinouks had invented in order to monopolize the trade; and we added that, if they behaved well, we, far from harboring antipathy toward them, would have much friendship for them."

Besides the tribes which have just been named, the establishment was frequented also by the Cathlamats, the Clemaks, the Tchilouts,[25] the Cathlaminimims and the Ouakikours.[25] Excursions were made from time to time into the country of the more neighboring indians, and their villages were visited in order to collect the largest possible number of pelts and to learn what the trade could procure in the places where the indian tribes assembled. Mr. R. Stuart went thus with Calpo,[26] a Tchinouk indian, as far as to 47° 20′ north and 124° west.[27] His absence lasted eighteen days. He found the country to be abounding in beaver, otter, sea-otter, elk, deer, bear and wolves, as also in fish of various sorts. The indians who inhabit this region were fewer, poor hunters and insolent. He thought, however, that a depot affiliated with the indians of Kodiak,[28] good hunters, would be advantageous, not only because they would easily kill many ani-[24]mals, the sea-otter among others, but also because it would make sure of the largest part of the fur trade to the north of Niouetic or of the Strait of Juan de Fuca.

The indians caused much inconvenience at the establishment by the thefts which they incessantly committed. Sometimes the stolen objects were returned by the chiefs, who usually showed zeal to effectuate these restitutions.

On September 7th, it was seen that the indians were coming in less number than ordinarily. This was about the time that they began to retire to their winter quarters. They hastened to get rid of the animals' pelts which they still had.

On the 26th, the house in which they were to live was finished, and they installed themselves in it. It was built of wood[29] and roofed with cedar bark. They had made some charcoal and various supplies for passing the winter. Game was not lacking during the late autumn; it brought pelicans, geese, ducks, and seals. They killed also some black bears. Sometimes, however, they were short of food.

On October 2nd, they launched the little vessel which they had built; it was named *Dolly*. After the 12th of that month, they sent it up the [25] river. It made several trips and was, among other things, very useful for transporting large pieces of building-timber.

On the 5th, they were agreeably surprised by the arrival of a canoe which had come from the outpost formed by Mr. D. Stuart on the Okannaaken. It brought several of his travelling companions, an Iroquois hunter[30] with his squaw and two children, and an American hunter[31] whom Mr. Stuart had advised to seek his fortune at the establishment. The travellers made a very satisfactory report, not only in reference to the pleasing, hospitable and honest nature of the indians who live above the falls of the Columbia, but also in regard to the aspect and products of the country.

The heads of the establishment were generally satisfied with all their men. Nevertheless, a certain Jeremie,[32] a man of turbulent nature, had caused them some annoyance. In July, they learned that, having made a packet of his belongings, he had hidden them in the woods and had hired four indians to guide him some distance up the river. They took him to task, and went with him to the spot where he had deposited his belongings. When they had exposed them to broad daylight, they were not a little surprised to find there many things belonging to various people and to the company. They reprimanded him, and asked him to sign a pledge of [26] better conduct in the future; but, as he persisted in his plan, they put him in irons and locked up all his property. Some days later, he wrote a letter of repentance. They pardoned him, and he resumed his tasks.

There were, it is said, some incorrigible men; Jeremie being of this number. On November 10th, it was learned that he had fled in company with two workmen named Pelleau,[33] and taken with him the clothes of some of his companions. Immediately, four people with two indians were sent in pursuit to try, with the aid of some natives to whom a large reward had been promised if they brought them back, to overtake them before they could pass the rapids. On the 14th, it was ascertained that the fugitives had reached the Clatsops' village with intention of gaining the Spanish colonies. An American and an indian were put on their trail. The first returned next day because the indian was unwilling to go further. Some other attempts to pursue them were fruitless. On the 20th, the first persons who had gone to search for them came back also, without having succeeded. However, because these persons had been told in the Tchilouits' village that the fugitives had been seen on its outskirts, they left there two of their number to watch for the fugitives. On the 24th, they brought them to the fort. They had found them imprisoned in the village of the Cathlana-[27]minimis. The chief of this tribe, who had arrested them some days before, would not free them without a large reward. On their arrival, they were put in irons.

On January 18,[34] 1812, there were seen to arrive at the fort two canoes in which were Messrs. Donald Mackenzie, R. McClellan, J. Reed and eight hunters. They had formed a portion of the party of Mr. Hunt, whom they had left, the previous 2nd of November, on this side of the Rocky Mountains among the Snake or Serpent indians. They had separated from the party in order to search for horses; and, seeing that they could not be of any aid to their companions, they had continued on their way. They had experienced unprecedented difficulties, and thought that, if Mr. Hunt and his party travelled during the winter, they would have suffered from dearth of food. The arrival of Mr. Mackenzie and his companions gave great pleasure to the fort's inhabitants, the number of which had been increased enough to impress the indians.

On February 15th, Mr. Hunt arrived with six canoes, which carried thirty men, one woman and two children (k). They had left, among the Snake indians, Mr. Crooks and five men,[35] whom fatigue prevented from continuing to travel. It was prob-[28]able that they had passed the winter amidst that tribe. As it was feared that they would have need of food, a canoe was sent, on March 22, to take them some, together with a lot of supplies. Mr. Reed and the five persons who manned it were afterward to make their way to Saint Louis, Missouri, and finally to New York in order to carry thither some despatches. That same day, Mr. R. Stuart also embarked with Mr. McClellan and some other people for the establishment[36] of Mr. D. Stuart, and a third detachment[37] ascended the river in a canoe in order to dig up some goods which had been cached.[38]

On the coming of spring, they occupied themselves with making excursions into the country in order to learn the resources it could furnish. Consequently, on March 31st, Mr. Mackenzie left with seven men and two canoes.[39] They had to examine the Oulamat's[40] neighborhood. All the parties sent to the interior were well armed, because it was necessary that they be in a condition to resist the indians always ready to attack.

Twice since their arrival, the Americans stationed on the Columbia's banks had heard some cannon-shots from the direction of the sea; but they had not seen any ship. However, they knew that Mr. Astor would be sending out new expeditions charged with bringing them trading

(k) The extract from the account of his journey will be found below. [*Editor's note:* see pp. 281-308.]

goods, munitions and [29] food. They accordingly were constantly on the watch; when, on May 7th, they learned that a ship had anchored off the mouth of the river. Messrs. McDougall and McClellan, in company with five others, descended the Columbia in order to ascertain the truth of this rumor. It was well founded, because, in the evening, the fort's inmates saw the ship. Mr. McDougall, on his return, related that he had seen it manœuvre to gain the river's entrance, and had heard a cannon-shot. On the 8th, the vessel fired several, to which they replied. They sent the *Dolly* to assist it in crossing the bar. Mr. McDougall went aboard, and found that it was *Le Castor* (the *Beaver*). It afterwards anchored in the river, landed the men destined for the establishment, and put ashore the animals it had brought.

Since the departure of Mr. R. Stuart and his party, there several times had been indirect news of them. In the beginning, it was said that all the party had been killed at the first rapids, later that they had had merely a skirmish with the indians and that these had been put to flight. Finally Mr. Pillet,[41] who had been sent with two men to the Cathlapouttes' territory to bring back an American named Pelton[42] who was on his way to the fort and whom they had kept prisoner for almost two months, returned with this Pelton on April 28. He stated that, a little below the [30] rapids, after Mr. D. Stuart and his party had made with the indians an agreement to carry his bales above the falls, these indians loaded the bales onto their horses and fled. Mr. Stuart told them to return. They did not heed him, and pursued their way toward the mountains. Then he threatened to shoot, and he fired a gun which killed one of the chiefs. A skirmish followed. Mr. Stuart was wounded in the neck, but not dangerously; and he kept on his way. Mr. Pillet said that the theft had been committed by the Tchilouts, a powerful and fierce tribe. On May 11, four canoes coming from Mr. D. Stuart's establishment arrived at the fort with him and Mr. R. Stuart. The thievery committed by the indians had compelled them to return, because they had made off with two bales of goods. They also had wounded Mr. Reed and had taken from him a package which contained important papers entrusted to his care. However, Mr. Stuart had bartered more than a thousand beaver pelts, which he had left with two of his companions. He had met, and brought in, Mr. Crooks and another American[43] who had had their goods stolen and who ever since had been living among the indians.

Mr. Mackenzie and those who had gone to explore the Oulamat returned on May 11. They made a very satisfactory report of the neighboring country. Game, beaver and fish abound there.

[31] Activity was redoubled at the American office after the arrival of the *Beaver*. They landed its cargo, took aboard all the bartered pelts, hastened to finish the work on the fort, and occupied themselves in making all necessary preparations for the journey which Messrs. R. Stuart, R. Crooks and R. McClellan had to undertake across the Rocky Mountains in order to return to Saint Louis, and thence to New York.

They left on June 29, 1812.

JOURNEY OF MR. HUNT AND HIS COMPANIONS FROM SAINT LOUIS TO THE MOUTH OF THE COLUMBIA BY A NEW ROUTE ACROSS THE ROCKY MOUNTAINS

[*Editor's Note.*—See maps facing pages 3, 235, 209, 127]

On July 18, 1811, Messrs. Hunt, Mackenzie, Crooks, Miller, McClellan and Reed, who were accompanied by fifty-six men, one woman and two children,[44] and had gone by water from Saint Louis to the Aricaras' village[45] on the Missouri, left there with eighty-two horses laden with merchandise, equipment, food and animal-traps. All travelled on foot except the company's partners and the woman or squaw. A route toward the southwest[46] was taken and they arrived on the banks of the Ramparré,[47] a small [32] watercourse which empties into the Missouri below the Aricaras' village. The name *Ramparré* comes doubtless from the French hunters, for it means furnished with numerous forts.[48] On the 18th, camp was made near a small stream[49] a short distance from its junction with the Big River or Ouenned-Poréhou,[50] which was crossed[51] on the 21st; and camp on the 24th was pitched on the banks of one of its tributaries.[52] They had travelled 67 miles, bearing a little more toward the west in the prairies where grass was knee-deep and the horses could graze to their satisfaction. The country was bare. Only a few cottonwoods[53] grew along the rivers.

Several members of the party being indisposed, a halt was made until August 5th. In the interim, Mr. Hunt visited a camp of some Chahays indians or Cheyennes. "I there bought thirty-six horses," says Mr. Hunt, "at a much better price than at the Aricaras' village. The camp was in the middle of the prairie near a little stream.[54] The indians used buffalo chips as fuel. Their tents are made of the skins of this animal well-prepared, carefully sewn together and supported by poles which are joined at the top; they can hold fifty people. These indians are honest and cleanly; they hunt bison; they raise many horses which every year they exchange at the Aricaras' village for corn, [33] beans, squashes and merchandise. They had a dozen beaver pelts, but they do not seem to know how to trap these animals.

"Having rearranged our baggage so that no horse would be overladen, we resumed travel on the 6th. We had horses enough to permit every two men to ride alternately, and six were allotted to the hunters whose duty it was to pursue bison. We crossed many ridges or detached hillocks composed of a red earth having the consistency of brick; other signs indicate also that they have been subjected to the action of fire; at the base of several are seen ashes and pumice stones. This rough country has scanty grass.

"It appeared that in these plains were at one time scattered trees; rotted remains of them are found; some stumps are still standing, and one recognizes from these vestiges that they were pines and oaks. On the 6th, camp was made on a tributary[55] of the Ouenned-Porêhou; on the 7th, in the plain near a pool of water. Buffalo chips served as fuel. Several of these animals were killed. They were all about us. As it was the rutting season, they made a frightful noise[56] like the sound of distant thunder; [34] the males tearing the ground with their hoofs and horns.

"We travelled 42 miles on the 6th and 7th. Later we somewhat slowed our pace in order that our hunters, who were behind us, might rejoin us. The country became mountainous and the water scarce. The hills were composed of white sandstone and ran from the southeast to the northwest. We here saw some big-horns.[57] We made fires on the summits to guide our hunters. At first we used buffalo chips, afterward we could use pine wood. (40 m. S.W.)

"On the 11th, there was crossed a range of mountains[58] like the preceding ones. The road was irksome because of steepness and the great number of stones. On the 12th, there were crossed two of the Ouenned-Porêhou's tributaries[59] coming from the southwest. One of them seemed to be the main branch. Many petrifactions were seen; several persons gathered them to use as whetstones. (27 m.)

"On the 13th, we marched in a more westerly direction, as we thought that our hunters were still to our right; and we crossed a confluent[60] of the Little Missouri, 300 feet wide, swift, muddy and filled with eddies. In the west, the mountains[61] seemed to bar [35] our route. Three of our hunters[62] returned at sunset." (12 m.)

On the 14th, camp was on a tributary[63] of the Little Missouri. The evening was very cold. At the north were mountains[64] covered with pines. They were crossed on the 15th. The country was extremely rugged; it became more so on the 17th, and a way out of these mountains could not be found.[65] A big-horn was killed; the flesh is good and much resembles mutton. These animals are usually found in the mountains where no other can go. Several were espied running and jumping on the edge of precipices. Black-tailed deer[66] also were seen. They are larger than the red deer and have very big ears. Their flesh is not as good as that of the red deer.[67] The tip of their tail is black.[68] They are found only in mountainous country. (45 m. S.W.)

On the 18th, it was necessary to leave the mountains and return to the broken country.[69] There they found the hunters, who had killed eight bison. After camp was made at the left of pine-covered mountains, Mr. Hunt and Mr. Mackenzie climbed the nearest ones. Their view extended in all directions. They saw far off in the west mountains[70] which appeared white in several places; they assumed that this was Mount Big Horn[71] covered with snow. [36] Below them numerous bands of bison wandered on the plain. (10 m.)

On the 19th, camp was made amid hills near a pond of limpid water. All around grew currants,[72] gooseberries[73] and thorny gooseberries[74] with yellow and red fruit. The clumps of cherry trees[75] showed sign of the paths used by black bear;[76] so that, with the slightest breeze moving in the bushes, one felt in spite of oneself a shiver of dread. However, only three of these animals had been seen as yet. (21 m. S.W.)

Halt was made, on the 20th, on a branch[77] of the Little Missouri which was regarded as the largest. The weather was cold and disagreeable. It froze during the night, the ice being as thick as a dollar. The country was high and rugged. It is the spot[78] which divides the waters flowing into the Missouri from those which discharge into the Yellowstone. (34 m. W.)[79]

On the 22nd, there was encountered a road which was supposed to have been used by the Crows or Absarokas in coming from the home of the Mandans.[80] The small river[81] on which camp was pitched, and which flowed toward the north, was without doubt a tributary of Powder River. On the 23rd, another branch[82] was encountered; but, before reaching it, the mountains and dry ravines[83] were crossed. The great heat, the bad road and the lack of water caused much suffering; several persons were on the [37] verge of losing courage. A dog of Mr. Mackenzie died of fatigue. Since travelling in these arid and naked mountains, no more bison were killed because they always stay near water. However, on the 25th, some were seen in the neighborhood. The hunters pursued them, and killed five. On the previous day, some of the voyageurs had eaten a wolf,[84] which they found very good. The camp was on a third tributary[85] of Powder River. (58 m. W.)

Its banks were followed for two days.[86] It flowed with water clearer than that of the previous tributary. Because many buffalo were killed, a halt was made on the 28th and 29th in order to dry their flesh at a fire. (18 m. S.W.)

On the 30th, the river was quitted and the camp pitched near Mount Big Horn,[87] which had been before us for so long a time. For several days we had been on the heights; our hunters had seen, the previous day, traces of indians; they discovered us first. On the evening of the 30th, two Absarokas came to our camp. The next morning, more of them arrived. They were all on horseback. Even the children do not go afoot. These indians are such good horsemen that they climb and descend the mountains and rocks as though they were galloping in a riding school. We followed them to their camp, which was near a clear stream[88] on the side of the moun-[38]tain. The chief came to meet us, greeted us in a friendly way, led us to his tents, and showed us a convenient spot for our camp. I made him a present of tobacco, knives and various trinkets for his men; and I gave him for himself a piece of scarlet cloth, some powder, bullets and other things. (26 m.)[89]

The day of September 1st was passed in buying robes and pelts; the jaded and injured horses were exchanged for fresh ones; a few of the voyageurs purchased some, which increased the number to one hundred and twenty-one—the most of them well behaved and capable of crossing the mountains.

On the 2nd, the journey was continued along the mountains,[90] and a halt was made near a small stream[91] which is said to be a tributary of Powder River. An effort was made, for half the day on the 3rd, to get out of the precipices and the arid mountains.[92] It was necessary to retrace the path and to regain the banks of the small stream.[93] Several very large elk[94] were killed. (21 m.)

"We had in our party," says Mr. Hunt, "a hunter by the name of *Rose;* he was a very bad fellow full of daring. We had been warned that he had planned to desert us as soon as we should be near the Absarokas, take with him as many of our men as he could seduce, and steal our horses. Wherefore, we kept close watch [39] during the night. Fearing moreover that, if despite our vigilance, he should succeed in fulfilling his evil designs, he would seriously cripple our expedition and that his schemes might be more extensive than we had supposed, we resolved to forestall him. On September 2nd, we had received a visit from some Absarokas of a band which was different from the one we had recently left and which was camped in the mountain. Consequently, I suggested to Rose that he remain with these indians, offering him half of his year's wages, a horse, three beaver-traps and some other things. He accepted these terms and immediately quitted his confederates, who, no longer having a leader, continued the journey."

Accordingly, Rose went to join the first Absarokas that we had met. Their chief, knowing that we had taken a wrong road, sent Rose on the 4th to tell us this and to place us on the right road[95] which crossed the mountains and which was shorter and better. We soon met the Absarokas, who were going the same way as we; this gave me a chance to admire the activeness of these indians on horseback. It was really unbelievable. There was, among others, a child tied to a two-year-old colt. He held the reins in one hand and frequently plied his [40] whip. I inquired his age; they told me that he had seen two winters. He did not talk as yet.

Camp was made at the headwaters[96] of the small stream of the preceding day, and the 5th was spent there to await the hunters' return. They returned in the evening. Some bison and a gray bear[97] had been killed. We were in the midst of Mount Big Horn,[98] thus styled because of the river of the same name which flows along its flanks that extend from northeast to [southwest].[99] It is an advanced spur of the Rocky Mountains; and is covered with pines, with many bushes and with plants which were in bloom. (16 m.)

We were joined on the 6th by eight indians and three families who were of the nation of the Flatheads and of that of the Snakes. In continuing our westerly route across the mountains and rocks, we encountered many beautiful bits of country, abundant springs, stretches of green grass, groves of pine, innumerable quantities of blooming plants; and yet it froze continually. We camped beside a stream[100] which runs toward the north and empties into the Big Horn. The ground was covered with gooseberries of two sorts, the best I have ever eaten. One of our men brought me some strawberries[101] which he had just gathered. We killed an elk and several black-tail deer. The bison [41] have been very common in these mountains, which for that reason resemble a continuous barnyard; but now not more than a single one is to be seen. We distinctly saw the third mountain[102] which is covered with snow; we avoided the first[103] by turning toward the south. (20 m.)

Having, on the 7th, descended to the plain,[104] we travelled on it until the 9th, when we reached the banks of the Big Horn, called here Wind River[105] because in winter the wind blows so constantly that it prevents the snow from lying on the ground. We twice camped beside this river. On the morning of the 8th, the indians, having received the price for a horse which they had offered us, left us to go to the home of the Arrô-polous,[106] a tribe of the Panis who live along the Platte River. One of our party left a gun at camp; the indians made off with it before he could return there. At evening, we were on the banks of a small river[107] which receives the waters of a stream[108] abounding in beaver.

The Big Horn in the place where we were camped is swift, clear and 300 feet wide. We could see below us the opening[109] in the mountains by which it escapes. It is a very narrow pass bordered on both sides by precipices. (45 m. W.)

On the 10th, we followed the banks of Wind River,[110] ascending it through a beautiful plain. Some [42] trees grow along the river, in which there are no beaver. Its freshets have covered its banks with gravel. We saw two bear, which we could not get near. Fish[111] were caught that much resembled the herring. On the 11th, we crossed a large tributary[112] of Wind River coming from the mountains[113] which rise in the south. For fire-making, while in the plain, we often used sagebrush, which here attains a considerable size. I crossed a clump of it that was as high as I when on horseback and was extremely thick-spread. The two sorts of gooseberries were very common. We saw numerous flights of robins and of other small birds. On the 12th, we had mountains to the north[114] and to the south;[115] they seemed to meet in the west.[116] We crossed[117] Wind River. The route was hilly. (38 m.)

From the 13th to the 15th, Wind River was crossed and recrossed;[118] as also were two of its confluents,[119] the larger of which came from the northwest. The country produced an abundance of wild flax[120] which is very like ours in its form, in the texture of its bark and in its seed pod; but this last is smaller and of a lighter color. The mountains drew nearer to each other. Consequently, the country was very rugged, the trail very winding between the heights. On the 15th, Wind River was quitted [43] and an indian trail[121] was followed southwesterly into the mountains. One of our hunters, who had been on the shores of the Columbia, showed us three immensely high and snow-covered peaks[122] which, he said, were situated on the banks of a tributary[123] of that river. (50 m. S.W.)

On the 16th, snow was frequently encountered; there were large patches of it on the summit[124] and on the slopes of the mountains exposed to the north. Halt was made beside Spanish River,[125] a large stream on the banks of which, according to indian report, the Spaniards live. It flows toward the west[126] and empties supposedly into the Gulf of California. We were surrounded by mountains in which were disclosed beautiful green valleys where numerous herds of bison graze; which made them much more interesting to us because, for several days, we had not seen a single one of these animals. I observed three different varieties of gooseberries:[127] the ordinary, with red fruit and low bush—very thorny; another, with yellow fruit, excellent and having thornless stems; the third with dark red[128] fruit, the taste of which is like that of our winter grapes. It is almost as large, stem very thorny. I saw also three kinds of currants;[129] one with red fruit, very large and palatable, bush from eight to nine feet high; another with yellow fruit the size of ordinary currants, [44] bush from four to five feet high; the third with handsome red fruit having somewhat the sweetness of the strawberry, though rather insipid, low bush. (20 m.)

On the 17th, we continued to follow the course of the river as far as to the opposite end[130] of the mountains. It seemed to abound in beaver and otter. In fact, the country for some distance down appears to be very favorable for hunting beaver. Geese and ducks are very common. (15 m. S.W.)

On the 18th, we left the river; and, travelling northwesterly, ascended a small stream[131] issuing from the mountains. Halt was made there to dry bison enough to last as far as to the shores of the Columbia and of rivers where we hoped to procure some fish. Some of our people, while hunting, met some indians who appeared much frightened and immediately took to flight. I ran after them with Mr. Mackenzie, Mr. McClellan and two other persons. It was not till the end of eight miles that we discovered them some distance away pursuing a bison. As soon as they saw us, they fled. We followed them and overtook two young men whose horses did not gallop as well as did those of their companions. They seemed at first very disquieted, but we soon reassured them. They [45] led us to their camp. It was a band of Snakes who had come into the neighborhood to dry meat; they had a large quantity of it which was very fat. They live in tents of skin, and possess many horses. Several of them, never having seen whites, were much pleased by our visit, gave us food and, in the main, a very hearty welcome. They had no pelts other than of bison and a dozen of beaver, which we purchased, encouraging them to kill more of these animals. We told them that we would return to them for trade. They seemed pleased. We bought from them nearly two thousand of dried bison meat which, with more than four thousand that our men had prepared, will load all our horses except six. (8 m.)

Having thereafter climbed a small mountain,[132] we arrived by a good road at a tributary[133] of the Columbia where it enters the fourth range, which consists of the mountains of this river. We had snow on all the heights to each side of us and in front of us. (15 m. W.)

The stream whose course we followed receives several others[134] and forms a small river.[135] We frequently forded it on the 25th and 26th. Its rapidity is so great that nobody could walk there without assistance. Our road has been very wind-[46]ing amidst small mountains and on the edge of the precipices which surround us. One of our horses fell with his pack into the river from a height of nearly two hundred feet, but was uninjured. (20 m.)

We emerged from these mountains on the 27th and halted at the confluence of a small river[136] with the one[137] we had recently seen. The Americans have named it Mad River because of its swiftness. On its banks, and a little above the confluence, are situated the three peaks[138] which we had seen on the 15th. We should have continued at that time to follow Wind River and to cross one of the mountains because we would have reached the headwaters of this river; but lack of provisions forced us to make for the banks of Spanish River.[139] (12 m. W.)

As this was the place where we had been led to hope that we might pursue our journey by water, we searched on the 28th for trees suitable for building canoes. Having ascended with a man some twelve miles on the other side of the river, I saw many indications of beaver, some signs of gray bear and a band of elk. On my return in the evening, I learned that nobody had been any more successful than I in searching for wood. The trees were too slender. They were of a variety of cottonwoods,[140] the leaf of which resembles that of the willow. There [47] were also some firs, but so full of knots that we despaired that our axes could manage them. The other trees we saw were cherries, small pines, serviceberries and cedars.

Accordingly, on the 29th, we moved our camp lower down because the trees there were more suitable: and we got ready to work; but I thought that we would be obliged to make some canoes out of two pieces. On the 30th, we set to work, and felled many trees that were not suitable. Nevertheless, as I feared that the river would not be navigable below the point[141] where it enters the mountains, Mr. Reed, attended by two men, set out downstream to explore it for a distance of four days' march.

Appendix A

The 1st of October, it rained in the valley and snowed in the mountains. Several of our men departed to catch beaver. That evening two Snake indians who had followed us from the Absarokas came to our camp. They made us fear that we would be unable to navigate the river. On the 2nd, Mr. Reed returned. At the end of two days' march he had been obliged to quit his horses, which were of no help to him in climbing the mountains and rocks. After an hour's effort to proceed afoot along the river, [48] he had been forced to relinquish his undertaking. An attempt to get through by means of travel across the highlands would have been an endless task. The river became very narrow. Its winding course was blocked by numerous rapids. Wherefore, it was necessary to search lower down for wood for the canoes with the hope of navigating; because, as far as he could see, the river continued to flow in the heart of the mountains. He had moreover noticed some signs of beaver and had seen two bears, one black and one gray.

All day long on the 3rd, rain and sleet fell. Everything was in readiness for crossing the mountain[142] which was regarded as the last. The storm ceased on the 4th, but all the mountains about us were covered with snow. We crossed Mad River—the water being up to the horses' bellies—and camped at the foot of the mountain. (4 m.) On the 5th, the mountain was crossed by an easy and well-beaten trail;[143] snow whitened the summit and the northerly slope of the heights. The Snakes served us as guides, although last year two[144] of our hunters had come into this region. (18 m.)

Halt was made near a small stream[145] which washes the northwest side of a beautiful plain[146] where we travelled on the 6th, and we camped by a river[147] which flows toward the northwest, it was crossed on the 7th. It receives several others,[148] and greatly enlarges. After [49] being joined by another[149] of equal size, it flows toward the west.[150] Numerous bands of antelope were seen. Wild cherries were common, they are the size of ordinary red cherries: they were not yet ripe. A dozen miles northwest of our camp is a hot spring.[151] I went there with Mr. Mackenzie. It is not erupting,[152] but constantly emits steam. (12 m.)

It was very cold all day on the 8th; the wind from the west blew with force, a little snow fell. We arrived at the fort of Mr. Andrew Henry.[153] It consists of several small buildings which he had erected so as to spend last winter there on a tributary[154] of the Columbia, 300 to 450 feet wide. We hoped that we could navigate it. We found some trees suitable for making canoes. On the 9th, we had already begun eight, all of cottonwood. This tree, the aspen[155] and some small willows are the only ones which grow in this neighborhood.

On the 10th, Mr. Miller, with four hunters[156] and four horses, left to go beaver-trapping. They took with them the two Snakes, and descended along the mountains in the hope of finding a band of indians from whom they trusted to obtain information useful for their hunt.

Every evening, we caught some beaver and some small salmon-trout.[157] On the 14th, we were [50] visited by a Snake who was half-dead from hunger and covered with tatters.

On the 17th, all being ready for our embarking, we cached our saddles in a spot which we showed to the two young Snakes who promised to care for them, as also for our seventy-seven horses,[158] until one of us should return. The poor devil whom we saw on the 14th came back with his son, who was even more ragged than he. We gave them food. They gathered up the paws and entrails of the beavers, and said good-bye to us. The inhabitants of this country must suffer greatly from the lack of game. Bison come here in certain seasons, their traces are numerous. There are also some elk and some very shy antelope. During our stay, the wind blew constantly from the west and often with great force. I noticed that it is the prevailing wind in these mountains, where it causes considerable havoc by upsetting large trees over a wide area and carrying their branches to great distances.

On the 19th, the cargoes being placed in our canoes, we embarked in them. The force of the current made us travel rapidly, and we were not long in passing the small river[159] of which I spoke on the 7th. After its confluence with Mad River, it became large enough so [51] that boats of every size could navigate it. Its water is a light green. As it has no name, I gave it that of *Canoe River*. Its banks are covered with small cottonwoods. Several signs made me think that gray bears had, within a few days, visited the thickets. Beaver, ducks and geese are very common here. It was cold, and snowed all day long. (30 m. S.)[160]

In proportion as we advanced, the river grew lovelier and wider; a space of 1200 to 1800 feet separated the two banks. On the 20th, we travelled 40 miles; but, during the last twenty of them, the bed of the river was intersected by rapids. There were two others a little further down. In passing there, two canoes filled with water. It was necessary to stop forthwith. I sent my canoe and one other to their assistance. The men were rescued. Many goods and provisions, as well as one canoe, were lost. We continued to have, on our left, the mountains parallel with the river. It was cold. We still had in sight the Pilot Knob[161] (summit of the pilot), seen on September 15th. (40 m. S.E.)

On the 21st, after passing two rapids, a portage[162] of a mile and a quarter was reached. The goods were carried on land, and the canoes were towed. The river is confined between two perpendicular mountains which, throughout nearly a half-[52]mile, allow it, in some places, only 60 feet of width and sometimes less. (6 m.) We had to guide our canoes through the rapids by a rope, and were not slow in reembarking on the 21st. There was a series of rapids, at two of which it was necessary to repeat the manœuvre of portaging. One of the small canoes filled and capsized, some goods were lost. (6 m.)

On the 23rd, the canoes were lightened in order to pass a rocky rapid. We afterwards encountered many others which were not dangerous, but the current was very strong. Beaver, geese, ducks were common. No trees were seen other than cottonwoods and willows. On the plain were prickly pears.[163] The prairies showed bisons' traces; they were old. From time to time, we saw numerous flights of magpies[164] and robins.[165] The mountains extend in different directions. (75 m. S.)

Toward the end of the day, the current lessened in force. Canoe River[166] receives, from each side, a small stream.[167] A band of Snakes and Chochonis[168] fled at seeing us. We found in their camp some small fish not more than an inch long,[169] some roots and seeds which they were drying for winter, some vessels woven of willow and grass for holding water, and a fish-net [53] very well made of flax or nettle. We left there some small merchandise and two knives. Having, a little further down, encountered three of these indians who were on a flimsy raft of reeds, we accosted them. They were wholly naked, except for a piece of rabbit-skin robe over their shoulders. Their bows and arrows were skillfully fashioned. The bow is of pine-wood, cedar-wood or bone, reinforced with sinews of animals. The arrow[170] is of reed or of well-trimmed wood, and is tipped with a green stone.[171] Halt was made at a waterfall[172] thirty feet high. (70 m.)

On the 25th, in order to avoid the waterfall, below which are some small rapids, we crossed to the southerly bank and proceeded on land. At the end of six miles, a rock dammed the river from one bank to the other;[173] but, as it was less high at the south bank, we let down the canoes by a tow-line. Several filled with water in crossing a series of rapids. We lost some more goods. The river was winding, the country uneven and rocky. The mountains crowded to the water's edge on the left or south bank. (12 m.)

On the 26th, the rapids were as yet rather numerous, but not very dangerous; the water in many places was quiet. We emerged[174] from the mountains, and made our way toward the northwest. Going [54] ashore to visit a camp of indians, these poor fellows fled at our approach. By making friendly signs, I persuaded one of them to return. He was on horseback and seemed better equipped than those I previously had seen. He had some trout and dried meat, which he traded for knives; but his fear was so great that I could not persuade him to indicate by signs the route I ought to take. He was concerned only in begging me not to deprive him of his fish and meat, and in consigning himself to the protection of the good spirit. (70 m.)[175]

On the 27th, the weather was gloomy and it rained in the afternoon. Only two rapids[176] were encountered in the morning. The river was nearly a half-mile wide.[177] Beaver were numerous. (40 m. S.W.)

On the 28th, our journey was less fortunate. After passing several rapids, we came to the entrance of a canyon.[178] Mr. Crooks's canoe upset, one of his men was drowned,[179] many goods were lost. (18 m.)

On the 29th, I went scouting with three men to investigate whether we could pass our canoes down the northerly side. For 35 miles, I followed the shores of the river, which continues to eat its way northwesterly through the mountains. Its bed is not more than from sixty to ninety feet wide, is full of [55] rapids and intersected by falls from ten to forty feet high.[180] The banks are precipitous everywhere, except in two places where I went down to get water. For supper we had only some fruits of the rose bushes, and then we lay down near the fire. We returned to camp on the 29th, very tired and very hungry. Those whom I had sent toward the south had found a spot where they thought we could launch our canoes after carrying them for six miles.

Our situation had become critical, we had food for not more than five days. On the 31st,[181] Mr. Reed and three men went downstream to endeavor to obtain horses and food from the indians and learn whether it was possible to navigate below the spot where I had been. Sixteen men with four of the best canoes went to attempt the passage. Afterwards, because the state of our provisions did not allow us to delay our march, we put to one side the most necessary things and began to dig some holes in which to cache the residue. Rain fell so copiously that we could not finish the holes.

On November 1st, we altered our plans. Our sixteen men had lost one of their canoes, as also their goods, in trying to [56] pass it down the rapids by means of a rope. The other three were stuck fast in the midst of the rocks. Seeing no means of continuing our journey by water, we made ready to go in various directions in quest of indians. The rain still hindering our work, we could not finish until the 2nd, and we deposited our baggage and goods in six caches.[182] Mr. Mackenzie with four men headed northerly toward the plains in hope of finding the Big River.[183] Mr. McClellan and three men descended along Canoe River; Mr. Crooks and three men[184] ascended toward its headwaters. I remained with thirty-one men, one woman and two children. We spread a net. Only one fish was found in it. I had our four canoes loaded, and the river was reascended. We lost one canoe in passing around a point in the midst of rapids. The cargo was salvaged. Our hunters, who rejoined us on the 4th, had caught eight beaver, which was a slight relief. Mr. Crooks returned. Having found the distance by land to be greater than he had expected; and, therefore having decided that he could not reach Fort Henry and get back this winter, he abandoned the undertaking. I halted at my camp of October 27th.

I spent the day of the 5th in making all the necessary arrangements for us to procure [57] food for several days until we should hear from Mr. Reed. We caught four beaver. We dried the tails and bellies. I had the dried meat[185] inspected and exposed to the air. On the 6th, despite our efforts, only one fish was found in the net. Two of Mr. Reed's men returned. After walking for two days, they had discovered that the river presented no change. Therefore, we judged with Mr. Crooks that the better course to pursue was to divide our party into two groups, each to go its own way. Consequently, I cached still further articles[186] and made the more necessary ones into packets of twenty pounds.

On the 7th, I returned to our camp[187] of October 28th; having thus wasted nine days in fruitless efforts. We caught eight beaver, but we have eaten the dried meat[188] because its quality is superior to that of these animals.

On the 8th, I again had goods cached and I distributed among all the people whatever of our provisions remained. Each person had five and a quarter pounds of meat. We had in addition forty pounds of corn, twenty pounds of grease and nearly five pounds of bouillon tablets. That was what must serve for the subsistence of more than twenty people.

On the 9th, I set out on the north [bank] of the river [58] with nineteen men, one woman and two children.[189] Mr. Crooks, with nineteen[190] others, marched on the south [bank]. It rained in the afternoon. We camped under the rocks on the bank of the river, and had much trouble in procuring water. (28 m.)

On the 10th, we travelled all day without being able to drink water other than that we found in hollows in the rocks. Finally we reached a spot where it was possible to descend to the river. Everywhere else its banks are formed of perpendicular rocks from 200 to 300 feet high. Its bed is intersected by rapids; but, in the intervening space, the water is quiet. Today it would be possible to navigate it for thirty miles. Some willows grew along the river. (32 m. N.W.)

On the 11th, having found a trail beaten by horses at the edge of the water, I preferred to follow it rather than again climb over rocks. Soon we met two Chochonis. They showed me a knife that they had received from one of our companions. One of them led us by a path that took us away from the river. We crossed a prairie,[191] and arrived at a camp of his tribe. The women fled so precipitately that they had not time to take with them such of their children as could not [59] walk. They had covered them with straw. When I lifted it to look at them, the poor little creatures were terror-stricken. The men trembled with fear as though I had been a ferocious animal. They gave us a small quantity of dried fish, which we found very good, and sold us a dog. One of these indians went with us. We were soon back at the river. It was bordered by their tents. We halted nearby. Some fifty men came to see us. They were very civil and extremely obliging. The river, as on the previous day, was intersected by rapids. (26 m. N.W.)

On the 12th, I visited some huts at which was a large quantity of salmon. These huts are of straw, are shaped like ricks of grain, and are warm and comfortable. We saw, at the door, large heaps of sagebrush which serves as fuel. I bought two dogs. We ate one of them for breakfast. These indians had good robes of bison skin, which, so they told me, they obtained in exchange for their salmon. On leaving them, we marched some distance from the river, and crossed a small stream.[192] We saw mountains[193] to the north. (16 m. N.W.)

On the 13th, camp was pitched at a spot where a small watercourse[194] issues from the mountains. (25 m. N.N.W.)

On the 14th, we came upon an indian camp of three huts. All around [60] was a vast quantity of the heads and skins of salmon, to which were still clinging pieces of flesh—the best having been hidden in the ground. None of these indians fled at our approach. The women are badly clad, and the children yet more shabbily. Nevertheless, each has a garment of the skin of bison, rabbit, badger, fox, or wolf, or perhaps of ducks' skins sewn together. These animals, with the exception of the rabbits, are rare in these plains. No bison have been seen there for a long time. (22 m. N.W.)

On the 15th, we purchased two dogs and a small quantity of salmon. Before us was a snow-covered mountain. The river seemed to enter there. Its banks were covered with the bodies of dead salmon, which emitted a horrible stench. Its bed, so far as my view extended, was devoid of rapids. We saw some horses. Their owners took great pains to keep them out of our way. The indians told us of some of our people who had passed by this spot. (28 m. N.W.)

Early on the 16th, the bed of the river showed itself again—constricted, full of rapids, and bordered with precipitous rocks. As food, we had only our parched corn and the remainder of our meat. We approached the mountains. On the 17th, I happily obtained a horse in exchange for an [61] old kettle; the indians not wishing any other of my goods. I obtained also two dogs. The country was devoid of wood, even the sagebrush had disappeared.[195] We camped on the bank of the river. (35 m. N.W.)

The baggage was put on the horse. There remained to us one quart (a litron[196] and a half) of corn and a little morsel of grease for each man. On the 18th, in following the river, we continued to march toward the northwest. (30 m.)

On the 19th, in accord with the advice of some indians whom we met, we changed our route and crossed the prairie,[197] where we found no water. Everything seemed to indicate that we would be no more fortunate on the following day. What vexation for men whose food consisted principally of dried fish! By good luck we bought a horse. (25 m. N.E.)

On the 20th, the rain, which had commenced to fall the previous night, gave us a little water. This alleviation was timely, as several Canadians had begun to drink their urine. (33 m. N.) It continued to rain all night.[198] On the 21st, at sunrise, we saw before us a river[199] which flowed westerly. Its shores were fringed with cottonwoods and willows.[200] Some indians had established their camp there. They had many horses, and were better clad than [62] those we had seen previously. They informed us that beaver are common further up in this small river. Very few of them are in the neighborhood of the camp. On reaching the huts, I lost my horse. An indian told me that it had been stolen from him.[201]

As it was necessary to provide for our needs, I bought some fish and two dogs. (12 m.)

The weather was constantly rainy. We could not make much progress. On the 22nd, we met some indians. From my observations and the few words I could understand, the distance from this place to the Big River was very considerable; but the indians told me nothing of the route I must follow. We obtained some fish, seven dogs and two horses. We followed the river.[202] (35 m. W.) On the 24th, we crossed it a little above[203] our Canoe River, which continued to flow toward the north. The mountains in front of us were everywhere covered with snow. (18 m. N.W.) On the 25th, despite the severe weather, our fatigue and our weakness, we forded another river[204] which came from the east. The water was waist-deep. (27 m.)

On the 26th, the hills began to appear. They stretched along the snowy mountains. We crossed another small stream[205] which flows from the same direction as the others. It [63] led us, on the 27th, to a defile[206] so narrow as to leave scarcely space enough to pass through. We frequently were obliged to remove the baggage from our horses and to travel in the water. On the previous evening, a beaver had been caught, which furnished us a scanty breakfast. We had supped off bouillon tablets. I therefore had a horse killed. My men found the flesh very good. I ate it reluctantly because of my fondness for the poor beast. (33 m. N.W.)

Early on the 28th, we arrived at some huts[207] of Chochonis. They had just killed two young horses to eat. It is their only food, except for the seed of a plant[208] which resembles hemp and which they pound very fine. I purchased a bag of it, as also some small pieces of horsemeat, which was fat and tender. Dreading a stay of several days in these defiles, I camped near the indians, in order to obtain a horse in exchange for some goods; but, in spite of all that I offered, I was unsuccessful. When the women saw that I insisted, they shrieked frightfully as though I had wanted to rob them. The indians told me of white men who had taken the same route as ours, and of others who had passed on a different side; which greatly assured me concerning Mr. Crooks and his company, especially when I learned that he still had one of his dogs, as I concluded that he had not [64] suffered too much from lack of food. The indians also said that I would sleep three more nights in the mountains and that, after six nights on the trail, I would reach the falls of the Columbia. However, I had little confidence in this talk, because it appeared to me that they were impatient to see me depart. (10 m. N.)

On the 29th, the bad trail compelled us to unload the horses, and at times to keep away from the river. We climbed mountains so high that I would never have believed our horses could have got over them. On the 30th, the mountains still further narrowed the bed of the river.[209] The summits displayed some pine trees and were covered with snow. We experienced the greatest difficulty in going onward because the steep rocks and the precipices projected to the very edge of the river, which flows toward the N.E. and toward the N.N.W. A black-tailed deer was killed, which made us a sumptuous repast. (28 m.)

On the 1st of December, it rained in the valley and snowed on the mountains. Climbing them in search of a passage, the snow was knee-deep. I saw many chokecherries, which were excellent because the frost had taken away their tartness. Snow fell so densely on the mountains where we had to go that we could see nothing a half-mile ahead of us. Accordingly, it was necessary to remain [65] encamped on the 2nd. The previous evening, a small beaver was caught. We had nothing more to eat. I killed another horse. (13 m.)

On the 3rd, it rained and snowed all day. We could advance only 9 miles. Our horses were unloaded to allow them to go along the river. The baggage was carried by hand. We travelled toward the northeast. On the 4th, it was necessary to leave the banks of the river and to climb the mountains. They stretched all around us, and were covered with snow. Pines and other green trees grew on the sides of some of them. The snow came above our knees. It was excessively cold. We were almost succumbing to its severity when, at sunset, we had the good fortune to reach a cluster of pines. We made a good fire, which comforted us. Although we marched all day, we were, because of the meanderings of the river, only 4 miles from our encampment of the preceding night.[210]

On the 5th, the abundant snow which was falling did not allow us to see three hundred feet ahead of us. We succeeded, however, in reaching the river's bank by letting ourselves slide. The sound of the running water guided us.[211] A horse with his pack fell some hundreds of feet in depth, but was not hurt. The weather was much less severe in the valley than on the heights. It rained there. The snow was [66] only ankle-deep. I killed another horse. (6 m.)

On the 6th, we had just started out, when—What was my astonishment and distress!—I beheld Mr. Crooks and his party on the other side of the river. I immediately returned to camp, caused a canoe to be made out of the skin of the horse killed on the preceding night, and sent enough food to our famished companions. Mr. Crooks and one[212] of his party came to us. Poor man!—he was well-nigh spent from fatigue and want. He told me that he had gone three days' march[213] further down; that the mountains[214] there are even higher and come closer to the river, which at that spot is compressed into a canal[215] not more than sixty to a hundred feet wide between precipitous rocks; and that it was impossible for men in their condition to proceed, because, for six days, their only animal food had been one of their dogs. Mr. Mackenzie and Mr. Reed with their party had gone on. Mr. Crooks had spoken[216] with them a few days earlier. They told him that Mr. McClellan, on leaving the small river, had crossed the mountains with the hope of falling in with the Flatheads. The river, at the spot where we were, flows almost easterly. Mr. Crooks tells me that it continues in this direction.[217]

I spent the night in considering my situation. I had to provide for the needs of more than twenty starving people and, in addition, give my utmost aid [67] to Mr. Crooks and his party. Notwithstanding all the discouraging reports to me concerning the region below here, I would have continued my journey on the mountains if it had not been, as I already knew from experience, that the depth of the snow would make the undertaking impracticable. It was necessary therefore, to my great regret, to retrace my steps, hoping to encounter in the meantime some indians on one of the three small rivers[218] above the mountains. I counted on buying from them a sufficient quantity of horses to feed us until we should reach the Big River, which I flattered myself to be able to accomplish this winter. I feared nevertheless that Mr. Crooks and some of his men would not be able to follow us. What an outlook! We must expect having nothing to eat for several days: because, on this side of the indian huts which we left November 29th, we have found only cherries; and perhaps there would be no more of them in the same places.

The skin canoe had been lost.[219] A raft was made, so that Mr. Crooks and his companions, with the remainder of the meat, might cross to the other side. The attempt failed. On the 7th, we were reduced to marching slowly, because Mr. Crooks was so feeble that he had great difficulty in keeping up with us. Most of my men had gone on ahead.

On the 8th, another raft was made; but, after [68] repeated trials, Mr. Crooks and his man[220] were unable to cross owing to the violence of the current. Therefore I was obliged to wait for them. Whereupon my men grumbled, saying we all would die of hunger; and importuned me in every way to go on. To add to my troubles, Mr. Crooks was quite ill in the night. Seeing that this mishap would delay for two days my arriving among the indians, I left three men[221] with him; and departed on the 9th with two others[222] to rejoin my party. I had three beaver skins, two of which I left with them. We supped off the third. The weather was extremely cold.

Early on the 10th, I overtook my men. There remained for us only one horse.[223] It belonged to Dorion, one of our Canadians. Killing it was suggested. Dorion would not consent. It was thought best to let it live until we should be sure that the indian huts were still at the same place. I the more willingly approved this plan since the poor beast was only skin and bones. We had not gone far when we encountered some huts of Chochonis who had come down from the mountains after we had passed. I cautiously approached to prevent them from hiding their horses. They had twenty of them. They sold[224] us five. I had one killed [69] immediately, and sent a man with a piece of the meat to Mr. Crooks. Several of my men had not eaten since the 7th, the day on which they had left me.

On the 11th, we had another calamity. One of Mr. Crooks's men[225] was drowned while crossing the river in a canoe which capsized with many goods. I had another horse killed. I left two of them for Mr. Crooks with part of the flesh of another, hoping that with this help he would be able to proceed to the encampment of the indians above us.

On the 13th, we arrived at the huts we had seen on our way down. The indians traded me a horse for an old tin kettle and some glass beads. They had refused a gun.

On the 16th, we emerged from the mountains,[226] and camped on the banks of the river[227] that we had crossed on the 26th of last month. Thus, for twenty days, we had uselessly tired ourselves in seeking a route along the lower part of the river.[228] The previous day, it had rained and snowed. The river contained drifting ice. The weather was extremely cold. By good luck, there were at this spot a dozen huts of Chochonis who had arrived since we had camped there. They told me that it would have been [70] [im]possible[229] for us to proceed by following the river. This news increased my anxiety concerning Mr. Mackenzie and his party. On the 17th, I ascended along the small river[230] and pitched my camp near that of some Chochonis, from whom I bought a horse and a dog. On the 18th, I procured another horse, a small quantity of dried fish, some roots and some dried, pulverized cherries. I spent the greater part of the day in getting information as to our route and as to the time it would take us to reach the Sciatogas.[231] The indians differed in opinion; they however agreed in saying that the trail was good, that it would take us from seventeen to twenty-one nights to get there and that, in the mountains, we would have snow up to our waists. I offered a gun, some pistols, a horse, etc., to whoever would serve me as guides. They all replied that we would freeze and urged me to remain with them during the winter.

On the 19th, I again tried to procure a guide. Though I sent to all the huts along the river, my efforts were fruitless. I nevertheless could not do without one, it would have involved a positive risk of perishing with all my people. To remain at this place was still worse after having travelled for so long a time and at such great expense. I ended by telling the indians that they spoke with a forked tongue, which is to say that they lied; I told them that they were women; in a word, [71] I used the expressions most likely to pique them. Finally one of them proved resolute enough to undertake guiding us as far as to the Sciatogas. These indians, according to the account of our Chochonis, live on the westerly side of the mountains and have many horses.

Therefore, I once more resumed my journey. On the 21st, two other indians joined our guide, who immediately led us to our Canoe River. We discovered there no reed canoes in which to cross. Accordingly two horses were slain, a canoe was made from their hide, and we crossed. I found on the other side thirteen[232] of Mr. Crooks's men. They told[233] me that, since we had left them, they had seen neither him nor the two men[234] who were with him. When all of us had crossed, which was not accomplished till the 23rd, my men regained courage. Those of Mr. Crooks's party were extremely weak and exhausted, especially four of them. They delivered to me a horse and various goods. Three men,[235] having expressed a wish to remain among the Snakes, I gave them the canoe and some goods. Next day they crossed the river, and I hope that they will not be slow in finding Mr. Crooks and his people.

My party now consisted of thirty-two whites, a woman more than eight months pregnant, her two children[236] and three indians. We [72] had only five wretched horses for our food during the passage of the mountains. On the 24th, I quitted the Canoe River, of which we all shall keep a very sad recollection. We[237] travelled westerly until the 29th, crossing some hills by a trail sometimes fairly level, more often not so, but always good. It snowed slightly and rained a little. On the 28th, we crossed a stream[238] which flowed toward the north. The mountains stretched on each side; on the left was the one[239] we had to climb; it ran from north to south, was well-wooded and covered with snow. On the 29th, there was a good trail in a level valley,[240] and the river[241] was crossed twice. (106 m. W.)

On the 30th, after quitting the small river[242] at the spot where it enters the mountains at the north,[243] we reached another lovely valley[244] several leagues wide and very long. A pretty stream[245] meanders through it and beaver seem to be common in it. We fortunately found there six huts of Chochonis, who had many horses. They sold us four of them, three dogs and some roots. They told me that we had yet to sleep three nights before arriving among the Sciatogas, and pointed out to me the gap[246] in the mountains by which we must pass. They added that there was not much snow there; but they [73] have so often misinformed me that I did not put much confidence in this news because on all sides the snow whitened the mountains. About dawn, the pregnant woman gave birth to a child.[247] Dorion, her husband, remained in camp with her for a day; then rejoined us on the 31st. His wife was on horseback with her newborn infant in her arms; another, aged two years, wrapped in a blanket, was slung at her side. One would have said, from her air, that nothing had happened to her. (21 m. W.)

My men urged me that, in order to celebrate the new year, we should not travel on January 1st, 1812. I willingly consented because most of them were very fatigued from having, each day, only a scanty meal of horseflesh and from carrying their packs on their shoulders across the mountains.

From the 2nd to the 7th of January, we traversed the valley, followed a small river[248] for some miles into the mountains, and climbed many pine-covered hills. On the heights, we had snow half-way up our legs, we sometimes sank to the waist, and we lacked water. On the 4th, we were on a point as lofty as the mountains which encompassed us on all sides. Some were wooded, all were snow-covered. The weather was cloudy and cold. On the 6th, we saw the sun [74] for the first time since entering the mountains; the snow much decreased; we could see in the west a region which seemed to be a plain. On the 7th, we encountered a small stream[249] which led us to an extremely narrow pass[250] between immensely high mountains. On every side, were seen horse-trails used by the indians in hunting deer, which must be very common because we have espied numerous bands of black-tail. The snow had entirely disappeared. Dorion's baby died.[251] At evening, several men had not reached camp. (68 m. W.)

The small stream[252] joined a larger one,[253] near which, on the 8th, we perceived a camp of Sciatogas and of Toustchipas[254] composed of thirty-four lodges. They had at least two thousand horses. Their lodges are of mats. They are clad in good robes of bison or of deer, have shirts and leggings of buckskin, and, in every respect, their clothing equals that of the best-equipped indian tribes. They have, in their households, some pots and kettles of copper, as also some other objects which indicate indirect communication with the inhabitants of the seacoast. They have also some axes. A cleverly made stone hammer is used to pulverize roots, cherries and other fruits, as well as fish. [75] Pointed bits of elkhorn serve instead of wedges for splitting wood. The women have caps of willow twigs very neatly made and ornamented with designs. The vessels for holding water are also of willow. They cook meat in them by throwing into them red-hot stones. At present, the copper pots have the preference; there are always three or four of them hanging in the lodge. (15 m. W.)

These indians made me very happy by telling me that some white men had arrived at the Big River, which is two days' journey from here. Apparently, in this neighborhood, grass grows all winter as the sides of the mountains were green.

All my men rejoined me with the exception of the Canadian, Carriere.[255] He had been seen, the previous afternoon, mounted behind a Snake indian on a horse near the lodge which we had passed when some miles from our camp of last night.

I cannot sufficiently express my gratitude to Providence for having let us reach here; because we all were extremely fatigued and enfeebled. There remained to us two horses, which were only skin and bone. At evening, we had as food only a small quantity of indifferent venison and some roots.

I stayed six days at this place. I bought there eight horses and two colts. We [76] ate two of them, and I delivered two to our guides on account of what I owed them. Several of my men also bought some. A number of men were ill—some from overeating, others from eating roots—; still others were lame. The last day, each person made himself moccasins and prepared for continuing the journey. I had sent two men to search for Carriere. They did not find him. This poor fellow had perhaps taken a hunting-trail of the indians and thus lost his way. The

Snakes having moved their lodges to another place, my men could learn nothing about him. The Sciatogas also transferred their lodges a day's march further down on the river.

On the 15th, we resumed travel and reached the Sciatogas' camp on the bank of the Euotalla.[256] They told us of a river situated higher up which they called *Oualla-Oualla*.[257] I suppose, according to Clark's map,[258] that it is the small river whose confluence with the Columbia he places near beds of shell-fish. From what I have learned, the Canoe River is the *Kemoenoum* of Lewis. (15 m. N.W.)

These indians had some venison, but they chose to sell it so dearly that I could not buy any. They hunt these animals by pursuing them on horseback and surrounding them. They use [77] the bow and arrow with singular dexterity and are excellent horsemen.

It rained so heavily during our stay on the banks of the Euotalla that the river swelled with prodigious speed. We were forced to break camp hastily. Three of our horses, attached to stakes on the lower land, were drowned. The indians were also compelled to move their lodges higher. I bought four horses from them. I wished to have a certain number because the indians told me that, on the Big River, I could obtain a canoe in exchange for one of these animals. They said too that in six nights I would be at the falls.[259]

On the 19th, I continued to descend the Euotalla. Beaver must be common because many places are full of their dams. Several of my men travelled on horseback, as I also did. We saw on the other side of the river some lodges of the Akaitchi indians[260] who dwell on the Big River. One of them swam to our camp. He gave me some very reassuring particulars concerning the whites who had earlier descended the river. (15 m. N.W.)

From the Sciatogas, who had again moved their camp lower down, I purchased still another horse; and I took leave of them. They are the cleanliest indians that I know of; like all the others, they are extremely proud. They do not eat either [78] dogs or horses; nor will they permit the flesh of these animals to be brought into their lodges. I greatly pleased them by stating that I would return to them with goods to barter for beaver. They already have some of these skins; and tell a very confused story of white men who come to trade, give them tobacco and smoke with them.[261] One of these men has, they say, a house on the Big River. My Canadians think that the reference is to a representative of the North West Company. We left the Euotalla. (12 m. W.)

Appendix A

On the 21st, we at last reached the banks of the Columbia,[262] for so long the goal of our desires. We had travelled 1751 miles, we had endured all the hardships imaginable. With difficulty I expressed our joy at sight of this river. It was three-fourths of a mile wide. Its shores were bare of trees; and were formed of pebbles and, in some places, of steep rocks. (10 m.)

They were inhabited by the Akaitchis, miserable indians who have neither moccasins nor hose; their clothing consists of only a scanty mantle of the skin of bison, deer, rabbit or fox or else of duck. They sometimes add to this a pair of sleeves of wolfskin. Their lodges are well made of mats, are in the [79] shape of the roof of a house, and are very light and warm. Holes dug in the ground and furnished with mats are the abode of the women. They usually are naked; some few have a scrap of robe which covers their shoulders, but all have around the waist a leathern belt which passes between their thighs and proves that they aspire to be decent. Also these indians are better provided with food than are the Snakes, for it seems that dried salmon abounds with them. They gave us a large quantity of fresh salmon-trout, which they catch at the mouth of the Euotalla. This fish is excellent. Their canoes are of pine-trunks split in two; consequently they are not raised at bow and stern. Having no sort of tool, they have recourse to fire for hollowing these trees.

I crossed the river[263] because I was told that the trail ran along the right or north bank. I left on the 23rd, after purchasing fresh fish and nine dogs. The trail along the river was very good. We settled ourselves near a camp of indians who had some fifty canoes. I bought nine dogs, which were very fat; and we made a delicious meal. Their flesh seemed to us well flavored, healthful and strengthening; whereas horsemeat, however well cooked, did not nourish, no matter how much one ate of it. The weather was fine and [80] very mild, like the fine days of October. (12 m.)

From the 24th to the 28th, we followed the river, which flowed almost due west. Its shores were usually bare. We frequently encountered huts of indians. They sold us some dogs. They placed such a high price on the meat of elk and of deer, that I could not buy it. Moreover, they caused us great inconvenience because they stole the ropes of the horses, which escaped and made us lose much time in recapturing them. Sometimes they took away these animals and hid them. These indians ate acorns; they told me that at a short distance from the river are found many white oaks. (57 m. W.)

On the 28th, the country became very mountainous. The indians seemed more prosperous. They talked to me of whites who had built a large house at the mouth of the river, had surrounded it with palisades, etc. They had not been there; but they informed me that the whites were in great trouble, expected a large number of their friends, constantly looked toward Big River and, when we arrived, would dry their tears and would sing and dance.

The mountains and rocks along the river became more frequent on the 29th. The indians whom [81] we saw had many horses. We began to maintain a guard during the night. (15 m.)

On the 30th, we camped opposite the mouth of Chochoni River,[264] named *Tou-et-Ka* by the indians. They had assembled in great number to dance in honor of our arrival. But this large crowd made me apprehensive, and I accordingly pretended to be indisposed and begged them to leave me alone. They complied with my wishes after a little while. (14 m.)

On the 31st, we passed the falls[265] of the Columbia, which we had perceived the preceding day. The principal one being on the south bank, I could not get a view of it. The bed of the river is blocked by rocks, across which the water violently plunges by several channels.

A village, called Ouaioumpoum, is situated on the river's north bank at the spot where the waterfall begins. The indians have a special name for each camp that is composed of more than one hut, and they are very fond of telling it to strangers.

I arrived early at the village of Ouichram[266] at the entrance of the long defile[267] in which the river has cut into the rock a canal from 200 to 240 feet wide and several miles long. This is the site of the great fishery of the Columbia. It re-[82]sembles one of the small fishing ports on the eastern coast of the United States. On both sides of the river are to be seen large flakes well made of interlaced sticks for drying fish. The ground is covered with the bones and heads of fish. In the springtime, when the waters of the river are high, the salmon come in schools so large that the indians catch them with dip-nets attached to the end of poles. They station themselves for this purpose on the tips of the most projecting rocks.

The indians of this place are the most intelligent I have yet seen. One of them knew several words of English; he told me that Mr. D. Stuart had gone on one of the northerly tributaries[268] of the Columbia to spend the winter there: he had seen him in his establishment. He recounted to me the catastrophe of Mr. Mackay and of the ship *Tonquin*.

Appendix A

We saw today some small white oaks. The country became more rugged and the mountains larger. A short distance below the falls, there is, on the left bank, a snow-covered peak which I began to see on the 20th of the month. I assume that it is the Mount Hood of Vancouver. (12 m.)

February 1st. Last evening a great many indians assembled near my camp. Not finding an opportunity to steal horses or goods, they devised an unusual stratagem to get something. They [83] informed us that some forty indians were coming from downstream to attack us and take our horses. We paid little attention to their talk. Later some of the village's chiefs arrived armed with knives, spears, etc., reiterating the story and adding that they wished to stay with us. I received them with extreme coldness, and gave them a pipe to smoke. Then I collected all my people and placed sentinels at different points. This measure produced the desired effect. The indians presently departed, and they brought to me a man who, so it was said, was the chief of the village the inhabitants of which were to attack us. They gave him all the credit for having dispersed the mob. I smoked again with them; and, shortly before daylight, they all returned to their homes. The rogues imagined that by frightening me I would have given them two or three horses to assure myself of the rest. As one of them had escaped on the previous evening and had not been found in the morning, I sold it for two bales of dried, pulverized salmon, each weighing seventy pounds. We camped on the hills amid bushes, pines and oaks. (10 m.)

I could procure only one canoe,[269] and for this I traded a horse. The indians have a great many [canoes]. They are very well made of pine [84] wood, raised at bow and stern; and some of them are able to carry three thousand pounds. Despite my injunctions that careful watch be kept, the indians had filched an axe. Emboldened by this success, several followed us on the 2nd and stole two guns; and, at eleven o'clock in the evening, though our horses were in our camp, made off with one of them. On the 3rd,[270] I embarked in the canoe with all our goods and sent my horses ahead.

I met my party at a village on the right bank at the mouth of the Oatarack;[271] and there purchased three canoes, each of which cost me a horse. While I was trading, the indians pilfered a hatchet and our last axe. They also made off with Dorion's horse. It was grazing near his tent, which this Canadian had had the wilful caprice[272] to pitch at some distance from ours. (9 m.)

Appendix A

On the 4th, the violence of the wind forced me, much against my wish, to remain among this gang of thieves. I obtained one more canoe in barter for a horse. The next day at a village[273] where I arrived, I traded the three remaining horses for two canoes. It seemed that the trail ends at this village. The hills changed to mountains, which for the most part are snow-covered. One sees here some pines; they fringe both sides of the river. [85] Cottonwoods, oaks and ash grow on the bank, with oaks on the most neighboring hills.

The extremely heavy rain and the storm detained me several days opposite an indian village. A Clatsop came to see us, and talked to me of the establishment at the mouth of the river, as also of Mr. Mackay's disaster.[274] He was the third one to give me this distressing news. This indian, who knew several English words, asked me for news of Messrs. Lewis and Clark and some of their companions. He already had heard of the death of Mr. Lewis. (26 m.)

On the 10th, the wind having abated, we embarked early. On reaching the commencement of the great rapids[275] (15 m.), I examined the portage on the left bank.[276] The trail was good for a mile. We landed all the canoes at ten o'clock, and were below the rapids[277] before one o'clock. They are very great; the water, in dashing against the rocks, produces some very high waves. No boat could pass, at least in the present state[278] of the river, which is much constricted between hills and rocks. There are at these rapids a second salmon-fishery, a village on the right bank and [86] three huts on the opposite side. The blue glass bead is the merchandise which these indians prefer. From this spot onward, the oaks and ash-trees become more plentiful; we saw a number of hazel-trees. The numerous streams[279] that fall from the mountain-tops down the rocks add to the beauty of the landscape. (16 m.)

On the 11th, some rapids[280] two miles in length forced us again to land our canoes. Finally, eight miles[281] from the great rapid,[282] we encountered the last one.[283] Below it, the river regains its usual width, which is three-fourths of a mile, and the hills diminish in height and recede from its banks. The intervening space is covered with pines, oaks, ash, cottonwoods, maples, hazels and willows. (12 m.)

On the 13th, I passed the mouth of Quicksand River.[284] It empties through the Columbia's left bank by two outlets which create a large sand-bar. Twenty miles further down and on the same side, the Columbia receives another river,[285] which is approximately 1800 feet wide. A large island[286] lies in front of its mouth. There are several small ones[287] a bit further down. The Columbia is here a mile and a quarter wide. On both sides of the vast rush-covered spaces, we saw sometimes small prairies and frequently ponds. Seals[288] were numerous. Much more distinctly than before, we saw the mountain which I [87] have already mentioned, and I no longer question that it must be the Mount Hood of Vancouver. For two days, the wind had blown violently from the east. It hailed, rained and snowed. (52 m.)

On the 14th, the mountains again drew close. We camped on the right bank at the mouth of a small river.[289] Indians talked to us of our fellow-countrymen's establishment, adding that we should have no more than one night to sleep before reaching there. (36 m.)

On the 15th, we passed several large islands.[290] The land on the left bank was covered with oaks and ash-trees, but all was inundated.[291] I stopped at some indian huts[292] where I found four of our fellow-countrymen who were bartering for sturgeon and were fishing for excellent small fish,[293] which were about six inches long. The indians call them *othlecan*, and catch many of them in the springtime. We camped on two low islands[294] near the left bank. (27 m.)

On our voyage, we frequently encountered huts of indians who sold us dogs, dried salmon, beaver skins, root of the ouapatou[295]—which is the ouapasippin of the Mississippi—and finally othlecans.

On the 16th, we started early. It had rained all night. The fog was so thick that we could see only the lowlands [88] and some small islands; all was covered[296] by it. It disappeared in the afternoon at high tide. I found that we were navigating along a large bay,[297] and shortly afterward I saw the fort of Astoria on the southerly bank. (30 m.)

I had the pleasure there of again meeting Messrs. Mackenzie and McClellan, who had arrived more than a month before, after having suffered incredible hardships.

In my journal I had entered the 16th[298] of February; here they reckoned only the 15th. It was a very real pleasure for travellers harassed by fatigue to rest in quiet and be surrounded by friends after so long a journey in the midst of savages of whom it is always prudent to be wary.

We had covered 2073 miles since leaving the Aricaras' village.[299]

Notes to Appendix A

1 *I.e.*, Taoutche-tesse or Tacootche-Tesse (indian name for the stream), the present-day Fraser River of British Columbia. *Bancroft*, XXVII (vol. I), p. 684; *Mackenzie; L. & C. Hist.*, p. 591.

2 This stream is largely a product of inaccurate geographic information. The text describes it as discharging into the ocean, while the accompanying map delineates it as a large southward-flowing river emptying seemingly into present-day Bellingham Bay in the state of Washington. Though no such watercourse existed, it is possible that the "Caledonia" of the text and map represents a distorted conception of present-day Thompson River, a confluent of the Fraser River.

3 Twenty-two, according to *Ross* [*A*], p. 13; twenty-three or twenty-four, according to *Franchere* [*A*], pp. 17, 18, [*B*], pp. 30, 31; twenty, according to *Astoria*, I, p. 49.

4 Eleven, according to *Franchere* [*A*], p. 17, [*B*], p. 30. *Ross* [*A*], p. 13, seemingly agrees with this; but *Astoria*, I, p. 46, states 12.

5 Eighteen, according to *Franchere* [*A*], p. 17, [*B*], pp. 30, 31. *Ross* [*A*], p. 13, seems to agree with this.

6 February 12, according to *Astoria*, I, p. 68; February 13, according to *Franchere* [*A*], pp. 38, 39, [*B*], p. 55, and *Ross* [*A*], p. 30.

7 Twenty-four, according to *Franchere* [*A*], pp. 62, 63, [*B*], pp. 84, 85, and *Astoria*, I, p. 78.

8 First mate Ebenezer D. Fox, sailmaker John Martin and three engagés, *i.e.*, Basil Lapensée, Ignace Lapensée and Joseph Nadeau. *Franchere* [*A*], pp. 17, 18, 64, 65, [*B*], pp. 30, 31, 86, 87; *Ross* [*A*], pp. 54-56.

9 Third mate (or possibly "maitre caboteur") Job Aikin, Aiken or Aitken, sailmaker John Coles, armorer Stephen Weeks and two Sandwich Islanders embarked. Aiken, Coles and one Sandwich Islander perished (*Franchere* [*A*], pp. 17, 64-70, [*B*], pp. 30, 31, 88-94; *Ross* [*A*], pp. 59-66; *Astoria*, I, p. 84). These cited pages suggest that possibly the ship's company contained two men each named Aikin, Aiken or Aitken: one of them being the third mate, the other of them the "maitre caboteur."

10 In variance with this assertion, *Ross* [*A*], p. 53, states that, during a storm at sea some days before, "all our live stock were either killed or washed overboard"; while *Franchere* [*A*], p. 74, [*B*], p. 98, avers that "The next day, the 27th, desirous of clearing the gangways of the live stock, we sent some men on shore to construct a pen, and soon after landed about fifty hogs, committing them to the care of one of the hands."

11 June 1, according to *Ross* [*A*], p. 81, and *Franchere* [*A*], p. 38, [*B*], p. 116.

12 August 5, according to *Ross* [*A*], p. 156. *Nouvelles Annales*' description of the *Tonquin's* destruction omits various details contained in *Ross* [*A*], pp. 158-166; *Franchere* [*A*], pp. 136-142, [*B*], pp. 180-188; *Fanning*, pp. 137-150; *Cox* [*A*], pp. 96-105, [*B*], pp. 63-67; *Mo. Gaz.*

13 Query: were these people of the North West Company? Or were they of the somewhat apocryphal party of Jeremy Pinch, for whom see *Fuller*, pp. 75, 76; *Clark* [*A*], pp. 122, 839, 840; T. C. Elliott's *The discovery of the source of the Columbia River* in *Ore. Hist. Soc. Quar.*, XXVI, p. 43.

14 This and the following paragraph supplement the accounts in *Franchere* [*A*], pp. 90, 91, [*B*], pp. 118, 119, [*C*], pp. 251, 252; *Ross* [*A*], p. 85; *Astoria*, I, p. 102.

15 This village was at the confluence of Warren Creek with the Columbia River in present-day Clatsop County, Ore. See note 3 on p. 39.

16 Present-day Okanagan River in state of Washington.

17 July 22, according to *Ross* [*A*], p. 103; July 23, according to *Franchere* [*A*], p. 93, [*B*], p. 122, and *Astoria*, I, p. 104.

18 See parallel account in *Franchere* [*A*], pp. 96, 97; [*B*], pp. 126, 127.

19 Styled "Kélémoux" in *Franchere* [*A*], p. 97, "Klemooks" in *Franchere* [*B*], p. 127, and today called "Tillamooks." See p. 336 *infra.*

20 A similar statement is in *Ross* [*A*], p. 97.

21 Styled "Concomly" or "Concomley" by other writers. For account of him see *MacDonald*, p. 74, f.n., as also the numerous sources cited in that f.n.

22 These indians were styled "Tchikélis" in *Franchere* [*A*], p. 94, "Tchikeylis" in *Franchere* [*B*], p. 124, and are today called "Chehalis." See p. 343 *infra.*

23 Present-day Baker Bay just inside Columbia's mouth and indenting its right bank. *Franchere* [*A*], p. 94, [*B*], p. 124; *Chart* no. 6151.

24 Query: is this possibly a garbled version of the Winship affair described by Stuart in his entry of July 1 (p. 29), and by him credited to the Hellwits (*i.e.*, Echeloots)? See p. 345.

25 The "Tchilouts" and "Ouakikours," Stuart styled respectively as Hellwits and Waakicums. See pp. 345, 363.

26 Known usually as "Coalpo," for whom see *Henry-Thomp.*, p. 782.

27 Query: was this the trip which *Ross* [*A*], pp. 79, 80, dates as apparently in May and limits to fifteen days?

28 In Alaska.

29 *Astoria*, I, p. 125, states that the house was of stone. That its foundation was of stone and that the walls were seemingly of wood appears from *Franchere* [*A*], pp. 94, 98, [*B*], pp. 123, 124, 129, and from Stuart's entry of June 29 (pp. 3, 4).

30 Ignace Shonowane, for whom see *Astoria*, I, pp. 126-129, and *Franchere* [*A*], p. 99, [*B*], p. 130.

31 Régis Bruguier. As a "respectable country merchant" in Canada, he had

been a trader among the indians on the Saskatchewan River, where he eventually lost his outfit. Having thereupon turned to trapping, he while in pursuit of beaver had gone into the Columbian region (*Franchere* [*A*], p. 99, [*B*], p. 130). See also *Astoria*, I, pp. 126-128, which styles him as "Regis Brugiere."

32 P. D. Jérémie, a Canadian engagé who, on July 30, 1810, at the south end of Lake Champlain, overtook and joined the party which under command of Alexander McKay was canoeing from Montreal to New York City preparatory to sailing on the *Tonquin* (*Franchere* [*A*], pp. 12, 17, [*B*], pp. 23, 24, 30). After his desertion as described in the text and in *Franchere* [*A*], pp. 100-106, [*B*], pp. 132-140, he remained seemingly unrecorded until December 18, 1814, when, being at Fort George (Astoria) and being by Henry termed a boat-builder, he shipped as an under-clerk aboard the British sloop-of-war *Raccoon* which sailed on December 31, 1814. *Henry-Thomp.*, pp. 773, 780.

33 Jean Baptiste Belleau and Antoine Belleau, Canadian engagés who on the *Tonquin* had reached Astoria (*Franchere* [*A*], pp. 17, 101-106, [*B*], pp. 30, 132-141). Jean Baptiste was a middleman in canoe no. 7 of the Grand Brigade which, April 4, 1814, left Fort George for the East (*Henry-Thomp.*, p. 875). Antoine, though registered as remaining at Fort George and as being one of the men who through venereal disease or other disablement were prevented from serving in that Grand Brigade, was a middleman in one of the two canoes which on May 1, 1814, left Fort George with express for Fort William. *Henry-Thomp.*, pp. 868, 869, 904.

34 January 10, according to *Ross* [*A*], p. 182; January 18, according to *Franchere* [*A*], p. 109, [*B*], p. 144.

35 *Astoria*, II, pp. 53, 56, 194, and *Franchere* [*A*], p. 216, [*B*], pp. 275, 276, identify these five men as John Day, Jean Baptiste Dubreuil, Jean Baptiste Turcotte, André LaChapelle and François Landry.

36 David Stuart's post on the Okanagan River.

37 According to *Ross* [*A*], p. 184, this third detachment was headed by Russell Farnham, for whom see note 41 on pp. 69, 70 *ante*.

38 Hunt's caches on the Snake River.

39 Seemingly this was the expedition to which Stuart referred in his entry of July 3 (pp. 31-33).

40 Present-day Willamette River.

41 Francis B. Pillet (sometimes mentioned as Pillette or Pillot), a Canadian who as a clerk had arrived at Astoria in the *Tonquin* (*Franchere* [*A*], p. 17, [*B*], p. 30), and for whom see *Henry-Thomp.*, pp. 757, 767, 783, 788, 825, 828, 832, 854, 860, 865, 872, 875, 899.

42 Archibald Pelton. For this crazed wanderer from the Missouri Fur Company's brigade see pp. CIV-CVI; *Henry-Thomp.*, p. 867, f.n.; *Franchere* [*A*], p. 113, [*B*], pp. 149, 150; *Cox* [*A*], I, pp. 91-93, [*B*], pp. 61, 62; J. Neilson Barry's *Archibald Pelton* in *Wash. Hist. Quar.*, XIX, pp. 199-201, as also his *Astorians &c.* in *Idem*, XXIV, pp. 221, 222. The text amplifies the accounts contained in these

cited sources and also ascribes to Pelton's arrival at Astoria a date later than the one these sources imply.

43 John Day, for whom see pp. xcvii-c.

44 This makes the party aggregate 65 souls instead of the 64 calculated in *Chittenden*, p. 904. Also the subsequent text, in harmony with *Astoria*, I, p. 235, states that Hunt now had 82 horses, whereas *Mo. Gaz.* and *Niles*, p. 265, assert the number was 80. The still later text has Hunt purchase 36 horses from the Cheyenne indians, while *Mo. Gaz.* and *Niles*, p. 265, give 40 as the number.

The text's "fifty-six men" were 11 hunters, interpreters and guides [*i.e.*, William Canning (Cannon), Alexander Carson, Martin H. Cass, John Day, Pierre Dorion, Jean Baptiste Gardapie (Gardipie, Gardpie, Gariepy), John Hoback (Hobaugh, Hobough, Hubbough, Hauberk), Benjamin Jones, Jacob Reznor (Rizner, Risner, Resner, Resnor, Reasoner), Edward Robinson, Edward Rose] and 45 Canadian engagés [*i.e.*, Charles Boucher, Bazile Brazeau (Brasseau, Brosseau, Brousseau, Brusseau), Pierre Brugere (Brugiere), Michel Carriere (Carrier), Antoine Clappine (Clappin), George Cone, Joseph Cotte (Coté), Joseph Delaunay, Pierre Delaunay, Jean Baptiste Delorme, Pierre Detayé, Louis Dinnelle, Jean Baptiste Dubreuil, François Duchouquette (Dechouquette), André Dufrene (Dufresne), Presque Felix, François Fripagne (Fripagnier), François William Hodgens, Charles Jacquette (Jacquet), Joseph Gervais (Jerve, Jervais), Jean Baptiste La Bonte, Louis La Bonte, André La Chapelle, Louis La Liberté, François Landry, Joseph Landry, Michel Lanson (Lançon), Louis La Valle, François Leclairc (LeClerc, Le Claire), Alexie LeCompt, Guillaume Le Roux, Charles Lucier (Lussier), Etienne Lucier (Lussier), François Marcial (Martial), Jean Baptiste Desportes McKay, Jean Baptiste Ouvre (Ouvrier), Antoine Papin, Jean Baptiste Pillon, Antoine Plante, Jean Baptiste Provost (Prevost), François Robert, Joseph Saint Amant, Louis Saint Michel or St. Michel, Jean Baptiste Turcotte, André Vallé]. Kenneth W. Porter's *Roll of Overland Astorians &c.* in *Ore. Hist. Soc. Quar.*, XXXIV, pp. 103-112, 286; J. Neilson Barry's *Astorians &c.* in *Wash. Hist. Quar.*, XXIV, pp. 221-224, 226-231, 282-284, 286-290.

The text's "one woman and two children" were Pierre Dorion's squaw, Marie L'Aguivoise (*alias* Aioe) Dorion, and her two offspring. See J. Neilson Barry's *op. cit.*, XXIV, pp. 226-229.

45 For site of this village see note 100 on p. cxxv.

46 *Astoria*, I, p. 236, states: "The course taken by Mr. Hunt was at first to the northwest, but soon turned and kept generally to the southwest . . ."

47 Present-day Rampart (*alias* Oak) Creek, which emptied through Missouri's right bank at a spot approximately six miles below the site of the Aricara villages and two miles above the mouth of present-day Grand River. Lewis and Clark referred to it, not only as "Rear par or Beaver Dam R.," but also as "Maropa" or "Maripa." Bradbury termed it "Marapa." *L. & C. Journs.*, I, p. 183; *L. & C. Hist.*, p. 158, f.n.; *Bradbury* [*A*], p. 109; *Geol. South Dakota.*

48 In the French text this word is *forts*. Does it refer to beaver-dams or indian strongholds?

49 Seemingly impossible to identify because in this locality several small streams emptied through Grand River's left bank.

50 Grand River, emptying through Missouri's right bank in present-day Corson County, South Dakota. It was the "Waterhoo" (*alias* "Wetarhoo," "Waterehoo") of Lewis and Clark and of Brackenridge; the "Palanata Wakpa" or "Ree River" of Warren and of Reynolds. *L. & C. Hist.*, p. 157, f.n.; *Brackenridge*, p. 267; *Luttig*, p. 65; *Geol. South Dakota*. See, however, *Nation*, p. 501.

51 Crossed to Grand River's right bank. *Astoria*, I, p. 237, states that on July 23rd Hunt camped on the bank of "Big river" (*i.e.*, Grand River).

52 Present-day Firesteel Creek, which emptied through Grand River's right bank in present-day Corson County, South Dakota. *Geol. South Dakota.*

53 See note 57 on p. 22.

54 This was either an eastward flowing confluent of Firesteel Creek or else one of the several nearby northward flowing confluents of Grand River.

55 Present-day Black Horse Butte (*alias* Black Horse) Creek, which emptied through Grand River's right bank in what is now Corson County, South Dakota. *Geol. South Dakota.*

56 For similar accounts see *Bradbury* [*A*], p. 182; *Brackenridge*, p. 263.

57 Mountain sheep, *Ovis canadensis canadensis* (*Shaw*).

58 This seemingly was the northern end of present-day Slim Buttes (longitude 103°) in what is now Harding County, South Dakota.

59 These two tributaries were, in the order of Hunt's crossing them (1st) present-day Sand Creek and (2nd) present-day south fork of Grand River; Hunt crossing this fork above its confluence with Sand Creek.

60 Little Missouri River itself. Hunt crossed to its left bank.

61 Present-day Powder River Range.

62 *Astoria*, I, p. 247, identifies these hunters as Pierre Dorion, Alexander Carson and Jean Baptiste Gardapie. This Gardapie was not improbably the —— Sardepie of *Astoria*, II, p. 44, and the B. Gardeipied (*alias* Gariépy) who was "ducent" of canoe no. 7 in the Grand Brigade which left Fort George (Astoria) April 4, 1814. *Henry-Thomp.*, pp. 872, 875; *Franchere* [*A*], p. 206, [*B*], pp. 263 *et seq.*

63 Seemingly this was present-day Boxelder Creek, which emptied through Little Missouri's left bank in extreme southwestern corner of North Dakota.

64 Powder River Range.

65 From August 15 to 17 Hunt was apparently wandering in the southern foothills of the Powder River Range.

66 Mule deer, *Odocoileus hemionus hemionus* (*Rafinesque*), which is commonly though confusingly termed Rocky Mountain black-tail deer.

67 Doubtless meaning the white-tailed deer, *Odocoileus virginianus macrourus* otherwise termed *O. americanus macrourus.*

68 The tail is snow-white except for a tiny tip of black.

69 Country east of Powder River Range.

70 Present-day Big Horn Range.

71 Seemingly present-day Cloud Peak (altitude 13,165 feet), highest peak of Big Horn Range. See *Quad. Cloud Peak. Astoria,* I, pp. 256, 263, gives August 17 as the date when Hunt first espied this mountain.

72 Apparently *Ribes sanguineum* (*Pursh*) and *Ribes aureum* (*Pursh*).

73 Apparently *Ribes grossularia.*

74 Respectively *Ribes rotundifolium* and *R. oxyacanthoides.*

75 Chokecherries, *Prunus demissa* (*Nutt.*).

76 *Ursus americanus* (*Pallas*). But *Astoria,* I, pp. 256, 257, asserts the animals were grizzlies, *i.e., Ursus horribilis* (*Ord.*); this assertion being consonant with the French text's description of the men's fear.

77 One of the headwaters of the Little Missouri River and probably either its so-called north fork or else present-day Prairie Creek. *Quad. Devils Tower.*

78 Watershed between Little Missouri River and present-day Little Powder River.

79 *Astoria,* I, p. 261, allots these 34 miles to August 20 and 21.

80 The Mandan indians (of Siouan linguistic stock) claimed, as their territory, so much of the right bank of the Missouri River as, beginning at site of present-day city of Bismarck, N. D., extended many miles upstream.

81 Little Powder River.

82 Present-day Powder River below Crazy Woman Creek's confluence with it—this creek so named because of a mentally deranged squaw. *Geol. Wyoming.*

83 Watershed between Little Powder River and Powder River.

84 Either gray wolf, *Canis nubilus* (*Say*), or that variety of coyote, *Canis latrans,* which is more specifically styled *Canis nebracensis nebracensis* (*Merriam*).

85 Present-day Clear Creek, a northeasterly flowing confluent of Powder River. *Geol. Wyoming.*

86 Hunt seemingly ascended Clear Creek to the vicinity of site of present-day city of Buffalo, Johnson County, Wyoming.

87 Cloud Peak. Hunt's camp, because of his having horses, was most likely on a stream; and, if so, was not improbably on either the north or the south fork of Clear Creek, or else was on either present-day French Creek or present-day Rock Creek. *Quad. Fort McKinney; Geol. Wyoming.*

88 Because of description in *Astoria,* I, p. 268, the camp was probably on one of the four creeks mentioned in note 87 *ante,* though presumably not on the one occupied by Hunt's camp; and, because of the topography, was very likely in present-day Mowry Basin lying at the junction of the north and south forks of Rock Creek. *Quad. Fort McKinney.*

89 *Astoria,* I, p. 268, gives this distance as 16 miles.

90 Hunt here was seemingly travelling southward along the easterly foothills of the Big Horn Range.

91 Apparently this was the north fork of Crazy Woman Creek.

92 *Astoria*, I, p. 271, shows that Hunt seemingly had been attempting to force his way westward across the highest section of the Big Horn Range.

93 North fork of Crazy Woman Creek. *Astoria*, I, p. 271, states that Hunt's camp of September 3 was within six miles of the site of his camp of the previous day.

94 Wapiti, *Cervus canadensis canadensis* (*Erxleben*).

95 This route which Hunt successfully followed across the Big Horn Range was, because of the topography, doubtless identical with the trail that, in after years, was used by indians and soldiers and that, according to *Yellowstone*, ran as follows: Starting on the southwesterly outskirts of the site of present-day city of Buffalo and at an altitude of approximately 4900 feet, the trail ran southwesterly until, having cut across successively the headwaters of (1st) various confluents of both the north and middle forks of Crazy Woman Creek, (2nd) the north fork of Powder River, it, at a spot approximately six miles south by west from the summit of present-day Hazelton Peak and at an elevation of 8337 feet, crossed the main divide of the Big Horn Range. Thence the trail, by descending present-day Canyon Creek (for the most part keeping itself two miles back from the left bank), reached this creek's confluence with present-day Tensleep Creek. There the trail turned southerly; and, meeting Nowood Creek at a spot just south of the mouth of present-day Otter Creek, crossed to Nowood Creek's left bank and ascended it to its headwaters. Thence the trail veered westerly; and, immediately before reaching present-day Bridger Creek (a southerly flowing confluent of present-day Bad Water Creek), the trail forked, each of the two forks later crossing Bridger Creek, encountering Bad Water Creek, and descending it to its confluence with present-day Big Horn River. Incidentally, the forks first encountered Bad Water Creek at spots respectively some 18 and some four and one-half miles below Bridger Creek's mouth. Hunt's text suggests that he used the left fork. *Quads. Fort McKinney* and *Cloud Peak.*

96 Headwaters of Crazy Woman Creek.

97 Grizzly bear, for which see note 73 on p. 23.

98 Assuredly *mont Big-Horn* of the French text means here the Big Horn Range, and not any one particular mountain in that range, although earlier in the text this same term had denoted present-day Cloud Peak. See notes 71, 87. Hunt was now some 25 air-line miles southerly of Cloud Peak. See *Quad. Cloud Peak.* Query: did not the French translator err in stating that the mountain range was named for the river? It seems probable that the range, as the abode of the mountain sheep, would have been the first to receive the name.

99 We have arbitrarily translated as "southwest" the French text's *sud-est,* which patently should have been *sud-ouest.*

100 Nowood Creek.

101 *Fragaria vesca.*

102 Query: does this mean present-day Hazelton Peak in the Big Horn

Range? See *Quad. Cloud Peak. Astoria*, I, p. 277, seems to suggest that this "third mountain" was a peak in the present-day Owl Creek Range.

103 Meaning probably the titanic wall consisting of, from north to south, Cloud Peak (13,165 feet), Mather Peak (12,410 feet), Hazelton Peak (10,307 feet) and the slightly lesser heights connecting them. *Quad. Cloud Peak.*

104 Seemingly the country immediately northeast of headwaters of Bridger Creek.

105 Hunt's styling as Wind River this section of the present-day Big Horn River was in accord with a Western custom which lasted till late in the 1860's and which specified, as Wind River, not only Wind River proper, but also so much of the Big Horn (formed by the confluence of Wind River proper and the Popo Agie) as extended from this confluence to the upper or southerly end of Big Horn River's upper canyon. See *Raynolds*, p. 82. The text shows that Hunt first encountered Big Horn River at a spot a short distance south of this upper end of the canyon and thus at approximately the mouth of Bad Water Creek.

Incidentally, "Big Horn River" is derived from the Absarokas' name for this stream, *Ets-pot-agie—Ets-pot* meaning "mountain sheep" or "big horn" and *agie* "water" or "stream" (*Raynolds*, p. 54). *Popo-Agie* is also an Absarokan name, signifying headwaters.

106 Arapaho.

107 Seemingly Bad Water Creek, which in days less cultured than the present bore the robust name of "Stinking Water."

108 Quite possibly Bridger Creek.

109 Southerly end of upper canyon of Big Horn River.

110 Big Horn River.

111 Quite possibly either the grayling, *Thymallus montanus* (*Milner*), or the whitefish, *Coregonus williamsoni* (*Girard*).

112 Popo Agie River at its confluence with Wind River. See note 105.

113 Southeasterly end of Wind River Mountains.

114 Owl Creek Mountains.

115 Wind River Mountains.

116 The Owl Creek Mountains blended into the Shoshone Mountains, which in their turn merged with the Wind River Range. *Holt; Quads. Fremont Peak, Younts Peak* and *Ishawood.*

117 Crossed to Wind River's left bank.

118 Between the mouth of Popo Agie River and the confluence of present-day Warm Spring Creek, the trail crossed Wind River eight times. *Yellowstone.*

119 It is impossible to identify both of these confluents because Wind River had many tributaries. However, we may well assume that the one described as coming from the northwest was so much of Wind River as lay above the mouth of present-day DuNoir River. See *Quad. Younts Peak*. This assumption is

supported by the statement which *Astoria*, I, pp. 277, 278, makes to the effect that camp on the night of the 14th was at the forks of Wind River.

120 Flax, *Linum perenne. L. & C. Hist.*, p. 423.

121 This trail, because running southwest, unquestionably led over present-day Union Pass. See note 152 on pp. 101, 102.

122 Present-day Teton Range, for details of which see *Quad. Grand Teton.*

123 Snake River.

124 Summit of Union Pass. See note 152 on pp. 101-102.

125 Present-day Green River. Hunt's point of initial contact with it, as *Yellowstone* and the local topography suggest, was doubtless at or near the spot where present-day Wagon Creek empties through Green River's right bank approximately in latitude 43° 21′ 40″, longitude 109° 59′ 25″. *Yellowstone; Wyoming Forest.*

126 Immediately east of Hunt's point of initial contact, the river flowed westerly for a short distance; but from this point of contact it flowed southerly. See *Wyoming Forest.*

127 For gooseberries in this general region, see *L. & C. Hist.*, pp. 379, 420, 440, 447, 448.

128 *Astoria*, I, p. 280, says purple.

129 For currants in this general region, see *L. & C. Hist.*, p. 419.

130 Meaning undoubtedly the valley's side furthest from Wind River Mountains. That Hunt descended Green River to a spot a few miles below the mouth of present-day Beaver Creek may be inferred from, not only the context, but also the reference which *Astoria*, I, p. 281, makes to "a mountain in the west," this mountain very possibly being present-day Lander Peak (altitude 10,456 feet), for which see *Quad. Afton.*

131 Seemingly Beaver Creek. *Wyoming Forest; Geol. Wyoming.*

132 Watershed between headwaters of north fork of Beaver Creek (this north fork being today styled North Beaver Creek) and headwaters of present-day Fish (*alias* Fisherman) Creek. *Teton; Wyoming Forest; Quad. Gros Ventre; Geol. Wyoming.*

133 Fish (*alias* Fisherman) Creek.

134 For numerous confluents see *Wyoming Forest; Quad. Gros Ventre; Geol. Wyoming.*

135 Present-day Hoback River.

136 Present-day south fork of Snake River.

137 Hoback River.

138 Teton Range, for details of which see *Quad. Grand Teton.*

139 The sentence seems to suggest (1st) that Hunt's original plan had been to cross present-day Twogwotee Pass and, having thus attained the headwaters of present-day Buffalo Fork, to descend that Fork to its confluence with south fork of Snake River (see *Geol. Wyoming; Yellowstone; Quad. Mt. Leidy*); and

(2nd) that the Twogwotee Pass was the one crossed by Robinson, Hoback and Reznor when, months before, they had journeyed eastward from Henry's Fort to their meeting with Hunt on the Missouri River.

140 See note 57 on p. 22.

141 Upper end of present-day Upper Canyon of south fork of Snake River. *Yellowstone; Teton.*

142 Present-day Teton Pass.

143 This was the route later taken in reverse by Robert Stuart. See his entries of October 2-7 (pp. 152, 153).

144 Seemingly the French text should have read *trois,* instead of *deux;* the three hunters being Robinson, Hoback and Reznor. *Astoria,* II, p. 12.

145 Present-day Trail Creek. *Teton; Targhee.*

146 Doubtless the flatland at site of present-day town of Victor, Idaho. *Targhee.*

147 Present-day Teton River. *Targhee.*

148 Teton River had numerous small confluents. *Targhee; Geol. Idaho.*

149 North fork of Teton River. *Targhee.*

150 Flowed westerly to its junction with south fork of Snake River.

151 Probably present-day Pincock Hot Springs, for which see note 4 on p. 168.

152 The French text's word is *brulante. Astoria,* II, p. 13, mentions the spring as "a hot spring continually emitting a cloud of vapor."

153 For site of Henry's Fort see note 16 on p. 169.

154 North fork of Snake River (known also as Henry's Fork). *Targhee; Geol. Idaho.*

155 See note 67 on p. 43.

156 Edward Robinson, John Hoback, Jacob Reznor and Martin H. Cass.

157 Trout, *Salmo clarkii.*

158 The horses had numbered 121 on leaving the Crow encampment east of the Big Horn Mountains (p. 284), and an additional horse had been purchased after crossing those mountains (p. 286). Miller's party, on its departure from Henry's Fort, had been given four of the animals (p. 290; *Astoria,* II, p. 16). It does not appear how many had earlier been left with the four men detached at the mouth of the Hoback. See *Astoria,* II, pp. 10, 11.

159 Teton River.

160 Though the river's course was actually south and southwest, the French text states merely "S."

161 Grand Teton (altitude 13,747 feet), the highest mountain in the Teton Range. *Quad. Grand Teton.*

162 This portage was seemingly at site of present-day town of Idaho Falls (sometime also known interchangeably as Eagle Rock or Taylor's Bridge), where there was a cataract 30 feet in height. The text's description is mislead-

ing to the extent that it mentions mountains as the constrictors of the river. The actual compressor is a lava flow lying between hills and through which the river has gnawed a channel with perpendicular sides. *Astoria*, II, p. 19; *Yellowstone; Bulletin* [*A*], p. 28.

163 See note 63 on p. 226.

164 Magpies, *Pica pica hudsonica.*

165 Robins, *Hesperocichla naevia.*

166 "Canoe River" (*Canoe-River* in French text), as used here and later in our translation, means present-day Snake River below its forks.

167 Present-day Portneuf River and a smaller and neighboring stream, Bannock Creek (in bygone days known also as Bannock River and Pannock River), emptied through Snake's left bank. Present-day Boone Creek emptied through Snake's right bank.

168 By "Chochoni" (*sic* in French text), as used here and elsewhere in our translation, is meant Shoshone.

169 *Astoria*, II, p. 21, states: "about two inches long."

170 *Astoria*, II, p. 21, states that the arrows were made "of the wood of rose bushes, and other crooked plants, but carefully straightened."

171 Query: might not this stone (*pierre verte* in French text) have been obsidian from present-day Yellowstone National Park?

172 Present-day American Falls. *Geol. Idaho.*

173 At this spot, which today is locally termed The Narrows, the bluffs abruptly constrict the river to less than half its normal width; and an irregularly shaped fault in the rock of the river's bed creates a rapid which, varying from four to ten feet in height, descends at its southeasterly end less steeply than at any other place.

174 The place of Snake River's emergence from the hills was apparently at the mouth of present-day Raft River. *Symons* [*B*].

175 While the French text, with palpable error, gives "70" as the mileage for this day and "40" as that for the following day, *Astoria*, II, p. 23, states "nearly eighty miles" as the aggregate distance for the two days.

176 Seemingly at lower end of site of present-day Lake Walcott, *alias* Minidoka Reservoir, which has been formed by damming the Snake. *Geol. Idaho.*

177 Because of text's description of river, this spot seemingly was in vicinity of site of present-day town of Burley, Idaho. *Geol. Idaho.*

178 Immediately below site of present-day dam at Milner, Idaho. See *Geol. Idaho*, as also note 65 on p. 122.

179 Antoine Clappine. See p. LXXXV; *Astoria*, II, p. 23.

180 Hunt, during this journey, actually passed Shoshone Falls (212 feet high) and Twin Falls (182 feet high), for which see note 53 on pp. 121, 122. His marked underestimate of height was due to the fact that, from his vantage spot on the rim of the canyon, he could have seen no more than the crests of these

particular falls, which descended into a deep rift in the floor of the main canyon.

181 October 30, according to *Astoria*, II, p. 26.

182 The later text mentions additional caching. *Astoria*, II, p. 30 and Stuart's entries of August 29, 30 (pp. 111-113) give the total number of caches as nine.

183 "Big River" ("Big-River" in French text), as used here and later in the text, means Columbia River.

184 This Crooks party purposed, so *Astoria*, II, p. 27, states, "retracing by land the weary course they had made by water, intending, should they not find relief nearer at hand, to keep on until they should reach Henry's Fort, where they hoped to find the horses they had left there, and to return with them to the main body."

That Crooks's companions numbered, not three (as stated in the text), but five (as stated in *Astoria*, II, p. 27) appears from the following tabulation:

The expedition, when leaving the Aricara village, numbered (p. 281 *ante*)		65
Deduct:		
Rose, who stayed with the Crows (p. 285 *ante; Astoria*, I, pp. 269-272)	1	
Carson, St. Michel, Detayé and Delaunay, who were detached at mouth of Hoback River (*Astoria*, II, pp. 10, 11)	4	
Miller, Hoback, Reznor, Robinson and Cass, who were detached at Henry's Fort (p. 290 *ante; Astoria*, II, pp. 14-16)	5	
Antoine Clappine, who was drowned (p. 292 *ante; Astoria*, II, p. 23)	1	
Reed and 3 men, who left Caldron Linn (p. 292 *ante; Astoria*, II, p. 26)	4	
McKenzie and 4 men, who left Caldron Linn (p. 293 *ante; Astoria*, II, p. 27)	5	
McClellan and 3 men, who left Caldron Linn (p. 293 *ante; Astoria*, II, p. 27)	4	
Hunt, 31 men, 1 woman and 2 children, who waited at Caldron Linn (p. 293 *ante; Astoria*, II, p. 28)	35	59
		6

This remainder of six consisted, accordingly, of Crooks and his five companions.

185 Doubtless the bison meat purchased by Hunt September 18 (p. 287).

186 See note 182.

187 The site of this camp and the location of nine of Hunt's caches may confidently be assumed to have been on the Snake's left bank and approximately two and one-fourth miles below the present dam at Milner, Idaho. *Astoria*, II, pp. 28, 30, 33, and the French redaction of Hunt's diary suggest that the camp

and the caches were near each other. Stuart tells us (pp. 111, 112) that these caches were not far from his own camp of August 29-30 and that this Stuart camp was on the left bank at a spot one mile downstream from where Crooks's canoe had been wrecked. Also we know (see notes 44, 65 on pp. 120, 122) that the scene of this wreck was one and one-fourth miles below the site of the Milner dam.

In conflict with this assumption, *Astoria*, II, pp. 23-25, 28, 30, 33, somewhat confusingly states that, when Crooks's canoe was wrecked, Hunt's entire party halted and "encamped upon the borders of the Caldron Linn" and that there they cached their surplus goods. The conflict is due to the fact that Caldron Linn is clearly shown by Stuart (entry of August 29, pp. 111-113) to have been some nine and one-half miles downstream from the scene of the wreck—*i.e.*, to have been the whirlpool at the foot of present-day Dry Creek Falls in the town of Murtaugh. However, the conflict is more apparent than real inasmuch as *Astoria*, though thus vaguely differing from Stuart as to the location of Caldron Linn, completely agrees with him in the description of its appearance. See Stuart's entry of August 29 (p. 112) and *Astoria*, II, pp. 23, 24.

Additional proof that Hunt's camp of October 28 was not at Caldron Linn is found in the French redaction of Hunt's diary, which (at pp. 292, 293) declares, in effect, that Hunt, after making caches October 31-November 2 in presumably the vicinity of his camp of October 28, attempted to reascend Snake River with four laden canoes and succeeded, with three of these canoes, in regaining the site of his October 27 camp in the neighborhood of the present-day town of Burley, Idaho (note 177), where he cached some goods and whence on November 7 he returned to the site of his camp of October 28, where he again made caches. It is highly improbable that, starting at Caldron Linn, he could have navigated laden canoes up Dry Creek Falls and the series of cruel rapids immediately above them.

188 See note 185.

189 This agrees with *Astoria*, II, pp. 33, 34.

190 That this number "nineteen" is correct and that *Astoria's* "eighteen" (*Astoria*, II, p. 34) is erroneous appears from the following tabulation:

After the death of Antoine Clappine, the people in the main expedition totalled		54
Deduct		
McKenzie, McClellan and their 7 companions who left Caldron Linn (p. 293 *ante; Astoria*, II, p. 27)	9	
Reed and 3 men who left Caldron Linn, though 2 of them returned thither (pp. 292, 293, *ante; Astoria*, II, p. 31); thus making Reed and 1 man as absentees	2	
Hunt's immediate party as stated in the text	23	34
		20

Accordingly, this remainder of 20 consisted of Crooks and his 19 men.

191 Seemingly in the neighborhood of site of present-day town of Hagerman (*Geol. Idaho*). Hunt's failure to comment on Shoshone Falls and Twin Falls (each of which he must have passed on November 10) is explained in note 53 on pp. 121, 122.

192 Apparently present-day Big Wood River (formerly known as Malade River). *Geol. Idaho*, as also note 18 on pp. 117, 118.

193 Either buttes south of present-day Camas River or else possibly southern end of present-day Sawtooth Range. *Geol. Idaho.*

194 Probably present-day Clover Creek near site of town of King Hill. *Geol. Idaho.*

195 The absence of sagebrush indicates the country in the vicinity of present-day Canyon Creek, which creek emptied through the Snake's right bank a short distance east of the 116th meridian. *Geol. Idaho.*

196 A now obsolete dry measure of capacity, being the sixteenth part of the old French bushel and equal to 1.43 pints.

197 Sagebrush plain west of Canyon Creek. See note 195. The later text discloses that, when probably a short distance west of the mouth of this creek, Hunt struck inland from the Snake and, going almost due north, encountered present-day Boise River at a spot near the site of the city of Boise, and that thence he descended that river along its left bank to just above its confluence with the Snake, where, again turning northward, he resumed his progress along the Snake's right bank. See also *Astoria*, II, pp. 37-39; J. Neilson Barry's *The trail of the Astorians* in *Ore. Hist. Soc. Quar.*, XIII, pp. 233, 234.

198 *Astoria*, II, p. 38, states "all day."

199 Boise River, for which see note 138 on pp. 99, 100.

200 See note 58 on p. 22.

201 *Astoria*, II, p. 38, states: "An Indian immediately laid claim to the horse of Mr. Hunt, saying that it had been stolen from him. There was no disproving a fact, supported by numerous bystanders, and which the horse stealing habits of the Indians rendered but too probable; so Mr. Hunt relinquished his steed to the claimant; not being able to retain him by a second purchase."

202 Boise River.

203 The French text's use of *au-dessous* ("below") instead of *au-dessus* ("above") is patently erroneous. Also we have the assurance of *Astoria*, II, p. 39, which states: ". . . crossed it just before its junction with Snake River. . . ." Accordingly, we arbitrarily translate *au-dessous* into "above."

204 Present-day Payette River, for which see note 142 on p. 100.

205 Present-day Weiser River, for which see note 143 on p. 100.

206 Seemingly this "defile" (*défile* in French text) was on present-day Mann Creek, a southerly flowing confluent of Weiser River. The text on this p. [63] as well as the subsequent text on p. [69] strongly suggest that Hunt followed Weiser River as far as to the mouth of Mann Creek, ascended this creek to its

headwaters, turned westerly across the headwaters of present-day Monroe Creek (a southerly flowing confluent of Weiser River), thereby reached the headwaters of present-day Wolf Creek (a westerly flowing confluent of Snake River), and descended that creek to its mouth approximately in longitude 117° 10′ 17″, latitude 44° 31′ 15″ (*Quads. Weiser* and *Pine*). By this route, Hunt would have made a short-cut across the base of the Snake's bend which began at Weiser River's mouth.

207 These huts, according to the later context, seem to have been on an upper reach of Mann Creek.

208 See note 120.

209 The Snake began to have a narrower bed at the mouth of its confluent, Powder River. *Snake Plan*, sheets F and G.

210 This description strongly suggests that Hunt's camp-sites of December 3 and 4 were respectively at the southerly and northerly ends of the Snake River's bend known today as the Oxbow, wherein the river, approximately in latitude 44° 57′ 40″, veered abruptly to the northeast and, in order to gain one mile of northing, flowed four and one-half miles around a hairpin turn (*Snake Plan*, sheet F; *Geol. Idaho*). Hunt here was at the southerly end of the so-called Seven Devils mountain range.

211 In the four miles of river bed between the Oxbow's lower end and the site of present-day town of Homestead, Ore., were four rapids. Three-quarters of a mile below that town's site were present-day Kerrs Rapids where the river was divided by an island into two very narrow channels. The text on p. [67] —*i.e.*, our p. 298—strongly suggests that this was the spot where Hunt encountered Crooks. *Snake Plan*, sheet F.

212 *Astoria*, II, p. 45, identifies this man as François Leclairc.

213 The mileage is not disclosed. However, Stuart in his entry of August 12 (p. 81) gives it as 30.

214 Present-day Wallowa Mountains, formerly styled Powder River Mountains.

215 It seems impossible to identify the particular river-stretch observed by Crooks at the end of his 30 necessarily sinuous miles of travel along the mountains flanking the narrowed Snake below Kerrs Rapids. Wholly commensurate with his mention of extreme constriction were at least three such stretches—the mileages hereinafter mentioned being measured along the Snake's channel:—*i.e.* [1] the stretch, some four miles in length, extending downstream from the mouth of present-day Doyle Creek (this mouth 11 miles below Kerrs Rapids); [2] the short stretch at the mouth of present-day Hells Creek (18½ miles below Kerrs Rapids); and [3] various sections of the stretch beginning 21 miles below Kerrs Rapids and extending to the mouth of present-day Rush Creek (this mouth 34 miles below Kerrs Rapids). *Snake Plan*, sheets E, F.

216 This conversation had been restricted to shouting across the river. *Astoria*, II, p. 46.

Appendix A

217 The river's course for many miles below this spot was approximately northeast. In the entire course from Huntington, Ore., to the mouth of the Clearwater River in Idaho (187¾ miles), there were only two due easterly flowing stretches (each of them one mile long) and four due westerly flowing stretches (respectively five, three and one-half, one, and one miles long). They all lay far below the Oxbow. *Snake Plan*, sheets A-H.

218 Seemingly the Weiser, Payette and Boise Rivers.

219 See *Astoria*, II, pp. 47 *et seq.*, for a similar account.

220 François Leclairc. See note 212.

221 *Astoria*, II, p. 48, states that two men were left with Crooks and Leclairc.

222 *Astoria*, II, pp. 49, 50, alleges that Hunt had three companions.

223 There must have been acquired somewhere another horse, concerning the acquisition of which both the text and *Astoria* are silent. Each of these sources, although relating purchases which (made November 17, 19, 22) totalled four horses and although mentioning (1) an indian's taking (November 1) one horse, and (2) the Hunt party's eating (November 27, December 1, 5) three horses, nevertheless avers that on December 7 the party still had one horse.

224 *Astoria*, II, pp. 51-53, states that "Five of their horses were eagerly seized" and also that "One of the chief dangers attending the enfeebled condition of Mr. Crooks and his companions, was their being overtaken by the Indians whose horses had been seized: though Mr. Hunt hoped that he had guarded against any resentment on the part of the savages, by leaving various articles in their lodge, more than sufficient to compensate for the outrage he had been compelled to commit." *Mo. Gaz.* and *Niles*, p. 266, add that, in exchange for the five horses, Hunt gave "three guns and some other articles."

225 *Astoria*, II, pp. 52, 53, identifies this man as Jean Baptiste Prevost.

226 Seemingly the hills lying between Mann Creek and Snake River. Their altitudes ranged from 900 to 4000 feet above the level of Snake River. *Quads. Weiser* and *Pine.*

227 Weiser River.

228 Snake River.

229 The French text, with patent error, states *possible* instead of *impossible.*

230 Weiser River.

231 See pp. 354, 355.

232 *Astoria*, II, p. 55, by using the expression "the thirteen men," implies that only 13 men of Crooks's immediate party were then on the Snake's left bank; whereas there were in fact 16—*i.e.*, the 13 in question and also the 3 additional men mentioned in note 235 *infra.*

233 *Astoria*, II, p. 55, states that the conversation was maintained by shouting across Snake River before Hunt crossed it. The text, in conjunction with *Astoria*, II, pp. 55, 56, while not disclosing the exact spot of Hunt's crossing the Snake, seems to imply that it was a short distance below the mouth of Weiser River.

234 *Astoria*, II, p. 53, identifies these men as John Day and Jean Baptiste Dubreuil.

235 *Astoria*, II, pp. 56, 193, identifies these men as Jean Baptiste Turcotte, André LaChapelle and François Landry.

236 *I.e.*, Hunt's Caldron Linn party (consisting of Hunt, 19 men, 1 woman and 2 children) together with Crooks's Caldron Linn party (consisting of Crooks and 19 men), after deduction of 1 man (Prevost) drowned and 6 additional men —Crooks, Day, Dubreuil, Turcotte, LaChapelle and Landry—left behind at Snake River.

237 The account beginning here is somewhat meagre as concerns geographical details; but, according to Stuart's entry of August 12 (p. 81), Hunt's route from Snake River to the Umatilla was identical with that later taken in reverse direction by Stuart and described by him in detail in his entries of August 1-12 (pp. 76-80).

238 Present-day Powder River, for which see note 70 on p. 94.

239 Present-day Blue Mountains, for which see note 77 on p. 73.

240 Present-day Baker Valley, for which see note 74 on p. 94.

241 Powder River.

242 Powder River.

243 Hunt seemingly quitted Powder River at the vertex of the hairpin turn which the river made at the northerly end of Baker Valley.

244 Present-day Grande Ronde Valley, for which see note 43 on p. 92.

245 Present-day Grande Ronde River, for which see notes 28 and 57 on pp. 90, 91, 93.

246 Near the present city of LaGrande and today known as The Narrows. See note 45 on p. 92.

247 The birthplace of the Dorion baby, apparently in the northerly end of Baker Valley, was probably in the vicinity of site of present-day town of North Powder, if Hunt's route was that later taken in reverse direction by Stuart. In conjunction with the text, see *Astoria*, II, pp. 59-61.

248 If Hunt was using the trail later taken in reverse direction by Stuart, this "small river" comprised (1st) Grande Ronde River above its exit from The Narrows, (2nd) its confluent, present-day Starkey Creek, and (3rd) the latter stream's confluent, present-day McCoy Creek. See Stuart's entries of August 1-5 (pp. 76-78).

249 If Hunt's trail and that later taken in reverse direction by Stuart were identical, this stream was present-day McKay Creek. See Stuart's entries of August 1, 2 (p. 76).

250 Probably present-day Sumac Gulch, for which see note 21 on p. 89.

251 The place of death of the Dorion baby is not disclosed. *Astoria*, II, p. 62, states merely that the baby died during the course of the day's march.

252 Apparently McKay Creek.

253 Present-day Umatilla River, for which see note 73 on p. 72.

254 Tushepaws (of Salishan linguistic stock), for whom see *L. & C. Hist.*, p. 583; *Hodge*, II, p. 853.

255 Michael Carriere, as to whose exact fate there is seemingly no record.

256 Umatilla River.

257 Present-day Walla Walla River, for which see note 84 on pp. 73, 74.

258 This *carte* of the French text, though unidentified by that text, was very possibly the Clark map reproduced in *L. & C. Journs.*, VIII, map 31, part II. For the French text's *bancs de coquillages* (beds of shellfish) see *L. & C. Hist.*, pp. 644, 646; *L. & C. Journs.*, III, pp. 131, 133.

259 Present-day Celilo Falls, for which see note 19 on p. 66.

260 *Astoria*, II, p. 67, styles these indians "Akai-chies." Their tribal identity is unknown. *Hodge*, I, p. 32.

261 For further details regarding these alleged whites see *Astoria*, II, pp. 65, 66.

262 Because of the text's statement that Hunt on leaving the Umatilla travelled westward and because of the route indicated on *Nouvelles Annales*' map (facing p. 270 *ante*), it would seem that he first encountered the Columbia at a spot west of the Umatilla's mouth. However, *Astoria*, II, p. 66, avers that the spot was "not far from the influx of the Wallah-Wallah."

263 Columbia River.

264 Present-day Deschutes River, which emptied through Columbia's left bank and for which see note 44 on p. 70.

265 Celilo Falls.

266 *Astoria*, II, pp. 69-71, 96, styles this "Wish-ram." Also see Henry J. Biddle's *Wishram* in *Ore. Hist. Soc. Quar.*, XXVII, pp. 113-130.

267 The upper end of the Dalles, for which see note 1 on p. 64.

268 Present-day Okanagan River in state of Washington.

269 *Astoria*, II, p. 73, states that Hunt "procured the requisite number."

270 *Astoria*, II, p. 73, states that the departure occurred on the 5th.

271 Present-day Klickitat River emptying through the Columbia's right bank, and for which see note 126 on p. 49.

272 The French text's word *simplicité* we have arbitrarily translated as "wilful caprice," it being the phrase employed by *Astoria*, II, p. 73, in describing this same event.

273 The text's mention of Hunt's horses suggests that the village was on the Columbia's right bank to which the animals had earlier been taken (see p. 306). If so, it was not improbably the group of huts which, at mouth of present-day Little White Salmon River, was noticed by Lewis and Clark. *L. & C. Journs.*, VIII, map 32, pt. 1, as also note 127 on p. 49 *ante*.

274 His death on the ill-fated ship *Tonquin*.

275 Upper Cascades of the Columbia, for which see note 92 on pp. 45, 46.

276 Robert Stuart, when making his overland journey, used the portage on the right bank. See his entries of July 6-11 (pp. 34-37).

277 Hunt had here reached the foot of Upper Cascades of the Columbia.

278 Low water, the spring freshet not having begun.

279 For these waterfalls, see note 91 on p. 45.

280 Lower Cascades of the Columbia, for which see note 92 on pp. 45, 46.

281 Distance exaggerated. Was actually some four and one-half miles. See note 92 on pp. 45, 46.

282 Upper end of Upper Cascades of the Columbia.

283 Hunt had here reached the foot of Lower Cascades of the Columbia.

284 Present-day Sandy River, which emptied through Columbia's left bank, and for which see note 81 on p. 44.

285 Present-day Willamette River, which emptied through Columbia's left bank, and for which see note 48 on p. 42.

286 Present-day Sauvie Island, for which see note 56 on p. 43.

287 Present-day Bachelor Island, Deer Island, Burke Island and Martin Island. *Charts* Nos. 6153, 6154, as also notes 53 and 42 on pp. 43, 41.

288 Harbor seals, *Phoca vitulina*.

289 Present-day Cowlitz River, for which see note 31 on p. 41.

290 Present-day Walker Island, Fisher Island, Crims Island. *Charts* Nos. 6152, 6153.

291 There is doubt as to whether the French text's *inondé*, as used here, referred to water or to fog. Though too early in the year for the Columbia's annual freshet, there may perhaps have been a local flooding. On the other hand, *inondé*, as employed in the following day's entry, clearly seems, from its context, to have related to fog.

292 For this Hellwit (Echeloot) village see note 20 on p. 40. Stuart (p. 30) states that Astorians were stationed at this village for purpose of procuring fish and game-birds.

293 Eulachon or candlefish, for which see note 104 on pp. 25, 26.

294 Apparently present-day Wallace Island, which is halved by a narrow channel. *Chart* No. 6152.

295 Wappattoo, for which see note 43 on p. 20.

296 See note 291.

297 Present-day Cathlamet Bay, for which see note 2 on p. 39.

298 *Franchere* [*A*], p. 114, [*B*], pp. 150, 151, state that February 15 was the date of Hunt's arrival.

299 The rest of the French version, which continues through p. 119 of *Tome* X and pp. 21-113 of *Tome* XII, has been excluded from our printed translation because, except in the particulars hereinafter mentioned, it amounts to no more than a mediocre rendering (principally metaphrastic, though, in part, paraphrastic, and, in other part, omissive) of Stuart's travelling memoranda.

The excepted particulars are represented by statements interpolated into the entries of November 2 (see note 34 on p. 201 *ante*) and April 4 (see note 83 on p. 227 *ante*).

Despite our thus refraining from printing an English rendering of the entire French version, we have reproduced (facing p. 270 *ante*) the map which is mentioned in *Nouvelles Annales*, X, p. 11 and which, in the French volumes, faces p. 21 of *Tome* XII.

APPENDIX B

INDIAN TRIBES MENTIONED BY STUART

APPENDIX B

INDIAN TRIBES MENTIONED BY STUART

In the matter of tribal names, the multiplicity of variant spellings has been due to the fact that, because the indians had no written languages, the recording of names was dependent on phonetic transcription by hearers of indians' talk.

When stating the reputed sizes of various Western tribes, the present appendix adopts the wording of the person who made the cited estimate. Since some of these estimates were in terms of "souls" and others in terms of "warriors," the reader should bear in mind that in early days the whites assumed that from one-fifth to one-quarter of a Western tribe's membership consisted of warriors.

For sake of the reader's eyes, this appendix fails to contain the numerous quotation marks which otherwise would disclose a very extensive indebtedness to the writings of Chittenden and Coues.

ABSAROKA, more commonly known as CROW

The indians of this tribe of, at most, some 10,000 souls called it Absaroka or Apsaroka, which is said to have signified a species of hawk. This name the early French fur traders translated into the term *Corbeau*, and accordingly they styled these indians *les Corbeaux*. The French appellation was later converted into English, thus pinning on the tribe the name of "Crow." Incidentally, the word Absaroka—this being its modern form of spelling—has in the past appeared as Absaroke, Absaraka, Absoraka, Aubsaroke, Absaruque, Upsaroka.

Although the above derivation is the one commonly accepted, *Clark*, p. 133, lists three other possible sources, all of them traditive. (1) In very early days, the tribe owned a pet crow to which was accorded marked attention and devotion. (2) During a fight between Grosventres (Minitari) and Sioux, some Absarokan braves sat on neighboring hills; and, at their refusal to descend and join in the combat, were asked why they sat up there like "a lot of crows." (3) The name may be a corrupted form of the local savages' term for "manifold," the first stomach of a herbivorous animal; and the Absarokas and Grosventres (Minitari) once quarrelled over the ownership of a bison's manifold.

The Absarokas belonged to the Hidatsa sub-stock of the Siouan family.

Their home territory in Stuart's time was principally the valley and watershed of present-day Wyoming's Big Horn River; but it extended thence easterly far enough to include, despite other tribes' resistance, the valleys of the Rosebud, Tongue, and Powder Rivers and also a strip on the bank of the Yellowstone River.

They had no fixed villages, and, as tepee dwellers and thoroughly restive nomads, were almost ever on the move, whether inside their own domain or else outside it during frequent raids and hunting excursions in every direction.

Essentially equestrian, they owned, in proportion to their numbers, more horses than did any other tribe in the Missouri River's watershed. Most expert of horse stealers and skilful of camp robbers among all the tribes in the West, thievery was with them a passion executed with consummate artistry and at times with sauciest humor.

Despite their pilferage of the animals and camps of the white man, they rarely killed him or waged war against him. On the contrary they courted, in a degree unusual among indians, the presence of such white-blooded or partially white-blooded men as they approved; and two such favorites, Edward Rose (of mixed descent from white, negro and Cherokee) and James P. Beckwourth (a mulatto), not only were adopted into the tribe but also were made sub-chiefs.

Among all the indian nations of the West, the Crows, though exacting and whimsical in business dealings, were the largest producers of bison pelts for the fur traders.

Their bitter foes were the Cheyennes, Arapahoes, Sioux, and the two Blackfeet septs known respectively as Siksikau and as Atsina (*alias* Grosventre of the Prairie), for which two septs see under BLACKFEET, pp. 334-336. The hostilities with these particular Blackfeet were well-nigh ceaseless save possibly, if tradition be accurate, during the few years in which an Absarokan band (the so-called River Crows), after Cheyennes and Arapahoes had ousted it from its home, found refuge within the bailiwick of the Atsinas.

More than half a century subsequent to Stuart's encountering the Crows, various of them through two decades acted most efficiently as scouts for the U. S. army in its several campaigns against the Sioux.

Chittenden, pp. 684-691, 852, 855-858; *L. & C. Hist.*, pp. 98, 198, 199, 1155; *Bonner; Fremont*, p. 30; *Astoria*, I, pp. 243-245; *Clyman*, pp. 39-43; *Clark*, pp. 132-138; *Hodge*, I, pp. 367-369; pp. 284, 285 *ante*.

Appendix B

ARAPAHOE, sometimes, as occasionally by Stuart, termed ARAPOHAY or ARAPAYHA

The Arapahoes (this name possibly derived from the Pawnees' word *tirapihu* or *larapihu*, meaning "trader") called themselves *Inunaina*, meaning "our people," and were of Algonquian stock.

The Arapahoes, the Atsinas (*alias* Grosventres of the Prairie, for whom see under BLACKFEET, pp. 334-336) and the Cheyennes (see pp. 340-342) were once close neighbors; the Arapahoes' home being either on the headwaters of the Mississippi River or on the nearby Red River of the North, the Cheyennes sharing this territory, and the Grosventres being on the Saskatchewan River of Canada. For some reason, probably because of pressure by the Sioux, they all migrated: the Cheyennes, the earliest to depart, moving southwardly; the Arapahoes, the next to leave, going toward the southwest; and finally the Grosventres of the Prairies pushing westward to the foothills of the Rocky Mountains.

The Arapahoes, in their migration, reached ultimately the upper stretches of the Missouri River, whence a portion of them (the later so-called Northern Arapahoes) veered to the headwaters of the Yellowstone River, while the rest of them (the later so-called Southern Arapahoes) made their way to the valley of the South Platte River in northeastern Colorado. Though continuing to occupy not only this valley but also the eastern watershed of the adjacent mountains, numbers of these Southern Arapahoes were wont to push westerly over the continental divide and thence to trap on streams as far westward as the Utes would suffer them to intrude.

The Southern Arapahoes (and it was with them exclusively and never with the Northern branch that Stuart dealt) were a wandering, tent-dwelling folk of some 2,500 souls. They were a brave, candid and usually honest people, much less given to beggary and thieving than were most other indians. Though in the main not aggressive or warlike and though ordinarily at peace with their indian neighbors other than the Utes on their west and Pawnees on their east, they could be sturdy fighters, and, during the earlier years of the fur trade, they were very hostile to the whites who entered their country.

In the matter of furs, they were extensive producers and astute traders.

After the year 1877, Arapahoes (both Northern and Southern) frequently served as scouts for the U. S. army, though prior to that year comparatively few of them rendered such aid.

The name Arapahoe is now carried by a county, two towns, two creeks and an important mountain range, all within the present-day state of Colorado.

Chittenden, pp. 852, 878, 879; *L. & C. Hist.*, pp. 56, 98, 147, 148; *Clark*, pp. 38-43; *Hodge*, I, pp. 72-74.

Black Arm, as styled by Stuart. See under caption of Uta, p. 363

Blackfeet

This equestrian tribe of Algonquian stock contained some 14,000 souls. It claimed for its home such of the present-day state of Montana's lands as were represented by the Missouri River's watershed above the mouth of Milk River, though the claim to so much of this area—the richest beaver country in the West—as lay westward of the Three Forks of the Missouri was frequently and vigorously resisted by other nations.

As regards the origin of the tribal name, there are two traditions. When the entire tribe was living in very early days on Canada's Saskatchewan River or possibly even to the north of it, discord arose within the tribe; and thereupon the Siksikau group, seceding, began its trek southward toward its ultimate home upon the upper reaches of the Missouri. During this journey, the migrants trudged across prairies which recently had been swept by fire; and the resultant sooting of their moccasins suggested to an encountered Absaroka indian that his own people's term for blackened feet would be a fitting name for the newcomers. Next came this term's direct translation from Absarokan language into French and thence into English. The second tradition is to the effect that the soil of the Blackfeet's early Canadian home was swart and therefore soiled their footwear.

The name Blackfoot is now borne by a river and a town in the present-day state of Idaho.

The tribe was comprised of four distinct bands:

(1) Siksikau (*alias* Siksika)—from *siksinam*, "black," and *ka*, root of *Oqkatsh*, "foot"—being the Blackfeet proper and living in the valley of the Milk River.

(2) Pikuni, being known otherwise as Piegan (this latter name from a chief who wore a robe badly dressed and spotted) and centering around the mouth of the Marias River.

(3) Kainah (*Ah-kai-nah*, "many chiefs" from *a-kai-im*, "many," and *ni-nah*, "chiefs"), being known otherwise as Kiara (*i.e.*, "old-time people") and as Blood and dwelling on the headwaters of the Marias and Milk Rivers.

(4) Atsina (whom *Clark*, pp. 39, 197, and *Hodge*, I, p. 113, allot to the Arapahoes instead of to the Blackfeet), calling itself *Aaninena*, which meant "white clay people." Its members were the so-called Grosventres of the Prairie or, as sometimes termed, Falls Indians—thus termed because reputed to have dwelt in earlier years at or near the falls of the Saskatchewan River. Their later country was the right bank of the Missouri River from its Great Falls to the Judith Basin. Not improbably all of Stuart's "Blackfeet" were Atsinas.

These Grosventres of the Prairie should not be confused with another tribe which, though also termed Grosventre (*alias* Minitari or less properly Minnetaree), was racially very different, being a Hidatsa sub-stock of the Siouan linguistic family and dwelling in permanent villages on the right bank of the Missouri near the mouth of Knife River.

As to why the title of Grosventre (*alias* Gros Ventre) was imposed upon either the Atsinas or the Minitaris, there is seemingly at present no satisfactory explanation beyond the meager one that, so the Minitaris claim, it was arbitrarily conferred by the white man. A weak tradition asserts that the Atsinas were dubbed Grosventres because of their alleged habit of running from one lodge to another in search of food with the result that their stomachs were always filled.

Because the four Blackfeet bands varied but little in dialect and closely resembled each other in physical appearance, they all were called Blackfeet by the white fur traders.

Nevertheless, in animus three of the bands were sharply differentiated from the fourth. Although the Piegans were customarily friendly to the whites, the Atsinas formed the most relentlessly hostile clan ever encountered by the whites in any part of the Northwest, and but slightly less inimical were the Bloods and the Siksikaus. So vicious were these last-named three bands in their treatment of the white man that they, under the generic name of Blackfeet, earned for themselves the sobriquet, "Scourge of the Upper Missouri."

Predatory, wandering extensively, raiding frequently their neighbors' territory and having their own territory invaded annually by such Shoshones, Nez Perces and Flatheads as came thither in quest of bison, all four septs of the Blackfeet were constantly engaged in warfare.

A portion of this warfare was grimly humorous inasmuch as it was provoked by the exercise of real affection. The Atsinas, having never outgrown their liking for their erstwhile neighbors, the Southern Arapahoes (for whom see under ARAPAHOE, pp. 333, 334), were accustomed every two or three years to visit these Arapahoes on the South Platte River. The route of the visitors, whether outgoing or returning, took them either directly through the country of their uncompromising enemy, the Crows, or else, as more frequently travelled in order to avoid the Crows, by way of the headwaters of Snake and Green Rivers and the mountains of northern Colorado. But the Shoshones along this alternate route, though less powerful than the Crows, equalled them in dislike for the touring Atsinas. And in response these jaunting Atsinas reserved for the Shoshones, as well as for the Crows, a hatred that was vitriolic. Accordingly, every two or three years, with their hearts replete with love for their friends and their quivers crammed with arrows for their foes, they would embark on their tender mission; and, mindful of the axiom that he who strikes first is he who strikes hardest, would leave behind them a trail reeking with arson and murder.

The present-day Gros Ventre range of mountains in Wyoming was given its name in commemoration of the fact that it lay near one of the above-mentioned routes of the sanguinary pilgrimages.

Chittenden, pp. 142-146, 850-855, 858; *L. & C. Hist.*, pp. 101, 148, 199, 200, 1105; *Clark*, pp. 68-73, 197-199; *Henry-Thomp.*, pp. 523, 524, 530, 733; *Hodge*, I, pp. 72, 73, 113, 508, 643, II, pp. 246, 247, 570, 571.

CALLEMEX or CALLEMAX, as termed by Stuart; but more commonly known as TILLAMOOK or, in plural form, TILLAMOOKS

This tribe, which Stuart credited with containing 200 men and with living on the Oregon seacoast about forty miles south of the Columbia River's mouth, was the *Kélémoux* and *Klemook* of Franchere, the *Killimux* of Alexander Ross's narrative, the *Clemak* of *Nouvelles Annales*, X, pp. 20, 23.

Appendix B

Coues, in a footnote to his *L. & C. Hist.*, states: "Callamox, Clark I 87; Kilamox, Clark I 89; Callemex, Gass, p. 180; meant for Killamucks, which is the same word as Tillamook, name of a head, bay, town, and county on the coast of Oregon . . . The Tillamook was a large and powerful tribe of the Salishan family, which lived on the Oregon coast 35 miles below Point Adams to below Tillamook Head. The tribe was also called Nsietshawus. There are [year of 1893] or were recently five Tillamook Indians living at Grande Ronde Agency, Oregon."

Ross [*A*], p. 87, [*B*], f.n. 13 on p. 102; *L. & C. Hist.*, p. 744; *Franchere* [*A*], p. 97, [*B*], p. 127, [*C*], f.n. 67 on p. 67; *Henry-Thomp.*, f.n. 25 on p. 858; *Hodge*, II, pp. 750, 751.

CATHLACKLA. See CATHLATHLA, p. 339

CATHLAKAHIKIT or CATHLAKAHEEKIT

This tribe, which Stuart rates as impudent and thievish and as having 150 warriors, he confusingly credits with living either at the Cascades of the Columbia River or else at the lower rapids of the Dalles in present-day Wasco County, Oregon. Though Lewis and Clark seem not to have noted it by any name reconciliable with that employed by Stuart, it very possibly was a subdivision of the Echeloot tribe of the Chinookan linguistic family. See *L. & C. Hist.*, p. 672; but see also *Henry-Thomp.*, f.n. 29 on p. 798; *Hodge*, I, p. 216; journ., p. 51 *ante.*

CATHLAKAMASS, as termed by Stuart; but more commonly known as CLACKAMA or CLACKAMAS

These indians, rated by Stuart as having 120 men and located by him as living at the mouth of the Willamette River, were credited by Lewis and Clark with inhabiting 11 villages upon that stream. They formed one of the Upper Chinookan (Watlala) linguistic tribes. Their name, spelled *Clukemus* by Henry and interchangeably *Clarkamus, Clark-a-mus* and *Clackamus* by Lewis and Clark, acquired eventually its modern accepted form of Clackama, pl. Clackamas; and, as Clackamas, is now used to designate a river, county, and town in the present-day state of Oregon.

The tribe in the year 1893 contained only some 50 or 60 souls, all living at the Grande Ronde Agency in Oregon.

Henry-Thomp., p. 811; *L. & C. Hist.*, pp. 711, 924, 932; *Hodge*, I, p. 302.

CATHLAMAT or CATHLAMET

The *Cathlama* of Clark, possibly the *Cathamux* of Ross, was one of the Upper Chinookan (or Watlala) tribes, and dwelt in a village at the confluence of Warren Creek with the Columbia River in present-day Clatsop County, Oregon. The tribe, which Lewis and Clark rated as 300 souls, is today extinct. Its name, in the modern accepted form of Cathlamet, is now borne by a bay in the state of Oregon and by a town in the state of Washington.

Ross [*B*], f.n. on pp. 102, 103; *L. & C. Hist.*, pp. 705, 711, 721, 907; *Hodge*, I, p. 216.

CATHLANAMENCIMEN or CATHLANAMINIMIN

These indians, rated by Stuart as having 60 men and located by him, as well as by Lewis and Clark, as living on present-day Sauvie Island at the confluence of the Willamette and Columbia Rivers, were by Lewis and Clark called interchangeably *Clannarminnamuns* and *Clannahminnamuns*, and by *Nouvelles Annales*, X, pp. 23, 26, were styled *Cathlaminimim* and *Cathlanaminimi*. They were a Chinookan tribe and, as early probably as the year 1840, became extinct.

L. & C. Hist., pp. 915, 931, 1249.

CATHLAPOOTLE

This tribe, credited by Stuart with having 180 men, was one of the Upper Chinookan (Watlala) group, spoke the Cathlamet (Katlamat) dialect, and lived in a village on the Columbia's right bank immediately above the lower end of present-day Bachelor Island. The tribe was by Ross termed *Cattleputle*, was by Henry designated as *Catlipoh* and *Cathlepuotla*, was by Lewis and Clark called interchangeably *Quathlapotle* and *Quathlahpotle*, and was the *Cathlapoutte* of *Nouvelles Annales*, X, p. 29. The modern accepted spelling is Cathlapotle. The name was a variant of *Gatlapotlh*, which in turn was derived from the name of the river Napotlh (*Yahkotl* on Stevens' map No. 3).

L. & C. Hist., pp. 711, 913, 914; *Ross* [*A*], p. 102; *Franchere* [*C*], f.n. 52 on p. 247; *Henry-Thomp.*, pp. 798, 821; *Hodge*, I, p. 217.

Cathlapooyay or Cathlapooyaa

These indians, the *Callahpoewah* or *Calapoewah* of Lewis and Clark, were estimated by Stuart to include 300 men. He located them as living on the Willamette River, immediately above its falls. Lewis and Clark assigned them to that same locality, and credited them with occupying 15 villages. Linguistically they belonged to the Kalapooian family. Only 22 of these indians were living in the year 1890, and presumably they are now extinct.

L. & C. Hist., pp. 932, 933; *Hodge*, I, pp. 187, 188.

Cathlasko or Cathlasco

Although Stuart rated these indians as having 150 men and located them as living in a permanent village at the Dalles of the Columbia River, Lewis and Clark failed to mention them. Possibly these indians were a sub-clan of the Echeloots whom Lewis and Clark found at the Dalles and rated as being one of the Upper Chinookan (Watlala) tribes.

L. & C. Hist., pp. 665-667, 672, 711, 787, 788, 944.

Cathlathla or Cathlackla

These indians, whom Stuart credited with having 80 men and whom he located as living on an easterly branch of the Willamette River above its falls, were possibly the *Cathlahaws* of Lewis and Clark. But to be so, they must, after Lewis and Clark found them at the mouth of the Willamette, have migrated up that stream. If identical with these Cathlahaws, they formed a sub-clan of the Calapooyan (*alias* Kalapooian) family.

L. & C. Hist., pp. 931, 932, 1263.

Cathlathlalla or Cathlathlala

This tribe, which Stuart rated as having 150 warriors, he confusingly credited with living either at the Cascades of the Columbia River or else at the lower rapids of the Dalles in present-day Wasco County, Oregon. The tribe was not mentioned by Lewis and Clark, who, as regards indians at the lower rapids of the Dalles, listed only the Chilluckquittequaws, Eneeshurs and Echeloots. Possibly the Cathlathlallas may have been a sub-clan of the Echeloots.

L. & C. Hist., p. 788; *Hodge*, I, p. 217.

CHEEPANCHICKCHICK. See CHIPANEKIKEKIK, p. 344

CHELWIT, *alias* CHILWIT. See HELLWIT, p. 345

CHEYENNE

The modern accepted spelling, Cheyenne, represents an evolution from earlier alphabetic attempts such as, for instance, Chienne, Chien, Schain, Chahay, Chajenne, Chayenne, Chaguyenne, Chaguine, Shyenne.

There has been a widespread assumption that the name was derived from the French word *chien* because the Cheyenne tribe had "dog soldiers." However, dog soldiers existed in other indian nations.

As to the meaning of dog soldier—in a militant tribe's selection of distinguishing titles for its various bands of warriors, recourse was had ordinarily to familiar entities such as dog, fox, raven, horse, war-club, bow-string and medicine-lance, though occasionally imagination went afield sufficiently to produce terms such as severally meant thief, old-chief, feather-head, black-mouth, crazy, strong-heart, afraid-of-nothing, etc. But, regardless of the actual title of a band, its members were commonly known to the whites as dog soldiers.

Consequently there seems to be scant assurance that there was any philological kinship between *chien* and Cheyenne indians.

A more probable etymon lies in the Yankton Sioux's word *Sha-en-na* (otherwise recorded as *Sha-ee-a-na*, *Shā-hī-yē-na* or *Sha-hī-ē-la*), an appellative by which these Yankton Sioux designated the Cheyenne indian.

Of this word, its initial syllable meant "red" and its final syllable was a diminutive used sometimes, as seemingly here, for mere euphony. This idea of red is consistent with the following theory and tradition.

According to the theory, *Sha-en-na* meant in effect, "speaker of an unknown language." The Sioux styled as red any language they did not comprehend, and the Cheyennes' language was entirely different from that of any of the surrounding nations.

According to the tradition, an indian one, the tribal name arose from the alleged fact that the first Cheyenne to be seen by the Sioux had red paint on his robe and on the skin of his body.

The Cheyennes' own name for their tribe was *Dzitsiista* (otherwise termed *Sa-sis-e-ta* and *Tsist-sis-ta*), which meant probably no more than "people" or "the people."

In very early days the Cheyennes lived on the Red River in either the northern part of the present-day state of Minnesota or the southern part of Canada. Ousted from there by the Sioux they retreated southwestward and forced their way through hostile nations to that section of the Missouri River's right bank which lay below present-day Big Beaver (*alias* Sand) Creek in Emmons County, North Dakota.

There they stayed awhile. But, again persecuted by the relentless Sioux, they resumed their southwestward thrust, to arrive eventually at the so-called Black Hills Country in the southwest portion of present-day South Dakota and the northeast portion of present-day Wyoming, the centre of their new territory being the river, which in common with Wyoming's capital, now bears their name.

They thus had become an isolated people. Themselves of Algonquian stock, they had Siouan nations to the east, Shoshonean nations to the west; also, in other directions, they were sandwiched between Kiowan tribes and the Middle Caddoans (Pawnees). However, in their newly acquired area they were ordinarily at peace with all their neighbors save only the Sioux.

Because of their superb horsemanship and great virility, they were efficient in battle. They were usually though not always on friendly terms with the whites; but, whenever opposed to them, proved "one of the greatest terrors of the frontier."

In their new home they relinquished their former habit of residing in fixed villages with cultivated fields and became somewhat nomadic. Discontinuing the practice of farming, they embarked whole-heartedly in the horse trade, obtaining their animals by capturing so-called wild horses and also by raiding tribes living south and west of them. They presently had a well-established business of selling horses to other indians and to the whites, and it was from the Cheyennes that Wilson Price Hunt, in the year 1811, acquired 36 of the horses needed for his journey to Astoria.

Appendix B

But their new home was not destined to be of long duration. Within two decades after Stuart's overland trip, numbers of them (afterward known as the Southern Cheyennes), unable longer to withstand both badgering by the Sioux and also temptation to enlarge the ambit of their horse trading and stealing, commenced to migrate in instalments to the country of the Southern Arapahoes. There, in the present-day state of Colorado, their name now designates a town, a county, a canyon, and a mountain.

The Cheyennes were rated by the white fur traders as among the most efficient gatherers of pelts.

United States troops, when campaigning against hostile indians in the Northwest, employed many Cheyennes as scouts. And in the decade of the eighties there was formed a military body which, as an integral part of the army and scheduled to act as an independent unit in the field, was except for its white officers composed entirely of Cheyennes and Arapahoes clad in the army uniform and carrying the American flag.

All this support of government was given despite the fact that, in the decade of the seventies, the Cheyennes' fealty was cruelly abused. In violation of a formal treaty between military officers and these indians, the civil officials caused many of the Northern Cheyennes to be transported to present-day Oklahoma and to be confined there upon a reservation. In a climate unfriendly to them and amid unfamiliar scenes they began to decimate, and all the while there was a yearning for the place of their former residence.

Despair having added itself to yearning, the prisoners decided to take affirmative action; and so, on September 9, 1878, they quitted their imposed reservation and, under the leadership of Dull Knife, began their tragic attempt to go home. Shouting no war cries, but merely crooning their tribal death song, they stumbled forward, broken in spirit. For some, the weaker ones, their song was promptly answered; and they were buried where they fell. The rest were presently captured and returned to the reservation.

Chittenden, pp. 852, 867; *L. & C. Hist.*, pp. 98, 147, 148, 168, 1188-91; *Grinnell* [*A*]; *Grinnell* [*B*]; *Hodge*, I, pp. 250-257; *Bronson*, pp. 127-197; *Wheeler*, pp. 274-286; *Remington*, pp. 22-48; *Luttig*, pp. 63-70, ed.'s note; *Clark*, pp. 98, 107, 354-356; *Mo. Gaz.*; *Nouvelles Annales*, X, p. 32, translated at p. 281 *ante*; *Astoria*, I, p. 242.

Appendix B

CHIHEELASH, CHIHEELEESH, CHEEHEELASH or CHEEHEELISH, as interchangeably termed by Stuart; but more commonly known as CHEHALIS

This tribe, which Stuart credited with having 234 men and which he located as living on the Oregon seacoast about 40 milés north of the Columbia's mouth, was of Salishan stock. It was the *Chickelis* of Ross, the *Tchikeylis* of Franchere, the *Chiehilths* of Henry, the *Chiltz* or *Chilts* of Lewis and Clark, the *Ichitchilich* of *Nouvelles Annales*, X, p. 21. Its name, in the form of Chehalis, is now borne by the county seat of Lewis County in the state of Washington.

L. & C. Hist., pp. 717, 761, 1252; *Franchere* [*B*], p. 124, [*C*], f.n. 65 on p. 256; *Henry-Thomp.*, pp. 855, 867; *Hodge*, I, p. 241.

CHINOOK

The present accepted spelling is Chinook, but in the past it has appeared as Cheenook, Chinuk, Tchinouk, Tshinuk, Tshinook, Tschinuk.

The name applies to each of the following two entities: (1) the entire Chinookan stock or family of numerous tribes as classified by Powell; (2) a particular one of these tribes, *i.e.*, the Chinooks most properly so called.

The Chinookan stock was divisible into two classes:

[A] Upper Chinookan (*alias* Watlala), composed of, among others, the following nine tribes: Cathlamet, Cathlapotle, Chilluckquittequaw, Clackama, Cooniac, Echeloot, Multnoma, Wahkiacum, and Wasco;

[B] Lower Chinookan, composed of two tribes: the Clatsop and the Chinooks proper.

The tribes of Chinookan stock lived, in part, on the Columbia River (chiefly on its right bank) from its mouth to the Dalles, and, in other part, on so much of the seacoast as extended southward for twenty miles below Point Adams and reached northward along nearly the whole extent of Shoalwater Bay.

The particular tribe commonly specified as Chinook proper was the one which Stuart designated by his term "Chinook" and which he credited with having 280 warriors.

This tribe lived at the mouth of the Columbia River, but now has probably no surviving member.

L. & C. Hist., pp. 710, 711; *Ross*[*A*], pp. 87-93; *Franchere*[*C*], f.n. 40 on p. 240; *MacDonald*, f.n. 48 and 49 on p. 78; *Hodge*, I, pp. 272-275; journ., p. 28 *ante*.

Chipanekikekik or Cheepanchickchick

This tribe, rated by Stuart as having 100 men and located by him as living at the Dalles of the Columbia River in present-day Wasco County, Oregon, was not listed by Lewis and Clark. But see under the caption of Cathlathlalla on pp. 339, 340.

Clatsop

This tribe, one of the two tribes of Lower Chinookan stock, was credited by Stuart with possessing 214 warriors. Its territory included not only the Columbia River's south shore westward from the site of Astoria but also all of Point Adams at that river's outlet. Though Lewis and Clark were offended by the tribe's lack of cleanliness and morality, they nevertheless gave its name to their own fort near the Columbia's mouth. Also a present-day county in the state of Oregon bears the name. The tribe, wellnigh extinct in the year 1893, is now in all probability nonexistent.

L. & C. Hist., pp. 711, 717, 730, 746, 747, 753, 757, 762, 766-769, 773-785; *Ross* [*A*], p. 87; *Franchere* [*B*], p. 99, [*C*], f.n. 39 on p. 239; *Hodge*, I, p. 305.

Cowlitsick or Cowlitsic, as termed by Stuart; but more commonly known as Cowlitz

This tribe, credited by Stuart as being "peaceably inclined" though "somewhat haughty and insolent" and as having 250 men, was of Salishan stock and lived in Stuart's day on the stream which, debouching through the Columbia's right bank in the present-day state of Washington, is now called Cowlitz River. Its remnants were, as late as the year 1893, settled on the Puyallup Reservation in the state of Washington.

The tribal name has been the victim of a variety of spellings: for example, Coweliske, Coweliskee, Cowleskee and Cowlitch; but, having eventually attained its modern form of Cowlitz, has in that form attached itself not only to the above-mentioned river but also to a neighboring county.

L. & C. Hist., pp. 698, 788; *Henry-Thomp.*, pp. 879, 880; *Hodge*, I, p. 355; journ., p. 30 *ante.*

FLATHEAD

Stuart's "Flatheads," because of the locality to which he ascribed them, were unquestionably not of the actual Flathead tribe (of Salishan stock) but instead were Nez Perces, for whom see pp. 347, 348. Also Hunt's "Flatheads" (p. 285), because of the locality in which he met them, were probably Nez Perces.

HELLWIT, CHILWIT or CHELWIT, as interchangeably styled by Stuart

Known today as Echeloot, it was the *Echelute* of Lewis and Clark, the *Whill Wetz* of Ross, the *Echeloot*, *Eskeloot*, *Eloot* and *Tilheillewit* of various other diarists, the *Tchilout* of *Nouvelles Annales*, X, p. 23.

This tribe was described by Stuart as being "200 Strong" and as living on the left bank of the Columbia River three miles below Oak Point (*i.e.*, at the mouth of Clatskanie River in present-day Columbia County, Oregon) except when each summer the tribe betook itself, for fishing, to an island in the Columbia River near the Dalles.

It was one of the nine principal septs of the Upper Chinookan (Watlala) stock, for which see CHINOOK, pp. 343, 344.

L. & C. Hist., p. 672; *Ross* [*A*], p. 104; *Henry-Thomp.*, p. 794; journ., p. 29 *ante.*

ILTHAKYEMAMIT or ILTHKYEMAMIT

Stuart rated this tribe as having 100 warriors and stated its permanent home to be at the Dalles of the Columbia River in present-day Wasco County, Oregon. The tribe was not included in Lewis and Clark's ethnic list, but see CATHLATHLALLA, pp. 339, 340.

Appendix B

KANSAS, styled KANZES by Stuart

Kansas, the tribe's own name for itself, implied a reference to the wind. The whites accorded variant spellings, as, for instance, Kanses, Cansa, Quonzai, Consa, Chonsa, Kenzia. Kaw, a nickname given by the French, served on occasion as a complete substitute for Kansas.

The tribe was of the Dhegiha division of the Siouan linguistic stock. It is thought that prior to the advent of the white man it was part of a large nation which included also the Kwapas, Omahas, Osages, and Poncas, and which dwelt in the Ohio Valley near the Wabash River. The Kansas, migrating from there, eventually settled themselves, it is said, in two villages which, on the right bank of the Missouri River, were respectively 37 miles and 66 miles above the mouth of present-day Kansas River. Later than this period, but before Stuart's time, the Kansas indians, already reduced in numbers and beset by the Sauks and Iowas, retreated up the Kansas River and erected on its bank two new villages. In Stuart's day the Kansas indians were rated as numbering approximately 1300 souls.

The Kansas were prone to war with all their indian neighbors; but on occasion they were at peace with the Otoes and the Missouris, with whom they intermingled to some extent. Though trafficking with the St. Louisan traders, they frequently plundered such of these traders as visited them and also committed depredations upon boatmen travelling on the Missouri River.

L. & C. Hist., pp. 34, 98, 517, 1234, 1258; *Chittenden*, pp. 870, 871; *Century*, XI, p. 560; *Hodge*, I, pp. 653-656.

MAHA, as styled by Stuart. See OMAHA, p. 349

MATHLANOB OR MATHLANOBE

These indians were rated by Stuart as having 80 men and were located by him as living on the upper end of Wappatoo (now Sauvie) Island in the lower Columbia River. Lewis and Clark make no mention of them. Stuart's "Mathlanobs," because of the site of their home, were probably of Upper Chinookan (Watlala) stock.

Appendix B

Missouri

These indians of the Tciwere division of the Siouan linguistic stock, though of little importance to the fur trade, are historically interesting in that, among other things, their tribal name (though in mutilated form) is borne by the great river on which they once lived.

The tribe assumed for itself a name which, as variously spelled by whites, was *Newdarcha*, *Neotacha*, *Neogehe*, *Niutatei*, etc.; and which is said to have meant "living at the mouth of a river," *i.e.*, the Missouri.

This native appellation, as carrying this meaning, seems to have been translated by some other nation (not improbably the Illinois) into the latter nation's tongue. And thus came the word *Oumessourit*, which Marquette in his map of 1673 noted as the tribe living on the *R. Pekittanoui* near its mouth. Thereafter the word was subjected to surgery at both its ends; and, emerging as *Messouri*, found itself presently as *R. Pekitanoui* or *R. des Missouris* on D'Anville's map of 1752.

In course of time the word *Pekitanoui* in its various spellings vanished from usage; but the word *Missouri*, by its mellifluence, made claim for linguistic permanence.

Between the dates of the maps of Marquette and D'Anville the Missouri indians, hard pressed by the Illinois, moved from their original domain near the Missouri River's mouth and installed themselves in a village which, on the stream's right bank, was four miles below the discharge of present-day Grand River in the state of South Dakota.

Subsequently, having been almost annihilated by smallpox and by wars with the Sac and Fox tribes, they dispersed; some of them to merge with the Kansas and Osage nations, the rest of them to hie to the Otoes' village on Platte River in present-day Nebraska and there make their home. Reckoned as inferiors by these Otoes, they were sometimes maltreated by them.

Chittenden, pp. 763, 875, 947; *L. & C. Hist.*, pp. 22, 23, 26, 62-65, 1257; *Century*, XI, p. 982; *Hodge*, I, pp. 911, 912.

Nez Perce, styled Flathead by Stuart

The Nez Perces, frequently called Chopunnish as well as by their own name Sahaptin, were of Shahaptian linguistic stock and numbered some 6000 souls. The name Nez Perce was given by French voyageurs, but the reason for doing so is now uncertain inasmuch as these indians seemingly neither wore nasal ornaments nor pierced their noses. Incidentally, the Nez Perces, prior to the white man's arrival in Oregon, practised to some extent the flattening of their children's foreheads. Because of this practice many early writers confused the Nez Perces with the Flatheads proper (of Salishan linguistic stock).

The Nez Perces, a brave and powerful people, inhabited the lower watershed of the Snake River, were essentially equestrian, and were physically well-developed. Their subsistence was both salmon and bison; and, for the purpose of obtaining the latter, they annually made excursions eastward to the Judith Basin of present-day Montana.

Deeply spiritual, the Nez Perces, as soon as they learned of the existence of Christianity, eagerly sought instruction in that religion; they offered for Christian missionary effort the most fruitful field among all the Western tribes. The historic delegation composed of indians seeking a copy of the white man's Bible and arriving at St. Louis in 1832 was probably composed of Nez Perces, though these delegates have frequentley been styled Flatheads.

The Nez Perces' contacts with all their indian neighbors except the Blackfeet were peaceful. As regards the white man, their relations with him were amicable from the date of their first encountering him until the year 1863. In that year the American nation, havocking its honor, repudiated the treaty which, made by Governor Stevens with the tribe in 1855, had afterward been duly ratified by the United States Senate. At the time of the repudiation, some of the Nez Perces accepted the offer of a substitute treaty materially decreasing the area of the tribal land, while others of them (popularly termed "Non-Treaty indians") smoldered till 1877 and then in defense of their guaranteed rights went on the warpath.

Among the chiefs of the Nez Perces was *Inmuttooyahlatlat*, commonly known as Chief Joseph. His indian name, meaning "thunder rolling in the mountains," was accordant with his nobility of face and figure and with his dignity and his intellect. He was a keen philosopher, speaking often in terms of whimsical epigram. As leader of the Non-Treaty indians throughout their campaign against the United States troops in 1877, he proved himself one of the ablest military strategists and tacticians America has thus far produced. Born about 1840 in eastern Oregon, he died September 22, 1904, at the Colville Indian Reservation in the state of Washington.

Chittenden, pp. 641-647, 888-891; *Clark*, pp. 269-271; *L. & C. Hist.*, pp. 583, 605, 606, 774, 988; *Hodge*, II, pp. 65-68; *Chief Joseph.*

Appendix B

Omaha, styled Maha by Stuart

This tribe, the *Maha* of Stuart, the *Maha* or *Mahar* of Lewis and Clark, the *Omawhaw* of Long and at the present time accorded the generally accepted name of Omaha, was termed by itself *Umanhan*, "those who went up stream or against the current." It was of the Dhegiha division of the Siouan linguistic stock.

For the tribe's possible origin, see Kansas, p. 346. At a later period and in the tribe's days of power—and it once was powerful—its principal village stood on the right bank of the Missouri River at a spot approximately 230 miles above the site of the present-day city of Omaha. Though cultivating there corn, beans and melons, the members of the tribe nevertheless were so bellicose as to terrorize their neighbors.

But, through both oppression by the Sioux and in the year 1802 an epidemic of smallpox, their numbers fell to about 400, if not to something less than 300. Thereupon, broken in spirit, they burned their village and sought a new abiding place, some of them to assume a more or less nomadic life in the valley of the Niobrara River, others of them to erect new villages in retreats found further southward on or near the Missouri.

The largest of these new villages was on the Missouri's right bank 100 miles above the site of Omaha.

Warfare, except as defensive, was abandoned, and, after the white man's coming, the tribe's members industriously devoted themselves to the gathering of fur. Though those remaining in the vicinity of the Missouri continued to dwell in fixed villages, their quest for pelts kept them from home for several months each year.

L. & C. Hist., pp. 9, 74-76, 98, 137, 138, 517, 1204, 1258; *Chittenden*, pp. 871, 872; *Neb. Hist. Trans.*, I, pp. 47, 48; *Clark*, p. 286; *Century*, XI, p. 758; *Hodge*, II, pp. 119–121.

Osage

This tribe (*Wazhazhe* being its name for itself), the earliest nation in the Missouri River's valley to have a regular trade with the whites, was of the Dhegiha division of the Siouan stock and quite possibly had the origin described under Kansas, p. 346.

In Stuart's time it was divided into the following three bands:

(a) The so-called Great Osages (an erroneous rendering of Highland Osage, "those who camped at the top of the hill"), boasting approximately 500 warriors and living in a village on the south bank of the present-day Osage River in the state of Kansas;

(b) The so-called Little Osages (an erroneous rendering of Lowland Osage, "those who camped at the base of the hill"), having some 250 warriors and inhabiting a village which lay some six miles from that of the Great Osages;

(c) The group which, containing some 600 warriors, seceded and thereupon settled on the Vermilion Creek in the present-day state of Kansas.

The members of these three bands lived in permament villages of huts. The Osages were of special importance to both the white fur trader and the early overland expeditions because of their extensive ability to supply horses, which they obtained during annual excursions to the southwestern plains. Though in the main friendly to the whites, the Osages were not above harrying small parties of trappers and hunters and also making many unprovoked assaults upon travellers on the Santa Fé Trail.

Chittenden, pp. 870-874; *L. & C. Hist.*, pp. 12, 98, 99; *Tixier; Century*, XI, p. 765; *Hodge*, II, pp. 156-158.

Otto, as termed by Stuart; but more properly known as Oto

These indians—whose native name (meaning "lovers of sexual pleasure") was rendered by Meriwether Lewis as *Waddoketahtah*, by Powell as *Watoqtata*, and by various others as *Watota*, *Wahtohtana*, *Wahtotata*, *Wadotan*, etc.—were called, by the French-speaking traders, *Othouez;* and, by English-speaking traders, *Otos*, *Otoes*, *Ottos*, *Ottoes*. The modern accepted form is Oto; plural Otoes.

They were of the Tciwere division of the Siouan linguistic stock; and were descended, it is said, from members of the Missouris' tribe in its early days.

In Stuart's time they numbered approximately 500 souls, including some 120 warriors.

Prior to his time they had lived on the right bank of the Missouri River about 20 miles above the mouth of the Platte, but, migrating thence, had installed themselves in the village at which Stuart visited April 13-16 (see his entries of those dates, pp. 233-237) and which lay on the right bank of the Platte one and one-half miles southeast from site of present-day town of Yutan. This village they shared with the Missouri tribe after that nation had been ousted from the river to which it gave its name.

The hunting territory of the Otoes and Missouris was the valleys of present-day Nebraska's Salt Creek and Little Nemaha River, as also the plains west of them.

Chittenden, pp. 874, 875; *L. & C. Hist.*, pp. 23, 24, 54, 55, 61-65, 99, 1258; Major A. L. Green's *The Otoe Indians* in *Neb. Pub.*, XXI, pp. 175-209; *Extracts from Diary of Moses Merrill* in *Neb. Hist. Trans.*, IV, pp. 160-191; *Clark*, p. 286; *Century*, XI, p. 767; *Hodge*, II, pp. 164-166.

Pawnee

In addition to the modern accepted spelling (Pawnee), the name has in the past appeared also as Pani, Pania, Panea, Pawnie, Pahnie, Panee, Panie and Panny. Possibly it was derived from the tribe's word *pa-riki* meaning a "horn" and thus alluded to the tribe's characteristic scalp lock which, stiffened by pigment, either stood erect or curved slightly backward.

The Caddoan linguistic family, to which these people belonged, was divided into three groups:

(a) Northern Caddoan, consisting of only the Aricara (*alias* Ree) tribe and living on the Missouri River in present-day state of South Dakota;

(b) Middle Caddoan, consisting of the four tribes each commonly called Pawnee;

(c) Southern Caddoan, consisting of the Caddo, Hueco (*alias* Waco), Keechie, Tawaconie and Wichita (*alias* Pawnee Pict) tribes living in the present-day states of Arkansas, Louisiana, Oklahoma, and Texas.

The above-mentioned Middle Caddoan group, *i.e.*, the strictly Pawnee nation, was self-split into four septs:

(a) Xaui (*Tsawe* of *Murray*, I, p. 283), more commonly known as Grand Pawnee (*i.e.*, the Pawnees proper), for which see *infra*. Stuart mentions this tribe (pp. 219-222).

(b) Kit-ke-hak-i (*Tskitkakish* of *Murray*, I, p. 283), more commonly known as Pawnee Republican or Republican Pawnee; so entitled, tradition says, because in approximately the year 1795 or 1796 its people seceded from the main nation and established a village of their own. This village was on that one of the Kansas River's branches which, by reason of the Kit-ke-hak-is' having thus lived on it, now bears the name Republican River. After the erecting of this village, they disintegrated into bands which settled at various other sites on the Kansas River; but in the year 1804 all of them, ejected by the Kansas tribe, journeyed to where they could settle beside the Grand Pawnees. Stuart mentions this Republican tribe (p. 238).

(c) Skidi (a name of seemingly unknown meaning), identical with the *Skere* of *Murray*, I, p. 283, as well as with not only the *Skeceree* and *Pawnee Loup* of Lewis and Clark but also the *Loup* and *Panimaha* or *Paneemaha* of other diarists. Stuart mentions this tribe (p. 221).

(d) Pit-a-hau-e-rat (*Petowera* of *Murray*, I, p. 283), more commonly known as Tapage, Tappage, Tappah and as Noisy Pawnee. "Noisy" is patently translated from the French *tapage*, but as to why the French thought these particular indians uproarious does not appear. The Tapages were also, for a while, termed Smoky Hill Pawnees because they once resided on the Smoky Hill River of Kansas.

The earliest known hunting ground of the Pawnees extended westward from the right bank of the Missouri River and was bounded on the north by the Niobrara River in present-day Nebraska, and extended southward to the Arkansas River. Tradition is that in still earlier days they had lived further to the south. In Stuart's time, however, they were distributed as follows:

The Grand Pawnees (having a membership of some 1600, including about 500 warriors) and the Republican Pawnees (numbering approximately 1400, inclusive of some 250 warriors)—the latter having already forsaken their earlier temporary home on the Republican and Kansas Rivers—lived in a village on the right bank of the Platte some 55 miles above its mouth. They used as their hunting ground both the Platte's right bank above their village and also the headwaters of the Kansas River. They trafficked habitually with the St. Louis traders and were rated by Lewis and Clark as being friendly to the white man. Though tolerant of the Otoes, Omahas, and Poncas, they were professionally hostile to the Osages, Kansas, Aricaras, Kiowas, Comanches, and Sioux. Stuart's entry of April 11 (p. 220) seems to show that in 1813 the entire village had moved for the time being to the vicinity of the Skidis' camp.

The Skidis (numbering approximately 1000, inclusive of some 280 warriors) lived on what is now known interchangeably as the Loup River or Loup Fork of the Platte. Their hunting ground was the Loup River's valley as well as the left bank of the Platte above the Loup's mouth. Because of the comparative isolation of their country, they were seldom visited by white traders, and therefore were wont to take their pelts to the Grand Pawnees' village on the Platte and there to barter with the whites.

The Tapages or Noisy Pawnees, boasting some 400 warriors, had earlier resided on the Kansas and Arkansas Rivers and for a while on the Smoky Hill River; but, repeatedly worsted in battles with the Osage tribe, they had already retreated to the banks of the Red River in the present-day states of Arkansas, Oklahoma, and Texas.

The Pawnees, wherever their distribution placed them, resided in fixed villages composed of tepees, and there they cultivated corn, beans, and melons; but they remained in their villages only when the need of sowing and harvesting prevented roving the plains in quest of bison.

Their men were notable for physical endurance, for ability to ride horses and to steal them, and for tenacious support of tribal consciousness.

Despite Lewis and Clark's favorable endorsement, the Pawnees as a whole were accused by Chittenden of being, during the period of the fur trade, such virulent foes of the white man as to create in the South the same intensity of dread as the Blackfeet produced in the North. The Pawnees, for several years, had with the Spanish Government a relationship akin to that which the Sioux had with the British—quasi-allies. However, in later years the Pawnees furnished a battalion of scouts which, as commanded by Major Frank J. North and his brother Luther H., gave long and efficient service to the United States army, being finally mustered out on May 1, 1877.

Various articles and bibliography in *Neb. Hist. Mag.*, X, pp. 159-261; *Chittenden*, pp. 868-870; *L. & C. Hist.*, pp. 55-57, 98, 144; Charles E. Deland's *The Aborigines of South Dakota* in *South Dak.*, III, pp. 267-592; *Pattie*, pp. 15, 16; *Gregg*, II, p. 300; Samuel Allis's *Forty Years &c.* in *Neb. Hist. Trans.*, II, pp. 133 *et seq.;* J. M. Thayer's *My Very First Visit* in *Neb. Hist. Proc.*, X, pp. 119-127; *Grinnell*, pp. 15, 281; *Long*, I, pp. 160 *et seq.; Clark*, pp. 279-294; *Murray*, I, p. 283; *Irving, John T.; Hodge*, II, pp. 213-216.

Ponca

This tribe—Ponca, according to usual spelling but formerly also called Poncah, Poncar, Poncaw, Ponka, Punka, Punkah, Puncah, Punkaw—was the *Poncara* of Lewis and Clark. It was of the Dhegiha division of the

Siouan linguistic stock but not of the nation known as Sioux proper or Dakota and described under SIOUX, pp. 359-362.

There is difference of opinion as to the early locus of these indians. Coues states (1) that they at one time resided on a branch of the Red River of the North (which would have placed them in either present-day northern Minnesota or southern Canada), and (2) that presently, being under molestation by the Sioux, they retreated to the right bank of the Missouri River. Chittenden on the other hand holds that, together with the Kansas, Omahas, Osages and Kwapas, they were separatists from a single large nation residing in the Ohio Valley; and that, on this alleged dissolution of the parent nation, they pushed westward to the Missouri River and ascended it.

When first seen by the white man they were settled in a fortified village in the northeast corner of the present-day state of Nebraska. This stronghold was situated on the Missouri River's right bank at the mouth of present-day Ponca Creek, a small stream lying 10 miles north of and flowing parallel with Niobrara River.

In this village they remained for several years. Eventually smallpox and the Sioux's continual harassment had reduced them to some 200 souls, and so they abandoned their home and its cornfields and took up their residence among the Omahas (for whom see p. 349).

The Poncas, despite occasional reputation for dishonesty, were always on friendly terms with the whites.

L. & C. Hist., pp. 106, 109, 1258; *Chittenden*, pp. 860, 871; *Clark*, pp. 286, 305, 306; J. A. Barrett's *The Poncas* in *Neb. Hist. Proc.*, II, pp. 11-25; *Century*, XI, p. 818; *Hodge*, II, pp. 278, 279.

SCIATOGA OR SCYATOGA

This tribe was encountered in the year 1811 by Wilson Price Hunt on the banks of the Umatilla River in present-day eastern Oregon.

The term Sciatoga, *alias* Shyeyetoga, Scietoga and Siatoga, was of Paiute (Shoshonean) origin, and, as translated into English, meant "camass eater"—*camass* being one of the variant spellings of the indian name for a bulbous lilacious plant of which there were two Western species, *Camassia esculenta* and *C. leichlini*. Since the term Sciatoga loosely included not only several different tribes of northern Paiutes (Shoshonean family) but also the Cayuses (Waiilatpuan stock), it lacked exactness in classification and accordingly fell into disuse. *Bradbury* [*A*], p. 231,

[*B*], p. 239; *Mo. Gaz.; Niles; Brackenridge*, p. 302; *Nouvelles Annales*, X, pp. 76-78 (translated at pp. 302, 303 *ante*); *Henry-Thomp.*, pp. 818, 819; *L. & C. Hist.*, pp. 603-606, 1038; *McArthur*, p. 65.

Because of (1) Stuart's description in his entry of August 12 (pp. 80-82), (2) the locality in which Hunt found his encamped "Sciatogas," and (3) the large number of horses which *Astoria*, II, p. 63, credits to this camp, it is probable that Hunt's and Stuart's "Sciatogas" were in fact Cayuses.

The Cayuses (the *Cajouses* of Ross, the *Caaguas* and *Kiooses* of Palmer, the *Caiilloux* of Hale, the *Cayooses* of Schouler, the *Kiuses* of Wyeth, the *Kayouses* of Townsend, the *Kyauses* of Work, the *Skyuses* of Farnham) lived in Hunt's and Stuart's time on the Walla Walla, Umatilla and Grande Ronde Rivers as well as on that portion of the Columbia which lay between the mouths of the Umatilla and the Snake. *McArthur*, p. 65; *L. & C. Hist.*, p. 1038; *Ross* [*B*], p. 137; *Palmer*, p. 53; *Wyeth, Nathaniel J.*, p. 231; *Townsend*, p. 147; *Farnham*, p. 150; *Hodge*, I, pp. 224, 225.

Though closely associated with the two neighboring Shahaptian tribes known respectively as Walla Walla and Nez Perce (for which see pp. 347, 348, 364), they were linguistically independent of them.

So efficient were these Cayuse indians in their horse-raising that, in later years throughout the entire Northwest, *cayuse* was the ranchmen's usual term for the type of animal which Southwesterners styled a *bronco*.

In 1847 the Cayuse indians perpetrated the so-called Whitman massacre, and they were removed in 1855 to the Umatilla Reservation in present-day eastern Oregon. Merging there with other indians, they gradually lost their tribal identity and language.

If Hunt's and Stuart's "Sciatogas" were not Cayuses, it is possible that they were not Sciatogas at all, but instead were of that Shahaptian tribe now known as Umatilla and for which see *L. & C. Hist.*, p. 606; *Hodge*, II, p. 866.

Shoshone (sometimes styled Shoshona, Shoshonay, Shoshonie, Shooshoonay, Shooshoonie, Chochini), otherwise termed Snake

The names Shoshone and Snake seem to have been as interchangeably used by Stuart as they later have been by other people, but see the query at the end of this section.

Inasmuch as some of the indians designated by Stuart as Shoshones were in all probability not of that special tribe although they were of Shoshonean linguistic stock, it is necessary here to give a summary of that linguistic stock.

It had twelve subdivisions as follows:

(1) Shoshone proper, known also as Snake and dwelling in the upper portions of the valleys of the Green and Snake Rivers and in the northern portion of the valley of Bear River, all these areas being in the present-day states of Wyoming and Idaho.

To this essentially nomadic tribe, Sacajawea (Sakakawea) of the Lewis and Clark expedition is said to have belonged.

Its members, because of their domain's meagreness in food, were physically inferior to the more easterly indians, so much so that in some localities they were wont to forego tepees and to shelter themselves within mere piles of sagebrush. Though subsisting in part on the sparse local supply of roots, seeds, berries, insects, reptiles and rabbits, they of necessity made excursions to the distant lower country of the Columbia's watershed in search of salmon and to the equally distant plains of the Missouri River in quest of bison. The hunt for bison forced them annually to invade the territory of the Blackfeet (for whom see pp. 334-336); but, on these ventures, they ordinarily went in force sufficient to defy their enemies and often were accompanied by auxiliaries from the Flathead and Nez Perce nations. Due to these methods of obtaining food, they acquired traits and customs characteristic of both the fishing and hunting tribes.

Though brave, active and shrewd, they, except such of them as during Chief Washakie's life were immediately under his control, were reputed to be suspicious, treacherous and jealous and also to be inveterate beggars and thieves.

Washakie [1804(?)-1900], a thoroughly reliable friend of the whites, proved on several occasions an important ally of the United States army in its indian wars. His band, most competently led by him, not only fought on the same side as the soldiers but also through many years furnished scouts to the troops.

He died February 20, 1900, at the Shoshone Reservation in Wyoming. His funeral, its religious part conducted by Protestant Episcopal clergymen, was under management of the United States army, and he was buried with the full military honors which army regulations prescribed for an officer having captain's rank.

The Shoshones as a whole were at peace with the Flatheads and Nez Perces at the north, as also with the white man after the first few years of his acquaintance; but they generally were at war with the Crows, Blackfeet and Utes. They were excellent horsemen and able warriors.

Before the white man's advent they, unlike the plains' indians east of them, were accustomed to poison the points of their war arrows; using for this purpose a mixture which, composed of pulverized ants and an animal's spleen, had been left in the sunlight until partly decayed. Arrows, when thus treated, were said to be no less deadly than were such of the Apaches' arrows as had been tipped with a paste of rotted liver impregnated with the virus of rattlesnakes.

They were efficient producers of furs, though not as productive as were various tribes to their east.

Stuart traversed their home territory.

The reason for the name Snake as attached both to these indians and to one of the rivers on which they dwelt is puzzling—in fact, presents two seemingly unanswerable problems. As concerns the river, was its name acquired from that of the indians or was it due to the extreme sinuosity of the river? As concerns the indians, was their name borrowed from that of the river? And, if not, whence came it? Alexander Ross, the Astorian fur trader, avers that it was due to the characteristic manner in which these particular natives, when confronted with a foe, concealed themselves, gliding like serpents through the sagebrush. On the other hand, not only are we told by Father DeSmet: "They are called Snakes by reason of their poverty, which reduces them to burrow in the ground like those reptiles and to live upon roots," but also we learn from Captain W. P. Clark that "In my investigations I was unable to ascertain positively why they were called Snakes, but one of their old men claimed that it was because they formerly ate serpents."

(2) Bannock (*alias* Bannack), which in early days was not infrequently termed Pannock or Pannack, appears as *Bonark* in *Jefferson*, Pt. III, and was derived from *Panaiti*, the tribe's name for itself.

These people, inhabiting the country bounded on the north by Snake River and on the south by Salt Lake, had as their centre the present-day Bannock Creek and Bear River in southeastern Idaho.

More virile, more warlike and less friendly to the white man than were the Shoshones, these Bannocks frequently attacked the trappers. Stuart's route took him through the heart of the Bannock territory.

(3) Tukuarika or Sheepeater (*i.e.*, eater of mountain sheep, *Ovis canadensis canadensis*), a small and insignificant tribe inhabiting the higher mountains within the region which is now occupied, in part,

by the Yellowstone National Park. This tribe's immurement on lofty heights and its dwelling there in caves and under sheltering rocks was, it is thought, the result of fearing local invasion by Blackfeet. Because of the isolation of its home, the tribe was so unprogressive that it restricted its clothing to skins and furs till long after neighboring indians had obtained blankets from white traders. Correspondingly dilatory as regards acquiring firearms and horses, it for many years unnecessarily limited itself to the bow as its principal weapon and continued to travel afoot. The Tukuarikas' food, however scanty at times, was almost epicurean for it mainly consisted of the flesh of mountain sheep.

The indians whom Stuart met on October 18, 1812 (p. 160), might, because of the place of meeting, be supposed to have belonged to this tribe, a supposition weakened, however, by Stuart's statement of their large numbers and negatived by their ownership of horses.

(4) Paviosto, dwelling in the southern part of the present-day state of Oregon and in the western part of the present-day state of Nevada.

(5) Saidyuka, dwelling south of the headwaters of the Willamette River in present-day western Oregon.

Not improbably it was members of this last-mentioned tribe whom Stuart designated as "Shoshonas" and "Shoo-shoo-nays" in his entry of July 3 (p. 33), as "Shoshonays" and "Shooshonies" in his entry of July 17 (p. 53). Also it is not improbable that the Walla Wallas' prisoner who, as described by Lewis and Clark, readily conversed with Sacajawea (Sakakawea) in her own dialect was a Saidyukan.

(6) Seven other subdivisions known severally as Chemehuevi, Comanche, Gosiute, Paiute (*alias* Piute or Digger), Tobikhar, Tusayan (*alias* Moki or Moqui) and Uta (*alias* Ute or Utah, for whom see p. 363). But all of these seven lived so far away from Stuart's path that he assuredly never encountered any of them.

Now as to the query reserved at the forefront of this section:

Did Stuart when using at times the word Snake and at other times the word Shoshone use them interchangeably? Or did he intend to differentiate among the encountered tribes of Shoshonean stock; and if so, how?

If we assume that he purposed distinguishment, we gain a puzzle. Presumably each of his "Shoshonays" of the lower Columbia was either a Paviosto or a Saidyuka. But what of his "Shoshones" and "Snakes" whom he met later in his journey?

One small lot of them may have been, as already stated, Tukuarikas; but what of the rest? As concerns the rest, did Stuart, when writing

"Snake" mean to specify the Shoshone proper or the Bannock; and, when writing "Shoshone," intend to designate the Bannock or the Snake? It is for the reader to decide.

C. L. Hall's *The Grosventre spelling of the name, Bird Woman* in *North Dak.*, I, pp. 69-72; *L. & C. Hist.*, pp. 183, 477, 478, 554-570, 973, 996, 1007; *Chittenden*, pp. 848, 884-888; *DeSmet Letters*, p. 217; *Clark*, pp. 47, 59-61, 334, 338; *Hodge*, I, pp. 128, 130, II, pp. 212, 555, 558, 606, 833.

Sioux

The name represents an evolution from the Algonquian word *Nadowessiwag*, meaning the "snakelike ones" or, in other words, the "enemies." This Algonquian term was erroneously transcribed by Nicollet in 1634-35 as *Naduesiu*, and by Hennepin in 1683 as *Nadiousioux*. Hence our modern accepted form Sioux, which has wandered through variant spellings such as Seaux, Seauex, Soux, Souex, Souix, Sieoux, Sieouex, Soeoux, Scioux, Scouex, Sceouex, Soues, Suouex, Soo, Soos, Sue, Sues, Couex, and Sicouex.

Sioux, particularly in its adjectival form, Siouan, had two significances. It denoted either (a) the entire lot of numerous tribes that spoke kindred dialects of a specific widespread language, or else (b) the particular one of these tribes that, though commonly termed *Sioux*, has also oftentimes been known by its self-selected name of *Dakota* (otherwise spelled Dahcotah, Dacotah and, less properly, Darcota, Darcotar, Dacorta) or, in Teton dialect, *Lakota*.

Stuart, in each of his references to the Sioux, restricted himself to this second significance and thus to this latter and single tribe, the Dakota. Accordingly, this tribe will be the only one to receive our comment, and, wherever later in this section the word Sioux appears, its meaning will be limited to this one tribe.

The Sioux in seemingly late prehistoric times migrated westward from territory east of the Mississippi River. When in the latter part of the eighteenth century they were first encountered by the fur trader, they were already settled on lands which are now embraced within the present-day state of South Dakota and the contiguous area around its borders.

The Sioux men being of stalwart physique and virile mentality, their tribe proved itself to be among the most aggressive and warlike in the West. It preyed upon all the indian nations surrounding it, and, in much later years, dared to attack large contingents of United States troops. The Custer massacre (June, 1876) and the Wounded Knee campaign (1889, 1890) were forceful expressions of protest against increasing domination by the white man.

Tent-dwelling nomads, the Sioux frequently wandered beyond the limits of their own country; but in extent of such vagrancy they were not the equals of the Crows, the Shoshones, or the Blackfeet.

For several reasons the Sioux were, to the fur trader, the most important of all the Western indians. Not only were they numerically the largest nation, but also their entire territory was a favorite feeding ground of the bison, and the Sioux were indefatigable hunters. Furthermore their territory contained many beaver, and the Sioux were expert trappers.

Because the Sioux inhabited both sides of the upper Missouri River, navigation there and traffic upon its northerly confluents were largely at their mercy. The American trader, in his earliest expeditions, met with such ardent opposition that more than one of these expeditions was forced to abandon its project and to retrace its course. Incidentally, the Sioux were then so much under British influence that in the War of 1812 they came very near taking an active part against the United States.

Abhorrent at seeing the white man obtain a foothold in their country, the Sioux also resented his effort at direct trade with other tribes in their neighborhood. They regarded these other tribes as enemies and did not wish them to be unduly benefited. In addition there was shrewd desire to exact a middleman's commission.

The Sioux were divided into three important septs:

(A) Yankton Sioux (more properly, it is said, *I-hanke-ya-ton-won-wa* meaning "farthest village"), its members numbering some 1000 souls and living in such part of the southern portion of the tribal territory as lay along the Missouri River and in the lower valleys of the present-day James, Vermilion and Big Sioux Rivers. Of all the Sioux, they were the least inimical to the white man.

(B) Yanktonai (*alias* Yankton of the Plains, or more properly, it is said, *I-hanke-ya-ton-won-ya* meaning "smallest village" or "farthest village" or "smallest band" of Yanktons), its members numbering some 2500 souls and occupying, on the east, the upper valleys of the James and Big Sioux Rivers and, on the west, a long stretch of the Missouri's valley. Treacherous, vindictive, adepts at ambush, and loathing the white man, they at times brought havoc to him and to his property.

(C) Teton Sioux, its members numbering some 5000 people.

Appendix B

Though *Teton* is probably a contraction of *Titonwan*, "prairie-dwellers," each of two inconsistent traditions seeks another origin for the name. One of them gives derivation from an alleged merger of two Dakotan words, *tinta* meaning "prairie" and *tonwon* meaning "village"—hence "prairie village." According to the second tradition, a chief having seceded from a main camp and having been later joined by other apostates, it became usual to say *Te-tona?*—an elliptical form for the question signifying "How many tepees has he?"

The Teton Sioux dwelt, for the most part, west of the Missouri River, and there overran the country as far to the west as the present-day Black Hills and to the southwest as the North Platte River. Their range at its north and south was bounded by the lands of respectively the Mandans and the Pawnees. In the early days of the fur trade these Teton Sioux were so inimical to the white man and were so accustomed to attack his boats that they were accorded the title, "Pirates of the Missouri." However, after tasting the initial profits from dealing with white traders they presently became more tractable.

This Teton Sioux sept was subdivided into seven bands known severally as:

(a) Bois Brulé, otherwise termed Brulé Sioux; but, in Teton dialect, known as *Si-chun-goo*, meaning "Burnt Thighs." Tradition furnishes the following two origins for this burning: (1) A chief and his war party, becoming intoxicated by whiskey, lay so near a camp fire as to be singed. (2) A chief and his companions, as an aid to digging artichokes from frozen ground, thawed the soil with an overspreading of burning brush. Presently the chief, dislodging an artichoke, found it very hot and thoughtlessly rubbed it against his naked thigh.

The Brulé Sioux lived on both sides of the Missouri near the mouths of the present-day White and Teton Rivers.

(b) Ogalalla (*alias* Ogallala and Oglala), this name, which means "throwing at" or "throwing into," being derived, it is said, from an alleged occurrence as follows: In an argument between two chiefs, one of them announced that, unless his opponent recanted, he would throw ashes or dirt in the opponent's face. The threat was fulfilled, and the opponent's followers were ever afterward impliedly designated as "those who had dirt or ashes thrown in their faces." The Ogalallas dwelt on the headwaters of the White and Niobrara Rivers.

(c) Uncapapa (*alias* Hunkpapa). This name, a corruption of *Hunka-pea* meaning "ends" or "outlet," refers to the fact that at mixed Sioux encampments—which, like other indians' camps, were ordinarily in the form of a circle having a gap or break in its circumference—the Uncapapas pitched their lodges at both ends of this break but did not close it.

(d) Minneconjou, a name meaning "planter by the water" and, according to tradition, given this band because a chief and his followers had farmed near a stream or lake.

(e) Sans-Arc, this being a French translation of *Itazipcho*, the Sioux's name for this band. As for the band's once being without bows, there are the following two traditions. (1) Some of its warriors, advancing to attack an Absarokan camp, were overwhelmed by an unexpected sortie and in their flight threw away their bows without having shot a single arrow. (2) At a very early period the band having been deserted by all its dogs, the medicine man announced that the dogs would return if all of the warriors' bows were placed on top of the lodges. The bows were thus disposed and the dogs made their return; but, before the bows could be recovered, enemies assaulted the camp and drove its unarmed inmates into flight.

(f) Two Kettle, this being an English version of *Oohenonpa* (meaning "two boilings"), the Sioux name for this band; a name due, it is said, to a chief's insistence that, when cooking some bison meat, part of the meat go into one pail and part into another.

(g) Blackfeet (this being an exact translation of *Sihasapa*, the band's name for itself), a people very different from the Blackfeet proper described on pp. 334-336. Though their name came probably from their wearing black moccasins, tradition gives two other sources: (1) A chief, jealous of his wife, compelled her to keep the soles of her moccasins blackened with charcoal so that he could trail her wherever she might go. (2) Warriors, when assailing Absarokan indians, allowed themselves to be the victims of a surprise attack in which they lost their horses. On their homeward walk, they crossed a country which had been swept by fire; and, their moccasins presently wearing away, the blackened stubble mutilated and tattooed their feet.

If Stuart had in mind any specific subdivisions of the Dakota indians when he phrased his apprehensive reference to them (p. 190), the subvisions which he indicated were not improbably the Ogalalla, the Bois Brulé, and the Yanktonai.

Chittenden, pp. 557, 863-867; *L. & C. Hist.*, pp. 70, 96-102, 316, 317; *DeSmet*, pp. 51, 58; Doane Robinson's *A History of the Dakota or Sioux Indians* in *South Dak.*, II, Pt. 2, pp. 1-523; *Clark*, pp. 73, 83, 256, 272, 273, 325, 341-348, 384, 385, 410; *Lewis and Clark*, table following p.

30; *Hodge*, I, pp. 109, 111, 166-168, 579, 580, 625, 736, 737, 868, 869, II, pp. 109-111, 136, 173, 453, 568, 569, 577-579, 736, 737, 988-990.

SNAKE. See SHOSHONE, pp. 355-358

UTA (*alias* UTAH), now more commonly known as UTE, styled also in early days as YUTA or EUTAW and seemingly identical with Stuart's "Black Arms" as described by him in his entry of Aug. 20 (p. 86)

The tribal name Uta meant, it is said, "those that dwell in mountains."

The tribe was composed of numerous septs, was of Shoshonean linguistic stock, was equestrian and predatory, and had no fixed villages. Dwelling in what today is a portion of northeastern Utah and of northwestern Colorado, its home territory included the valleys of Grand River and lower Green River and was bounded on the west by the Wahsatch Mountains. From this home territory trails led into present-day New Mexico. The tribe's members were industrious in fur gathering, were relatively thrifty and were comparatively little addicted to thievery and other forms of dishonesty. Though not innately belligerent, they were brave when war was necessary. Their eastward excursions for bison brought them into frequent collison with the Southern Arapahoes, the Cheyennes and other eastern tribes. In 1879 the Utes warred against the whites, toward whom in earlier years they ordinarily had been friendly.

The State of Utah, one of its counties and an important mountain pass in Colorado are each named for them, while the name of one of their chiefs is borne by the city of Ouray in Colorado.

Chittenden, pp. 887, 888; *L. & C. Hist.*, p. 479; *Dawson; Clark*, pp. 386-392; *Hodge*, II, pp. 874-876; *Burton*, p. 272.

WAAKICUM, as termed by Stuart; but more commonly known as WAHKIACUM

This tribe, which Stuart credited with having 66 warriors and which he located as living at or near the confluence of the Elokomin River with the Columbia River in present-day Wahkiakum County, Wash., was called by Lewis and Clark *Warciacum*, *Warkiacum* and *Wahkiakume*, by *Nouvelles Annales*, X, p. 23, *Ouakikour*, while Alexander Ross termed it *Wakicum*, and Wilkes styled it *Waikaikum*. It was of Upper Chinookan (Watlala) linguistic stock, and, since the year 1850, has had no existence as a tribe. Its name, in the form of Wahkiacum, is now borne by the county mentioned above.

L. & C. Hist., pp. 700, 701, 705, 711, 740, 781, 906, 1250, 1263; *Ross* [*B*], p. 102; *Franchere* [*C*], pp. 39, 40, 45, 52, 53, 65, 67; *Wilkes*, *Narr.*, V, p. 120; *Hodge*, II, p. 890; journ., p. 28 *ante*.

Walla Walla

These indians, whom Stuart rated at 200 souls, were of Shahaptian linguistic stock. He termed them "good Indians," while Lewis and Clark said concerning them: "We may, indeed, justly affirm that, of all the Indians whom we have met since leaving the United States, the Wollawollahs are the most hospitable, honest, and sincere." Part of them lived on the river which, located in the present-day states of Washington and Oregon, now bears their name. The rest of them occupied sites not only on the Columbia's left bank adjacent to the mouth of the Walla Walla River but also on the Columbia's right bank opposite that mouth.

In this tribe's native language, the word *Walla*—if that is the way the white man should have spelled it—signified "running water." Also, in that same indian language, the iteration of any word had diminutizing effect. Accordingly *Walla Walla* meant a "small swift river," and such, in fact, was the Walla Walla River.

How spell the name? Lewis and Clark used indiscriminately these forms: *Woller Woller*, *Wollah Wollah*, *Wollaw Wollah*, *Wallow Wallow*. But the citizens of the present-day state of Washington have authoritatively settled the matter by entitling the river, a county, and a city, all of them, as Walla Walla.

L. & C. Hist., pp. 606, 669, 973-977, 980; *Hodge*, II, p. 900.

INDEX

EXPLANATION OF SIGNS

† If attached to

(1) name of person, indicates member of Stuart's overland party,

(2) geographical name, indicates that the entity either lay in the route of Stuart's party or was mentioned by Stuart,

(3) name of indian tribe, indicates that the tribe either was encountered by Stuart's party or was mentioned by Stuart,

(4) name of an animal, bird, tree &c., indicates that the entity was mentioned by Stuart.

* Has, for Hunt's overland party and for mention by Hunt, the same significance that the sign † has for Stuart's party and for mention by Stuart.

‡ Indicates person who sailed in ship *Tonquin* from New York to Astoria.

¶ Indicates person who sailed in ship *Beaver* from New York to Astoria.

§ If attached to

(1) name of person, indicates member of Missouri Fur Company's brigade,

(2) name of fort, indicates ownership by Missouri Fur Company.

Index

Index

Index

Index

Index

Index